# VICTORY AT SEA

# VICTORY AT SEA

### NAVAL POWER AND THE TRANSFORMATION OF THE GLOBAL ORDER IN WORLD WAR II

## PAUL KENNEDY

*with paintings by*
## IAN MARSHALL

Yale UNIVERSITY PRESS
NEW HAVEN AND LONDON

Published with assistance from the Kingsley Trust Association Publication Fund established by the
Scroll and Key Society of Yale College.

Yale University Press books may be purchased in quantity for educational, business, or
promotional use. For information, please email sales.press@yale.edu (U.S. office) or
sales@yaleup.co.uk (U.K. office).

Maps by Bill Nelson.
Designed by Amber Morena.
Set in Minion Pro type by Motto Publishing Services.
Printed in Slovenia.

Library of Congress Control Number: 2021945484
ISBN 978-0-300-21917-3 (hardcover : alk. paper)

A catalogue record for this book is available from the British Library.

This paper meets the requirements of ANSI/NISO Z39.48-1992 (Permanence of Paper).

10 9 8 7 6 5 4 3 2

*To Cynthia and Jean*

*From Paul and Ian*

# Contents

# Paintings by Ian Marshall

# Maps

# Charts and Tables

## Charts

## Tables

# Preface

The present work is, first and foremost, a book about naval history; it tells a story of naval battles, maritime campaigns, hard-fought convoys, amphibious landings, and strikes from the sea during World War II, and of the state of navies for a brief while before and after that. But as well as being a study of a mere ten years (1936–46) of maritime affairs, it is also a work that grapples with the larger story of the rise and fall of Great Powers in recent times. This is a naval tale, to be sure, yet in addition it is an analysis of power shifts in the international system at the time of the greatest hegemonic war in history. It is a study in the causes of historical change using the compressed time frame of a single decade, but this brief period was a very special one; *at no other time in history did the naval balances of power change as much.*

To be more specific as to the author's deeper intent: this work offers a novel attempt to trace and measure the dynamic growth of the United States of America, through the prism of its swift attainment of naval mastery at the close of the war years, to be the number one world power by 1945. The convoy struggles and the battleship shootouts described in detail here, then, are presented as the surface events of a larger struggle for world power; beneath and behind those naval campaigns, huge alterations were taking place in the international ordering of the leading countries of the globe. Perhaps only a few perceptive observers of the time saw it, but what was occurring was a seismic shift in the world order. *Victory at Sea* is about warships and navies, from beginning to end, but it is also about that extraordinary shift in Great Power history.

---

A few years ago I really did not think I would be writing another work about World War II, especially not one about navies. I was drafting a new introduction and conclusion to a twenty-fifth anniversary edition of my earlier book, *The Rise and Fall of the Great Powers,* and also collecting materials for a possible study of Kipling's imperial thought. That would be plenty. But a conjuncture of circumstances occurred, beginning with various surgeries that kept me close to home and away from the UK libraries that I wished to work in. It was during those nontraveling months that I offered to write the foreword, and later an accompanying text, to my friend Ian Marshall's planned new collection of his original paintings of *Fighting Warships of the Second World War.* For a little while, I could take time away both from Kipling and from my reflections on what had been happening to the Great Powers since the first edition of *Rise and Fall.* It would be easy to compose a simple narrative of the maritime events of the period 1939–45. And it would be fun to work with a renowned maritime artist (Ian had just been elected the president of the American Society of Marine Artists). With the support of Yale University Press, a publisher who would respect the need to integrate Ian's paintings into the specific chapters and narrative of this book, I commenced drafting.

After a further year or so, when I had returned to teaching at Yale, other changes had occurred. The first was Ian's sad and unexpected passing, at home, just before Christmas 2016. He was an artist of remarkable and original talent, as those who possess his beautiful books on *Armored Ships, Flying Boats, Cruisers and La Guerre de Course* and *Passage East* well know.[1] He had been painting almost to his very end, however, and sending fresh naval portraits from his studio to me as well as detailed, fully researched descriptions of all the works already completed; it seemed only proper—indeed, I was compelled—to finish and have published our joint project. I miss his gentle manners, his great professionalism, and his remarkable erudition in the realms of maritime history and warship design. Each painting is not only a fine work of art but also an understated display of Ian's impressive topographical and historical knowledge.

The other major change from the original plan was an intellectual one, which had slowly taken shape while I was thinking about and drafting the middle chapters of this book. The more I saw the story unfold, from those early successive blows by the Axis on the Anglo-American navies (Norway, the Fall of France, Crete, Pearl Harbor, Manila, and Singapore) to the amazing turnaround of fortune in the midst of this gigantic conflict, the more motivated I was to return to probing the deeper reasons for the transformation. Ian's illustrations alone, even as I was choosing where to insert them, were telling us something here. One painting for the year 1940 showed a battle-worn destroyer disembarking British troops after the Dunkirk disaster (painting 17); another, for late 1941, portrayed the HMS *Prince of Wales* and HMS *Repulse* in Singapore harbor just days before their destruction by Japanese naval airpower (painting 26). Yet the paintings for the year 1944 show something quite different, like that one of rows of American fleet carriers stretched across their anchorage in Ulithi Atoll, an image of limitless naval power (painting 41). In a mere two years, more or less, the world had changed.

Something had happened to cause this huge alteration in the maritime balances, and it simply wasn't enough to state that the US Navy was by now sending more and more new aircraft carriers to the Pacific and therefore was able to advance. Somewhere around the middle period of this great war at sea, more exactly as the critical year of 1943 unfolded, a massive shift in the global balance of power took place, a change of fortunes that was both reflected in and helped by alterations in the naval balances themselves. Obviously, this was not the first time that epic, interacting transformations in history had occurred. Century after century, great conflicts between the powers really did change the relative position of states, just as they changed the nations themselves. Had not the distinguished sociologist Charles Tilly, writing of Europe's rise in early-modern times, coined that reciprocal phrase, "War made the State, and the State made War"?[2] In our case we might say: *Naval events led to Allied victory and changes in the distribution of international power. Yet it was the inherent, unfolding distribution of power that determined the outcome of naval events.*

Another study of early-modern Europe cast its influence as I struggled to write a book both of narrative history and of deep structural changes over time. My mind was drawn back to that seminal work of the great French scholar Fernand Braudel, *The Mediterranean and the Mediterranean World in the Age of Philip II.*[3] This was also an age of epic struggles like Lepanto, the Spanish Armada, and the revolt of the Netherlands—which he referred to, famously, as "history of events" or "events-history" (*l'histoire événementielle*); but underneath those clashes of navies and armies were the deeper structures of history, both the unalterable conditions of geography, climate, distance, and size and the steady, irreversible shifts in economic power, productive output, and technological improvement. And by the close of this sixteenth-century Mediterranean world, Braudel reminds the reader, the centers of production and the pace of events were moving toward northwest Europe and the Atlantic. In a somewhat similar way, it can be argued, during the course of the twentieth century a primarily European-centered international order shifted outward, toward newer powers in America and Asia, and the chief player in and beneficiary of this particular global change was the United States of America.

This is neither to push the analogy with Braudel's lifelong work too much nor to hide the fact that *Victory at Sea* devotes a far greater proportion of its pages to naval actions and campaigning than did *The Mediterranean World*. This present work is overwhelmingly one of narration—and illustration—of national fleets and their maritime conflicts across and under the waters of the globe during the six years of World War II. The Braudel analogy is used, as all comparisons should be, only to make one think better about the shape and purpose of the original project; and as such, it works well here. There are two levels of analysis in *Victory at Sea* that are not separate but are intrinsically related: the winning of the hegemonic World War II cannot be understood without knowledge of its maritime side, and in turn the vast surge in the achievements of the Allied navies cannot be comprehended without the reader's recognizing the underlying seismic shifts of this time.

———————

The basic narrative here is easy to summarize. In the period before 1939, as chapter 2 describes, there were six major or considerable naval powers (Britain, United States, Japan, France, Italy, and Germany). The Royal Navy was still the world's largest, if only just ahead of the US Navy, and the three Axis fleets of Japan, Italy, and Germany were preparing for their future challenges to the maritime status quo. The European war that broke out in September 1939 was a decidedly limited one (chapter 4) because of the huge preponderance of the British and French navies over Germany's. But the maritime balances changed dramatically following Hitler's conquest of Norway and the rest of northwest Europe, the Fall of France, and Italy's entry into the war. For one lengthy, dramatic year and a half (chapter 5), the Royal Navy struggled to hold off the combined Italo-German attacks at sea. Then an even more dramatic change in the maritime balances occurred with the Japanese attacks upon the American and British positions in the Pacific and the coming of what was now truly a world war.

The struggle for naval mastery raged fiercely during the next two years and more, in all the major oceans and seas of the globe, across the surface, in the air, and under the water, and the substantive chapters 6 and 7 strive to recapture for the reader those epic contests. This was the greatest naval war the world had ever seen, with the year 1942 itself laying claim to being the "fighting-most year" in all of naval history. Despite gains in the Mediterranean, though, the overall naval picture was hardly a promising one for the Allies. At the onset of 1943 the US Navy was down to a single fleet carrier in the Pacific War, and German U-boats were poised to launch their largest-ever offensive against the critical Atlantic convoy trade. Changes had to come if the Allies were to prevail.

The changes came in 1943. World War II defies easy summary, but the key to an eventual Allied victory, essentially, was to get the increasingly vast numbers of American and British Empire fighting men and munitions across two oceans so that the combined armies (along with the Russians) could crush Italy, Germany, and Japan. This involved two elements, sea power *and* a productivity revolution. In the sea-power story (chapter 7), the struggle for control of the North Atlantic was won by the defending forces, quite dramatically, in May and June of that year, with severe U-boat losses. North Africa was consolidated, Malta relieved, and Italy defeated. Things moved more slowly in the Pacific fighting, but victories in the Gilberts, the Solomons, and northern New Guinea confirmed an American advance that would not be thrown back. Yet the year 1943 meant more than just another saga of hard-fought convoy battles, amphibious landings in the Mediterranean and Pacific, and the sinking of a German battle cruiser off Norway. It was the year in which the sheer productive muscle of the United States, which had existed in latent form and in so many measures before that time, at last *realized itself* in all of the arenas of the world war, as the pivotal chapter 8 demonstrates. In place of the dearth of fleet carriers, new powerful ones began to stream across the Pacific from June onward. Over the Atlantic, high above the now-secured convoys of supply ships and troopships, flew thousands of US aircraft on their way to their new bomber and fighter bases in southern England. Landing craft and Liberty ships poured out of American shipyards. Even the Royal Navy's hard-fought defeat of the U-boats in 1943 could not have been imagined without the productive American force behind the ultra-long-range B-24 patrol planes, the escort carriers, the mass-produced miniature radar sets, the homing torpedoes, and Lend-Lease stock for Canada's and Britain's production of escort vessels. By the year following, this flow of munitions to the fronts had become a flood, producing in turn the victories of Leyte Gulf and Normandy (chapter 9). And behind all this military hardware and productivity was a financial, tax-raising strength bigger than anything known to history. Allied naval predominance was assured because of a surge in the American economy that dwarfed that of all its rivals. It was not just a story of more and more warships; it was also a tale of a new international order emerging. *Victory at Sea* was affirmed, with the clear winner of the war being the United States of America.

---

After 1945, then, the naval landscape was completely different from that of a mere ten years earlier. The navies of Japan, Germany, Italy, and France had been either totally destroyed or massively reduced in size. Only two countries possessed a large fleet, and one of those, that of the Royal Navy, found itself rapidly falling behind America's enormous naval force. The situation was analogous, many scholars suggest, to the situation in 1815 after the Napoleonic Wars, when the British fleet had emerged as number one, well ahead of the rest, although on this occasion the American predominance was far greater. In this new narrative, the 1939–45 struggle had been the latest of the half dozen or more "hegemonic wars" that political scientists identify as having occurred over the past five centuries,[4] except this time the capital city of the new hegemon lay outside Europe, three thousand miles to the west. The New World had not only come to the rescue of the Old, as Churchill had hoped; it had actually replaced it.

In creating a structure for this book I sought to reconcile that natural tension between length (the unfolding story) and depth (explanation and diagnosis). The outline below provides a map of how this was attempted. The first three chapters are preliminary, ground-clearing ones. The detailed account of "Warships and Navies before 1939" in chapter 2 was written especially with the general reader in mind and functions as a gateway to the narrative. The third chapter discusses the elements of geography and economic power and introduces some of the classic theories about understanding sea power. The three substantive chapters that follow (4–6) narrate the great war at sea until close to its turning point; here, then, is this book's "history of events." And while the fighting narrative continues into the lengthy chapter 7 (on 1943), that particular chapter is linked with the critically important deep-structures analysis of chapter 8. The book then returns to the story of the maritime campaigns of 1944 and 1945, detailing the predominance of Anglo-American sea power. At the very end, the audit given in chapter 11 tries to offer just that.

Methodologically, this is a study of a basic reciprocal action—how sea power influenced World War II and how World War II affected sea power. It is obviously not the first time I have grappled with this very large question of the relationship between naval and military actions and larger historical forces. Decades ago, in an early study, *The Rise and Fall of British Naval Mastery* (1976), I tried to analyze, albeit in chronological form, the story of British sea power in relation to its relative economic strength in the world. In another early work, *The Rise of the Anglo-German Antagonism 1860–1914* (1980), I sought for the first time to intersperse narrative and deep-structural chapters while looking at one of the largest issues of pre–World War I diplomatic history.[5] While I was not dealing with navies, I was honing my intellectual curiosity about how to understand and explain change over time. Then, after many detours through the thickets of Great Power history, global trends, and the United Nations,[6] I returned to another analysis of historical causation—a look at how some key problems of World War II were solved—in my book *Engineers of Victory* (2013).

The subtitle of that particular book made its focus clear: *The Problem Solvers Who Turned the Tide in the Second World War*.[7] It, too, was an exploration of different levels of causality, showing how Allied planners, scientists, and engineers overcame tactical and operational obstacles to victory at sea, in the air, and on land through developing newer weapons and methods of war. And it, too, paid particular attention to the pivotal year of 1943, when naval escorts at last had radar, ultra-long-range aircraft closed the Atlantic gap, fleet carriers streamed into Pearl Harbor and escort carriers into Liverpool, and landing craft finally became available in large numbers. Of course the present *Victory at Sea* has its own purpose—to narrate the story of the great maritime war of 1939–45—but it is also interested in a *how* question: how was the flood of long-range Liberator patrol aircraft, escort carriers, landing craft, fleet carriers and their fighter planes, radar sets, and homing torpedoes that had joined the Allied navies and air forces from 1943 onward made possible? The answer, again, takes us back to the vast surge in US industrial and technological performance by the middle stages of the war. The weaknesses of the British and American navies before that time—the limited capacity against U-boats of little corvettes like HMS *Pink* (painting 8), the vulnerability of their battleships to Axis aerial and submarine attack, the restricted offensive strength of Admiral William Halsey's fleet when he had only the carriers USS *Saratoga* and HMS *Victorious* (painting 39), and the frequent heavy losses taken by the Malta convoys—were all things of the past by the end of 1943. As chapters 9 and 10 here show, the question after that date was not *whether* but *when*. When would the victory at sea occur?

A concern with timing also explains the chronological beginning and end of this study, which was roughly the decade between 1936 and 1946. The year 1936 was a time when classical naval power was operating as normal and when traditional battleship-centered fleets appeared unchallenged. It was also an important date in foreign affairs. The Abyssinian Crisis in the Mediterranean, Japan's growing expansion in East Asia, the virtual collapse of the League of Nations, the end of the Washington and London naval limitations treaties, and the resumption of newer fleet building by all the larger nations provide good starting points for this story. After a decade and a half of peace and disarmament, sea power was again coming to the fore, with battleships still regarded as the best indicator of naval strength and influence—nicely captured, then, in Ian Marshall's portrait of the British capital ships HMS *Hood* and HMS *Barham* anchored in the historic Grand Harbour of Malta during the latter part of the Abyssinian Crisis (painting 1).

A mere ten years later, the overall strategic landscape for navies and naval affairs had been altered in no less than four remarkable ways. First, the multipolar maritime balance of the 1930s had gone, with the elimination of the Italian, German, Japanese, and almost all the earlier French fleets; second, there was the end of the era of the big-gunned surface vessel, the battleships and heavy cruisers, most of which were being towed off to the scrapyard; third, there was the advent of the atomic bomb, which challenged the utility and roles of all traditional armed services, navies, armies, and regular air forces; and, finally, there was a new world maritime order, dominated by an American economic and military power larger than anything the world had ever seen. Whatever the newer challenges the postwar era might bring, one Great Power had the resources to handle them and was keen to demonstrate that. In one symbolic showing, at the close of our narrative account, throughout August and September 1945 a huge US Pacific Fleet was anchored right across Tokyo Bay as the sun set each evening behind Mount Fuji (painting 49). The naval war had come to its close. And a new world had arrived.

# PART I

## Setting the Stage

**PAINTING 1.  HMS *Hood* and HMS *Barham*, Malta, 1938.** Symbolizing British sea power in the Mediterranean, the lengthy battle cruiser *Hood* and the modernized battleship *Barham* lie at anchor in the Grand Harbour. Both were sunk in the intense fighting of 1941, but Malta itself was held.

# ONE

## Prologue

### *Sea Power and the Sweep of History*

The soft, warm waters of the Mediterranean lapped gently against the sides of the two great warships anchored across from each other in Malta's historic Grand Harbour in the summer of 1938. The fifteenth-century porticos of the Knights of St. John stood out behind the vessels. An Admiralty tug moved close by, and small boats occasionally went back and forth to the landings, but little else stirred. The world was quiet at that time, so it seemed, although not fully at peace. A keen-eyed observer might have noticed that across the top of the *Hood*'s and *Barham*'s giant gun-turrets lay several brilliant stripes; they had been painted on to indicate to aircraft flying above that both vessels, and all other British warships in the Mediterranean theater, were neutral in the Spanish Civil War still on at this time. The international arena was not entirely clear, then, of the clouds of war. That struggle for Spain was still being fought out, albeit only on land and in the air. The Italian war against Abyssinia had recently come to an end. Hitler's Third Reich had moved without contest into Austria in the Anschluss of March 1938. In the Far East, Japan's armies were advancing through great swathes of China. All of the Great Powers were now rearming, though some at a far slower pace than others. Still, probably only a few experts on foreign affairs at this time thought that they stood on the brink of a war that would be larger than that of 1914–18. And none of them conceived that they were only a few years away from a watershed, a near-complete break in the international system as a whole. How hard it is, given the usual blur of weekly events, to guess what comes next.

It was scenes like the one in Malta's Grand Harbour that encouraged a broad sense of stability and security in Britain and the West, regardless of the fighting in Spain and distant China and despite the Fuehrer's disquieting speeches. Indeed, there was such a long list of reasons to as-

sume that things were unlikely to change very soon that it is intriguing to
note them in bullet-point form, if only to enhance the starkness of the impending transformation.

- A Eurocentric world order still prevailed, except in the Western
  Hemisphere.
- The British Empire still appeared to be the number one world
  power in 1938.
- Malta was just one very important fleet base in a global imperial
  network.
- Sea power was still the main, and easiest, measure of world
  influence.
- Battleships and battle fleets were still the way to measure that
  influence.
- The Royal Navy was still the leading navy in the world.
- Aircraft did not (yet) have the range and destructiveness to
  dominate.
- The USSR was far away, and only Berlin and Tokyo really worried
  about it.
- The United States' interest was also far away, turned to the Pacific.
- Japan was a threat, yet only in its region, not an existential danger
  to the West.
- The League of Nations was finished, but European diplomacy
  would sort things out.

To put this in another way, it was still a world in which, say, a British Army officer, schoolteacher, missionary, or rubber planter could take
berth on a British India passenger ship all the way from Southampton to
Bombay (via Gibraltar, Malta, Suez, and Aden) and see only British ports,
British ships, and British influence. It was a world that Disraeli might
have known. A mere twenty years later, by 1958, that whole world would
be evaporating; thirty years later, by 1968, it would be gone. Yet thirty
years is such a small stretch in the sweep of human history.

The chief reason why these scenes looked so reassuring, and the situation so unthreatened, was that a similar picture could have been seen
in the Grand Harbour for *generations* beforehand, going back via those
mid-Victorian black-and-white photos of the Mediterranean Fleet decked
out for a royal visit, to the aquatint illustrations of an even earlier time,
showing Nelson's squadrons in the outer roads. Malta's waters had somehow always reflected the tides of power. Various western European kingdoms from the Normans onward had contested control over the central
Mediterranean both among themselves and against Arab and Ottoman
opposition to the East. Of course, there had also been, generation after

generation, Braudel's Mediterranean world of the natural seasons in their unchanging rhythm, the patterns of local life looking similar from one region and hillside to the next.[1] But the history of events in this sea had been important too, and in the modern age what that story of wars, diplomacy, and kingdoms showed above all was the steady decline of the non-European order after 1800 or so. A continual struggle for supremacy among the European states had spilled outward to place its stamp on much of the rest of the world, and that struggle had now arrived along the shores of North Africa and beyond. From Algiers to Jamaica to Rio to the Cape to Jakarta, European peoples were coming to impose control. The earth, or at least those parts of it accessible to the influence of sea power, was falling under the domination of the leading Atlantic maritime nations, and there was little that could be done to halt it. Merchants, capitalists, missionaries, engineers, and even schoolteachers might be pouring out of the Home Counties to Cairo and Calcutta, but ahead of them had advanced the redcoats, and behind them were the intimidating barrels of navy guns. The scene in Malta's Grand Harbour was tranquil because, well, the West had won.[2]

This, of course, was the American author Alfred Thayer Mahan's historical message, drummed into his readers' minds in volume after volume. No doubt he overstressed the ubiquity and importance of naval affairs and did not recognize that European sea power's influence was specific to time and space and thus not universal.[3] Yet the fact was that in this particular time and space, from the sixteenth to the twentieth century, and in the waters that ranged from the Caribbean to Aden, the naval nations of Europe had been taking more and more of the world, showing what another scholar termed "the impact of Western Man."[4] While the extent of the economic divergence between Europe and the rest of the planet is still warmly debated among its historians, there was no doubt that by the more forceful measure of maritime power, the world's balances had shifted and continued to shift as the nineteenth century unfolded and industrialization grew.[5] It was the West's gunboats that were steaming up the Yangtze and Niger in these decades, and not the junks and dhows of the East sailing up the Thames or the Hudson. Among the many "revolutions" that it is said Europe experienced after 1600 (such as the Commercial Revolution and the Scientific Revolution), there is surely one, the Military Revolution at Sea, that explains how the Europeans did it: through organized, state-financed and state-built fleets of warships struggling for command of international trade and markets and through pushing to acquire the adjoining coastlands and, eventually, their hinterlands.[6]

The long nineteenth century, from 1789 to 1919, seemed to confirm that Europe's economic, technological, and maritime dominance was growing stronger. The Industrial Revolution, which was just beginning to unfold in Britain at the time of the Napoleonic Wars, had spread widely across the continent one hundred years later. The age of iron had given way to the age of steel: steel mills, steel warships, steel locomotives, and giant steel shells.[7] As productive and industrial power expanded, from northwest Europe to the Mediterranean shores, Europe's political footprint also surged, across to North Africa, through the Levant, and into the Near East. In the 1920s and 1930s, with the French, Italian, and British acquisitions affirmed through treaty, the colonial powers could push on, employing their same manufacturing prowess to construct large new commercial harbors, naval bases, and docking facilities along both the European and African shores. The French built a huge naval base on an old Arab settlement at Mers-el-Kébir. The port city of Beirut boomed, commercially and culturally, as the Paris of the Levant. Old Benghazi harbor was drastically altered by the same dedicated Fascist planners who were modernizing Italy's larger home ports. Marseilles and Genoa grew fast, in active rivalry with one another.

There was even a demographic aspect to this story, rarely thought about by historians of navies and world power. Despite the hemorrhaging of European peoples by the double blow of World War I and the 1918 flu epidemics, overall population numbers were still lurching upward; hence the curious fact that Europe's share of total world population reached its highest point (22 percent) only as late as the year 1928 before rapidly falling away in the decades following.[8] This meant, too, that the continent's leading nations were still exporting people as well as capital, goods, infrastructure, and governance to their colonies. If British emigration in the interwar years went chiefly to Australia, South Africa, and America, significant flows of French and Italians moved to Algiers, Oran, Tripoli, Benghazi, and surrounding areas, constructing (along with the boulevards, civic buildings, and railway stations) new harbors to allow passenger ferries and cargo vessels to dock. The European world order of the 1920s and 1930s was both symbolized and actualized by these ports as well as by fleet bases and the warships within them. In the "Mediterranean world" of the late 1930s, where even the physical landscape was being changed, three large navies (namely, of France, Italy, and Britain) might be seen visiting the various harbors and crisscrossing the waters from north to south and west to east in much the same way that at least four navies (Japanese, British, French, and American) steamed in and out of the Chinese ports and those further south; meanwhile, in a smaller way, Dutch warships cruised through the East Indies, and gunboats went up and down African rivers. Much of the world still seemed to be Europe's oyster; the Nazis' complaint was only that they didn't have a share of it. That was also the Japanese position, though they were taking steps to amend the order of things in the Far East. As for Americans at this time, trading and banking out of Singapore and Jakarta, and with US gunboats getting refueled and restocked in Hong Kong, there was no need to upset the colonial applecart; one had the benefits of empire without its costs. And, after all, the United States already did have some imperial assets (in the Philippines, Guam, Samoa, and Puerto Rico), nearly all offering overseas naval bases.[9] In 1938, there simply was no need to acquire more.

The picture of sleek and massive vessels lying in their well-protected harbors was not just a British phenomenon, therefore, but a far broader one. To keenly nationalistic populations, nothing seemed more exciting than to catch sight of their own warships, either in home ports or when they traveled abroad. Thus, while a British patriot might thrill at spotting a Royal Navy battleship in the Channel or off Aden, an Italian could feel pride at the flotillas of Mussolini's new navy anchored off Taranto, Naples, Trieste, and elsewhere. Straining one's eyes through the windows of any train approaching Naples, for example, a traveler could pick out, beyond the cranes and dockyards and customs and emigration halls of this fast-growing port, many of the most impressive warships of the Regia Marina.[10] What better confirmation was there that sea power was important?

However eye-catching and pretty these images of Western warships, there was nothing artificial about their fighting power or the determination of their political leaders to deploy force where necessary. The *Zara* had already intervened in the latter part of the Spanish Civil War, and it was to be deployed again in April 1939 when Mussolini struck at Albania. Nor was there anything artificial about those British battleships anchored in Malta and the deterrent purpose behind their deployment. Their 15-inch guns were real, and deadly, and promised enormous destructive power. And there were a lot of them. To the thousands of British sailors who swarmed into the very British pubs and teashops around Valetta and Sliema harbors, and to the tens of thousands of Maltese who were employed in the great repair yards, there was no apprehension that this Royal Navy–dominated world was a mere generation away from its end; how could there be, when for ages nothing had changed? The only possible challenger could be another European naval power, Italy, with its warships and harbors admittedly not too far away. But even that challenge, if it happened, was surely going to be a limited, regional one, an upset neither to traditional forms of navies nor to the Eurocentric world order.

In sum, then: where, really, was the evidence back in 1936 or 1938 that any of the geopolitical and military assumptions listed in those bullet points above might be wrong? Was there any challenge to the idea that Europe was still the most important part of the world, with London, Paris, Berlin, and Geneva its most important capital cities as compared to distant Tokyo, self-isolated Moscow, obscure Beijing, and a still provincial-looking Washington, DC? Or that (regardless of Wall Street's financial

**PAINTING 2.** Italian heavy cruiser *Zara* and its sister ships, *Fiume* and *Pola,* Naples, 1938. Italy built the most elegant warships of all, as shown here in the 8-inch-gunned heavy cruisers of the *Zara* class. All three were sunk by British battleships in night fighting in the Battle of Cape Matapan. See also painting 25.

heft) the British Empire was the number one world power, with its maritime bases galore, and the Royal Navy the world's leading navy, with the
fleets to occupy them? Or that battleships were still the most important
type of vessel in any navy, and thus battleship tallies remained the proper
measure of relative strength? Or that the order of things in this Grand
Harbour scene wouldn't change, at least in the foreseeable future? It was
true that from time to time in history, empires rose and fell, but there was
no evidence of that happening anywhere soon.

What, then, might cause this political landscape to alter, and alter drastically? The 1920s turned out to be more of a decade of Great Power recovery and military stabilization than of change following World War I's
convulsions. The "Russia Danger,"[11] whether czarist or Bolshevik, had
been pushed into a corner. The French Third Republic, which was close to
being smashed by 1917 or so, had been shored up—or had shored itself up.
The British Empire, which had buckled but not been broken by the strains
of mass warfare, found itself territorially enhanced in the peace settle-
ments and in the curious state of looking much stronger than it felt.[12] Italy had preserved its narrow place in the big boys club, and all that Mussolini wanted was a better position in it. Japan's navy, which by 1917 had
been carrying out antisubmarine patrols in the Mediterranean, was now
to be seen only in Far Eastern seas. And the American giant, which in
1918 seemed poised to be the sole arbiter of the struggle for "mastery in
Europe,"[13] had gone into serious, grumpy retreat—from League of Nations membership, from a guarantee to France, and from much else except for its pressing to have Allied war debts repaid. As the 1930s began, with the Powers striving desperately to stabilize their stock markets
and currencies, the broad political desire for conservatism that was latent in Baldwin's Britain, Tardieu's France, and Hoover's America had if
anything grown and was hardly going to be replaced by a cautious, isolationist Roosevelt. There seemed to be no grand, unfolding sweep of history occurring here, as the Powers made clear when agreeing to a further freeze on naval armaments at the 1930 London Naval Conference. If
World War I had let many genies out of the bottle, the intention in these
postwar years was to stuff as many of them back in as possible.

Moreover, while there certainly were some hints of transformations to
come in the military-technology fields by the late 1930s, it is easy to exaggerate their impacts. The problem was that within the post-1919 navies
and armies there had occurred a general swing back to conservatism parallel to that in the realms of politics and diplomacy. It may sound odd
to argue it thus, but it probably was the case that World War I's fighting had not lasted long enough, ironically, or been intensive enough to
cause real breakthrough technologies and structures to prevail. Some of
the newer, disruptive systems (submarine, torpedo, and aircraft) were un-

folding swiftly in the first decade of the twentieth century, but even they had not come into a state of full development before the conflict occurred. In a curious way, the Great War's fighting had been so "great," that is, large-scale, that it tended to slow things down, even to freeze the military struggle on land and at sea before airpower really could show itself. The western front became too big and entrenched so very soon, and the armies that fought on it became far too large, for Blitzkrieg to be successful. The firepower revolution of high-explosive shells was huge enough to wipe out battalions but not to blow holes through layers of trenches and tangled barbed wire, and the machine gun turned out to be the supreme weapon of defensive warfare. Tanks arrived in too-few numbers, and a little late. The internal-combustion engine (in the form of army trucks) hardly showed up. The long-range heavy bomber was about to come into wide use but hadn't yet done so. Aircraft carriers were too new and lacked speed, length, and the proper more-powerful planes. Amphibious operations were messy failures, and unpromising. The vast numbers of battleships in the Grand Fleet and High Seas Fleet in the cramped waters of the North Sea made for cautious tactics and conservative outcomes. The one truly revolutionary naval instrument of war, the U-boat, had been shut down by vast numbers of naval escorts and the Allied adoption of convoys; and submarines were thought not to be such a threat in a future war because of the invention of ASDIC (sonar). When the British and German admirals went home after 1919 to fight a memoirs war, it was with an enhanced belief that large battle fleets still were key, and most of their US and Japanese counterparts said amen to that. Conservatives chiefly prevailed at the top of the armies and navies, to the disgust of radical theorists of war like Sir Herbert Richmond, Sir Basil Liddell Hart, J. F. C. Fuller, and Billy Mitchell.

Still, the images of maritime power as represented in the majestic forms of the HMS *Hood* and HMS *Barham* at anchor in Malta, or by the elegant and impressive shape of Italian heavy cruisers in home ports in 1938, were by no means anachronistic. The full broadside of the *Barham* weighed fifteen thousand pounds, for example, and its high-explosive shells could be thrown at targets over twenty miles away. And so long as other admiralties clung onto large numbers of heavily gunned capital ships and after 1936 were in fact building more of them that were bigger and faster, then it behooved one's own navy to do the same. Destroyer flotillas could keep submarines from getting close to one's battleships, and the bomber aircraft of the age didn't seem all that strong or destructive. Was there any other weapon around to challenge the all-big-gunned warship?

There was perhaps one. A very different form of capital ship 6,500 miles to the east had also been showing the flag in its home waters and in the near abroad during the late 1930s. The Japanese aircraft carrier *Kaga* was

**PAINTING 3. Japanese aircraft carrier *Kaga* at Kure Naval Base.** The Japanese carriers *Kaga* and *Akagi* were built on the basis of hulls that had been intended for very large battleships and therefore had a speed of 30 knots. *Kaga* took part in the attack on Pearl Harbor, but it and three other carriers were destroyed at the Battle of Midway (see chapter 6), and with that the core of Japanese naval power dissolved.

not as elegant as those Italian heavy cruisers, nor was its "punch" seem-ingly as hefty as the 15-inch shells of the *Hood* and *Barham,* yet it was a very deadly man-of-war and, in its own way, the possessor of immense destructive power. Laid down originally as a battleship for the Impe-rial Japanese Navy (IJN) in 1920 (and thus almost a contemporary to the *Hood*), *Kaga* was completely rebuilt in the years after the Washington Na-val Treaty to allow it to become one of the IJN's very large fleet carri-ers, displacing some 33,000 tons and with a main flight deck of over eight hundred feet. It was modified yet again in the 1930s to give it a newer pro-pulsion system and make it an even more impressive warship.

To put this in another way, the Japanese Navy was so thoroughly re-building its slightly older carriers that by the approach of World War II they were as fast and effective as any of the modern British or Ameri-can vessels, and they carried at least as many torpedo-bombers and dive-bombers, if not more. And if one considered it, the total punch of the 500-pound and 1,000-pound bombs and 1,200-pound torpedoes borne by the seventy or so bomber planes of such a fleet carrier was enormous. What is more, these Japanese vessels were not hidden away from for-eign eyes. Even before its second refit, *Kaga* had been in action in Chi-nese waters at the time of the 1932 Shanghai Incident; and in the year 1937 alone, while attacking many targets after Japan commenced its larger op-erations in China, it steamed some thirty-three thousand miles in active service.[14] In 1938–39 and beyond, while the navies of the European states were rather less at sea, the IJN was ordering all six of its fleet carriers to practice repeated group maneuvers in order to perfect launching multiple aircraft at the same time against distant targets, whether on land or at sea. There was, then, a newer form of very-long-range naval warfare in the off-ing, even as those towering older battleships swung at their moorings in Mediterranean harbors or occasionally went to sea to carry out gunnery practice. Yet who was to know, at this particular moment in history, what the fate of each of these warship types was going to be?[15]

Carrier task forces were starting to be assembled and trained on either side of the Pacific by around 1938, even if they could not or did not exist in Europe. And every navy was now straining to construct more-powerful submarines. Yet it was hard to surmise that these disruptive weapons sys-tems would assume a much bigger role in maritime affairs when the larg-est expenditures of all navies in the run-up to World War II were brand-new battleships and very heavy cruisers. Perhaps a transformation would occur, though, if there came about another "total war," with the three re-visionist Powers throwing immense aerial and naval resources into the task of breaking the West's stranglehold; with the Third Reich mobiliz-ing not just big surface vessels but also hundreds of U-boats for a renewed Battle of the Atlantic; with Japan striking at America's main fleet in order

to gain control of the Western Pacific; and with Italy and Germany determined to choke Britain's Mediterranean pipeline. If all that happened, if
there was a manic, large-scale attempt to change the world order, a maritime fight far larger than that which had taken place in World War I, then
there would be, of course, a far greater likelihood that the existing strategic landscape would itself dissolve during the new hegemonic conflict.
With huge warship losses therefore likely on all sides—losses on a scale
that had been suffered in the French Revolutionary and Napoleonic Wars
but not in the 1914–18 war at sea—many of the familiar names that were
seen in the fleet harbors of the Powers during the peacetime years of the
1930s would not survive. They would have disappeared, then, along with
the comfortable maritime world suggested in the above Grand Harbour
scene.

Warship scenes of this time tell the acute observer an awful lot about
the Great Powers, it can be argued, because they reveal their naval priorities and expenditures, and because the fleet deployments of the late 1930s
inform us what their respective governments thought to be the most vivid
manifestations of strength and influence in this age. They tell us relatively
little, though, about the relative economic weights of those nations, were
they ever to be mobilized for a serious and long-lasting struggle. But if,
of course, intense mobilization of national power for such a total war did
come about, then the navies of the world—along with the air forces and
the armies—would have to be greatly transformed. Lenin's "locomotive of
war" as the mover and disrupter of things would have arrived once again,
with even greater propulsive force. And the grand sweep of history would
bear down on the sea power of the age.[16]

How does one know, the renowned Cambridge diplomatic historian
Zara Steiner famously asked as she composed her great two-volume study
of the interwar years, when one era is over and a new era is slowly beginning?[17] How does one guess, at a time of relative placidity, that one
is crossing or at least approaching a watershed in world history? The individual can't, was her answer. How, then, could the captain of a visiting French or Italian naval vessel, paying a courtesy call in Malta's Grand
Harbour in 1936 or even 1938 and seeing the great warships HMS *Hood*
and HMS *Barham* across the bay, guess that within ten years all such vessels would be gone and the Eurocentric world order would be over? That
there would be no more great naval guns left, save for as museum pieces
or on mothballed vessels in a few faraway US ports? That the extensive
networks of the naval bases owned by the European colonial powers, like
Dakar, Alexandria, Singapore, Saigon, and Malta itself, were only a decade or so away from extinction, after having been the prized strategic
chess pieces of all navies since the age of Blake and Napoleon? He could
not. Nor, indeed, had we been there, could we have guessed.

**PAINTING 4. USS *Texas* visiting Portsmouth, England, 1938.** A nice sideways view of the modernized American battleship visiting Europe in the summer before war broke out. She fought off North Africa (Operation Torch), Normandy, Iwo Jima, and Okinawa and is now a museum ship in San Jacinto, Texas. In the background is the British light cruiser HMS *Emerald*.

# TWO

## Warships and Navies before 1939

The naval policies of the Great Powers of the world in the 1930s were established and executed by a very small number of men, all of whom were to be found in their respective capital cities or in their major fleet bases in nearby home waters. Each of the navies had a political minister of sorts—a secretary of the navy, a first lord of the admiralty, a minister of marine—who was nominally head of the service and its interface with the central government itself, be it the cabinet or the head of state. Each of them also had a premier naval officer (again, with various titles, such as first sea lord, chief of naval staff, chief of naval operations, or Oberbefehlshaber der Marine), possibly with some sort of formal admiralty board, but in any case with other senior naval officers responsible for procurement, shore establishments, personnel, budgets, communications, intelligence, and so on. Depending of course on the overall size of the navy in question, other senior officers would command home and overseas fleets, and some would be in command of the larger naval ports themselves. Navies were like large business establishments, with extraordinarily complex networks; and thus a huge naval base such as San Diego, Dakar, or Hong Kong might have been a long way away from the home admiralty, yet it was in fact part of a worldwide web. The small number of men at the top who proposed and carried out their country's naval strategy knew all that, because they had seen a lot of their navy, both ashore and at sea, during their rise from second lieutenant to admiral. Even the biggest navies, like the British and American ones, possessed a senior officer corps small enough for each member to know, or at least know of, all the others. When the time came for the prime minister or president to select the next senior commanding officer, only a very limited number of candidates stood in the wings. But that was indeed as planned.

As the head of the navy and his colleagues strove to execute each nation's policy, they were acutely aware that they operated within a particular context, constrained both physically and politically. Each sought to
attain the best possible outcomes for their own armed service, and each
knew the difficulty of attaining what they wanted fully, or even partly.
Each admiralty had pretty much complete command over what went on
*within* their own service and also had a dominant role over the types of
warships they would build; but the further one went outside those particular arenas, the less they were in control of events, of course. It may
help, therefore, to think of the naval policy and position of the Powers
as being a set of concentric circles, with the admirals and their warships
and fleets at the center but always linked to and unable to escape from
the larger correlation of things—the entire navies themselves, their geographical position, and their economic and technological foundations.
Few if any of these first sea lords or grand admirals could quote Alfred
Thayer Mahan's classic *The Influence of Sea Power upon History, 1660–
1783*, verbatim, but each would have understood his argument that a nation's maritime strength was a much more complicated affair than mere
warships and fleets, that there were some "General Conditions affecting
Sea Power"[1] that had remained critical even into their own modern, industrial age.

Yet while it would be too narrow to look only at the characteristics of
warships and the size of navies in the interwar era, it probably does make
sense to begin with such an examination in the present chapter and then
work outward and look at the larger geographic, economic, and strategic
contexts later, in chapter 3.

## Navies in the Era of Naval Restrictions

In the world of the 1930s there were six large fleets, although they differed very much in size. The top two navies in total tonnage, as established back in the Washington Treaty of 1921–22, were the American and
British ones, although the Japanese Navy had made remarkable strides in
its attempts to narrow that gap by the end of the decade. Three other nations, France, Italy, and, though very late in the day, Nazi Germany, also
boasted modern fleets of war by 1939, even if their overall tonnages—and,
more important, capital-ship numbers—were far behind. Crudely put, the
"Washington system" had given the Royal Navy and the US Navy each
about 30 percent of the world's battleships (and big-gun firepower), the
Japanese around 20 percent, and the French and Italian navies each about
10 percent. This was very much a "multi-polar naval world"[2] and thus not

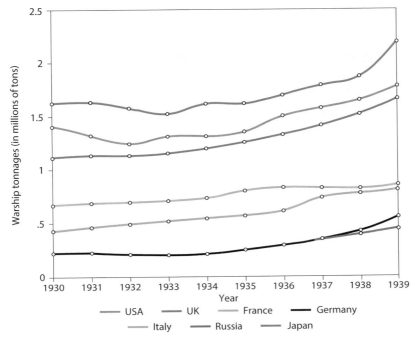

**CHART 1.** Overall warship tonnages of the Powers, 1930–39. Data was compiled by Arun Dawson, from Crisher and Souva, *Power at Sea: A Naval Dataset, 1865–2011,* accessed February 13, 2020, https://qualitativedatarepository .github.io/dataverse-previewers/previewers/SpreadsheetPreview.html?fileid =2453823&siteUrl=https://dataverse.harvard.edu&datasetid=66002&dataset version=1.0.

greatly different from that of the 1900s or, indeed, of the eighteenth century. This global distribution of maritime power had been very different at the height of the Pax Britannica, say, around 1860, and it would look very different again after 1945, when another single naval Power, the United States, would stand out. But in the 1930s a half-dozen navies jostled, unevenly, for power. Little wonder that all their admiralties found long-term strategic planning, and their warship procurement orders, so demanding a task.

Measured simply in terms of fleets and ships, the Royal Navy's position in 1939 was impressive. Its overall tonnage, when all the smaller warship classes are included, was roughly 2,185,000 tons, rather higher than America's 1,778,000 and Japan's swift-growing 1,661,000 tons, and way ahead of Italy and France's about 850,000 tons each.[3]

All these Powers, including Japan, had been belligerents during World War I and were still grappling with the huge shock waves caused by that conflict; but they had all existed as sovereign nation-states for a lot longer than that, and thus their basic strategic position was also a longer-lasting one. Britain and Japan, both island empires absolutely dependent on overseas food and supplies, regarded naval security as vital and felt that after 1919 no less than before. The United States, expanding across the oceans, claimed a similar need, albeit less plausibly, and during the 1930s it hadn't fully built up to its full tonnage entitlement. France and Italy and Germany were "hybrid powers" in this regard, wishing to make claims for their own proper share of naval power but being compelled by geography to be much more concerned about their respective capacities on land and in the air; Germany's naval desires were constrained additionally by its general disarmament following Versailles 1919. To a large extent the fleet ratios hammered out in the Washington and London treaties reflected this broad picture: two very large, egoistical, coequal naval powers at the top; a third, upwardly striving, not so far behind; two more medium-sized navies; and a badly reduced sixth player. (The newly founded Soviet Union, first enmeshed in a civil war and then in its internal reconstructions, was not yet interested and is not covered here.)

Yet while an international system containing five or six jealous Great Powers pointed to the coming of yet another competitive, multipolar era in world history after 1919, an unchecked naval arms race did not take place this time. As it happened, one new and great political factor also existed that curbed the navalists everywhere: the demand for *large-scale disarmament*. The unbridled enthusiasm for warships that characterized publics and politicians before World War I had been shattered by the horrid costs in blood and matériel thrown up by that conflict. In its place, there now existed an equally strong repugnance against all forms of militarism, nationalistic pride, the undue influence of bankers and weapons manufacturers, and, perhaps especially, arms races. If expensive rival construction plans on land and at sea had played a major role in triggering the war—and this was a widely asserted claim—then surely the best thing to prevent a repetition in the future would be to severely restrain defense expenditures. The monies thus saved could be used either to pay for much-needed social programs, war pensions, and the like or to pay down the truly alarming totals of national debt.

But to the economizers of the 1920s it was not enough to force generals, admirals, and air marshals to agree to reductions in defense totals alone, for cunning arms designers might find a way to step around purely financial limits. Neither was it enough, in considering naval restrictions, to push for some type of simple numerical ratio among, say, capital ships, along the lines of the abortive Anglo-German "naval holiday" talks before 1914. Instead, actual warship types—the first target because it was thought that fleet limitations were much easier to arrange and patrol than armies and air forces (battleships were large, easily visible things, after all)—would be ruthlessly cut back in both qualitative and quantitative ways. It would be the most purposeful arms reduction agreement in all of history, and its advocates were very proud of that fact.

The naval agreements concluded in Washington in 1921–22, which were enacted along with other international treaties concerning fleet bases and the preservation of the status quo in the Pacific / Far East, are easy to summarize here. The fact that admirals in all five navies felt so passionately that they had been betrayed by their own devious political leaders indicates that serious sacrifices were involved and that this cutback truly was unique and universal. There was, to begin with, a restriction placed on the overall tonnage of each country's capital ships: Britain and the United States were permitted up to 525,000 tons in battleships and up to 135,000 tons in carriers; Japan 315,000 and 81,000 tons, respectively; and France and Italy 175,000 and 60,000 tons. Then came the qualitative constraint. No battleship, apart from a few identified exceptions, should displace more than 35,000 tons or carry a main armament caliber of more than sixteen inches; no carrier should displace more than 27,000 tons overall. Not all smaller warship types had specific constraints immediately, though by the time the world had entered the 1930s, international treaties would have restraints on cruisers in both the heavy and light categories, on destroyers, and even on submarines.[4]

The mathematics of all this in terms of numbers of warships in the fleet was easy to see. If the upper size of capital ships was no more than 35,000 tons displacement, then the related constraint of an overall limit of 525,000 tons meant that Britain and the United States could only possess fifteen large battleships each, while Japan's total of 315,000 tons gave it nine such vessels. Both the Royal Navy and the US Navy therefore had to scrap a lot of older dreadnoughts and pre-dreadnoughts to get down to size, cancel ambitious building projects on the stocks, cut down the length of certain battleship designs (*Nelson*-class), and convert other large vessels into carriers (HMS *Courageous,* USS *Saratoga*). By the same token, an upper limit of 135,000 tons in carriers meant, effectively, only six such vessels for the British and American navies, with a mere four for Japan and three each for Italy and France.

The politicians of Washington imposed one further, and amazing, naval restriction on the Great Powers' battle fleets: in addition to certain ships getting scrapped or greatly modified, there was also to be a ten-year naval holiday before any of the existing heavy ships could be replaced. Later, at the 1930 London Naval Conference, this "freeze" was extended for another five years. Today's admirals, not to mention the military-industrial complexes that rely so heavily on government orders, would

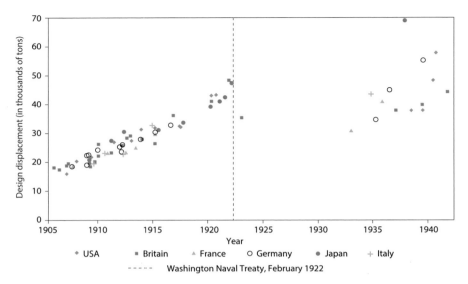

**CHART 2.** The battleship-building "gap" of the 1920s and early 1930s. Reproduced from Keating, "File: Battleship Building Scatter Graph 1905 Onwards. png," Wikimedia, last modified December 29, 2011, https://commons.wikimedia .org/wiki/File:Battleship_building_scatter_graph_1905_onwards.png.

be amazed at having to accept, in such a total form, a fifteen-year gap in major warship construction. But the political unpopularity of armaments firms (the "merchants of death") and the horror of having one's armed forces sucked into battle again could not be gainsaid. And, after all, both the British Army and the US Marine Corps were reduced to being small colonial police forces, so navies were *relatively* lucky, and many of them (except Japan) did not even build up to their full treaty allocations. Still, the overall result of this naval holiday was stunning and is well captured in the above "battleship-building scatter graph," where the contrast with the frenetic pre-1914 naval race could not be more marked (see chart 2).

Not all of these restrictions were upheld to the letter, although the breaches would not become clear until much later on. Generally, the American and British and French navies kept their newer, replacement craft within or slightly over treaty limits when fully laden, whereas warships of the revisionist states of Germany, Italy, and Japan were almost always in excess of tonnage limits, the Japanese heavy cruisers egregiously so. While this seemed to give them a clear advantage in one-on-one surface fighting over, say, the less protected British vessels, their evasion of the treaties turned out to benefit them much less during the 1939–45 campaigning than might have been thought, if only because torpedoes, mines, and hostile submarines and aircraft turned out to be far more lethal than the enemy's surface ships and simply knew no difference when it came to the tonnage size of, say, their cruiser targets.[5]

The London Naval Conference of 1930 tidied up some loose ends: there was a slight adjustment of the 5:5:3 ratio for heavy warships in Japan's favor, and a lengthy Anglo-American quarrel over the maximum size of light cruisers and cruiser totals overall was settled in Washington's favor. Restrictions were also imposed on the maximum displacement, gun caliber, and overall tonnage totals for destroyers and submarines, although with some exceptions because of French and Italian objections. The latter countries both opposed overall displacement totals for submarines and destroyers, since they saw in possession of large numbers of such vessels a sort of equalizer to the leading capital-ship navies. In general, also, France and Italy went for larger-sized (2,000 tons plus) destroyers, and so later would Nazi Germany. The results, again, were powerfully armed but top-heavy warships that tossed in all directions during very rough seas when sent out to fight.

There were other significant matters that naval staffs could not ignore but found more difficult to handle. While their fleets had been shaped by history and tradition, as explained earlier, they were also fashioned by their more current concerns: who would the likely enemy be, and how, consequently, did one prepare for that particular conflict? Even if the enemy was known with some certainty, what sort of war did you plan to pursue in order to defeat them, or at least avoid defeat? Did you intend to fight defensively, or aggressively? And with or without allies? Would your main enemy itself have allies and thus force a dilution of your naval assets? Even when you'd built your warships, how and where would you deploy them?

As we shall see, many of the naval setbacks and warship losses experienced by these belligerents in World War II were caused by misjudgments made in the interwar years. The Italian Navy desperately hoped it would be able to engage only the French fleet but not have to fight the Royal Navy in the Mediterranean. Grand Admiral Erich Raeder counted on Hitler's promise of war *not* happening in 1939 and was left with a half-built fleet. The Royal Navy's plans didn't of course envision the sudden fall of France; even worse, they underestimated the German U-boat threat, and they quite underestimated the Japanese Navy. Both American and Japanese battleship admirals looked forward to fighting a grand "second Jutland," this time in Pacific waters; neither foresaw how carrier-borne aircraft would cripple such ideas.

All these considerations, it should be borne in mind, had to be blended with the eternal challenges to warship designers concerning that quartet of desired attributes: speed, endurance, offensive power, and defensive strength. Every vessel design strove to possess all four characteristics, but they could not, logically, possess each in equally satisfactory measure. Was that any different from what history had taught? A multistory Spanish galleon boasted of great firepower, but it was a hopeless sailor in the wild gales of the Atlantic; and a Mediterranean galley might be swift and formidably crewed, but it could not withstand a volley of cannonballs. Such design trade-offs still remained in the 1920s.

And all these normal challenges to naval engineering and design now had to be forced into the iron corset of strict numerical and size controls dictated by the Washington and London treaties.

Moreover, ships' designers had to react to newer technologies, especially the rising power, speed, and range of aircraft. The years 1890–1918 had already thrown up many challenges to a surface warship's security, most noticeably in the form of the naval mine (Dardanelles) and torpedoes fired by submarines (Battle of the Atlantic), and now there was this new threat from the air, which admiralties (despite their own conservative admirals) could not dismiss. Should the secondary five-inch armament be replaced by newer multibarreled Bofors and Oerlikon guns? Wouldn't carriers have to be given both the power and range to keep up with the main fleet and be given decks lengthy enough to land faster and faster aircraft types? If so, should they be built from scratch or converted from existing battle cruisers? And since carriers themselves now became large, attractive targets for the enemy's own carrier and land-based aircraft and thus needed their own expensive defenses, should they be equipped with fighter-aircraft squadrons as well as torpedo planes and bombers? Finally, how could they ever be guarded from U-boats except by a screen of escorts? The consequence of all these ponderings was an ironic one: both battleships and aircraft carriers, being large and very expensive naval assets, needed in turn an expensive array of lesser warships and aircraft to protect them.[6]

Admiralty planners also faced the question of the timing of any later increases in the size of navies to comply with the treaties' rules. Scrapping a dozen warships might not take much time, but rebuilding a fleet was a different affair (as Admiral John Fisher used to lament before 1914, you cannot have a new battle squadron merely by the passing of a Supplementary Estimate). Such was the design and building time required for large warships that governments had to order weapons systems that would need five to six years to achieve entry into full high-seas service, which is why contemporary observers and also later scholars thought the additional five-year freeze imposed by the London Treaty was a disaster. As the planners waited and waited for that treaty's validity to end, they tinkered with gun sizes, displacement sizes, and engine types. The re-armament programs of the late 1930s were for all navies a mad dash to make amends, to catch up. So many of the fighting warships that feature prominently in the following chapters—for example, *Essex*-class carriers and *King George V*–class battleships—were not to join their fleets until well into the war even though they had been authorized in, say, late 1930s estimates.

## The Warships of the Age

Although every fleet contained one or two hybrids or oddities, by the 1920s there were five major warship types (battleships, carriers, cruisers, destroyers, and submarines), so that a country's relative naval power could be easily understood (see table 1).

The battleship, that direct descendant in the industrial age of Nelson's original line-of-battle ship, remained at the center of all interwar navies. While severely affected by the Washington and London treaty limitations, its actual design stayed much the same, being less shaped by new technologies than other warship types were. By the eve of World War I, the basic features of the *Dreadnought*-type battleship were already in place: a heavy armament (12-inch to 16-inch) of uniform caliber with smaller guns for close-in fire, under unified direction control; a wraparound armored belt, particularly protecting the magazines and other vital parts; usually a turbine-engine propulsion system, which produced immense horsepower; and a fuel-fired energy source. With this rough uniformity, it was possible to lay down warships in classes, so that coherent squadrons could be formed.[7]

**TABLE 1.** List of Warships of the Leading Navies in 1939

| Type | Great Britain | United States | Japan | France | Italy | Germany |
|------|------|------|------|------|------|------|
| Capital ships | 15 | 15 | 9 | 7 | 4 | 5 |
| Aircraft carriers | 6 | 5 | 5 | 1 | — | — |
| Heavy cruisers | 15 | 18 | 12 | 7 | 7 | 2 |
| Other cruisers | 49 | 17 | 27 | 12 | 14 | 6 |
| Destroyers | 179 | 215 | 112 | 59 | 61 | 22 |
| Submarines | 57 | 87 | 59 | 78 | 106 | 65 |

Data from "Naval Strength of the Leading Powers, September 1939 (Completed Ships Only)," in *Jane's Fighting Ships 1939*, xiii.

Battleship designers thus followed the aim of providing their vessels with the necessary firepower, protection, speed, and range, sometimes making last-minute changes at the news of what other navies were doing to advance their latest types. After the 1906 arrival of the *Dreadnought* set a new standard, battleships increased incrementally rather than fundamentally in the years before and during World War I. The larger gun calibers, higher speeds, and greater displacement size obviously led to far greater expenditures; some traditional shipyards became too small to build the new 700- to 800-foot-long vessels; and naval workforces everywhere multiplied in size. All this interacted with the many political and territorial rivalries among the Great Powers, creating the famous pre-1914 "naval races." And although the American and Japanese battle fleets also expanded swiftly in the pre-1914 period, the maritime center of gravity remained firmly Eurocentric. This inadvertently produced one truly significant consequence: future battles were expected to occur only a few hundred miles or so from the European coast or at least their bases, so virtually all European heavy warships were relatively short-ranged in their endurance and would remain so into World War II itself, a fact exposed during the chase and sinking of the *Bismarck* in 1941 and in the later difficulty British and French battleships had maintaining long-distance Pacific operations.

The story of larger guns leading to a larger length/beam and thus to a greater displacement and thus to a continual upward spiral in warship size obviously came to a halt with the advent of the drastic Washington Treaty regulations, detailed earlier. Various battleship-building plans were abandoned, while certain ships found their eventual size and speed much different from their first design specifics. Perhaps the best-known example here of a heavy-warship design altered by treaty can be seen in the shape of Britain's only two 16-inch-gunned battleships of the Washington era, HMS *Nelson* and HMS *Rodney*.

One can observe from painting 5 how altered the *Rodney* and *Nelson* were to fit the terms of the Washington Treaty—putting the three main 16-inch turrets forward saved a significant amount of weight, but those design changes took so long to effect that *Rodney* was not completed until 1927, a rare example of a heavy warship being launched during the "holiday" period. For many years it was the mainstay of the Home Fleet, and when war came it had a remarkable campaign career (Norway, Bismarck chase, Malta convoys, Sicily and Italy, and D-Day bombardments). It steamed 160,000 nautical miles during the war—perhaps a heavy-warship record—and surely repaid its original builder's cost of £7.6 million many times over. Back in the 1920s, though, it seemed a very expensive vessel.

There was one other notable feature about these battleships of the

World War I era and of those completed in the early 1920s: most of them were *slow,* with top speeds ranging from 20 to 25 knots. High-speed turbine engines were hugely expensive in any case, and heavy armor protection greatly added to a ship's weight, of course. In the case of the *Nelson*-class, the British Admiralty sacrificed speed for firepower and protection. It could not have caught the Bismarck had the latter not been crippled by torpedoes, and it would always be left behind by the faster Italian battleships. And, like the other older British capital ships, it remained at home when the Royal Navy sent a force of fast battleships and carriers to the Pacific for the final year of the war against Japan.

Although they could not build new battleships during the fifteen-year Washington hiatus, most navies were able to take in hand the best of their World War I capital ships and modernize them substantially while avoiding pushing the vessel's overall displacement over treaty limits. The US Navy did this for most of its battleships, the Italians did it for their four smaller battleships in the *Cavour*-class, the French for the *Bretagne*-class, and the Japanese for all of theirs.[8] The wartime USS *Texas,* shown at the beginning of this chapter, was heavily rebuilt in 1925–26, with new boilers, new masts, and better secondary gunnery, and it also was to have an outstanding campaign record during World War II. Perhaps the most successful example here was the British Admiralty's rebuilding of the five 15-inch-gunned *Queen Elizabeth*–class "fast battleships" of 1913–15, turning them into modern-looking vessels, as painting 6 suggests, although their speed (around 23 knots/25 mph) was not so great.

As with many other battleships, the heavy artillery here was arranged into eight main 15-inch guns in four centerline turrets, two being superimposed. This provided excellent fields of fire and avoided some of the mechanical complications of multiple mounting. The *Bismarck* and *Tirpitz* battleships had a similar layout, as did the Japanese *Nagato*-class vessels and the classic *Colorado*-class US battleships (albeit with eight 16-inch guns). The main alternative gunnery layout would be to equip a battleship with nine heavy guns arrayed in three triple turrets, two forward, one aft. There was really nothing quite like these dreadnoughts in regard to mobile, intimidating gunpower. A battleship fired a greater round of shells than an artillery division and could do so while moving at 15 or 20 knots! One of the *Rodney*'s salvos ripped away the front turret from the immobilized *Bismarck;* three years later, off the Normandy beaches, another of its salvos hurled German tanks into the air while they were more than ten miles inland. A month later, the USS *Texas,* engaged in the same D-Day bombardments and crushed the German fortifications at Cherbourg; the following spring it was blasting at Japanese positions on Iwo Jima and Okinawa. It is interesting to note that all of the older American and

**PAINTING 5.** HMS *Rodney* passing under the Firth of Forth bridge, 1942. HMS *Rodney* and HMS *Nelson* were the only two 16-inch-gunned battleships in the Royal Navy, their turrets all located forward so as to keep the ships within Washington Treaty tonnage limits. Its incredible battle career began with actions off Norway and included sinking the *Bismarck,* participating in the Malta convoys, and covering the Sicily and Normandy landings.

I. H. M.

PAINTING 6.  HMS *Queen Elizabeth*, Grand Harbour, Malta, 1936. Like so many of the other British, French, Italian, Japanese, and American battleships of the WW1 era, she was greatly modernized between the wars. Repeatedly taking part in Mediterranean actions, she was sunk while in the Alexandria harbor, raised again, and ended the war bombarding Japanese positions in Southeast Asia.

British battleships settled comfortably into this role of supporting troop landings, and their fire was deemed to be much more accurate than that of the faster, modern battleships that occasionally joined in bombardments before rushing off to another mission.

The same pattern of providing "upgrades" during the Washington and London Treaty years was also true of the various battle cruiser classes in these navies. In Japan, for example, the four *Kongo*-class fast battle cruisers (the *Kongo* itself, ironically, having been built in Britain back in 1913) received not one but two significant upgrades during the 1930s and proved themselves to be formidable fighting ships throughout the Pacific War. They were not large ships, however, displacing only 23,000–26,000 tons for their 14-inch guns. Similar-sized and repeatedly redesigned French battle cruisers (the 13-inch *Dunkerques*), German 11-inch-gunned battle cruisers (*Scharnhorst*) and pocket battleships (*Deutschland*-class), and the Italian *Andrea Doria* (12-inch guns, 21 knots, 26,000 tons) were much less impressive than the Japanese vessels. Without exception, they failed at least one if not more of the necessary requirements of ample firepower, protection, speed, and endurance.[9] The *Scharnhorst*'s rapid destruction by the battleship HMS *Duke of York* in December 1943 is a good example of the price that these "demi-" battleships paid; against 14-inch radar-controlled gunnery, the German 11-inch-gunned vessels had no chance. Even the full-size (15-inch-gunned) British battle cruiser HMS *Hood* proved to be too thinly armored against the plunging fire of the *Bismarck*.

Every admiralty, really, was waiting for the treaty limitations to be denounced—Japan and France would certainly not tolerate restrictions after 1936, when the London Treaty expired—in order to advance to much more powerful heavy warships. Still, the fact was that few nations possessed the full resources, including large enough construction bays, to lay down the super-battleships of the navalists' dreams. To be sure, the new classes of fast, modern battleships that joined the fighting after the war began—the five British *King George V*–class vessels (35,000 tons plus), the German twins *Bismarck* (40,000 tons at least) and *Tirpitz*, and the Italian *Littorio*-class quartet (40,000 tons) were decidedly more satisfying to their naval commands than treaty battleships. But one would probably have to go to the very last of the Japanese and American World War II super-battleships to witness the apotheosis of these sacred vessels.[10] The *Yamato* and *Musashi*, described in chapter 8, were utter behemoths, extreme examples of what had begun almost forty years ago as Admiral Fisher's "dreadnought gamble." Yet neither giant ship had a chance against massed aerial attacks.

The second most powerful category of gunned armored warships, the cruiser, was also brought under treaty limitations at Washington and again (and very contentiously) at the London talks in 1930. This type of vessel, the descendant of Nelson's frigates via many design routes, was not strong enough to stand in the line of battleships but, being swifter, was ideal for reconnaissance, gunboat diplomacy, protection of trade, and, conversely, raids on enemy merchant shipping. Cruisers divided into various classes, with geography and history once again determining admiralty choice. Britain, with its extensive transoceanic trade routes and half of the world's merchant shipping, needed lots of lighter cruisers, with protection being sacrificed for endurance. Most other navies, expecting to fight closer to home and perhaps in conjunction with their battle fleets, preferred heavier cruisers with larger armaments, more protection, and less range. While it was impossible for Britain, the United States, and Japan to agree on an overall tonnage total (and therefore numbers) for cruisers at Washington, they were able to agree on an upper limit of 10,000 tons displacement and a maximum 8-inch caliber for the main armament of the heaviest cruisers. The negotiators also agreed that the class called "light cruisers" should carry not more than 6.1-inch guns, although in practice many navies chose lesser calibers (5-inch, 5.5-inch, or 6-inch) for their guns, which they placed in various numbers and gun-turret layouts.[11]

It is not hard to have a certain sympathy for a country's warship designers during this time as they sought to create the optimal heavy cruiser under all of these contending demands. Their basic armament of 8-inch guns, plus lesser armaments, plus the fire-control towers, plus crew space and storage space, and finally, plus the boiler and engine rooms already ensured that a ship's displacement target of 10,000 tons would be filled, with the cruiser's weight distributed over a hull size roughly six hundred feet in length and fifty-five feet in breadth. But more difficult decisions remained. Should it have turbine engines for speed, or diesel for range? Should it build fuel tanks for an endurance of just four thousand miles (at steady speed) or create more space for a range of twelve thousand miles? Should it protect the upper levels from horizontal fire and its decks and turret tops from vertical fire, even if that increased the superstructure tonnage and made the vessel top-heavy in North Atlantic storms? Each choice brought disadvantages as well as hoped-for benefits.

Thus, the Royal Navy's urge for endurance and economy showed up well in the design of their classic *County*-class cruisers, 8-inch-gunned warships set with four twin turrets and possessing an enormous cruising range. With its long, flush sidelines and its low-slung superstructure, a craft such as the HMS *Dorsetshire* carried this simplicity to perfection.

Since the British planners' main concern had been to assure the future safety of the Empire's worldwide shipping routes from enemy raid-

**PAINTING 7. HMS *Dorsetshire*, Simonstown Bay, South Africa.** Here the sweeping lines of the classic 8-inch-gunned *County*-class cruisers can be seen. She was involved in many actions in the Atlantic, including torpedoing the stricken *Bismarck,* but a year later was sunk by a massed Japanese carrier air attack in April 1942. Simonstown was the chief (and very safe) Royal Navy base for southern ocean waters.

ers, its 1920s construction program included fifteen such large cruisers. As scouts, their reach was enhanced by carrying seaplanes, and as combatants, their main armament was indeed the 8-inch gun, to match the largest of likely hostile cruisers. The foremost considerations were speed, endurance, seaworthiness, and habitability for long periods at sea. In addition, the high freeboard hull endowed *County*-class cruisers with structural rigidity and made a steady gun platform in heavy seas. This advantage was shown to great effect in May 1941 when the *Dorsetshire,* leaving a convoy in mid-Atlantic, had the range to join its fellow cruiser *Norfolk* in shadowing the *Bismarck,* joined in the general firing when the German battleship was immobilized, and then dispatched torpedoes into the hull of the hapless vessel to finish it off. Yet the *County*-class's light-armored protection—only the magazines had solid "box" armor around them—meant that these ships were extremely vulnerable to aerial assaults. When the *Dorsetshire* left Simonstown (as in painting 7) to join the Eastern Fleet in early 1942, it and its sister ship HMS *Cornwall* came under severe and repeated attack from dive-bombers from Japanese carriers, and both cruisers were swiftly sunk, with heavy loss of life south of Ceylon as they sought, in vain, to get out of range. The lessons of Norway and Crete—without adequate air cover, warships were doomed—were reaffirmed here.

One might make an extreme contrast between the low, slim lines of the *Counties* and the powerful, initially impressive and muscular shape of those heavy cruisers built about ten years later by the Germans, such as the *Prinz Eugen,* or the Japanese heavy cruisers of the *Mogami* class. The latter two both stood much taller out of the water because of their massive superstructures; unsurprisingly, they also had a displacement at full load of 15,000 tons, far above those of the treaty cruisers. In fair weather, they both could probably overpower a *County*-class ship, although their top-heaviness in stormy waters would hurt them. The same was to be true of the heavy cruisers of Mussolini's navy, those elegant vessels of the *Zara*-class like the *Fiume,* which were also well over treaty displacement totals.

Geography had forced other considerations on Italian designers here. With a long, extended coastline on both sides of the country and trade lines to Italy's colonies in Africa, the Regia Marina had the unenviable task of defending them all. Worried about direct shootouts with the better-trained Royal Navy, the Italian aim was to seek action only under favorable circumstances. This explains their key performance characteristics, such as faster speed and 8-inch guns modified to shoot at greater ranges than could the *County*-class vessels—if their foe pressed toward them, they would move off at high speed. They also carried much more protection, with 6-inch armored belts and 3-inch decks, so when these vessels, with their handsome superstructures, appeared from the early 1930s onward, they received very favorable comments—except from the German naval representatives in Italy, who privately thought them to be only "fair-weather warships."[12] It did not help that these warships, like the rest of Mussolini's navy, had very little gunnery practice, and none at night.

In all, as these remarks suggest, cruisers turned in a mixed performance during World War II. The large German vessels were picked off, one by

one—the *Blücher* by Norwegian shoreline guns and torpedo batteries off
Oslo as it attempted to land troops during the invasion of April 1940 and
the remainder, later based in Norwegian or home waters, steadily obliterated by RAF Bomber Command. (In other words, no German cruisers
were destroyed by *other* cruisers or by any enemy warships.) As we have
noted, the Italian cruisers were cramped, physically and psychologically,
and many were to be sunk in nighttime battles with the Royal Navy. Individual Japanese and American cruisers fought well in individual encounters (with the Japanese getting the better of it) all the way to the confused
Leyte Gulf battles of 1944, but otherwise the Pacific War was not so suited
for this class of warship. There were no convoy routes to contest, and US
cruisers, along with the older battleships, steadily became used as preinvasion bombardment vessels and/or antiaircraft protectors of American
carriers. Only the British cruisers, heavy and light, seemed to have fulfilled all the envisaged roles, from assisting in major surface battles (*Graf
Spee, Bismarck* chase, *Scharnhorst,* Matapan) to being continually deployed in the defense of trade from the Gibraltar routes to the Arctic convoys. The losses in these heavy cruisers—HMSs *Exeter, York, Canberra,
Dorsetshire,* and *Cornwall*—were correspondingly high, and those in light
cruisers were even greater.

   Ten years after Washington, the arms negotiators sought to get a grip
on warships *smaller* than light cruisers in armament or displacement. It
was of course agreed that there were simply too many minor actors, perhaps thousands of them across the world—sloops, corvettes, patrol boats,
landing ships, monitors, minesweepers, torpedo boats, and others—to do
much about them. On the other hand, World War I had already suggested
that destroyers were too important, too lethal, for consideration not to
be given to restrictions on their numbers, size, and striking power. This
ship's origin was as a protector of one's own battleships against enemy
torpedo boats, but the larger ones were then equipped with their own torpedoes for attacks on surface warships, guns fore and aft as standard armament, and, finally, with depth charges for attacks on U-boats. By 1919,
therefore, the destroyer was already a small general-purpose fighting ship,
with the larger ones (fleet destroyers) being given great speed so as to be
able to keep up with battleships and carriers. In anticipation of the newer
fast battleships and carriers, their size and power—and expense—would
increase by leaps and bounds as World War II approached, but most navies entered the conflict with many of their destroyer flotillas of an earlier age.

   The restrictions of the Washington and London treaties regarding their
destroyers were indicative of the different positions of the Powers. There
were limits on total destroyer tonnages only for the British, American,

and Japanese navies (the French and Italians refused to join). And, with a few exceptions made at the London Naval Conference, destroyers were limited in their displacement to 1,850 tons and in gun size to a 5.1-inch caliber, yet again this applied only to the three largest navies. Although such limits would be cast aside when many admiralties—Japanese, French, Italian, and German—laid down the super-destroyer classes in the late 1930s that were almost the size of light cruisers, one senses again and again that some of them became too overloaded, too muscular. While British fleet destroyers were lower slung and displaced less (the famous *Tribal*-class were about 1,800 tons, the superb American *Fletcher*-class about 2,100 tons), the reason was that Admiralty and US Navy designers sought to produce a type that was a really good sailer in all oceans and could therefore go after an enemy battleship in the heaviest sea.[13] German vessels armed with 5.9-inch guns looked intimidating, but that almost guaranteed that they would tip and yaw in North Atlantic waters.[14]

All the powers ended up, as table 1 shows, with considerable numbers of destroyers completed by 1939: the US Navy with 215, the Royal Navy with 179, Japan with 112, France with 59, Italy with 61, and Germany with 22; in Raeder's view, of course, this was far, far too few. Yet every admiralty complained incessantly about not having enough numbers, and given all the demands that would be made on "the workhorses of the fleet," they were all right. As Nelson had put it in a different era, there could never be enough frigates when fighting a great war.

What was lacking in the obsession to have big destroyers fast enough to keep up with the battle fleet and launch mass torpedo attacks on the enemy's battleships was consideration for building smaller, slower destroyers that would escort merchantmen and conduct searches for enemy submarines; the vessels that, later on, the American Navy would term "destroyer escorts," the Royal Navy frigates and sloops. Again, the British Admiralty, with its smaller destroyer types, was something of an exception here. Yet there was some method in the prioritization of the bigger boats. Since it took five to six years to complete a new fast battleship and perhaps two years for a heavy cruiser, when the end of the Washington and London Treaty restrictions at last allowed a great surge in warship building after 1936, it made a lot more sense to devote a nation's resources (for example, steel, wiring, gun shops, and shipyard workers) to the larger projects, including fleet destroyers. The smaller vessels really could be built in a hurry—when the British Admiralty switched to its immediate war needs program as late as July 1939, it started ordering dozens and then hundreds of the famous *Flower*-class corvettes; in less than a year the first ones were headed out to sea, underarmed and underpowered yet a vital stopgap measure.[15]

**PAINTING 8.** *Flower*-class Corvette HMS *Pink* in heavy seas, 1943. The British Admiralty put in a rush order for hundreds of these small escorts when war broke out; they performed vital duties until the larger sloops (see painting 47) came along. HMS *Pink* played a heroic role in Convoy ONS-5 in May 1943.

Submarine development and policy in the interwar years is a different story again. Here was another disruptive and alarming weapon offering a form of "asymmetric warfare," in this case a smaller-sized item of technology that could destroy a huge battleship and was an ideal tool for a medium-sized naval power to contest the sea routes, as the U-boats had well shown in 1917. Unsurprisingly, then, the British government would have welcomed the total abolition of submarines at the Washington Conference—it had already managed to compel the defeated Germans to give them up—but the French and Italians absolutely refused to accept proposals to restrict the number of U-boats, through which they hoped to rectify their disadvantage in larger warships. At the London Naval Conference, however, submarines were limited to maximum displacement of 2,000 tons and a gun size of 5.1 inches, and there was a maximum tonnage limit on submarine fleets for the first time. Still, it was going to be very hard for naval intelligence departments to estimate the effectiveness of other countries' submarine fleets in these years of peace. Many navies had laid down class after class of U-boats in very small batches, as if experimenting with the designs—Italy's impressive total of 104 submarines by 1939 turns out, on inspection of the data collected in *Jane's Fighting Ships,* to be composed of no fewer than nineteen (!) different classes built and six more classes being constructed. No one knew what the reported Soviet total of "approximately 130" boats really meant. Of Germany's total, 32 were in fact "coastal types" of 300 tons displacement and little range; Vice Admiral Karl Doenitz had only a very few Type VII vessels by 1939. The French Navy had a full thirty submarines of the impressive *Redoutable-*class, which were large, fast, and had great range, but wasn't quite sure of their function—probably to scout for the surface fleet. Japan had large numbers (59) but didn't think submarines were commerce raiders; America had even more (87), but as it turned out, they had hopeless torpedoes, even worse than the German ones. No one seemed to know about the extraordinary range and power of the Japanese 23-inch "Long Lance" torpedoes that were also given to the Imperial Japanese Navy's (IJN) submarines. No one knew how submarines would fare on the surface as naval air patrols and Coastal Command airpower developed. It was an odd fact that the Royal Navy had the smallest submarine fleet (57), but it may actually have had the most useful bunch.[16]

When one thinks of those lengthy periods of naval history where there was a relative stability and consistency in warships' design—the whole eighteenth century, for example—it is not hard, then, to have some sympathy for naval designers of the turbulent first four decades of the twentieth century. The age had begun with the launch of the fabulous HMS *Dreadnought,* whose far larger displacement, all-big-gun armament, steel armor, and turbine propulsion seemed to make these new battleships the apotheosis of sea power for the foreseeable future. Thus, a navy's relative strength was always to be measured in terms of how many dreadnought and pre-dreadnought battleships it possessed, and it was quite simple to move on to advanced dreadnought types like the *Queen Elizabeth*–class. So it was a cruel historical irony that just as Admiral Fisher's great battleship design came to the fore, a whole number of truly revolutionary technologies also emerged that were far smaller in size and less expensive to build—for example, torpedoes, submarines, naval mines, and, later, the bomber—yet could challenge the capital ship's security.[17]

Then there was that other potentially transformative weapons system: the aircraft carrier. The first airplane had only flown in 1903, and the first very primitive carriers for naval missions were just appearing in the last year of World War I—at that stage they were small and not close to the tonnage limitations imposed in 1921–22. These were, literally, flattops, like the original HMS *Argus* or its American equivalent, the USS *Langley,* shown in painting 9. Their aircraft had a fixed undercarriage so they could take off and land on the deck, making them wholly different from float aircraft that existing seaplane tenders lifted in and out of the water. Also, for the first time ever, the planes could be stowed, via an elevator, on a lower deck. No independent operations were envisaged for them at this time; rather, the aircraft could be used for long-range scouting, as the carrier was seen as an auxiliary to the battle fleet.

As painting 9 suggests, the USS *Langley* was built on top of a different ship, a very large coal carrier (HMS *Argus,* for its part, was built on top of a small ocean liner). Thus, these early carriers looked ramshackle and were clearly experimental vessels. When the war ended their chief role was to assist in training the first and second generations of American naval pilots, mainly spotter pilots, although there was some early practice with the dropping of small bombs. They also operated as testing beds for advances in carrier design and for working out the complications of arrestor cables and launch pads; and the first-ever catapult launches took place off the *Langley*'s decks. By the late 1930s it was with the Pacific Fleet but redesigned as a mere airplane tender, and when war broke out, it found itself carrying reinforcement aircraft for the ABDA (American-British-Dutch-Australian) Command. While engaged in such duties it was found and sunk in February 1942 by waves of dive-bombers of the superefficient Japanese Naval Air Command—a cruel irony for such a pioneer in naval aviation history.[18]

The next stage in aircraft carrier development was to create far longer flight decks for planes by drastically converting certain British, Japanese, and US battle cruisers that would have needed to be scrapped under the

**PAINTING 9.** USS *Langley,* Hampton Roads, 1924.
The early small carriers like *Langley* trained generations
of US naval airmen—less than two decades before the
great fleet carriers of World War II.

I. H. M.

**PAINTING 10.** USSs *Saratoga* and *Lexington,* Puget Sound, 1936. The largest carriers in the world (converted battle cruisers), they were very fast and could carry up to ninety planes. While the *Lexington* was lost at the Battle of the Coral Sea, the *Saratoga* fought throughout the war.

new Washington Treaty requirements, when capital-ship numbers had to be trimmed. The Royal Navy did this with the HMSs *Glorious, Courageous,* and *Furious,* the Japanese Navy with the *Akagi,* and the US Navy with the *Lexington* and the *Saratoga,* both enormous battle cruisers.

This pair were extremely large vessels, 880 feet long, and with enormous machinery; both could reach 33 knots and had an operating range of ten thousand miles, and they kept the guns of an 8-inch heavy cruiser! Intended by ambitious American planners to be the world's largest-ever battle cruisers and faster than any other warships afloat, save perhaps HMS *Hood,* they ended up as the sort of super-carriers of their era. They could operate more than eighty aircraft, an amazingly high number. Both warships spent their careers almost entirely in the Pacific, where in prewar exercises they played a leading role in evolving the whole technique of US naval air operations. As is well known, they were providentially absent from Pearl Harbor at the time of the Japanese attack—and made history because of that.

It is not hard to see in this illustration an early example of the notion of *clustering* carriers so that their aircrafts' combined force would be of great hitting power and thus quite decisive. Indeed, already in the decade before the war, this became the doctrine of both the US and Japanese carrier fleets. This idea of carriers operating without battleships and by implication becoming strike forces in their own right was of course resisted by the more traditional admirals in all navies, even as the size of this branch of the service was steadily growing.[19]

Since the Japanese Navy, even with its new fleet carriers of the 1930s, kept to a completely flattop design, it was only with the completion in 1938 of the American carriers USSs *Yorktown* and *Enterprise* and the British carrier HMS *Ark Royal* that the classic shape of this warship type appeared. In less than two decades, then, a new and completely game-changing sort of major vessel had arisen. In the entire history of the evolution of ship types, that was an astonishingly swift transformation.

While the only one in its class, the *Ark Royal* was going to be the Royal Navy's prototype for the six *Illustrious*-class fleet carriers, which were laid down before the war but not completed until 1940–43. It was not a fully armored ship, but its flight deck was of 1-inch steel. It formed the upper strength component of the hull, which incorporated a lower armored deck, belt armor alongside the vitals, and extensive underwater subdivision against torpedoes. Trading protection for striking power, British carrier designs had much more armor plate than their Japanese and US equivalents but correspondingly fewer aircraft—the *Ark Royal* carried only about sixty planes, the USS *Yorktown* around ninety, and the *Akagi* sixty-six plus reserves. One further and critical distinction here is that both the American and Japanese navies could independently procure their own planes, whereas the unhappy Fleet Air Arm could not.[20]

Regardless of the disdain of the more traditional service officers, it was becoming clear by the end of the 1930s that governments and admiralties both viewed carriers and their striking capacity as having a deterrent effect and therefore as important strategic chess pieces. Thus, as the setting of the Grand Harbour of Malta in painting 11 suggests, by basing this and other carriers there, London was signaling that there was a new type of guarantor of Britain's imperial sea-lanes, and that here was a warning to Mussolini's navy. The same message was intended with America's decision to move a considerable part of its carrier fleet from the West Coast to Pearl Harbor.

But if aircraft carriers posed a new threat, it was also true that they and all surface warships were in turn threatened by the swift evolution of land-based airpower. The years from roughly 1930 to 1940 saw the engine power, speed, carrying capacity, and range of all planes, including the modern two-engined and four-engined bomber aircraft, greatly increase. So while it was true that the striking power and reach of the newer Japanese, American, and British carriers rose greatly, so too did the nascent threat to their entire navies from other aircraft (from Stuka dive-bombers to the later high-level B-17s), which represented a completely new factor. The result was to pare back the advantage of the larger naval powers. Thus, even if the combined Anglo-French surface fleets stood in great superiority over those of their likely enemies in European waters in 1939, what did that mean if hostile land-based airpower could threaten their security and their maritime effectiveness up to one hundred or more miles off the coast? Who really would command the Mediterranean, or the North Sea? What did it mean in the Pacific and in Southeast Asia if numerous Japanese land-based air flotillas threatened the Allied maritime control of the Philippines, Hong Kong, and Singapore? Was naval power going to be enough?

## The Navies of the Six Powers in 1939

How did each of these six nations fare, in their efforts to be secure at sea? It is clear that, while striving to create the most appropriate mix of warship types to meet that aim, the admirals of *La Royale*—the French Navy—had found themselves far more constrained than their equivalents in Washington, Tokyo, and London. The astronomical losses of capital, material,

**PAINTING 11.** HMS *Ark Royal*, Grand Harbour, Malta, 1938. The Royal Navy's most famous fleet carrier, seen here as it is towed out of the historic Grand Harbour of Malta shortly before the war's outbreak. This warship achieved great battle distinction in Atlantic operations, the destruction of the *Bismarck*, and Malta convoys before it was sunk by *U-81* in November 1941.

and human life caused by the Great War made large-scale spending on new and increasingly expensive vessels seem out of the question; as it was, the anemic French economy went into another downspin in the mid-1930s just as those of rival powers were improving. The diplomatic agreements of the preceding decade (the Versailles, Washington, Locarno, and Dawes and Young plans) had locked the world into an uneasy truce and made arms spending impossible and improper. Yet when that international house of cards swiftly collapsed during the years following, the nightmarish rise of a manic and militarized German dictatorship meant that a heavy proportion of the inadequate sums France could afford for defense had to go toward its army and its air force. What was left available for naval spending had to be allocated toward warships, personnel, and modern bases that would answer the country's most immediate strategic demands. A huge battleship-building program was therefore out of the question, but France did seek to upgrade its older treaty capital ships and to launch two modern battle cruisers; and a lot was allocated to fast cruisers (19), large destroyers (78), and many (86) submarines rather than to aircraft carriers (only 1).

The specific shape of the European diplomatic scene after 1935 also conditioned France's naval posture. More and more, its maritime assessments during the late 1930s operated within a strategic quartet—Paris, Berlin, Rome, and London—that was, in its way, a classical example of "navies in multipolar worlds."[21] The German dimension, as noted, loomed larger than anything else simply because the growing Nazi threat was an existential one—and assumed to most likely be another catastrophic land attack (like those of 1870 and 1914), joined now by heavy aerial assaults from the Luftwaffe. Still, the rise of Hitler's Kriegsmarine—especially in the form of the long-range, commerce-raiding pocket battleships of the *Admiral Scheer*–class, backed by the later *Scharnhorst*-class battle cruisers—did concern naval planners in Paris, hence the construction of their own, larger *Dunkerque*-class battle cruisers. The greater part of their attention, however, went southward, toward the far larger danger posed by the Italian Navy's 8-inch-gunned cruisers, destroyer flotillas, scores of submarines, and, in the background, its newer battleships. Thus the navies of France and Italy went into a separate naval race of their own. Had they actually entered a one-on-one war in the Mediterranean in 1939, it would have been interesting to see what the result would have been—after all, they had been accorded equal tonnage at the Washington Naval Treaty; they had both roughly built up and modernized to size; neither had special warfare advantages (for example, radar, aircraft carriers, night-fighting competence, and Ultra); and each was haphazardly supported by an air force and air bases on either side of the Mediterranean. Neither had yet received any newer battleships in 1939. While the French Navy felt it was superior, and probably was, the result of a Franco-Italian naval struggle would most likely have been inconclusive for quite a while, until the weaker Italian economy buckled.

Italy's chances would have been far greater, of course, had France also had to fight against Germany, which was what the Rome-Berlin axis was very much about. Yet as war approached in 1939, the idea of a separate Franco-Italian fight, or the prospect that France would be standing alone against Italy and Germany, if that was ever a worry, had withered away. London and Paris would fight together. Great Britain itself, and more specifically the Royal Navy, thus constituted a huge reinforcement to France's naval position, both against the Kriegsmarine and, if necessary, against the Regia Marina. There was no way a German surface force could push down the English Channel and attack the French coast in these circumstances, while the possible future threat posed by German commerce raiding in the Atlantic and beyond could only be episodic, to be countered by Anglo-French searching groups. Meanwhile, Mussolini's navy, should it go to war, would be relatively easily checked by the French fleet in the western Mediterranean and the British in the eastern Mediterranean (and at Malta).

In 1939, therefore, the Regia Marina was strong, but not strong enough. It had only four modernized battleships (the *Littorio*-class vessels would begin coming during the next year) and had never been permitted a carrier. Like France, it was more impressive in other regards, possessing around 20 heavy and light cruisers, almost 60 destroyers, around 60 very dangerous large torpedo boats, and an enormous fleet of 106 submarines, with naval bases (and air bases) along the Italian coastline, in Sardinia, and in North Africa. This was clearly not enough, though, and Italy's disadvantages did not stop there. Its likely foes, especially those British naval forces in the Mediterranean, enjoyed technological and operational benefits that would compensate for any apparent smaller numbers. By 1940, the British had the inestimable boon of shipborne radar. And the code breakers at Bletchley Park often permitted British admirals to know of Italian fleet movements. The Royal Navy forces always included an aircraft carrier, sometimes two; even before the war broke out, each side knew that that would be a huge bonus. British warships were training for night fighting, something the Italian squadrons lacked; and, overall, the former's warships had much more battle practice. Had Italy possessed a large and modern naval air service (like Japan's), things might have been very different; but it did not. Had those 106 submarines really been top-notch operationally, that also might have tipped the balances; but they were not. The Italian Navy did pay a lot of attention to antisubmarine warfare, as British submarine losses in the Battle of the Mediterranean would testify, but again, that was not enough.[22]

Every nation's admiralties (except Japan's) cursed the fact that the fighting came before the arrival of their newer post–"Washington naval holiday" battleships—their *Littorios, Richelieus, King George Vs,* and *North Carolinas*—regardless of the fact that the other navies had been similarly disadvantaged. All suffered from the awkward fact that these newer classes of capital ship, larger and much more sophisticated than their World War I predecessors, took years to be built by shipyards that themselves usually needed modernization. And the navy least ready for war when Hitler attacked Poland in September 1939 was, ironically, the Reichsmarine itself, under the direction of the resourceful if pessimistic Raeder. There were no fast battleships in sight yet—the *Bismarck* would not be ready until mid-1941—but the two new *Scharnhorst*-class battle cruisers were almost ready for service, and the three ingeniously designed pocket battleships (*Deutschland*-class) were poised for the Atlantic. Germany's two new heavy cruisers, six light cruisers, and twenty-two large, fast destroyers were all impressive, just simply too few. The much-vaunted Plan Z program for a truly North Atlantic fleet (ten battleships, half a dozen carriers, and so on) was years away, and made impossible by the early coming of war. There remained Doenitz's small yet promising fleet of around 25 U-boats, again too small to be of real strategic import, just dangerous.

In retrospect, one might wonder whether the German Navy would have achieved more if the material and personnel resources devoted to battleships, battle cruisers, and heavy cruisers had been allocated instead to the construction of massed flotillas of destroyers, E-boats, and especially U-boats (including accelerated production of the more revolutionary types).[23] Of course this would have been a huge morale blow to its surface-officer corps, but the fact is that the only time the Kriegsmarine approached being "strategic" during World War II was in 1942 and 1943, when its U-boats were sufficiently large in number to ravage the Atlantic convoys. But three years earlier, as Doenitz readily admitted, the size of the German submarine fleet was too little, the boats were too small, and the geographical limitations—hemmed in by the North Sea—made sustained operations west of the British Isles incredibly difficult. The Royal Navy alone was massively superior. The addition of a hostile French Navy plus the announcement of Italy's neutrality simply made the odds look laughable. And no help was forthcoming from the Far East. On learning the news of the British and French declarations of war in early 1939, Raeder noted in the official War Diary that they knew at least "how to die gallantly."[24]

Compared to those three European navies, the IJN of the late 1930s was massive, successful, strong in many fields, and seemingly well prepared for modern maritime warfare. It was one of the only three carrier navies, and the best organized one of all, with its vessels being clustered to form what was essentially a carrier task force. And that force was in training to be able not only to unleash tightly coordinated attacks on enemy targets like fleet bases but also, perhaps even more remarkably, to carry out very-long-range missions in midocean. The IJN also contained a significant array of modernized battleships and battle cruisers even before the giant *Yamato*-class vessels came to join the service. Its heavy cruisers were heftier than any others, threw a larger broadside, and (like other Japanese warships) had great night optics. Its speedy, large destroyers were all equipped with the powerful and very-long-range Long Lance torpedoes—in fact, all Japanese heavy cruisers, light cruisers, destroyers, and submarines were loaded (almost overloaded) with very large torpedoes, with the intention of inflicting the first blows in any surface battle.[25]

Because the IJN possessed an air force completely separate from that of the army and did not have the Fleet Air Arm's awkward relationship with the RAF, it was able to purchase, train, and control its own air fleets. Most of its dive-bomber and torpedo-bomber squadrons were first-class, and the Zero fighter was better than anything possessed by the West in the Pacific arena. Finally, in addition to a large force of carrier-based planes, a considerable number of similar squadrons were based on land, on Japanese airstrips in Southeast Asia, and on the Pacific island bases. Such squadrons could be switched from sea to land operation, depending on the tactical opportunity. The IJN Air Service also had a considerable coastal command reconnaissance division. There was nothing as good elsewhere.[26]

By the time Japan commenced war across the Far East, the inventory of active warships available to the IJN included 10 battleships, 6 fleet carriers and 4 light carriers, 18 heavy cruisers and 18 light cruisers, 113 destroyers, and 63 submarines. All told, this was about 70 or 80 percent of the fighting strength of each of the two greatest navies, those of Britain and America, but Japanese planners assumed that in any shootout their forces would have greater discipline and fighting "punch" vessel for vessel and that those other two navies would not be able to concentrate their entire fleet in the Western Pacific. These were not incorrect assumptions at the time.

Yet Japan's naval power did suffer from some very serious disadvantages. Although it was an island state like Britain and equally dependent on the safe flow of huge amounts of imports, it had, peculiarly, not done much to develop its antisubmarine warfare capabilities. Moreover, while its own submarine fleet was a sizable one, it was to train those boats using a rather questionable doctrine: in the pursuit of the enemy's hard-to-catch main fleets rather than as commerce raiders. It was way behind the West in the development of shipborne radar and would find that a great drawback in nighttime battles and, more generally, in positioning itself for combat. And it had no equivalent to the Allied possession of signals intelligence, whereas their American foes enjoyed the advantage of reading the enemy's diplomatic and military-naval codes. While the IJN was undeniably the most powerful surface navy in East Asian waters, these would be damning weaknesses if and when it came to confront an even greater maritime nation across the Pacific.

Moreover, as the shrewder of the senior IJN officers like Admiral Isoroku Yamamoto were well aware, Japan's true naval effectiveness was constrained by certain larger background forces outside of the service's control. The first and completely inalterable problem lay in Japan's peculiar geographical situation as a mountainous, forest-covered archipelago at the far end of the Eurasian landmass. The conundrum it faced was that while it enjoyed the freedom of action that came from being a very long distance from any other large naval force, it was by the same token a considerable way from the places it wished to conquer and then hold. Even if it achieved success at first strike, it was probably going to be a strain to control for many years an arc of territories ranging from Burma and Singapore around to the Solomon Islands and up to Alaska.

The second problem was Japan's deficits in raw materials, the very sinews of war. It would of course not have needed to go conquering abroad had it been better endowed with the natural resources required for a modern industrial society. It was a revisionist power on account of its weaknesses, not because it was strong. It was totally dependent on imported oil, and it was the West's embargo of that product (in July 1941) that was going to cause Tokyo to elect for war. But it was also lacking in rubber, timber, wheat, tin, copper, and many other ores, even if its annexation of Manchuria had given it some coal and iron reserves. Its stockpiles of these critical materials would not last very long once war began, and a state of heavy fighting would naturally undermine its wartime output, in some areas rather swiftly. Capable though it was of producing effective modern ships, carriers, and planes, that was all being achieved under forced peacetime conditions and under great strain to its national economy. If it started to lose significant naval and aerial assets as the fighting unfolded, there would be little "surge capacity" left.

As a final point, the Japanese Navy had a terrible problem with its sister service, the army, which was a decidedly more powerful political force nationally. This meant not only that the Japanese Army (and Army Air Force) naturally consumed a large share of the defense budget—just as in France, Germany, the USSR, and Italy—but that it was the generals and not the admirals who decided on the timing and direction of Japan's outward thrust. As it was, the direction preferred by Imperial General Headquarters was westward, to territories on the Asian *continent*, not down to Malaya or the South Seas. While General Hideki Tojo and the Japanese military were slowly coming to agree with the navy that war with the Anglo-American powers might be necessary, that change of mind occurred only because their huge military operations in China in turn demanded a secure supply of oil and metals from the south, which the West might well deny.[27] If Tokyo ever began an all-out war southward, though, the strategic flaw was stunning—here would be a country of only limited resources launching a huge campaign of overseas conquest, yet with so many of its military forces tied heavily to a continental war.

Things would be better, of course, if Japan possessed naval allies able to help out and even to fight side by side against the common foe. Here again, geography was a disadvantage, in that it was a good six thousand miles from its Axis partners in Europe; should they be at war together, neither it nor they possessed any bases at all to connect the three Fascist navies. And while it was true that the threats posed by the Italian and German navies were helping to keep most of the Royal Navy in European waters, the fast-growing US Navy was probably not going to be deterred from assembling a large maritime force in the Pacific. To Western eyes, Japan's geopolitical position seemed enviable. To the more pessimistic planners in Tokyo, the country seemed fated to having to oppose two land powers (China and, more distantly, Russia) as well as compete with two larger sea powers (Britain and America). The consolation was that its navy was now a formidable force, offensive minded, willing (and able) to take casualties, and hard to beat. Whether that was going to be enough remained to be seen.

---

The naval foe that Admiral Yamamoto worried most about was the United States. Clearly, it was America's longer-term military potential that chiefly concerned him; having been the Japanese naval attaché to the United States in the 1920s and traveled across the entire country, he was in no doubt as to how much richer and better resourced this nation was. Still, in the late 1930s—say, in 1938—American naval strength offered a rather uncertain picture, mirroring the very mixed and messy maritime-power distribution of the age. Just as the US economic advantage had been set back most by the great tariff wars of the Depression, so had it been the American navalists' gigantic battleship-building plans that had undoubtedly been the most damaged by the Washington limitations and naval holidays. For all the country's greater productive strength, its navy was not in the lead at this time. The Royal Navy was larger and occupied a far better position across the world's waterways, and the Japanese Navy was probably better equipped and prepared, at least ship for ship, than was the US Navy.

America's still-fledgling maritime position was determined more than anything else by its internal politics. As the country recoiled from World War I, domestic opinion had become firmly isolationist, and the various Neutrality Acts of the mid-1930s simply reemphasized that fact; FDR's occasional attempts to alter the situation usually produced a wave of criticisms and left him denying that he had wanted any change at all. Fortunately for the administration, strengthening the US Navy could be presented as merely a defensive measure and as such found support among many in Congress. Yet in addition to internal reasons, there was the simple fact that the Royal Navy was usually seen as a barrier to any European incursion into the Western Hemisphere; by the 1930s, amid the growing concern about Nazi Germany's ambitions, this geopolitical calculation remained. In consequence, even those Americans sympathetic to Britain and France saw no reason for their country to step into the front lines. A sizable battle fleet could be built, of course, but it was not until the very end of the decade that more than modest naval increases were authorized.[28]

And even when that happened, the first new American battleships to be built, that is, the USSs *North Carolina* and *Washington,* were not completely post–Washington Treaty vessels. Like the Royal Navy's *King George Vs,* their displacement and heavy armament had been entangled in the continued restrictions of the earlier era; it took years before the US Bureau of Design eventually settled on the larger 16-inch guns for this and all of the later American capital ships. The 1939 edition of *Jane's Fighting Ships,* striving to keep up with the many bulletins issued about these vessels, included these sentences: "Delays in laying down these ships have been due to changes in design, late delivery of materials, and necessity for extending and strengthening building slips. . . . It is quite likely that further modifications may be made in the course of construction."[29] (As it was, the USS *North Carolina* would be commissioned and join the fleet in

April 1941.) Another late, brief entry in that same edition of *Jane's Fighting Ships* noted that further congressional authorization had been given to two *Iowa*-class battleships of much larger displacement and speed, with the cost to be in the unheard-of "region of $100,000,000 apiece."[30] (They were commissioned in February 1943.) Thus the problem was the same. The "new" US navy was unlikely to be available in large numbers before the international tensions of the age exploded into outright war. Why would a revisionist Japanese power wish to wait that long?

So it was that the American battle fleet of 1939, like the other Powers' battle fleets, consisted of a cluster of older warships laid down at least twenty years earlier, with varying main armaments (12-inch to 16-inch) and constrained displacements (generally around 31,000 tons). In all, and having decided against having battle cruisers, the navy had fifteen relatively slow battleships, some significantly strengthened, others undergoing long refits (and therefore unavailable), and still others unmodernized and weaker, a classic pre–World War II navy. By contrast, if it were to come to a fight against Japan in the Pacific or a shootout with warships of the newer German Navy in the Atlantic, American admirals could at least take comfort in possessing eighteen 8-inch-gunned heavy cruisers, a substantial number, that were rangy enough for long-distance scouting and fast enough to run away if they encountered larger forces—fast enough, too, to serve as escorts to the US carriers. Since they still lacked ship-to-ship radar, whether they could handle the even more powerful Japanese heavy cruisers, with their better optics, looked dubious. The American fleet possessed significantly fewer light cruisers, not having the Royal Navy's needs in that class.

The smaller warships of the US Navy also reflected the country's unique strategic position. Being an entire continent in size and completely self-sufficient in foodstuffs and most forms of raw materials (except rubber), the service had given little thought to commerce protection and was hostile to the idea of convoys. Therefore, its numerous fleet destroyers (over two hundred) were precisely that, the best of them being speedy and heavily gunned vessels designed to fight alongside the battleships and to protect the carriers; there was, however, a long "tail" of older, four-stacker destroyers of much less worth. And there were hardly any destroyer escorts, and nothing like the later frigates, corvettes, or sloops of the actual war itself. The US Navy of the 1930s was a large firepower navy—the navy of Mahan, not of Corbett (see chapter 3)—and saw ample justification for being so, given the shape of the IJN and the threat of the new German heavy ships. Antisubmarine warfare was a neglected area until the Battle of the Atlantic broke out. And while some warships had minesweeping tackle, the US Navy had *no* minesweepers; the Royal Navy, prudently, had forty-four, and Italy and Germany had over twenty. Finally, by the same token, the American submarine force of this period (around sixty-five of them) was designed for the fight against the main Japanese battle fleet, and it contained many larger boats than those in Doenitz's navy; the idea of attacking the Japanese merchant marine came only after 1942.

Unless one were a dedicated carrier warfare enthusiast, it would be difficult to see that the US Navy's flattops represented the most powerful striking element in the fleet in 1939. Visually and tactically, it didn't look like that—while everyone envisaged American battleships being deployed as a fleet, the carriers were used individually, as scouts, or to provide planes for aerial patrol over the battleships. Even when two carriers were at sea together, the general idea was that it would be smarter tactics for them to operate far apart to confuse a likely enemy. Battleship admirals frowned on junior carrier captains who wanted to operate differently; thus, while some dedicated carrier officers (William Halsey, Marc Mitscher, and John Tower) were rising into flag positions, they were not yet able to have the sort of carrier task force fleet that would emerge in the war itself.[31] Still, in sheer material terms, the US Navy, like the IJN, probably did possess a totally new form of sea power within its ranks here. There were five full fleet carriers in 1939: the two converted battle cruisers, the *Lexington* and *Saratoga;* and three late-design vessels, the *Enterprise, Hornet,* and *Yorktown.* They were all very fast and each one carried over eighty planes. Yet they could not be a great naval force when, in addition to being deployed for scouting, they were split between the Atlantic and Pacific commands.[32] It was true, however, that the navy was able to enjoy its own aircraft-procurement ordering, which made it much better off than the Fleet Air Arm. What all this meant was that if the IJN's carrier navy was the best in the world at this time, the American Navy's carrier arm was not too far behind, while the British had decidedly slipped into third place.

It is amazing to see, in retrospect, how fast this picture of rather restrained American naval power changed. The fact was that in the summer of 1939 the US Navy was just one year away from receiving a tremendous longer-term boost through legislation unhindered at last by any treaty restrictions, fueled by a threatening turn of world affairs, and agreed to by a very frightened Congress. Its time was coming, but it was certainly not there when Hitler's forces began their attack on Poland.

Compared to all the other navies described earlier, even that of the Americans, the situation of the Royal Navy at the close of the 1930s must have seemed an enviable one. It was the only *worldwide* naval service, just as the British Empire after 1919 was the only worldwide imperial system. While World War I had destroyed national exuberance, caused immense losses of life in the fighting, and shifted the global financial balance away from London to New York City, the Empire's territorial reach had become even greater following its takeover of many Ottoman and German colonies.[33] The self-governing Dominions, even in a newer constitutional relationship, were still part of the system—which meant that places like Esquimalt, Halifax, St. John's, Simonstown, Durban, Perth, Sydney, Darwin, Auckland, and many lesser harbors were Royal Navy ports to a greater or lesser degree. The Indian raj remained just that, and its security was more than ever the focus of British strategic attention, so within this imperial orbit lay all the ports from Bandar Abbas in the west via Bombay, Colombo, and Calcutta to Rangoon in the east. Then there was that unequaled and endless string of harbors that Admiral Fisher had so crowed about, most acquired in the eighteenth-century wars against France, a few in the early Victorian era: Bermuda, Jamaica, Gibraltar, Freetown, Lagos, Ascension, Mombasa, Malta, Alexandria, Aden, Singapore, Hong Kong, and Fiji—all connected by a secure, "all-red-route" network of underwater cable communications laid down at the beginning of the twentieth century. In the geographical measurement of sea power—as discussed further in chapter 3—the British advantages seemed very large indeed.

As for the actual ships and warship types, the Board of Admiralty of 1939 had created a navy of some 15 post-dreadnought capital ships (12 battleships and 3 full-sized battle cruisers), 7 aircraft carriers (3 rather small), 15 heavy cruisers, 41 light cruisers, and 8 antiaircraft cruisers. Destroyer totals range widely depending on the method of counting, from around 113 "modern," or "fleet," destroyers to around 175 overall, including many older ones, but essentially Britain had more of this class than anyone else apart from the United States. There were 55 modern submarines plus a multitude of fleet auxiliaries. A full two hundred thousand naval personnel—officers, ratings, and reserves—were in the service, but the capacity to recruit and train many more, from the merchant marine, the Empire, and the ranks of retired sailors, was also large.

The Admiralty also had the world's largest warship tonnage on order, including the five *King George V*–class battleships, six *Illustrious*-class carriers, and almost two dozen cruisers. When those *King George Vs* arrived, they would reinforce the existing cluster of fifteen capital ships—that is, the two 16-inch-gunned battleships, the *Nelson* and *Rodney;* the five modernized dreadnoughts of the *Queen Elizabeth*–class, all with eight 15-inch guns; the three fast though lightly armored battle cruisers HMSs *Hood, Repulse,* and *Renown,* again with eight 15-inch guns; and the five unmodernized Royal *Sovereign*-class vessels.[34] This seemed a battle fleet with the firepower to achieve total command of European waters and, when needed, to send a substantial force to Singapore; at least, that was the Admiralty's hope.

More than any other class of warship, it was the serried ranks of cruisers that Admiralty planners saw as a sort of glue holding the imperial networks together and consequently paid so much attention to the design of. As noted earlier, the core heavy cruisers of the pre-1939 years, the so-called *County*-class, looked somewhat puny and thin-skinned compared to the muscular, high-super-structure profiles of their competitors. But their low-slung design made them better sailors in very stormy weather; they had an enormous range at sea; and their heavy armament was a full eight 8-inch guns plus torpedo tubes. And with float seaplanes and (very soon) radar, they were rather well equipped to carry out most operational functions. Joining them came their eventual successors, the dozen or so 6-inch-gunned *Town*-class cruisers, to be followed shortly after by a further array of so-called *Crown Colony*–class cruisers. A whole panoply of smaller, older cruiser classes were good for limited trade-protection roles or as destroyer leaders.[35]

However many destroyers they possessed, Admiralty planners still doubted whether it would be sufficient to defend a worldwide empire in the event of hostilities breaking out in more than one place. This fear animated their thinking about overall numbers as they strove each year to scrap the many older, smaller World War I–era boats and to design vessels fast and powerful enough to keep up with and protect the navy's battleships and carriers. Even during the economies of the Depression years, each year London laid down at least one new flotilla (eight destroyers of the class plus a destroyer leader), with each group usually bigger than its predecessor. To repeat, the overall total of these vessels by 1939 looked impressive; and yet again, the Admiralty wondered whether they would ever have enough. Moreover, the more powerful the newer destroyers became, the less suitable they were, ironically, for slow-ish and long-range convoy duties, as would soon be shown. Overall, though, it is clear that the Royal Navy had paid considerable attention to its cruiser and destroyer forces.

When it came to Britain's aircraft carrier force, a different picture emerges, one in which the navy's early material and technological advantages here were slowly lost. The tonnage constraints of the Washington Treaty fail to explain this—after all, the US Navy was in the same bind, and the other three navies suffered from even greater tonnage limitations. One big reason was the severe economic constraints after 1919, although of course Japan was just as badly hit and managed to produce a far better carrier fleet in the end. Admiralty indecisiveness and unwillingness to build a standard large-framed vessel clearly played a role. Thus, while Britain boasted seven carriers in 1939, six of them were either too small, too slow, too old, or all of the above. Their dates of completion give the game away: *Furious* (1917), *Argus* (1918), *Hermes* (1919), *Eagle* (1921), *Glorious* (1925), and *Courageous* (1925)—only the *Ark Royal* was modern. Most of them carried only a small number of planes, and the aircraft themselves were a poor medley of types: too few, too weak, too underpowered, or equipped with smallish bombs and smallish torpedoes. The struggles with the Royal Air Force over aircraft design and with securing resources to permit Coastal Command to protect home waters was a terrible drawback that lasted well into the war; and it is a tribute to the Fleet Air Arm and Coastal Command that they were able to perform as well as they did. Historians' descriptions of this messy story range from the polite to the painful to the withering.[36]

In contrast to the Royal Navy's interwar record on carriers, the service did take both submarines and antisubmarine warfare most seriously. It had been an early pioneer in submarine developments and design and in torpedo technology, in part because of Admiral Fisher's enthusiasms, although the interest was more broadly felt. During World War I it had been able to deploy its own boats aggressively against German warships and commerce in the Baltic and against the Austro-Hungarian Navy in the Adriatic. While the submarine branch had to remain small after 1919, it was not neglected. By 1939 it possessed no less than fifty-three modern boats, with another two dozen being built. Because it was smaller in number than all the other navies, the Royal Navy's submarine branch gets little coverage in the literature, but its standard *S*-class boats were ideal for North Sea and Mediterranean waters and carried a large complement of torpedoes that worked far more effectively than the American and German ones.[37]

In the same way, following the loss of the dreadnought HMS *Audacious* in the first month of World War I, the Royal Navy paid high regard to the potential threat of U-boats and naval mines to its own battle fleet. And it had been scarified by the devastation inflicted on British merchant shipping during the 1917–18 Battle of the Atlantic and had spent the following years seeking to ensure that such losses could not occur again. Forbidding the German fleet to possess U-boats lasted only until the advent of the Third Reich, when the threat emerged again; and while it is true that the Royal Navy's antisubmarine-warfare planners were too blasé in assuming that the new ASDIC device had solved the underwater detection problem and brought security, at least they always gave commerce protection a very high priority. The consequence of all this was that, in addition to the many destroyer flotillas that could be pressed into commerce protection, the Admiralty also controlled a wide variety of smaller surface-escort vessels, sloops, patrol craft, torpedo boats, and even armed trawlers. It also possessed no fewer than forty-four minesweepers, far more than any other navy, to keep its seaways open.

How did the Royal Navy look overall, then? Although there were some significant weaknesses (especially with the carrier navy), this was on the whole a pretty balanced fleet, numerous in capital ships and unequaled in cruisers yet also not neglectful of important smaller types like destroyers, submarines, and even minesweepers. Comparatively, the Royal Navy looked and was stronger than any other naval power of the time, not by much more than the US Navy, but the latter's reach extended only between, say, Bermuda and Manila, while Japan's did not go south of the approaches to Shanghai. France's and Italy's navies were obviously a long way behind and canceled each other out, while Hitler's Reichsmarine was a distant sixth. Britain's naval reach started at Portsmouth and ran to the Cape of Good Hope, and from there to Hong Kong and Sydney.

Yet that was not the same as the measure of British naval effectiveness in the world at the end of the 1930s, and for three major reasons—reasons that those planners at the Admiralty and the Committee of Imperial Defence worried about so much.[38] The first concern, although perhaps less strongly felt than the others, was of the danger posed to the Royal Navy's warships from hostile airpower, wheresoever it be located. While it was more difficult than ever to judge how serious a threat land-based aircraft were to large warships—and Western naval intelligence about Japan's capacities here were severely deficient—the Admiralty was sufficiently concerned by 1937 to begin laying down a new class of what were virtually antiaircraft cruisers, the *Dido*-class, bristling with dual-purpose 5.25-inch armaments. They were also beginning to add more and more anti-aircraft weaponry (quick-firing 4-inchers, Oerlikon heavy machine guns, and later Bofors pom-poms) to every new or rebuilt vessel. The point of Britain's possible vulnerability here was of course not lost among military planners in Germany, Italy, and Japan: the huge tonnage advantage of the Royal Navy might be considerably reduced or even negated altogether if it became vulnerable to modern bomber aircraft capable of striking up to 150 to 200 miles out to sea. Unlike the mine and the torpedo, those other threatening weapons of asymmetrical warfare, this one could only really be countered by superior British airpower, not more warships.

The second concern was for Britain's overall security, which was threatened not merely from the rising danger that the Luftwaffe posed to na-

val vessels but from an even more fundamental threat: a Third Reich that
dominated all its neighbors in Europe would make an Allied victory in
any future conflict impossible. The course of World War I had already
shown that the Royal Navy, however superior on the seas, could not by
itself bring down a massive German land power. For a full twenty years
after 1919, Whitehall planners had avoided confronting that awkward
grand-strategic issue, but from early 1939 onward they began to wrestle
once more with the core problem: to achieve victory, the British side would
have to prevail over German land power *and* German airpower. But how?
This was not a matter that could be addressed by having a few more new
battleships join the fleet. As it was, the British government had conceded
that point on the eve of war as it made preparations for army divisions and
some RAF squadrons to be shipped over to France once again. In another
total war for the mastery of Europe, navies could only do so much.[39]

The third factor reducing Britain's naval advantage was that, from at
least 1936 onward, the Empire had had to plan for the possibility of war
against not one or two but as many as three hostile Powers. Although hoping to the end to reduce those odds by diplomacy, London faced a strategic challenge that it had not had since the late 1770s. Having the largest
surface navy in the world was no guarantee of security if you had to divide your fleet three ways. The sheer speed of the deterioration in Britain's
security was shocking. In 1930 it was still on reasonable terms with Japan,
Italy was a friendly guarantor of the Locarno accords, and Germany was
a humbled Weimar Republic. Only five years later, Japan was a threat to
the Far Eastern order, Hitler's Germany was on the move, and because of
the Abyssinian Crisis, Italy changed from being a friendly Power to also
becoming a potential foe. The worried Admiralty memos to the cabinet of
1935–36—warning that if the Royal Navy found itself in a Mediterranean
war, both Japan and Germany could take advantage elsewhere—glaringly
showed the dilemmas of facing too many potential foes arraigned in different parts of the globe.[40] Just how many of Britain's limited capital ships
(some were in lengthy refits) should it retain with the Home Fleet, and
how many should it station at Malta, as opposed to the numbers required
in Far Eastern waters? Where should the precious few carriers be, or the
few operable squadrons of Coastal Command aircraft?

Throughout the rest of the 1930s, therefore, the Admiralty had no
choice but to engage in what seemed like a continual reassessment of this
new multipolar naval world. Just as in the global financial and credit system that undergirded the British Empire, a crisis in one part sent shock
waves throughout the whole. Since the plain fact was that the Royal Navy
could not be strong everywhere, Whitehall finally concluded in the sum-

mer of 1939 that it must keep a large fleet in the Mediterranean vis-à-vis
Italy at the cost of tacitly abandoning the Far East. From this time onward, the order of importance put home waters in first place, with the
Mediterranean second; the Far East, including the Singapore base, was a
distant third.[41] If the Italian threat forced the Mediterranean Fleet out of
Malta, it would only go to Alexandria. All these were hard but necessary
decisions.

How ready was the Royal Navy when World War II began? Iconoclastic scholars like Correlli Barnett, writing in the aftermath of Suez and the
end of Britain's empire in Asia, saw only the many weaknesses, the back-
wardness, and the imperial overstretch.[42] More recent naval historians
of the interwar years have been kinder in their assessments, and indeed
some have argued that Great Britain was still the most powerful maritime nation in the world in 1939—"Britannia Rules the Waves" is Professor Evan Mawdsley's summary[43]—given that the Royal Navy, in its overall tonnage, fleet personnel, dockyards and bases, ships at sea, and ships
under construction, remained larger than any other navy, even that of the
United States. With America deliberately sidelining itself and Germany
and Japan merely regional players, the British Empire remained the only
country that might be termed a "Super Power."[44] Yet by the strictly naval
measure of overall warship tonnage—as shown in chart 1 (chapter 2)—
that argument looks as if it has pushed things too far. The Royal Navy
was strong, alright. But it was not properly ready. And the test ahead was
larger than any it had met before.

Finally, it is worth recalling that the navies of the Great Powers were
not the only institutions—and, certainly, not the only armed service—
grappling with the political, economic, and technological confusions of
the late 1930s. War was coming, because two revisionist and authoritarian
regimes were no longer willing to tolerate existing borders, and a third
(Italy) would expand if it saw the chance. A gigantic economic depression
had ruined trade, devastated industries, hurt treasuries, and cramped
budgets, and yet nations now had to pursue last-minute, large-scale rearmament in order to survive, and they had to decide which military
spending items merited priority. Technological and scientific advances of
the most extraordinary sort were challenging all the older ways of doing warfare, and it was difficult to see which breakthroughs were going
to be the most critical. All three main services, army, navy, and air force,
strove desperately for effectiveness at every level—strategic, operational,
and tactical.[45] Each service urgently pushed its own vision of things and
argued its own vital needs.

The admirals of 1939 were not alone, then, in being alarmed, frustrated, and worried about the future. Still, some of their navies were better placed than others to withstand the strains of total war. Great individual surprises would occur as the fighting unfolded, especially in 1940–41 when France fell and Pearl Harbor was ravaged. Yet how each of the world's major navies fared overall in the course of this conflict ought not to have been such a great surprise, for their respective strengths and weaknesses were generally apparent before even the first shot was fired.

**PAINTING 12.** *Luetzow* and *Scharnhorst,* **Narvik fjord, 1943.** The German seizure of Norway in 1940 broke through its earlier geographical confines and gave their large warships—here a pocket battleship and a battle cruiser—access to the Arctic and the Atlantic. *Scharnhorst* was sunk at the Battle of the North Cape, and *Luetzow* was crippled by RAF bombers in 1945.

# THREE

## Geography, Economics, and Geopolitical Writings

The admiralties of the 1930s surely did not read Karl Marx, but some of their members probably knew of his famous remark that "men make their own history, but they do not make it as they please." They make it, the phrase continues, "under circumstances existing already, given and transmitted from the past."[1] For whatever the number and quality of the battleships and destroyers they possessed, each of the six great navies described above had to operate within contexts not of their making, within inherited constraints that they, as a simple armed service, could not bend to their own advantage. And of all the "circumstances existing already," it was the elements of geography and of economics that had the greatest influence here. Sea power was, after all, a very material thing.

More specifically, every naval planning staff operated knowing that their country's prospects were significantly affected by the larger interacting forces of geographical situation, technology, and economics. Geography was an existing given, of course, because it provided both the spatial opportunity for and the unyielding physical constraints on every navy, large or small. It was true that modern technology had been able to provide a significant variable, because steam propulsion eliminated a vessel's dependence on wind and tides, while the coming of aircraft offered further mobility to the armed forces. But distance—whether the too-cramped distances of the Dunkirk shores or the incredibly wide distances of the central Pacific—was still a terribly important factor. And economics, or more specifically, the productive capacity of the nations, brought another interacting variable into this mix, because as the 1939–45 war was to show so very often, victory in battle wasn't simply the result of geographical advantage or of one navy's technical ingenuity. Massive industrial heft, and thus massive productive power, was always required. One radar set was not enough; a radar-equipped flotilla of destroyers was different. The hordes of heavy bombers that shrugged off the Atlantic's distances, the dozens of new carriers racing across the Pacific, all confirmed the old understanding: a country's maritime power had to rest on strong productive foundations.

## The Influence of Geography on This Six-Nation Conflict

All these general points (including even a bit on the impact of wireless telegraphy) had been discussed decades earlier in a remarkably wide-ranging 1902 article, *Considerations Governing the Disposition of Navies,* by the great naval strategist Alfred Thayer Mahan. The political conditions of the time were in immense flux—the Boer War had just ended, the Anglo-Japanese Alliance had just been signed, the United States was moving into the Caribbean, war clouds were rising in the Far East, and the German Navy's battleship size was being doubled—but Mahan was much more interested in the larger and longer-term aspects of how and where naval power was distributed. As he explained it, "tradition and routine," not to mention a preference for their basic geographical home location, kept most navies in their predictable place, where defense of their national interests was easiest. Nonetheless, he went on, there did occur from time to time an "assignment of force follow[ing] changes in political circumstances."[2] Thus, world affairs had caused Imperial Russia to deploy more battleships to East Asia in recent years, while the Royal Navy now had far fewer squadrons in American waters, France had beefed up its Mediterranean presence, and so on. In all such periodic redistributions, however, the admiralties of the Powers still needed to take account of some larger geographical facts, like the centrality of that line of human activity that ran from Gibraltar to Suez, to Aden and beyond; or the way the British Isles always acted as a "giant breakwater" to the northern European states; or the sheer distances across the Pacific. To Mahan also, geography was destiny (which is why, of course, he could be optimistic about America's future). And it was precisely because he wrote more in generalities and avoided going into the specifics of the world circa 1902 that his remarks were of a transcendent value, pertinent for the naval-political circumstances of the late 1930s as well.

Even before that decade had arrived, the Great Powers had experienced how geography worked to the disadvantage of some of them and the advantage of others. From beginning to end, World War I had been a struggle between geopolitical haves and have-nots. Thus, after Turkey joined the Central Powers in November 1914, the tsar's regime found itself cut off from assistance from its allies via the Black Sea as well as the Baltic, with its armies subject to an annual battering from the Germans; when it broke militarily and the revolution came, there was really nothing that a distant West could do. By contrast, Japan, with no powerful neighbors to constrain it, took much advantage of its distance from the European war. Turkey's decision to join in was also a fatal one for itself, for not only had it large wars to fight on its Russian and Balkan fronts, but it had opened its near-eastern territories to invasion by the French and the British. Italy should have stayed out; it could never fight its way through the Dolomites and Alps, and it ended the struggle a victor in name only. France found itself, as in 1870, the subject of a huge German military occupation of the northern third of the country; on this occasion it didn't collapse, due to its own extreme exertions plus the help of very large British Empire and US armies, but it was a war in which its own navy had a relatively small role to play. Germany was pinned into the eastern North Sea, as Mahan had forecast (see below), just as the Austro-Hungarian Navy was pinned into the upper Adriatic—only the newfangled U-boats gave Berlin the chance to strike out at Anglo-American naval mastery, but that effort was too little, too late. The United States had a fairly easy time of the war at sea, simply because of its distance from Europe and because it came in very late. But the Royal Navy found it harder to achieve a sweeping maritime victory than it had anticipated: it picked up most of Germany's scattered colonies easily enough and hunted down its few overseas squadrons, but it found amphibious operations (Gallipoli) disappointing and was surprised that the German economy withstood the maritime blockade so well; and it was embarrassed that the British nation was clearly upset at the result of Jutland. Then came the damage caused to Allied shipping by the U-boats in the Atlantic—until the latter were defeated by convoys and a huge mobilization of new escort forces—that revealed that the enemy had found one way, with a very recent technology, of partially getting out of the North Sea.[3] Its own geographic advantage had been muted here.

When, twenty years later, the various admiralties of the nations pondered how they would fight a second global conflict, they struggled once again to understand and exploit the role of location and distance. Much more than before, they all could see that the newer weapons of aircraft and the submarine might alter the conditions of surface naval warfare, but to what extent would that occur, exactly, if every combatant employed the same newer technologies? In any case, whatever the newer weapons systems might do, there still remained certain basic geographical verities. Five-sixths of the surface of the globe was water, and the distances between New York and Glasgow (3,200 miles) and San Diego and Tokyo

(5,600 miles) were so vast that it was axiomatic that geography would play a critical role in naval grand strategy in both oceans in a future war, and in so many ways. The strategic benefits conferred to the British by their bases at Scapa Flow, Dover, Gibraltar, Freetown, and Cape Town; the stark directness of the convoy "run" from Halifax to the northwest British ports; the military difficulties faced in supplying Malta; and the challenges confronting any island-by-island-hopping campaign across the Pacific would each play an important role. While all this was obvious, though, it would be folly for any belligerent to take its geographical advantages for granted.

If it was among the three least of the naval powers that the force of geography was most keenly felt, that was because they of course were the countries with the most limited choice in moving their navies around, or actually no choice at all. Hybrid nations—those with significant land frontiers and thus physical constraints—have by definition never really possessed the luxury of concentrating solely upon the maritime realm; even the Dutch and the Portuguese, even the Venetians, had to look landward at some times during their long periods of glory.[4] Land frontiers were almost always a weak point, and this was so even if the nation in question was large and populous. Perhaps this was the deeper meaning of the aphorism "geography is destiny," which Napoleon is said to have murmured as he marched fatefully into Russia. Land powers could never escape the drive to be secure on land.

Geography was certainly destiny for that later regime of France, the Third Republic, as explained in the chapter preceding this one. Tied at the hip to an expanded Nazi Germany that possessed a much bigger population and far larger industrial base, France had invested as much as it dared into its relatively modern, midsized navy by the end of the 1930s. If it could hold off a German landward assault, as it had managed to do in 1914, it could certainly handle the far smaller Reichsmarine, even without the help of the Royal Navy; if, however, it could not resist the German Army and Luftwaffe, then its maritime power would crumble in any case. France's survivability as a Great Power simply did not depend upon the sea. By contrast, aggressions by Italy, in whatever form they took, could never be fundamental.

Italy's own naval prospects were also much affected by geography, albeit in different ways. It had neither an intimidating Germany nor an ominous USSR along its land borders, and it was always wonderfully protected by the large mountain range of the Alps to the north. Weak states lay across the Adriatic to the east, and the French and Italian armies sort of canceled each other out in Savoy. Its coastline boasted many fine harbors, to which could be added the large islands of Sardinia and Sicily—plus the colonial territories it had acquired in North Africa.

Nonetheless, Italy's overall strategic position in the twentieth-century configuration of the Great Powers was not strong. In any global layout of the larger empires, its own cluster of possessions appeared modest, a batch of lands around the small Mediterranean. It was in truth a regional and medium-sized power that was, moreover, completely locked into the Middle Sea, even more than Germany was locked into the North Sea. Its only chance of escaping from being "prisoner in the Mediterranean," Italian nationalists fantasized, was to have possession of the Straits of Gibraltar and control of Egypt. But that was the second geopolitical problem, because since the mid-eighteenth century, when Italy was just a medley of small kingdoms and city-states, a far more unified and industrialized power (Britain) had purposefully pushed itself into the Mediterranean and by the late nineteenth century had established a line of imperial communications and commerce right through the sea. Physically, that line might appear as a very slim and perhaps vulnerable one, yet all would depend on how vigorously the British Empire intended to hold on to it. By 1939 the air and land reinforcements being sent from London to the Egyptian garrison and the strengthening of the air defenses of Malta suggested that the fighting would be hard. In any case, there was also the very large French military position in the western Mediterranean to take into account. Little wonder, then, that the Italian government decided to stay neutral when the war over Poland began. In sum, had Mahan devoted any space to Italy's dilemma in his 1902 essay, he might have said as he did of Germany, that here was the country's "initial disadvantage of position," to be overcome by superior numbers. Yet such numbers were never to be forthcoming.

The geostrategic and political situation of Nazi Germany and its navy in 1939 was different again, being significantly more cramped than all of the five Washington Treaty countries. Twenty years earlier its brand-new Weimar government had had to swallow the unheard-of disarmament clauses of the Versailles peace settlement (no aircraft, no U-boats, no capital ships, a miniscule army, and so on), and after 1933 the Nazi remilitarization gave priority to the Luftwaffe and the army. Economically, the country had the second-biggest industrial base in the world, and thus it could, in theory, construct a very large battle fleet indeed. But that was something for the 1940s, as Hitler kept reassuring an anxious Admiral Erich Raeder. At the close of the 1930s, its array of modern warships was very small indeed—individually dangerous because of fine German construction standards but overall still a small fleet, about one-quarter the size of France's.

If that was the numerical situation, then geography simply made things worse. It was in Mahan's 1902 essay that the classic formulation of Germany's geographical disadvantage appears: "Sea-defence for Germany, in case of war with France or England, means established naval predominance at least in the North Sea; nor can it be considered complete unless extended through the Channel and as far as Britain will have to project hers into the Atlantic. This is Germany's initial disadvantage of position, to be overcome by adequate superiority of numbers."[5] Thus were Germany's, even Nazi Germany's, maritime prospects circumscribed. No one could imagine an "adequate superiority of numbers" over the Anglo-French fleets for another decade, if at all. Until then, geography boxed the Reichsmarine into a very limited field of play.

Or did it? If Germany's problem here was a positional one, then why not see whether the very geopolitical positions themselves could be changed, by international agreements or (much more likely) by decisive military force? Such was the argument advanced in a strikingly iconoclastic book, *Die Seestrategie des Weltkrieges (The Naval Strategy of the World War)*, published in 1929 by the retired German rear admiral Wolfgang Wegener.[6] Earlier, Wegener had been one of the many critics of Admiral Alfred von Tirpitz's scheme to construct an ever-larger High Seas Fleet and then defeat the Royal Navy's Grand Fleet in a decisive battle in the central North Sea. Such a plan was mistaken, Wegener felt, not just because Britain would keep building ever more warships but also because the British didn't need to send their fleet into mine- and submarine-infested waters. After 1917, and in any future war, the Royal Navy could be content to hold on to the two exits from the North Sea and continue to throttle German overseas trade. So the only way to change this situational weakness was to amend geography itself by taking over Denmark and Norway. With this one blow, the German Navy would escape from its North Sea prison and be able to base powerful commerce raiders, plus lots of U-boats, in Norwegian harbors. And maybe, if the times were right, it might also advance in the southern North Sea and be able to base its U-boats into Zeebrugge and the other Belgian ports, as had been done back in 1918. This was a very ambitious "Atlantic-oriented strategy," Wegener admitted. All that was needed was a bold navy leadership and a new, strong Fuehrer of Germany willing to challenge Britain's naval mastery in a very different way.[7]

Did the British Admiralty and its intelligence department understand that these notions of Wegener, of how a future Germany might escape from its geographical "trap," were beginning to seep upward in the Kriegsmarine throughout the 1930s, especially after the intensely nationalist Admiral Raeder tightened his grip on the service? The answer is a "yes, but . . ." Successive British naval attachés and the specialist naval journals in London tracked what was going on in all significant foreign fleets, and with ever-greater interest after the end of naval shipbuilding limitations. Yet that itself was a problem: there were also critically important changes in the Italian Navy to be followed, plus the intentions of Japanese shipbuilding programs to be assessed, new destroyer types announced by France, reports on main US fleet movements, the fierce debates about aircraft versus battleships, and plans for imperial naval coordination. In the midst of all this, an eye had to be kept on what was happening in post-Weimar Germany, but until the Reichsmarine really had a lot more large warships and a lot more submarines (for Raeder held U-boat expansion down), it was hard to think that Berlin could undertake as huge an operation as the capture of Norway, and virtually off the shores of Scapa Flow.

This point, that the British had the fleet base of Scapa Flow located close to an area of what would be serious naval operations in World War II, is worth examining further. Of course the Royal Navy *was* set up for serious action here, Scapa being one of the historic naval bases of the whole British Empire. But that was simultaneously both the geographical strength and the worrying geographical problem for British grand strategy in a world in which not one but three revisionist Powers had commenced a serious buildup of their naval forces to advance their territorial ambitions. Exactly how one viewed the global scene in the 1930s depended, as it ever did, on where in the international landscape an individual Power was located. More specifically, what appeared as an extraordinary network of imperial domains and strongpoints to an outsider's eye could look more like a sprawled-out array of half-protected imperial liabilities to an overworked British planner. It was Wegener's distinction to see that the weak geographical position Germany occupied might be escaped from, by actions very close to the home waters of Britain's naval power if it was distracted elsewhere. Even "number ones" cannot control everything.

Yet being number one is almost always better than being number three or number five. So, in comparison to the constricted geographical circumstances all the European Great Powers found themselves in, the British seemed downright blessed. To German nationalists of the nineteenth century like Heinrich von Treitschke, an inherent, almost unfair, geostrategic advantage had been conferred upon Britain when those islands were unified under a single political entity in the sixteenth and seventeenth centuries. Thereafter, everything seemed to go right for the Hanoverian and Victorian nation, relatively speaking: all of its rivals reduced themselves through protracted land wars; the surge in Atlantic and other transoceanic trades boosted British ports and industries; its demographic spurt interacted with its coal-mining boom, its factory movement, and the great growth of its cities (London above all); and healthy state finances allowed it to outspend any rival in wartime, even Napoleonic France.[8] If the late Victorians in their turn so often rejoiced in their country's favorable

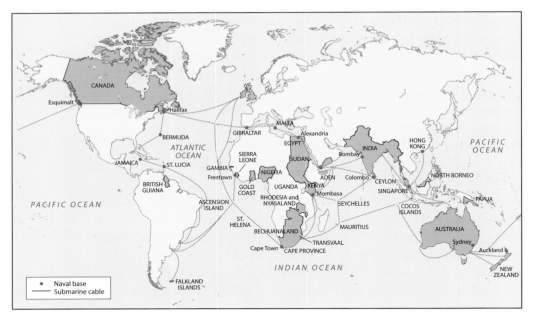

**MAP 1.** The interconnected British Empire: Naval bases and submarine cables, ca. 1900.

geographical position and the favors that brought, they had good reason to do so. And if Mahan, in the very first portion of his *The Influence of Sea Power upon History, 1660–1783,* stressed the overriding importance of location in explaining Britain's rise, his readership probably knew that already; it was just that no writer before him had so lucidly shown the connections between geography, navies, trade, and economics.

In fact, the enormous geographical advantage enjoyed by the British seemed so obvious to Mahan that when he returned to this topic in his 1902 essay on the disposition of navies he hardly spent much space describing it at all. The hyperpatriotic imperialist and navalist media of the age could do all that in any case, or maybe it could be left to such flamboyant publicists as the influential Admiral Fisher. There were "five keys that lock up the world!" the admiral used to boast to his journalistic pals[9]—Dover, Gibraltar, Alexandria, the Cape, and Singapore—and Britain held them all. Add to this a so-called All Red Line underwater cable communications system that no other Power could possibly replicate,[10] and London seemed to command a worldwide security system that looked invulnerable.

This global layout of the British position, illustrated in map 1, secured already by 1900 and still in existence in 1939, calls for two further, perhaps obvious remarks. First, it suggests a strategic world order that was firmly centered on London (or Dover), and it pointed to an intricate arrangement of imperial naval assets stretching west and east of the Greenwich meridian. Because it is such a British world map, then, what also hits the reader in the eye is the key place of that long arterial spine running from Gibraltar to Malta, Alexandria, Suez, and Aden and then on to Bombay, Colombo, Singapore, and Perth. This was indeed that "vital strategic Line" governing the disposition of navies to which Mahan had drawn attention in his article.[11] It will also be noticed, then, that the giant region of the Pacific Ocean has been consigned to the two ends of such a map; it is therefore cut in half and falls off the page. This is, in a way, a very truthful map, for British imperial power did peter out eastward of Singapore and also no longer extended significantly around the tip of Latin America and into the Pacific (the Falklands were thus a sort of farewell point). Still, anywhere between the Jamaica base in the west (77 degrees west) and Sydney in the distant east (151 degrees east), a giant chunk of the world measured in territories and trade, was essentially within the Royal Navy's orbit, albeit with one critically important proviso. The blunt fact was that a sufficient number of modern Royal Navy warships always had to be available for all the pertinent stations—the Channel Station, the Gibraltar Station, the Mediterranean, the South Africa Station, the Indian Ocean, and the Australia Station—in order to make a global naval strategy effective. Without strong fleets stationed in that great array of harbors, the latter would be, in Correlli Barnett's mocking phrase, "like sentry-boxes without sentries."[12]

Were there enough "sentries" to operate from Britain's many naval base sentry boxes, or at least to be so deployed as to have control in the most important of the stations listed above? The full list of the active warships of the Royal Navy in all categories in 1939 is given in table 1. From this total the Admiralty would immediately have to deduct around one-quarter of that strength to account for vessels undergoing major refits, suffering collision damage, or having new equipment fitted. Thereafter, it disposed of its major fleets very much along the general principles adumbrated in Mahan's essay, namely, with regard for traditional regions on the one hand while attempting to account for newer threats in the international system on the other. In practical terms, deciding which cruiser squadrons or submarine flotillas should be on which station or how many capital ships should go to the Mediterranean Fleet was a daunting task, a global strategic juggling act that no other navy had to do. Aphorisms like those of Frederick the Great to his generals (avoid being "weak everywhere, strong nowhere") didn't really help if warship numbers were insufficient. A service tradition of ruthless prioritization of fleet distribution certainly did.

This meant that the Admiralty was always going to give priority to the defense of the home islands and the surrounding waters—the Channel, the Nore, the North Sea, and the Atlantic ports. Since 1914 it had always seen Scapa Flow as its main battle fleet (the Home Fleet) base, not that that anchorage possessed huge ship-repair infrastructure like Newport News or the Clyde, but it did represent the best geographical compromise in the face of various threats and contingencies. When based at Scapa, the fleet would be safe from German air attacks, yet it could be sent south if a serious invasion threat arose. It should ordinarily be able to prevent large enemy warships getting into the Atlantic, but if that did happen, battleship and cruiser squadrons would be swiftly dispatched from Scapa to give pursuit. Warships from the Home Fleet could, obviously, be used to cover any convoys to North Russia. Destroyers from the Home Fleet might conceivably be sent to assist in the Battle of the Atlantic, should those critical commerce routes ever be in danger of being completely disrupted. It was to Scapa Flow that brand-new warships from the Tyne, Clyde, and Belfast were first ordered to report for working up and fleet training. Finally, it was from this central pool of naval vessels that the Admiralty could assemble and empower an ad hoc force (Force M, Force H, or whatever) to pursue an enemy pocket battleship, escort a troop convoy to the Mediterranean, or reinforce Gibraltar.[13] And whenever such operations were complete, most of the warships involved would return to the Home Fleet. This was a situation quite different from that of the 1914–18 war at sea (where 90 percent of all battleships stayed with the Grand Fleet for 90 percent of the time).

If the British Admiralty's threat assessment here was basically correct, and it was also correct in identifying a strong Home Fleet as key to its overall battle-fleet deployments, this did not mean that the Royal Navy had covered all operational contingencies, even in home/Atlantic waters, let alone further afield. One grave question, already flagged above, was whether any of the essentially "offshore navies" were ready to handle well-mobilized, land-based airpower as it sought to drive fleets a long way back from the Continent. If they could not, which was probably the case at least early on, what might the result be? On the one hand the destructive power of aircraft had given an advantage to early-mobilizing Powers such as Germany (and Japan) by the late 1930s, yet on the other hand Britain's island geography plus a superior Royal Navy meant that it couldn't be defeated easily, so it was possible that the next Anglo-German war might turn itself into a stalemate, not along another western front on land but down a lengthy north-south "front" one hundred miles off Europe's shores.

One final question concerning strategic geography here was whether either side was ready for a renewed Battle of the Atlantic, for another giant tussle between U-boats and Allied escorts similar to, though more developed than, that of 1917–18. Purely in terms of position, the advantage would always lie with the British, for the main flow of oceanic supplies (foodstuffs, armaments, and men) could be directed toward the great western ports of Belfast, the Clyde, and Liverpool, all equipped to receive and distribute such tonnage. German raiders, whether large surface ones (*Scharnhorst* and *Bismarck*) or submarines, had a considerable way to travel—and thus to open themselves to counterattack from British bases—to get at those Atlantic routes, even if Hitler seized additional European coastal positions on the lines that Wegener was arguing. This would still be true even if a sullenly unhelpful Éamon De Valera was going to keep Eire neutral in the next war and thus deny the Allied warships and merchantmen those harbors like Berehaven and Cork that they had been able to use freely in World War I; for British logistical planners could with some difficulty reroute all trans-Atlantic shipping to steam around the north of Ireland into home ports. In this theater of fighting, as in all the others, of course, positional advantage could well be neutralized either by new technologies or by one side's application of brute force, but overall geography would tend to favor the British in any reenactment of the Battle of the Atlantic.[14]

Each belligerent was under no illusion that this would be the most significant struggle of all in the West. Each side had put into place structures, commands, and leaders (Western Approaches Command, Oberbefehlshaber der U-boote, and RAF Coastal Command) that reflected this. Each side harnessed intelligence offices, new code-breaking departments, science labs, and statistical teams to try to get things right. Each was going to engage in a gigantic shipbuilding race—producing large numbers of Allied merchant vessels versus numbers of new U-boats versus numbers of newer escort vessels—because at the end of the day this really was a battle of attrition, to be measured more in years than in a single season of campaigning. And if the higher politics and diplomacy of a future war should bring the Americans in—at first as targets for U-boat attacks but then with later US shipbuilding resources—the game would get even bigger.

While the great bulk of Allied shipping for war in Europe crossed the "broad commons" between the New York–Halifax harbors and those of the western British Isles, two significant branch routes would carry supplies further, the first to North Russia, the second into the Mediterranean (Malta and Egypt). In the period before the United States was fully in the war, both spur routes involved convoys originating from the United Kingdom itself, usually from the Mersey or the Clyde, and of the two the

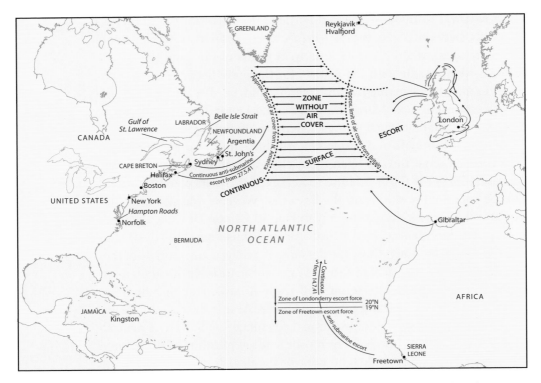

**MAP 2.** The Battle of the Atlantic: The mid-Atlantic air gap, until mid-1943.

northern was clearly the simplest geographically. Traders and fishermen
from Scotland and England had gone up to northern Norway and to the
ports of North Russia for many generations; during World War I it had
been a rather precarious link to tsarist Russia and then, after the 1917 revolution, to the forces fighting the Bolsheviks. Still, there were few if any
contingency plans developed at the British Admiralty for convoys along
this seaway prior to 1939, and for good reason. It was assumed that in the
event of war Norway would once again declare its neutrality (which it
did), so that the areas offshore would not see very much, if any, belligerent activity. And while diplomatic relations between Britain (and France)
and Stalin's USSR oscillated greatly in the late 1930s, few conceived of a
time when the Royal Navy might be required to convoy merchantmen to
North Russia with supplies to assist in a gigantic Nazi-Soviet war!

In the event that such a convoy route was required, however, the physical challenges were well known in advance.[15] The distance from the Clyde
to northern Russia was not such a great one, but the weather conditions
at sea were awful for most of the year, and in midwinter the line of polar
ice pushed dangerously south, forcing vessels to transit fairly close to the
Norwegian coastline. In the summer, by contrast, it was light virtually

throughout the entire day, leaving the merchantmen clearly exposed to any predator. None of this mattered much during the international crises of the late 1930s, when the Admiralty's attention was focused almost entirely on events in the Far East and Mediterranean. What could change all this would be northern Norway falling to a hostile power—not very conceivable given its proximity to the great base at Scapa Flow—or the further unlikely contingency of Neville Chamberlain's government desiring to convey aid to Stalin. The route to North Russia was not headline news.

In contrast to this neglect, planning for the defense of Britain's imperial trade routes through the Mediterranean Sea grew more and more intense during the second half of the 1930s. As noted above, they had been provoked by Mussolini's attack on Abyssinia in 1935, and they seemed even more necessary by 1939, when Il Duce was demanding French concessions over Savoy and Corsica and in April actually invaded Albania. Geographically, a war between Britain and Italy seemed a tough one for each side. The Royal Navy appeared to have the greater task, of protecting merchant shipping along that lengthy thin line between the Mediterranean "narrows," with hostile sea and air bases on each side. But Italy also faced the challenge of trying to run its oil tankers and troopships from ports like Naples and Taranto to its garrisons in Libya against inevitable disruption from RAF bombers based in Egypt and Malta, not to mention the Royal Navy itself. Each combatant, it is fair to say, tended to overestimate the military effectiveness and readiness of the other.[16] The difference was that a Mediterranean naval air struggle was really the only thing the Regia Marina had to worry about; to the Admiralty in London, this was just one of its many strategic headaches prior to 1939, albeit a major one.

Ensuring Britain's vital sea line of communications here was affected by two further aspects, one positive and one very tricky. The positive element here was the probability that the large French fleet (plus the French Air Force operating out of Tunisia, Corsica, and metropolitan France itself) would be involved in any clash with Italy and thus be an intimidating presence. Indeed, if France were also at war, then the British role in the Mediterranean might be more of a supporting than a frontline one. But the second aspect really gave the Admiralty planners cause for pause: it was that, unlike in 1914, they could no longer make battle calculations based on the capacities of their surface fleets alone. In such narrow confines as the waters of the central Mediterranean, and with visibility usually so good, just how vulnerable would heavy warships now be to enemy bombers? To what extent would the Royal Navy's possession of aircraft carriers be decisive? Plus, how important was Italy's huge lead in numbers of submarines? Might each side's battle fleet be driven from the center, rather as the Grand Fleet and High Seas Fleet were kept out of the central North Sea after 1916? Here, clearly, was a possible case where radical new weapons technologies could significantly impact traditional maritime geopolitics and the naval balance itself. If war came to the Mediterranean, the prospects for severe ship losses for each side were very high.

And they would be high because these were waters over which the British had determined to stay and fight. By the late 1930s any earlier ideas about withdrawing from the Mediterranean and "closing it off" at either end had been rejected as too defeatist, and too dangerous. To be sure, a lot of merchant shipping (especially the critical oil tankers) would be redirected along the Cape route; that was not the point. The strategic point was that allowing Mussolini's Italy to dominate the eastern Mediterranean might lead to the collapse of British influence in Yugoslavia, the Balkans, Greece, and even Turkey and be a threat to the Levant (Palestine) and perhaps even to the hold on Egypt itself. The decision to fight for Malta, even if France couldn't help, and when necessary to run convoys to it from either east or west, set the scene for what was going to be called the Battle of the Mediterranean. While the Royal Navy's heavy ships would be pulled back from Malta due to their vulnerability to air attack, a very substantial battle-fleet force, with a carrier, was to operate aggressively out of Alexandria. So it was that very close to the eve of the war, Britain privately decided that the Mediterranean Fleet was to be regarded as second in importance only to the Home Fleet itself.[17]

That of course left the waters east of Suez to occupy a decidedly secondary status, even if such would never be admitted in Whitehall itself, since it ran counter to twenty years of acceptance of the famous Jellicoe Report (1919) recommendation that the Singapore Base be treated as second in importance only to the home islands.[18] Britain's severe difficulties in implementing its declared Main Fleet to Singapore strategy are of course well known. The more interesting point, geopolitically, is that if Whitehall found itself unable to put a first-class battle fleet into the Indian Ocean until late in a global World War II, then it might not be alone. It could turn out that no one else was able to do so either. Neither the United States nor France had significant interests in these waters, Italy couldn't get through the Suez Canal, and Germany was simply too far away. So, too, was Japan, at least a Japan that had primarily to deal with an American naval challenge in the Pacific. By default almost, the Indian Ocean, which had become a "British lake" during the nineteenth century, looked as if it would remain a British lake both into and probably throughout the next great conflict the Empire would have to fight. That itself, of course, was a huge strategic and commercial bonus. The British position in Egypt and the eastern Mediterranean could be sustained along these Indian Ocean routes, Persian Gulf oil exports could be maintained, Indian Army divisions could be shipped westward, and the Australian trades were kept in no danger. When the gathering storms eventually cracked into the fury and turbulences of open war, very few things went right for British imperial grand strategy as western Europe fell into German hands, France collapsed, Italy jumped into the fight, the Balkans and Greece fell, the Battle of the Atlantic intensified, and even Singapore and the Eastern Empire surrendered. As Britain fought on and the Atlantic sea-lanes were maintained, therefore, it was also a huge relief that the Indian Ocean remained relatively uncontested (interrupted by one single Japanese carrier raid in 1942). The so-called tyranny of distance, which meant that the Royal Navy's presence here was far lighter than it wanted it to be, was keeping the other large naval forces from the Indian Ocean altogether.

One may disentangle all of the above discussions with this summary: as war approached in 1939, it was more than likely that the Royal Navy, along with the Royal Air Force, had it within its power to defend the home islands and, in a war against Germany alone, to hold the Atlantic. If it was also called upon to protect a route to North Russia, it could do that as well. Maintaining a full line of communication through the Mediterranean against Mussolini's navy and air force would be much more difficult, although Britain had considerable assets there, and trade might well need to be rerouted around the Cape. Unless it suffered from some huge defeats, it should be able to hold on to the Near East, the Persian Gulf, East Africa, and India. But holding on to the Far East in the face of serious Japanese naval and aerial attacks, even if the London government faced no European campaigns, might well be too much. Should war against the Axis occur, then, it really would be helpful to Britain's imperial future if much of the German war machine was tied down along its Eastern Front[19] and if the Japanese war machine had to grapple with the Americans in the Pacific. Geography counted for a lot in war; so, too, did having allies.

This same conviction about the value of allies also dominated the thinking of President Roosevelt and most of his key military advisors. It was true that being situated three thousand miles from the Old World and a full six thousand miles from East Asia had bestowed the most incredible good fortune upon the United States in military-strategic terms. It really was geographically secure from either naval blockade or aerial attack, despite the alarmists' agitation about both German and Japanese designs on the hemisphere. Yet even if the challenge of existing in a multipolar naval world came easier to the United States than to any other Power, that did not stop particular strategists in Washington from worrying about which foreign threat was the greatest and about where to place what they felt were their still-inadequate naval assets. As such, these worries were the continuation of the Atlantic versus Pacific debate over maritime priorities that had so preoccupied the planners from 1897 to 1921.[20] The elimination of the High Seas Fleet plus the freezing of the Japanese Navy at an inferior size by the naval treaties did of course greatly reduce that concern, and for a while during the 1920s the US Navy department seemed more agitated about the size and numbers of British cruisers than anything else. But the Manchurian Crisis of 1931–34 and then Japan's opposition to prolonging any naval limitations after 1936, and all this just as the Nazis had come into power, forcefully revived the old strategic dilemma. Should one divide the battleship force between the Atlantic and Pacific fleets (the greatest strategic heresy of all, to some pundits), and if so, in what proportions—one-third in the east, two-thirds in the west? If, however, one kept the fleet together, then to which ocean did one commit all the big ships (remembering that there would always be two to three of them under reconstruction at any given time)? What if most of the battle fleet had been allocated to the Pacific, and Britain was conquered? Alternatively, what if one committed those large warships to the Atlantic, and Japan went on a rampage in the Pacific? Polishing up War Plan Orange (versus Japan) and War Plan Black (versus Germany) in these years did not solve this problem but, rather, emphasized it. Americans were still some time away from the hugely expensive step of building a navy strong enough to be unchallenged in both oceans. Whatever the isolationists maintained, then, the logical conclusion pointed in the opposite direction: with a potential enemy threat in both oceans, it really was important to look for a naval ally, and that could only be the British.

Both geography itself and some earlier key episodes in American naval history—the War of 1812, the Civil War at sea, and World War I—had endowed the US Navy with a grand array of fleet bases and repair and construction sites along its entire eastern coastline: Portsmouth, New Hampshire; Boston; New York City; Philadelphia; Baltimore; Annapolis; Norfolk; Newport News; Charleston; and down to the Caribbean ports. Assuming British friendship, protection of that coastline was flanked by the bases of Halifax and St. John's to the north and Bermuda and Jamaica in the south. It was difficult to conceive that anything other than an incidental U-boat shelling could breach that long but formidable security line. It was also difficult to conceive the need for significant planning for convoy escorts along the Eastern Seaboard and even more difficult to imagine the Caribbean sea routes into Galveston, New Orleans, or Mobile requiring future naval protection. By contrast, it did seem plausible to worry about Nazi political influences gaining ground in Brazil and other South American states, with possible maritime activities also developing.[21] Even then, though, it was hard to do much planning without coming back to that basic question: what would be the position of Great Britain, and where would the Royal Navy be? Such a lot of US preparation for hemispheric defense hung on that factor.

There was one further aspect to the distances and dimension of the great North Atlantic basin. Wide though that sea was, there was nothing, no array of dangerous reefs, no chunk of neutral territory, between those bustling East Coast harbors and the strategic ports of western Europe, Cherbourg and the Normandy coast, North Africa, Gibraltar, and the entrance into the Mediterranean. If ever it was necessary, to use Churchill's phrase, to call upon the New World to come to the aid of the Old, there would be nothing geographically to stop that happening. Perhaps American politics would forbid it or lines of U-boats stop it, but it did seem that nature had disposed both the ports and the productive industries of the United States to be tilted in this very direction.

Clearly that could not be said so easily of America's other flank. And it was not just in terms of geography that the Pacific, and the Pacific War that was fought across it, was sui generis. The gigantic struggle that began with the attack on Pearl Harbor and ended with the dropping of the atomic bombs was different from any other major war in history—different in its dimensions and topography, different in the weapons systems and support systems (carrier airpower, landing craft, and fleet trains) that emerged to be the war-winning ones, different even in the sorts of fighting units (Marine Corps, Seabees) that had to be put together. It was geography that demanded that the country emerging victorious here would have to become a special sort of maritime power. The combatant that understood that first, and better, would be the victor.

It was also true that such an epic fight across the vast stretches of the Pacific Ocean was likely to take place while another war that began earlier, in 1937, was fought for control of the rimlands of East Asia and Southeast Asia, ranging from the Korean Peninsula at one extreme and down via Indochina and British Malaysia to Burma at the other—that is, along a north-south axis, roughly. But that war, launched to achieve Japan's self-proclaimed "Greater East Asia Co-Prosperity Sphere," was essentially a land war, fought in jungles and up lengthy river valleys, and didn't look too different from many an earlier Asian war of conquest by distant imperial rivals. It certainly would not have seemed much different to the Indigenous Javanese and Vietnamese if their Dutch and French rulers left and the Japanese marched in.

Yet war across the Pacific was something else: geography made that so, and in turn it impelled the responses that would grapple with the challenge of extreme distance and space. The vastness of this ocean stunned all the early explorers. There was, really, nothing at all in its middle latitudes, and while this is true of the middle of the other oceans (for example, the Indian), the distances from one side to the other in those seas are simply not so far. Had it not been for the outcrops of rock of the Hawaiian archipelago, themselves a good 1,400 miles north of the equator, there would have been nothing substantial across some seven thousand miles of ocean. No aircraft of the 1930s could cover such distances, nor could many warships other than cruiser types (and that at economical speeds, unlikely in wartime). This in turn made possession of the Hawaiian sea and air bases such an incredibly important asset, and it also explains why a few other small island groups (the central Solomons, the Gilberts, the Marianas, and Okinawa) came to have such strategic importance. Yet "possession" of a group no longer meant just a flag hoisting and a few colonial troops, as it had a half century ago; the seizure of one or another island now would take a substantial amphibious force, the creation of air bases, and a sea-denial capacity. The geography of Melanesia and Micronesia demanded the forces of long-range warfare and technology; and long-range war and technology in turn would conquer this vast Pacific geography.

The combatants pretty well knew all this, even before the actual war itself. The British, the least of the three large players here, understood shortly after 1919 that the furthest east they could create and, hopefully, maintain a main fleet base was at Singapore; the China Squadron based on Hong Kong played certain roles, visited the Chinese Treaty ports, and kept piracy in check but could never be an equal to a rising Japan. The real question, so far as an anxious Admiralty was concerned, was whether the Singapore base itself, even if construction of it was never completed, would be of much value if pressures in Europe prevented a battle fleet from ever being deployed there. It was therefore not surprising that the late 1930s and early 1940s witnessed London wistfully suggesting the stationing of an American squadron in Singapore as a novel deterrent force against Japan, since Britain itself could not provide the ships. Even in the age of the long-range sail the Royal Navy had found naval operations on the far side of the world a real stretch for it. Now it was far more difficult, so maybe it was better to have American warships steaming in and out of Singapore harbor than hostile Japanese?

Of the two main contenders for mastery in the Pacific, the decision-makers at Imperial General Headquarters in Tokyo were also somewhat daunted by this ocean's sheer dimensions, at least the area that stretched away from the larger outer island groups like the Philippines, the Celebes, and New Guinea. Their army's steady aggressions southward had already extended Japanese control over much of South China's coastline and French Indochina, so it was not a terrific thing for their planners to assemble forces that might one day move on Malaya, Singapore, Java, and Sumatra. It was also true that Tokyo had acquired Imperial Germany's island colonies (Carolines, Marshalls, and Marianas) in the 1919 peace settlement, although it actually hadn't invested much in their garrisons. Yet going much further afield than that did not seem to make any sense to an army already deeply engaged in the conquest of central China—French Polynesia had no known value, and an invasion of the Hawaiian Islands, even if some in the navy urged it, was judged to consume too many divisions. Rather conveniently, then, the Japanese military drifted toward a war plan where they imagined that, in a struggle with the Anglo-American powers, they should run rampant for the first six months, conquer what was necessary, create an extensive perimeter rim around the Western Pacific, and then expect the United States to discuss peace terms. That looked attractive politically, and it seemed very appealing geographically.

The Japanese High Command might have been further encouraged had they understood how much their American counterparts wrestled with this problem of strategic geography during the 1920s and 1930s. In very rapid order, at least as measured in the larger historical context, during the nineteenth century the United States had seen the closing of the frontier and its emergence as a nation with a Pacific shoreline that was thousands of miles in length, which was both an opportunity and a vulnerability. The laying of the transcontinental railway system on the one hand and, especially, the opening of the Panama Canal (1914) on the other had greatly reduced the amount of time needed to transfer military reinforcements—and fleets—from the advanced, industrial East Coast to the still-developing Western states should some challenge occur in the Pacific. Even so, and despite all the efforts of the Department of the Navy to establish fortified harbors in California, Oregon, Washington State, and the outlier of Pearl Harbor itself, the fact remained that the United States faced an extraordinarily demanding geostrategic dilemma if it sought to ensure that its national interests were simultaneously secure in two quite different oceans of the earth. To be sure, America was not alone in facing such a dilemma (Imperial Russia had felt a similar tug between defending its European shorelines and its Far East possessions, and the British Empire faced an analogous challenge in trying both to defend India and to preserve the European balance), but the task was no less difficult logistically just because other Great Powers faced a similar tension.

As noted earlier, the successful conclusion of World War I and the terms of the various Washington naval treaties appeared to resolve America's security dilemma after 1922, yet that sense of peace lasted scarcely a decade. Years of further ponderings led to President Roosevelt's eventual order to have the overwhelming bulk of the US battle fleet be based in the Pacific Ocean. Even that decision, important though it was, did not resolve the navy's next problem: where in the Pacific should that be? Should it be in the relative safety of West Coast ports from San Diego to Puget Sound? Or should the Pacific Fleet, all or some of it, instead be based at Pearl Harbor, a massive 2,500 miles to the west but obviously more of a warning to the Japanese? Or third, should it be deployed even further afield, in East Asia (Manila), which was approximately another 3,500 miles west of Hawaii? Even if the broad Washington consensus was against the latter option as being too risky (which is why the planners would later decline the British idea of basing warships at Singapore), the fact remained that the Pacific's huge expanse had left the US Navy with this second dilemma, that of San Diego versus Pearl Harbor. The bolder of the two options would of course be to station the main US battle fleet in Hawaiian waters, but even then it would be some days from the action if the Japanese did sweep down upon the Philippines and Hong Kong— so far away, in fact, that no one in the leadership could imagine that Pearl Harbor itself would be the aggressor's first target![22]

Assuming that a Japanese-American conflict in the Pacific was coming, there were two other points about the geography of this vast tract that both sides' planners bore in mind. The first point was the appalling, continuously stormy weather across the entire North Pacific, which not only made major fleet action difficult; it made maritime warfare impossible. The second was that the entire southeast quadrant of the Pacific, from French Polynesia stretching eastward toward the west coast of South America, was simply out of range as well as being unimportant to the Japanese High Command. It therefore followed that the operational range for the US forces in the Pacific was between a line that went directly westward from Hawaii and a second line heading southwestward via island groups (Samoa) toward Australia and New Zealand. In planning terms nothing much mattered to the north or to the south of that long strategic segment; and nothing much did happen when war came, except that the islands of French Polynesia prudently elected to be on de Gaulle's side and that there was the brief Aleutian campaign of 1943.

Certain operational conclusions also followed from any broad geographical understanding of both the limits and the opportunities of war fighting in this theater. With so few outcrops of land occurring in this ocean, and the distances between them being so great, it was clear to all that a future struggle for the Pacific would be very much a *positional* war, with the belligerents striving to get control of those land areas. Japan's planners therefore intended to take the Philippines, Singapore/Malaya, the Dutch island archipelago, and New Guinea to assure a large protective zone and then perhaps also take Midway and the Solomons. So, the United States in turn had to think of positional warfare across the central Pacific via various island groups like the Gilberts, Marshalls, and so on. Consequently, from 1919 onward a few thinkers in the US Marine Corps (Earl H. Ellis, most prominently) had begun to advocate for the necessary logistical planning regarding advanced base operations in Micronesia and involving both island hopping and the necessary weaponry and vessels for amphibious operations. Somewhat later, procurement officers in the navy's bureaus began to see that refueling and sustaining very-long-range cruises by the Pacific Fleet might require modern forms of supply ships—the early fleet train, in other words.[23]

Far less thought was given, however, to other types of warfare. Very little attention was paid to the practical defense of sea-lanes (for example, through a convoy system for merchantmen), in part because so relatively little shipping flowed directly across the Pacific at this time, in part because the Japanese Navy had given no indication that it itself regarded commerce raiding as important, and finally, in part because US naval doctrine in general didn't pay much attention to convoy operations. American shipping up and down its western coastline was too far away from Japan, and Australia's and New Zealand's export trades angled westward, around Cape Town to Britain, and were just as far away. It was true that, by contrast, Japan had a valuable overseas merchant marine to be defended or attacked; but if an attack were to take place, it was anticipated that it would be by American submarines operating out of Subic Bay, always assuming of course that the Philippines would not fall.

The quintessential sort of naval fighting that was hoped for and planned for in the Pacific theater was that between the two navies' great battle fleets. Until very late in the day during the 1930s, both the Japanese and American services were very much dominated by "battleship admirals" who had always encouraged their successors to follow suit. Even when carrier officers made it to flag rank, they were still in a distinct minority; and during most of the peacetime years the aircraft carriers themselves would be engaged in individual journeys and flight practices, not task force operations. The battle fleets on each side of what the US Navy termed "War Plan Orange" would, however, be practicing repeatedly for a giant engagement, a second though much more decisive Battle of Jutland somewhere in the western Pacific Ocean. And with an overwhelming big-gun victory achieved, it was thought, the defeated side would give way. This was Mahan's intellectual vision, after all, and Japanese battleship admirals were as much Mahanians as were their equivalents in the American fleet.[24]

## The Economic Variable: Technology and Production

There was no way, then, that the geographical variables of distance and size could be wished away; the simple fact was that they disadvantaged Italy, France, and Germany while conferring advantages on Japan, Great Britain, and, above all, the United States. Since the coming of the Industrial Revolution, however, persistent human invention—Professor David Landes's *Unbound Prometheus* discusses this[25]—had had the effect of greatly reducing the time taken for humans to travel lengthy distances across land and sea, including, of course, for warlike purposes. The invention within a short period of time of the steam engine, the railway, electricity, the internal-combustion engine, and, finally, aircraft led to a transportation revolution unimaginable to earlier generations. Explosive growth occurred in the transportation by sea of bulk goods once the coming of the reciprocating engine could propel vessels forward whatever the contrary tides and winds, and even more when improvements in shipbuilding techniques created ever-larger cast-iron and then steel hulls. Moreover, the bulk goods themselves changed from older items to those needed by modern industrialized societies: steel, machinery, aluminum, rubber, electrical goods, and petroleum. Some industrializing societies, and Britain in particular, also became huge importers of foodstuffs (wheat, beef, tropical fruit, and vegetable oils) such that by the 1930s entire steamship companies focused individually on the transport of Argentine frozen beef, New Zealand lamb, West Indian bananas, and so on. The result of all this, as the global economy picked itself up from the Great Depression, was a gigantic network of trade flows,[26] with thousands and thousands of merchantmen at sea on any given day of the year, as seen in the historical chart in map 3.

This striking representation of the world's largest merchant fleet steaming the high seas—each dot indicates a single vessel—was a statement of confidence in the British imperial trading system as, say, the London Chamber of Commerce would have viewed the world in late November 1937. It might also be seen as a declaration of confidence in unfettered oceanic commerce; thus, merchant ships coming from the Southern Hemisphere steamed directly and individually across the center of the Atlantic rather than being herded into convoys to be escorted northward via Freetown or to hug the American Eastern Seaboard until reaching Halifax. To planners in the British Admiralty, though, with sharp memories of what the U-boats had achieved a mere two decades earlier, an illustration like this confirmed what a huge logistical and military challenge they would face if or when a second war at sea had to be fought against a revived German Navy. To the submariners surrounding Karl Doenitz, who was al-

**TABLE 2.** Size of the World's Major
Merchant Navies, 1939

| Navy | Gross tonnage |
| --- | --- |
| British Empire | 21,000,000 |
| Norway | 4,800,000 |
| France | 2,900,000 |
| Greece | 1,800,000 |
| Netherlands | 3,000,000 |
| United States | 9,000,000 |
| Italy | 3,400,000 |
| Germany | 4,500,000 |
| Japan | 5,600,000 |

Data from Milward, *War, Economy, and Society,*
*1939–1945,* 146.

ready by this time the senior commanding officer (Fuehrer) of the U-boat arm, each of those dots represented a potential target. And there were certainly a lot of them.

For the fact was that Great Britain still possessed the world's largest marine by far, even if it had been overtaken in certain other economic realms. After all, much of Germany's merchant fleet had been lost or confiscated by 1918, neither France nor Italy had large commercial fleets, and the US merchant navy suffered from uncommercial rates and the fierce opposition of its own agricultural and industrial lobbies to any imports (unless it was goods that they themselves did not produce), so it was rather isolated from world routes. Among the large naval powers, only Japan possessed another sizable merchant fleet, although it also just traded regionally.

Table 2 merits a little further comment. While it is true that Britain's merchant navy remained the world's biggest in the 1930s, it was less so than before 1914, when it possessed around 60 percent of the global total. Both during World War I and especially in the later years of peace, a small yet important number of medium Powers like Greece, Panama, Poland, the Netherlands, and Norway, seeking to generate foreign earnings, had built up their own merchant fleets staffed mainly with their own national crews. The unintended consequence of the existence of these newer merchant marines was that when the Nazi war machine struck out in conquest of so many of Germany's neighbors, those fleets were ordered to report to their governments-in-exile in London and thus to join the British maritime effort. But that was clearly not foreseen before the war itself.

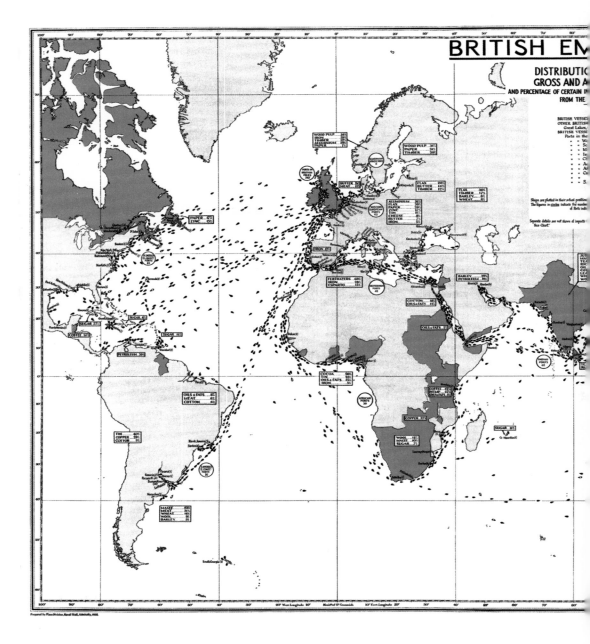

**MAP 3.** Worldwide chart of British Empire shipping, November 24, 1937 (historical chart, originally prepared by HM Admiralty).

All national shipping fleets, whether of commercial vessels or of warships, required substantial shipbuilding and ship-repair industries, and here the situation was a rather similar one. None of the six Powers lacked a shipbuilding base, for all had been involved in the various "naval races" of the pre–World War I era, and each, too, had striven at that time to con-

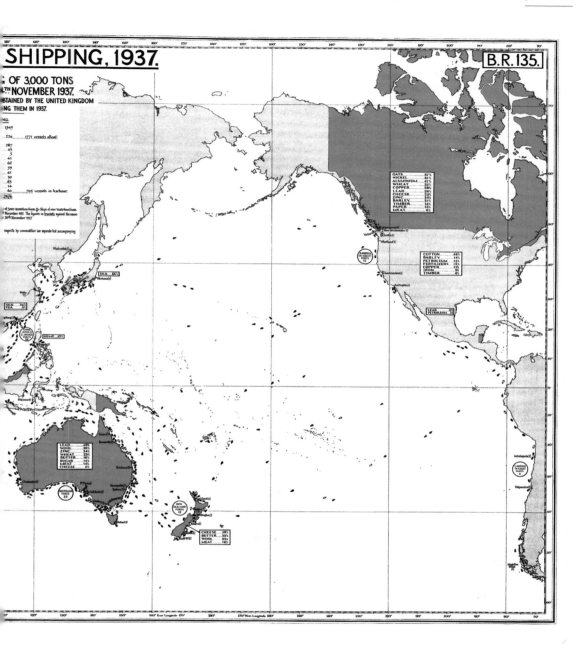

struct a modern merchant marine, including ocean liners. With very few exceptions, shipbuilding was done by private firms, albeit with various forms of subsidy and support and in the lean years of the Depression with government small-warship orders and repair contracts just to keep them going. The spurt in fresh heavy-warship orders after 1937 thus came to shipyards that already had the slipways and skilled (if often unemployed) labor waiting. Just a glance through the trade advertisements in, say, *Jane's Fighting Ships 1939* shows the national champions: the big Italian yards at Genoa and Trieste, for example; the Japanese firms at Kure and Yokosuka; the big French shipyards at Brest, St. Nazaire, and Lorient; and those familiar German names at their North Sea and Baltic locations. Thus, the massive imperial shipyard of the kaiser's era at Wilhelmshaven became the Kriegsmarinewerft-Wilhelmshaven of Nazi times, producing among many other vessels the famous pocket battleships *Admiral Scheer* and *Graf Spee*, the battle cruiser *Scharnhorst*, the battleship *Tirpitz*, and dozens of Type VII U-boats. Meanwhile, of the four fast battleships of the *Roma*-class ordered in the late 1930s by Mussolini's government, two would be built at the Ansaldo shipyard in Genoa and two in Adriatic shipyards. All of these large shipbuilding programs went more slowly than their admiralties wanted, sometimes due to a lack of skilled craftsmen, high-grade steel, or funds, but every one of the Powers regarded this industry as strategic and deserving much support.[27]

This was no less the case with regard to the British shipbuilding industry, despite what seemed at the time like the broad collapse of work at the Clyde, the Tyne, Barrow, and the other industrial centers. It is not clear, therefore, that the size of the naval cutbacks in the 1920s caused serious delays or, at least, more serious delays when rebuilding commenced for the Royal Navy than it did anywhere else. Overall, as noted in the previous chapter, no nation seemed to be able to produce a ready-for-action battleship in anything less than about five years from authorization to fleet readiness, so new warships authorized under the 1936–37 and 1937–38 programs usually were not in service until as late as the Fall of France. What the British Admiralty did during the lean years was to dole out its limited purchases as strategically as possible, keeping the smaller coastal yards going with the annual order of destroyers and light cruisers and the larger yards with the big reconstruction jobs (like the modernization of the *Queen Elizabeth*–class battleships). When at last the green light for post–Washington Treaty rearmament was given, the allocation of contracts for the new *King George V* battleships and *Illustrious*-class carriers showed the same intention: that is, to keep at least six large shipyards going as the vital underpinnings of Britain's global, imperial policy.[28]

All those large yards—John Brown and Fairfield on the lower Clyde, Vickers-Armstrong and Swan Hunter on the Tyne, Cammell Laird, and Harland Wolf—were privately owned, albeit integral parts of the British "warfare state." The structure of control therefore differed from the situation in the United States at this time, where an important cluster of four large and various smaller government-owned shipyards (Norfolk Navy Yard, Philadelphia Navy Yard, New York Navy Yard, and so on) existed alongside privately owned shipyards, also large and small in size (for example, the Newport News yards, building most of the carriers at this time). Although this may have been an expensive commitment—like the protectionist legislation insisting that US-flagged merchantmen contain only American crews—and state shipyards usually had higher costs, their existence provided competition for the private companies in bidding for warship contracts. Moreover, the pro-navy attitude of FDR, the use of some New Deal legislation to boost shipyard jobs, and the supportive Vinson-Trammell Act of 1934 meant that American shipbuilding was pretty busy even during its isolationist years.[29] When the huge naval increases of 1939–40 were announced, much of the basic infrastructure, at least for building new battleships and carriers, was already in place, and the contracts were distributed to state-owned and privately owned yards alike. The first four *North Carolina*–class battleships' contracts went each to a different yard, two government and two private—there was a method here.[30]

As the warship builders' yards across the world went into a much higher tempo of launchings during the last years of peace, the demand for every critical component associated with naval vessels (turbine engines, screws and rudders, electrical wiring, gun placements, optical instruments, and so on) just soared. Above all, steel production surged, as it was needed for a warship's hull, decks, superstructure, and gun turrets. From the Franco-Prussian War of 1870 onward, steel had been the best measure of world power, with its multiple military applications for railways, rifles, cannon, engines, warships, trucks, and tanks. In this respect, at least, not much had changed as the new war approached, for while the 1939–45 conflict would indeed be characterized as the "Wizard's War" (of, for example, radar, homing torpedoes, and proximity fuzes), the huge new battleships laid down in the late 1930s each required their tens of thousands of protective Bessemer steel.[31] Like the size of a nation's total population, the amount of its steel output was regarded as one of the great indicators of its military potential (see table 3).

That the German and American steel production should be ahead of all others would come as no surprise to any economic historian of industrialization in the West; when the age of iron production shifted to that of high-quality steels, those two countries developed a far larger output than the rest even by 1913, and the same was true for that related and absolutely critical industrial product—machine tools. Here the German advantage was remarkable, even over that of the United States, and quite a way ahead of Britain. But this of course had been the success story of post-Bismarckian Germany, which in many regards was replicated in its prowess in the other industries of the Third Industrial Revolution, such as chemicals, electrics, optics, and automobiles. The supposedly punitive peace treaties of 1919 had done nothing to take those innate strengths

**PAINTING 13.** Battleships USSs *Oklahoma* and *Nevada*, Charlestown Navy Yard, 1935. Here is the traditional US battlefleet navy of the interwar years in Boston Harbor, across the bay. These 14-inch-gunned sister ships had a very different war experience: *Oklahoma* was irretrievably damaged at Pearl Harbor, whereas *Nevada* survived and was active during the war (including D-Day and Okinawa operations).

**TABLE 3.** Population and Steel Output of the Powers, 1939

|  | Population (millions) | Steel output (millions of tons) |
|---|---|---|
| Great Britain | 48 | 13.2 |
| British Dominions | 20 | 2.6 |
| France | 42 | 6.2 |
| United States | 132 | 51.4 |
| Germany | 76 | 23.3 |
| Italy | 44 | 2.3 |
| Japan | 71 | 5.8 |
| USSR | 190 | 18.8 |

Data from W. Braakhuis, "Assault on Europe 1939," accessed June 12, 2020, http://www.euronet.nl/users/wilfried/ww2/1939.htm, a collection of data on the year 1939, useful because it also includes the population and steel statistics for the Dominions as well as the usual powers.

away from a defeated Reich, so they could all be resuscitated through heavy Nazi defense spending, with giants like IG Farben and Krupp Industries at the fore.[32]

And then there was Fokker and Messerschmidt and Boeing and Grumman and de Havilland and Mitsubishi Air Industries. One further, very significant measure of military-industrial strength by the late 1930s was of course airpower, and thus the size of the air forces of these six naval nations. For while shipping fleets and shipbuilding capacities remained critical indicators of a Great Power's comparative naval strength, just as they had been before World War I, the swift development of bigger and longer-ranged bomber aircraft brought a completely new and possibly transformative factor into play. Naval mines, torpedo boats, and coastal submarines had already made it far too dangerous for large warships to come close to a hostile shore,[33] but the newer threat posed to fleets by swarms of land-based bombers (dive-bombers, high-level bombers, and torpedo-bombers) was greater still, even if some admirals continued to dispute that fact. Of course, those bombers needed to be assured of protection by their own fighter forces and therefore enjoy their own local air superiority, which is why the overall aircraft production of these nations was such a critical and anxiously observed matter (see table 4).

It is not difficult to see how these figures translated into the power politics and strategic opportunity of the time. By 1938, the year of Munich, both Germany (significantly) and Japan had a larger plane output than did the United Kingdom, while Italy's figures were considerably bigger than France's. Aircraft quality was another thing, to be sure, and each nation's proclaimed total disguised a long list of slower aircraft types, many trainer aircraft, and so on, but there was no doubting that the Axis powers had stolen a lead here—the sharp increase in British output in 1939 was a sign of the Chamberlain government's belated recognition of that worrying fact. Those raw totals disguised much else too, like the British move to the world's first radar-controlled aerial defense network, the extremely high quality of the Japanese Naval Air Force, and the Italian fuel shortages. Finally, the United States' extremely large *commercial* aircraft-building capacity (which could swiftly be converted to use for building bombers) is quite invisible here, so that all that is seen is its miserably low output of military planes. Still, if politicians in the three Western democracies had these figures in their minds—in the year of Munich, the combined Axis plane total was roughly twice as much as theirs—they surely had one further reason to seek to avoid going to war.

That very low American output of military aircraft was a reflection of, more than anywhere else, a nation still wedded to the path of peace even into the late 1930s, and of a Congress yet to be persuaded of the need to spend much of its national income on the defense budget. This led to the curious fact, remarked on by some contemporaries, that whereas the United States possessed the largest economy in the world by far and was indisputably one of the Great Powers, it allocated a much smaller proportion of the country's overall wealth to the military than anybody else did (see table 5).

Nothing better reveals the distorted nature of the Fascist states' militarized economies than these comparative statistics, which was under-

**TABLE 4.** Aircraft Production of the Powers, 1932–39 (nearest hundred)

|  | 1932 | 1933 | 1934 | 1935 | 1936 | 1937 | 1938 | 1939 |
|---|---|---|---|---|---|---|---|---|
| United Kingdom | 400 | 600 | 700 | 1,100 | 1,900 | 2,200 | 2,800 | 7,900 |
| United States | 600 | 500 | 400 | 500 | 1,100 | 900 | 1,800 | 2,200 |
| France | (600) | (600) | (600) | 800 | 900 | 700 | 1,400 | 3,200 |
| Germany | 36 | 400 | 2,000 | 3,200 | 5,100 | 5,600 | 5,200 | 8,300 |
| Italy | (500) | (500) | (800) | (1,000) | (1,000) | (1,500) | 1,900 | (2,000) |
| Japan | 700 | 800 | 700 | 1,000 | 1,200 | 1,500 | 3,200 | 4,500 |

Data from Kennedy, *Rise and Fall of the Great Powers*, 324, with an explanation of the Italian and French figures on p. 590 n. 139. Soviet totals not reproduced here.

**TABLE 5.** National Income and Percentage Spent on Defense, 1937

|  | National income ($bn) | Percentage on defense (%) | Defense spending ($bn) |
|---|---|---|---|
| United States | 68 | 1.5 | 1.0 |
| British Empire | 22 | 5.7 | 1.3 |
| France | 10 | 9.1 | 0.9 |
| Germany | 17 | 23.5 | 4.0 |
| Italy | 6 | 14.5 | 0.9 |
| Japan | 4 | 28.2 | 1.1 |

Data from Wright, *Study of War,* 672.

standable enough, for if one was out to revise the territorial status quo, it was necessary to spend a lot on the weapons of war in the first place. Thus it was that, by straining itself to the uttermost, Japan (whose central government budget was almost entirely devoted to the military) was spending about as much on defense, slightly over $1 billion, as the far, far richer United States. Hitler's Germany, moreover, was spending around three times more than Chamberlain's Britain and almost four times more than Roosevelt's America. Of course it was a good moment for Berlin and Tokyo to run the risk of war! But one blindingly obvious fact was also clear from these figures: both the British Empire and, much more so, the United States had a very large "surge capacity" for arms spending if they moved their economies into a state of total war. A Britain willing to spend, say, 15 percent of national income on defense would have almost caught up to the Third Reich's outgoings, while an America allocating a similar percentage on defense would be outspending everyone else.

Although it merits more analysis later (see chapter 8), one final confirmatory statistic is worth mentioning here. In terms of sheer industrial and technical muscle, the United States had possessed the capacity to create the world's largest navy since early in the century, and after 1919 its relative productive power simply grew more, even if damaged for a while by the Depression. By 1937, it contained 41.7 percent of what was termed "the relative war potential of the powers" as compared to Germany's 14.4 percent, the USSR's 14 percent, and Britain's 10.2 percent—or Japan's 3.5 percent.[34] These figures (albeit with their suspicious exactitude) are of course a later, postwar calculation and were not known at the time. What was understood by all was that the United States was still in a condition where it much preferred to spend on butter rather than guns.

Thus, an examination of the economic and technological correlation of forces between the Powers would indicate that the West's lead here was not as great as it would seem from the clear advantages that Britain and the United States possessed in the geographical realm. The former scene was more mixed due to Nazi Germany's sizable assets in steel production and ball bearings (and in many other aspects of "relative war potential") and to the greater readiness for combat possessed by the German and Japanese armed services, especially in their air forces. While the gap between the status quo and the revisionist Powers had been partially closed by their earlier rearmament, though, it remained an open question whether the have-not naval states would be able to achieve their aims if total war occurred with the richer and more productive Anglo-American nations.

## Strategic Thinkers and the Winning of Naval Wars

There was nothing simple about all that is described above. The roles of geography, economics, and technology, the interrelationships between them all, and then the relationship of each to sea power makes hard any attempt at synthesis and generalization. The many differences both in geography and in economic condition between the six great naval nations induces a need to qualify almost immediately any general remark that might be made about how navies operate or about what strategic feature is the most significant. If generalizations about the nature of sea power are risky, then, it would be a bold author who would claim to have detected certain immutable "laws" concerning naval affairs and navies that were applicable to all ages. And yet that is indeed what Mahan did early into his most famous work, *The Influence of Sea Power upon History, 1660–1783*. As he very well knew, important changes did occur from time to time in warships' sizes, armaments, and propulsion—Mahan must have been aware of the great alterations in the character of the US vessels that passed under his windows at the Naval War College, where he wrote and taught—and he was swift to admit that changes in the "instruments" and weaponry of navies did alter tactics in wartime. Yet still, he argued, for all such transient changes, "the old foundations of strategy remain, as though laid upon a rock." The principal elements affecting the growth of sea power in nations belong to "the unchangeable, or unchanging, order of things, remaining the same, in cause and effect, from age to age."[35]

Was it because Mahan was a child of the nineteenth century and the positivist search for general laws that his conclusions about the essence of sea power were so firm? Or was it simply that his *Influence* books covered a cluster of historical campaigns where one could demonstrate that victory derived from major fleet battles (the Seven Years' War and the

Napoleonic Wars)? Whatever his intellectual provenance, Mahan made it clear that naval mastery was achieved by decisive battles on the high seas and that the winning navies needed a large and central force to implement that strategy. The contemporary French preference for *guerre de course*—commerce raiding—was, he felt, a nitpicking strategy that could never achieve a complete victory in war. If the Royal Navy wished to stay at the top in the face of all of the challenges to it at century's end, it would need to keep the biggest and best battle fleet; and if his own United States wished to become a great naval power, then it, too, would have to create a large battleship navy, not a fleet of cruisers.[36]

The influence of Mahan's *Influence* on admiralties and admirals across the globe after its initial publication in 1890 is very well known. The naval lobbies in aspiring new sea powers—Japan, Germany, and Italy—seized upon it gratefully; the expansionists of his own United States in this decade rejoiced at having their own prophet of maritime navies and large fleets; and the British Navy, both the subject and the beneficiary of Mahan's many writings about the importance of the sea in world history, rewarded the American author with adulation and emulation. The international scene was favorable for just such a book as his. An intensification of the scramble for colonies—including coaling stations and warship bases—in Africa, Asia, and the Pacific was accompanying a boom in international commerce and capital flows, a dizzying rise in industrial output and newer technologies, and a great spurt in expenditures on both armies and navies by the leading European states, joined now by the United States and Japan.[37] Navy budgets surged overall just at the same time that warships became far larger, faster, much more heavily armed, and clad with far more armor. By the time of World War I those "super-dreadnoughts" (for example, the *Queen Elizabeths* and the *Colorado*-class) were far more powerful and expensive than their predecessors of 1890—how satisfying it was, therefore, that there existed grand intellectual and historical arguments showing that all successful states needed strong sea power in order to advance, or just survive. "The poor French!" exclaimed Kaiser Wilhelm II on learning that Paris had backed down before a navally bigger Britain in a colonial quarrel of 1898. "They have not read their Mahan!"[38] Germany, by contrast, should learn that lesson and build up the strongest navy possible. But so, of course, should the Japanese, the Italians, and the Americans.

The results of the Spanish-American War (1898) and the Russo-Japanese War (1904–6) confirmed Mahan's teachings—victory went to the nation winning the main conflict at sea—and World War I did not undermine them; the losers in 1918, after all, were the Central Powers with their cramped naval effectiveness, the winners those Anglo-American-Japanese battle-fleet nations. If there were to be lessons learned by the victors concerning the inconclusive results of some World War I naval battles like Jutland, that was precisely the point: how to improve signaling at sea, how to improve warship protection—all that would help to make the future fight between their respective armadas more decisive.[39] The fact that the critical Washington Naval Treaty focused so clearly on the size and number of *battleships* was just another affirmation of how important sea power was to world politics and of just how—through capital ships—the leading nations were to be measured. Thus, the naval ministries of the 1930s were not just making their own history under the context of material and geographical constraints, they were doing so under the decided influence of received ideas about how to fight the next war at sea.

Clearly, the Japanese and American battleship admirals found it easiest both to imbibe and then to utilize Mahan's theories about navies, since they were intent upon gaining a great Pacific Fleet victory in the next war, which would secure for their country that "overbearing power on the sea which drives the enemy's flag from it, or only allows it to appear as a fugitive."[40] And the secondary naval powers, France and Italy, wrestled with this Mahanian insistence upon the critical importance of the big battle fleet as best they could: by building their own fine new post–Washington Treaty capital ships, if only a few of them, while also constructing lots of lesser weapons (torpedo boats, destroyers, and submarines) that might blunt the power of larger battle fleets in any actual fighting. Then, in the case of the German naval leadership of Admiral Raeder, who had an occasional vision of 100,000-ton battleships (!), there existed someone with a Mahanian, and Tirpitzian, belief in large central battle fleets without much hope that such could ever be acquired, at least for a long while.

It was ironic, then, that the nation that was the epitome of Mahan's lessons on sea power, Great Britain, also turned out to be the one least suited for *simply* having a battle-fleet-centered navy.[41] Any one of the others, as we have seen, would have been a much better match. Yet Britain, and the sprawling empire it possessed, was a quite different kind of maritime nation and had been for at least a century beforehand, when its economy started to switch from agrarian protectionism to industrial free trade—that is, when it could no longer feed its population from domestic sources but instead relied upon overseas supplies, together with its great strength in warships to defend the sea-lanes in times of war. British manufactures would surge outward to both imperial and foreign markets, while vast amounts of foodstuffs, fuel oils, and raw materials would be transported to the homeland in the world's largest merchant fleet, its security guaranteed by the presence of patrolling cruisers and flotillas of smaller Royal Navy escorts. The true essence of British naval strategy was therefore the preservation of the oceanic lines of communication, because the ultimate aim of the nation's grand strategy—in the Clausewitzian sense—was the security of the British Isles themselves. If the imports got through, even after tough fighting, that purpose was achieved. If they got through without battle, the same was true, but even better. A clash between the battle fleets was only really important if the victor could then throttle Britain's trade lifelines; and thus an enemy pocket battleship at loose on the high seas was a danger only when it began opening fire on the merchantmen. The Royal Navy was always imagined to be powerful enough in capital-ship numbers to deal with such dangers, but in addition to that it really needed a second navy, a very large number of light cruisers, escort destroyers, and such vessels designed for trade protection. If war broke out, this second navy would decidedly not be with the battle fleet. Sea power, from this perspective, was about getting merchant ships safely to port.

The naval writer most closely associated with such arguments was of course the British official historian and strategist Sir Julian Corbett. Not someone in search of grand historical "laws" like Marx or even Mahan, Corbett simply used his deep study of England's naval past, and especially of its great maritime achievement in, say, conflicts like the Seven Years' War (1756–63), to inform his views of what the best strategy might be for Britain in the contemporary age.[42] As he saw it, like Venice or the Dutch Republic but even more so, the British Empire relied upon command of the trading routes for its economic survival. It followed from this circumstance that the real "historical strategy of Britain" (Sir Basil Liddell Hart's phrase) was to ensure that the many maritime lines of communication to and from the home islands, their population, and their industries were kept secure. If Britain's navy could guarantee that, and thus keep its economy robust and protected, then that would in turn safeguard its state finances, keep its credit high, and allow the state to raise an army, subsidize its allies, and aid its colonies. This was a much larger concept of what sea power constituted than the simple notion of winning a battle-fleet action. It was to follow for Corbett, then, that the navy's eventual victory in the Battle of the Atlantic in the critical years of 1917–18—thus keeping its overseas commerce and then the US armies flowing into British harbors—was a much more important component of the Empire's grand strategy than what had happened at the Battle of Jutland, just one of the points that caused this writer to be seen with suspicion by traditionalist admirals.[43]

One further very significant operational consequence of Corbett's thought, again based on his studies of the Napoleonic Wars at sea, was that he was not averse to the use of convoys in wartime to protect British commerce, even if they were clumsy to organize and slowed down the faster merchantmen and their shipping companies. On the contrary, he felt, if an enemy's capacity to sink large numbers of civilian ships was great, then it should be the Royal Navy's prime purpose to protect all seaborne trade, by organizing and then fighting the convoys through. It was, moreover, a silly distraction of Britain's naval strength to go looking for commerce raiders across the ocean's giant stretches; such raiders, whether the great French raiding frigates or German U-boats, would be drawn to the convoys like wasps to honey, and could be confronted—and destroyed—at that time. And if they chose not to attack, if they couldn't get close, or even if a convoy fight was eluded altogether and the merchant ships got home unhindered to Portsmouth and Liverpool, then the strategic victory was Britain's.

This all made perfect sense and, as we shall see, by 1940 or so it was a policy generally pursued by the British Admiralty, even if some senior officers (and Churchill) yearned for shootouts against enemy capital ships on the high seas. But the high commands of most of the other naval powers still regarded the essence of maritime warfare as being a large-scale Mahanian clash of their main battle fleets and therefore organized their forces along such assumptions. In a smallish way, though, Germany and Italy were willing to run coastal convoys, and the latter also saw the need for convoys to and from North Africa. France always provided strong naval escorts for its troopships, but not for much else. Finally, there was the very odd case here of Japan, which, while having an economy as heavily dependent for its survival on overseas commerce as Britain, made no serious preparation for the protection of its merchant fleets. Corbett, had he lived to see that, would have shaken his head.

The mixed condition of the six large naval powers by the eve of World War II defied the idea that there might be a single authoritative work on the lessons of sea power that would suit all. If the majority of them preferred a roughly Mahanian emphasis on a battle-fleet strategy, it was because it seemed to fit their circumstance best. And if the Royal Navy paid more attention to the defense of trade in 1939, it was not only because commerce protection mattered but also because there was no single large enemy battle fleet—no High Seas Fleet—against which it could array its own heavy warships. It made sense, really, to suppose that if a truly global conflict opened up between the three Axis powers (and their navies) on the one hand and the Anglo-American (-French) naval nations on the other, then the maritime campaigning would differ from sea to sea: chiefly a fight over the trade routes in the Atlantic; some bruising, close-in shootouts over Malta and Libya convoys in the Mediterranean; and most probably large-scale surface encounters between US and Japanese battleships and carriers in the Pacific. Rather than one form of naval war, there might be many, leading to a very mixed and complicated narrative indeed.

---

Is it possible to draw some general conclusions out of the many points made above, aside from the mere truism that both geography and economics had an influence on sea power? Yes, to be sure: for, from the evidence assembled here, it seems clear that the three revisionist nations of the 1930s and their navies had the odds set against them, in regard to both their geographical position and their relative economic power. Sorely lacking in most of the raw materials needed for modern industrialized warfare, not possessing any of the great fleet bases on the world's major highways, and together having only around one-third of the combined shipping and ship construction holdings of the Anglo-American maritime countries, the leadership in Berlin, Rome, and Tokyo might well have been deterred from their desire to upset the status quo. But dissatisfied have-not nations do not always act as Rational Economic Man, and besides, in the narrower military correlation of forces, the Axis possessed certain points of strength that seemed to have game-changing potential: as noted, the Luftwaffe of 1939 had considerably greater striking power than any rival, and the Japanese Naval Air Force of 1941 possessed a far bigger punch than any other. In addition, the indices of the shifting balances of global strength suggested that it would be better to strike soon, before the United States gave up its isolationism and spent much more on its armed forces and perhaps also before the USSR recovered from its self-inflicted damage. By taking swift aggressive action while the other side was far less ready to fight, ambitious Axis leaders hoped in turn to seize new geographical positions and economic assets and thus become considerably stronger. Another hegemonic war was looming into sight, then, in which, once again, navies, whether the flotillas fighting in large-scale fleet actions or the U-boats and escorts struggling to dominate trade routes, would play a critical role.

# PART II

Narrative of the
Great Naval War,
1939–42

**PAINTING 14.** HMS *Warspite* in action, Narvik fjord, April 1940. In an amazing action, the veteran battleship was sent right up the fjord to wipe out the entire German destroyer flotilla, but the Royal Navy could not prevent Hitler's seizure of Norway.

# FOUR

## The Early War at Sea
*September 1939–July 1940*

In contrast to the Pacific War two years later, the naval struggle in the West had rather cautious and scattered beginnings in September 1939. The neutrality of half of the maritime powers (Italy, Japan, and the United States) plus Germany's geographic disadvantage and limited fleet assets accounted for that. World War II in Europe began, after all, as a war over Poland. The Third Reich attacked its eastern neighbor, and the British and French Empires, in accord with their military guarantees, declared war on Germany. America and Japan stayed neutral because this was not their war, and Italy stayed neutral (despite Mussolini's earlier promises to Hitler) because Rome was desperately anxious not to fight overwhelming Anglo-French naval forces in the Mediterranean. And the USSR, as noted earlier, was throughout the entire war an insignificant force on the high seas, and in any case had just cut a deal with Hitler to stay neutral. In 1939, then, the war at sea was a distinctly limited one.[1]

While nominally three naval powers (Britain, France, and Germany) were combatants here, in fact the French fleets played only a relatively small role in the nine months before the Republic's dramatic defeat on land, and surrender. The possibility of any hostile move by Italy kept the greater part of the French battle fleet, and its submarine forces, in the Mediterranean, while smaller flotillas remained stationed further afield to protect France's colonies in West Africa and Southeast Asia. After war broke out in western Europe, sizable naval forces were deployed to escort the flow of army reinforcements from North Africa to the French homeland. Still, the French admiralty deemed it important enough to base some of its fast, modern squadrons at Brest and Cherbourg to add to the Royal Navy's "hunting groups" in Atlantic waters. Thus, by October 1939, two considerable French task forces were deployed in the hunt for the *Graf Spee* and other German commerce raiders.[2]

The chief contestants were, though, the British and German navies, those old foes of 1914. Strategically, it seemed that not much had changed. With the Netherlands, Denmark, and Norway once again neutral, how could it have? Warships of Dover Command closed off the Channel. German minelayers laid a great screen around Heligoland and further west; British minelayers laid fields off the German ports and islands. Occasionally, they bumped into each other in the mists, since neither side had radar, and a scrap ensued. The larger Royal Navy (now named the Home Fleet rather than the Grand Fleet) assembled at Scapa Flow, while smaller vessels patrolled the Norway-Scotland line. The small Polish Navy, except for that part of it that had been sent out of the Baltic, was smashed by the Luftwaffe, with Britain or France unable to do anything about it. A few German raiders were out on the high seas, as had been the case in 1914, but the greater part of Hitler's Kriegsmarine was confined to Wilhelmshaven and Kiel, just like the Kaiser's Hochseeflotte back then—the biggest difference being that there was no real German High Seas Fleet in 1939, only half a dozen battle cruisers and pocket battleships, plus cruisers, twenty modern destroyers, and several flotillas of submarines. At this very early stage in the war even the revolutionary capacity of aircraft was limited, through geographical distances across the North Sea and by cloud cover on most days and blackouts at night. All this made finding the location of military and naval targets difficult for each side's air forces. On some days, RAF medium bombers dropped propaganda pamphlets on Hamburg, though when they began to be shot down by German fighters, Bomber Command switched to nighttime raids. This was not really a Great Power conflict at all, and it was certainly hard to think in Mahanian categories of decisive fleet battles for control of the global commons when one side didn't have a fleet.

What Germany did have, however, was a resourceful commodore of submarines, Vice Admiral Karl Doenitz, and a small cluster of U-boat captains eager to take advantage of any possible weaknesses in the Anglo-French command of the sea. The first blow they struck occurred as early as September 17, 1939, with the sinking by *U-29* of the large fleet carrier HMS *Courageous* as it was engaged, ironically, on an antisubmarine patrol southwest of Ireland. This was not just a grim human disaster (518 sailors' lives were lost) but a larger blow and lesson to the Royal Navy. Here was "asymmetric warfare" indeed, a 730-ton warship destroying a 22,500-ton one, and the latter sinking within fifteen minutes of the submarine's torpedoes hitting home. Admiral John Jellicoe's anxieties about the security of his battleships in the North Sea in the years after Jutland had to be relearned; from now on every large, precious capital ship should go to sea only if accompanied by a bevy of escorts—the *Courageous* only had two destroyers at the time of *U-29*'s attack. An even more questionable aspect to this story was the very idea (chiefly Churchill's as First Lord) of forming carrier groups as so-called units of search and sending them out to find elusive enemy submarines, a proverbial needle-in-the haystack operation indeed. Three days earlier the HMS *Ark Royal* had probably been saved from a similar fate when the torpedoes fired at it by *U-39* exploded prematurely. At the *Courageous*'s sinking, the Admiralty now abandoned this fatuous search-and-destroy scheme, but it had lost one-sixth of its precious carrier fleet.[3]

An even worse blow to the Royal Navy's pride, and a further loss of its capital-ship strength, came less than a month later, when the resourceful submarine captain Guenther Prien carefully guided his *U-47* through the inadequate underwater defenses of the main British naval base at Scapa Flow and attacked the battleship HMS *Royal Oak* resting at anchor. When early strikes all failed due to defective magnetic torpedoes, Prien calmly reloaded and fired again. Three torpedoes blew apart the 15-inch-gunned dreadnought in a mere thirteen minutes, with huge British casualties. The U-boat carefully picked its way out and steamed safely home to Wilhelmshaven, to great German fanfare and the Fuehrer's immense jubilation.[4] Here, as elsewhere across the British Empire, the harbor defenses of the major fleet bases—Scapa, Gibraltar, Alexandria, Trincomalee, and Singapore—were quite inadequate, if they existed at all after decades of low military spending. In consequence, the Home Fleet, battered by these two early losses, was for a while sent to anchor in various Scottish lochs, even in the Clyde, obviously a dangerously long way away if required in the North Sea or off southern Norway.

After these twin early blows against the British home battle fleet, a quieter time ensued in northern waters for a while. A quick, successful raid by the battle cruisers *Scharnhorst* and *Gneisenau* near Iceland in November netted them the sinking of a Royal Navy auxiliary cruiser (*Rawalpindi*) before caution prevailed and they raced back to harbor. This sort of swift excursion, clearly, would be typical, rather than any large-scale fleet sally across the North Sea; in both surface warfare and in submarines, the German challenges to British naval mastery would have to be episodic, opportunistic, and brief. The fleets of the two sides had to get into a more prolonged fight to reveal each side's mettle, but that was still six months away. The German aerial threat to British naval power would be fully revealed only when Hitler's ambitions turned west. As for the U-boat menace, while it was ultimately going to be far greater than it had been even in 1917, there was simply not enough firepower on the German side to offer a strategic threat. Still, the achievements of just a few resourceful U-boat captains were already scary enough, and their clever and increasing habit of countering the Allied convoy system by nighttime attacks on the surface (and thus undetectable by ASDIC) was a great headache. As was well known, the torpedo's explosive power was greater than any shell, and the basic Type VII submarine that Germany had developed was showing itself to be a remarkably capable weapons system—give Doenitz three or four times as many of them, and the situation for the Allies might be dire.

The naval scene further away from Scapa Flow and Irish Sea waters was also a challenging one for British Admiralty planners. As it happened, World War II at sea began earlier than its formal first day of hostilities, September 3, 1939. Some weeks previously, in anticipation of being cut off by the British naval blockade, German surface raiders in the form of secretly armed merchantmen were already taking up positions along the trade routes. A sufficient number of these clandestine raiders would be in action against the Allies' extensive and exposed long-range shipping routes in the first few years of the war, which thus forced the Admiralty to arm dozens of merchant ships of its own as well as to deploy great numbers of its cruisers on trade-protection duties. If Admiral Erich Raeder hoped that these ancillary raiders would consume a great deal of his enemy's attention, he was correct, but by their very nature they had to flee as soon as a regular British or French warship came into sight. Far more dangerous, clearly, would be a sortie by larger forces, such as the pocket battleship *Graf Spee,* which had also been dispatched early on to the distant waters of the South Atlantic and Indian Oceans and commenced its attacks on trade as soon as it received the signal that the conflict in Europe had begun.

## The Epic of the *Graf Spee*

Since on any day of the year there were thousands of British and Allied merchant vessels at sea, including dozens of them independently steaming across the South Atlantic and the Indian Ocean, the pocket battleship *Graf Spee* was able to prowl successfully on this traffic, sinking or capturing vessels over a very wide area indeed, and always moving on. As historian Stephen Roskill records it, "After sinking the *Clement* off Pernambuco on the 30th of September the *Graf Spee* crossed the South Atlantic and on the 5th of October found her second victim, the SS *Newton Beech.* . . . The *Graf Spee* sank or captured three more ships on the trade routes from the Cape of Good Hope between the 5th and 10th of October and then returned to her cruising ground in the center of the South Atlantic where, on the 15th, she fueled again from the *Altmark* and transferred to her the crews of her victims."[5] In even greater detail (see table 6) does the official British naval history record the extraordi-

**TABLE 6.** British and French Navy Hunting Groups, October 1939

| Force | Composition of hunting group | Area of operations | Diverted from |
|---|---|---|---|
| F | *Berwick* and *York* | North America and West Indies | Halifax |
| G | *Exeter* and *Cumberland* (*Ajax* and *Achilles* later) | Southeast coast of America | South Atlantic |
| H | *Sussex* and *Shropshire* | Cape of Good Hope | Mediterranean |
| I | *Cornwall*, *Dorsetshire*, and *Eagle* | Ceylon | China |
| K | *Ark Royal* and *Renown* | Pernambuco | Home Fleet |
| L | *Dunkerque*, *Béarn*, and three French 6-in.-gunned cruisers | Brest | |
| M | Two French 8-in.-gunned cruisers | Dakar | |
| N | *Strasbourg* and *Hermes* | West Indies | *Hermes* from Plymouth |

Data from Roskill, *War at Sea*, 1:114. Thus, the total out searching for the *Graf Spee* was fifteen cruisers, three battle cruisers, and two carriers. All British battle cruisers, although less well protected than a battleship, carried 15-inch guns.

nary array of British and French warships spread across this vast space, their patrols, and the enemy merchantmen they picked up as they swept the seas, week after week, in search of this raider. In all, there were established eight powerful hunting groups, each a mix of battle cruisers, carriers, and cruisers, all relatively fast vessels therefore, with the Royal Navy's battleships left in the North Atlantic to cover the large homeward convoys from Halifax against attack from the *Graf Spee*'s sister vessel, the *Deutschland*.

Here were the larger contours of naval history. To later scholars of the workings of sea power, Roskill suggests, the details offered about "the ocean-wide strategy"[6] that led to the eventual tracking down of the pocket battleship ought to be of greater interest than the flood of popular works on "the Battle of the River Plate." That was the later title given to the epic shootout that occurred on December 13, 1939, between the *Graf Spee* and three British cruisers, HMSs *Exeter*, *Achilles*, and *Ajax*, which was followed by the pursuit of the damaged raider into the waters off Montevideo and its eventual scuttling. To be sure, the story of that engagement is a compelling one.[7] The squadron that engaged the *Graf Spee*, one heavy and two light cruisers under Commodore Henry Harwood, was one of the less powerful of the hunting groups, but it was brilliantly and aggressively handled against an indecisive opponent. Like Nelson at the Nile (1797), Harwood divided his warships into two attacking forces in order to split the enemy's fire. While the *Exeter* was so badly hammered by 11-inch shells in the exchanges that it had to pull out of the battle and limp off to the Falklands for repairs, the German raider also took some damage to vital parts.

Enough 6-inch and 8-inch shells had hit the *Graf Spee* to knock out its main range finder, destroy its food galley, damage the water-filtration system, and tear a hole in its bow, thus causing its commander, Captain Hans Langsdorff, to order his vessel into the neutral harbor of Montevideo for repairs. And when that occurred, the British devised ways to keep things on hold while summoning far larger forces into the area. When the sensitive, aloof Langsdorff elected to sink his own vessel rather than give further battle and have the *Graf Spee* devastated by enemy shells, the Royal Navy was presented with a much-needed morale boost, helping greatly to compensate for the loss of the *Royal Oak* and *Courageous*. Both during the war and long after it (for example, in the classic 1956 movie) did the Battle of the River Plate enter the pantheon of the great naval fights of modern times.

The larger structures of the Allied hunting network were, indeed, remarkable. Even if the pocket battleship had been more forceful in the first encounter, sunk the *Exeter,* and then steamed toward the high seas, it is hard to think that its days would not have been numbered. Damaged in its fresh-water and food supply systems, the German warship would have had little real chance. A large proportion of the British and French naval forces was being thrown into the South Atlantic, while the *Graf Spee,* lacking any of the Allies' refueling stations (Dakar, Freetown, the Falklands, and Capetown) and unable to use neutral ones, would have crossed and recrossed the southern oceans, like a fox without a hole, until its oil bunkers were empty and the hunters caught up with it.[8] Such, after all, had been the fate of the famous and considerably larger German East Asia Squadron of 1914 (whose commander was, ironically, Admiral Graf von Spee), destroyed at the Battle of the Falklands. The so-called *guerre de course* raiding strategy, epitomized by the famous French frigates in the age of sail, had far less chance of overall success for Hitler's Kriegsmarine, crippled by its inadequate numbers, logistical support, and geographical constraints.

Students of the great battles of the age of sail would be struck by one further thing, which was the sheer *vulnerability* of the modern ironclad warship whenever it came to fighting. The line-of-battle ships of Nelson's day, even the frigates, took an enormous amount of punishment before they were destroyed; usually, they would still be afloat (and recoverable!) even after all their masts had been blown away and their crews annihilated. The twentieth-century armor-plated naval vessel, curiously, could be knocked out much more swiftly. Of course the immense destructive power of TNT, whether in an 8-inch shell or an 18-inch torpedo, was responsible. Yet again, newer warships seemed to have many more vulnerable parts than did the old USS *Constitution* or HMS *Victory*. One torpedo hit to the *Bismarck*'s rudder crippled that giant. One shell knocked out the *Graf Spee*'s range finder. A single torpedo was enough to blow a 130-foot hole in the side of the *Ark Royal* and sink it. The *Hood* was blown up by a single plunging salvo. The USS *Wasp* perished within hours of Japanese torpedoes hitting its fuel tanks. The *Roma* was wiped out by a single glider bomb. The ocean in wartime and the skies above it were dangerous places wherein an enemy might lurk. As the possibility of battle approached, therefore, commanders were usually wise to proceed cautiously until it was clear what lay ahead.

At this stage, it was the German raiders into the Atlantic who had to take account of this fact; for however intimidating they appeared to an Allied merchantman, they in turn were immensely susceptible to damage from a glancing shell, a submarine's single torpedo, or a British destroyer's desperate ramming action tearing a hole in the side. As the Admiralty soon discovered, the mere presence of even an older battleship with a convoy would cause much faster German warships to steer clear (this was indeed the Kriegsmarine's firm instruction to its captain), for one 15-inch salvo could cripple it badly. Even if only partially hurt, a damaged raider almost always needed to go and find repairs. It would be lucky, indeed, if it scraped home.

By the onset of 1940, the tally of major warship losses for each side had not changed. The loss of the *Royal Oak* was the least significant, because the British preponderance in battleships was so large and the vessel itself was slow and unmodernized. Losing a full fleet carrier like the *Courageous* was quite another matter, given the strategic flexibility of such a vessel and the still-considerable striking power of its Swordfish torpedo planes. The *Graf Spee*'s sinking may have seemed less of a blow to the German Navy—here was a hybrid vessel, not even a proper battle cruiser—but Raeder had far too few heavy warships at his disposal to afford this loss. More to the point, the sheer size of the Admiralty's response to the *Graf Spee*'s intrusion into the South Atlantic and the precious imperial trading system, and its impressive creation of powerful hunting groups at so many points—the Cape, Freetown, the River Plate, Pernambuco, Jamaica, Perth, and so on—showed that the odds would always be tilted against any future long-range German incursion. With the exception of the *Admiral Sheer*'s cruise (chapter 5), no later raid by German warships upon the Allied convoys, whether by the *Luetzow*, *Scharnhorst*, *Gneisenau*, or even the *Bismarck*, ever got out of the North Atlantic.

**PAINTING 15.** **Damaged *Graf Spee* off Montevideo, 1939.**
Damaged in many ways by the spirited British cruiser action
at the Battle of the River Plate, this famous German pocket
battleship was scuttled off the harbor rather than allowed to
take further action.

More promising, potentially, to Hitler's hopes of defeating the Allies at sea had to be the interruption of Britain's lines of communication across the North Atlantic by Doenitz's U-boat forces. The issue here was clear: if ever the submarine blockade of the British Isles succeeded, the war in the West would be won. In fact, during the 1939–40 season of U-boat warfare, the prospect of that happening was virtually impossible. First, geographically, the only way the submarines could get out to the central Atlantic was via that long and dangerous journey around Scotland. Second, and most important, Doenitz's U-boat arm simply had far too few vessels to come anywhere close to paralyzing the mass of Allied merchant ships moving in and out of British ports, whether in convoy or single sailings. And the enemy's defensive capacities, even if it had various flaws, were both wide-ranging and growing faster than Germany's own capacity to inflict losses. Roskill's useful statistical tables here, on the shrinkage of the size of the U-boat fleet as the early months of the war unfolded, are compelling. At the war's beginning, Doenitz had forty-nine "operational" submarines in his fleet, of which probably only twenty-nine were really oceangoing. By the end of the year the total force had shrunk to thirty-two; it popped up a bit by March (forty-six boats), but the next few months of combat knocked it down to twenty-eight by July 1940. As if to add insult to injury, this numerical weakness was aggravated by the all-too-frequent failures of the German torpedoes to explode. All this meant that Allied merchant-ship losses, while palpable, were far below being strategically important. In the first seven months of the war, from September to March, the average monthly loss of Allied merchant shipping was around 200,000 tons, a long way from Doenitz's hopes and intentions.[9]

## The Fall of Norway

If the naval balance of power between Germany and the West was to be decisively altered, therefore, it could come about only through a significant change in the land war, a much bigger expansion of the U-boat campaign on commerce, or both. But that double transformation in fortunes was still many months away as the year 1939 ended, and each side appeared to settle into the winter period, that of the so-called Sitzkrieg (Sitting War), or Phony War. The Nazi security apparatus took draconian control of Poland. Moscow and Berlin steadily carved up the rest of east-central Europe in line with the secret clauses of the Molotov-Ribbentrop Pact, and there was simply nothing that Chamberlain's and Daladier's governments could do about that. French reserve units beefed up the regulars behind the Maginot Line or were sent to reinforce the Franco-Italian border. The

British Expeditionary Force (BEF) once again crossed the Channel and deployed into northern France but not into a neutral, hopelessly frightened Belgium. The small western states of Denmark, Norway, and the Netherlands hoped their declarations of neutrality would buy them continued independence, even as they watched Stalin seek to bully Finland into territorial concessions and then stumble embarrassingly during the first part of the Red Army's attacks during the (December–March) "Winter War."

If the USSR-Finland conflict showed how ineffectual Russia's divisions were for campaigning over frozen terrain, there was, once again, nothing that the Western nations of Britain and France could do to alter things in northeastern Europe. Their air forces lacked both range and power. A small joint Allied expeditionary force might possibly have been landed somewhere, but that would have involved transgressing either Norwegian or Swedish neutrality, and in all probability would have had no more effect than the abortive North Russia interventions of 1918–19. That the French and, more reluctantly, the British Army Commands actually got expeditionary forces ready for some sort of strike by March 1940 did not make the prospects for success any greater—they may have been lucky, really, that the Finnish government asked Moscow for a cease-fire and negotiated concessions. In addition, Stalin's economically autarkic Russia was unblockadable. Sea power had next to no influence over continental heartland matters, and the Russian-Finnish borderlands were surely in that zone. Moreover, all the press reports that the British and French were planning action in Scandinavia clearly had their effect on an excited Hitler, who resolved that he at least *was* going to do something.[10]

The quiet winter months in the West were broken dramatically by the German offensive against Norway beginning on April 8–9, 1940, which was unusual and historic for many reasons. During World War I it was generally the Allied sea powers who sought to escape from the military stalemate of the western front by operations along the flank (such as Gallipoli, Salonika, and Palestine), but in this later war it was Hitler who struck out and succeeded in the major peripheral campaigns, from Norway to Greece, with the British limiting themselves to mere commando raids after their first disastrous year of the war. The Fuehrer's decision to add all of Norway to his swathe of conquests suggested boldness to the point of recklessness, and many higher members of the Wehrmacht were worried that they were going too far, too fast. Moving through Denmark would be a relatively easy, small-scale land campaign, most agreed, while the Netherlands simply hadn't the territorial depth for a lengthy fight against invasion, even though the Dutch defenders would put up a struggle. But was not Norway, especially in its Atlantic and northern parts, simply out of German reach, being almost in Scotland's backyard? Admiral Raeder was quite candid in saying so in his March 9, 1940, memo to Hitler, where he admitted that trying to gain Norway in the face of "a vastly superior British Fleet . . . is in itself contrary to all principles in the theory of naval warfare." Yet the admiral then went on to say that a victory could be achieved provided there was surprise at the outset, boldness of execution, and the highest levels of organization.[11] Here, indeed, was German military effectiveness at its best, unencumbered by the Fuehrer's later delusions and showing not only that Prussian staff tradition of meticulous planning in advance but also a remarkable level of interservice cooperation, at staff level as well as at the front, where no less than five simultaneous landings would be attempted.[12] How else could they have hoped for victory, especially on the seas, against Anglo-French fleets that were six, eight, maybe ten times larger and against navies that possessed battleships as well as that new weapon of war, fleet aircraft carriers, when Germany had only two and none, respectively?

In addition to demonstrating bold and meticulous organization, moreover, the Wehrmacht possessed the advantage of significantly more effective airpower. Thanks to the Third Reich's early heavy spending on the Luftwaffe, the latter already possessed a far more powerful and available *bombing* delivery than either the British or the French Air Force in 1939. RAF bomber squadrons still had very little real destructive capacity at this time, and while the Fleet Air Arm's carrier squadrons had some offensive capacity, the aircraft were old and the numbers were few.[13] The French Air Force was not going to be able to defend its homeland in the following month, so it was absurd to think it could play a role as far north as Norway. By contrast, the Luftwaffe, which had already picked up many significant tactical lessons from the aerial campaign against Poland, planned to deploy 290 bombers, 40 Stuka dive-bombers, 100 modern fighters, 30 coastal patrol aircraft (to cooperate with the navy), and 40 of its invaluable long-range reconnaissance aircraft. It also was committing no fewer than 500 Junkers transport planes for the rapid deployment of the army's assault forces, including some parachute battalions.[14] Maybe all those "principles in the theory of naval warfare" to which Raeder referred were now far less relevant in the face of the transformative impact of the new technology of airpower. For twenty or more years, the argument had rolled on about whether aircraft had really changed things at sea. Now the real test was at hand, and the results, considered historically, were remarkable. Less than four decades after the Wright brothers first flew, the Luftwaffe was transporting an invading army hundreds of miles through the air to seize key points, blunting the enemy's counterattacks by shooting down his aircraft and bombing his air bases, attacking and

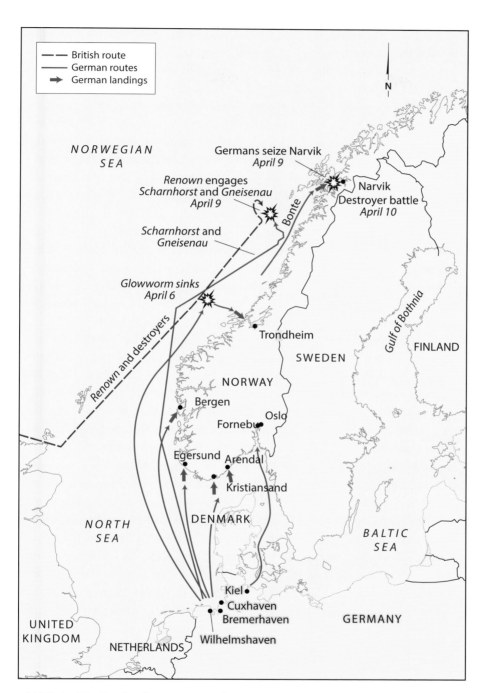

**MAP 4.** The Battle of Norway, April 1940.

sinking the enemy's destroyers and supply ships, and deterring his larger warships from coming close to Norway's southern shores.

Still, events might not have gone so badly for the Allies had they themselves not been so operationally and strategically indecisive, unsure as to where the key military objective was, ordering their expeditionary forces from one place to the next, disembarking troops one day and reloading them only days later, and piling up intelligence mistakes to an extraordinary degree. To all these confusions one might add the many erratic interventions of the First Lord of the Admiralty himself, Winston Churchill, who sought to take almost hour-by-hour control in the face of this stunning German blitzkrieg. It is not the intention to detail here all the mistakes by British decision-makers Churchill, Chamberlain, and others or to spend much time on the few occasions where the Anglo-French forces got things right. The facts were that the Wehrmacht caught them completely off-balance and that they never recovered from the size and boldness of the German strikes. Indeed, for much of those confused weeks in April and May 1940, the Home Fleet was endeavoring to offer protection to landing operations at three different points along the lengthy Norwegian coast while still trying to cover for a German heavy-ship raid against the Atlantic convoy routes.[15] At some times, too, the Home Fleet was required to release vessels to cover the possibility of action in the southern North Sea or, more distantly, in the Mediterranean should Mussolini also undertake aggression. Very occasionally, the Admiralty played its cards right. Thus, the renowned British battleship HMS *Warspite* was returning to its Mediterranean station in early April when it was ordered to turn around and steam up to the Narvik fjord—to devastating effect in the Second Battle of Narvik (see below)—and then immediately afterward to be redeployed to the Mediterranean, where two months later it could participate in the Battle of Calabria. But most of the time the Royal Navy deployments seemed to be in the wrong place, to be inconsistent, or (in the later stages) to be successful only in recovering Allied troops from the various failed landings up and down the Norwegian coast: "half-prepared" and "half-baked" was Lloyd George's withering description of these operations in that historic House of Commons censure debate that brought down Chamberlain's government on May 10.[16]

The overall Norwegian campaign was a disaster for the British and French governments and frustrating for the various military contingents who had been ordered to seize, and then later to abandon, a whole range of critical objectives. Which one, it might be asked, was key—Andalsnes? Trondheim? Namsos? Bergen? Still, there were moments when the inherently superior strength of the British naval forces could be brought successfully into play, as in the First and Second Battles of Narvik, where the

German planners simply overreached themselves, gambling the greater part of their destroyer strength on a risky effort to secure that strategically vital harbor in the far north. The first of these clashes, on April 10, was something of an epic in small-ship warfare, with the captains on each side showing great aggression, initiative, and fighting spirit and with the initial surprise attack of Bernard Warburton-Lee's destroyer flotilla being checked when they in turn were ambushed by the larger German warships lying in the side valleys—did any other naval fight in World War II take place, one wonders, in circumstances akin to this one, in the tight, ice-coated corridors of a fjord?[17]

The Royal Navy's destroyer losses in that fight were equal to the German (two each were sunk, though the Germans also lost various merchant ships), yet the fact was that the British ended up with control of the mouth of Narvik fjord and could therefore "bottle in" the remainder of this large Kriegsmarine flotilla, which was in any case suffering from a severe shortage of fuel. So, here was a rare occasion in this confused overall campaign where the British Admiralty actually *knew* where the enemy was, and for the Second Battle of Narvik it took no chances. Escorted by destroyers and guided by its own spotter aircraft, the massive shape of the battleship HMS *Warspite* steamed up the fjord on April 13, slowing down at necessary points to blast at the next target. With three of the German destroyers sunk by this gunfire, the remaining five simply flooded themselves and evacuated their crews; after all, the latter could at least join up with their expeditionary forces on land and continue the fight. But as a naval gamble, it was all over. Not one of the ten German fleet destroyers committed to the Narvik expedition ever came home.[18]

The Kriegsmarine's losses in this campaign were considerably larger than that, however; it lost the brand-new heavy cruiser *Bluecher* to Norwegian coastal fire off Oslo, the light cruiser *Koenigsberg* to RAF Skua dive-bombers (the first time this had happened in history), and another light cruiser, the *Karlsruhe*, to a British submarine. The pocket battleship *Luetzow* was heavily damaged by another sub, the heavy cruiser *Hipper* had its side ripped by the destroyer HMS *Glowworm*'s ramming, and by the end of the campaign the battle cruisers *Scharnhorst* and *Gneisenau* had also returned home damaged. These were significant losses not only in absolute terms but much, much more as a proportion of the Kriegsmarine's relative size. By the middle of May 1940 Raeder's navy still had many dangerous E-boats and submarines, plus of course the ever-formidable Luftwaffe, but it no longer possessed a surface fleet, at least for now. Still, he had gained for his Fuehrer the key asset of Norway, as he had promised.

Drawing a balance sheet of each side's overall losses and gains after the Norwegian campaign is a more complicated exercise than one might think. It was a decided shock and humiliation for Britain to lose strategic control over a territory that was largely so much closer to its own coasts than it was to Germany's. And it was thus a supreme political irony that the parliamentary uproar over the failures of the campaign led to the collapse of Chamberlain's government in late May 1940 and to the advent of Churchill, whose advice and interventions throughout the whole affair, as noted above, had so often been wrongheaded and silly. The Royal Navy's destroyers had fought boldly and well in virtually every encounter with the enemy, but apart from *Warspite*'s actions in the Second Battle of Narvik its main fleets were never really able to come to grips with its enemy. Keeping its larger vessels well away from the Luftwaffe, it found its absolute losses were not very severe overall—one aircraft carrier sunk by the German battle cruisers near the end (HMS *Glorious*), plus two cruisers and seven destroyers sunk. But as we have seen, the far smaller Kriegsmarine lost far more warships, and when the fighting was all over, Raeder's surface navy had been reduced to an all-time low. Even if Germany's control of Norwegian harbors helped it somewhat in the forthcoming Battle of the Atlantic and in its capacity to disrupt the future Arctic convoys, the acquisition of this huge, long, and mountainous land was to tie down a very large number of German troops (approximately 300,000) for the rest of the war. That was much larger, it might be noted, than the number of frontline Afrika Korps troops that Erwin Rommel would ever have at his disposal in his critical campaigning against the British armies in Egypt.

The heavily reduced German Navy did not, of course, stop fighting in European waters; each side sought to mine and countermine the North Sea and used submarines, surface craft, and planes to attack the other side's vessels. Losses due to mines rose sharply on each side, even if neither navy was willing to risk deploying larger warships in the area. The Germans called this sort of struggle *Kleinkrieg* (petty warfare), but it was punishing enough. On the night of May 9, for example, the destroyer HMS *Kelly* (commanded by Lord Louis Mountbatten), which had just returned to the fleet after being badly damaged by a mine in February, was attacked through the mists by German E-boats and hit amidships by a torpedo near the entrance to the Skagerrak. Towed through night and day by a fellow destroyer and then by tugs and heavily escorted by cruisers and destroyers, the stricken warship was eventually brought to its own shipbuilders on the Tyne.[19] Here was a typical, rather than untypical, casualty of these North Sea naval clashes.

After the conquest of Norway by Germany, King Haakon VII and his government were brought to London to join the governments-in-exile of so many of the other European nations whose lands had fallen into the

**PAINTING 16. HMS *Kelly* limping into the Tyne, 1940.** Badly damaged by German E-boats in a furious fight in the North Sea, Lord Louis Mountbatten's warship nearly sank and was towed back to its builders for repair (a scene witnessed by Paul Kennedy's father). The *Kelly* was sunk by massive Luftwaffe attacks off Crete in 1941.

Nazi orbit. With Norway now fully part of the Allied war coalition, the numerous shipping lines of its merchant marine could be integrated into a single organization (Nortraship) and added to the West's overall carrying capacity. This turned out to be, in fact, a huge addition to British maritime resources in the future battle of the sea-lanes, for the Norwegian merchant navy was the fourth largest in the world and by far the most modern, with many fast diesel-engine ships and numerous oil tankers, already the main carriers of the RAF's vital aviation-fuel supplies.[20] It was a grand irony that Hitler's land aggressions across Europe gave Britain such unexpected yet badly needed relief even as the Battle of the Atlantic was about to enter a more severe phase. Still, if any country needed strategic consolation at this time of the war, it was the battered British government in London.

## Disaster in the West, April to June 1940

A mere hundred or so miles south of where the *Kelly* was attacked, and only one day later, highly skilled German paratroops and glider crews landed precisely on the tops of the Dutch defenses and Belgian fortresses. This operation on the morning of May 10 was merely the first stroke of the Wehrmacht's amazingly bold move into the Low Countries and marked the latest stage in Hitler's aggressions against his neighbors. Overwhelming German airpower crushed the obsolete Belgian and Dutch air forces as it had done the Poles in the East. There was of course very little that British and French naval power at the time could have done to prevent such things happening. Nothing short of huge carrier task forces, with enough aerial capacity to put a sustained protective cloak over the Dutch-Belgian land forces and air bases and shoot down the oncoming waves of Luftwaffe bombers and paratroopers, would have done the trick. But such massive naval air capacity was not to appear in this war until the arrival of the vast US carrier task forces during the second half of the Pacific campaigning, off the Mariana and Caroline Islands, in 1943–44. There were certainly no forces like that available to the Allied Supreme Command when Germany had struck through the Low Countries four years earlier, nor had the British and French navies ever assumed they had any obligation to think in such terms. Their task, after all, was to keep the seas, not to alter the balance of military power on the land around the borders of the Third Reich.

Then, the dramatic breakthrough of the German panzer columns at Sedan on May 14, 1940, and the subsequent drive of the forward units all the way to the Channel in a mere ten days transformed the entire military situation in the West. Most of the French Army, some of it still fighting well, fell backward on Paris, while the entire BEF, together with the French First Army, was bundled toward the Channel coast. Within another week, Lord Gort, commander of the British troops, was envisaging a complete pullout via the Dunkirk ports. The rout—for that is what it was—was complete.[21] These were extraordinary military circumstances for Winston Churchill's brand-new government to inherit.

The new situation thus altered the Royal Navy's role from the simply secondary one of keeping secure the army's supply lines from southern English ports to the much more critical and desperate one of rescuing as many of those battered Allied divisions as possible. Under better military circumstances, perhaps, the considerable BEF of 1940 might have remained on the continent, a sort of large "wedge" along the Belgian coast and steadily reinforced from the sea, just like Wellington's army when it had fallen back to defensive lines around Lisbon after Napoleon's armies swept across Spain in 1810. But there was no Wellington present on this occasion, and in any case the Luftwaffe's aggressive bombing and constant harrying of Allied troop movements changed everything. Even when Heinz Guderian's tanks were ordered by the German High Command on May 24 to cease their advance for a few days, German dive-bombers and medium bombers were pounding away in fulfillment of Hermann Goering's boast that his air forces could finish things off. While that proved not to be true, what the Luftwaffe's punishing attacks did was to destroy all the harbors, staithes, and other landing facilities along the entire coast. Dunkirk itself was a town full of collapsed buildings, its harbor full of sunken vessels and fallen cranes. Thus, when Admiral Bertram Ramsay of Dover Command took direct control of naval forces and operations at this time, he saw that the only thing left was to try to withdraw as many Allied troops *from the beaches* and any small mooring points as possible—little wonder that the British planners thought they would be lucky if sixty thousand soldiers could be rescued.[22]

Although a whole armada of smaller craft steamed to the rescue—involving hundreds and hundreds of yachts, trawlers, tugboats, Channel steamers, and so on—the Royal Navy chiefly relied upon its destroyers for the core of this aptly named Operation Dynamo. With their combination of high speed (they could return to Dover and back in a day) and relatively shallow draught, such warships could be directed to stand off the Dunkirk beaches and half-broken piers and in that way retrieve as many of the retreating British and French soldiers as possible. Extracting an army from land to sea while under fire had long been regarded by professionals as the most difficult and risky operation of all, and the Germans managed to make this evacuation especially onerous: long-range artillery was brought up to batter the Dunkirk pocket, E-boats were sent south to harry the British ships at night, and above all, there was the unrelenting assault from the sky by Luftwaffe bombers. Originally envisaged as speedy escorts for the British battle fleet, Ramsay's destroyers were now being asked to function as a sort of reverse amphibious boat, pulling an entire army back from the shore, and with only a few days and nights in which to do it before the Wehrmacht resumed its advance. This was far more dangerous than even the Norway fighting.

As it turned out, the worst few hours of all for the evacuating destroyers and the exhausted British troops occurred on May 28–29, when one disaster seemed to follow another during the middle of that night. On this occasion the danger came from German E-boats rushing out of the dark, loosing off torpedoes, and equally rapidly disappearing. Just after midnight one such attack torpedoed HMS *Wakeful,* and as the destroyer swiftly sank it dragged down not only a large number of the crew but, even more tragically, hundreds and hundreds of war-weary soldiers who had been sent to quarters below deck and could not escape.[23] This desperate situation was spotted by a sister destroyer, HMS *Grafton,* which was returning from Dunkirk with an already very heavy load of troops.[24] By the time the *Grafton* stopped to pick up *Wakeful*'s survivors, however, the submarine *U-62* had come across this crowded scene and fired two torpedoes at the stationary destroyer before itself disappearing. The first torpedo missed, but the one that did hit caused a series of internal explosions, inflicting further large casualties among both the soldiers and the naval crew—the bridge itself blew up, dramatically, killing the ship's captain and many others. The middle part of the stricken vessel still floated, however, and there were still survivors aboard when shortly afterward a *third* Royal Navy destroyer, HMS *Ivanhoe,* arrived to help.

*Ivanhoe*'s story here is nothing short of epic.[25] It was an attractive *I-*class destroyer of the mid-1930s (1,390 tons displacement, four 4.7-inch guns, and torpedoes), one of the Royal Navy's classic workhorses of the sea, a vessel that had done offshore interdiction patrols during the Spanish Civil War, been in repeated action during the Norway fighting, and then was very successfully engaged in minelaying operations off the German and Dutch coasts when it was redirected to Dunkirk waters to help in the evacuation. On May 29 it was carrying 930 grateful soldiers back to England, to which total it would now add the survivors of the *Grafton.* Since the latter's condition was hopeless, *Ivanhoe* torpedoed its hulk and sent the destroyer to the bottom before itself getting back to Dover. By this stage, though, the Admiralty was becoming frightened at losing any more of its invaluable fleet destroyers (the plan was for these 36-knotters to fight alongside heavier Royal Navy warships if any invasion of England was to come), and it therefore ordered the *Ivanhoe* to pull out of the Dunkirk scene. *One day later* that decision was reversed, however, and the *Ivanhoe* was sent again across the Channel, bringing another 1,290 troops back to Dover on May 31. By the day following, June 1, this extraordinary ship was again off the Dunkirk piers, picking up another load of (chiefly French) troops, when the Luftwaffe attacked it with a melee of bombs.

There was a bitter irony about this date. The Glorious First of June is commemorated each year by the Royal Navy to mark its victory over the French fleet off Ushant in 1794 near the beginning of the Revolutionary and Napoleonic Wars. The results of the fighting in this year of 1940 were to be far less glorious for the service, however, although the performances of some of its destroyers and crews were remarkable. One heavy bomb crushed most of the *Ivanhoe*'s upper deck, with many casualties among crew and soldiers, and flooded two of its boiler rooms—but didn't sink it. The story gets more amazing. The destroyer HMS *Havant* and the minesweeper HMS *Speedwell* took off all the troops and the many wounded, but most of the *Ivanhoe*'s crew stayed on board, since boiler room number three was still intact and the warship could thus make its way, slowly, back to Dover on its own power. The story was a far less happy one for HMS *Havant*. Loaded down with five hundred troops from the Dunkirk beaches and now carrying the *Ivanhoe*'s wounded and previously evacuated soldiers, it was attacked by two Stukas, damaged irretrievably, and had to be sunk by its escort. Among those killed on the *Havant* were some British soldiers who had been sunk, rescued, and then sunk again in the same afternoon! Two other Royal Navy destroyers, HMS *Keith* and HMS *Basilisk,* were sunk by the Luftwaffe off Dunkirk on the same day, by far the worst in terms of warship losses.[26] Nearby was the classy 5-inch-gunned French destroyer, the *Foudroyant,* which, having also just picked up hundreds of troops from the Dunkirk staithes, was attacked by such a swarm of Heinkels and Stukas that it turned over and sank in shallow water, its hull visible to all.[27] Above this melee was another one, as squadron after squadron of Hurricanes and Spitfires were desperately sent in by RAF Fighter Command to try to blunt the Luftwaffe's offensive—twenty-four German planes were shot down over Dunkirk that day and many others damaged (though not the hundreds famously claimed by Churchill to the House of Commons).

Not by coincidence, it was on this disaster-filled day of June 1 that London informed a bitterly disappointed Norwegian government that it would be withdrawing from all its operations in that country, including the advance on Narvik. The Allied military catastrophe in Belgium thus dealt an end to their operations in the north. The German generals themselves could hardly believe that all this was happening. And as if this British tale of woe was not enough, on June 8 the carrier HMS *Glorious,* participating in the pullout from Norway and with its deck completely loaded with rescued Hurricanes and unable to fly any off, was caught and sunk during a sneak, brief sortie by the battle cruisers *Scharnhorst* and *Gneisenau*—a Parthian shot indeed by Raeder's own badly depleted navy, even if the destroyer *Acasta* managed to ram and tear open the *Scharnhorst*'s side.[28] These were unbelievably dramatic days for both the British and German navies.

The *Ivanhoe*'s saga did not end with its Dunkirk encounter. After its exhausted crew had brought their battered vessel into Dover, it was sent north for lengthy repairs, and by late August, remarkably, it was back in action off the Texel (Dutch coast). Alas, this was an operation that went badly wrong during the night of August 28, when its squadron of destroyers crashed upon a newly laid German minefield. Struck by a mine that blew off its front end, the *Ivanhoe* attempted to return home, but as it lay in the water, it was then attacked by E-boats and further damaged. With its crew removed, it had finally to be sunk by one of its own side, HMS *Kelvin,* on September 1, 1940. Finishing off a fellow vessel whose condition was hopeless was an almost commonplace task during these brutal, close-in struggles; it was deemed quite undignified to let an empty warship drift, and there was the added fear that the enemy might capture it, possibly seizing documents, equipment, or other valuable material. The North Sea, for centuries a graveyard to the ships of many a great naval war, was now claiming many more victims; turbine-driven, steel-plated destroyers and feisty E-boats now joined the wrecks of ironclad cruisers and timber-framed frigates in the sand and mud.

If this quadruple destroyer saga (*Wakeful-Grafton-Ivanhoe-Havant*) portrays a Royal Navy off Dunkirk being badly hurt by the ferocity and deadliness of the German attacks by air, submarine, and surface vessels, that picture is, surely, correct. Overall, of the thirty-nine British destroyers engaged in this campaign, six were sunk and no less than nineteen were badly damaged—little wonder, then, that the Admiralty was worried at the loss of such critical naval assets just as all of western Europe was falling into German hands and the British home islands themselves were now exposed to threat. Yet such a focus on these amazing naval struggles might miss another part of the Dunkirk story, that is, the near-miraculous evacuation flows that also took place during exactly these days. On the very day and night of May 30, as the *Wakeful* was sunk, over 47,000 British soldiers were brought back across the Channel, and on the day following, some 54,000 more. On May 31 the total recovered from France surged to 68,000 British and French soldiers, and on June 1—that is, in the midst of HMS *Ivanhoe*'s many travails—another 65,500 men were brought back. Thus, during those embattled four days alone, 232,000 Allied soldiers were rescued from German capture—this was a full 65 percent of the Dunkirk recovery total of 338,226 men.[29]

Even while losing such an awful amount of their critical equipment (445 tanks, 2,400 artillery pieces, and tens of thousands of trucks and other vehicles), those troops, once they had recovered from that ordeal, were going to be a substantial addition to Britain's home garrison should any future invasion occur. And when those British Army regiments were not needed in such a defensive role, then they would, once reequipped, be ready for deployments in Egypt, Iraq, and India as the year 1940 led into 1941. Indeed, many of those battered units from the Dunkirk campaign would later be found fighting all through the Alamein and Tunisian campaigns, the D-Day landings, and the march into Germany in 1945.[30] The Royal Navy's losses in those extraordinary days of late May 1940 were severe, therefore, and as Churchill himself repeatedly said, "wars are not won by evacuations"; but to the historian of Britain's long sweep of continental campaigning, this was certainly not the first time that an expeditionary army had had to be unceremoniously pulled back from France and the Low Countries only to return later, when the tides of war had turned.[31]

There had been no major British warships involved in the Dunkirk operations and therefore no losses of cruisers and carriers, as was the case in both the Norway and Greece campaigns. No larger German vessels were ever sent to the lower North Sea either, so the bulk of the Royal Navy was held back, in Britain's many western and northern ports. The navy's destroyer losses off Dunkirk were large enough, of course, especially when added to those suffered at the First Battle of Narvik, but despite the Admiralty's worries they actually were not a huge enough percentage of the whole to be critical, and it was remarkable how swiftly British repair yards could put together even the most battered warship (the *Ivanhoe* was back in action within three months, and HMS *Kelly*, an extreme case, was back at sea by December 1940). By contrast, as we have seen, Raeder had lost a full half of the German Navy's twenty fleet destroyers during the Norway fighting, and only a very few of the remainder were fit for action during the second half of the year. The other damages suffered by his surface fleet, most particularly those to his battle cruisers *Scharnhorst* and *Gneisenau* in the late stages of the Norway campaign, meant that, even had he thought of risking heavy vessels off Dunkirk, there were really none available for fighting.

Nor did he have a surface fleet ready during those summer months when British fears of an invasion were at their height and weather conditions the most suitable. Raeder would thus have to wait for a repaired navy and for some brand-new reinforcements (for example, *Bismarck*) over the next year, but well before then the British shipyards were at last beginning to turn out their own post–London Treaty warships. The battleship *King George V* joined the fleet in late 1940, and its sister the *Prince of Wales* shortly after that; the new carriers HMSs *Illustrious* and *Indomitable* also reached the fleet in 1940. All ten of the new *Town*-class cruisers had already joined the service, and some of the brand-new antiaircraft (*Dido*-class) cruisers were working up to readiness.[32] Curiously then, regardless of all the disasters that had taken place off western Europe and in the Atlantic by this time and whatever challenges were now to unfold for the Royal Navy in the Mediterranean, the Anglo-German naval balances in surface ships were even more skewed in Britain's favor than they had been before the Norway-to-Dunkirk calamities transpired.

Nor was this the time, as noted above, for Doenitz's ambitious U-boat arm to adjust those balances, even if it was gaining valuable forward bases

PAINTING 17. British destroyer disembarking troops at Dover after Dunkirk. This unidentified Royal Navy destroyer was one of many that repeatedly ferried exhausted British and French troops back from the Dunkirk beaches—often twice in one day.

in Norway and France. Here, again, the Kriegsmarine was not ready to exploit the new geography of the war. With the Nazi economy at this stage far from being fully mobilized for total war, and priority of production given to the German Army and the Luftwaffe and then to surface warships, Doenitz's arm was lucky to be able to have more than twenty boats at sea (and that included the Baltic) at this time. And then there were the losses to enemy action, small at first but rising the more the fighting had intensified off Norway and the Low Countries. Nine U-boats were lost in 1939, and a further sixteen in the first six months of 1940.[33] But the overall striking power of Doenitz's submarine arm was weakened even further by the widespread incidence of defective torpedoes. As it turned out, Prien's experience of firing so many dud torpedoes during his Scapa Flow saga was not uncommon; at this time, maybe half of all the torpedoes fired in action failed in one way or another.[34] Alas, for Raeder this conjuncture of German naval weaknesses—the surface fleet hardly existing, the submarine fleet so small—lay in such contrast to the obviously dazzling power and successes of the German Army and to what seemed to all to be the mind-boggling strength of the Luftwaffe. This was not a good time to expect the Fuehrer to spend much more on the Third Reich's modest naval branch.

Still, this relative weakness of the navy was easily hidden by Germany's overall staggering successes during the first nine months of the war. To contemporaries and later historians alike, the overwhelming impression must have been how effective and dangerous the Wehrmacht's armed forces had shown themselves to be, again and again. Crushed into defeat after 1919, Germany had reemerged like the proverbial phoenix. In campaigns from Poland to Norway, its army, from tanks to paratroops, had been unstoppable. And even in the war at sea, despite the many problems described above, despite its restricted geographic location and its relatively small number of surface vessels and submarines, the German Navy had thrown a real challenge to the numerically far larger Allied navies— in dangerous attacks on the oceanic trade routes, from the North Atlantic to the South, by surface warships and clandestine raiders; in the brutally effective thrust to seize Norway and its harbors; and in assisting, at least in part, the Wehrmacht's takeover of the western shores of Europe from Denmark to the Spanish border. If the German submarines had proven to be less successful than Doenitz had hoped, they nevertheless had struck a few dramatic blows against the Royal Navy; and now that they possessed French and Norwegian bases, even with a limited number of vessels the U-boat threat looked as if it could only increase. Not appreciating the significant German weaknesses, from the unreliability in torpedo design to the amazingly low percentage of the submarine fleet that was actually

combat ready at this time, the British Admiralty saw only enemy ingenuity and threat by mid-1940. It was thus unsurprising that all thoughts in
London were focused on the prospect of the Wehrmacht's next dramatic
leap, across the North Sea and Channel and onto the beaches of England.

Above all, though, there was the daunting threat of a German airpower
that appeared to be able to project itself a hundred miles, perhaps several
hundred miles, out from the land and over the sea. Since this was entirely
new in the annals of warfare, the extent of this transformation in fighting
was not yet fully known, nor were the means of countering it understood,
let alone worked out. For over half a century, the Mahanian school had
presumed and written about an "influence of sea power" that could prevail against all nations and societies accessible to strong offshore navies;
at the same time, advocates of amphibious blows against an enemy, such
as Admiral John Fisher, had talked boldly about the British Army being
"a projectile launched from the sea."[35] Now, instead of the territories of
the hegemonic land power being threatened by a naval foe, it looked as if
a large and effective air force such as the Luftwaffe might be able to push
away the Atlantic maritime nations, maybe keeping them at bay forever.
"The historical strategy of Britain," as described by the military strategist Sir Basil Liddell Hart even at this time,[36] looked less and less applicable in the era of modern, fast aircraft capable of carrying 250-pound and
500-pound bombs. Clearly, anyone who intended to assault and conquer
an enemy's shores at any future stage in this war would also need to have
established command of the air as a prior condition. Fortunately, this truism applied as much for any intended German invasion of the British
Isles as it did for any future Allied attempt to reenter Europe. Here, then,
would be the German Air Force's next test.

One more general thought is worth offering about the Luftwaffe's pum-
meling of the Royal Navy's warships during these early clashes off Norway and the coasts of France. It was, obviously, the first time in history
that warships operating offshore had ever encountered large-scale aerial
attacks, and from fast, modern planes such as Goering's massed fleets of
Messerschmitts, Dorniers, Heinkels, and Junkers. There had been nothing like it during World War I, and the Manchurian, Abyssinian, and
Spanish Civil War contests of the 1930s also offered little guide as to what
might come. The Allied forces operating off Norway and (especially) the
Franco-Belgian coast were neither well prepared nor well equipped for
what the German Air Force could do. Handling the speed and angle of
attack of the Stuka (Ju-87) dive-bombers was a special challenge. Most
Royal Navy guns had only a 45-degree elevation, and none of them had
enough modern antiaircraft armaments (the warships that survived the
various 1940 operations would soon have a cluster of Bofors and Oerlikon

guns welded, in great haste, to their upper decks). There was no operational doctrine for sustained aircraft-carrier or escort-carrier coverage of amphibious landings or withdrawals. Short-range fighter aircraft (Hurricanes and Fairey Battles) based on English airfields carried far too little fuel for continuous patrols over the Dunkirk beaches and onloading warships. In short, this was a novel, lopsided struggle, not ships versus forts (Nelson's adage) but ships versus planes, and the warships of the time were simply not equipped to protect themselves or the British and French soldiers they were striving to evacuate.

No separate statistics exist on the Allied troop losses to Luftwaffe attacks on them as they stood in their patient lines along Dunkirk's beaches or in the many rescue ships that were either sunk or badly damaged by German aircraft as they sailed back to England. All were part of the far larger losses suffered by the British and French forces during the overall May–June "Battle of France." The French Army, which continued to fight for some days after the Dunkirk evacuation was declared complete (June 4), took 360,000 casualties overall, including as many as 85,000 dead. The BEF lost 68,000 men (dead, wounded, and captured) in the entire campaign and, as mentioned above, absolutely all its military equipment, from 445 tanks and 2,700 artillery pieces to 20,000 motorcycles. In addition to the six Royal Navy destroyers sunk, the French lost another three, all to devastating aerial attack. About 200 other, smaller British and Allied vessels were sunk. The Luftwaffe probably lost some 240 aircraft during the overall French campaign, chiefly (156 of them) on the Dunkirk front. RAF Fighter Command lost 127 aircraft in Dunkirk operations.[37] For the first time, the German Air Force had met an equivalent, and some of their more thoughtful strategists, like Adolf Galland, were drawing some obvious conclusions. For the moment, though, the Germans could claim an undoubted victory—"the greatest battle in the History of the world," boasted Hitler—and assert control of Europe's western border from the North Cape to the Spanish border. Whether it could expand further outward, beyond the English Channel, Gibraltar, and North Africa, was quite a different matter.


## "Westward, Look, the Land Is Bright!"

It was of course not just along the European side of the Atlantic that the political landscape was shifting fast during June and July 1940. The stunning news of the Fall of France and the entry of Italy into the war led to a near panic in Washington that this would be followed soon by a surrender by Britain and the possible Nazi seizure of the French and British navies and then even by a German push toward the West Indies and Brazil.[38] This in turn led to dramatic responses by the Roosevelt administration and by a now thoroughly alarmed US Congress, which abandoned all of its earlier political reservations about excessive naval spending. The timing here could not have been more exquisite. On the afternoon of June 17, 1940, the head of the US Navy, Admiral Harold Stark, was scheduled to appear before the House Naval Affairs Committee with a request for the gigantic sum of over $4 billion for warships, aircraft, and shipyard and port installations, an annual increase far larger than in any previous year. But that same morning, congressmen would read in their newspapers of France's decision to stop fighting and to ask Nazi Germany for surrender terms. A shaky Britain seemed on its own, and the Atlantic had never looked so narrow. So upset was Congress by all this news, and so eager to receive the navy's request, that by the end of the afternoon the measure was approved, without any contrary votes, for the next stages. When the monies were fully tallied up and the authorization to this bill concluded in the following month, the total had risen to a staggering $8 billion. No other power could have afforded this amount of money, and this for just *one* branch of the US armed services. The naval shopping list itself read as follows: 4 *Iowa*-class battleships, 5 *Montana*-class super-battleships, 18 *Essex*-class fleet carriers, 27 cruisers (including 14 *Baltimore*-class very heavy cruisers), 115 (eventually 175) fleet destroyers (including the powerful *Fletcher*-class), innumerable fleet auxiliaries, supply vessels, and so on. Additionally, ordnance works, naval base construction, and additional shipbuilding facilities were needed, in the United States and further afield.[39]

Here, at last, was the two-ocean navy that American expansionists had argued for during the whole century hitherto. In terms of overall naval tonnage (1,325,000 tons), this act alone authorized building the equivalent of virtually the entire Imperial Japanese Navy, and (depending on how one counted the laying-down dates) of about eight to ten times Hitler's Kriegsmarine.

It is worthwhile, therefore, to tease out a little further the sheer naval power and ambition that was implicit within this expansion act. The construction data was of course pretty clear to any naval expert. The *Iowa*-class battleships, when available, would already be superior to the *Bismarck* and the *Tirpitz;* they were somewhat longer and broader and a few knots faster than the huge German vessels, and they had more heavily armed ($9 \times 16$ inch to $8 \times 15$ inch) main guns that were to be radar controlled. They would indeed be more powerful, vessel for vessel, than the newest battleships of any European navy. Yet the five *Montana*-class super-battleships to follow would be much larger again, displacing over

70,000 tons and carrying twelve monstrous 16-inch guns.[40] Chiefly intended to take on the Japanese *Yamato*-class behemoths in a Pacific clash, these *Montanas,* even just two if deployed with attendant heavy cruisers and destroyers in Atlantic waters, would have neutralized any threat from a possible *Bismarck* incursion and thus ensured American naval mastery along the Eastern Seaboard and beyond.

While this increase in the traditional weapon of battleships appeared decisive enough, the real power shift implied in this congressional spending act lay in the authorization of no fewer than *eighteen* aircraft carriers—all *Essex*-class fast fleet carriers—together with fifteen thousand new planes for the US Navy alone. While vast new battleships were of course critical for America's sea power, Admiral William Pratt had assured the traditionalists among his audience that he and his planners had no doubt that airpower—and aerial dominance over the oceans—was the instrument of the future.[41] With funds also authorized for fast fleet oilers and supply ships and a host of additional fast *Fletcher*-class destroyers, the new fleet carriers would have the range to strike far and wide. Indeed, it was possible to imagine a future force of, say, six or eight such carriers (with or without the battlewagons) being able to determine the maritime balances in the North Atlantic even as the navy carried out separate and extensive operations in the Pacific. They would certainly make the Western Hemisphere safe from any Axis naval penetration, which is why even US isolationists voted for the act. The only snag was that all of this was at least two years away.

Precisely because this was the great American navy of the future, then, the new measure could not assist Britain's desperate strategic position around July 1940, which is why Churchill would press his friend Roosevelt for more immediate, practical measures such as destroyers-for-bases, the transfer of army equipment (machine guns and artillery pieces), and Lend-Lease. Still, the larger message of this new shipbuilding program should have been clear to any reflective strategic thinker, since an American navy of this size pretty much foredoomed all German and Italian maritime ambitions. Ironically, these many signs of the unleashing of America's huge productive powers reinforced in the Fuehrer's mind the conviction that unless he somehow very soon controlled all the resources of continental Eurasia, including those of the USSR, he would never be able to take on the American colossus in a later struggle for world mastery—thus his idea of soon turning against Russia.[42] And in Tokyo, even more clearly, the prospect of a gigantic US Navy emerging by as early as 1943 (the first *Iowa* and *Essex* ships would be active by then) seemed to give Japan only an approximately two-year window of opportunity to press forward in the Pacific and Far East with any prospect of success. And that conclusion itself assumed, as Admiral Isoroku Yamamoto was to argue to the Japanese High Command, that some ruthless preemptive blows to cripple Anglo-American strategic assets would have to be delivered soon.[43] Much more than before, then, after the passing of the Two-Ocean Navy Act both Tokyo and Berlin felt that they were running out of time and had to act. Although it may not have been completely understood by any of the participants in this drama until much later, the Fall of France, the Two-Ocean Navy Act, the Battle of Britain, Operation Barbarossa, the unfolding Battle of the Atlantic, and Pearl Harbor, all occurring during the long seventeen months between June 1940 and December 1941, were all strategically connected, all part of a larger struggle for global mastery to which the turbulent 1930s had been a mere prelude. Very few observers, one suspects, may have grasped the full dimensions of these many changes in the global landscape, but to those in the US Navy charged with building the new Rooseveltian fleet, the way ahead was much less complicated: all that was needed now, really, was to launch those battleships, carriers, and cruisers as fast as possible.[44]

There was one chief player in this global drama who certainly felt that the collapse of France and the future attitude of the United States in this struggle were intimately bound together. In Churchill's mind, the former was a truly historic event and, as an intense believer in the power of the French Army, he was much shaken by it. To his inventive mind, then, Germany's arrival on the other side of the Channel and North Sea called not only for immediate and intensive home-defense measures but also for a larger global response. On June 4, 1940, already, the prime minister made one of his greatest political speeches, his magnificent address to the House of Commons, describing the gravity of the post-Dunkirk scene and insisting that Britain would fight without flinching: "We shall fight on the beaches . . . fight on the hillsides," until, as he then put it, "in God's good time, the New World would come to the rescue of the Old."[45] Still urging the French to fight on, offering in desperation even a permanent Anglo-French union, the prime minister was already looking over his shoulder and across the Atlantic. After France's complete collapse two weeks later, the need to keep—to increase—American support became Churchill's great strategic priority, second only to survival itself, indeed an integral part of it. But he was well aware that many in the United States, including in its government, doubted whether a battered Britain had the will and the strength to fight on. Washington's urgings that, if Britain fell, it should promise to send its fleet across the Atlantic and out of Nazi hands, showed how doubtful the American government

PAINTING 18. Bombardment of the French battleship *Richelieu*, Dakar, 1941. The Royal Navy repeatedly sought to cripple the vessels of the Vichy Navy through bombardment and air attacks. Though frequently damaged, *Richelieu* survived to have an amazing wartime career after it joined the Allied side in 1943.

was at this time. But what the United States feared about possible German control of Britain's fleet, Churchill in turn, and much more immediately, feared about possible Nazi control of France's.

Cruelly, therefore, the fate of the Vichy French Navy, still the fourth largest in the world and ordered by the Compiegne surrender document of June 22, 1940, to be "demobilized and disarmed under German and Italian control," became a critical part of the new British government's striving for survival, for desperately restoring the disastrous and unexpected change in the naval balances, and for proving to Roosevelt that the island nation could match the German threat with equal ruthlessness and decision. By the beginning of July, Churchill had persuaded his Cabinet that if France's admirals declined the invitation to join in the fight against the Axis or at least to demobilize their ships, then the latter would be sunk. Whether the prime minister had in memory Nelson's ruthless preemptive destruction of the neutral Danish Navy at Copenhagen in 1804 to prevent it joining Napoleon's coalition is not clear.[46] What is clear is that Britain, to preserve its own threatened maritime security, was now prepared to sink the fleet of its own former close ally. How ironic that it was Churchill, the most Francophile among the English politicians, who was making this decision for "Operation Catapult."

The July 3–6 sinking of the French fleet at Mers-el-Kébir and other North African ports is one of the best-known, and perhaps saddest, naval actions of World War II.[47] Certainly, Admiral James Somerville at Gibraltar and Vice Admiral Andrew Cunningham at Alexandria and the other Royal Navy senior officers who were given orders by London to begin shooting all felt so. With the French fleet moored along the outer mole, they were clear targets for the powerful battle squadron (*Hood, Resolution,* and *Valiant,* all 15-inch gunned) that had been sent from the Home Fleet and designated as Force H. The two older French battleships *Provence* and *Bretagne* were sunk on July 3, the latter with terrible loss of life (over one thousand officers and crew) when it blew up, and the modern battle cruiser *Dunkerque* was badly damaged, but its sister ship *Strasbourg* made a successful escape to Toulon. Another large British battleship-carrier force arrived off Dakar on July 8 and, with a torpedo attack by aircraft of the carrier HMS *Hermes,* hurt the new battleship *Richelieu.* Two weeks later, the French warship was further damaged by shelling.

Apart from the few lesser warships that either joined de Gaulle's Free French side or agreed to be interred in Alexandria and the French West Indies, the rest of the French Navy, chiefly clustered at Toulon, became bitterly resentful and had to be considered as hostile by the Royal Navy. While the Vichy French government in Algeria and Morocco regarded the British with great enmity, its fleet now lay to the north and could not constitute a close threat to the Malta convoys, then just beginning. And while Italy's entry into the war brought another major change in the European naval balance of power (chapter 5), the British had shown that they were going to clamp down tightly on the western Mediterranean and fight with the greatest resolve. Hitler was amazed by this action, and Mussolini and his admirals were greatly worried; but, most important, the Americans were impressed.

---

By the second week of July, with Operation Catapult sadly over, HMS *Hood* and most of the rest of Force H were steaming northward from Gibraltar again, promptly recalled for duty in home waters at this time of the Cabinet's fears of a possible German invasion of eastern England. The first phase of the maritime struggle, so relatively balanced during the seven Phony War months, and so incredibly turbulent and violent during the next mere quarter of a year (early April to early July), had come to its close, and in the North Atlantic and North Sea waters all actions by major forces ceased; even U-boat and convoy fights were minimal. When fleet actions by the Royal Navy next occurred, they would be in the central Mediterranean, and against a new belligerent.

Taken overall, the first nine months of the war at sea had been a poor one for British naval power. The carrier *Courageous* had been sunk by a single submarine, the battleship *Royal Oak* destroyed in its own home base, and the carrier *Glorious* blown to bits by surface raiders. The Royal Navy's strength in cruisers was hardly touched, but the number of its all-important fleet destroyers that were sunk and badly damaged off Norway, the Dutch coast, and Dunkirk was severe. Merchant-ship losses in all waters were sustainable, so far, but it was easy to imagine that that situation would not last for long given the new geographical conformation.

Losing Norway was a severe setback. The Fall of France was a colossal defeat. Italy's entry into the war would tighten the screws. Britain, battered as never before, had lost its only expeditionary field army and looked very weak. It is true that in the far west a huge military giant was awakening. But in the early summer of 1940 it seemed to many observers an open question whether the Royal Navy and the Royal Air Force could hold their enemies at bay until the time, if it ever came, when the United States would at last be a belligerent in this world war.

**PAINTING 19. HMS *Sheffield* off Gibraltar, 1941.** In this superb and symbolic painting, the British cruiser stands off Gibraltar, which was its Force H base for so long. These classy 6-inch-gunned *Town*-class cruisers fought in all oceans throughout the war.

# FIVE

## The European War at Sea
### *July 1940–December 1941*

I n June 1940, with the French Empire collapsed and Italy entering the war in the Mediterranean, Britain faced a strategic situation more dire than any it had encountered since 1805, when Napoleon's Grand Army lay encamped near Calais. Vigorously rejecting ideas of a negotiated peace, Churchill urged the nation to fight on, relying upon its moral strength, its domestic material resources, its aerial defenses, and its Navy. The cartoonist David Low captured this defiant sentiment in his well-known sketch of "Very Well, Alone," of June 18, 1940, a mere twenty-four hours after Pétain surrendered. A strong-jawed British Tommy, equipped with only his rifle, stands on a storm-washed rock and defiantly waves his fist in the air.[1] But of course Britain was never, ever entirely alone. Its huge empire was mobilizing itself for war, and to such an extent that the prewar planners could scarcely have imagined.[2] Its vast merchant fleet was being added to by a large number of vessels flying the Dutch, Norwegian, Polish, and (slightly later) Yugoslav and Greek flags, just as the Royal Air Force's pilot strength was to be enhanced, not only by many British Dominion squadrons but also by hastily recruited units of Polish, Czech, Free French, and American volunteers. And in the background, as we shall see, there was to be the steadily growing and ever-less-neutral intrusion of US naval patrols into Atlantic waters, plus the September 1940 destroyers-for-bases deal and then the flow of Lend-Lease supplies after March 1941.

Still, in those months when German invasion barges were being gathered in Channel ports, with the whole line of the Atlantic from the North Cape to the Pyrenees in German hands, with Luftwaffe bombing attacks at London and the southern English ports growing, with the critical Mediterranean route now threatened by Italian aircraft and the large Italian fleet, and with General Rodolfo Graziani's army advancing from Libya on Egypt, the overall situation was shocking. So, even if there were considerable British and imperial assets to be considered in the overall strategic net assessment, there is no doubt that the events of May–June 1940 had led to a huge negative shift in power, toward the Axis and away from Britain itself. It was not surprising that, even across the Atlantic, the Roosevelt administration began to worry about the security of the Western Hemisphere.[3] In this immediate crisis situation, the capacity of the Royal Navy to fight, from the close-in Channel waters and right across the Atlantic and through the Mediterranean, was absolutely vital. Overall, the service did extraordinarily well, but at very heavy cost to itself. Soon, Churchill was to offer fulsome and public praise to the aircrews of RAF Fighter Command for their heroic role during this period of the island nation's "finest hour," but the parallel naval achievement was equally gallant, and no less important.

## The Atlantic Struggle Intensifies, 1940–1941

Germany's military and geographical gains vis-à-vis Britain by the summer of 1940 were breathtaking. As noted in chapter 4, it was not simply that the armed forces of key European states—Norway, Belgium, the Netherlands, and above all, France—were removed from the sum total of anti-German forces; it was also that the Third Reich had now gained a huge positional advantage, breaking out of the strategic box that had hemmed in its Wilhelmine forerunner. In the whole sweep of modern European history, it is hard to think of a geopolitical change as large as this one. It was less than fifteen years ago (see chapter 3) that Wolfgang Wegener's book *The Sea Strategy of the World War* had called for Germany to counter its geographical weakness in a future war with England by obtaining naval bases in Norway and in western France.[4] What had seemed purely speculative and impossible at that earlier time, now—amazingly— had happened, and both the Luftwaffe and the Kriegsmarine swiftly moved into bases in their newly acquired territories.

Thus, while most eyes were focused on the Battle of Britain during those key months following July 1940, it was also the case that the Battle of the Atlantic had entered its second stage, one that showed off Germany's great new advantages.[5] The biggest gain, obviously, was that Karl Doenitz's U-boats could now be based in harbors outside the North Sea, in the multiple moorings of the Norwegian fjords and in the strongly defended French ports of Cherbourg, Brest, and the Gironde. And, while a smaller matter, Axis blockade runners now found it easier to run supplies to Germany via France than they had earlier, when they had had

to steam past Scotland and into the North Sea. Almost equally important as the new U-boat advantage was the fact that the Luftwaffe could
place its air forces along the Atlantic coastline. This included a few squadrons of the long-range Focke-Wulf Condor bomber that could shadow,
report upon, and very frequently attack Allied convoys when they were
still well out into the Atlantic, although the most frequent danger was
the attacks by dangerous medium bombers (Dorniers and Heinkels) on
Britain's coastal convoys as well as the vital Gibraltar routes. Finally, although Admiral Erich Raeder had only a few heavy warships ready for
combat at this time, existing units like his battle cruisers *Scharnhorst* and
*Gneisenau* could make a sortie and then retire into French or northern
Norwegian ports following their convoy raids—they did not need to cross
the North Sea, as previously. Of course, had the Third Reich possessed at
this time something like the massed squadrons of the former imperial
High Seas Fleet or the futuristic giant Plan Z navy, then the great maritime war after 1940 would very likely have had a Mahanian look to it. But
instead of an epic Anglo-German fleet encounter somewhere in the Western Approaches, there was to unfold a less dramatic, much longer-lasting,
and far more complex struggle for control of the sea-lanes to and from the
United Kingdom.

In this struggle Britain and its navy still retained immense geographical and material advantages, despite the fall of Norway and France. To begin with, there were the multiple resources of the home island itself. To a
worried British public in the summer of 1940 suffering under increased
aerial attack, shocked by the return of the shattered troops from Dunkirk,
and watching with alarm the hasty erection of anti-invasion barriers,
the country appeared surrounded, weak, and encroached upon from all
sides by German threats. To a sober-minded senior German general like
Fritz Halder, chief of the army staff,[6] the British Isles appeared more like
a giant porcupine, its many Channel ports full of destroyer squadrons,
the eastern shores protected by minefields and gun emplacements, and
the whole country containing serried ranks of RAF fighter and bomber
squadrons controlled by a sophisticated headquarters. Nor was it all that
vulnerable to German aerial pressures on the economic front. Although
it was a wrenching business, the main flow of its imports from the world
could henceforth come in via Glasgow and Liverpool rather than Southampton and London. Moreover, the country's main shipbuilding centers
and battle-fleet bases and "shadow" aircraft factories lay a long way to the
northwest, and with formidable antiaircraft defenses all the way. Defeating Britain was simply a far larger proposition than anything the Third
Reich had encountered before, and, quite frankly, Berlin simply had not
figured out how to do it.

The German invasion plans and movements of 1940—Case Yellow (*Fall Gelb*)—were never really pushed after their initial preparatory stages for another reason, a political one, because Hitler's own preoccupations shifted, to his rising quarrels with the Soviet Union about the disposition of land and resources in eastern Europe. But it is worth noting all the physical difficulties facing the German High Command when it contemplated the invasion of Britain, if only because the Allies would in their turn have to overcome a similar array of challenges when they considered a large-scale invasion of North Africa, Italy, and France. Thus, the German Army wanted a broad array of landing spots, but the German Navy protested that it was not strong enough to offer protection for such a large operation. Its landing barges, tugs, and other craft were scattered throughout many Channel ports, and assembling them—and they were already coming under RAF attack—in such difficult waters would be a bosun's nightmare. Even if the Luftwaffe achieved complete command of the air, it is clear that any attempted invasion of southeast England (German forces could not possibly reach further) would be a horribly difficult and bloody affair, especially on the obstacle-strewn beaches. But the fact was that, in any case, Hermann Goering's vaunted air flotillas simply could not crack the dense networks of aerial defenses that Britain possessed by 1940, from its comprehensive radar-detection network to its rising number of RAF Fighter Command squadrons. To repeat, for the first time the Third Reich was now fighting another truly Great Power.

Thus, while the dangerously efficient divisions of the German Army had come to the shores of the Atlantic, they would go no further westward. Geopolitically, this was of huge significance. The Wehrmacht could turn its attention further south, which it did by the late spring of 1941 as it entered the Mediterranean fray to assist Italy; and it could turn its attention to the east, as it did by June of that year, driven by Hitler's manic desire to destroy Bolshevism. Yet already after, say, September 1940 it was left to Germany's aerial and naval forces to achieve the task of reducing to surrender the main enemy in the west, Britain, and the chances of being able to attain that aim were dubious to say the least. The tide had already turned in the air war. If the Luftwaffe could not prevail over the skies of southeast England during the long sunny summer months, why should anyone assume that its unescorted bombers could bring a highly scattered and more distant British industry to its knees in the nighttime raids, in overcast weather, in the winter months that followed?

The chief task of defeating the United Kingdom had therefore to be carried out by the German Navy by strangling the British Isles in a counterblockade to the Royal Navy's own blockade of the Third Reich. To achieve this, Germany possessed three significant operational instruments of war:

its long-range naval air forces; the Kriegsmarine's own array of surface vessels, from powerful, fast warships to cleverly disguised merchant raiders; and, perhaps the most dangerous threat of all, the still-growing U-boat flotillas.

It has to be said immediately that Germany's naval air forces were not enough to alter the course of the Battle of the Atlantic, certainly not by themselves. The losses such aircraft inflicted were sometimes significant, and of course they were very important in their roles of spotting Allied convoys at sea and directing the U-boats to such targets—but only if they themselves had spotted anything in such vast regions.[7] How many squadrons of FW-200 Condors, one wonders, flying at extreme range from their bases in France, would it have taken to achieve continuous air command over the huge stretches of the North Atlantic? Clearly, there were never enough. Moreover, the Condors' effectiveness was soon going to be challenged by equipping convoys with primitive air defenses, as when single Hurricane fighters were launched by catapult from specially equipped merchantmen to drive off or, if possible, shoot down the snoopers (the Hurricane then ditched close to the ship, with the pilot, hopefully, being picked up). And the situation became much worse for the Focke-Wulfs at the end of the following year, when the Royal Navy at last received its long-awaited escort carriers. The very first of these, for example, the aptly named HMS *Audacity,* repeatedly employed its Marlet fighters during a Gibraltar home convoy in December 1941 to drive off and shoot down the slower-maneuvering Condors. Even though the escort carrier itself was sunk later in that convoy fight, the addition of this new element showed that the writing was on the wall: in fact, by the time this well-protected convoy had reached the United Kingdom, two Condors had been destroyed and no less than five U-boats sunk.[8] From then on, whenever a convoy was important enough to be given continuous air protection, whether by these carriers or by increasing numbers of Coastal Command planes, it was going to be safe from aerial attack.

All this merely hinted at how much more damage could have been inflicted had the air fight over the Atlantic not been left to a few dedicated, understrength squadrons and if, more generally, the Luftwaffe's chief strategic aim been devoted to bringing Britain to its knees. Yet how could that ever be after the Battle of Britain? For a few brief months after October 1940 there was something like an aerial balance in the West, and then things changed abruptly by the beginning of the next year. From that time on, Goering's vaunted *Luftflotten* had to be juggled between its Mediterranean and Balkan, its western, and then its Russian fronts,[9] and the Third Reich was already revealing its fatal inability to prioritize strategically.

This left the task of defeating Britain chiefly to the vessels of the Kriegs-marine, which was a task far beyond its capacities. The German Navy's surface raiders—whether of the clandestine type or the heavy warships proper—were always too few at any given time in the fight. The geograph-ical and physical difficulties they encountered across the North Atlantic arena were huge. And the foe, far from being exhausted or even badly weakened by the Fall of France, seemed to be mobilizing substantial in-depth and concentric forces that reached right across the oceans.

It followed from all this that Germany's clandestine armed merchant-men surface raiders, being only moderately armed themselves, had their best chances when they came upon individual Allied merchant vessels on open seas. Obviously, they could never take on a convoy protected by warships, and they were also in danger if they unintentionally encoun-tered an armed British auxiliary cruiser. They were usually stronger than the latter, but even there the risks of damage during a shootout were high, and taking on the 8-inch guns of a *County*-class cruiser was unthinkable. Thus they had to patrol warily, like foxes on a wide heathland, looking for their opportunities between the enemy's daunting array of naval bases and escort flotillas on either side of the oceans. For all the romanticiza-tion in later literature about these disguised oceanic highwaymen, their actual sinkings were never large enough to affect the overall story; and only for a few months in late 1940 did they inflict much damage.[10]

The threat posed to Allied shipping in the Atlantic by regular German warships was something else. They were much faster than merchantmen, so when they came upon a convoy, they could swiftly sink a consider-able number of the fleeing flock, as was demonstrated by the hugely suc-cessful cruise of the formidable 11-inch-gunned *Admiral Scheer*. In No-vember 1940, shortly after reaching the Atlantic, it came across a convoy south of Halifax and sank five merchantmen plus the escorting armed merchant cruiser SS *Jervis Bay,* and then for months afterward it ram-paged in the South Atlantic and Indian oceans, returning only to Ger-many in April, having sunk seventeen ships of 113,000 tons.[11] Yet that was an exceptional cruise, and, as always, Raeder's surface fleet was much less powerful than the list of warships under his command might have sug-gested. For example, the German fleet destroyers, or those left after the Norwegian fighting, were too "short-legged" to stay in the mid-Atlantic for long as well as being too top-heavy for the giant oceanic rollers. The Kriegsmarine's heavy cruisers of the *Hipper*-class also lacked the endur-ance for long-range raiding, and while the battle cruisers and the pocket battleships (*Panzerschiffe*) like the *Admiral Scheer* were ideal in that re-spect, their 11-inch armaments and lesser armor meant that they always had to run fast if they encountered a 15-inch-gunned British battleship on convoy duty. Above all, though, the slow pace of the Kriegsmarine's construction and repair schedules plus frequent bombing or mine damage meant that Raeder was never able to send to sea more than a few of the warships nominally under his command. The whole story of German surface raiding in World War II was, therefore, one of an irregular succession of single- or, at the most, twin-ship sorties to attack the convoys.

One highly successful example of an attack on British commerce in the North Atlantic, which began from Kiel and ended in Brest, came in an extended raid carried out by the fast battle cruisers *Scharnhorst* and *Gneisenau* between January and March 1941. After sinking a number of unescorted Allied merchantmen east of Newfoundland, the German warships raced far to the south, seeking to disrupt the Freetown convoy traffic (and working there in conjunction with U-boats). Whenever the bulky shape of a British battleship was sighted, though, they swiftly ran from their slower but heavier-armed foe. These really were hit-and-run tactics. Thus, while they rendezvoused repeatedly with their own oilers and sank many further merchantmen in the middle Atlantic and then back in North Atlantic waters, they continued their policy—Raeder's strict order—of never running the risk of being hit by a 15-inch shell. There were many grumbles at this ultracautious tactic; could not two fast, nine 11-inch-gunned modern battle cruisers take on an ancient World War I slow battleship like HMS *Ramillies*? Yet there was also a logic to Raeder's policy, as was evident from the *Graf Spee*'s story in the previous chapter. If either vessel, or the *Admiral Scheer,* were to be hit by a single 15-inch shell in the boiler rooms, where would it go for repair? Clearly not to North America or the Caribbean, nor, practically, to any harbor in Latin America, in which case they might be interned. If they limped into the Vichy port of Dakar, then Force H and the Royal Navy's carrier aircraft would surely come after them. This was ironic: German heavy warships were powerful, impressive, and incredibly well-built craft, with competent commanders and crews, but, as noted before, they dared not suffer much damage while on the high seas.

Before the *Scharnhorst* and *Gneisenau* anchored in Brest on March 23, 1941, they had sunk twenty-two ships of 115,000 tons, temporarily disrupted the entire convoy system, and exposed the Admiralty's folly of allowing groups of "dispersed" merchantmen to steam unescorted, whether throughout their journey or after partial naval protection had been withdrawn.[12] The one consolation to a highly disturbed British Admiralty and a furious Churchill was, of course, that once they returned to ports in Europe they could be subject to RAF bomber raids and to Royal Navy submarine patrols. In April the repeatedly unlucky *Gneisenau* had its stern blown off by a torpedo dropped by a Coastal Command torpedo-bomber, but when moved into dry dock it was then hit by a Bomber Command attack. And the *Scharnhorst*'s engines, worn by heavy cruising, needed serious repair and also had to stay in the dockyard. Yet now that the Luftwaffe had lost aerial control over the English Channel, if it ever had it, Brest was a terrible place in which to have to station German warships.

However severe the disruptions these raiders caused to Allied mercantile traffic in early 1941, then, they really did not last for very long. Even when nearby convoys were ordered to go about for a while in the North Atlantic when raiders were loose, many others were slowly advancing through distant waters, from Buenos Aires and Montevideo, around the Cape, and across the Indian Ocean. For example, there were over twenty convoys at sea and, of course, many, many more unescorted sailings heading toward British ports when the Kriegsmarine attempted its most famous disruption of the Atlantic routes, that by the giant new German battleship *Bismarck* in late May 1941. Obviously, all of those convoys were put on hold by the Admiralty, or even sent back to port, while those that had enjoyed the escort of a battleship (HMS *Rodney*) or heavy cruiser (HMS *Dorsetshire*) saw the latter ordered to join the pursuit. But when this disruption was over, the traffic resumed its sailings again.

The *Bismarck* venture was Admiral Raeder's largest effort to disrupt such traffic. Attended by the heavy cruiser *Prinz Eugen,* the great battleship steamed out through the Denmark Strait and into the North Atlantic, and in a brief but epic exchange on May 24, 1941, the German warships sank the Royal Navy's largest vessel, the HMS *Hood,* while also damaging the Royal Navy's newest battleship, the HMS *Prince of Wales.* Plunging shells brutally destroyed the British battle cruiser in this exchange, just as they had wreaked havoc upon Beatty's battle cruisers at the Battle of Jutland exactly twenty-five years earlier. Encouraged by this remarkable feat, the German commander Admiral Günther Lütjens chose not to return to base but instead to take the *Bismarck* further into the Atlantic to ravage the merchant convoys.

In the famous and tense chase that followed, the British threw everything into the area, although given the concurrent fighting in the Mediterranean, in fact that wasn't really very much—two capital ships in the Home Fleet (*King George V* and *Rodney*) and a battle cruiser (*Renown*) and carrier (*Ark Royal*) with Force H at Gibraltar, plus a second carrier (*Victorious*), attached cruisers, and destroyers as well as those others called from convoy duties. But for once, luck broke in London's favor, and a second round of torpedo attacks by *Ark Royal*'s Swordfish aircraft managed to cripple the *Bismarck*'s rudder and thus disable the ship's steering. Unable to fire properly in the rolling waves, and assaulted by destroyers, cruisers, and then the Home Fleet's battleships, a burning *Bismarck* scut-

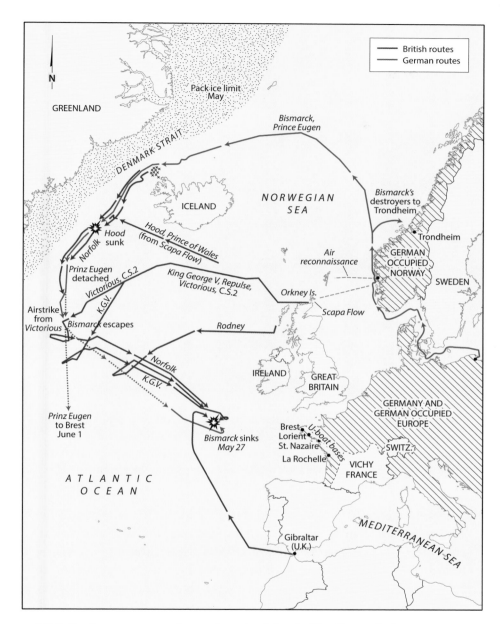

**MAP 5.** German encroachment into the Atlantic: The *Bismarck* chase, May 1941.

tled itself on June 1, to Churchill's enormous relief.[13] Had the giant vessel reached Brest unscathed and, with the *Prinz Eugen,* joined up with the repaired battle cruisers *Scharnhorst* and *Gneisenau* for future raids, the Royal Navy might really have been hard-pressed to hold on to their North Atlantic convoy routes.

Yet that hypothetical "if" was never to happen, simply because the

**PAINTING 20.** The *Bismarck* under attack from Fairey Swordfish torpedo-bombers, 1941. Only three days after sinking HMS *Hood* in the Denmark Strait (on May 24, 1941), the great German battleship's steering was crippled by torpedo attack. The Swordfish look miniscule compared to the warship itself.

Kriegsmarine itself had discovered, just as had the Italian Navy in the Mediterranean, that it had emerged to challenge the Anglo-American control of the seas just as the aircraft was demonstrating its growing influence over both land and sea operations everywhere. It was not, of course, that either Germany or Italy lacked airpower themselves, but they did not have enough of it or of the right sort, while their opponents did. Overall, the British possessed far too few carriers during the first half of the war, yet, still, their presence so often tipped the balance. At Taranto and at Cape Matapan, as in the *Bismarck* strike, even a small number of carrier-based torpedo-bombers, however slow, were a huge threat to any enemy fleet at sea or in harbor, simply because the torpedo itself was such a devastating weapon. But so, too, of course, was the heavy (500-pound or 1,000-pound bomb), whether it was being dropped on Royal Navy ships off Crete or, as was now to be the case, on German vessels as they rested in the harbors of western France.

As the *Bismarck* was being sunk, the *Prinz Eugen,* which had been de-tached for separate raiding, escaped into Brest, joining up therefore with the battle cruisers *Scharnhorst* and *Gneisenau.* Yet their potential threat to the Atlantic seaways, and thus the importance of German heavy vessels that Admiral Raeder always liked to emphasize to Hitler, was again and again blunted by British bombing attacks. A month after *Prinz Eugen*'s ar-rival, it was hit and badly damaged below deck following a Bomber Com-mand attack; and in late July, fifteen RAF bombers caught the *Scharn-horst* and damaged it with five bombs. Repairs were always made, of course, but just how long would it be before the three warships were more seriously damaged or even destroyed in these exposed harbors? As is re-counted in further detail below (chapter 6), the matter was resolved in February, when they made their bold and successful Channel Dash back to the Baltic and northern ports—this was also to fulfill the Fuehrer's in-sistence that they be brought back in order to protect Norway. This bold German operation, steaming during the night past the great fortress of Dover itself, no less, was a superb example of high-level naval staff plan-ning,[14] and when news of the successful journey broke, it caused a huge outcry in the British press. Yet however humiliating that operation was to the Royal Navy and the Royal Air Force (its various commands had sent hundreds of bombers and fighters aloft, which launched a number of limp attacks), the Kriegsmarine was, as Raeder sadly noted in his diary, mak-ing a strategic retreat. All those French harbors that seemed so danger-ously close to the English coast when they fell into German hands in 1940 had clearly turned out to be far too close to RAF Bomber and Coastal Command squadrons. Being so vulnerable to heavy air attack, where else could his battle cruisers go but back home?

The story then got worse for the German surface fleet. Even as the *Scharnhorst* steamed along the Dutch coast on the night of February 12, it hit a mine (dropped by the RAF a few hours earlier), was stopped in the water for a while, then only limped into Wilhelmshaven for extended re-pairs. Far worse, and to Raeder's utter dismay, within a month of its hav-ing reached a purportedly safer abode, the *Gneisenau* was smashed by a vengeful Royal Air Force attack; its front foredeck zone was destroyed, and it was essentially a wreck for the rest of the war. A short while later the *Prinz Eugen* was badly damaged in its stern by a torpedo from the British submarine HMS *Trident,* and even when repaired, the heavy cruiser was chiefly used for cadet training and later for coastal-support operations in the Baltic. The German effort to dispute British naval mastery by means of surface warships, although it had been temporarily scary on two occa-sions in 1941, was over within less than two years of the outbreak of war.

After the *Bismarck* episode, no heavy German warship ever went into the North Atlantic again, let alone into those southern waters cruised by the *Graf Spee* early in the war. This dimension of the Anglo-German naval struggle ended, then, before the US Navy had even entered the conflict and could bring its own heavy ships into the equation. What remained in the Kriegsmarine after February 1942 was a significantly reduced surface force of one large battleship (the *Tirpitz*) and the *Scharnhorst,* plus a few others, all being sporadically damaged by bombs or torpedoes and then repaired to rejoin what was in essence merely a Baltic-Norway-based fleet. The German heavy warships remained a sufficient danger to later Arctic convoys for the British and American navies to take it seriously.[15] But Hitler's surface navy was never again a threat in the Atlantic itself. That could be offered only by Doenitz and his U-boats.

From this time onward, three further factors began to tilt in Britain's favor. The first was Hitler's Operation Barbarossa attack on Russia from June 1941 onward. While this seemed to have little directly to do with sea power, in fact its significance was great. Having entered a life-or-death struggle with the Soviet Union, Germany began to throw a huge and increasing share of its land-based military power *eastward* and could scarcely tolerate any distractions. This did not of course reduce the existing number of Admiral Doenitz's submarines or the production of newer U-boat types from German shipyards in that immediate summer of 1941, but it was the case that a very large number of Luftwaffe bomber and fighter squadrons were also pulled from their Atlantic and Mediterranean commands and sent east. Even the ferocious bombing campaign against the Royal Navy's warships off Crete (see below) was very severely reduced when the assault on the USSR began. In the longer term, then, Berlin's commitment of so great a proportion of its resources to Operation Barbarossa obviously affected the war at sea, because it left so *relatively* little for other sorts of campaigning. As scholars of Germany's strategy have pointed out, had the Third Reich at this time chosen to allocate significantly more resources to the campaign against Allied shipping—say, triple the number of long-range Focke-Wulf Condor squadrons and triple the number of new U-boats—the story could have been a very different one. But since the Third Reich's industrial output could not meet every demand, Doenitz's needs seemed to pale by comparison with those of the Battle of Stalingrad. Was it ever likely that U-boat construction would be higher than in fourth, or sixth, place in either Hitler's or Albert Speer's priorities?[16]

The contrast with Britain's own assessment of its strategic purposes could hardly be greater. The more the size of the war on the Eastern Front became clearer, the more the threat of a German invasion of the British Isles, already unlikely by the end of 1940, fell away. Among other things,

**TABLE 7.** UK Aircraft Production, 1939–42 (nearest hundred)

| 1939 | 1940 | 1941 | 1942 |
|------|------|------|------|
| 7,900 | 15,000 | 20,100 | 23,700 |

Data from Overy, *Air War*, 150.

Royal Navy destroyer groups, hypothecated for anti-invasion operations, could now be redeployed, while more and more RAF fighter and bomber squadrons could be sent to the Mediterranean. An even larger point was the geopolitical one. After June 1941, obviously, the Third Reich found itself fighting one fully Great Power to its east while it faced another to its west; and while it could have chosen to divide its productive assets along roughly fifty-fifty lines, Hitler himself had clearly prioritized the fight against the USSR. Britain, for its sake, never ceased to regard the defeat of Germany as its number one aim. With the Italian challenger always seen to be a second-order foe, and the Far East given (whether wisely or unwisely) a lowered priority, Churchill's government always regarded the fight against Germany on sea, air, and (less directly) land as primary and thus commanding an overwhelming share of the British Empire's fighting resources. This was reflected more than anything else in the huge investments allocated to British aircraft production by this time, which itself became the second major military change in London's favor. By mid-1941 the Royal Air Force was growing very rapidly indeed. Those numerical weaknesses in aircraft that had made British governments in the 1930s so timid and had so hamstrung the RAF in the spring and early summer of 1940 during the fall of Norway, the Low Countries, and France were steadily decreasing. As the Battle of Britain was blunting the Luftwaffe's power in the west, there occurred in those same months and in those following a real step-up in aircraft production, as at last the country's long-term investment in the industry paid off, with the overall numbers shown in table 7.

This was not a perfectly satisfactory story as far as the direct campaign against the U-boats was concerned, however, because so great a proportion of the RAF's rising budget was in fact to be consumed by the enormously expensive strategic-bomber campaign against the Third Reich and, secondarily, by the air war in the Middle East. Still, by the summer of 1941 RAF Fighter Command possessed many more squadrons than hitherto and felt itself ready to turn from a defensive to an offensive posture. In consequence, it was confident enough to order its famous Spitfire "sweeps" over France that, while not the grand success against the Luftwaffe claimed for these operations at the time, was a sign of the changed aerial balance. Almost in parallel with these fighter sweeps, moreover, were Bomber Command's growing operations against enemy economic targets, including German and French ports, railway lines, and shipbuilding yards. And as these attacks grew in number and in size, forward-located harbors like Brest and Cherbourg, and the German heavy warships sheltering in them, were now just further RAF targets. The weakest aspect of this story on the British side was, as noted before, that there were still disgracefully few long-range bomber and reconnaissance squadrons allocated to Coastal Command for the direct fight against the U-boats, yet the larger shift in relative Anglo-German airpower was indisputable.

Finally, there was the American factor. If the United States had essentially played the role of an offstage actor during the first twelve months of the year, it now steadily and circumspectly entered the struggle in what was a series of most unneutral steps masterminded by a deft American president who explained them all as being measures to defend the nation's security. The largest of those measures (like the destroyers-for-bases deal) are commonly known, but there were many smaller ones, institutional, local, and personal, occurring all through this time, and some of them told a lot about the larger story. When, for example, the battleship HMS *Rodney* was detached from a westward convoy on May 29, 1941, to join in the hunt for the *Bismarck,* it was not only carrying its own spare parts for a substantial refit in the Boston Navy Yard, but it also had on board the Assistant US Naval Attaché, Lieutenant Commander Joseph Wellings,[17] returning to Washington to report on his time in London. Regarded virtually as a fellow participant in the fight, Wellings was invited to join the *Rodney*'s own captain, Dalrymple-Hamilton, and several other senior naval officers on board, in "war gaming" where the *Bismarck* might be going, and guessing (well before the C-in-C Home Fleet did) that it might be looping back to take refuge in Brest. A day later the attaché had an amazing ringside seat while watching the *Rodney*'s 16-inch guns and the *King George V*'s 14-inch guns tear the Bismarck apart. After refueling back at the Clyde, HMS *Rodney* (with Wellings still a guest) resumed its journey to the Boston yard, where not only were its engines to be refitted but its antiaircraft armament was also to be substantially increased. As Wellings himself traveled on to DC to complete his report, he was virtually mobbed by fellow American naval officers wanting to hear his story! In other words, while President Roosevelt continued to assert publicly that his chief aim was to keep America out of the war, all the practical evidence, large and small, was of a distinctly unneutral position, to the benefit, very clearly, of a hard-pressed Royal Navy.

As early as September 2, 1940, Roosevelt had authorized the destroyers-for-bases deal whereby the United States was permitted to establish new air and naval establishments in the Caribbean and Newfoundland in exchange for handing over fifty older American destroyers to the Anglo-Canadian navies. While it was going to take a while for those vessels to be of much use, Churchill was clearly pleased at the symbolism of it all. Even more practical, and aggressive, was the steady extension of the US naval patrol zones into the Atlantic, almost always justified by reference to an action by a U-boat that appeared to transgress American neutral rights or was interrupting US-escorted merchantmen—the shootout between the *U-652* and the destroyer USS *Greer* south of Iceland in September 1941 was typical here. The so-called Western Hemisphere Security Zone—within which US warships and planes were free to attack any unidentified vessels, that is, U-boats—was pushed ever eastward throughout the year. In early July 1941, a force of US Marines took over from Britain the garrisoning of Iceland, and an American air base was established at Keflavik, while only slightly later a US air base was also installed in Greenland. Were these the acts of a neutral Power? For a long time, and frequently because of the Fuehrer's concerns, the Kriegsmarine had sought to tread lightly here, trying to avoid attacking US-flagged merchantmen and warships, but by the fall of 1941 that fiction was no more. The most dramatic—and deadly—evidence of this came, famously, with the sinking of the destroyer USS *Reuben James* by *U-552* on October 31, when a torpedo blew the entire front of the ship off and killed one hundred crewmen. It is worth noting that the *Reuben James,* along with four other American destroyers, had been escorting a convoy eastbound from Halifax to Iceland. This was no longer a surrogate war, a phony war, or a "backdoor to war," as the earlier American strategies were sometimes described. It was real war, and it was taking place sometime before Pearl Harbor occurred.[18]

It has always amazed historians that the usually aggressive Fuehrer held himself back for so long at all of these acts of American support for Britain—for they were indeed blatantly unneutral in both intention and result. The record shows, though, that even he seemed to agree that having to fight both the British Empire and the USSR was enough enemy to handle during the second half of 1941. Still, when news arrived of the Japanese attacks on Pearl Harbor and the Philippines, with the likelihood that most US fighting efforts would be directed to the Pacific, it really was not surprising that he was then most willing to declare war on the United States (on December 10, 1941) in support of his Axis partner. The shadow struggle with Washington was now at last a fully open one.

There were lots of ways prior to that time in which the Roosevelt administration sought to give aid to Britain while formally keeping out of

**PAINTING 21.** American four-stacker escort destroyers, Halifax, 1941. The most dramatic nonneutral action of the American government was its destroyer-for-bases deal of September 1940. While most of these fifty older warships needed refits, some of them (easily recognized by their four tall funnels) had joined the Canadian and British fleets on convoy duty by 1941.

**PAINTING 22. HMS *Warspite* under repair at Bremerton yards, 1941.** When the veteran British battleship was damaged in the Crete campaign, it steamed across the world to be repaired on the US West Coast—before America was at war. The same Bremerton shipyard later repaired the casualties of the Pearl Harbor attacks.

the conflict, but perhaps its most remarkably unneutral measure was the way that the meaning of Lend-Lease was interpreted and extended to pay for the repair of so many damaged Royal Navy warships by American shipyards. On March 11, 1941, the US Congress had agreed to this Act for the Defense of the United States, and in the next years the measure allowed for huge sums of aid (weapons, munitions, raw materials, foodstuffs, and civilian supplies) to go to Britain, Free France, Russia, and many smaller allies, without which they could hardly have sustained the struggle.[19] Yet the ship-repair policy was even more dramatic than sending provisions, for by it the Roosevelt government simply deemed that British and Commonwealth warships damaged in the fighting could be repaired in American yards *and paid for in Lend-Lease dollars*. This was, really, an extraordinary win-win situation for both countries, since it meant that the great US shipyards at Bremerton, Philadelphia, Brooklyn, and Boston, still working up to full capacity as 1941 unfolded and still reaching out to recruit an ever-larger workforce, found themselves gaining more income and greater experience by repairing a long list of the Royal Navy's battleships and aircraft carriers.[20]

One final, almost too obvious remark stands out here: a facility like the giant Bremerton repair yard was totally bomb-free, just of course as all of North America's military-industrial complex was bomb-free. By contrast, the shipyard areas of the European combatants, from Gdynia to Genoa but perhaps especially the French Atlantic harbors, were on the front line, their cities' air-raid sirens wailing night after night as enemy bombers came in. For all the reasons noted above, the German heavy warships in port were a special target from 1940 to 1942 and beyond, and they suffered repeated damage—the ill-fated *Gneisenau* was just the best example here. But British battleships, battle cruisers, and carriers in this crucial period, even if damaged in action at sea, could limp across the Atlantic to these completely secure US shipyards, get repaired and refitted, and emerge in better shape to resume the fight.

These larger political and military factors, from the growth of British airpower to Hitler's fateful turn on Russia to the increasingly unneutral actions of the United States, pointed to the tides turning against Germany. Yet all of these setbacks, together with the weakening of Germany's surface navy, simply made it all the more important for the submarine war against the Allied sea-lanes to succeed. Throttling British overseas trade, or at least so reducing the amount of food and raw materials reaching the home islands that Churchill's government would be forced to call for a negotiated peace, should have been Germany's number one strategic aim after June 1940. Even when Barbarossa was launched a year later, it still should have stayed as the coequal number one aim. And the German submarine arm should therefore have been allocated the resources that reflected that priority. Yet the reality was to be far, far different.

The Battle of the Atlantic was, as a Wikipedia piece on that topic puts it, "all a numbers game,"[21] and a multisided one at that. Ostensibly, and in most of the standard accounts, it was the number and tonnage of merchant vessels sunk each month that was the vital statistic, while the other, obviously, was the number of U-boats sunk. Merchant ships and U-boats, then, formed the two parts of a double-entry ledger (see chart 4 in chapter 7). Another important figure was the absolute number of the operating U-boats that Doenitz could put out to sea, month by month—it is hard to argue that the fight against the submarines was over once America entered the war without at least discussing the huge rise in effective U-boat numbers operating in the Atlantic as late as April 1943. And there is another, Corbettian consideration: some thoughtful later studies suggest that the focus might be on the sheer number of convoys and individual merchantmen who got across the vast Atlantic without seeing a single U-boat. As a variant of that question: was the amount of supplies reaching Britain always going to be sufficient to sustain the population's needs (including also Fighter Command and Bomber Command's requirements) during the early war efforts and then, after 1943, also sufficient to support the buildup of a three to four million invasion army? Then there was the merchant tonnage-added versus tonnage-lost story: did the simple tally of tonnage sunk by Doenitz's command make much sense unless one measured that against the huge early surge of Allied shipping (especially Norwegian) acquired after the fall of western Europe, and later against the post-1942 surge of US Liberty ships and tankers?[22] If all of these measures were represented as lines across a master monthly grid running from the Fall of France to the Normandy invasion, one would note how many of them fluctuated wildly even in the course of a single year.

And they would fluctuate so heavily also because the Battle of the Atlantic was so big, the patterns so mixed, the tempo so changeable, and the number of significant variables so many. The seasonal weather conditions explain a lot; there were no great convoy fights in January when huge Atlantic gales made a U-boat's task impossible. Merchant-ship losses in the mid-Atlantic also dropped severely when German submarines were directed to the Mediterranean or to the Florida coast. Reading B-Dienst's codes—or losing that ability—made things less or more difficult for the Admiralty, although the importance of Ultra has been exaggerated in many earlier writings. Putting more merchantmen into convoys, having the "fast" convoys go faster, adding an escort carrier to a convoy, and giving the escorting warships their own radar (chapter 7) were all critical variables; closing the mid-Atlantic air gap may have been the single most important change of all. Then there were all the variables on the German side: simply having torpedoes that worked *or that did not work* was a critical factor during the first two years of the war. Stressing the sheer flood of new US ship production that entered the story in 1943–44 may be a less important factor here since the U-boat challenge to the Atlantic routes was essentially broken by the grand fights of May–July 1943. The reader may thus be forgiven if the main thread of this tale is often hard to follow: it was, after all, the most complex campaign of the entirety of World War II.

Thus, it was hard to expect there would be much of a fight over the convoys in the late spring and early summer of 1940, when the maritime battle was so desperately being fought around Dunkirk; and Doenitz himself did not expect much from the Atlantic campaign then. But it did become a much more serious struggle that fall, when the U-boat bases had been set up in western France, and his band of submarine captains, being coached to operate in packs, now included some of the most aggressive and capable naval fighters of the war. It helped their cause that British escort numbers were still woefully thin, that those warships might often accompany the convoys only part of the way before the latter dispersed, and that many escorts lacked the speed of U-boats running on the surface. The Royal Navy's destroyer flotillas, depleted after the Norway and Dunkirk campaigns, were desperately needed for the Mediterranean and for the Home Fleet, while the newer categories of sloops, frigates, and destroyer escorts were not yet ready. Sometimes even large convoys were sent out from Halifax with two or three escorts and reinforced only when it looked like an attack was impending or was actually under way. Air coverage was weak and inconsistent at this time because Coastal Command itself was weak. Disliking convoy, hundreds of merchantmen still preferred to sail alone, and while a great number of them were fast enough to make the run to Glasgow or Liverpool unchallenged, many others paid the price for being unprotected. It was not surprising, then, that the U-boat commanders referred to the months from late 1940 until about April of the next year as "the First Happy Time."[23]

The consequences were miserable, frightening, and most deadly for the Atlantic convoys of these months, and deeply worrying to the Admiralty. Again and again, the resulting tragedy showed how devastating a wolf pack could be when it was brought together against targets with such inadequate protection. The worst story of all involved the slow Convoy SC-7, which crossed from Nova Scotia to Liverpool in the first half of October 1940. Once alerted by an advanced patrolling submarine, Doenitz's headquarters at Kerneval (Lorient, in Brittany) ordered a group of his best captains into the attack. In the pitch darkness of October 17–18, the slaughter was unrelenting, with the bolder U-boats running rampage right amid the convoy itself—the legendary Otto Kretschmer sinking six merchant ships within two hours, and other submarines attacking from all sides. A frightening 20 ships out of the 35 didn't make it to British harbors, and those U-boats that had still a few torpedoes remaining turned on a couple of better-escorted fast convoys (like HX-79) and managed to sink another twenty vessels. Now the figures were looking simply awful: in a mere quarter of a year, wolf packs in the Western Approaches sank around 140 British and Allied ships.

And those were the losses to U-boats alone. When Raeder and Doenitz also added in the sinkings inflicted by the large surface warships during this time (see above), by the half dozen or so ingenious, clandestine German (*Hilfskreuzer*) auxiliary raiders like the *Atlantis, Komet,* and *Kormoran*,[24] and by the Luftwaffe's long-range aircraft, the numbers really soared. In that regard April 1941 was the most awful month, with 616,000 tons being sunk: 323,000 by German aircraft alone and 249,000 by German and Italian submarines.

Still, the facts remained that the British Isles were never cut off by the German maritime blockade and that months like April 1941 were exceptional: winter storms once again bit heavily into the U-boats' chances of seeing anything, the long-range Condors' kill record was soon curbed by better aerial defenses for the convoys, the auxiliary raiders were steadily hunted down as 1941 unfolded, and the surface raiders were either being pounded in Brest or had gone home. Above all, the noted German submarine victories that gave occasional cheer to the Fuehrer really did depend upon the exploits of a very small cluster (say, a dozen) of U-boat "aces." As it was, fortune was soon to turn against Doenitz rather swiftly and cruelly in March 1941, when he lost numbers of his key U-boat aces to furious British destroyer counterattacks during convoy actions. The redoubtable Joachim Schepke's *U-100* was forced to the surface through depth charging during the night of March 16 and was then sliced in two by HMS *Vanoc,* one of the escorts to the Halifax fast convoy HX-112. That group of forty-one merchantmen included many oilers and was therefore given very heavy protection, and it was during the four-day battle that even the extremely resourceful Kretschmer met his match—*U-99* had penetrated the convoy and sank four oilers in less than an hour; then depth charges from the vengeful destroyers crushed the submarine's engines and steering, so that he and his crew had no alternative but to abandon ship (and become British prisoners for the rest of the war). Worse still, although no news had yet come in to Doenitz's headquarters, it was becoming clear that the legendary *U-47,* that hero vessel of the sinking of the *Royal Oak,* had been sunk (with Guenther Prien and all its crew) during the chaotic fighting around another convoy, OB-293, ten days earlier.[25] This was not some freakish bad luck, although these convoys were unusual in the amount of protection they enjoyed. The escorting warships were not slow, old corvettes but fast, heavily armed destroyers equipped with HF-DF and even early radar and commanded by very experienced officers such as Captain Donald McIntyre. If this was an indication of the future, then Doenitz would have to reply with countermeasures of his own: with many more submarines, with better detection equipment, and with greater air support. And with fewer distractions, like the dispatch of so many of his best boats to the Mediterranean.

In the tumultuous middle months of 1941—of course, it was also the time of the Battle of Crete, the Bismarck action, and every month two dozen convoys having to cross the North and South Atlantic en route to British shores—the Royal Navy was soon to find itself distracted with yet another call for its resources, in the form of the Arctic convoys to North Russia. Hitler had launched his giant land assault on the USSR on June 21, and Churchill immediately offered an alliance—and aid—to Britain's long-term ideological and imperial rival. And the Admiralty would just have to work out how to get this done. Here was the clearest way in which the grand strategy of the British Empire showed at this time. London's highest political (that is, Clausewitzian) aim was of course the complete defeat of the German-Italian Axis using all possible means, and yet that was clearly a long way off in the straitened circumstances of early 1941. Having a huge Great Power like the Soviet Union suddenly in the fight was a godsend to Churchill, provided Hitler did not crush his eastern foe first, which initially seemed quite a worry to the prime minister (as it did to Roosevelt). Possessing no army with which to launch a D-Day type of landing in Europe, Britain had to help by the only means it could: intensifying the bombing of the Third Reich while also dispatching military supplies to North Russia via convoy. These were not great amounts, certainly, but they were all meant to count—Hurricane fighters, Matilda tanks, and artillery, all originally destined for the Middle East or Malaya but now needed to help stem the Wehrmacht's advance on Moscow.

The famous Arctic convoys to North Russia were soon to match the Mediterranean convoys in sheer difficulty: they had to beat off persistent enemy attacks by nearby aircraft, by packs of submarines, and by heavy warships.[26] But the operational problem was made even worse by the weather—as noted above, in summertime there was virtually twenty-four hours a day of light and thus no cessation of air attacks, and in winter the ice packs pressed the convoys south, to run so much closer to enemy-held northern Norway. There was no worse convoy run, so the British were lucky in the early stages that it took the Germans until 1942 to position their forces in this region for attacks.

The first British convoy, oddly named Operation Dervish, left Liverpool via Iceland on August 21, 1941, and arrived in Archangel ten days later, with rubber, tin, Hurricanes, and RAF personnel. No interference from either the Luftwaffe or the German Navy took place; Churchill was delighted at the propaganda coup, and Hitler furious. Later receiving their famous PQ designation (Iceland to North Russia), these convoys, albeit small at this stage, sailed at around two per month for the rest of the year and into 1942. Steadily, then, the totals of tanks and aircraft reaching Archangel built up; they were then sent south, many to be deployed in the critical struggle around Moscow that midwinter.[27] It would be a while yet before substantial US Lend-Lease began to flow toward Russia, although some American merchant ships were already in the convoys.

The result was that the Royal Navy found itself stretched three ways, from Arctic convoys in the north to Mediterranean convoys in the south, with, as ever, the gigantic task of getting all the Atlantic convoys to their destinations. Little wonder that Admiralty planners were grateful that so large a proportion of the German heavy surface navy was damaged or sunk, and they were grateful too that the Japanese had not yet moved. Not yet.

All things considered, during the second half of 1941, things had eased a bit, though not much, for the Atlantic and overseas convoys. Not only had the threat from the German surface navy gone, but the U-boats were clearly finding it much harder now than during the First Happy Time. The vital fast convoys (with most of the oil tankers) were steaming faster, there were more air patrols (including American ones) over the oceans generally and more air cover near the convoys, and Doenitz still had too few submarines and too few experienced captains left to really throttle the sea-lanes. While things did not look comfortable from the Allied perspective either—the complaint was always that there were insufficient surface escorts and far too few long-range aircraft—the tally of monthly merchant-ship sinkings by the U-boats in these months was indicative that the advantage had swung back to the defenders. Certainly, Allied losses of, say, 202,000 tons of merchant shipping in September 1941 and 124,000 tons in December were far short of Doenitz's desired target of 900,000 tons sunk per month. The existing and newer U-boat commanders would just have to work harder, and more cleverly, to crack this nut.

By the last few months of 1941, the pattern had become clear: U-boat attacks would almost always be at night, they would be on the surface to avoid detection by ASDIC, and they would be launched in packs, stretching the capacity of the defending warships to their limits. In reply, the Admiralty would place more and more merchant ships into fewer but larger convoys, which made more sense operationally and statistically. Of course, the planners would try to route the convoys so as to avoid the wolf packs altogether (which was why the battle between the Ultra and B-Dienst decryption teams was so important), but if that were not possible then the convoys would have to be fought through, and with ever-newer weapons and technologies. And while the tempo of this fight sometimes ebbed, its intensity was likely to grow—the planned increases in U-boat numbers made that so. Any temporary dip in the overall Allied losses of merchantmen was not an indicator of an easy future.

That canny realist Doenitz could have felt only moderately optimistic, then, as the year 1941 closed. If the actual battle over the convoys in the North Atlantic had become tougher after the First Happy Time, he was perhaps beginning to sense great opportunities for his submarines to inflict destruction on the traffic along America's Eastern Seaboard, against the Arctic convoys, and even in the western Mediterranean. His additional U-boats would include many that were larger and longer ranged, while the long-range Focke-Wulf Condors, with better-trained crews, would remain a great asset. The total tonnage of Allied merchantmen sunk in the extraordinary year of 1940 (3.9 million tons) had, despite the relatively small number of active U-boats at sea and the frequent diversions out of the North Atlantic, gone up to 4.3 million tons in 1941 and would hopefully increase further in the year ahead. His major limitation remained as always the still relatively small number of operational U-boats with experienced crews after the loss of so many aces. At year's end Doenitz still had only about forty to forty-five operational vessels, more than two whole years after hostilities in the Atlantic had gotten under way, even as he waited in anticipation for the new ones.[28] And there were now those other factors for him to worry about. The Americans, at last emerged from their half-phony war, would throw more and more into the struggle to help the British. The Royal Canadian Navy was becoming a real factor in the western convoy zones. Finally, as he reflected in the Kriegstagebuch (the "Daily Operational Diary"), his service's old nemesis, the Royal Navy, was showing itself as tough and resourceful as ever in steadily bringing to the battlefront newer technologies, tactics, and resources. There would be no dramatic collapses like the Fall of France to the overall strategic balance after December 1941, so the grim struggle between convoys and U-boats would continue, with only rare delays and diversions, until one side or the other cracked.

## The Mediterranean Cauldron

In contrast to its concerns nearer home, the British Admiralty had, understandably, not given much attention to Gibraltar and the western Mediterranean in the period preceding September 1939, nor did it, indeed, in the nine months following. Its priorities had properly been directed instead to the hunt for German raiders in the Atlantic and then, overwhelmingly, to the unfolding Norway debacle. The waters to the east and west of Gibraltar were, after all, supposed to be safely in the hands of the powerful French Navy. The fortress and harbor had a secondary (that is, non–main fleet) base status and were deemed much less important than either Malta or Alexandria, where Vice Admiral Andrew Cunningham's powerful Mediterranean Fleet resided, deterring any Italian move toward the great colony of Egypt. Gibraltar, rather like Freetown or Jamaica, could supply the hunting groups going after the *Graf Spee,* but, really, it offered little more than that. It hadn't done much in World War I, either.

The dramatic geopolitical happenings of June 1940 changed all of this, in two historic military ways. The first was that the shockingly swift Fall of France had convinced Mussolini at last to abandon Italy's neutrality and to come into the war against Britain, rather fondly assuming that London would soon negotiate some cease-fire with Berlin even as a crushed France was handing over Savoy and perhaps various colonies to Rome. And the second was that the French government's prevaricating reply to London's demands to neutralize its navy had led by early July to the Admiralty's decision to send a large naval force to the Gibraltar area, from which it launched its destructive assault on the French vessels at Mers-el-Kébir. When the *Hood* and other warships returned home after that operation, therefore, and all sides—Britain, Italy, the new Vichy France, and the Third Reich—assessed the altered strategic landscape, it was patently clear that the Gibraltar base was no longer in some secondary category. As its geographical importance became clear, it stepped far closer to the front lines. It separated the southern harbors of Vichy France from its western ones. It blocked German warships in the Atlantic from gaining access to the Mediterranean and Italian warships from gaining access to the Atlantic (even their submerged submarines ran considerable risks in passing these straits). It was one of the few strategic keys—the others were Scapa Flow, Dover, and Alexandria—to keeping Axis power confined to mainland Europe until, if ever, the larger global balances tilted more favorably in the British Empire's favor.

Hence the establishment of the Royal Navy's famous Force H, no longer simply one of the eight or so hunting groups going after those early German raiders but now a Gibraltar-based fleet in its own right—flexible, fast, and powerful. It could always be reinforced substantially from the Home Fleet[29] when the need called for it, as frequently happened when large-scale cover was required for a Malta convoy. But it could also be summoned back into the North Atlantic urgently, and at virtually a day's notice during the extreme crisis of the *Bismarck* chase. It was Force H's *Ark Royal*, after all, whose Swordfish torpedo planes had crippled the German battleship's rudder and led to its end; yet just before *and* just after that dramatic operation, this same naval group was to be found escorting critical convoys that were going to Malta and Alexandria. And it was the carriers and heavy ships of Force H that, so frequently in 1940 and 1941, launched attacks on Italian positions at Sardinia, Genoa, and Naples to distract and weaken their foe.

Why was it not the Italian Navy that was on the strategic offensive in the Mediterranean during these months after France fell and when Britain clearly feared invasion across the North Sea? After all, Italy's fleet (as detailed in chapter 2) was a very considerable one: its main force of four

**PAINTING 23. Italian battleships *Littorio* and *Giulio Cesare*, 1940.** The handsome new battleship *Littorio* fought in many actions against the Royal Navy, was sunk at Taranto, was recovered, and fought again. It surrendered into Malta in September 1943. The older and smaller *Giulio Cesare* fought in early actions and also survived the war.

older dreadnoughts was just receiving the first of its fast, heavily armed *Vittorio Veneto*–class battleships, and it had a large number of heavy and light cruisers and destroyers and supposedly the world's largest number of submarines. It was backed up by a very large air force. It possessed significant naval bases all along its coastline and in North Africa. Geographically, Italy sprawled across the center of the Mediterranean, virtually cutting it in half. Weren't these waters really mare nostrum? Was it not destined to be the Second Roman Empire of Mussolini's ambitions?[30]

Yet despite the bombast of Mussolini's early war speeches, the coming of hostilities in June 1940 was not viewed happily by the Italian Naval High Command. What appeared as terrible, weakening blows to the British strategic position at that time were not necessarily seen as such by Italy's admirals. The prisoner in the Mediterranean complex of the prewar years still prevailed, along with an extremely high respect for the Royal

Navy. Geographically viewed, things seemed daunting. Looking outward from the Bay of Naples the admirals saw only obstacles. A thrust toward Gibraltar, containing British squadrons of aircraft, submarines, and the heavy surface warships of Force H, maybe with half the Home Fleet just behind, seemed completely out of the question. Pushing a fleet into the eastern Mediterranean, on the other hand, risked a certain encounter with Admiral Cunningham's powerful battleships *and* aerial assaults from his ever-dangerous carriers—so why not leave it to the Italian Army to capture Egypt first? Malta was viewed not as a beleaguered isle waiting to be taken but as a well-held fortress, defended by a sizable garrison, heavy artillery, dangerous submarines, unknown minefields, RAF fighters, and light cruiser and destroyer flotillas even when the main Mediterranean fleet had been forced to leave it. Counting only heavy warships as key, and waiting for the addition of the newer battleships to its fleet, the Regia Marina greatly neglected the potency of its submarine arm, which despite its impressive numbers was low in morale, prestige, and efficiency. Denied a carrier fleet of their own, the admirals worried, rightly enough, about going into battle against an enemy that did have them and were dubious about receiving the right support from the Italian Air Force, from whom they had received little cooperation in the past. Nor, finally, had the fleet received any practice in night maneuvers or night fighting. These were already serious disadvantages, but had they known about the British advantages both in radar and in decryption, they would have felt even more intimidated. This was not a navy that planned to be cruising off the approaches to Malta. What may seem curious to the reader, then, is how highly many British admirals rated the disruptive potential of the Italian Navy, and for how long into the conflict, when the Italian admirals' perceptions of their chances against the Royal Navy were almost the polar opposite.[31]

If all this gave an operational advantage to the British, it was also because London was heavily investing a lot of its scarce resources in this theater, neglecting, among other things, to shore up its Far Eastern possessions. Considering the altered strategic scene after the Fall of France, the Admiralty had decided to concentrate its capital ships (battleships, battle cruisers, and carriers) in two theaters of war. The first was in the Home Fleet, not only because that force was always fundamental to Britain's homeland security but also because it was from the main base of Scapa Flow that squadrons could be sent out to North Russia, the Atlantic, the West Indies, and even to the South Atlantic when German raiders prowled there. Thus, while making its new home in Gibraltar, Force H could always still be regarded as an outlier of the Home Fleet, one that would be pulled back to the North Atlantic (as in the *Bismarck* chase) when it was not giving cover to the Malta convoys. The second most powerful British naval force was to be the Mediterranean Fleet, in keeping with Churchill's conviction that the British Empire had to show itself strong across the entire Middle East. By August 1940, for example, Cunningham usually commanded three or more battleships, a carrier, and flotillas of cruisers and destroyers, now based on Alexandria because Malta really was too precarious. If the Italian commander in chief was daunted by the thought of always being situated between two Royal Navy fleets, then he was right to be daunted. If he went westward against Force H, he would not know whether Cunningham's ships might be approaching Taranto; if he ventured south of Crete into the eastern Mediterranean, what might happen further west? Perhaps there would be a Force H carrier raid on the Italian coast and a bombardment of, say, Genoa. Both happened frequently in 1940–41.[32]

The first year of the Anglo-Italian naval struggle in these waters showed the Regia Marina's apprehensions to be perfectly justified in many regards. Even when its many cruiser and destroyer units skirmished rather well, as they did during the confused and desultory naval Battle of Calabria on July 9, 1940, the fleet's heavy-ship gunnery was universally poor, and it may have been lucky that the *Warspite*'s damage to the battleship *Giulio Cesare* on that occasion was not more severe.[33] Their superior speed, helped by smoke screens, saved the Italian ships on that occasion, as they did on many more, but it was clear that seeking a fight with the full Mediterranean Fleet was not advisable. In addition to the impressive range of the British 15-inch guns (the *Warspite*'s shell hit the *Giulio Cesare*'s funnel and ammunition boxes from over 26,000 feet away), there was the daunting matter of the British carriers—how could one match the tactical flexibility and unpredictability that they brought?

As it turned out, simply worrying about what damage a British carrier might do did not translate into being prepared to meet an actual strike, such as the one that came, dramatically and without warning, on the night of November 11, 1940. A mere twenty-two Fairey Swordfish carrying torpedoes and bombs flew 150 miles from Cunningham's sole aircraft carrier, HMS *Illustrious,* and brilliantly attacked a whole array of Italian battleships and cruisers anchored in the southern main base of Taranto. This long-range carrier strike upon an enemy fleet in port was a first in naval history (and as it turned out, one that was carefully if secretly studied by the Japanese Navy as it planned its own surprise strike on Pearl Harbor). The Swordfish aircraft themselves were the same slow, vulnerable, open-cockpit biplanes that would also be sent against the *Bismarck,* yet it didn't matter: throughout World War II, torpedoes, whether launched by submarines or aircraft, even these slower types, showed they could blow

**PAINTING 24A AND B. Pen sketch of HMS *Illustrious* and its Swordfish torpedo-bomber.** The *Illustrious* was the first of the classy and effective fleet carriers in this war, and it was her "Stringbag" Swordfish planes that struck the Italian fleet in Taranto in November 1940. The *Illustrious* fought all through the war, including in the Pacific, and was in the Royal Navy until the mid-1950s.

a hole in the side of even the largest surface vessel. In two hours of their runs across Taranto harbor, the attackers managed to sink the new battleship *Littorio* and the veteran *Conti di Cavour* and damage a third, the *Giulio Cesare,* while other Swordfish armed with bombs also damaged two Italian heavy cruisers.[34] As it happened, being attacked while in shallow anchorage meant that two of the Italian battleships were able to be refloated, repaired, and sent to sea again (just like many of the US battle-

ships sunk after the Pearl Harbor attack). Nonetheless, the larger point was there: from the time of Taranto onward, the battleship was no longer the queen of the oceans; that distinction had clearly come to belong to the fast fleet carriers. Cunningham himself, although by career a battleship admiral, recognized that the Fleet Air Arm now constituted the core of any navy's striking power. And of course only three nations in this war found themselves possessing this weapon.

Nevertheless, the Italian Naval High Command was still willing to send out two battleships and supporting warships only days later to try to deter the British from a mission to fly fighter reinforcements off carriers to Malta. And an even larger Italian sortie was made on November 27, leading to a fast and complicated set of shadow-box exchanges with, on this occasion, Force H at the Battle of Cape Spartivento.[35] Therefore, despite the morale blow of the Taranto operation, neither navy was really dominant in the central Mediterranean, and the Italians continued to have an easier time maintaining their flow of supplies to North Africa than the British did to Malta. While the Regia Marina would neither push aggressively toward Gibraltar nor venture against Cunningham in the east, it was at least holding its own in the middle. It was certainly doing a better job than the Italian Army, which was being drubbed for its rash moves against Egypt in late 1940.

In this situation, then, Malta became more and more the central point of the entire Battle of the Mediterranean. Looking at this theater from a distance, it was clear that the British, by clinging on to Gibraltar, Malta, and Egypt, were also holding on to the southern rimland of Axis-dominated Europe overall. With Franco staying doggedly neutral, Gibraltar could be assaulted only from the sea, an impossible operation for Italy without carriers, with Force H there, and with the Home Fleet behind it. And an amphibious assault on Egypt, with its huge British garrison, was out of the question. But as for Malta? Was it not as vulnerable as its small size and precarious position between Italy and Libya suggested? Its fall would have been a real disaster for the British, but for various reasons, and despite their possession of substantial land, naval, and air resources, both the Italians and later the Germans held off from attacking the island. Admittedly, it would have been a major, difficult operation to undertake, since not only would any amphibious landing need to be a large one, and ready to face heavy resistance along the shoreline, but would also provoke powerful British counterattacks from the west and east. On the other hand, Italian forces *were* capable of inflicting repeated heavy damage on the garrison and people of Malta through bombing, while their surface warships, submarines, and air squadrons would try, when the opportunity seemed worth the risk, to interrupt every convoy and thus bring the island to surrender by starvation. And the more successful they were in neutralizing Malta, the easier was the military task of maintaining the supply links to North Africa.[36]

The biggest difference between 1940 and 1941 in the Battle of the Mediterranean was that the Germans arrived on the scene. Their coming, however, was never as consistent in either time or size as Mussolini might have hoped or as the British feared. Hitler very often indicated that he thought this theater of the war should basically be left to his partner—to the frustration of the likes of Admiral Raeder and Field Marshal Erwin Rommel—and even when the Fuehrer agreed to commit forces to the region, they could often be switched out of it; for example, the aerial pressures on Malta lessened when the Luftwaffe was relocated to Greece, and in turn their threat to the British in the eastern Mediterranean diminished when those same Luftwaffe squadrons were pulled out to the Russian front. Nonetheless, when German forces were operating in this theater, their actions always had painful, decisive effects on land, in the air, and at sea.

An early sign of this, and a warning that the relatively even period of struggle between Britain and Italy was over, came with the arrival in January of the Luftwaffe group Fliegerkorps X into southern air bases (Sicily and Calabria). Intended by Hitler to "stiffen up" the Italian fight against the British for a while, this particular group of several hundred modern medium bombers, dive-bombers, and fighters were all antiship specialists and had already shown their efficiency in the Norway campaign. They now wasted no time in moving onto the attack. On January 10, 1941, sailors on a large-scale Malta convoy—weirdly code-named "Operation Excess"—noted various preliminary though ineffectual bombing runs against the British warships by Italian aircraft before the new carrier HMS *Illustrious*'s radar spotted two large, tightly grouped flights of Ju-47 Stukas purposefully headed its way. With its own fighter defenses distracted and in the wrong place, the carrier took six direct hits by 1,000-pound and 500-pound bombs that created multiple fires, wrecked aircraft below, and cut the power for a while; it is hard to think that any American, Japanese, or older British carrier could have survived such bombing, but the all-steel decks, sides, and elevator lifts of the *Illustrious*-class vessels had created amazingly tough warships. Fighting off further aerial attacks, and to the amazement of the Fliegerkorps X pilots, the carrier limped toward Malta, escorted by a pair of destroyers. On the day following, coincidentally, a squadron of twelve Stukas spotted and then, coming out of the glaring sun above, tore apart the cruiser HMS *Southampton* a little to the south of Malta while also badly damaging its sister ship HMS *Gloucester*. "We could not but admire the skill and precision of it all," wrote Cunningham ruefully of these Luftwaffe squadrons. "There was no doubt we were watching real experts."[37]

As the *Illustrious* was being hastily given temporary repairs in the Malta dockyards, the Luftwaffe struck again on January 16, with forty-four Stukas and seventeen Ju-88 medium bombers. While the carrier was only lightly hit this time, saved again by its armor plating, hundreds of houses and churches all around the Grand Harbour of Valetta were smashed—the *Illustrious* Blitz, as it was termed—and the ordeal of the people of Malta had begun.[38] These aerial onslaughts on the island would last for another two years, often with an intensity that equaled the Luftwaffe's blitz on London. As for the aircraft carrier itself, it slipped away on

January 23 to Alexandria, then to Durban for repairs in the dry dock, and then to the Norfolk Navy Yard for full repair plus multiple improvements, again made under the Lend-Lease arrangements.[39]

The coming of Wehrmacht forces to the Mediterranean thus set up a sort of three-way minuet between the Italian, British, and German players that would last until 1943. Usually, the very large naval fleets and army divisions of the British Empire would inflict heavy damage on their Italian opponents, but then the British would overstretch themselves or be diverted elsewhere. Then, relatively small but highly efficient German units would attack and disrupt the British positions, compelling a withdrawal and a licking of wounds until reinforcements allowed a fresh round in the fighting. The Fliegerkorps X's arrival from January onward, the advent of Rommel's Afrika Korps regiments and early campaigning in late March, and the large inrush of German submarines into Mediterranean waters after September 1941 all conformed to this pattern.

In late March 1941, it was again the turn of the British to inflict very severe damage on the Italian main fleet at sea, the latter having come out only on the mistaken German intelligence that most of Cunningham's battleships had been badly damaged by the Luftwaffe. Nothing could have been further from the truth, and thus a set of favorable circumstances allowed the Royal Navy one further success: a victory in the battle that took place off Cape Matapan (southwest Greece) on March 27–29, 1941—coincidentally, at the very beginning of the Greece campaign on land. A cat-and-mouse game between Italian cruisers, an advance group of British cruisers, the Italian fast battleship *Vittorio Veneto*, and then the main British battle fleet (HMSs *Warspite, Valiant*, and *Barham*) might have led to a desultory result but for torpedo aircraft—again!—from the new carrier HMS *Formidable*, which had joined the Mediterranean Fleet to replace the *Illustrious*. One aircraft strike damaged the Italian battleship and sent it home to base; more seriously, a second wave of carrier torpedo-bombers managed to hit the heavy cruiser *Pola*, destroying its power and bringing it to a halt. While the rest of that cruiser division was detached to give escort to the *Pola*, they were unaware that they were being tracked by the radar of British warships. Trapped unsuspectingly in the dark, they were suddenly subject to point-blank 15-inch gunfire from the radar-equipped British battleships.[40]

Every one of the Mediterranean Fleet's strengths was in play here—Ultra intelligence from Bletchley Park that had given advance notice that the Italian fleet was at sea, the ace card of carrier aircraft using torpedoes, the incredible advantages of shipborne radar and the element of surprise, the British training in night fighting, and finally, the complete imbalance in destructive power once the battleships opened fire. The Italian heavy cruisers, *Zara, Fiume,* and *Pola,* were swift, modern, powerful, and beautifully designed, among the very best of their type in the world; but on that night they simply had no chance, and the rest of the Italian fleet was perhaps lucky to have escaped a little earlier. It may be worth noting here that, along with the later sinkings of the *Bismarck* and the *Scharnhorst,* this success at Matapan constituted the Royal Navy's only three battleship victories during the six long years of World War II.[41]

While the Matapan defeat intimidated the Italian main fleet and kept it in harbor, the rest of the conflict continued unabated, with, as ever, each combatant trying to throttle the other's respective convoy runs. Italy's supply lines to its North African ports were repeatedly attacked by British submarines, by RAF bombers, and by cruisers and destroyers based on Malta. Royal Navy convoys heading to Malta from either Gibraltar or Alexandria were always subjected to intense assault from Italian and German aircraft, surface warships, motor torpedo boats, and submarines. Each side liberally, almost recklessly, laid wide swathes of deadly mines. The British ferried desperately needed aircraft spares to Malta inside submarines and on extremely fast minelayer-destroyers. Older carriers like the *Argus* and *Furious* were escorted several hundred miles out of Gibraltar and then launched squadrons of relief Hurricanes and Spitfires on a one-way flight to Malta. Italian cruisers and destroyers in turn were escorting oil tankers and supply ships to North Africa. At no other place in the war at sea was there such a remarkable cross-cutting fight, so it is perhaps not surprising to learn that by mid-1943, when this brutal contest was over, the floor of the Mediterranean to the east and west of Malta was littered with warships, some visible through the very clear waters. Given the size and needs of the massive Italian military presence in North Africa and then the gasoline and munitions needs of Rommel's Afrika Korps, the convoys to the Libyan ports had to be run much more frequently than did the Malta convoys. By one estimate, an Italian division consumed 10,000 tons of goods every month, which implied an almost continuous run of merchant-borne supplies that might be exposed to the attacks of the enemy's surface ships, submarines, and bombers. Yet these supply runs, however precarious, however likely to provoke attack, simply had to be made. Of what use was the Afrika Korps without shells and fuel? And of what effectiveness was Malta without a constant supply of food, gas, and Spitfires?

This relatively balanced situation was again disrupted, and massively, from April 1941 onward by dramatic events in the Balkans that rapidly spilled southward, through Yugoslavia (which was swiftly attacked and conquered on Hitler's orders when an anti-Axis government came to power in Belgrade) and then into Greece (which was already fighting Italy

**PAINTING 25.** *Zara* **and sister ships, Cape Matapan, 1941.** Following earlier actions against the Royal Navy, the Italian heavy cruisers found themselves trapped in a night action off Cape Matapan (Greece) against superior British battleships. The *Zara*, *Fiume* (see painting 2), and *Pola* were all sunk, in the Italian Navy's largest defeat at sea.

in its western provinces). Churchill's gallant desire to aid Greece brought the Eighth Army's advances in North Africa to a halt, as over thirty thousand troops and their equipment were embarked and sent to fight alongside Britain's new ally. Unfortunately for this scheme, neither the Greek Army nor the British, Australian, and New Zealand expeditionary troops were capable of withstanding the powerful, fast-moving, and much more battle-hardened Wehrmacht brigades. Worst of all, the Allies simply lacked the airpower to take on the much larger and more modern Luftwaffe squadrons; the Greek Air Force's much older planes and the few Hurricane squadrons hastily sent to operate from Crete or that were operating from a single carrier had no real chance against the enemy's five hundred and more bombers and fighters—including, once again, the antiship specialist squadrons of Fliegerkorps X, temporarily transferred from Sicily.[42]

Pulling the battered British Empire troops from southern Greece to hastily erected positions in Crete and then shortly afterward trying to extract them back to Egypt exposed the Royal Navy to by far the fiercest and most prolonged set of air attacks it had ever experienced—conditions were much worse than in Norway and still worse than off Dunkirk. The number of days of intense aerial attack on the British warships was about three times longer than at Dunkirk; their room for maneuver in the narrow harbors and the thin stretch of waters between southern Greece and the island of Crete was minimal; the heavily overcast and protective North Sea clouds obviously were not here; the number of Luftwaffe bombers (especially those terrifying Stuka dive-bombers) was much larger; and the German bomber pilots and crews were now incredibly experienced. The British regiments on Crete and the British ships that ferried them had no squadrons of RAF Fighter Command to fly across the Channel and dispute control of the sky. Thus it was that destroyers that had fought hard and survived in northern waters during 1939–40 found themselves only a year later being torn apart by a familiar enemy. Lord Louis Mountbatten's HMS *Kelly*, now repaired and serving in the Mediterranean Fleet, was caught in the open by no less than twenty-four Stukas on May 23, 1941, just south of Crete. Wrecked by the first bomb, it turned over and lay belly-up for a mere thirty minutes, then disappeared. Nearby, its fellow destroyer HMS *Kashmir*, directly hit by another Stuka's 1,000-pound bomb, was gone within two minutes. This was carnage.[43]

And it was not just destroyers this time, for every larger warship in the eastern Mediterranean came under air and submarine attack. So while it was all very well for Cunningham to declare that "the Navy will not let the Army down," the blunt fact was that the close-inshore convoying and rescue attempts by the Mediterranean Fleet's cruisers and destroyers and the offshore "cover" provided by the main battle fleet exposed them all to repeated aerial attack. Then there were the many sneak attacks by German E-boats and Italian MTBs. Perhaps nothing captured this vulnerability to Axis power more than the sad sight of the heavy cruiser HMS *York,* which lay for days, half sunk and half exposed in the harbor at Suda Bay after attack by Italian torpedo boats, until a little while later, when it was finished off by German bombers. By the time the last of the shattered British battalions had been pulled back to Egypt in early June, the Mediterranean Fleet had lost three more cruisers (HMSs *Gloucester, Fiji,* and *Calcutta*) and seven destroyers, with another seven cruisers and eight destroyers damaged. Slightly further afield, the carrier *Formidable* and the battleships *Warspite* and *Barham* were also badly damaged and had to limp away from this campaign; temporarily patched up, the heavy ships were all sent off to America for repair. One source claims that "for the British, the Battle of Crete was the costliest naval engagement of the entire war."[44] After it, Cunningham was left with a fleet of only two battleships and three cruisers to face an Italian main fleet of four battleships and eleven cruisers plus many flotillas of destroyers. Some cheer, though not much, was provided to sailors by the news from home that the *Bismarck* had been sunk.

The British venture into Greece and Crete had been a humiliating and very damaging defeat, including a prestige blow for Churchill personally. Perhaps nothing could have changed things once an enraged Hitler decided to divert so many first-class army divisions and air squadrons into the Balkans even as the Wehrmacht made itself ready for the invasion of the USSR. In consequence, by the time the Greek and Cretan campaigns were over, the British military position in the Mediterranean and North Africa had been weakened in many ways. The Eighth Army had been forced to divert and then lose significant numbers of men and equipment. The Royal Navy's Mediterranean Fleet was more than halved in strength. Worse still, even while the Germans were devoting the bulk of their forces to the colossal Operation Barbarossa, they had now arrived in force—and with air bases—along the Mediterranean's northern shores as well as on Crete itself, making the whole eastern Mediterranean a much more dangerous place to sail in. And while German U-boats were now supporting the Italian war efforts at sea, the initial small Wehrmacht reinforcement to the Italian forces in North Africa was by August 1941 expanded and formally constituted as the Afrika Korps under Rommel, whose aggressive forward moves against a British Eighth Army depleted by this Greek diversion were now going to pose a far larger threat to the British hold on Egypt.

Considered more broadly, the British failures in Greece and Crete on the one hand, and the German failure of its biggest Atlantic sortie (that is, by the *Bismarck* and *Prinz Eugen*) on the other, was more than a chronological coincidence. Each pointed to certain conclusions about the tangled matter of sea power *versus* land power at this stage in the struggle between these two large and relatively well-organized combatants. There was, again, nothing in London's historical, peripheral maritime strategy that could match the brutal and well-integrated Nazi blitzkrieg on land and air. Indeed, the latter was never more impressive during World War II than in the early summer of 1941, with this example of fast-moving German Army brigades and devastating Luftwaffe squadrons tumbling Yugoslav, Greek, and British Empire forces into the sea before being pulled northward to join the drive through the Ukraine. Perhaps Churchill was right that the British had to commit to the Mediterranean and Middle East theaters of war, taking out Italy first, and then build up strength for the next stages of the struggle, hopefully by then with American participation. Yet the fact is that the prime minister, not yet grasping the new realities of warfare and perhaps clinging to older memories of the Salonika or Palestine campaigns, had unnecessarily exposed underpowered RAF squadrons, British and Commonwealth Army brigades, and Cunningham's precious battleships, cruisers, and destroyers to loss and defeat, and he had diverted the Empire's limited resources from the solid stronghold of Egypt to fight in vain in the slender toeholds of southern Greece.

Yet, at the same time, it was also true that Hitler had lost the first round of his renewed campaign in the West. The Fall of France had not been followed by the Fall of Britain. The British Isles were now impregnable, unless the U-boats found a way to throttle supplies. And the Fuehrer's savage attack on the USSR was, ironically, a huge relief to the British strategic position. While the greater part of Germany's war machine was now devoted to the struggle in the East, more and more British Empire resources, especially army divisions and aircraft squadrons, were being sent to Egypt. In sum, Britain *would* blunt the German position in the Mediterranean in due time, but that would be more than a year later, and by then of course the United States was in the war and Allied sea power and productive strength would permit a huge buildup of aircraft, armor, and infantry under Bernard Montgomery's command. And that buildup in turn could take place only because the maritime lines of reinforcement back in the Atlantic had not succumbed to the assaults of Doenitz's U-boat flotillas. For about one month in mid-1941, though, with the Greece/Crete debacle at its worst and the *Bismarck* loose in the Atlantic, the situation for Britain must have seemed grim. It was hardly the case, really, that 1941 was, as a later historian has described it, "the year Germany lost the war."[45]

Moreover, far from there being any slackening after the fall of Crete, the central Mediterranean battles were undiminished, since the two convoy flows had to be maintained regardless of operations elsewhere. Thus, a large British convoy (Operation Substance) successfully reached Malta in mid-July, while Royal Navy carriers (HMSs *Furious, Victorious,* and *Ark Royal*) also made repeated sorties from Gibraltar into the Mediterranean to fly off Hurricane reinforcements for Malta and Egypt. An even larger Malta convoy operation in September (Operation Halberd), which involved a heavily reinforced Force H putting out from Gibraltar and throwing a close screen around a dozen fast merchantmen to deter the Italian navy, was a great success; only one merchant ship was lost, and 80,000 tons of vital supplies were delivered. Royal Navy submarines, together with the light cruiser and destroyer forces based in Malta itself, were inflicting heavy losses on Italy's own precious north-south supply routes to Tunisian ports. In early November, in the so-called Battle of the Duisburg Convoy, an entire group of seven large German and Italian merchantmen, plus one destroyer, was sunk in night fighting by a small contingent of British light cruisers and destroyers.[46] A month later, in the violently fought Battle of Cape Bon, two Italian cruisers carrying vital aviation fuel were surprised and sunk in the dark by British destroyers attacking from each side.[47]

Yet all of these smaller victories, while hurting the Axis armies in North Africa and keeping Malta going, hardly compensated for the blows dealt in return by the Germans and Italians. In late November, while Cunningham's Mediterranean main fleet was cruising off Alexandria, the battleship HMS *Barham* was blown out of the water by three torpedoes from the German *U-331,* with great loss of life. A little earlier, on November 13, in another dreadful blow, the legendary and invaluable carrier *Ark Royal* was sunk by another German submarine, the *U-81,* close to Gibraltar; one torpedo was enough to tear a vast hole in its side and cripple its power, and the blow was fatal. In mid-December, the extraordinarily successful and flexible Malta-based cruiser squadron, Force K, joined at the time by another small cruiser/destroyer group, Force B, steamed across a large minefield laid by the Germans months earlier and was reduced to a shambles. After this, and while the flow of Italian supplies to North Africa surged, British surface warships were again pulled out of operating from Malta. The final blow of the year came on December 19, just a short while after the Royal Navy's loss of the *Prince of Wales* and *Repulse* off Malaya, when a team of three Italian midget submarines brilliantly succeeded in crippling Cunningham's two remaining battleships, the HMSs *Valiant* and *Queen Elizabeth,* anchored in Alexandria harbor. For a while at least, until they were repaired, the Mediterranean Fleet hardly existed.[48] In its worst period ever, then, the Royal Navy lost four capital ships (*Barham, Prince of Wales, Repulse,* and *Ark Royal*) and had two more badly damaged in the space of two months. In the calendar year of 1941 itself, more-over, the service had also lost nine of its invaluable cruisers, a full eight of them in the Mediterranean. This was far worse than anything that hap-pened in World War I.

Had it not been for the even greater and more amazing events of De-cember 1941—the entire American battleship fleet was wrecked in Pearl Harbor, the Wehrmacht was at the gates of Moscow, and Japanese troops were pouring into Malaya, Thailand, and the Philippines—those British losses in the Mediterranean would have seemed truly crushing. Instead, they were simply some of the very hard knocks that the Royal Navy and its Axis foes were inflicting on each other as the struggle for mastery in the Mediterranean intensified. Severe though these setbacks were to a ser-vice that had already taken so many hits earlier in the year, they did not affect the all-important Battle of the Atlantic. And they were almost com-pletely detached from the dramas that were unfolding six thousand miles farther east of Suez, as a new naval challenger entered the war.

## War Comes to the Pacific and Southeast Asia

There had been an uneasy quietness in international affairs across most of Asia during those first two eventful years of World War II in Europe. For their various reasons all the Great Powers preferred things to remain un-changed. After declaring war on Germany in September 1939, France and Britain simply wanted their colonial empires in the East to stay unchal-lenged, and Hitler had no time for anything other than European con-quests. Japan's leaders were upset by the new Nazi-Soviet Pact, and its military had been surprised and bruised by the Red Army's robust de-fense during the Manchurian border clashes of 1938 and 1939; in any case the Japanese generals had further tough campaigning to do in China proper. Stalin's attention was chiefly focused westward—after Barbarossa, exclusively so. And the United States had no cause to disturb things in Asia. After much consideration, it pushed its main Pacific Fleet forward to Pearl Harbor (instead of San Diego), but the West's naval presence in the main ports of East Asia—Hong Kong, Manila Bay, and Singapore—was otherwise limited to cruiser squadrons, almost as if it were, say, the year 1910.

This relatively tranquil political situation had already changed a bit fol-lowing the Fall of France, though, for that gave Tokyo the opportunity to press the new and weak Vichy regime to permit Japanese forces to oc-cupy the northern half of French Indochina (North Vietnam). And when the negotiations took too long, the Japanese military forcibly moved in regardless in September 1940, and the French defenders had to sue for peace. Neither Washington nor London did anything then, and the Japanese themselves decided not to push further. Hitler's attack on the USSR changed all that, and a month later, in July 1941, Japan took its boldest step yet by announcing a so-called joint protectorate with a helpless Vichy government over all of southern French Indochina, including naval bases like Cam Ranh Bay. At one fell swoop, it now controlled strategic positions outside and south of Hong Kong and Manila and several thousand miles closer to the critical oilfields of the Dutch East Indies. It was also now dangerously close to northern Malaya, and this at a time when the British were reeling from Crete, and German armored columns were plunging through the Ukraine.[49]

The West's response, led by President Roosevelt, to Japan's new aggression was unusually tough: the United States, the British Empire, and the exiled Dutch government (still controlling the Dutch East Indies) instituted a critical oil embargo. Given Japan's acute dependency on imported fuel supplies, of course, this economic move was a military ultimatum to Tokyo—step backward from your aggressions, or in six months' time your naval and military activities (including your operations in China) will grind to a halt. From Japan's perspective, if the West could blatantly turn its vital oil supplies off and on at whim, then it was imperative to have complete control of one's own fields—meaning, those of Southeast Asia, especially in the Dutch East Indies—and to seize them within six months or so. In retrospect, and given the intransigence of each side, one can see that this set the timetable for war beginning in or around December 1941.[50]

Yet if getting control of the critical oilfields of the Dutch East Indies was key to Japan's basic security, then ensuring that America and Britain could not stop that move in turn triggered a logical chain of steps flowing all the way from the Palembang petrol refineries up to Manila and on to Pearl Harbor. Tokyo had to assume that a forcible seizure of the Dutch and North Borneo fields, defiantly breaking Roosevelt's embargo, would cause a further strong response from the West, such as a naval interdiction of the shipping routes. If that was the case, then one would have to take out the American naval and air bases in the Philippines, seize Hong Kong, and neutralize the great Singapore base (hence all the training of Japanese Army units for amphibious operations, and the practice for large-scale aerial bombing attacks during the fall of 1941). But, the Imperial Japanese Navy (IJN) planners argued, how could one risk sending troop convoys south when there was such a latent threat from the great American battle fleet in Pearl Harbor and another from the Royal Navy's Force K being assembled at Singapore? Strategic necessity led remorselessly, ineluctably, to the decision to disable the US battleships, and that would best be achieved by catching the American fleet in harbor, as the

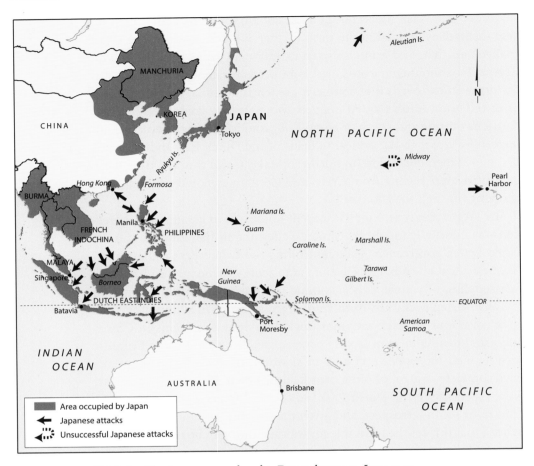

**MAP 6.** The Japanese onslaught, December 1941–June 1942.

British had done at Taranto. If the diplomats wanted to hand over a formal declaration of war, then so be it, provided it was made just as the attacks were unfolding and not before then.

The whirlwind flow of bombing strikes, amphibious landings, and other actions that took place across the waters of East Asia during the final month of 1941, masterminded by the new head of the IJN, Admiral Isoroku Yamamoto, secured Tokyo's aims to a remarkable extent. It all testified both to Japan's careful planning and preparations and to the highly effective quality of its naval, aerial, and land forces. Nothing, really, was going to stand in its way; if the enemy fought back, as in the Philippines, that would not be for long. Japan's brilliant blows on December 7–8 of that year constitute one of the greatest acts in the history of modern international power politics, more important than the Fall of France, perhaps as important even as Hitler's gigantic invasion of the USSR itself.

Considering the global scene as a whole near the end of 1941, the American strategic situation was clearly lopsided, being very secure in the Atlantic yet worryingly exposed in the Pacific. With the battleship *Bismarck* sunk and the other heavy German warships damaged by bomber attacks, there was no practical prospect of a Nazi venture toward the West Indies or Brazil. And all of Roosevelt's unneutral naval steps of the previous months (Atlantic patrols, the garrisoning of Iceland), but especially the declarations of no-go zones, had pushed the U-boats away into the mid-Atlantic, where they could tussle with British airpower and sea power. Operation Barbarossa pulled Hitler further to the east, and Mussolini was held in the Mediterranean. By contrast, there was much less security at the far end of the Western Pacific, and even less so in East Asiatic waters.[51]

The tyranny of distance was the culprit here, as it ever had been. Hawaii was about as far westward as the US Navy wished to station its heavy ships, leaving General Douglas MacArthur's American garrisons in the Philippines vulnerable—tethered goats, really—should Japan choose to strike. Perhaps the new B-17 squadrons would re-alter the balance when they arrived, but that was unclear. What was clear was this: the Atlantic front was secure, for all of Roosevelt's and Stimson's claims that America lay threatened, but the Pacific front was certainly not. That may not have been a completely bad thing in FDR's complex, tortuous juggling of foreign and home affairs in those tense months of late 1941. The Japanese militarists might decide not to knuckle down to the oil embargo but instead to lash out. So be it; if war came to the Pacific, the United States would have to take some losses, for example, in the Philippines, but Japan would certainly be defeated and punished for its aggression; and war in the East might also at last provoke Germany (Roosevelt's chief foe) to come in. Is this what the president was thinking when he told Churchill, in a phone conversation on December 8, that "today all of us are in the same boat"? The coming of war at last removed all the uncertainties and compromises of the preceding three years.

Even so, when the Japanese massed air attacks took place on the US fleet at Pearl Harbor, the actual event seems to have been as much a surprise to Roosevelt and Stimson as it was to all on the Hawaiian bases (and revisionist efforts to prove that somehow the president knew it was going to happen still fail to find the evidence). An attack on anywhere else in East Asia, of course, would have been far less of a surprise, since all British and American intelligence data at the time suggested that Japan was planning major military moves by the end of the first week of December. As it was, the Japanese attacks, launched simultaneously on December 7 and 8, happened in three places—Hong Kong, the Philippines, and Pearl Harbor itself—all of course to ensure that there was no interruption to the main purpose, the conquest of what C. L. Symonds calls "the southern resource area."[52] And the Allied assessments were indeed right, for also in those same two or three days invading Japanese armies were carried un-interruptedly southward, toward Luzon, Thailand, and northern Malaya (the landings there actually took place just as the first bombs exploded in Pearl Harbor—Tokyo's timing was impeccable). This was a huge, impossibly bold venture, spread over thousands of miles. Among all these actions, though, it was the attack on Pearl Harbor that counted the most.

The story here is very familiar. Most of Pearl Harbor, as with most of Hawaii, was fast asleep that Sunday morning. Radar detection of a large flight of incoming planes was falsely interpreted as being B-17s from the US mainland and not the 183 massed Japanese high-level bombers, dive-bombers, and torpedo-bombers. The sinking of a Japanese midget torpedo at the harbor entrance did not get the right attention. Most American planes were lined up on their tarmacs, unprepared, the crews asleep or in town. And the American battleships were also lined up, anchored together two by two, with most of the crews, like the local Hawaiian population, mainly asleep. Shortly after 7:40 a.m., that peace was shattered as the bombs of the attacking planes ripped into their targets. The battleship USS *Arizona* was the most spectacular casualty, its magazine detonated by a massive bomb (actually, a 16-inch armor-piercing shell) dropped from ten thousand feet. Torn apart, it sank within minutes; some 1,177 men lost their lives. More bombs crushed the *Tennessee* and *Maryland*, while torpedoes took out the *West Virginia* and *Oklahoma* and badly damaged the *California* and *Nevada*. As the first great force of attackers flew off, a second assault of 170 aircraft moved in to try to finish off the partially damaged battlewagons and sink any other warships around.[53]

Many smaller vessels were indeed sunk or hurt, and 190 US planes destroyed. But it was the American Pacific battle fleet that counted, and it had been devastated in the swiftest possible time. By 10:00 a.m. it was all over, the Japanese mobile striking force now steaming quickly for home rather than launching further attacks. Whereas the Japanese naval planners assumed that they might lose two out of the six carriers deployed, in fact they lost a mere 29 aircraft and 64 men. It was about the most disproportionate engagement of the entire war. Four US battleships were sunk, two permanently, and three were heavily damaged (and 2,403 American servicemen were lost). As a tactical strike, the Japanese assault on the US battle fleet at Pearl Harbor was brilliant. Operationally, the plan had been virtually flawless. Politically, however, the consequence was dire, for it aroused the entire American nation and brought it united into the war.

The Japanese attack had been focused overwhelmingly on the big and obvious targets, the American battleships. Yet what was not hit in this aerial blitz has been deemed by many historians to be at least as important. The submarine base, and US submarine headquarters, remained intact. The critical oil storage facilities and the reserves of aviation fuel were completely missed, and yet it is difficult to see how Pearl Harbor could have functioned as a fleet base if the great tanks that held its petroleum supplies had gone up in flames. The naval repair yards, the cranes, the welding shops, and the power lines and water pipes were all undamaged. Of course they were not as extensive and comprehensive as those at Bremerton or the Boston Navy Yard, yet by being left intact these facilities could begin doing patch-up repairs to the damaged American warships almost immediately; while many a later vessel, returning after fierce action, could get attended to here (thus, the carrier USS *Yorktown*, damaged in the Battle of the Coral Sea, could be hastily patched up in the Pearl Harbor dry dock and sent out to fight again at Midway). But that leads to the most important American asset that escaped being hurt or sunk in this historic raid: the Pacific Fleet's three carriers, all of which were elsewhere when the Japanese planes attacked, all of which could be dispatched on their own raids against the enemy's midocean island positions almost as soon as the New Year arrived, and all of which pointed to the war's future. Even if the US battleships had remained intact, this great struggle across the Pacific's wide expanses would have steadily shown that the fast-carrier arm was the most important. But the battleship versus carrier fight that had simmered among the American admirals had now been settled, at least for a while.[54] The fact that the US battle fleet had been eliminated while the carriers were intact caused the newly arrived commander in chief, Admiral Chester W. Nimitz (ironically, a battleship man), to rely upon the latter to start the naval counteroffensive. This whole transformation of war was to turn carrier admirals like William Halsey and Frank Fletcher into American heroes almost immediately, and yet who remembers the names of US battleship admirals in this war?

Then there was the geopolitical aspect, and here again the American situation was not as bad as may have been thought. With the Philippines and Guam fallen, the United States had been tossed entirely out of the Western Pacific, whereas through these successes the Japanese had buttressed their existing holdings in the Marshall, Marianna, and Caroline Island groups. Any American recovery after these early losses was going to be an extremely long haul. Still, the most important strategic point was that the Japanese had not taken Pearl Harbor itself. Had they done so,[55] they would have thrown the American forces back another three thousand miles and made any trans-Pacific recovery plan so much more difficult. That would have altered not only the entire chronology of the Pacific War but also perhaps the war's structure—would there have even been a Central Pacific Command if the Japanese had made Hawaii virtually impregnable and if the only way the United States could reinforce Australia was via the Cape? The retention of Hawaii meant that there was such a command, essentially a navy-dominated one, with a separate Southwest

Pacific Command established under MacArthur. By keeping the huge physical base resources of Pearl Harbor, which in the future was to be free from hostile air attacks, the United States remained a central Pacific power. Moreover, after its strike on Pearl, Japan's drive was to the south. All of these factors were going to give Washington invaluable time and space as it mobilized its domestic resources for its strategy of recovery.

In this respect, it was to be the British who were hit much more substantially by Tokyo's move to war, because its losses across the Far East were total and included a huge swathe of territory by the time the initial six-month Japanese offensive stage was over. Few imagined that Hong Kong could be held for more than a few days or weeks, and the unlucky garrison there was just a token one. (Fighting by its garrison ended on Christmas Day.) But the ease of the Japanese amphibious landings into southern Thailand and the Malay Peninsula in early December was a real surprise, harbingers of the further swift advances and successes of 1942. Those were the losses on land. To the students of sea power, there was the immense shock of the loss on December 10, 1941, of the battleship *Prince of Wales* and the battle cruiser *Repulse* on the high seas, and after only a few hours of aerial attacks.

The story of the destruction of Force Z, such a signal event in the Royal Navy's history, has been narrated and analyzed hundreds of times,[56] and only the more salient points need to be noted here. It goes without saying that no one in London thought that the Japanese could drive down through Southeast Asia with the boldness, speed, and efficiency with which they did or that such a combination of mishaps would occur to render the British capital ships unprotected from the air. It is also fair to argue that if the Admiralty was going to protect Singapore and Malaya with any heavy warships at all, committing a small group of faster vessels (a new battleship, aircraft carrier, and battle cruiser) was far better than a division of slow *R*-class battleships, which after some debate were very wisely kept back in the Indian Ocean. But the whole concept started to come unstuck when the Force Z aircraft carrier, HMS *Indomitable,* ran aground in the West Indies and was therefore in repair in early December, a good eight thousand miles away. Relying instead upon air coverage from the few RAF squadrons based on Malayan airfields was a very weak alternative. Above all, no one on the Western side, either in Hawaii, in Singapore, or in the entire vaunted Anglo-American intelligence and decryption bodies, had any comprehension of how well trained and deadly the Japanese Naval Air Force's squadrons—whether those based on the carriers or those based on land in French Indochina—really were. It took a mere three days, from December 7 to December 10, to discover it.

Learning of the Pearl Harbor attacks and then also receiving word that a Japanese invasion flotilla was headed toward the coasts of Siam, Admiral Tom Phillips, a Churchill favorite, determined to sail north with Force Z, investigate, and give battle. Alerted by a patrolling Japanese submarine of this move, squadron after squadron of the 22nd Naval Air Flotilla was sent to catch the warships, which had only a small destroyer escort. Still, to big-ship advocates, going back all the way to those who had derided Billy Mitchell in the famous 1923 bombing trials, the vessels of Phillips's command should have been able to look after themselves. They were fast ships, they contained experienced crews, they were steaming in open waters (unlike, for example, as off Crete), and they had massive antiaircraft capacities: the modern antiaircraft guns of the *Prince of Wales,* for example, were estimated to fire seventeen thousand shells per minute. Yet even this was not enough to beat off the swarms of Japanese aircraft, chiefly torpedo-bombers, although the first attacks were delivered by high-level bombers as part of a combined attack from all heights and directions. Maneuvering a battleship to avoid being hit was impossible when multiple torpedoes were approaching (the sinking of the giant *Yamato* four years later is anticipated here). Among the torpedoes slamming into the side of the HMS *Prince of Wales* was one that blew off its entire propeller shaft and sent the ship turning in circles. It is worth noting again both that all Japanese torpedoes, whether those deployed by surface warships or those carried by their planes, were far larger than those in other navies and that, unlike their German and American equivalents, Japanese torpedoes really worked. A short while later, a second wave of torpedo planes caught up with the fast-steaming battle cruiser *Repulse* and tore into its side, causing it to roll over within an hour. A good two thousand crew members of the two big ships were picked up by the British destroyers, but Phillips himself did not survive.[57] And the Japanese troop transports continued unhindered toward their landing spots.

The whole attack upon Force Z cost the IJN a mere eight aircraft. Little more need be said. Here was a new era in naval warfare, confirming that even the most powerful surface warships could no longer operate at sea in the face of an enemy's air forces *unless* they also possessed strong aerial defenses. In all, this was a much more dramatic statement about sea power's future than the sinkings of anchored warships in Pearl Harbor or Taranto.

It all fitted together. In a mere thirteen months of naval history in late 1940 and 1941 there had taken place a number of actions—Taranto, Crete, the Bismarck crippling, Pearl Harbor, and the sinking of Force Z—that combined to say that the age of the dominance of the heavily gunned, armored warship at sea was over. Anything that floated on water was a target, vulnerable to attack from the air. At the time, in the struggle for primacy in East Asia that was taking place as December 1941 unfolded, it was Japan's aerial power that prevailed. What remained to be seen was

**PAINTING 26. HMSs *Prince of Wales* and *Repulse*, Singapore, 1941.** The new battleship HMS *Prince of Wales* and the veteran battle cruiser HMS *Repulse* were about to leave on their fateful voyage in December 1941. Despite evasive actions, both were sunk by Japanese land-based planes in just a few hours on December 10 off the Malay coast.

whether it could retain that mastery of the skies in the battles that lay ahead.

In strategic terms, nothing could have been worse for Britain's global position—and perhaps to the Royal Navy in particular—than the crescendo of lethal attacks launched by the Japanese armed forces on Western possessions in the Pacific, East Asia, and Southeast Asia that December and in the months following. From the Abyssinian Crisis onward, the main fear of the British Chiefs of Staff had been that one day they would have to face a threefold challenge, from an enemy based in northern or western Europe, another in the Mediterranean, and a third in the Far East. In their many memoranda of these years, the Admiralty always conceded that that was an extreme scenario. But now it had come about. Of course, in the sheer tally of capital ships sunk by Japan's strikes, the US Navy had lost far more, and yet America's overall strategic position in the Pacific Ocean was not really destroyed but merely set back. Great Britain's overall strategic position in Southeast Asia was hit in a much bigger way, in fact, by an irrecoverable blow.[58]

Where did things stand, then, with the American and British navies at the close of 1941? The situation was not very encouraging. The lessons of Pearl Harbor and the HMSs *Prince of Wales* and *Repulse* sinkings could be understood immediately, but that did not mean that the battered Allies could do much about it. The advantage was completely with the fast-roaming Japanese forces, and it was hard for the Americans and British to do anything other than try to limit the extent of their enemy's advance. Similarly, in the Mediterranean and Atlantic theaters of war, the task seemed simply to try to withstand the many further onslaughts of Axis might. What did appear blindingly clear was that without command of the air, nothing could possibly work, and yet that was at least a year or more away. If and when the time came for the Anglo-American navies to push back their enemies' gains, they would undoubtedly have to advance their forces (via amphibious landings in the Southwest Pacific, further Malta convoys, and other operations) into hostile air zones. This meant that they in turn would have to blunt the enemy's airpower over the sea approaches as the first prerequisite. Although their own British and American air chiefs, committed to long-range strategic bombing, were little interested in such campaigning, in fact winning command of the air around the peripheral rimlands of southern and western Europe and over the island groups of the Western and Southwest Pacific would be the single most important Anglo-American activity of the next two years of fighting.

---

Viewed overall, the eighteen months between the Fall of France in June 1940 and Pearl Harbor in December 1941 were probably the most kaleidoscopic in all of Great Power history. An Anglo-French lineup against Germany turned, after a mere nine months, into a German-Italian lineup against Britain when France was no longer a player. A year later, after Barbarossa, it was the Berlin-Rome axis against a London-Moscow alliance. Five months later still, following Japan's actions against America and Britain and Hitler's declaration of war against the United States, it was the three Fascist powers against Churchill's so-called Grand Alliance of the British Empire, the Soviet Union, and the United States. After that, there would be no further changes until Italy fell out of the war late in 1943. And if one added Japan's campaigns in China to the geographic area that was at war, a full 80 percent of the world was now involved.

There is one further interesting remark to make about these kaleidoscopic eighteen months following the Fall of France—a side comment about the rise and fall of the Great Powers. It began with a blow from the sea and the air, in the devastation of the French fleet at Mers-el-Kébir. And it concluded with an even greater blow from the sea and air, with the devastation of the US battle fleet at Pearl Harbor. Yet the difference in the consequences of these two strikes could not be bigger. The first confirmed the end of France's independent power: German actions had crushed its land and air forces, and now British actions had greatly eliminated its effective naval power. No such thing happened to the rising United States when it was struck by Japan. While it lost a collection of older battleships in Pearl Harbor, it remained strategically secure and politically so aroused that it would not cease until it had utterly punished the aggressor through the use of overwhelming force. Little wonder that the prime minister, initially amazed at the many Japanese attacks, rejoiced at all that had happened.

The British Admiralty's eyes, and Doenitz's, remained glued to a giant plot, which showed that fighting for control of the Atlantic continued unabated. And in strong second position came the fierce battles for control of the Mediterranean. That would not change. But after December 1941, the zones of battle became wider and wider still. A vast new area of combat, from the Aleutian Islands virtually to East Africa, had now opened up. Two new major naval players, Japan and America, had made this a truly global struggle. London and Washington could at last openly plan for the joint prosecution of war against the Axis, as witnessed by Churchill's rush across the Atlantic, where he spent Christmas 1941 and some days afterward in the White House. Force Z might be sunk. Singapore might be threatened. But that was not the main thing. The United States was at last in the war.

**PAINTING 27.** SS *Ohio* **limps into Malta following Operation Pedestal, August 1942.** A historic scene showing the much-battered American tanker virtually being carried into Malta by two Royal Navy destroyers following the greatest convoy battle of the war. The *Ohio* was beached on land and the vital oil supplies taken off the ship just hours before it broke in half.

# SIX

# A War in Every Sea

## *1942*

The year 1942 was the fighting-most year in all of naval history. More battles were fought in this year than at the time of Lepanto, the Armada, or Trafalgar, and over a far wider extent of ocean. Throughout 1942 the unrelenting Battle of the Atlantic continued, with its heroic and epic outlier in the Arctic convoys. In the Mediterranean theater the Royal Navy's convoys included the most important and fiercely fought one of all, Operation Pedestal, following which, in what might seem a really remarkable change of roles, there occurred in November 1942 the giant Allied invasion of the North African ports and littoral. By the end of the year, despite a very large Italian fleet still in existence and frequent enemy air and U-boat attacks, the Royal Navy was, somewhat shakily, back in control of both the eastern and western Mediterranean.

The change of fortune in the fighting across the Pacific, southeast Asian, and Indian Ocean waters after the first six months of 1942 was even more remarkable, in fact quite dazzling. For almost half the year the Japanese assaults had flowed outward, overwhelming American, British, Dutch, and Australian forces and territories from Hong Kong, the Philippines, and Guam to the entirety of the Dutch East Indies, much of New Guinea, and Burma. Japanese carrier forces raided and punished with impunity in the Indian Ocean. It was only by midsummer, after the American holding successes at the Coral Sea and Midway, that the Japanese push into Pacific waters came to a halt. And it was not long afterward that their tentative amphibian landings in New Guinea and Guadalcanal met up with military resistance.

In the grand scope of Anglo-American strategy, one could say that by the end of this year, one Axis foe, Japan, was being held in check, while the beginning of an Allied counteroffensive was occurring against the other two. German armies had been roundly battered at Stalingrad and El Alamein, and the first Allied landings had succeeded in North Africa. But more than that could not be said. The Battle of the Atlantic was still being contested, with each side bringing in further resources. The strategic bombing campaign was hardly under way, and many setbacks were ahead there. The Western Allies were a very long way from the invasion of France, still less the defeat of Germany in the field. But Allied sea power had by the end of 1942 established that their foes would advance no further. The losses had been heavy, and the fighting ferocious.

## Atlantic, Arctic, and Caribbean Waters

The Battle of the Atlantic remained absolutely critical throughout the year 1942, although to most historians of World War II it would be those events elsewhere—Midway, Stalingrad, Alamein, and Torch—that would be more exciting and command more attention. There was no dramatic *Bismarck* chase across the North Atlantic in the middle of the year as had happened in 1941, and no sudden collapse of the U-boat effort as would happen in the middle months of 1943. The adjective that is most used about the struggle over the Allied convoys in the Atlantic campaign is "unrelenting" (and also "grim"). There was much in this fight, scholars have pointed out, to remind one of the land struggle along the western front during World War I. Each side's push for victory was held off by the other. Each side lamented that they had insufficient force to finish the job, even as they poured more and more equipment and men onto the front. Each side's losses mounted. Statistical data of this grinding clash were keenly scrutinized.[1]

In this particular campaign, then, statistics were always part of the critical rock-paper-scissors game described earlier. Could enough convoys get through to sustain the British Isles and deepen the Allied strategy for recovering Europe? Could the U-boats sink enough merchant ships that Hitler's strategy would be winning? Could Allied naval escorts and aircraft destroy enough submarines that Karl Doenitz would have to admit defeat? This had been true even earlier, of course, as we have seen in previous chapters, so the only question was whether those already large losses of 3.2 million tons of Allied merchantmen in 1941 would spiral further upward. With the newer U-boats of 1942 possessing a far greater range, the game could now be played out across a very broad field of battle indeed. Viewed in the largest sense, Sir Julian Corbett's wisdom seemed so pertinent: command of the sea lines of communication being the essence of sea power, what really mattered was to get supplies safely to the other side.

In this theory, then, hunting and sinking U-boats themselves was secondary. Of course, to British, Canadian, and American frigate captains, and especially to Captain Johnny Walker, RN, and Admiral Ernest J. King, USN, all yearning to see the German submarine threat crushed, that would seem a sort of strategic nonsense—instead, you should just smash lots of U-boats and you would have safe and secure sea-lanes, and in addition those U-boats would never emerge as a threat later and in other places. To the statisticians, the essence of it all lay in the monthly shipping losses, as measured against the goods getting through to Britain and against the incoming additions to the Allies' available pool of vessels for the Atlantic routes. It hardly needed to be said that the many calls to provide shipping for elsewhere, to the Middle East, Indian Ocean, and Pacific, would also be easier to fulfill if the shipping demands in the North Atlantic were less heavy.

It is instructive to compare the geographical reach of the convoys and of the fighting in the overall Atlantic Ocean between the beginning and end of 1942. Of course the Admiralty had always recognized critical routes other than the Halifax-to-Liverpool one, such as the grain and beef traffic from the River Plate, oil traffic from Trinidad, the Gibraltar run, the food supplies from Australia and New Zealand, and the Freetown nodal point. What the year 1942 witnessed, though, was not just an increase of ships' numbers along those older routes but also the emergence of vast flows of goods to destinations that didn't exist or were rarely used in prior years. Thus, the shipping traffic going directly from America's East Coast and Gulf ports to North Africa, nonexistent at the beginning of 1942, would be very wide by December of that year, reflecting US troops and supplies pouring into the western Mediterranean. Very large, too, although not brand-new, would be the flow of merchant ships carrying British Army divisions, tanks, artillery, and perhaps boxed fighters from the United Kingdom itself and around the Cape to Madagascar, Egypt, and India. The great planning plot in the Admiralty's underground situation room in London would on each day show dozens of convoys at sea across the North, Central, and South Atlantic.[2] Critical also were the *returning* convoys, bringing back the merchant vessels and their invaluable crews so that they could be fully reloaded in Baltimore or Savannah with fresh supplies and then sent again to sea.[3] The pressures on the escort vessels and their weary crews were thus unrelenting; if the sailors got a few days off in Liverpool while the return convoy was assembling, that was the norm.

The Battle of the Atlantic, as it unfolded in 1942, really took many forms, all tracked by the Admiralty officials deep in their London Plot Room. Their immediate concern was about the further incursion of German *heavy* warships into the Atlantic, but that was actually over by March

1942, with the confinement of Admiral Erich Raeder's surface Kriegsmarine to home waters and Norway after the Channel Dash—although
it took some time for a permanently anxious British Admiralty to realize this. Their second worry was over the Allied convoys to North Russia
during 1942, because their fate was so unpredictable. One of those convoy
operations was the disastrous Convoy PQ-17, which lost most of its merchant vessels to German attacks. On the other hand, there was great relief
in the admiralty at the German failure to destroy Convoy JW-51B during
the Battle of the Barents Sea, and at intelligence hints of the crisis between
Hitler and the leadership of the German Navy. Their third area of concern, which occurred somewhat earlier in the year, was that America's entry into the war meant that a virtually unrestricted submarine warfare
was carried out during the first months of 1942 against US and (chiefly)
British shipping along the eastern coastline and across the Caribbean, until proper defensive measures were put in place. As that flood of losses was
staunched, though, there came the new strain, after October, of escorting
both British and American divisions and equipment to the North African
theater of war. And all the time there was that central plot, tracking the
continuous convoy supply to and from the British Isles, the most important strand of all. The organizational demands here were just astonishing.

The first aspect of this tale, that of the threat to Allied sea routes posed
by Germany's surface navy, petered out swiftly after January 1942, to Britain's great relief. The threat, after all, had seemed a very considerable one
until then, simply because the presence of German heavy warships in
Brest, so close to British coastal waters as well as to the North Atlantic
commerce, had no equivalent in either the Mediterranean or Pacific campaign stories. The German forward strategy here had compelled the larger
British navy to keep a more powerful number of warships ready to protect the Atlantic routes and had often forced convoys to be diverted or
halted. In an ideal scenario, at least to Admiral Raeder (and the Fuehrer along with him), Berlin would order into the Atlantic all of the nation's intimidating surface warships, the heavy cruisers *Hipper* and *Prinz
Eugen*, pocket battleships like the *Luetzow*, speedy battle cruisers like the
*Scharnhorst* and *Gneisenau*, and, finally, the giant battleships *Bismarck*
and *Tirpitz*, with U-boat forces on each flank and a massive aerial armada
above. In the resultant shootout, British naval mastery would at last be
broken. Yet, as we have seen, Raeder's ideal never occurred, because not
more than a couple of those warships were fit for sea at any one time.
What was left was a piecemeal strategy: either hit-and-run raids by the
battle cruisers or the dangerous (and disastrous) cruise of the *Bismarck*.

Still, to the Admiralty, equipped with only partial intelligence about
the condition of Germany's warships, another large-scale surface raid re-

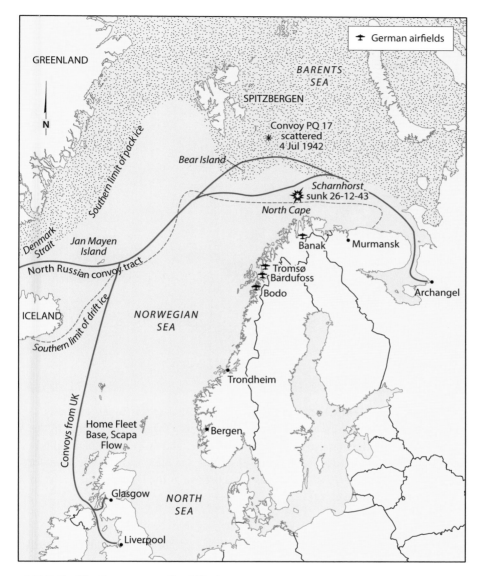

**MAP 7.** Northern routes for Allied convoys.

mained as a nightmare. Hence the anxiety about keeping the Home Fleet at Scapa Flow strong enough to counter any combination of the big German surface vessels; hence the constant worried calculation about sending battleships to join operations in the Mediterranean or to join the Eastern Fleet if the core squadron at Scapa Flow became too weakened. In sum, the heavy guns of the Kriegsmarine compelled London to allocate a large stock of its own heavy cruisers, battle cruisers, and battleships, especially the new, fast *King George V*s, to home waters. (And every new ar-

**PAINTING 28.** HMS *Anson* in the Tyne, 1942. By 1942 the Royal Navy was receiving new battleships and carriers, and the tides of war were turning. In the background are the massive shipyards of the Tyne. The 14-inch-gunned capital ship would steam up to join the Home Fleet in Scapa Flow and provide cover for many Arctic convoys. HMS *Anson* also was present at the Japanese surrender in Tokyo Bay (see painting 49).

rival from the shipyards, like the HMS *Duke of York* or the *Anson,* would be greeted with obvious joy and relief at the Home Fleet's base at Scapa Flow.) Later on, and from time to time, worry about a deficit in heavy ships would lead Churchill and the Admiralty to ask Roosevelt and King to station some American battleships in the Atlantic, sometimes indeed with the Home Fleet.

Yet in reality the German strategy of a forward fleet came to a dramatic end when those warships based in French ports returned to Norwegian and Baltic waters. The spoiler here, as we have noted before, was the Royal Air Force's bombers. Even when located in Norwegian and home ports, German heavy vessels were vulnerable to Scottish-based air raids, but in western France they had just become too easy a target, both to Coastal Command torpedo attacks and, even more, to the RAF's bomber squadrons, now including Lancasters. Repaired again and again, the German vessels were then bombed again and again. As noted earlier (chapter 5), a month after reaching Brest in June 1941, the *Prinz Eugen* was badly damaged by a Bomber Command raid, and among the cruiser's many compartments destroyed was its vital gunnery transmitting station. With the RAF's overall striking power so obviously getting larger, the big German ships had to be removed; and in any case Hitler was at this time convinced that Norway might soon be invaded. Getting away from Brest, then, was just a matter of when. In February 1942, after clever clandestine preparations, the partially restored *Hipper* along with the *Scharnhorst* and *Gneisenau* made their famous Channel Dash, humiliating the Royal Navy by steaming chiefly unscathed past Dover and Folkestone and into home ports.[4] The British embarrassment was huge, but the reality was that this phase in German naval history was over, and all its heavy warships were from then on boxed into a narrow portion of northern Europe, just as their powerful Italian equivalents were boxed into a few Italian harbors much further south. It was still open to the Kriegsmarine to attack Arctic convoys, but never again would they contest the waters of the North Atlantic. It was ironic—in 1940 the German navalists' dream of getting access to the high seas had at last been realized, but it was with a surface fleet too small to do much and in a situation where they were so vulnerable to enemy airpower.

Germany's prospects were different, though, in the waters to the north. With the coming of Hitler's attack on the USSR, Arctic convoys had clearly become of vital importance strategically, and yet it was extraordinarily difficult and dangerous for the British fleet to ensure their safety in practice. Out of the very great fear that Russia might collapse in the face of the repeated Nazi onslaughts, Roosevelt and Churchill felt that these voyages must be undertaken if at all possible—and Stalin demanded no less—although it was clear that the burden would fall overwhelmingly on an already overstretched British merchant marine, Coastal Command, and Royal Navy. The success of those early Arctic convoys, carried out in late 1941 before Germany's forces had been mobilized to deal with them, was unlikely to be repeated in 1942. By then many more enemy air bases and U-boat harbors flanked the convoy routes, and it was of course in those same northern ports that the remaining heavy warships of the Kriegsmarine were increasingly based, even if they were also subject to raids from RAF bombers. In this positional struggle, at least, Germany had the advantage. However the Admiralty sought to prevent it, losses were inevitable, and the only question was whether those losses would be enough to halt the convoys altogether.[5]

Given these acute difficulties, the reader cannot help being struck by how relatively successful (with one exception) the Allied convoys to North Russia were during 1942. At first, as we have noted, this was simply due to the German High Command paying little attention to these sailings—if the USSR was going to be swiftly smashed by Operation Barbarossa, and Murmansk seized in the process, why bother? Consequently, the record shows that only one of a total of 103 Allied merchant ships sent in convoy to Russia was lost before spring 1942. By the summer, of course, the Wehrmacht had indeed understood that stopping the Red Army from receiving new supplies was very important, but by then so had the Admiralty, which began committing powerful escorting resources to match the larger supplies of wartime materials being carried. Thus, the convoy PQ-16 that sailed from Iceland on May 21 was an unusually big one, with thirty-five merchantmen, escorted by close-in flotillas of destroyers and frigates and tugs but also by an experienced cruiser squadron in middle distance and by the battleships USS *Washington* and HMS *Duke of York,* plus carefully arranged submarine escorts and aerial protection. But the German heavy ships did not rise to this bait—had they done so, the fight might have been stupendous—and a large portion of the convoy got through safely (in its last two days it was joined, interestingly, by three Russian destroyers and six Russian Hurricane fighters—the latter brought to the Red Air Force in earlier convoys).[6]

Yet the next convoy, intimidated by the fear that the giant *Tirpitz* was at sea, turned out to be a disaster—in fact, the greatest convoy disaster of the entire war. Convoy PQ-17, comprising thirty-four merchant ships that sailed from Iceland to Archangel in July, was also as powerfully supported as its predecessor: close-in smaller escorts with the merchant ships, the First Cruiser Squadron some way off, and the Home Fleet's battleships (HMS *Duke of York* and USS *South Dakota*) giving distant cover. But it was all to no good. The Admiralty felt it could not risk its expensive capital ships to air and U-boat attack and had to keep them some way from the convoy itself (the same policy of distant escorting as with the Malta convoys). Then, fearing that the *Tirpitz* was at sea, London issued various contradictory orders to the convoy commander, and the exhausted and troubled First Sea Lord himself (Admiral Dudley Pound) gave the fateful and controversial directive for the merchant ships to scatter and make their individual ways to safety. No longer defended, the flock was simply torn apart by U-boats and the Luftwaffe, although the *Tirpitz* itself, which set briefly to sea, was recalled. A terrifying number of twelve vessels was sunk on July 5 alone, two on the 6th, four on the 7th, and one on the 10th. Of the thirty-four merchant ships, chiefly American, that had set out, only eleven made it to port—an unsustainable percentage and of course an utter breakdown of the principle of convoy. A total of 153 merchant sailors of many nationalities lost their lives.[7]

There was another bad way to tally this disaster. The records show that these sunken merchantmen were carrying to their Russian allies some 3,350 motor vehicles, 430 tanks, 210 bombers, and almost 100,000 tons of general US cargo. How useful would more than 200 modern aircraft have been to the Red Air Force in the summer of 1942? All of this equipment had been assembled in America, a testimony to the country's growing productive powers, but what did this avail the Allied effort if, like the oil tankers sunk by U-boats off the Florida coast somewhat earlier in the year, the actual war material could not get into use? Here, to repeat, was the greatest strategic challenge to the British and American navies throughout 1942—how to protect the supply routes so that the required amounts of weapons, men, and munitions could be got safely to the theaters of war. So very often, and to great chagrin, vital supplies were sunk by enemy aircraft or submarines a mere one hundred miles from their destination, after having been shepherded over three thousand miles of ocean.

In the short term, the disaster of Convoy PQ-17 did exactly as the Germans had hoped it would and prevented any relief being given by sea to Russia until mid-September, by which time merchant fleets were assembled again and critical Royal Navy forces had returned from supporting Mediterranean operations.[8] The July losses had made the Admiralty determined to protect the next convoy, which it did by giving PQ-18 a huge destroyer screen and formidable antiaircraft protection, including Hurricanes of the highly effective escort carrier HMS *Avenger*. Since the German heavy warships did not emerge and the U-boats played a relatively small role, the chief assault upon the convoy was left mainly to coordinated mass attacks by the Luftwaffe. Although the latter sank thirteen out of the forty merchantmen, they suffered the unsustainable loss of forty-one aircraft (including thirty-three torpedo-bombers, which was most of their air group). This was an enormous turnaround in fortunes, scarcely noticed amid the continued controversy over the fate of PQ-17, and perhaps more Allied convoys might have been sent along this route, but in fact most activity fell away for the remainder of the year. The Luftwaffe squadrons had to be sent to the Mediterranean front, Doenitz needed all his U-boats in the Atlantic, and the Home Fleet's battleships and carriers also had to go south to partake in Operation Torch.[9]

Then, at the New Year, things went further wrong for the Kriegsmarine. A small convoy of fourteen ships, JW-51B, plus escorts was sent to Russia in the dead of winter, hoping to be helped by the severe lack of visibility—as indeed it was. That factor plus faulty information, mixed signals,

**PAINTING 29.** USS *Hambleton*, **Pentland Firth, Scotland, 1942.** One of the many *Gleaves*-class destroyers built in the expansion of the American fleet in the late 1930s, the USS *Hambleton* spent some time with the British Home Fleet and is seen here acting as radar picket for the battleship HMS *Duke of York*.

and confusion of purpose caused a powerful intercepting force including the pocket battleship *Luetzow* and the heavy cruiser *Hipper* to hesitate in their mission and not push their attack through against a superbly handled and aggressive close escort of British destroyers and light cruisers. The German flotilla returned home empty-handed, none of the merchant ships were sunk, and the Royal Navy duly celebrated this escape as the Battle of the Barents Sea. Reports of this setback led to Hitler's furious denunciations of the navy and his demand that all heavy German warships be scrapped. For a while following Admiral Raeder's resignation over this crisis, things hung in the balance. Then the newly promoted head of the service, Admiral Doenitz himself, managed to persuade the Fuehrer to rescind that order, but the fact was that Germany's major warships would normally now stay in harbor, where they were to risk even further damage from Bomber Command attacks.[10] In sum, therefore, the anticipated German assault by surface warships upon the Allied convoy system in Arctic waters really only lasted for six to nine months in 1942 before it was contained. And the single belated attack, a full year later by the *Scharnhorst,* would lead to a true disaster.

Just as the Royal Navy's escort squadrons were being shifted from sea to sea in this long, hard war, so also were the Kriegsmarine's U-boat flotillas—with the latter of course very often preceding the former. Sometimes packs of German submarines were ordered to (and recalled from) various waters because of the Fuehrer's strategic whims rather than direction from Doenitz's command. The story of the U-boats' campaigns in 1942 was, therefore, a geographically wide-ranging one. Many were kept in Norwegian waters out of Hitler's apprehension of a British invasion, others were dispatched to support Italy in the Mediterranean theater, and yet others were sent to prowl off Freetown or the River Plate. However, in the first six months or so of 1942, the U-boats' biggest campaign was to mount a hugely successful assault upon the newly vulnerable merchant shipping routes off the Eastern Seaboard of the United States and the Gulf of Mexico.

Doenitz's intentions here in this new target area were very clear, the logic cold-blooded, and the execution impressive, ruthless, and deadly.[11] By the beginning of 1942, fighting against the well-trained British escort groups in the stormy North Atlantic was becoming a difficult matter for his boats (for example, the Allied frigates and escort destroyers had better weapons, there were more Coastal Command aircraft around, and the merchant ships themselves were getting better armed), so why not, after America's entry into the war, move the area of attacks to the far more vulnerable flows of vessels as they emerged from the ports of the southern half of the United States, or even better, to that stream of oil tankers and food ships as they sailed from Venezuela and the Caribbean up along the Florida and Georgia coastlines? Why not do it, ruthlessly and easily, as those coastlines were still beaming with light, as if the nation were not at war? And why not do it while the American naval authorities from Admiral King downward declined to have the merchantmen (with chiefly British vessels and crews) protected by a convoy system? It was as if the three years of convoy experience of this war and the two years of 1917–18 counted for nothing. There was also of course the American need to switch warships into the Pacific during the critical months of early 1942, plus unexpectedly large delays in their escort-destroyer–building program, but nonetheless the very heavy Allied losses in American waters caused by a relatively small number of U-boats could have been substantially reduced.

Those sinkings during the so-called Happy Time amounted to many thousands of tons and were the more serious because, as even General George C. Marshall was drawn to point out, so many of them were oil tankers, whose final destinations were likely to be Allied bomber airfields in eastern England, the fuel bunkers deep under the vital harbors of Gibraltar, or the diesel depots for the tanks of Bernard Montgomery's Eighth Army—perhaps even the diesel depots for the tanks and trucks of Georgy Zhukov's Guards divisions in the East. Still, if the situation here was critical during the early months of 1942, it was not yet disastrous. Slowly, steadily, convoy arrangements were put into effect all along the American coast, and merchantmen were instructed to move from one protected "box" to the next until they reached the better arrangements of the New York–Halifax patrols. By midsummer many more small patrol ships became available to keep the U-boats underwater. More American patrol aircraft came on hand. New arrangements were made in the structure of the zonal command system, with the US Navy taking over responsibility for securing these regions and assembling large escort forces for that. Within a short while, too, large American bases were being created across the West Indian islands, northern Brazil, and Liberia. This was chiefly to support the impending huge American troop activity in the Mediterranean, but the end result was that much more aerial activity arrived over the Caribbean, the Brazilian coast, the Azores, and the sea routes to West Africa.[12] The U-boats no longer had it easy.

Even more important was Hitler's persistent belief—mentioned above—that the decisive battle area would be off the shores of Norway, and thus his pressure on Doenitz to concentrate all new U-boats there, to counter an Allied invasion that would never come. As early as January 1942, eight brand-new (and improved) submarines were ordered north to protect the approaches to Norway—what they could have done instead, operating off the well-lit harbors of Miami, is all too imaginable. Still, the existing U-boats that were sent to the American coasts did enough damage to push the total monthly tonnage of Allied merchantmen sunk from 200,000 to over 300,000 by April 1942; and in June the total sunk ran up to the terrifying total of 600,000 tons, that is, very close to what at the time seemed the breaking point. However, it was in that very same month that Doenitz brought this more distant campaigning to its end. In yet another twist to this ever-changing tale, feeling that he now had enough additional U-boat resources to concentrate on and *break* the North Atlantic convoy system at the center, he sought a return to the main battle area. The lesser campaigns afield were to be reduced, patrols in Arctic waters could be suspended in the summer months, and everything could be returned to the core theater.

In Doenitz, the Allies clearly faced one of the smartest and best organized of the higher German leaders. His almost daily assessments in the staff war diary of the submarine war, and often of the war itself, were incredibly candid and level-headed and are a pleasure to read. Having shown flexibility and intelligence in shifting his U-boat attacks on the Allied system to the Gulf trades, he would now again focus on the North Atlantic. What mattered always to him was the number of ships actually destroyed in any given theater and how close that brought him to defeating the convoy system overall. Each Allied merchant ship sunk diminished the whole, a universalist approach shared, more gloomily, by the Admiralty planners and statisticians. And by the second half of 1942 all the logic pointed to concentrating the submarine attacks on the critical North Atlantic routes once again. In the first place, there still existed that critical air gap south of Iceland that Allied aircraft were still unable to close—did Doenitz guess, one wonders, how brief a window of opportunity he had before the American and British air forces might actually have very-long-range bombers equipped with all the necessary detection equipment and improved depth charges? The second point, which he well knew, was that any U-boat operating in the gap obviously needed to travel only one-half the distance than if it operated in the Gulf of Mexico and only one-third the distance than if sent to patrol off the Cape. Third, German industry was now virtually mass-producing U-boats, whose numbers available to him were rising month by month. The new crews might be raw and brittle, but there was no real shortage of boats, and RAF Bomber Command's efforts to destroy this production were never sustained enough. Given that Doenitz's boats were now also becoming much better equipped—for example, with a radio detector on each vessel that could identify when it had been picked up by Allied radar—and given also that, in the most dramatic of all the changes of fate, Bletchley Park lost its capacity to read en-

emy messages *throughout this period* just as Germany was to decrypt almost instantaneously all Admiralty directives, the overall situation for
Allied shipping in the second half of 1942 worsened once again.

That this did not result in a complete interdiction of trans-Atlantic traffic, however, was also due to a number of factors. Many an individually
sailing merchant ship and many a smaller convoy did get through; there
were just so many ships carrying cargoes to and from Britain in any given
month (slow convoys, fast convoys, Gibraltar convoys, speedy oil tankers,
and the ocean liners) that it was impossible for Doenitz's force to throttle
all trades in 1942 even with more submarines at sea. The dense Atlantic
fogs and the storms that obliterated the U-boats' vision helped a convoy's
chances. If the weather was truly impossible and a convoy had to turn
back, it was safe for another day, and the U-boats had a fruitless patrol.
And a single air attack on a submarine, be it by a Hurricane fired from a
merchantman's catapult or by the swoop of a Catalina or Sunderland, often sent the attacker into a deep dive, to discover hours later that the convoy was nowhere in sight. Each single encounter, with its own story, contributed to the monthly tallies and to the general picture.

And so, while the picture by the end of 1942 was ominous for the Allies because of the buildup of U-boat strength, there still was the prospect
of a great easing as soon as the American shipbuilding industry really got
into its stride, with the hoped-for huge increases in launchings. At this
stage in the struggle, it was hard to puzzle out where things stood overall.
Different history books on the Battle of the Atlantic, offering assessments
of where things were by the close of 1942, are *radically different in tone*
and presumption, making the task of the later author a difficult one.[13] The
basic statistics are indisputable: throughout 1942 the total of Allied merchantmen losses to enemy action was a staggering 7,790,000 tons, and of
that 6,266,000 tons were to submarines. The German heavy warships,
now a mere memory, had been cleared out of the North Atlantic. Eighty-
seven U-boats and twenty-two Italian submarines had been sunk in 1942,
but the operational strength available to Doenitz at year's end was now
an impressive 212 boats, with many more being laid down, launched, undergoing trials, and so on. American yards alone had launched 5.2 million tons of shipping in 1942 and were primed to double that number in
the coming year. (But how much of that would Admiral King order to the
hard-pressed Southwest Pacific?) Every statistic had a different shape: if
the awful November 1942 total of 768,700 tons sunk could be carried forward through 1943, Doenitz would be close to his deeply desired total of
900,000 tons per month, over 10,000,000 tons a year. Yet if the December
total of the far smaller 316,500 tons averaged out later, the North Atlantic
route was saved.[14]

And just at this time, there came a new element to affect this giant story of Allied convoys versus German U-boats in 1942: the opening up of the North African front after the November invasions of Morocco and Algeria. Hitherto it had been chiefly a story of Royal Navy convoys across the Atlantic to Britain and then further Royal Navy convoys of troops, tanks, and other munitions outward from the homeland—the Gibraltar convoys, the Freetown convoys, the Middle East convoys, and the North Russia convoys—with the United Kingdom acting as some sort of vast bellows, sucking in and pushing out, and the Admiralty arranging its convoy system accordingly. In consequence, even at the beginning of 1942, pursuing the Battle of the Atlantic was overwhelmingly an affair of the British, Canadian, and smaller Allied navies (with growing American assistance to Iceland and in the West Indies). That was obviously no longer the case by December 1942, for Operation Torch meant that there now had to be a colossal and uninterrupted flow of American munitions and men steaming across the Atlantic directly into North Africa and the Mediterranean from southern US ports, and this *in parallel to* the primary flow across the North Atlantic that would sustain the British Isles, permit the future giant Anglo-American strategic bombing campaign, and ensure the planned invasion of France. The plots on the naval planners' wall charts had to be expanded again. The Battle of the Atlantic was becoming larger than ever before.

## Malta and the Inland Sea

The Battle of the Atlantic was not the only great campaign demanding the Admiralty's constant attention that year. The ferocity of the naval-cum-aerial battles for control of the eastern and western Mediterranean was also extraordinary, the aircraft and submarine losses on both sides being severe and the warship and merchant-ship losses of the British being extremely heavy each time they sought to relieve the beleaguered and heavily bombed outpost of Malta. Many of these losses occurred during the three great naval operations of the year—the second Battle of Sirte (March), the twin convoy battles of Harpoon and Vigorous (June), and then Pedestal (August)—but there were also many individual losses to submarine and air attack on both sides and during the frequent Italian efforts to supply their North African bases. The large Italian aerial and naval assets were also reinforced by the Luftwaffe, whose J-87 and J-88 bombers proved, just like the Japanese Naval Air Force's bombers in the East, to be so deadly in attacks upon ships at sea. For the first eight months of that year the British were badly on the defensive, with the change coming rather suddenly and more due to the vast deployment of Allied land power and airpower consequent on the El Alamein and Torch victories than to any naval battle or further Malta convoy operation.

Malta's position, as we have already seen, was strategically unique, and by 1942 the situation was critical for both sides. Either the Axis could manage one last surge[15] of force that would carry Erwin Rommel and his German-Italian armies forward into Cairo, smashing the center of the British position in the Middle East, or the gathering strength of offshore Anglo-American naval and aerial power would display itself in this theater and develop North Africa as a springboard for a counterattack on Italy. Either way, possession of the island base was essential. If the British continued to use its submarine and air bases to attack the Italian convoys, that would exacerbate the Axis armies' existing weaknesses in fuel and ammunition, just as Montgomery's stocks were swelling. Each side knew that the outcome of this year's battles would be decisive—in London, for example, the Cabinet more than once anxiously considered if and when Malta might have to be surrendered—which is why they threw virtually everything they had into the fray. It is worth remarking on the tenacity and aggressiveness of Italy's air squadrons, smaller naval squadrons, and E-boats in the 1942 battles, given the swift nature of its surrender just one year following.

To this day, then, the reader can only stand amazed at the determination, despite appalling losses, of the Royal Navy's fight to keep Malta supplied and operational and at the unrelenting ferocity of the Italian and German attacks upon the convoys and upon the island itself.[16] Every Malta convoy suffered disproportionate losses, with the Admiralty wincing but reluctantly accepting that often a mere one-quarter or one-third of the cargoes would get through. The fleet actions occurring at the Second Battle of Sirte (March 1942) proved this point. Even with the Mediterranean Fleet's heavy units so damaged that it lacked both battleships and carriers, a convoy of four merchantmen (Convoy MG-1) was sent out from Alexandria under considerable cruiser and destroyer escort. The latter's surface-action performance, through smoke screen, launching multiple torpedoes and racing into gunnery action against the probings of far heavier Italian warships, was a remarkable display of David-versus-Goliath aggressiveness, one of the greatest in the war, and succeeded in pushing away a mighty new battleship and two heavy cruisers. But the merchant ships that were not sunk en route were, disappointingly, swiftly torn apart by air attack in Malta harbor, which had by now become inoperable; and only 5,000 tons of the 26,000 tons of supply were landed there, with the Royal Navy having nine of its warships sunk or badly damaged in this effort. The Royal Air Force on Malta was virtually annihilated.

**PAINTING 30.** Submarine HMS *Upholder* departing into the Mediterranean Sea, 1941. Part of the famous Tenth Flotilla and based on Malta, HMS *Upholder* was the most successful British submarine of the war, sinking

I. H. M.

93,000 tons of shipping. She herself was sunk, probably by enemy action, during her last patrol in April 1942.

Overstretched by the losses in the Indian Ocean, Atlantic, and North Cape, Britain's Mediterranean naval strategy was then completely inactive during April and May of 1942, even as the submarines of each side were constantly looking for targets.

The Royal Navy's desperate effort to reverse this situation through the double-pronged Operation Harpoon-Vigorous of June turned out to be just dreadful. Operation Harpoon was a run by a convoy from Gibraltar to Malta, a ten-day epic that endured attacks from over two hundred aircraft and a force of Italian cruisers and destroyers that were repeatedly beaten off. Two of the six merchant vessels reached Malta; the other four were sunk, as were two destroyers, with four other warships badly damaged. Overall, this part was judged by the British to be a victory (!). The much larger convoy attempt from Alexandria—Operation Vigorous—was not. From almost the beginning this convoy and its escorts came under unrelenting attack from enemy E-boats, submarines, and, again, highly skilled Italian and German bombers, a purgatory then compounded by the news that an Italian battle force was also at sea. Fear of having the merchant ships torn apart by 15-inch and 8-inch shells caused the British naval leaders to order the convoy to and fro four times before eventually ordering a return to Alexandria. Six merchantmen were sunk, and the Royal Navy also suffered the loss of the destroyer HMS *Bedouin*. On land, Rommel's Afrika Korps had pushed so far into Egypt that the rather panicked new commander in chief of the Mediterranean Fleet, Admiral Henry Harwood, ordered his warships to abandon Alexandria for the Palestinian ports of Haifa and Acre. The surrender plans for Malta were again urgently debated.

But the British could not contemplate the defeat of their entire Mediterranean strategy, and Churchill especially, who pinned so much on winning decisively in this theater, insisted on a renewed and even greater effort being made, even if it meant a significant weakening of the Indian Ocean and the Home Fleet. Thus additional forces were assembled for Operation Pedestal (August 10–15), which was to be the largest, most ferocious, and bloodiest convoy operation of all of World War II. The historian would have to go back to Tromp and de Ruyter's desperate convoy escort battles up the English Channel during the Anglo-Dutch Wars three centuries earlier to find its equivalent. No less than two battleships, the long-serving HMSs *Rodney* and *Nelson,* three aircraft carriers, and three cruisers provided the larger escort to the cruiser and destroyer group, which in turn provided closer escort to the fourteen merchant ships, including four vital oilers. Most of this force came from the Clyde, and after six days at sea, it pushed past Gibraltar and into the Mediterranean.[17]

There is no way that a ship steaming from Gibraltar to Malta can avoid many hours in that central stretch of water triangulated by Tunis and Tripoli, lower Sardinia, and western Sicily; newly constructed Axis airfields abounded, and Italy and Sicily provided numerous submarine bases. Italian heavy vessels used Taranto, Naples, Genoa, and other ports. There was also no way, in the British Admiralty's grim estimation, that their battleships and carriers dared come into Malta itself—that was a fading interwar memory. When their Ultra intercepts told them that the Italian main fleet was not coming out this time, then, at a position roughly north of Bizerte, the main escorting force turned back, leaving the merchantmen to be escorted by that closer group of 6-inch cruisers and destroyers until, a day or so later, they also hauled off to Gibraltar, leaving the much smaller escorts (light cruisers and destroyers) to continue on the final 150-mile-plus ordeal to Malta. So the early stages of the Axis submarine and air attacks not surprisingly focused on the plum targets of the larger British warships, achieving great success: the carriers *Eagle* (sunk) and *Indomitable* (badly damaged). Then the cruisers became the targets, with two damaged and two sunk, one of the latter (HMS *Manchester*) by intensive German E-boat and Italian motor torpedo boat attacks at night. In the daytime the bombers poured out of a brilliant sky, at night the E-boats came in close, and all the time enemy submarines probed and attacked.

This threefold gauntlet decimated the merchant ships during the final stages of their run to Malta. On the night of August 12–13, six of them went down, while others took much damage. One of the latter, the American-owned fast oil tanker the SS *Ohio,* became a legend. It was hit by a first torpedo from the daring Italian submarine *Axum* (which also damaged two Royal Navy cruisers in the same salvo) and a second by a crashing enemy aircraft; then it was covered in smoke and giant plumes of water from multiple near misses from bombs; and then it stopped in the water, appearing foundered, with its crew partly taken off. But it did not sink, and so vital was its cargo that a decision was made to tow it by placing a steel hauser under its belly and having two destroyers give it an underarm carry, slowly steaming on for another hundred miles. At one stage a well-aimed German bomb broke the tow, which was then restitched. When the battered vessel eventually limped into the entrance to the Grand Harbour of Malta, it was the morning of August 15, the great holy Feast of the Assumption. Most of the devout Maltese population had been at mass, but then many of them slipped out of the churches and raced to the battlements as word grew of the "miracle." The crowds cheered and cheered. A brass band played. The *Ohio* was cautiously berthed and a precious 10,000 tons of its cargo off-loaded before it broke and sank. In all, five of the merchantmen had made it. The losses to the incredibly overstretched Royal Navy were one carrier sunk as well as a heavy cruiser, an antiaircraft cruiser, and a destroyer (and a carrier and two cruisers damaged). But the population could eat, and the Spitfires could be refueled.

Was Malta worth all this? In his wonderful though idiosyncratic history of the Royal Navy in World War II, the well-known British military historian Correlli Barnett repeatedly inveighs against the strategic folly of committing so much of the nation's limited resources in fighting to retain the island and, indeed, against Churchill's heavy investment of men, weapons, and money into the entire Mediterranean and Middle East. Barnett sees this as a romantic imperial illusion and a waste of resources that could otherwise have been deployed for a more direct war against the Third Reich.[18] This author is unconvinced. As will be described below, there was simply no way that an invasion of western Europe could have taken place before 1944—that is, not before the Battle of the Atlantic and (especially) the air war over Germany was won. Also, the loss of Malta in 1942 would have delivered a huge blow to the Allies' North African plans—Egypt would have most probably gone, Torch could hardly have taken place, and Italy would not have been so threatened.

As it was, with Malta held, and refueled, by Pedestal, a breathing space had been gained by August 1942. One might also note, however, a more limited rearming of Malta's garrison in these months by less dramatic means. To meet the island's emergency, Royal Navy submarines were used repeatedly to convey vital aircraft engines and other parts. Even more was carried by the super-fast light cruisers (minelayers) such as HMSs *Manxman, Welshman,* and *Abdiel,* all of which engaged in solo swift runs from Gibraltar and back. Above all, there were the multiple unobtrusive missions by the small older carriers, HMSs *Furious, Eagle,* and *Argus,* which were escorted to a fly-off point as far as five hundred miles from Malta; at that stage groups of Hurricanes and Spitfires would be launched to make a one-way flight to the island's air bases. The most remarkable of these reinforcing trips was made by the fast carrier USS *Wasp* no less, on loan following a desperate appeal by Churchill to Roosevelt. In April 1942 it picked up forty-seven Spitfires from the Clyde, and a few days later, under heavy escort, flew them off to Malta—a "first" assist by the US Navy in the Mediterranean in this war.[19]

Almost all those aircraft were destroyed on the ground by the Luftwaffe, but a month later, *Wasp* reentered the Mediterranean to fly off another forty-seven Spitfires. The *Eagle* itself (before its sinking during Pedestal) made three unnoticed trips in May and June, dispatching seventy-two Spitfires in all. The ancient *Argus* made many others. Moreover, from the east the massive growth in British resources both before and during the El Alamein battles meant that Maltese and forward Egyptian air bases were receiving more and more squadrons of Beaufighter, Hudson, and Welling-

ton bombers. The air balance of power was swiftly turning, and with results. The Italian convoys to Tunis were paralyzed, U-boats driven underwater, and Axis MTBs and E-boats relentlessly punished, and their
inadequate harbor facilities were battered further. None of this could have
happened, of course, had Malta been surrendered earlier in the year and
turned into a substantial Luftwaffe air base.

The end of the story (after a full thirty-five convoys were run to Malta
between 1940 and 1942) was anticlimactic. A group of four merchant ships
was successfully escorted from Alexandria to Malta in Operation Stone-
age in November 1942, with only the cruiser HMS *Arethusa* damaged; in
December a five-ship mission supplied the island in Operation Portcullis,
once again from Alexandria—the only convoy operation ever to be unscathed. It is again remarkable that the Allies—the British really—were
supplying Malta from the *east,* meaning that the merchantmen had had
to sail all the way around Africa to begin with. By November, of course,
Gibraltar and its straits were far too full of invasion shipping to permit
any Malta convoy to pass through.

The invasion in question was that of French North Africa, a move made
only after President Roosevelt's decision to commit US forces to this operation ended a year of Anglo-American quarreling about just where to take
the battle to the Axis. The actual operations, from November 8 onward,
were a massive advance on what until then had been a naval war: now
very large armies were being committed on the ground against the Vichy-
held ports of Casablanca, Oran, and Algiers. The sheer size of the invasion
fleets bluntly said that this was a venture that would and could not fail; as
some of the planners admitted, memories of the distant Gallipoli operation of 1915–16 had never fully left their minds. Every aspect had been re-
hearsed again and again. The larger of the two invasion fleets (with fifty
thousand Anglo-American troops in four convoys, two fast, two slow) and
vast escorting flotillas was sent south from the Clyde. The sketch in map 8
captures the sheer complexity of it all.

That Britain could still do this while now in its fourth year of the war
was a sign that it was a Great Power yet. Equally significant to the historian is the fact that by simultaneously dispatching another great Allied
armada (thirty-five thousand troops)—this one coming across the entire
Atlantic, from Norfolk, Virginia, to Casablanca—and providing the bulk
of the invasion troops for the assault on Algiers, the United States was
showing that its historic commitment would be huge and decisive. It had
now committed itself to a southern European return strategy, at least for
the next year until all of North Africa was in Allied hands. After Algeria its troops would march on Tunis and Tripoli, joining up with Montgomery's armies coming from the east. And then perhaps there might

**PAINTING 31.** "Spitfires for Malta" USS *Wasp*
at Greenock, April 1942. On two vital occasions the
US carrier was loaded with Spitfires in the Clyde and then
took them into the Mediterranean to fly off to the relief of
Malta. The *Wasp* itself was sunk by the Japanese submarine
*I-19* during the Guadalcanal campaign in September 1942.

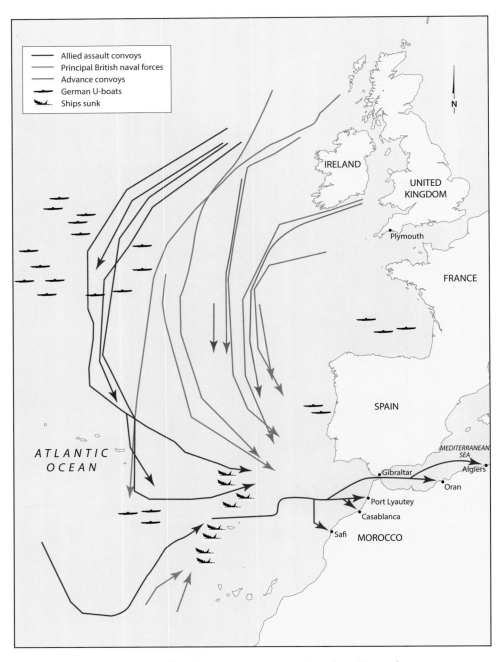

**MAP 8.** Operation Torch: The invasion convoys, October–November 1942.

be Sicily. All this meant that even after the initial Torch operation, there would continue to be a second vast convoy stream crossing the Atlantic, from the US southern states toward the Mediterranean theater.[20] But first, North Africa had to fall.

In one very important way the Allied planners for Torch, and of course the participating troops, had it lucky. These first efforts at unleashing a vast amphibious force—always regarded as the most complicated and hazardous military operation of all—took place against the armed services of Vichy France, and not against the far more experienced and ruthless troops and aircraft of Nazi Germany. Certain proud Vichy French units fought boldly, and while those opposing the American invasion along the Casablanca coast had little prospect against overwhelming force, the defenders in the ports of Oran and Algiers swiftly crushed the impudent British try at rushing destroyers with commandos on board into their harbors. But their superior commanders were already negotiating a compromise cease-fire followed by a political deal that would bring Admiral François Darlan to power. With this resistance lapsing, the Allies had made a huge first step toward victory in the West, however far away it seemed—and was—by the end of 1942. That the twin armada forces had been separate ones from beginning to end, from their ports of origin to the actual landings and move from the beachheads—so that there were no confusions over different British and American equipment, radio systems, and even military jargon—was also a lesson that could be taken forward to all later operations.

The complex amphibious landings threw up a myriad of operational lessons large and small. The original basic wooden landing craft (the popular Higgins boats and the flat-bottomed tender from the Louisiana oilfields) splintered on most shorelines and possessed no front ramp. While the Algiers and Oran operations were each orchestrated by a specialized Royal Navy Command ship, the headquarter vessel for the Casablanca operation was located in the heavy cruiser USS *Augusta,* which had to be diverted into action against a threat from Vichy French destroyers— carrying a frustrated General Patton away with it! The need for large beaching craft to get tanks directly onto the shore became obvious to all. The use of submarines to guide the invasion force in its final stages, the need for a beachmaster to control the landing forces and direct them off the beach as swiftly as possible, the importance of total command of the air above the invading warships and troops, the extraordinary value of uninterrupted shortwave radio communication—all these and a hundred other points became more and more obvious to Allied commanders and could be borne away to be studied again before the next great amphibious operation.

Torch was a brilliant example of strategic deception. The Axis thought a very large Malta operation was in the offing and were taken quite by surprise. When the real purpose became clear, nothing could be done apart from a few bold U-boat strikes against some landing ships and escorts. Probably nothing more could be done in any case. Northwest Africa lay outside Hitler's orbit, the Vichy French were unreliable allies and quick to defect, and the Italian fleet did nothing against the very large Royal Navy group (Force H again)[21] screening the twin Algerian landings. The only resistance was put up briefly by certain Vichy French naval and air units and by a couple of U-boats. A massive 107,000 Allied troops were committed here, and the casualties were around 480 dead. Overall Allied shipping losses for Operation Torch included the escort carrier HMS *Avenger,* four destroyers, and a few merchant ships—fewer casualties than in many a Malta convoy. In no other Allied operation in the war was so much achieved strategically at such little cost. And while it was true that the Anglo-American land offensives very quickly stalled by early 1943 when German military opposition showed itself, the sheer momentum of the Torch thrust meant that a third, southern front against Axis-held Europe was now an undeniable, uncomfortable fact for the German High Command to confront.

There was a side consequence to the Torch invasion that ended a latent threat and brought about a huge alteration in the maritime balances; and yet it is relegated to a brief note in most histories, including the official naval histories of World War II: the elimination, through scuttling, of the remainder of the very large Vichy French fleet still resting at the base at Toulon. Allowed its quasi independence under the 1940 armistice agreement with Berlin and augmented by those warships that had escaped the British shellings at Oran and Mers-el-Kébir, this force's existence as a fleet in being had frequently worried Royal Navy planners—it was considerably larger than Force H at most times, for example. When the Anglo-American assault on North Africa prompted Hitler to order the occupation of the remainder of France and then to further order the seizure of the Toulon fleet, the French skeleton crews managed a dramatic and almost total self-destruction of their ships, especially the most modern ones. The result was actually epic in scale: three capital ships, seven cruisers, eighteen fleet destroyers, twelve torpedo boats, and fifteen submarines were scuttled, plus dozens of smaller vessels—fifty-five fighting ships in all and thus far larger than what remained of the Kriegsmarine.[22] The Germans gained only a few warships but could never really use them. Hitler was satisfied that at least the Free French would not acquire the fleet, and de Gaulle was correspondingly furious.

Although some British officers from the Mediterranean Fleet might have been saddened at this end of the French Navy, the result was a strategic bonus. The Toulon scuttling was not as large as the sinking of the High Seas Fleet at Scapa Flow in June 1919, but the result was much the same: a threat to the Anglo-American command of the sea had been eliminated. Within less than another year, the same would be true of the even larger Italian Navy, and by that time the German Navy itself was a mere Norwegian-based remnant. The six Great Power navies that had entered World War II had, by halfway through the struggle, become merely three. *Victory at Sea* had become an affair of the big guys.

## The Japanese Onslaught, Then Midway, and the Transformation of Naval Fighting

In the third battle area in which command of the oceans was being fought for, that is, in the Pacific War, the age of fleet carrier warfare commenced. One senses that this change in the composition of navies was hardly noticed, however, in the other two (say, by Doenitz, or even by Churchill), and perhaps understandably so. In the Battle of the Atlantic, the long struggle of the convoys against the U-boats had to go on, and with grim similarity. And in the Battle of the Mediterranean the Royal Navy's forces would be thrown in, time and again, to the reinforcement of Malta, with the hope of changing the larger strategic balance regarding Egypt and North Africa. But in this third naval struggle the situation was clearly different again. To begin with, in 1942 Britain and the United States were not the dominant naval powers, sending out their fleets to maintain their command of the sea. In the Pacific realm they confronted a naval power stronger and better equipped, for after Pearl Harbor the Allies definitely had the weaker fleets. Moreover, the naval warfare they waged chiefly involved something new: independent long-range carrier operations, moving over vast distances to strike the enemy's resources, harbors, merchant shipping, and, of course, naval forces. It involved carriers seeking to crush the enemy's carriers, hybrid air-sea power in a contest against the foe's own hybrid air-sea power.

All this was swiftly made manifest in the Japanese Naval Air Force's quadruple knockout blows to the Anglo-American positions of December 1941—at Pearl Harbor, in the buffeting of Hong Kong, in aerial assaults against Manila and the destruction of US airpower in the Philippines, and in the sinking of the HMSs *Prince of Wales* and *Repulse*. In regard to the Philippine and Malaya-Singapore-Indonesian campaigns of January to May 1942, the story then became a military-amphibian one, of successive Japanese Army landings without much opposition and of pushing coalition American-Filipino, British-Australian-Malayan, and then even Dutch garrisons ever further back and into eventual surrender. Without command of the air, the Philippines were indefensible against more modern and more flexible Japanese invasion forces that possessed considerable equipment for amphibious landings, much better than any in the West. Lightly armed and ill-trained Filipino forces were scattered along the coastlines and had little chance of success wherever the Japanese Army chose to invade. The bulk of General Douglas MacArthur's own army was sited around Manila, an open city with a large, sprawling civilian population that could not really be defended. Disease made a nonsense of any formal numbers—by March, only around one-fifth of the American troops could fight, MacArthur had left for Australia, and more Japanese troops, artillery, and tanks were arriving to mop up the Allied garrisons. Despite the withdrawal to Corregidor, there would be no real fighting on, as occurred at Leningrad or in the Caucasus. When MacArthur "returned" to the Philippines, it would be well over two years later and under entirely different circumstances, when Japanese power was essentially drained by fighting across the Pacific.[23]

In the American prewar strategic planning there never had been any hope of holding on to the Philippines in any case; they were simply too far away, too surrounded by superior Japanese armed forces in Taiwan, South China, Okinawa, Indochina, and the mandated islands. By contrast, the British planners, and especially Churchill himself, had assumed that the grand imperial possessions of Singapore-Malaya would be held and had thus dispatched military, naval, and aerial forces to hold the line. Unfortunately, the story of the fall of Singapore was one where the military forces deployed just did not match up with the operational realities of the situation. Sir Basil Liddell Hart explains it best when he notes that the British Empire ground forces (all eighty-eight thousand of them by 1941) had been sent "to guard airfields that contained no adequate air force, and that these airfields had been built to cover a naval base that contained no fleet."[24] Here was an operational setup that had made a lot of sense in the 1920s and yet didn't by the early 1940s. Admiral John Jellicoe's famous 1919 report asserted that a major battle-fleet base had to be built at Singapore to assure the future defense of the British Empire in the Far East, and so, after fits and starts, it was. But land-based airpower advanced so greatly over the next two decades that by the eve of World War II it was clear that the great harbor could be protected only by a significant air force, and thus an array of airfields for those squadrons was constructed up the Malayan Peninsula. Alas, the demands of the global fighting by late 1941 meant that the required fleets of RAF bombers and especially fighters were directed elsewhere—to the Middle East and North Russia—or retained in England itself. When the Japanese attacked Malaya, they had *four times as many* aircraft, most of them superior in quality. The Japanese infantry were also of superior quality to the mixed British-Australian-Indian-Malayan units, and they possessed light tanks, logistical equipment, and a flow of supplies. Numerically, the two sides looked fairly equal, but in reality the gap was a wide one.

The Philippines were going. Malaya went. Singapore went on February 15, a dreadful blow to Churchill. The Dutch East Indies were next, their resources primary targets for Japan's imperial ambitions. Here the Japanese amphibious forces could be amply supported by their navy's many heavy cruisers, light cruisers, and fleet destroyers, all usually well supported from the air. So, just as the British and American land defenses respectively in Malaya/Singapore and in the Philippines were falling swiftly to the Japanese Army's expeditionary forces in February and March 1942, their hastily assembled local naval flotillas also crumbled against enemy attacks. This was scarcely surprising when Japanese surface groups had so much more firepower, speed, and coordination during naval encounters, including some that occurred at night. At the Battle of the Java Sea of February 27, 1942, in particular, the coalition of ABDA (American-British-Dutch-Australian) cruisers and destroyers under the Dutch admiral Karel Doorman found themselves repeatedly pummeled by 8-inch cruiser shells and salvos of the deadly Japanese Long Lance torpedoes as they endeavored in vain to reach the enemy troop convoys heading for Java. On March 1, another assembly of ABDA warships, the Australian cruiser *Perth,* the American cruiser *Houston,* and the River Plate veteran HMS *Exeter,* with an American and a Royal Navy destroyer, were all sunk as greatly superior Japanese aerial and naval forces closed in.[25] A few days later, Java surrendered, and the Dutch East Indies and all their resources were in Japanese hands. The rout was complete, and the Japanese were ready to pursue further.

Even as compared with all that had gone before, the Imperial Japanese Navy's (IJN) push into the Indian Ocean in April 1942 and its carrier aircrafts' ravaging of so many targets on land and at sea was staggering in its boldness, range, and punitive power. And the reason for this, undoubtedly, was the bunching together of the carriers so they could form a large strike force. The Japanese vessels themselves were very fast, speedier than any battleship. They were usually accompanied by an oiler or two for refueling, which gave them extra range. The aircraft were of the most modern sort, the benefit of the IJN never having become subordinate to any land-based army air force during the interwar years. The aircrews were extremely well trained and enjoyed great prestige among the officer corps, even more so after their Pearl Harbor victory. Although individual carriers could be dispatched on a particular mission, the air squad-rons could also be clustered if an operation called for it: the twenty-five dive-bombers of one carrier would become the seventy-five bombers of three carriers, and thus a force almost impossible to resist. Here was the Luftwaffe's blitzkrieg, only that it was deployed at sea against very vulner-able targets—slow-moving merchantmen, or the flat deck of a single en-emy carrier, or lines of battleships anchored in port. Here was an air force elite so well trained that when its dive-bombers, high-level bombers, and torpedo-bombers were thrown together against a target, they had good chances of demolishing even fast-moving, heavily equipped warships—the sinking of the *Prince of Wales* and *Repulse* was the irrefutable proof of this.

The powerful Japanese armada that pushed into the Indian Ocean in early April 1942 also contained many of the traditional sorts of surface warships as backup, with three battleships, six cruisers, and more than twenty destroyers acting as escorts. On the other side of the Indian Ocean, Churchill and the Admiralty had ordered substantial British naval forces into this theater, but unfortunately most were old and slow World War I–era battleships, the deployment of a Jutland-age navy, so to speak. Really, they had no prospect of deterring or holding their own against those five Pearl Harbor carriers, with Admiral Nagumo again in overall command and the aggressive Captain Fuchida leading his super-efficient naval air force squadrons. Unable as yet to locate the American flattops in the cen-tral Pacific, the Japanese carriers had been directed to the west, through the Malay barrier. Symbolically, it was the first great naval incursion from the "East" since the Chinese admiral Cheng Ho's fleets in the 1410s. This was tremendous history in the making, and while the Japanese carriers would not stay long in the Indian Ocean, the British, upon their return in 1944–45, would not dominate those waters for very long either.

From the Royal Navy's own perspective, then, the story of this Japa-nese "raid" of April 1942 was unrelentingly dismal. Its *R*-class battleship forces in the Indian Ocean were too scattered, too slow, and always inef-fectual; the Fleet Air Arm aircraft on the two modern carriers were an-cient and embarrassing; and the numbers of cruisers and destroyers were far too low. The senior naval leadership at this time was poor and seemed to lack the fighting grit that was seen in the Mediterranean in this crit-ical year. Often the individual British units didn't have a chance: thus, the renowned heavy cruiser HMS *Dorsetshire* and its sister HMS *Corn-wall* were obliterated in less than an hour by a sudden Japanese carrier air attack on the morning of April 5, 1942. Ten months earlier, ironically, the *Dorsetshire*'s torpedoes had been deployed to finish off a traditional kind of enemy, the battered *Bismarck,* in the North Atlantic. Now the cruiser seemed to be caught up in a completely new, bewildering form of war at sea, like the *Prince of Wales* and *Repulse* just before it, heavy warships surrounded and "stung" to death by what seemed like a swarm of hornets. Attacked by no less than fifty-three "Val" dive-bombers, the two cruisers were each hit eight or more times and had no chance; over four hundred seamen were lost.[26]

Two days later the elderly British carrier HMS *Hermes* suffered the same fate. Japanese warships meanwhile scoured the Indian Ocean, sinking thirty-one British merchant ships with a total tonnage of 154,000 tons. An aerial armada of 180 Japanese carrier aircraft ravaged Colombo, the capital of Ceylon, and later assaulted the great naval base of Trincomalee, though it found few targets there, for the Admiralty was hiding some of its warships in the Maldive Islands and kept its slow battleship force even further back, in East Africa. The symbolism here for the British was just awful: Hong Kong, Singapore, Penang, Trincomalee, and Rangoon were like an array of gigantic imperial sentry boxes built to preserve the Empire, but all of them were now missing their sentries. Naval harbors without navies, as Nelson remarked, were just futilities.

How World War II might have unfolded had Nagumo's unscathed and powerful fleet pushed further, toward East Africa and the Suez Canal, is one of the great "if onlys" of the war itself. It didn't happen, but it is not difficult in retrospect to imagine the Japanese seizure of Aden or Mombasa, even if by a few battalions. Unless they could have counterattacked swiftly, the British would have had to cease all convoy sailings into the Indian Ocean, and, with no ships able to get to the Suez Canal, Britain's hold on the entire Middle East would have suffered a huge blow. Where would Alamein, even Torch, have been then? How could Malta have been reinforced by convoys from the East any longer? Indeed, frightened by these possibilities, the British assembled enough forces to execute a rather impressive amphibious operation of their own, seizing Vichy French–held Madagascar in a long-range strike (from the Clyde) in May 1942.[27] Encouraging though this was, in fact the Indian Ocean crisis was already over, for the attack on Ceylon had been the farthest west that Japanese sea power would stretch. Having thus demonstrated its ferocious striking power, Nagumo's fleet had turned eastward for refueling and for its destiny in battle against the carriers of the US Navy. That was not long coming.

These successes of the Japanese Navy had reached much further than the Army High Command had envisaged and probably even wanted—every distant province or ocean group that was conquered required another occupying garrison to be diverted from the critical China campaign. And the distances were so vast—how many divisions would it take to conquer Australia, for example, and what was the strategic point? Still, Imperial General Headquarters did agree that after all their amazing conquests, some further divisions were needed to hold the perimeter ring. It also agreed that steps would have to be taken to cut the maritime routes between the United States and the Southwest Pacific. Troops would therefore be dispatched to take Midway in the central Pacific plus certain of the Solomon Islands and Port Moresby in New Guinea. As it happened, then, those next expeditionary forces would find themselves engaging the forces of the refashioned American command structure: the new Central Pacific Command (Admiral Nimitz) and the Southwest Pacific Command, where General MacArthur had established himself after leaving the Philippines. It followed that both the US Army and US Navy leaderships in Washington (General Marshall and Admiral King) would want the utmost support to be given to these theaters. Defensive lines were being drawn here, just as they were on the ground in North Africa and around Stalingrad, with the Allies bracing themselves to hold their positions and directing more reinforcements to these fronts.

When the rival American and Japanese carrier forces both entered into the Battle of the Coral Sea (May 6–8), they were as evenly balanced as imaginable: two fleet carriers and 120 aircraft were on each side, with about a dozen cruisers and destroyers as escorts.[28] In the annals of independent carrier warfare—in fact, in the whole history of sea power—this relatively small engagement claims great importance. No side ever *saw* the other's fleet, though at one stage they must have been only seventy miles from each other. On the 7th the Americans sank the light aircraft carrier *Shoho*—in ten minutes—and on the next they badly damaged the fleet carrier *Shokaku*. But they missed finding the *Zuikaku*, whose aircraft in turn tore apart the giant, powerful USS *Lexington* and also damaged the *Yorktown*. The US Navy therefore lost the most in carrier numbers, yet the Coral Sea has always been accorded an American victory, since the Japanese postponed their assault on Port Moresby while their foe's repair teams effected an amazing recovery job on the *Yorktown*, making it fit to fight at Midway, whereas the *Shokaku* was not.

It was less than a month afterward that a far greater carrier air battle took place to the west of Hawaii and around the small island of Midway. Perhaps the IJN should have paused in its drive into the central Pacific here, but, really, why should it do that? It was still far superior in every category of warship to Chester W. Nimitz's reduced fleet, and in taking Midway with a small expeditionary force and provoking the Americans to come and fight again, there lay the best chance of destroying the remaining US carriers and thus being unchallenged across the whole ocean.

Perhaps even Hawaii would fall easily after that, and the whole strategic perimeter would be established.

In the first week of June 1942 Nagumo's carrier force, with a vast battle fleet some way behind it, advanced upon Midway, a move that US naval intelligence detected. This was not the only time in the Pacific War that Japanese planners would set up a complex trap for their American enemy and in which superior detection and code breaking helped Nimitz's Central Pacific Command to prepare his own carriers for a cautious operational defense. With American scouting aircraft and submarines deployed across the area, the weaker combatant thus had good prospects of spotting the Japanese forces before their own carrier flotillas were spotted. It was, interestingly, just twenty-six years after the Battle of Jutland, where the rival British and German fleets had striven to discover where the opponent's battleships were. Now, by contrast, the question was, where are the enemy carriers? As Japanese and American squadrons converged, cloudy weather and radio silence meant that each side was not exactly sure.

The subsequent battle between the two fleets, then, like that of the Coral Sea, was one fought at a distance and with aircraft bombs and torpedoes, not battleship shells, being the decisive projectiles. And although there was a sheer frenzy of mutual aerial attacks during a day of chaos, this encounter produced a result that is regarded, along with, say, Salamis, the Armada, and Trafalgar, as one of the greatest naval victories in all of history.[29] In none of those earlier great encounters, full of drama though they were, did the fortunes of war change as swiftly as happened at Midway. Unsurprisingly, then, tactical naval historians recount the Battle of Midway almost as reverentially as Civil War buffs detail the unfolding of the rival sides' armies at, say, Gettysburg—minute by minute, almost second by second. The appointed high time in this case was 10:26 a.m. on June 4, 1942, when Japan's military enterprise was stilled in its tracks as three fleet carriers, the *Akagi, Soryu,* and *Kaga,* were ripped into flames by American dive-bombers who had spotted them through a hole in the clouds below and dove down to attack. With the Japanese fighter defenses distracted by earlier combat, the carriers were completely vulnerable to bomb after bomb and were aflame within minutes, each ship's crew suffering numerous casualties.

So it was that tactical blows inflicted by only a few dozen dive-bombers turned an entire strategic gambit on its head, although in truth the battle could have gone the other way had each side's carriers and attacking aircraft been at a slightly different position and had the cloud coverage also been different. While the three Japanese carriers were sinking, further

**PAINTING 32.** Japanese carrier *Shokaku* at the Battle of the Coral Sea, 1942. Engaged here in the first carrier battle in history, the *Shokaku* itself was damaged, although its planes helped to destroy the USS *Lexington*. After fighting many other battles, the *Shokaku* was sunk at the June 1944 Battle of the Philippine Sea.

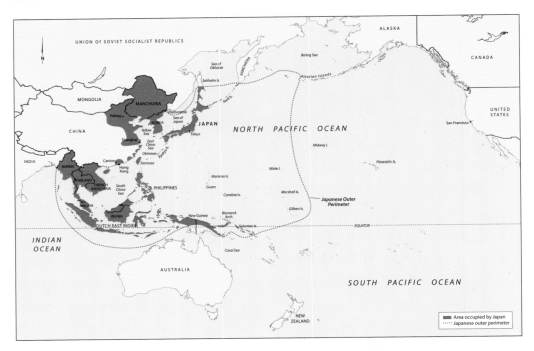

**MAP 9.** The Japanese Empire's expansion at its peak, 1942.

American air squadrons were still looking for more targets and turned to sink a fourth carrier, the *Hiryu,* although ironically the USS *Yorktown* was also attacked and critically damaged at this time by the *Hiryu's* own patrolling planes. A seagull on this day might well have spotted four Japanese carriers and one American carrier slipping into the waters of the mid-Pacific, their crews abandoning ship, rescue destroyers staying close by them, and smaller vessels (and a Japanese heavy cruiser) also sinking, while up in the sky aircraft from each side who had lost their home carrier were searching for another deck to land on or just ditching in the ocean beside a friendly warship. It was, and is, an amazing tale.

With the destruction of four fleet carriers and one light carrier, with the fleet carrier *Shokaku* still badly damaged by the fight in the Coral Sea, and with the loss also of so many planes and highly trained crew, Admiral Isoroku Yamamoto decided he must revert to the defensive, at least in the central Pacific. He possessed the largest battle fleet in the world, including the mighty *Yamato,* but now was wary to move. Thus it was that six months of extraordinary victories and conquest had come to an end, exactly halfway through 1942. By some measuring, the Japanese outer rim, from the Indian-Burmese border to the middle Aleutians, ran an extraordinary 14,200 miles and thus gave the Japanese many takeoff points if it wished to go further, to cut the American-Australian connection, for example, or to go on to Alaska. Yet it might also be seen as an unequaled case of overstretch, should Japan's foe have the resources to penetrate it. It therefore remained to be seen which side would take the initiative once they had gained their breath.

After Midway, the only serious campaigning that took place along that fourteen-thousand-mile line during the second half of 1942 was in the Southwest Pacific. Up in the north, in the Aleutians, Japan had taken a couple of islands, but fighting went quiet there until the American recovery efforts the following year; at the other far end, along the Assam-Burma border, General William Slim's tired divisions were in no shape to move. At Pearl Harbor, as mentioned, Nimitz was prudently awaiting his new fleet. However, the Battle of the Pacific now bitterly intensified in the southwest, where the two sides repeatedly clashed on and around the island of Guadalcanal in the Solomons group and in Papua New Guinea, where MacArthur's Australian-American armies had begun their first advance against the Japanese invaders.

The New Guinea campaign was not a naval one, of course, but one fought instead across mountain ranges and tropical jungles. As such, it can be picked up in 1943–44 (chapter 7), which is when MacArthur's forces increasingly undertook leapfrogging amphibious moves. But the great struggle for Guadalcanal and the Solomons did involve repeated fights at sea, with major losses of carriers, heavy cruisers, a battleship, and many destroyers suffered by the two rival navies in nighttime and daytime clashes every month between August and November. Here was a story equal to the great Mediterranean Sea battles of 1940 and 1941, a bruising blow-by-blow maritime tussle that seemed much more traditional and understandable than the almost surreal victory of Midway.[30]

The Guadalcanal fight started as early as August 1942, and then the pace of escalation in the fighting was astonishing. At the beginning the two sides simply stumbled into conflict—this was not a premeditated Torch invasion. Feeling for a more secure strategic lodgment in this part of the lower Pacific, they came to clash in an obscure, largish, jungle-clad island called Guadalcanal, located two-thirds of the way down the Solomon Islands chain and only just within Nimitz's Pacific Command area. Just as the Japanese were establishing a small, rough air base there (soon to be called Henderson Field), the US Marines arrived on the same beaches—and each side reached for their guns. Both commands sent reinforcements to push the other into the sea, with neither getting a full measure of what numbers the foe had landed. Ferocious land fighting took place, even across the runway and rim of the air base itself. Still, the US Navy planners, with the advantage of being able to read the Japanese messages, steadily knew that they had a good chance to beat off the enemy's repeated attempts to get control of the Solomons, whereas Tokyo never fully grasped the significance of what was happening here. In retrospect, one can see that the Japanese should have either committed much larger aerial, naval, and troop contingents from their great base at Rabaul and sent them earlier on or left Guadalcanal alone while continuing to strengthen their island defenses elsewhere.

Japanese forces fought gallantly and determinedly to get Guadalcanal from August 7 (the date that the First US Marine Division landed under their noses) until February 4, 1943 (when Imperial General Headquarters decided on evacuation), and along with this six-month struggle on land went a blow-by-blow fight at sea. No sooner had the Americans landed at Guadalcanal than the Japanese sent in a powerful naval response, and at the nighttime Battle of Savo Island (August 7) they crushed the US warships escorting the amphibious force; four heavy cruisers were sunk and another badly damaged—in fact, the navy's worst losses in a surface shootout during the entire war. Yet the Japanese did not get at the transports, so the amphibious force remained unscathed and was thus able to hold on. While the Marines lodgment fought off two further Japanese attacks on land, another naval fight—the Battle of the Eastern Solomons—took place on August 24, but as a chiefly carrier-to-carrier contest that saw the loss of the Japanese light carrier *Ryujo* and over seventy of their aircraft and crews. The latter blow was important; here also, as at Coral Sea and Midway, the Japanese Naval Air Service was steadily losing the bulk of the highly trained crews it had possessed eight months earlier. Yet the situation still seemed critical to Nimitz, because the USS *Wasp* was sunk by a Japanese submarine in mid-September, and the carriers *Saratoga* and *Enterprise* were now badly in need of repair. Moreover, the Japanese regrouped their forces and decided to commit their Combined Fleet under Yamamoto, with a huge force (four remaining carriers plus four battleships) sent to cruise off the northern Solomons and await the outcome of the land struggle for Henderson Field. In one further naval encounter, the Battle of the Santa Cruz Islands (October 26), the USS *Hornet* was sunk and the *Enterprise* damaged, while the Japanese *Shokaku* and *Zuiho* were damaged. In early November the Japanese tried even harder, in the two surface-action clashes of what became known as the Naval Battle of Guadalcanal. The first clash saw the Japanese lose the battleship *Hiei* in exchange for the loss of two US cruisers, while the second (on November 13 and 14) saw the radar-controlled guns of the battleship USS *Washington* devastate a second Japanese battleship, the *Kirishima*, at night.[31] Thus it was that one small island had suddenly become a critical strategic

**PAINTING 33. USS *Hornet,* San Francisco.** The famous American carrier triumphantly returns to San Francisco after launching the Doolittle Raid on Tokyo in April 1942. Shortly afterward, it played a critical role at Midway but was sunk after repeated attacks by enemy planes during the Battle of the Santa Cruz Islands, October 1942.

point, leading to each combatant pouring in more and more forces until at last one side judged its losses to be intolerable.

In this case, it was the Japanese who decided to pull back. Fighting for Guadalcanal and control of the air and waters surrounding it had become a bleeding sore for a frustrated Japanese High Command. However many reinforcements they had committed to this fight—and from Tokyo headquarters these islands must have seemed a long way away, and not so vital after all—it never seemed enough. They had lost battleships, carriers, cruisers, tens of thousands of combat troops, and hundreds and hundreds of aircraft, with no prospect of victory in sight. So, on February 4–7 the Japanese garrison at Guadalcanal was secretly withdrawn, with the Americans not knowing what was going on until they discovered empty trenches and beaches. This marked the limit of Japan's tide of expansion in the Southwest Pacific. In fact, they would advance no further anywhere except, ironically, on the Chinese mainland. After a long period needed for rebuilding, training, reinforcement, and planning, however, the Americans would.

Each side was discovering how very different it was, really, to do fighting across the vast realms of the Pacific when perhaps 95 percent of the campaign arena was not dry land. It was unlike any other theater of the war. Far-removed and minor rocky outcrops were bitterly contested, airfields were thrown onto coral reefs, distances were enormous, and an amphibious capacity was everything, provided of course such landings as occurred were securely protected from air attack. Here was a gigantic campaign that placed supreme value on such newer items of war as landing craft, construction battalions, oil tankers, and escort carriers—each contestant could never get enough. And since each side desired to move their own forces long distances by sea and then attempt to throw the other off balance, good naval intelligence was also at a premium. In all these respects as well as in a simple count of warships, the Japanese Navy was steadily losing the massive advantage it had possessed in the aftermath of Pearl Harbor. Even so, except in those fierce clashes around Guadalcanal, US forces were not yet ready to advance until the second half of 1943 brought that great surge of reinforcements that would transform the war itself.

It was ironic, really. By any comparative measure of military conquests—Caesar's, Frederick's, even Napoleon's—the Japanese had done astonishingly well, and over a far wider extent than any previous conqueror. But in the mind of their own most successful commander, Yamamoto, they had not achieved their strategic purpose. They had rampaged around the Pacific for the first six months well enough, as he had promised they could. But then they had stalled and could no longer move forward. Politically, they had not compelled their foe to consider a negotiated peace—indeed, far from it. Truly, Roosevelt and Churchill could now enjoy their Christmas with far greater ease than had been the case in 1941, a mere twelve months earlier. That was surely not so true in Tokyo, Berlin, or Rome.

# PART III

## The Critical Year of 1943

**PAINTING 34. U-boat under attack by RAF Sunderland flying boat, 1943.**
A rare painting by Ian Marshall of an air-sea action, it shows an RAF Coastal
Command Sunderland (probably equipped with radar) swooping down on an
unsuspecting U-boat; after this time more German subs were sunk by Allied
planes than by warships.

# SEVEN

## Allied Control of the Seas

*1943*

A s with the great 1942 maritime struggle that predated it, the year 1943 was in essence three different wars at sea, three distinct forms of naval struggle, fought in three separate arenas. In the North Atlantic, the gigantic battle by the U-boats to strangle the convoy lines to and from Great Britain reached its climax, with Karl Doenitz's wolf packs being forced to pull back after June and more permanently by the end of the year. In the Mediterranean, Anglo-American fleets took command of most of the inland sea and moved huge amphibious forces into Europe proper via Sicily and on to Italy, knocking out Mussolini's Fascist state in the process. And in the Pacific, there was a relative lull in naval fighting in the Central Pacific Command area (compared to the fleet battles that had happened in 1942 and would occur again in 1944) until almost the very end of the year, when Chester W. Nimitz's forces burst through the Japanese perimeter lines and took the Gilbert Islands. Further south, General Douglas MacArthur's own thrust advanced throughout the year by more limited hops and some fast-fought destroyer actions in the Southwest Pacific Command area, north of New Guinea, and in the South Pacific. Military atlases of the war show arrows pushing outward in almost all directions from Germany, Italy, and Japan in the 1939–42 period, but later pages show the arrows going in the opposite direction, from the world outside and toward the Axis capitals.

Overall, then, by the close of 1943 the maritime situation was much more firmly in Allied hands than it had been twelve months earlier, but the victories were very separate ones, fought by different types of fleets, each to a different pattern and pace. What held this all together was the unique structure of the Anglo-American joint direction of the war—political, strategical, and operational—with a British military liaison office in Washington but with the overall directions for future campaigns being provided by critical summit meetings of the prime minister, the president, and the Combined Chiefs of Staff, especially those at Casablanca (January 1943), Quebec (code-named the Quadrant Conference, August 1943), and Cairo (Sextant Conference, November 1943). It was at these meetings of the highest level that Roosevelt, Churchill, and the Chiefs would give authorization, for example, for the further strategic bombing offensive against Germany; also at these meetings, they would make further decisions, after receiving the Admiralty's reports on the Atlantic struggle, on naval allocations and shipping resources. Not surprisingly, the Chiefs often quarreled, especially over the best way to weaken and then defeat Germany, but historians who focus on Anglo-American differences regarding, say, the size of the Mediterranean commitment, miss the larger point: that this merging of the Alliance's political and military leadership really was intended to create a true grand strategy. From these remarkable conferences, then, came the overall decisions about the size, the direction, and the speed of the campaigns themselves. Through this singular process, the mission to destroy the Axis powers was prioritized.[1]

Thus it was that at the first of the 1943 conferences, at Casablanca, the Combined Chiefs had readily identified winning the fight against the U-boats as the first priority, approved of the increased tempo of the strategic bombing campaign, listened to reports on the situation in the Pacific, and stipulated further moves into Tunisia and the Mediterranean itself.

## Triumph in the Mediterranean

The end to the bloody three-year fight (June 1940–July 1943) for control of the Mediterranean was to a very large degree presaged by the Allied seizure of Morocco and Algeria in November–December 1942.[2] For unless German land and air forces in North Africa could undertake decisive counterblows against Bernard Montgomery's large armies advancing from the east and Eisenhower's growing coalition force from the west, they would find themselves at an ever-increasing disadvantage as the military balances tilted against them. German fighting efficiency had often allowed its forces to prevail against larger odds in the past and did so again with some surprising operational upsets against green Allied units (for example, in the Kasserine Pass, February 1943); overall, though, by this stage in the war its blitzkrieg operations no longer worked so well. The Wehrmacht's opponents just had too much strength in depth everywhere from Stalingrad to El Alamein, the Allied air forces were now pressing hard and growing larger, and the Third Reich's internal lines of communication were too overworked. The German Army was still a master at switching large numbers of its highly trained forces over long distances to stabilize a threatened front, and they showed that by rushing eight German divisions into Tunisia between November and January. Yet while this seemed a huge reinforcement to Erwin Rommel's Afrika Korps, the fact was that Hitler overreached himself here by dispatching troops that often lacked fuel and equipment and, critically, lacked command of the air and the sea. Ironically, the Germans now did the reverse of what Churchill had done in his bold Greek-Cretan foray of 1941 and similarly risked being made hostages to fortune—as indeed they became.[3]

With North Africa completely under Allied control by the end of May, the Anglo-American navies and amphibious forces were freed to strike again and again. In July 1943 the cluster of commanders who had supervised Operation Torch were back in charge of the huge invasion of Sicily. In September the same command organization, with many of the same players, oversaw the invasion of Italy proper. Scarcely three years after Dunkirk and two years after Greece, the sea god Neptune was advancing upon the European landmass from the south. Nor would the invaders be checked, as they had been in those earlier campaigns. Although their shipping would receive some nasty blows from Luftwaffe attacks, from this time onward the Allied commanders could assume general command of the air, with ever more squadrons of fighters and bombers flowing into this theater, just as was happening in the Pacific. At the onset of the Sicilian invasion, for example, some 3,500 planes were available for operations, compared to the Luftwaffe's roughly 900 aircraft (though probably only half of those were actually ready to fly). Under this umbrella the Allied navies in the Mediterranean, chiefly the Royal Navy, took steps to ensure uninterrupted maritime control. Malta itself, whose future had been so uncertain just a short while earlier, now received an inflow of fresh troops, planes (600 fighters alone), and naval flotillas and became a springboard for the next Allied move, whichever direction it would take—to Sicily, or to Italy proper, or to southern Greece. The main British harbors of Gibraltar and Alexandria teemed with battleships, aircraft carriers, cruisers, destroyers, admirals' flags, and admirals' boats.

Relatively speaking, then, the Allied invasion of Sicily in July 1943 (Operation Husky) was an easy one, with most of the landings along the southern and southeastern beaches being uncontested and turbulent waves and winds causing more of a challenge than any defending forces.[4] Yet it was, symbolically, a giant step—from Africa into Europe. So it was ironic that the Wehrmacht did not offer much resistance, as it was to do further east in the Dodecanese and Rhodes and all the way up the Italian Peninsula. In this case, the same German High Command that had committed an entire army to fight for Tunisia was now cautious of a forward-defense posture in Sicily, where it initially stationed only two scrap divisions. And the Italian Army was by this stage virtually finished, its leaders in Rome scheming how to get rid of Mussolini and then how to switch sides. Acutely conscious also that they had lost command of the air over most of the Mediterranean theater, neither the German nor Italian forces in Sicily and southern Italy were in any condition to fight a major campaign.

But the Allies were. Having accepted that many practical obstacles (and Churchill's opposition) ruled out an invasion of France in 1943, Roosevelt and the American Chiefs now agreed that Sicily was open for conquest by the vast Anglo-American armies encamped all along North Africa's shores plus the many fresh troop convoys still pouring in from home ports. In this operation the Allied military commanders were determined to take no chances, preferring to err on the side of caution—Correlli Barnett compares it to a hammer being used to crack a walnut.[5] To some war-weary British battalions who had fought since the Cyrenaica campaigns of 1940–41, there may have been amazement, or perhaps grim satisfaction, as they watched the many fresh divisions and air squadrons arriving into this theater; from this time on, they would never be fighting without the odds being heavily in their favor. General Eisenhower, again appointed to have control of this Anglo-American endeavor, could order unprecedented numbers of aircraft, warships, and men into the fight, even more than at Torch.

When Admirals Bertram Ramsay and Henry Kent Hewett raised their flags over this massive double-headed venture, then, approximately 800 major ships (and 2,500 ships and vessels together if one counts the landing craft, tugs, and lighters) converged on Sicily in convoyed armadas from the west, south, and east. On the early morning of July 10, they began to land seven full infantry divisions—three American (66,000 troops, when support units are counted) along the central south coast and four British Empire (115,000 troops) around the southeast corner of the island—on generally open beaches. It was to date the largest amphibious operation in history and actually was a larger operation, at least in that initial phase, than Overlord in the following year. There were also extensive nighttime parachute and glider operations—the first the Allies had ever attempted—in advance of each of these amphibious operations. In a foreshadowing of Normandy, the gusty winds that night caused many of the American and British airborne forces to land far from their targets (and some to crash into the sea), although all of this, ironically, caused confusion among the unprepared defenders. Rough waves disrupted the American beaches, scattering and damaging hundreds of small craft, but even that did not prevent the majority of the seasick GIs from gratefully

**MAP 10.** Allied invasions of Sicily and Italy, July–September 1943.

disembarking and pushing inland. When the only really serious counterattack occurred, mounted by the hastily assembled Hermann Goering
Division near Gela, US naval gunfire from the cruisers and destroyers offshore was repeatedly called upon to check that move. Once consolidated
on land, the American units, urged on by the dynamic General Patton,
romped ahead toward Palermo on the west of the island, leaving Mont-

gomery's divisions to move more slowly through the eastern hills, including around the stony volcanic slopes of Mount Etna. By late July, however, German reinforcements and the tough terrain slowed down the entire Anglo-American advance toward Messina.

The Allied navies had it easier. Even without any battleship encounters with the Italian fleet, there were subsidiary roles for sea power, precisely in the amphibious action of landing these armies on an enemy shore and in giving bombardment support to Allied troops on the beachheads. In addition, the navies always had the supporting task of protecting the full flow of troop reinforcements and supplies to the battlefields from submarine and aircraft attack over the next few weeks, until the enemy's final withdrawal from Sicily. There was no larger role, of course, not even the sort of fighting that had occurred between American warships and Vichy French flotillas off North Africa back in November, because the Italian main fleets, waiting for orders that never came, did not emerge from their harbors. Even at this stage in the war, it might be noted, the Italian Navy was still the fourth-largest maritime force in the world, comprising in theory a full 6 battleships, 7 cruisers, 48 destroyers and torpedo boats, 50 submarines (plus the formidable 20 German U-boats), and almost 150 Italian and German E-boats.[6] It was true that much of that fleet was short of fuel and had not been out to sea or fired a shot in anger for a long while, and many of its captains must have guessed that political negotiations were probably under way to effect some sort of armistice. Still, even if a general sallying forth was very unlikely, it was always possible that some Italian units might be more aggressive than the rest.

So the Allied fleets had to be intimidating, and duly were. In the eastern Mediterranean, or at least to the east of Sicily so as to screen that part of the Italian battle fleet lying in Taranto as well as to suggest a move on Greece, there steamed a vastly enhanced Force H. It consisted, symbolically and most appropriately, of those veteran battlewagons HMSs *Nelson*, *Rodney*, *Warspite*, and *Valiant*, together with the carriers *Indomitable* and *Formidable*, the Twelfth Cruiser Squadron, and a host of destroyers. To the west of Sicily there was another covering squadron consisting of the fast battleships HMSs *Howe* and *King George V* and their destroyer escorts. Royal Navy submarines lay off the major Italian bases in the north, and lighter cruiser forces stood in the middle waters.[7] Prodded by Churchill and seeing no major risks in the other naval command areas at this time,[8] the Admiralty had been willing to shift the greater part of the Home Fleet into the Mediterranean for this operation and to draw down its Indian Ocean fleet. It was important to get everything right.

Given the dominance of Allied air and sea power here—in all, during the whole Sicily campaign, German and Italian aircraft and submarines managed only to sink three destroyers and about a dozen merchantmen and to damage the carrier HMS *Indomitable* as well as a number of cruisers and destroyers—many historians have wondered whether their naval leaders (especially Admiral Andrew Cunningham himself) might not have acted more forcefully near the end of this campaign by preventing the German defenders from extracting across the Straits of Messina so much of their equipment and so many of their troops during the middle days of August 1943. As it was, the tough resistance that the German Army units steadily offered as far-larger Anglo-American divisions pressed them into the northeast corner of the island, and the professionalism with which the German and Italian evacuation commands protected and shuttled the greater part of these battalions to the mainland without very much loss, took a certain shine off the Allied conquest of Sicily. They had made this vital strategic step forward, to be sure, but they had not really defeated a German Army in the field (by contrast, the epic Battle of Kursk was just at this time winding down), and around forty thousand tough German soldiers and lots of equipment—ten thousand vehicles!—had escaped into Italy to fight another day, as certainly they would.

After Sicily came Italy. The predictable Anglo-American political and strategic tussle over whether more campaigning in the Mediterranean would not further delay the invasion of France had been settled at the Quadrant Conference (Quebec) in mid-August. Churchill's pressures were hard to resist, and in any case continuing military and logistical deficits (uncertainty about the Battle of the Atlantic and lack of control of the air over Europe) made Normandy landings impossible any time during 1943—so why not, it was argued, use the many army divisions and landing equipment already in the Mediterranean to knock Italy out of the war before ordering their recall to Britain? The operational consequence, then, was a huge combined Anglo-American assault (under General Mark Clark) against the Italian coast south of Naples at Salerno, with two smaller all-British landings under Montgomery along the foot of Italy.[9]

Apart from the amphibious operations themselves, the naval side to these invasions was marked by another significant action—the surrender of the entire Italian battle fleet during September 9–12, 1943. As we have seen, there had been no really large-scale fleet battles in the Mediterranean during the three years that followed Italy's entry into this second conflict, though the threat from the Regia Marina had always forced the British Admiralty to keep powerful forces at both Gibraltar and Alexandria. On September 2, 1943, that threat disappeared. With Mussolini being obliged to hand over power and a new Italian government (Badoglio's) secretly eager to switch sides, the only real issue was whether its warships could get away to Allied harbors before an irate Hitler realized what was happening and ordered their seizure or sinking.

The Italian Navy's escape succeeded, although not quite completely. The story of the Taranto squadron's initial part of the journey was unusual, to say the least. Here again were historic warships—the battleships SS *Andrea Doria* and *Caio Duilio,* three cruisers, and a destroyer—sortieing from a harbor that had witnessed so many ups and downs during this war, although this time they were not heading to attack a Malta convoy but rather to be interned *in* Malta. But at the same time as the Italian vessels emerged, a Royal Navy force centered on the battleships HMSs *Howe* and *King George V* and carrying the first cohorts of invasion troops, all of them at action stations, was steaming inward! What a curious sight that must have been for some high-flying spotter aircraft. The American official historian Samuel Morison later mused that one accident or trigger-happy move might have led to a "minor Jutland," but nothing untoward happened and the Italian flotilla sailed on to its internment. It was just one of the quirkier and more absurd moments in Fascist Italy's misjudged war.

Meanwhile the main Italian fleet had sortied from La Spezia and consisted of the flagship, the new 15-inch-gunned battleship *Roma;* two other battleships, the *Vittorio Veneto* and *Italia* (formerly the *Littorio*); three light cruisers; and a destroyer squadron, soon joined by three more cruisers from Genoa. By this stage, the subterfuge that they were sailing to fight the Allies had worn too thin, and on the afternoon of September 9, vengeful Luftwaffe attacks took place, including one by a bomber squadron employing for the first time the frighteningly effective FX-1400 guided bomb (the Fritz)—in a way, the world's first air-to-surface missile. It took one such projectile hitting the *Roma* amidships and detonating its magazine to destroy the big warship and kill over 1,300 members of its crew, including the commander in chief, Admiral Carlo Bergamini. Despite this loss, and two hits on the *Italia,* the bulk of the force sailed on around the western tip of Sicily, where they met up with British warships and were escorted into Bizerta. Some smaller Italian vessels, including many of the submarines, turned themselves in to other Allied harbors during the days following. Among the crews of the veteran battleships HMSs *Valiant* and *Warspite* during these events may have been a few long-serving sailors who had witnessed the surrender of the High Seas Fleet into Scapa Flow back in June 1919. When the Italian vessels from Taranto finally anchored at Valetta, Admiral Cunningham sent his famous message to the Admiralty: "Be pleased to inform their Lordships that the Italian Battlefleet now lies under the guns of the fortress of Malta."[10] One wonders whether even that tough, unemotional fighter was not, underneath, amazed and moved at the turn of events—after all, it had been less than two years ago that Italian frogmen had badly damaged his battleships and left the Mediterranean Fleet without a single capital ship. Now it was all over.

The land campaign that followed the actual invasion of Italy at this time was far less easy and belied the code name of the main move, Operation Avalanche. The Allied landings of September 3–9 came in three distinct places. A large force of British Empire troops (Eighth Army) crossed the undefended Straits of Messina and slowly advanced along the "toe" of Italy, while a second British invasion was brought into Taranto to occupy the "heel." The advances here were slow and rather predictable. The German forces planned only a delaying strategy, and they did it very well. Occasionally they resisted hard, causing the British Empire divisions to pause and gather strength in typical Montgomery fashion; and then the defenders slipped away overnight, always leaving a legacy of booby traps, ruined bridges, and blocked highways. Brindisi had been taken on September 11, and Bari shortly thereafter, but Foggia, with its air bases, was not captured until the 27th. Moreover, the hoped-for linkup by this advance with the battered forces at Salerno was not made until September 17, when the beachhead crisis there was pretty much over. In addition, no thought was given to employing Allied sea power more aggressively and, for example, landing a substantial amphibious force further up Italy's Adriatic coast, much to the ire of the prime minister.

If the advance of Montgomery's Eighth Army up the eastern coast disappointed by its slowness, the landings at Salerno by Clark's Fifth Army achieved no advance at all. On the contrary, this large force (55,000 came ashore initially and another 115,000 followed) was swiftly punished by a German tank and infantry counterattack so decisive that by the 13th it had almost driven a wedge to the sea. Desperate to avoid being humiliated by a much smaller enemy, the Allied generals and admirals (Eisenhower, Alexander, and Cunningham) agreed to throw in everything to stem the onslaught: unrelenting aerial attacks, battleship bombardments, paratroops, further infantry divisions, further tank units, and even a flotilla of amphibious vessels bound for India. By the 16th, this punishment was too great, and the German units began a step-by-step withdrawal further up the peninsula to new defensive positions that they were preparing north of Naples. That great seaport, badly smashed by the retreating troops, was occupied only on October 1. When the huge numbers of sunken cranes, locomotives, ships, trucks, and other equipment were cleared from the harbor's floor, it became the main throughway for the Allied armies, and Salerno reverted to a quiet coastal plain, albeit one littered with military debris. There was no doubt which side's armies had performed better, and indeed this whole tussle on land so impressed Hitler that he now fully

**PAINTING 35.** Italian battleship *Vittorio Veneto*, La Spezia, 1943. This fast, impressive, and heavily armed (nine 15-inch guns) Italian battleship partook in many actions, all inconclusive, and was damaged at Cape Matapan by submarine and by allied bombing, yet it survived to surrender (to Malta!) in September 1943.

accepted Albert Kesselring's strategy of holding on to as much of Italy as possible for as long as possible. By the onset of winter, then, this very large force of American and British Empire troops was still a long and painful way from Rome. "The sequel to the invasion of Italy had been," in Sir Basil Liddell Hart's understated words, "very disappointing."[11]

It is worth noting that two significant advances in firepower had appeared in these months, one advantaging the German defenders, the other the Allied invaders. The first and more dramatic innovation was the German deployment of those Fritz-X guided missile bombs from its Dornier squadrons. The sinking of the *Roma* and the considerable damage inflicted on the battleship *Italia* on September 9 was not the only blood drawn by this new weapon, for on the 16th another such attack struck HMS *Warspite* while it was part of the bombardment operation off Salerno, destroyed one of its rear turrets, and forced it to be towed back to Malta. There was of course nothing in the Allied armories to protect against such a weapon, for the German bombers could launch it well outside the range of antiaircraft fire.[12] Such blows, together with the destruction these guided bombs inflicted on Allied merchant ships in a few later raids and the contemporaneous use of a slightly different type of radio-controlled bomb (Hs 293) on the Gibraltar home convoys (see below) all suggest that had the Third Reich allocated more resources to developing and mass-producing this type of weaponry, it might have made impossible—certainly, made far less easy—Allied access to German-held shores. The same might be said, of course, of the slightly later technological developments in ultrafast submarines and snorkel-type U-boats, of German catch-up work on radar, and of its V-1 and V-2 missile programs. All came too little, too late, sacrificed chiefly to the yawning demands of the war on the Eastern Front.

The second firepower development was also new, although it has been far less noticed by scholars, even naval writers: the reversal of the historical advantage that shore-placed gunnery had had in duels with offshore warships. "Ships against forts," Nelson had famously opined, "was folly." By 1943, at least so far as the European theater of war was concerned, that was no longer the case. Better fire-control instruments to account for a ship's roll, the coming of radar-controlled gunnery, better numbered target-zone grid maps, and specially trained spotter aircraft: all this—combined with the crushing weight of a full salvo fired by a battleship or heavy cruiser or even with the quick-firing artillery of fleet destroyers—turned the scales. The repulse of the Hermann Goering Division's assault at Gela was just a foretaste of this, as the punishment inflicted upon the German tanks behind the Salerno beaches well confirmed. Some accounts talked of a heavy tank flying into the air after being struck by a 15-inch shell or an artillery position being blown to pieces, and when General Heinrich von Vietinghoff reported that he was being forced to call off the attack on the Allied beaches, he made specific reference to the power of the naval gunnery. The larger implication lay just ahead: when, eventually, Anglo-American armies would be cast against the so-called Atlantic Wall of western France, the maritime powers would have the capacity to breach even the heaviest shore defenses. This could not be said of an earlier time.[13]

Sea power had shown its "influence," then, in these repeated demonstrations of Anglo-American naval might in the waters around Sicily and Italy during 1943. But by the later stages of this campaign, things appeared much less dramatic and important than the fighting for command of the sea that was taking place in the Atlantic and Pacific. There had been, obviously, less and less of a naval enemy to give battle to, while the Allied armies that were placed ashore had difficulty in moving swiftly or securing victories that looked like real breakthroughs. General George C. Marshall thus had good cause for his continual concern that Mediterranean operations could take too much attention and resources from the promised invasion of France, even if the campaign in Italy was also engaging increasing numbers of German divisions. Nevertheless, since the great Normandy invasion could not have occurred before the early summer of 1944 in any case, there was one sense in which the Sicily-Italy operations in this period *were* decisive—they knocked Mussolini's Fascist regime out of the war and brought the Italian fleet to surrender. After that, it was time to move on. By late October 1943, the renowned Force H was disbanded, and Admiral Cunningham was on his way to London to become First Sea Lord.

The Italian Navy's messy surrender a month earlier was a sad ending to the story of that service's efforts in World War II. The conflict was one that most of the Italian admirals had not wanted to fight, and on many occasions they fought it only halfheartedly. While the Italian Navy possessed many impressively designed warships, it never escaped from certain key weaknesses, as was shown again and again in its tussles with the Royal Navy, namely, its lack of radar and regular air support, its lack of training in night fighting, its great deficit in cryptographic intelligence, and always of course the cramped geographical circumstances in which it was forced to operate. It fought rather better in defense of its convoys to North Africa than is sometimes suggested, and its midget submarine and sabotage arm was always scary. Overall, the threat posed by the Regia Marina had worried the British since well before the war and, evidently, had concerned Admiral Cunningham right until the end. Like the German heavy ships in the north, Italy's battle squadrons in this campaign played a critical negative role as a fleet in being, both of them compelling London to keep by far the greater part of its major warships in European waters for two years after the Pacific War started, which reduced the Indian Ocean Command to secondary status and made the naval struggle against Japan even more of an American action than it otherwise might have been.

The Regia Marina's departure from the scene by late 1943 was of course symptomatic of something far larger. Its elimination, on the heels of the scuttling of the French fleet's remains and the reduction of the Kriegsmarine to a few heavy vessels in the north of Norway, marked the disappearance of that six-sided naval landscape with which the war had commenced.[14] Of course, the Italian, French, and German navies had never been up to the size of the Big Three as established in the Washington and London treaties. Yet for the first four years of this war they had played a distractive part. Now it was down to the remaining three: a remarkably doughty and still growing Royal Navy, with a global reach despite all its losses; an Imperial Japanese Navy (IJN) that retained great firepower but was poorly structured for the unfolding Pacific war; and a US Navy that was gaining its full, daunting size. It had taken some time to show it, but by 1943, history was at last favoring the big battalions.

## Victory in the North Atlantic

Among the many decisive turning points that historians declare to have occurred during World War II, the transformation of fortunes that took place during 1943 in the Battle of the Atlantic can surely claim prominence among them.[15] After all, this primal struggle had been going on for nearly three and a half years, with the advantage swinging back and forth, though with Allied merchant-ship losses having steadily mounted as the Kriegsmarine put more and more U-boats into the battle. Perhaps one might have imagined that 1943 would see much the same story, just at a rather heavier pace: more U-boats available, more shipping losses and more replacements, more desperate defensive measures by somewhat more escort forces; in other words, more of everything, but no severe break in the narrative. Instead, the tide turned in the Allies' favor, and very fast indeed, in the space of about three months. At the beginning of this short struggle for supremacy, after the March tallies of merchant ships sunk were reported, the Admiralty really did fear that the U-boats were gaining the upper hand tactically and that therefore the vital North Atlantic sea line of communication was in danger of being cut. If these losses got worse, as a later official assessment dryly put it, "we should not be able to regard convoy as an effective system of defence."[16] Yet a mere three months later, by June 1943, it was Doenitz who was candidly admitting in the naval staff war diary that the Kriegsmarine had suffered a very bad defeat and that he must in consequence pull his submarines from North Atlantic waters.

What is even more fascinating about this story, to the scholar of causal links between daily fighting on the one hand and the deeper structures of war on the other, is that the change of Allied fortunes in the struggle against the U-boats represents perhaps *the best example*—better even than the reinforcement of new American warships arriving at Pearl Harbor in the same year—*of where vast improvements in one side's material-technological power at the base really did translate into sustained changes at the top, in the battleground itself, at the hard edge of war*. Because the base itself moved, the respective position and fortune of the national contenders also altered. Marx and Braudel would have been delighted to know this.

No sign of an Allied victory suggested itself when the year 1943 began. As it happened, the waters in the North Atlantic were so rough during that winter—huge waves actually snapped an elderly bulk-ore carrier in two—that little activity could be undertaken; January's low total of 215,000 tons of Allied shipping (and only forty-five ships) lost said little about the overall conflict when storms forced so many convoys back to port, and fifty-foot-high waves made visibility for the U-boats impossible.

Relative inactivity helped the German side most, of course, for in that time Doenitz could receive more new vessels—around twenty a month were now being launched—and his staff officers could train more crews. The previous year's losses of eighty-seven submarines over the entire twelve-month period was tough to bear, but those figures were completely sustainable, and now his U-boat fleet was almost doubling in size. By March he had no less than four wolf packs operating in different places in the North Atlantic, often with as many as seventeen or eighteen vessels each, all closely connected by wireless, all waiting for directions that would send them into attack.

The story of the critical convoy struggles of March–June 1943 is familiar to naval history specialists—there are, indeed, complete books given over to the story of a single convoy's fight—but they are far less known even to well-read general students of World War II. There was no epic, single, sharp battle, no Midway or *Bismarck* chase or Leyte Gulf, just a grim, unrelenting, merciless fight between two extraordinarily determined and extremely well-organized foes, on the seas, under the seas, and above the seas, all year round. Rather than trying to detail every one of the twenty

I. H. M.

PAINTING 36. Liberty ships at sea, 1943. The Battle of the Atlantic was the longest campaign of the entire war, and at its heart was the unrelenting fight between the Allied merchant convoys and the U-boats. Approximately thirty-two thousand British seamen lost their lives during the war, as did approximately eight-thousand-plus US seamen.

or more Atlantic convoy "rounds" of these three months of 1943, the best way to show the transformation of fortunes might be to select and summarize three critical clashes: first, the U-boats' successful ravaging of the HX-229 and SC-122 double convoy of mid-March, that is, the one that caused such concern at the Admiralty; second, the remarkable story of Convoy ONS-5 running the gauntlet through three entire wolf-pack lines in late April and early May, with considerable merchant-ship losses but also with a far higher price paid than before by the submarines; and third, only slightly later in May, the double convoys SC-130 (to the United Kingdom) and ON-184 (from the United Kingdom) pushing off the German attacks so easily that, while the U-boats never got a blow in and lost five of their number, the two groups of merchantmen reached their respective destinations with no losses at all. Convoy defense had come of age. The change of circumstances was stunning.

Convoys HX-229 (initially fifty ships, though some pulled back, and five escorts) and SC-122 (sixty ships and eight escorts) left New York on the 5th and 8th of March 1943, respectively, and limped into Liverpool on March 23. By the time the faster convoy almost caught up, this cluster of over one hundred merchantmen constituted the largest escorted group of the war hitherto; and when the results became known, German public radio declared the event to be "the greatest convoy battle of all time."[17] For once, Nazi propaganda was entitled to its jubilation. Because German B-Dienst was easily penetrating the slack Allied Cipher No. 3, an alerted Doenitz could line up three wolf packs of some forty-one U-boats for this attack, and even though HX-229 initially slipped through the first line, that pack (appropriately code-named "Raubgraf," or "Robber Baron") moved swiftly on the surface, caught up with the convoy by March 16, and then launched a devastating number of attacks—no fewer than eight merchantmen were sunk in less than eight hours of carnage, with most escorts diverted to picking up survivors. Convoy SC-122's own first encounter with the enemy (the second wolf pack) came when *U-338*, amazingly, sank four ships from a single spread of torpedoes. Attacks continued upon both convoys through the next two days until March 19, by which time various fresh escorts and air cover had arrived to bring the exhausted merchantmen into Liverpool and a very satisfied Doenitz ordered his U-boats to disengage.

Only one submarine was lost in this entire battle, to an air attack; no U-boats at all were sunk by the very weak and generally inexperienced convoy escorts, which is remarkable. The unfortunate HX-229 lost thirteen ships totaling 93,500 tons, and SC-122 lost a further nine ships of some 53,700 tons—in other words, close to 150,000 tons of precious war goods (sheet steel, ores, oil, and grain) were all in these merchant ships' inventories.[18] Some three hundred civilian merchant seamen died in this catastrophe. There had been only brief air cover over the critical mid-Atlantic "gap," and the newer escort carriers were not yet ready. These two convoys had been terribly weakly protected, therefore, and paid the price. Simply launching more new merchant ships wasn't going to solve this problem.

Of course, a lot of supplies still got through to the United Kingdom. On the positive side, then, it could be recorded that "42 of the 60 ships in SC 122 reached their destinations, as did twenty-seven of the forty ships of HX 229."[19] Yet the attrition of over thirty vessels out of a hundred was a simply awful loss for the Allies, both in that human sense as well as in the destruction of the shipments of such a lot of wartime supplies and of the valuable ships themselves. Statistically, the figures were now frightening. Later analysts might point to the three or four contemporaneous convoys (for example, to Gibraltar, from Freetown, or in the very northern Atlantic) that got through without any or many losses in those same two weeks. But in parts of Whitehall, the worst conclusions were being drawn: that is, if there was another major convoy at sea that Doenitz's command had detected and was determined to attack, and if the wolf packs could be pre-positioned to make contact with it, then the Germans now seemed to have the capacity to inflict losses so much heavier than before that they might actually make this route unsustainable. Evading the lines of submarines seemed less and less possible, lighter days and calmer seas were just ahead, and British industrial-intelligence data confirmed that many more U-boats were "working up" for their first missions. Gloomily, Churchill told his War Cabinet on March 18, 1943, that the country's naval resources "were stretched to the uttermost" and were "inadequate to meet the enemy's concentration of U-boats." In a phone call with Roosevelt, pleading for more American long-range aircraft, he said much the same. Perhaps this is what the postwar Admiralty assessment (see above) of it being less possible "to regard convoy as an effective system of defense" was referring to, which implied that merchant ships might simply return to the prewar situation of individual sailings by vessels when they could. At the Board of Admiralty, though, the mood was grim but not defeatist. To Admiral Dudley Pound, the First Sea Lord, the sheer size of the German presence in the mid-Atlantic meant only one thing: "We can no longer rely on evading the U-boat packs and, hence, we shall have to fight the convoys through."[20] As with the critical Malta convoys of the previous August, everything now had to be thrown into the fray.

With many U-boats pulled back to port to be rearmed and refreshed, the struggles slackened a little in April 1943, only to be resumed with even greater intensity in May. And of all the ferocious convoy battles that occurred in that month, none was more epic than that of ONS-5, the slow convoy that sailed from British ports to New York in the three weeks between April 21 and May 12. Ironically, then, this was not a convoy actually laden with precious supplies for Britain but a body of almost empty ships returning to America to take on further supplies; but Doenitz, having just missed an eastbound convoy (the lucky SC-127) had determined that this new one was to take the full brunt of his reassembled wolf packs, so the fight was to be great.

And so it was: a pounding, relentless, almost continuous battle that has attracted much attention from historians not only because it marked a real turning point in the Atlantic campaign but also because of its stunning, Homeric nature—one entire book on it is called *The Fiercest Battle,* and there are many other works that examine the tale of this convoy on a virtually hour-by-hour basis.[21] This time, the sides were to be more evenly matched, although the odds still seemed tilted in Doenitz's favor. The Kriegsmarine had no less than fifty-eight fully armed U-boats clustered in three wolf packs in the North Atlantic at this time, and two of them (forty-two boats) were arrayed right across Convoy ONS-5's track. On the other side, though, there was a cluster of up to a dozen well-experienced warships, destroyers, sloops, corvettes, and a US Coast Guard cutter, all commanded by the formidable Captain Peter Gretton.

As it turned out, despite the appalling weather conditions, a full thirty U-boats managed to get close enough to launch torpedo attacks against this single convoy and its varied escorts as they slowly approached the Newfoundland coast at the beginning of May. It was a battle that seemed to have everything: dense fogs, crashes between U-boats and destroyers, a Force 10 gale that scattered many of the ships, exhausted escort vessels almost running out of fuel and depth charges and being detached to Iceland, a worried Admiralty that rerouted fresh warships toward the fray, and, finally, the story of one group of five merchantmen that accidentally detached from the rest in the fogs and were heroically defended for days by a single corvette—the remarkable HMS *Pink* (painting 8), under its just-promoted and seasick-prone commander, Lieutenant Robert Atkinson—until it reached safe harbor, with scarcely any fuel left in the little warship's tanks.[22]

An in-depth analysis of this battle, then, allows important general conclusions to be drawn about the entire U-boat-versus-escorts war. Doenitz's flotillas were horribly mauled—seven submarines were sunk, another seven seriously damaged, and many others partly hurt. Moreover, almost all the U-boat losses (six out of seven) in this particular encounter were inflicted by the surface escorts; bad weather had again reduced flying by both Coastal Command and the Luftwaffe to a minimum, and

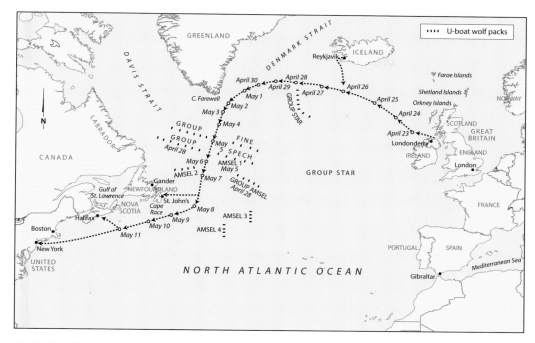

**MAP 11.** The greatest convoy battle: Atlantic Convoy ONS-5, April–May 1943.

the Admiralty's aerial counteroffensive of escort carriers and many more very-long-range Liberators was only just assembling. Determined and repeated attacks by a dozen or so truly heroic U-boat skippers could and did get through the convoy screen and sink ships, but at a massive price, because now at last they could be detected. In the fogs and darkness of the single night of May 5–6, the new technical device of centimetric radar, fitted even on some corvettes, made an immense difference. For example, "HMS *Vidette* made radar contact at 5,100 yards. . . . (*U-531* sunk), HMS *Loosestrife* made radar contact at 5,200 yards. . . . (*U-196* sunk), HMS *Pelican* made radar contact at 5,300 yards. . . . (*U-438* sunk), and so on." Most of the U-boats mentioned were sunk by depth charges, but one was destroyed by the new forward-firing Hedgehog.[23] *These terse battle summaries are for the naval historian to savor, because they show the exact times and the exact distances at which each U-boat had been sunk that night and by which Royal Navy warship.* (For this reason a fuller extract is given in appendix A.) It was at the news of these heavy losses that Doenitz finally ordered his wolf packs to disengage before they suffered further. In the entire naval war, it is hard to find a better example of a novel technology immediately making a difference to the fight.

There are other conclusions to be drawn. Bletchley Park's recovery of the capacity to read German naval codes by this time clearly helped the

Admiralty: it knew that a major U-boat assault was assembling (just as German intelligence knew when a convoy was assembling), and later on it could read Doenitz's bleak order for disengagement. But even if Allied naval intelligence had not been functioning, the battle would have been fought and presumably would still have gone the same way. And while the invaluable HF-DF radio detection system located the position of many U-boats at a distance, it was clearly less important in the actual fighting than the new miniature radar systems. The larger "Atlantic plot" surrounding this battle is also of the greatest interest. Excluding ONS-5, there were no fewer than eight Allied convoys (some 350 merchant ships) in the North Atlantic at that time, although four were just arriving at or leaving US East Coast ports and two were off British ports, and thus all of them could have been ordered home if the Atlantic became more dangerous. Another two were routed well to the south. But Doenitz, as we have seen, had chosen to make an example of this one as a taste of what was to come, and, ironically, it turned out to be just that. Thirteen precious merchant ships were sunk (nine British, three American, and one Norwegian), to the total of 63,000 tons, but as it happened, this was to be the last convoy in which significant numbers of such cargo vessels were sunk. Thereafter the story is, amazingly, often a tale of *more* submarines being sunk per encounter and per month than merchantmen. Perhaps the final word on this great fight should be left to Stephen Roskill in his official history: "This seven-day battle, fought against thirty U-boats, is marked only by latitude and longitude, and has no name by which it will be remembered; but it was in its own way, as decisive as Quiberon Bay or the Nile."[24]

The third example of a convoy encounter in this critical time, number SC-130, occurred only two weeks later and was another North America–to–United Kingdom operation, notable as being one that many scholars would identify as the convoy that went right, one that was challenged by a mass of U-boats but was so well protected that it got through without any cost. Ultra decrypts had picked up a gap between the wolf packs through which these merchant ships would be directed, but as so often happened, U-boat Command had spotted that move and directed its submarines onto the convoy. Yet, alerted by the Admiralty, the latter was ready, and by this stage its many additional layers of defense were tight—a squadron of close-in naval escorts, a surrounding "hunter-killer" group, and Liberators and Hudsons overhead in continuous daylight patrols. Consequently, *none* of the thirty-eight merchantmen were lost, but four further U-boats were, all in the area south of Greenland. On May 19, *U-954* was sunk by an RAF Liberator, *U-209* was lost soon after to frigates HMSs *Jed* and *Sennen* of the First Escort Group, *U-381* after that to the destroyer HMS *Duncan* and corvette HMS *Snowflake* of the B1 convoy escort group, and *U-258* to another RAF very-long-range Liberator (from the same highly successful 120 Squadron of RAF Coastal Command).[25] At roughly the same time, another Allied convoy, ON-184, was sailing in the opposite direction with forty-two ships, accompanied also by the escort carrier USS *Bogue,* whose Avenger aircraft sank *U-569* on May 22.[26] Thus, when spotted and attacked by aircraft in all daylight hours, swiftly counterattacked by the close-in escorts when they attempted to approach the convoys, pursued for hours or even days by the support escort groups, and harried by the escort carrier's planes, even the most determined submarine commanders started to waver. Others, new and intimidated by this defensive blitz, went home after experiencing only initial depth charging and sustaining small damage. The statistics here, and the tactical situation, were now absurdly tilted in the Allies' favor: two convoys had sailed, with a total of eighty merchant ships at sea, and none were lost, but five U-boats had been sunk, most of them new boats though with experienced crews. One of them, the *U-954,* had included in its crew Doenitz's own son, Peter, yet he showed no outward sign of that loss. After exhorting his captains to stand firm for several more days, the admiral reluctantly ordered all of his submarines to leave those waters, go south, or come home. "We had lost the Battle of the Atlantic," he flatly stated in his later memoirs.[27]

Even at the time, and with breathtaking calm, Doenitz (or his assistants) had also written into the naval staff war diary his conclusions about why the Allies had now turned the tables. Extracts from these remarks read as follows: "Enemy radar devices operated from both air and from surface vessels very greatly hampered the operations of individual U-boats." So it was clear that Doenitz had concluded that the Allies then had, essentially, their new miniature radar sets. "The enemy's air force can now provide air-cover for . . . the whole area of the North Atlantic." This forced submarines to submerge, so they fell "hopelessly astern of convoys." Furthermore, there were "new methods of location" against submerged U-boats with "more powerful depth-charges" and an "increasing number of escort vessels available to the enemy." Above all, though, it was "the enemy Air Force" that was decisive. Constant air coverage stopped U-boats concentrating ahead of Convoy SC-130 and, in the case of Convoy ONS-184, simply "precluded all contact."[28]

It is important for the reader to understand the full importance of Doenitz's candid statements here in explaining the *causality* of the Allied victory and the German defeat in the battle of the convoys. No one came closer to him in knowledge of the verities of this grand campaign. Submariner himself, he had thought about and planned for the U-boat offensive against Britain well before the war broke out; he had urged on his "band of brothers," those U-boat aces, to that very end, mentored all of them, and tracked their successes and failures; and he had repeatedly, though so often in vain, pressed Hitler as well as the Navy High Command to allocate far greater resources to the U-boat Service than it ever was to receive. After all, what might have transpired if Doenitz *had* had three times as many boats at sea by 1942, a not impossible outcome if the required steel and electricity had been diverted from, say, a portion of German tank production and if the two-hundred-division German Army had been a division or two less? It was Doenitz who, as we see here, had the temperament to be able to cold-bloodedly analyze the statistics of each side's losses and gains in the triangular convoys-submarines-escorts struggle and to describe what was going on, better in fact than any other military commander in the war did in their own respective campaigns.[29]

To Doenitz, then, it was plainly the combination of newer military instruments and enhanced escort forces that had entered the Battle of the Atlantic in these months of April–June 1943 on the Allies' side that was decisive, not some bad luck attending his wolf packs grappling with a couple of convoys or the fact that there were many more merchant vessels being launched in American yards. Certain things had happened at sea, and very swiftly, that had greatly tilted the odds, and he was prepared to list these items because he believed it was important to do so: a larger number of surface escorts had become available to the enemy's commanders; there was improved tactical conduct in the naval war, plus their greatly improved radar and other detection techniques; and above all, "the Allies' far greater power in the air." These were the decisive points, and he could see that they were proving to be far too much for his U-boat fleets. By early June 1943 he had lost too many great submarine commanders, and with them, too many of their valuable trained crews (see table 8). He really had to pull the remainder away from the North Atlantic convoy routes, send them to less dangerous waters, or bring them home for refits while he considered whether—and, if so, how—there was any way of regaining the advantage that he once believed to have been within his grasp.

It was these cold statistics—twice as many U-boats lost in the second third of 1943 as in the first—that counted in Doenitz's calculus. Thus, he would have been dumbfounded to read later statements by Western historians that the surge in US shipbuilding output—the flood of Liberty ships and others just being launched—assured *inevitable* victory in the Atlantic campaign to the Allies in any case, or that he and his Submarine Service had no real chance of ensuring that the flow of supplies to Britain could have been terminated, or that the fact that such a large number of convoys reached the United Kingdom without being attacked meant that the challenge his Service mounted never really threatened the island nation's ca-

**TABLE 8.** The Rise in German U-boat Losses, 1943

| January | February | March | April | May | June | July | August |
|---------|----------|-------|-------|-----|------|------|--------|
| 7 | 18 | 15 | 17 | 44 | 16 | 38 | 25 |

Data from Helgason, "U-boat Losses during 1943," accessed February 6, 2020, https://uboat.net /fates/losses/1943.htm.

pacity to fight or its command of the sea. Yet such statements abound to-day. "The Atlantic sea route was never as seriously threatened by Hitler's U-boat fleet as is sometimes suggested. . . . From the spring of 1942 it is difficult to envisage Britain being forced to surrender," one distinguished scholar concluded.[30] Even John Ellis, who makes magnificent use of Al-lied and German battle-loss statistics and of Doenitz's naval staff war di-aries and is at pains to stress how tough the fighting in the Atlantic actu-ally was, becomes overly impressed by the sheer numbers of US merchant ships launched and at one stage asserts: "Once America joined the fray there was nothing he (Doenitz) could do to prevent the U-boat arm from becoming strategically marginal."[31]

Such claims don't seem right, at least not when stated so baldly, as if shipbuilding production totals could or did alone win the Battle of the Atlantic. To be sure, the sheer explosion of American shipping output in 1943 looks fantastic, mesmerizing almost, since the newer monthly totals were of course much larger than before, indeed substantially larger than Doenitz's target of sinking 900,000 tons of Allied shipping each month. So why not assume that this US production boom settled the struggle and made the U-boat Service strategically marginal? But that is the statisti-cian speaking, not the naval historian. There is no consideration of the critical fact that Allied merchantmen, whether in existing convoys or as newer replacements, had so often to be fought through a gauntlet of en-emy attacks and that the U-boats in the central North Atlantic simply had to be sunk or driven away before their power increased even further. Above all, no consideration is given to the point that, having lots of ad-ditional merchant vessels (if ships' crews could be found for them, given the heavy personnel losses) wouldn't have solved the issue if Doenitz had been able to increase his forces to six or even eight large packs of U-boats at sea by the fall of 1943, because the Allied naval and air forces actually hadn't crushed the earlier groups. It was precisely because the escorting warships and Coastal Command's bombers *could* sink enemy subma-rines in sufficient numbers, and precisely in these months, that the Bat-tle of the Atlantic had been won. What the flood of new Liberty ships, oil

PAINTING 37. Convoy with HMS *Campania* tossing in the Arctic spray, 1944. From 1942 onward, escort carriers, like the British-built *Campania*, gave protection to Arctic convoys even in terrible weather. When air cover was provided to the convoys, the U-boats' chances of success were negligible.

tankers, grain ships, and refrigerated meat ships arriving uninterrupted by U-boats by *late* 1943 did mean was that the United Kingdom's supply crisis in critical fields (for example, bunker fuel) was solved, that the British industrial war machine could continue and even increase, and especially that the huge buildup of supplies for the invasion of France and further advances in Italy could be further expanded.[32]

But a mere surge in ship launchings alone could not have achieved victory in the Atlantic, any more than could, for example, a surge in B-17 output have won the air war over Germany if the Luftwaffe was capable of decimating the Eighth Air Force's bombers each time they flew.[33] If Doenitz's U-boats had not been beaten squarely, in mid-Atlantic waters, during certain key May and June 1943 convoy battles, the story *would* have been different.

Chart 3 confirms this point, and may be perhaps one of the most remarkable examples of what Edward Tufte termed "the visual display of quantitative information."[34] It is a later reconstruction of the records that tracked and totaled each day *the availability for combat* of every one of Doenitz's U-boat fleet.

While they did not possess this exact later graph, both the Admiralty's plotting room and Doenitz's own U-boat headquarters had this sort of critical outline very much in mind. It was a truism that the more submarines were on active duty against the convoys, the greater the prospect of a German victory, and by this stage Doenitz was operating with a vital if very rough 300 U-boats in total; 100 in action, statistical assumption. In his calculation, the Service needed to possess a total of 300 boats because, given the wear and tear of this demanding oceanic struggle, he could hope for only around a third of them (perhaps slightly more) to be on the high seas and ready to receive his radio orders to go into action at any given time. About 100 more would just be coming into service, receiving training and warm-ups in the Baltic with their new crews, or being repaired—after a single fierce convoy battle, perhaps as many as a dozen or more would have significant damage that required weeks of repair. Finally, about 100 boats would always be en route to and fro, and not only to North Atlantic waters but also to the Caribbean, the dangerous Mediterranean, and the Indian and South Atlantic oceans. This was, then, a huge, unrelenting, almost global operation, in its way one of the greatest of the entire war.

Thus, given the size of the forces mobilized by the British, Canadian, and American navies against the submarine threat, it was an enormous organizational achievement by the German U-boat Service to push the number of operationally active boats ever upward throughout 1942 and into the next year. Doenitz finally achieved the astounding, if brief,

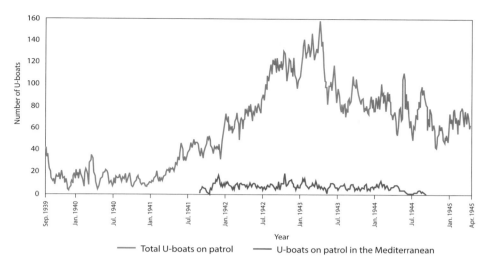

**CHART 3.** Daily U-boat availability for combat, 1939–45. This remarkable data is taken from Helgason, "U-boat Force Combat Strength," accessed February 4, 2020, https://uboat.net/ops/combat_strength.html. Note also a very fine map in Roskill, *War at Sea,* 2:374, showing the location of all U-boats in transit, the four U-boat wolf packs, and the location of individual U-boats sunk on May 1, 1943.

highest-ever total of 159 submarines out on the sea by April 29, 1943, as shown in chart 3. To be sure, that figure included vessels in transit, so the lines are blurry (after all, a U-boat headed to distant waters could attack a closer-in convoy if the chance occurred, but one returning would no longer possess torpedoes), yet it is probable that 80 or 90 submarines were ready for combat somewhere on the oceans on that day, chiefly in the North Atlantic. The irony of the date must therefore strike the reader as remarkable. It was, literally, exactly halfway between the savaging of the March convoys by the U-boats and the savaging of the U-boats themselves by the Allied aircraft and warships escorting the May convoys— on April 29, the very highest point of U-boat availability at sea, the critical Convoy ONS-5 was steaming into the first wolf-pack line (map 11). The falloff in the number of U-boats available just after that date—with 35 lost in a month and at least as many damaged and needing to leave the fray— is also evident in chart 3.

In sum, had the panoply of many newer elements of antisubmarine warfare *not* come into play at this very moment in the Battle of the Atlantic, it surely could have been possible for Doenitz, with twenty newer boats being launched every month, to increase his active clusters of very large wolf packs in the critical waters west of Ireland and south of Iceland and Greenland, ready to tear apart easy summertime convoys. His great foe, the British Admiralty, had certainly feared as much, and at first could not believe Doenitz's agitated exhortations to his U-boat commanders as their May attacks faltered. When he ceased his urgings and instead ordered them out of North Atlantic waters—one can imagine the British code breakers giving out a sort of Waterloo victory call ("La Garde recule!" one might say)—the naval war had moved on, never to return to that springtime crisis. It really *had been* possible, though only with Herculean effort and massive resources, to beat off one of the most ferocious campaigns ever launched by one of Germany's best-organized fighting services against its foes.

Despite all that, the submarine threat did not totally disappear. Regardless of his clear disappointment in June 1943, Doenitz, the fighter, simply would not give up completely on the North Atlantic, and the technical resources of the Nazi war machine were still very impressive. During the lighter days of July the number of Allied merchantmen lost went up again, and by October this amazingly resourceful admiral sent his U-boats back into North Atlantic waters, this time equipped with the brand-new Gnat homing torpedoes, deliberately seeking to kill off the naval escorts as their first target. (Ironically, then, the merchant-ship losses themselves at that time were not so great.) For a brief while that tactic seemed to work, and five destroyers were sunk while escorting a couple of hard-fought convoys, but the Allied planners had been preparing a novel electronic decoy device that neutralized the Gnats' threat, and after that the sheer aerial and naval power of the escort groups and their newer detective capabilities proved to be far too much. The mid-October convoys ONS-206 and ONS-20, for example, were covered by no less than *three* very-long-range Liberator squadrons.[35] In the second half of 1943 U-boat losses went up again, to twenty-six in October and nineteen in November, essentially eliminating for good Doenitz's strategic hopes for this renewed campaign. Indeed, during four of the last six months of 1943 submarine losses were regularly higher than the number of merchant ships sunk, which was, as noted above, a complete turn in the story. After the end of this year, the loss to a U-boat of an Allied merchantman traveling inside a North Atlantic convoy was a rarity. Submarines might still be dangerous around home waters and off Canada's shores or still achieve sinkings in more distant seas, but they never again went back to the main battleground in significant numbers. The 1943 figures speak for themselves, as seen in chart 4.

Further south, a separate and somewhat smaller campaign also took place in 1943, as reconstituted clusters of U-boats battled a newer force, that of the US escort carriers and destroyer groups who were protecting convoys on the North African run across the middle Atlantic.[36] Ever

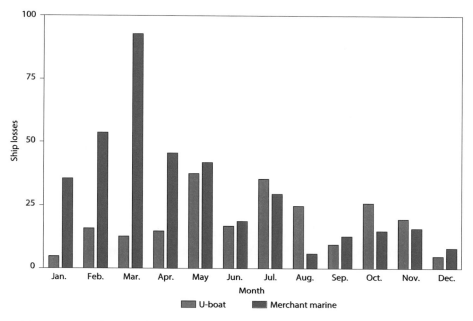

**CHART 4.** U-boat and merchant-ship losses in the North Atlantic, 1943. Data from Kennedy, *Engineers of Victory*, 43.

since the Torch landings the previous November, and with the presence in the Mediterranean theater of rising hundreds of thousands of American troops requiring a vast new oceanic supply chain, the US Navy and its forceful chief, Admiral Ernest J. King, had become much more invested in the Battle of the Atlantic and the destruction of German submarines. A March 1943 Anglo-American-Canadian conference had agreed upon two separate naval control zones, with a new Atlantic Command (Tenth Fleet) of the US Navy taking over the southern routes, which was probably just as well, since the two chief admiralties pursued very different strategies. In London, there continued to prevail the Corbettian notion that getting the merchant ships through unscathed was the prime objective and constituted ipso facto a strategic success; the home island would be secure, and vast material resources for the future D-Day operation and eventual defeat of Nazi Germany would be assembled. It was enough therefore to have evaded or beaten away the U-boats, although of course also very satisfactory if many of the latter were sunk in the process. To the very aggressive and impatient naval directors in Washington, this was insufficient; the American Navy and its new escort carrier task forces were directed toward an active search-and-destroy campaign, which included using top-secret Ultra intelligence to surprise U-boats refueling from milk-cow submarines in remote Atlantic rendezvous.[37] As it turned out, the British concern that this aggressiveness would *at last* cause Doenitz to realize that his supposedly unbreakable encrypted messages were being read was never realized. To the very end he believed that it was the enemy's increasingly wide aircraft patrols plus some super, new long-range radar that accounted for these remarkable detections. The Allies' luck held.

At the end of the day, though, the result was the same: the U-boats' relocation to attack convoys further south also led to unsustainably heavy losses. Ironically, when the first group of around seventeen submarines was pulled away from the North Atlantic run and reassembled, it was named Wolfpack Trutz (Defiance). But simply being more defiant was to no avail. Whether it was in active defense close to their US-to-Gibraltar convoys or in the risky over-the-horizon surprises of a U-boat refueling rendezvous, the Tenth Fleet's new escort carrier groups—centered on the USSs *Bogue, Santee, Card, Block Island* (the only American carrier sunk by a submarine), *Guadalcanal,* and *Core*—inflicted heavy damage on the U-boats and their supply vessels all through the second half of 1943. Again and again, the reader is struck by how many newer weapons technologies and additional fighting forces were coming into the Allied fleets in this great watershed year. Not only were there numerous US escort carriers with their faster destroyer escorts (not corvettes or sloops), but these far-better-equipped carriers could now dispatch the speedy F4F Wildcat fighters to strafe the U-boats while the Avenger bombers came in low with depth charges and the Fido airborne acoustic torpedoes. Even submarines fitted with heavy antiaircraft pom-pom guns found themselves overwhelmed. Thus, by the end of the year another twenty-four U-boats, including at least five U-boat tankers, had been sunk by escort carrier forces. If these numbers never approached those sunk by land-based (Coastal Command) aircraft overall, the message was the same—the strategic balance really had shifted. By October a disappointed Doenitz had pulled most of his boats from this route and devoted his attention to getting better detection and offensive systems for his fleet, although even that was to be in vain.[38] As one historian (David Syrett) of the 1943 defeat of the U-boats points out, Doenitz's switching the concentration of attacks from one theater to another—from North Atlantic to North African or Gibraltar routes or to distant waters like the Brazil coast and the Indian Ocean and then back to the British Isles—was less a sign of being in control of things, like a Frederick the Great probing an enemy's lines for weaknesses, and more a repeated retreat from the tougher main battlegrounds, itself a sign of defeat.[39]

In other words, a new U-boat zone of attack was not necessarily an easier one, as was demonstrated by the intense naval and aerial battles in the *third* Atlantic battleground, around the UK-Gibraltar convoys, also in the second half of 1943. After the Fall of France in 1940, this route had always been a very precarious one, for it was not only vulnerable to U-boats based in the nearby Atlantic ports but well within range of numerous Luftwaffe squadrons of Dornier, Heinkel, and Focke-Wulf bombers located along the Bay of Biscay. Geographically, the advantage was Germany's, and both aerial and U-boat attacks could be pressed home with great intensity, sometimes with three lines of waiting U-boats. Against one large Gibraltar home convoy, the German attackers consisted not only of those lines of U-boats (well over twenty) but also a surprise daytime attack by twenty-five Heinkel 177s firing off the new radio-controlled glider bombs. Yet these renewed assaults came too late, and all were determinedly beaten off. Not only were the Gibraltar convoys now protected by many more powerful surface warships and escort carriers, but Coastal Command at last had the aerial resources to throw into battle whenever it was alerted that a U-boat group was assembling. Sunderland and Wellington bombers equipped with sophisticated acoustical systems patrolled over the Bay of Biscay at night, swooping down upon the U-boats on the surface and then blinding them with the new powerful Leigh Lights. German submarines equipped with heavier antiaircraft guns and attempting to fight their way out to the Atlantic found themselves in furious battles, and always with the danger that the Allied aircraft would swiftly call in surface warships. One amazing shootout took place between five U-boats and four Polish-flown Mosquito fighter-bombers. On occasion the fighting was so close that destroyers and sloops crashed into and sank some U-boats. Luftwaffe patrols found themselves being ambushed and becoming the hunted. On some occasions, lifeboats with the survivors of sinking merchantmen, escorts, and submarines and of ditched aircraft were in the water together! The tally of U-boat losses in these 1943 Bay of Biscay / Gibraltar–run fights steadily rose; ten were lost in the November battles alone. And the Heinkel 177 attacks did not last long before those squadrons were rushed to stabilize Germany's deteriorating situation in the Mediterranean after the surrender of Italy.[40]

Ironically, the last fight of the year between German and Allied naval forces in this area—an encounter aptly named the Battle of the Bay of Biscay[41]—was a furious, storm-torn surface fight between the Royal Navy cruisers HMSs *Glasgow* and *Enterprise* and a force of four German destroyers and six large torpedo boats that had been sent out from French ports to escort the blockade runner *Alsterufer,* which was returning from the Far East with critical supplies of tungsten and rubber. Here, too, Allied firepower was simply too much for Doenitz's side. While long-range B-24 Liberator bombers sank the blockade runner itself, Ultra decrypts allowed the Admiralty to put out a net of cruisers to spring the trap. Caught off guard, the German destroyers and torpedo boats fought fiercely, even in an Atlantic gale, but the radar-controlled 6-inch guns of the cruisers were too much. Three of the German warships, including the destroyer *Z-27*, were sunk, and after this time in the war no more surface blockade runners managed to make a successful run to relieve the Fatherland.

While the commercial and troopship traffic from America's southern ports to the Mediterranean had soared throughout 1943, the convoy traffic to North Russia witnessed a lesser tempo.[42] The recently opened supply route via the Persian railway system, although extremely lengthy and elaborate, reduced the urgency of getting Western supplies to Stalin's forces by the traditional Atlantic convoys, and the quietly operated trade into Siberia—in Russian-flagged merchantmen, for Japan and the USSR were still of course neutral through these years—made a huge difference to the task of getting American aircraft, trucks, tanks, guns, and ammunition to the Soviet war machine.[43] But the main reason for the reduction in Arctic convoys was that the bad experiences of 1942 (the destruction of Convoy PQ-17, the unexpectedly strong damage repeatedly inflicted by the Luftwaffe as well as by the U-boats, and the still-looming presence of the *Scharnhorst* and *Tirpitz*) had caused Churchill to insist that this trade be suspended, at least during the lighter summer months. And so it was between March and November 1943, to Stalin's anger and his many protests about uneven sacrifice. By the time the last few convoys of the year did sail to Archangel, however, the overall strategic outlook of the war, especially that on the Eastern Front, was very much changed.

The final month of the year did, however, bring a long-hoped-for gain to the Royal Navy in Arctic waters and another blow to Germany's limited heavy-warship fleet. On December 26, 1943, after two exciting days of pursuit, the remaining effective battle cruiser *Scharnhorst* was caught and sunk by the new battleship HMS *Duke of York* plus a force of Royal Navy cruisers and destroyers.[44] It was an action in which, from Doenitz's perspective (as head of the overall German Navy), everything went wrong. The British convoys went unscathed throughout. The large German destroyers were too top-heavy for the huge Arctic swells and were sent home, and the Luftwaffe was also partially cramped by the foul weather. As had happened in the almost-simultaneous Battle of the Bay of Biscay, Ultra decrypts alerted the Admiralty as to German intentions, and superior British radar, especially on the cruisers, helped to keep track of the *Scharnhorst* despite its frequent changes of course. Shell damage slowed the battle cruiser down, and it was surrounded. Its sinking off the North Cape, despite gallant efforts to fight back, marked the last attempt by Germany's surface fleet to dispute Allied naval mastery and was in fact the last-ever battleship action in Western waters during this war. *Sic transit gloria.*

## The United States Advances in the Pacific, Slowly

Events in the Pacific War during 1943 were altogether less dramatic and decisive than those in either the Mediterranean or the Atlantic, chiefly because Nimitz was still waiting for the surge of new carriers, battleships, and other craft from US shipyards. This lesser pace of things in the central Pacific stood in contrast to the Japanese-American carrier-led fleet actions in 1942, such as in the Coral Sea and at Midway, and those in 1944 in the Philippine Sea and Leyte Gulf. The battles that did take place in the Southwest Pacific Command region during 1943, though sometimes sustained and intense, were more local, chiefly involving cruisers and destroyers, plus each side's *land-based* air forces, in battles surrounding landing operations, island garrisons, and maritime supply missions. The end result was a steady pushing back of the Japanese perimeter line of defense, in the entire Solomon Islands and around Rabaul and the Bismarck Archipelago, as the year unfolded. Meanwhile, up in the far northern Pacific, there took place the much easier reconquest of Japan's recently acquired Aleutian Islands. It was not until the arrival of the first new fleet and light fleet carriers at Pearl that Nimitz could authorize early small-scale raids on Japanese-garrisoned atolls from August 1943 onward and then, when far larger US forces were ready, order the important seizure of the Gilbert Islands in November.[45]

Such a relative lack of action in the central Pacific should have allowed plenty of time for the Japanese to recuperate and to amend their allocation of forces, had they wanted to do so. But there was the rub. The Japanese leadership, torn by its traditional divide between the oceanic-focused navy and the continent-centered army, found itself in more and more of a quandary by early 1943. While the generals were still determined to push forward in their gigantic China campaign, the admirals were urging that a much larger threat to security might be coming across the seas, even if the enemy still appeared to be a long way from Tokyo. But those distances were indeed great, and the Imperial General Staff was not paying proper attention here. And the truth was that the Japanese Empire was still at virtually its greatest extent at the beginning of this year; it was hard to see, really, where the dent in the perimeter line representing the loss of the Solomons was on any large-scale map of Japan's conquests (see map 9).

Geographically and thus operationally, then, it appeared as if Japan still had the advantages of being able to move its forces along interior lines, shuttling army divisions from, say, China to New Guinea or from Okinawa to the Gilberts should its foes attempt a serious breach of its new empire. But of course that depended upon whether Imperial General Headquarters was willing to allocate substantial army divisions to be a mobile central reserve or whether it would merely trickle brigades to the Pacific on a piecemeal basis. And regardless of troop numbers, there was also the critical factor of airpower, since both sides were still scrambling to appreciate how significant the aerial factor was, still trying to get further fighter and bomber squadrons into the Pacific. If the Japanese commanders at the peripheries of the so-called absolute defense line lost control of the air, then all their ground forces and naval flotillas, large and small, would soon be powerless.

Things would only be worse, moreover, should Japan's enemies attack along more than one axis, for that could either leave individual garrisons alone to be overwhelmed by larger assailing forces or run the risk of shuttling reinforcements from one threatened point to another and fall between stools in doing so. By contrast, provided they received additional strength, the United States and its allies, Australia to the south and the British-Indian Empire to the west, were placed in a better position for future comebacks, ironically because of the very extent of the Japanese area of conquest. On the map, the size of Japan's new realms looked daunting, for who could imagine anyone being able to crack a zone of conquest so large and whole as this? But then, the Nazi empire also still looked enormous at the beginning of 1943, until the Allied advances, from the Ukraine to Algeria, exposed its many weaknesses. So was it here. By pushing outward in so many directions, into China, Burma, the Dutch East Indies, the Southwest Pacific, the central Pacific, and Alaska, and then garrisoning that gigantic perimeter so relatively thinly, Tokyo made itself a hostage to fortune.

Indeed, the Allies could in theory launch counteroffensives from a range of at least four different takeoff points, as illustrated in map 12. But those four alternative routes were not equally promising, as Liddell Hart and other strategic commentators pointed out a long time ago.[46] While the distance between Chinese (nationalist-held) bases and Japan was theoretically the shortest, the supply lines from the United States *to* such places was impossibly long, going as they must across the Pacific, into British airbases in India, and then over the Himalayan hump. And any drive by British forces from the India/Burma direction, while it might have coincided with Churchillian hopes of also reconquering Malaya, Hong Kong, and the rest of the Empire en route to defeating Japan, was the furthest way off and belied the British lack of resources. The trans-Pacific routes were altogether more plausible, and inevitable, and not just because they were shorter: Japan had shocked and humiliated America by its aggressions against Pearl Harbor, and those blows were going to be returned, and Tokyo vanquished, by a gigantic strategy of reconquest, by pouring men, ships, and aircraft from America's productive base, from the military-industrial heartland and the colossal shipyards, and from

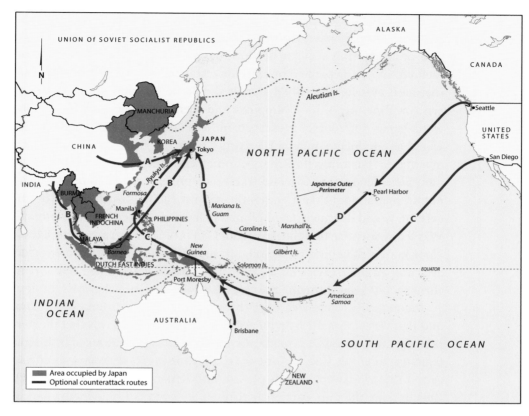

**MAP 12.** The four options for Allied counterattack against Tokyo, after 1943.

the great West Coast naval and air bases into the Pacific realms. Furthermore, even if the Solomons or the Ellice Islands looked an awfully long way from the United States, they were also a great distance from Japan itself, and thus this campaign would very much turn on which side could best master the tyranny of distance. With the Japanese already checked and then knocked back a bit in the second half of 1942, the struggle for command of the Pacific would be an extended one, with victory going to the masters of logistics, supply chains, and inherently greater productivity.

America's "return road to Tokyo," as some wartime commentators like to call it, did not mean driving *straight westward* across the central Pacific Ocean, as map 13 might suggest. There really was no large piece of land, no east of England, no North Africa, on which to base some vast American comeback force, as was being planned for the European-Mediterranean theaters; and that might be why some US military leaders, like Eisenhower (anticipating direction of sixty army divisions) and Spaatz (dreaming of controlling four thousand heavy bombers), were always more interested in the German war—after all, there didn't seem to be much place for large-scale Sherman tank operations on coral islands. So it was a fair point also for MacArthur's planners, citing the advantages of their large Australian supply bases, to warn against the untried and precarious option of attempting a major drive across a region possessing such small toeholds of land separated by extreme distances and to argue instead that the main axis for the Allied assault should be via New Guinea's northern coastline on to the Philippines and then (possibly via Formosa) toward Japan. Of course, it escaped no one's attention that such a drive would be conducted under a US Army Command region with the imperious MacArthur himself in charge, something that Admiral King and the navy were determined to avoid. Their own preference had to be for trying out an operational thrust across the central Pacific, which, however uncertain, would definitely favor Nimitz's Hawaiian-based naval command. Was it any surprise that the American Chiefs of Staff and an interested yet aloof Roosevelt behind them voted to support *both* lines of advance, thus avoiding an interservice clash, with the additional argument that a twin thrust could keep throwing the Japanese defenders off balance?

Theoretically, there was a *fifth* return route by Allied forces to Tokyo, and that was across the North Pacific. The only problem was that the perpetually atrocious storms made possession of the island bases of little strategic use to either side. In June 1942, a Japanese expeditionary force had seized the windswept islands of Attu and Kiska in the Aleutians, which thus became the only part of the United States to fall into enemy hands. But the occupation had no significance, for Japan advanced no further eastward, nor was the United States in any great rush to drive the invaders out. The isolated Japanese garrisons there simply became one of many that its navy had to supply across the wide Pacific. By the following March, the growing American fleet strength allowed an interception by a force of cruisers and destroyers, in turn provoking the only naval action in these waters of the entire war. Initially, the gunfire of a more powerful Japanese flotilla (two heavy and two light cruisers) brought the cruiser USS *Salt Lake City* to a standstill, but a vigorous destroyer defense, with torpedoes and smoke screens, caused an unusually timid Japanese admiral Boshiro Hosogaya to pull away and the supply operation itself to be abandoned.

Apart from this single action, given the grand name of the Battle of the Komandorski Islands,[47] nothing else happened until two months later, when a substantial US amphibious force of twelve thousand men was landed on Attu under the cover of a naval force that included three battleship veterans of Pearl Harbor, the USSs *Pennsylvania*, *Idaho*, and *Nevada*, plus six cruisers and nineteen destroyers. The fighting on land was ferocious and lasted several weeks before the defenders were eliminated, a story that would be replayed time and again as the Pacific War unfolded; the tale involved an isolated Japanese Army garrison, heavy bombardments by the offshore squadrons, large-scale amphibious assaults, and a fanatical re-

**PAINTING 38.** USS *Salt Lake City* **at the Battle of the Komandorski Islands, 1943.** Shown here is the fast American heavy cruiser in action against the cautious Japanese flotilla in this sole naval action in the northern Pacific. Although severely damaged, she survived and went on to fight in more naval actions than did any other US warship in the Pacific campaign.

sistance that so often ended in a suicide charge. Attu was completely retaken by the end of May. Shortly afterward Imperial General Headquarters prudently decided to withdraw its Kiska garrison, but storms and mist so obscured the move that the later American invasion force had no idea it had taken place. In late July and early August its battleships, cruisers, and destroyers bombarded beach installations and the XI Army Air Force strafed and bombed all over the place. On August 15, a huge invasion force (initially thirty-five thousand troops) landed unopposed and then went in search of their enemy. Even the patriotic US official historian Morison concedes that the whole thing was "mildly ridiculous," and it is clear, at least in hindsight, that the whole American investment in the Aleutian campaign—about a hundred thousand men were employed overall—could have been far better directed to assisting MacArthur's Southwest Pacific Command in its much tougher advances of this time.[48]

Ridiculous or not, the disproportionate forces deployed in the Aleutians campaign were a harbinger of what was to come. As 1943 unfolded, American troops, aircraft, and warships began to stream into the Pacific theater, and the narrow balance of military advantage that obtained at Midway and Guadalcanal became a thing of the past. Not all of these re-inforcements arrived at the same pace, however, and thus it was only in the second half of the year that Nimitz felt he had enough new carriers to make significant moves on the Gilbert Islands and beyond. This would be the first time in history that large-scale amphibious operations would be undertaken against an enemy who possessed strong air squadrons in a network of island bases *without* the support of one's own land-based aircraft. A couple of well-placed bombs from Japanese aircraft operating from Truk or Rabaul could easily cause great damage to US warships, and if several carriers were knocked out, it was easy to imagine an operational reversal to Nimitz's task forces and to the strategy of an independent drive across the central Pacific. Not all American admirals, it might be noted, liked this growing emphasis on the carrier arm, and all through 1943 var-ious subgroups quarreled among themselves over how far the fleet should become carrier-centric, with senior aviator officers in charge of the major fleet divisions and operations and with battleships (even the most modern ones) pushed into supporting and bombardment roles.[49]

Although the outcome of that debate would not be clear until early 1944, after the spectacle of the Marianas Turkey Shoot itself, the carrier lobby had two great elements in its favor. The first was the coming of so many new weapons systems into the American fleet at this time; the sec-ond was the continued caution of the Japanese in the Pacific theater in those very same months. If any aspect of the US war campaigning ben-efited from the explosion in its industrial productivity (see chapter 8), it was here. The mid-1943 combination of new weapons systems and tech-nologies for hard-hitting, long-range carrier warfare constituted a wa-tershed in naval history that was even greater, perhaps, than the coming of HMS *Dreadnought*. Clark Reynolds, the chronicler of the fast-carrier story, sums it up enthusiastically: "The fast carrier task force, then, would be initiating several new pieces of equipment in battle: the *Essex*-class heavy carrier, the *Independence*-class light carrier, the F6F Hellcat fighter, multi-channeled VHF radios, and the PPI and DRT radars. Supporting these ships would be the proximity-fused 5-inch/38cm shell, an arsenal of 40mm and 20mm anti-aircraft guns, and a host of new and modern-ized older battleships, cruisers, and destroyers."[50] All that was needed to add to this were the new fast oilers and supply ships of the fleet train, and then these entire flotillas of US aircraft carriers would scarcely have a geographical limit to their striking range. That, at least, was the vision of the aviator admirals as they stood on the brink of a forward strategy that many of their more traditional colleagues still doubted.

Yet this sudden freedom to attack far and wide across the central Pacific was also made possible by their enemy's caution. In theory, there was no reason why the IJN could not have carried out a whole series of aggressive "spoiler" strikes in 1943 even if Tokyo's overall decision was for the strategic defensive until the next year. It certainly had sufficient carrier forces of its own (the big carriers *Shokaku* and *Zuikaku,* and the *Zuiho*) for aggressive operations out of Truk, moves that could be supported by bomber squadrons based on Rabaul plus a network of island airstrips. But as the year unfolded, the tendency for caution among the IJN seemed to build up, clearly reinforced by a sense of loss at Admiral Isoroku Yamamoto's death in April, the drain on naval-aviator losses from the Southwest Pacific fighting, and the tendency to emphasize Rabaul's *defense* as key to their strategy, especially as Admiral William Halsey's forces moved closer to envelop it from the south. Occasionally, Tokyo would order its Combined Fleet of battleships and carriers toward the central Pacific in the hope of catching the Americans, but all these turned out to be uneventful sweeps.

As Japan stood almost still, Nimitz's carriers became bolder, all the time gaining the experience of group handling. In late August, the minor Marcus Island (much closer to Japan than to Hawaii) had its air base and weather station pounded by squadrons from the carriers *Yorktown, Essex,* and *Independence* with minimal resistance. In early September an amphibious American force covered by two carriers seized the small airstrip on Baker Island. Later in the same month the carriers *Lexington, Princeton,* and *Belleau Wood* launched heavy aerial attacks upon Tarawa. Small in scale, each of these operations added new tactical features that would contribute to the larger successful advance: a forward-positioned submarine (to pick up downed US airmen) was now provided for each strike; refueling the fleet at sea before and after a day's strike was practiced and perfected; the complications of radar control and radio communications with so many aircraft in the sky at the same time were wrestled with; and these task groups really did maneuver as a single force, with the carriers in the center surrounded by a protective screen of battleships and cruisers and then by a circle of destroyers.[51]

When the American assault upon the Gilbert Islands finally came, then, between November 2 and 5, it should have been a relatively easy, even if major, step forward by the attackers, for Tokyo had decided to leave the garrison of 4,800 men there to fight to the last man, and Nimitz's assemblage of covering forces was by this stage overwhelming. Instead, Operation Galvanic turned out to be remarkable for its two wildly different features. The first was indeed the absolute supremacy at sea and in the air of the giant naval screening force, TF 58, as it steamed around the islands, blocking any possible Japanese interference from the west and covering the actual bombardment and amphibious forces themselves. But the second was the shocking difficulty of the assault and thus the losses encountered by the US Marines as they attempted their landing across the coral reefs of Betio at Tarawa Atoll. The latter setback was no threat to the eventual outcome of the advance, and as an operational stroke the American seizure of the Gilbert Islands was a vindication of the strategy of a direct central Pacific drive toward Japan. Yet the casualties upset the American High Command as well as the public back home.

The reasons for the heavy losses suffered by the Second US Marine Corps Division on the reefs of Tarawa were overwhelmingly tactical. Preinvasion intelligence had failed to take into account the buildup of the Japanese land fortifications (following, ironically, the air strikes of September), with a network of dug-in positions that proved impervious to bombing attacks and even to the very heavy naval bombardment on the days before the landings. The assault took place on a neap tide, which meant that the waters over the coral reefs were even shallower than normal—a mere three to four feet in depth—so that the Higgins landing craft could not bring their men and equipment across them, whereas most of the very small number of amphibious troop carriers that could be deployed were soon hit and disabled by Japanese defensive fire. Pinned down a thousand yards from shore, the marines were forced to crawl their way in, suffering the highest-ever casualties *proportionately* (that is, proportionate to the short time of the action and to the area of the fighting) in the Corps's long history. Americans back home were shocked at the newsreels of dozens of dead bodies strewn across coral reefs, and from his headquarters MacArthur declared it "a tragic and unnecessary massacre," making plain again that he felt the strategy behind this operation to be a waste.

Of course it was not. The marines' casualties were 1,000 dead and over 2,000 wounded (the losses at Anzio, by contrast, were 43,000 overall), and Betio was taken within three days, although US efforts were very much helped by the Japanese commander's decision to order his remaining troops to stage suicidal Banzai charges against the superior American firepower; only 17 of those 4,800 defenders surrendered. And the ragged performance of the inexperienced US Army division (11,000 men) in conquering the smaller nearby island of Makin a few days later was also a cause for concern at Pacific Command headquarters and in Washington. Yet it very soon became clear why the seizure of the islands had been harder than expected and that important lessons could be drawn for the *next* amphibious landings. When those came, it was certain, there would be even more preparations, better intelligence, much more preinvasion bombardment, a far bigger landing force, and so on. Operation Galvanic was a salutary lesson, not unlike the Dieppe Raid in some ways.[52]

The seizure of the Gilberts was the first very-large-scale *naval* operation conducted by the Pacific Fleet since the Battle of Midway, and the sheer size of the covering force showed that a cautious Nimitz and his staff were determined to take no chances of a Japanese intervention. Thus the landing force for Tarawa was accompanied by three battleships, three heavy cruisers, five escort carriers (for close-in air attacks), and twenty-one destroyers, and that for tiny Makin by four battleships, four heavy cruisers, four escort carriers, and thirteen destroyers. But the most impressive show of force lay further afield, in TF 58 itself, with no less than *thirteen* fleet and light fleet carriers, subdivided into four virtually independent groups.[53] The latter was a brilliant idea operationally, for it meant one of those flotillas could be sent westward to screen against any movement from Truk, another deployed in the direction of Rabaul, and so on, yet all four could be summoned back under Admiral Raymond Spruance's tighter control should a full-scale battle with the Japanese Combined Fleet appear likely.

Had the Japanese battleships moved forward to contest this Gilberts operation, of course, then a great naval encounter between the two foes might have taken place eleven months prior to Leyte Gulf. Yet it was not to be, and the chief reason for the IJN's decision to decline battle here was, significantly, the blow that a far smaller group of American carriers, temporarily placed under Halsey's South Pacific Command, had just struck against the enemy's aerial and naval force at Rabaul on November 5. The damage to so many of Japan's heavy cruisers and other warships there was bad enough, but even worse was the decimation of so many of the experienced and irreplaceable carrier aircrews by the new Hellcat squadrons. Without carrier air cover, the imposing Japanese battle fleet that was available dared not move forward. Thus, a victory occurring in one US Command area had proved beneficial to the invading forces operating in another. By moving along two lines of advance, the Americans kept confusing their foes. Finally, the fact that the Gilberts operation had been undertaken without needing land-based aerial support meant that the navy's thrust through the central Pacific atolls had been proved doable and would continue. The Marshall Islands, the Carolines, and even the Marianas beckoned next, and if MacArthur's Southwest Pacific Command could not keep pace with such advances then it would clearly lose its claims for strategic prominence.

US naval operations around the Gilbert Islands did not go completely unscathed. The Japanese submarine *I-175*, in a bold act, snuck close enough to the warships operating off Makin on November 23 to torpedo the escort carrier USS *Liscome Bay*, which blew up instantly. Only three days earlier, an attack by a group of Japanese torpedo-bombers had managed to inflict heavy damage on the light carrier USS *Independence* operating off Tarawa; it survived but was knocked out of action for over seven months. This latter blow provoked the extreme carrier air advocates to protest against their vessels being tied to defensive operations, and thus the internal debate over command and control of these new task forces rumbled on as the year ended, with various of Nimitz's admirals being promoted and others moved around in the process.[54] The Japanese High Command had of course no idea of such internal rows; all it saw, or foresaw, was a likely American advance upon the Carolines or Marshalls once 1944 arrived.

The story further south was a different one. There were numerous reasons why the American advances went slowly through the areas of the Southwest Pacific (MacArthur's) and South Pacific (Halsey's) Commands during 1943. The geography of it was complicated throughout; supplies of the right weaponry, including naval and amphibious forces, were initially insufficient; and there were arrays of Japanese garrisons and bases in the immediate way and also further back. MacArthur's American and Australian army divisions still had the long slog along the eastern shores and mountains of New Guinea and were tied to this step-by-step coastal approach, rather like the British Army up the Italian Peninsula. Offshore, the island-based push by South Pacific Command found itself confronting one Japanese-held island after another as it moved northward after the Guadalcanal campaign—there were determined garrisons at Santa Isabel, Vella Lavella, Kolombangara, Empress Augusta Island, New Britain, and many smaller islands. While this whole movement was grandiosely called Operation Cartwheel, suggesting some swift cartwheeling strike over the main Japanese base of Rabaul, the official US naval volume here lists dozens of landings, sea battles, and air strikes that were part of this advance.[55] It was sometimes difficult to recall that the whole purpose of this twin drive, with its many fast-and-furious fights, was simply to breach the Bismarck's barrier so as to be able to advance into the open Pacific and across to the Philippines.

While the American naval buildup to the southwest Pacific area grew only slowly in early 1943, the same was not true of US airpower, for Hap Arnold, head of the USAAF back in Washington, showed himself willing to funnel an ever-increasing number of fighter, medium bomber (B-25), and even heavy bomber (B-17) squadrons to the Fifth Army Air Force (MacArthur's aerial branch, under Lieutenant General George C. Kenney). There was no real strategic bombing campaign in the Pacific War at this time, of course, not until the attacks on Japan's cities from the newly established Mariana bases after late 1944. But each side's air forces, reinforced by fresh squadrons from the homeland, were used aggressively to attack enemy warships and disrupt convoys at sea, to raid land installations and amphibious landing sites, and to tussle for air supremacy against the other side's fighters. For the first year of the war the advantage had clearly lain with the Japanese, but by 1943, at least after the addition of the long-range Lightning, Thunderbolt, and Hellcat squadrons to the US armory, the balance of advantage in the air war changed rapidly. More than that, the American side had increasingly better intelligence as to their enemy's intentions, partly because of their knowledge of the Japanese military codes but also because of their huge commitment to long-range aerial reconnaissance (a lesson from the disaster of Pearl Harbor) and because of the growing deployment of radar to anticipate and counter immediate attacks in the air and at sea. The shift in the Pacific War balances was not to be counted in carriers alone.

One dramatic example of the US Air Force's use of superior intelligence in these months was shown in the devastation of a critical Japanese troop convoy in the Battle of the Bismarck Sea in early March 1943. The aerial attacks resulted in the virtual slaughter in full daylight of an entire fleet of eight troop-carrying transports plus half (four) of the escorting destroyers that were headed from Rabaul to reinforce the Japanese position in Papua. Low-level machine gunning and skip bombing from Marauders, higher-level bombing by B-17s, rocket attacks from Australian Beaufighters, and a scattering of the Zero escorts by the new P-38 Lightnings led to a devastation of the convoy that was finished off by MTB attacks that night and further bombing the next day. An impressive 335 Allied aircraft had been committed to this fight, and only 5 were shot down, whereas Japan had lost 8 ships, over 3,000 men and perhaps 30 planes. No further large-scale reinforcement of New Guinea by sea would ever be attempted. It had been less than a year since the Japanese Naval Air Service, like the Luftwaffe's Luftflotte X, had dominated the air.

Worse was to come for Tokyo. In late March, Imperial Japanese Headquarters had sent Admiral Yamamoto himself, together with a large-scale reinforcement of navy bombers and fighters, to regain the initiative across the Bismarck Sea and the Solomons. Here both sides lost ships and aircraft in repeated tussles, but the biggest victory was achieved on April 18 by long-range American fighters (P-38s), which, alerted by code breakers,[56] were able to ambush Yamamoto's aircraft as it was coming in to land at Buin, New Georgia. No one survived the crash. No other Japanese admiral matched him for intelligence, insight, and quality of mind, so it was an enormous blow.[57] Perhaps not surprisingly, a couple of subdued months followed these transformative shootouts in the southwest Pacific theater. In that time, the American-Australian ground forces were growing exponentially, while by July, MacArthur's air forces were about 1,000 planes strong and Halsey's contained a very sizable 1,800 aircraft.

If the Southwest Pacific Command became used to displaying its growing *land-based* airpower in this time, it was because that was the only type of airpower it possessed. During the first half of 1943 there were, actually, no American carriers in the Pacific other than Halsey's veteran USS *Sara-*

*toga,* operating near Guadalcanal. Nimitz himself still had *no* carriers in Pearl Harbor. There were, remarkably, more Royal Navy aircraft carriers at Gibraltar at this time than US boats in the entire Pacific. This explains the remarkable circumstance in which, for a few months (between May and July 1943), the new British fast carrier HMS *Victorious* joined the USS *Saratoga* to operate under Halsey's command, patrolling all July off New Georgia as part of Cartwheel and earlier to screen MacArthur's forces' "jumps" along the New Guinea coast from possible interruption from the four remaining Japanese carriers. The interlude was a brief and complex operation—the Fleet Air Arm pilots left their own planes behind on the West Coast and flew US aircraft, and the *Victorious* operated only fighter patrols during their joint ventures against the Japanese—but this experiment closed a definite carrier gap for a brief while, no setbacks occurred, and the amphibious landings received their due protection. By August the US Navy's shortage in carriers was over, Pearl Harbor was filling with many new boats, and HMS *Victorious* was headed home again. It was another testament to the ubiquity of the long-range carrier, for the warship's previous actions had been in Operation Torch, and the following one would be in strikes against the *Tirpitz.*[58]

By September 30, 1943, Imperial General Headquarters had once again redefined its absolute defense perimeter in the Pacific. Since Tokyo still had no proper realization of the giant size of the American forces now assembling against it and its military leaders were still focused on the Asian mainland, there remained a full thirty-four Japanese Army divisions in China and another cluster in Manchuria at this time, compared to only five (with one on its way) in the entire Southwest/South Pacific. Moreover, even those units on the outer side of the defense line, that is, in the Solomons and Rabaul area, were optimistically supposed to fight on for at least another six months. To this end, in October 1943, the Japanese again sought to stabilize the line—indeed, to counterattack by sending another large force of heavy cruisers and destroyers plus several hundred more navy aircraft to Rabaul. Instead of realizing its purpose, though, the move provoked a dramatic double counterstrike. First, Halsey achieved a hugely damaging action against Rabaul on November 5 with all his carrier aircraft while having American land-based fighters provide cover for his ships. And this strike was followed by another on the 11th, when a three-carrier attack from Nimitz's Central Pacific Command came south briefly to inflict another blow.

The attack by Halsey's carriers on Rabaul demonstrated a really significant increase in the power of mass, long-range aerial strikes from the sea. While it did not sink any enemy capital ships as, say, at Pearl Harbor and Taranto, it pretty much destroyed Japan's naval and aircraft assets here and wrecked considerable parts of this major base. There was, after all, something dramatic about that November 5 early-morning appearance of massed dive-bombers and torpedo-bombers swarming in from over the horizon while the Hellcats saw off so many Zero fighters, just as there was something prophetic about Rear Admiral Montgomery's *Essex*-group being switched from the central Pacific to carry out the crippling November 11 attacks, then racing back to participate in the Gilbert Islands operation only a few days later. There was no equivalent to this type of power projection anywhere else in the war. And more than just clobbering a major Japanese *base*, these particular attacks directly hurt major parts of the IJN itself, crushing so many of the navy's renowned fleet of heavy cruisers and reducing such a major part of that service's misused carrier aircrews that the *Shokaku, Zuikaku,* and *Zuiho* lost all their offensive power during this critical turning point in the conflict. The purportedly ominous Combined Fleet thus became, as the historian Clark Reynolds noted, a force of battleships without their accompanying cruisers and of carriers without their aircraft.[59]

Another sign of the steady assertion of American military supremacy in these waters was the growing exploitation of ship radar, a consequence of the novel miniaturization of the Allies' radar systems that allowed for their installation on smaller fighting vessels and aircraft. Possession of radar equipment on larger British and American warships had already allowed Cunningham's battleships to smash the unsuspecting Italian cruisers at Cape Matapan, the *Norfolk* and *Suffolk* to track the *Bismarck,* and the USS *Washington* to creep up on and then devastate the battleship *Kirishima* in the Second Naval Battle of Guadalcanal. By this stage in the war, though, the Allied advantage had become much more ubiquitous, on the one hand giving those Royal Navy escorts the instruments to detect and sink four U-boats in a single night when escorting Convoy ONS-5 in the North Atlantic but on the other hand allowing Captain Moosbrugger's flotilla, a mere three months later, to crush Japanese destroyers eight thousand miles away in the Pacific. Naval fighting at night, due to this unique Allied technology, was becoming a one-sided affair.

This was witnessed again when American cruisers and destroyers intercepted a Japanese force trying to disrupt an amphibious landing at Empress Augusta Bay on November 2, 1943, and sank a cruiser and destroyer in the process, and yet again on November 23 at the midnight Battle of Cape St. George, when Captain Arleigh Burke's flotilla mauled a raid by the Tokyo Express for the last time in this campaign, sinking another three enemy destroyers with torpedoes and gunfire. When retaliatory Japanese air attacks were launched the day after these night actions, they also were picked up by Allied radar (and other intercepts) and suffered heavy damage—seventeen Japanese planes were shot down during a November 3 bombing attack on retiring US destroyers, with no major

damage to the latter.[60] Tokyo may have lost no further capital ships in its lengthy campaigns in the Southwest/South Pacific theaters during 1943, but the reduction in the numbers of its cruisers, destroyers, and aircraft was enormous. And time and again, the Americans had known that the Japanese were coming. Japan was now fighting blind.

This massive shift of advantage toward Allied sea power and against the Axis that took place as the year 1943 unfolded was *not* shared by the American Submarine Service. This was of course a huge disappointment to US submariners and their admirals, because much had been expected

**PAINTING 39.**
**USS *Saratoga* and HMS *Victorious*, Nouméa, May 1943.** In an amazing and rarely known act of cooperation, the new British carrier (given the code name USS *Robin*) came to reinforce Admiral William Halsey's flagship in the Southwest Pacific during mid-1943. The *Victorious* operated the fighter squadrons, the *Saratoga* the heavier bombers.

of them. The insular Japanese economy was as dependent on imported raw materials and foodstuffs as Britain itself (and it had a far less organized convoy-protection system), and the lengthy routes between Japan's main naval harbors abroad, from Manila to Singapore to Truk, also offered prime opportunities for any aggressive US submarine captain. Yet the Pacific distances were vast, early intelligence about Japanese shipping movements was poor, the enemy's fast-moving battle fleets were difficult and well-protected targets, most of the 1941 US boats were rather antiquated, and above all, American submarines were equipped with a seriously faulty weapon of attack—their very own magnetic torpedo. The sensitive detectors of the latter simply blew up prematurely, to the fury, naturally enough, of the submariners. Yet even when that flaw had been corrected by a return to the older-fashioned contact torpedoes, so many of the latter didn't work either because of their weak, fragile contact tips. The thud of a torpedo hitting the side of a Japanese warship or merchant vessel yet failing to explode was a common occurrence throughout 1942 and much of 1943.

The story was a miserable one, compounded by a failure in the leadership of the US Submarine Service to make corrections, and it took the most vehement protests from senior, experienced submariners about their dud warheads to get the naval authorities at Pearl Harbor to do proper testing and at last rectify the problem, but that was not until almost two years into the war. By that stage, the American submarines were far larger, with a much longer range; they were faster and much roomier inside and carried a greater arsenal (and even radar). Yet without effective torpedoes the submarines' "punch" didn't work. Clearly, a better-equipped and better-directed US sub force in Pacific waters might have made a far greater impact, and much earlier, in hitting enemy naval traffic operating out of Truk and Rabaul or in crippling the oil traffic from Palembang. Even in January 1944, the Japanese still had over 300,000 more in tanker tonnage than they possessed at the beginning of the war.[61]

Ironically, the Japanese story was far worse, because its own very considerable force of modern submarines was deployed in the most mistaken way throughout the war, defying all strategic sense. After all, if Japan was to maintain its advantage following its early success it had *to defeat and deny any US comeback across the Pacific.* This meant cutting that huge flow of the enemy's traffic to Australia and, even more, to Hawaii; in other words, the IJN's submarine force had to do in the Pacific what Doenitz's wolf packs were doing, so dangerously, in the Battle of the Atlantic. Yet, as mentioned earlier, commerce warfare was never a part of Japanese submarine doctrine, and the force was directed primarily against American warships on the high seas and thus against fast, difficult, elusive targets. The occasional big successes (sinking the carrier *Wasp* in September 1942, for example, or that very late attack on the Makin amphibious landings that sunk the USS *Liscome Bay*) disguised the harsh fact of Tokyo's generally wasteful use of its submarine arm, a waste made even worse by turning the larger boats into supply vessels for isolated Japanese garrisons. Of course, even a well-orchestrated Japanese submarine campaign might not ultimately have stemmed the great surge of US military power across the Pacific after 1943, yet it could have done far more than it did.[62]

As the year gave way to 1944 in the Pacific theater, therefore, both of the main advances were moving on. With the Gilbert Islands operation complete, many of Spruance's TF 38 units were taking a short recuperation, while others were still ranging and striking against smaller Japanese targets in Micronesia. Further south, the ring really had closed around Rabaul, which suffered almost daily bombing raids from land-based American squadrons; by February 1944 Japan was to recognize this reality by pulling its remaining aircraft and ships back to Truk in preparation for the next thrust against the Empire's perimeter. And it was also a measure, symbolically, that Halsey's South Pacific Command was itself dissolved at that time and he himself brought back to Hawaii in preparation for the next westward strikes. Before very long, those Melanesian outcrops—Guadalcanal, Tulagi Beach, and Empress Augusta Bay—would fall quiet again, just as quiet as the sands of El Alamein and the limestone outcrops of the Kasserine Pass. All the fighting, with its soldiers, warships, and aircraft, had gone to the north.

The circumstances of the great war at sea were, then, very different by December 1943 than they had been at the year's beginning. Viewed thus far, the overall unfolding of this lengthy struggle in the larger Atlantic (including the Arctic and Mediterranean) and across the Pacific Ocean was taking the form of a gigantic human ebb and flow: the first wave, that outward surge of the various German-Italian-Japanese forces to challenge the Allied command of the sea, was only effectively stopped after four years of fighting in the West and almost two years of battle in the war against Japan. Then the tides did indeed turn. By the end of 1943, Fascist Italy was no more, and almost all of the waters of the Mediterranean were under the control of Allied air forces and the Royal Navy. The main German U-boat campaign in the Atlantic had been crushed. The Indian Ocean no longer saw even smaller Japanese warships in it. And in the Pacific, Tokyo's strategic perimeter rim was buckling under two giant American counteroffensives that were now accelerating in speed and range.

Yet the tides of the war had turned not merely at the surface level of fierce U-boat-destroyer battles off Newfoundland, amphibious landings on the Sicilian shores, and bitterly contested aerial battles over Rabaul. They had also turned, in a profounder historical way, at the level of mass mobilization for war, as the global balances themselves underwent great alteration. Behind the Allied advances in all the major campaign areas described in this chapter, another set of advances was under way in the realms of weapons production and the creation of newer and more-powerful instruments of war, which in turn led to vast increases in Allied ships, planes, guns, and tanks that, with far larger numbers of sailors, airmen, and soldiers to man them, were now committed to the struggle. These shifts in the productive balances were not just changing the face of World War II, as the next chapter will seek to show, but were going to be large enough to alter the strategic landscape of the twentieth century itself.

**PAINTING 40.** *Essex-*class carrier USS *Intrepid.* Claiming the longest career of any modern US carrier, the *Intrepid*—launched six days before Pearl Harbor!—fought throughout the Pacific War and survived repeated damage from kamikaze attacks. Planes from the *Intrepid* helped crush the giant battleship *Musashi* at Leyte Gulf. A veteran of the Vietnam War also, the carrier is now a museum ship in New York Harbor.

# EIGHT

## The Shift in Global Power Balances

*1943–44*

O n the early morning of June 1, 1943, to the cheers of the dockside observers, the new American fleet carrier USS *Essex* steamed slowly into the great naval base of Pearl Harbor. The warship had been so named after a historic, battle-scarred frigate of the War of 1812 and was now the first of a brand-new class of fast carriers—hence, the "*Essex* class"—authorized under the congressional expansion schemes of 1939–43. The modern vessel would also have a combat-rich experience and occupy an equally prominent place in US naval history.

It is worth repeating that, when the *Essex* joined Chester W. Nimitz's Central Pacific Command, there was only *one* American carrier operating on active duty in the entire ocean—the USS *Saratoga*—out of the six large fleet carriers with which the US Navy had begun the war. The *Lexington* had been lost in the Coral Sea, the *Yorktown* at Midway, the *Hornet* in the battles off Santa Cruz Island, and the *Wasp* to a Japanese submarine.[1] The many actions the *Saratoga* had been carrying out under Admiral William Halsey's Southwest Pacific Fleet in early 1943 were historically more interesting because, as noted above (chapter 7), some of them were carried out in conjunction with the new British fast carrier HMS *Victorious,* loaned by the Admiralty to help make up for the desperate American shortage in these vessels. Ironically, then, although not using them aggressively, the Japanese actually had more carriers in the Pacific in the first half of 1943, even after the Midway losses. By the time the *Victorious* returned to the Home Fleet in late 1943, however, the American navy's carrier shortage in the Pacific theater was over. The USS *Essex*'s arrival at Pearl Harbor was simply the harbinger of what was to come—the creation of the largest aircraft carrier force in history, and thereby of a new order of sea power that completely eclipsed the four-hundred-year era of the all-big-gun warship.

The *Essex*-class ships were impressive vessels indeed, a testimony both to American design and productivity.[2] They were the first carriers to be designed unencumbered by the tonnage constraints of the naval limitations treaties or, for that matter, by tight fiscal limits, and the American planners took full advantage of such freedoms. Two features especially stood out. They were extremely speedy vessels, boasting a high speed of around 33 knots, with powerful turbine engines that could sustain that pace for long distances; they could move a very long way toward or away from the enemy in any 24-hour period. What's more, this capacity hinted that such fast-carrier forces really shouldn't be held back by operations with slower battlewagons. Considerably longer and broader than the previous (*Yorktown*-class) boats, the new vessels boasted a second and most formidable feature, namely, the large number of aircraft that could be contained on board each of them: thirty-six Grumman Hellcat fighters, thirty-six Curtiss Helldiver dive-bombers, and eighteen Grumman Avenger torpedo-bombers. This lethal combination of ninety planes per carrier, jokingly called "the Sunday Punch," was more than any Japanese vessel carried and many more than those aboard the steel-deck-protected British fleet carriers. And since the Pacific Fleet was organizing these warships to operate in a task force cluster of four or six carriers together, it meant that each such group could put into the sky literally hundreds of aircraft for a single strike.

## The New American Navy

The new navy, then, would be able to field *multiple* fast-carrier task forces once the home shipyards had built it enough boats. In that flurry of congressional authorizations before and after the Pearl Harbor attacks, an amazing total of thirty-two large fleet carriers were ordered, although eight of them were later canceled once the outcome of the war had become clear. What is also noteworthy is that the navy invested in numbers of *light fleet carriers* (CVLs) as well, rapidly and very successfully converting eleven of them from *Cleveland*-class cruisers and then sending them also to the Pacific War to operate, each with their 45 planes, alongside the larger carriers. As early as August 1943, for example, the first two CVLs were operating with the *Essex* against Japanese-held atolls.[3] A subgroup of two fleet carriers and one light fleet carrier, possessing in total around 230 aircraft, was an incredibly flexible and powerful subunit to be deployed as Nimitz's fleet moved steadily against successive Japanese positions. As these vessels poured into the Pacific by the beginning of 1944, they must have fulfilled the largest dreams of those rising carrier admirals of the 1920s, like Mitscher, Turner, Halsey, and King himself.

As if this were not enough, both the Central Pacific and Southwest Pacific Commands called for ever-larger numbers of escort carriers to meet a variety of different operational demands. These smaller, more primitive converted carriers were ideal for escorting troopships and other convoys to the various theaters of war, and they were to be particularly useful in giving continuous cover over landing beaches when the larger carriers were called away for operations against the Japanese fleet. By taking what was initially a merchant-ship hull and placing a flat deck on top of it— the Royal Navy had started doing this in 1940—American yards could of course mass-produce a simple escort carrier both swiftly and cheaply, which were ideal features in the desperate circumstances of the two-ocean war of early 1942. But already the creative genius of Henry Kaiser, soon to become famous chiefly for his Liberty ships, had obtained from his friend Roosevelt permission to build an entirely new class, the *Casablanca*-class, from the bottom up. They would draw 11,000 tons, steam at 20 knots, and carry 28 planes, a 5-inch gun, and smaller armaments, and they would operate as a jack-of-all-trades covering every new amphibious operation as well as the escort duties mentioned above. Kaiser's scheme was symptomatic of the entire story of American wartime expansion. One single shipyard, in Vancouver, Washington State, was swiftly converted from building Liberty ships, and its twelve slipways were then used to construct the *Casablanca*-class. In amazing time—in less than two years (November 1942–July 1943) and by recruiting a workforce thirty-six thousand strong—this program was complete, and *fifty* such vessels had been launched from that yard. Overall, the United States launched no less than 122 escort carriers (CVEs) during the war.[4] Most of the earlier, slower ones were, like the hundreds of other smaller escort warships built for wartime needs, scrapped or sold shortly after the fighting was over. Many a wartime shipyard, it is also worth noting, was swiftly closed after 1945. American-style mass-production warfare had built into it a lot of future mass obsolescence as well. There was a grim ruthlessness to all this.

If after Pearl Harbor the aircraft carrier was recognized as the new capital ship and the United States had already planned to have a bigger carrier navy than anybody else, it always had a formidable competitor in Japan. In the years before the war, as noted in chapter 2, three navies—the Japanese, the British, and the American—were in contention to build the most effective carrier fleet, and it is clear that by 1940 the Imperial Japanese Navy (IJN), with its ten carriers, had the edge. It was its service that had invented the operational concept of fast, wide-ranging carrier *groups* whose clustered air squadrons could deliver devastating blows on even the largest enemy ships, as was proved with the sinking of HMSs *Prince of Wales* and *Repulse* in December 1941. In the first seven months of the war, the Japanese Navy's carrier-based squadrons had run rampant, from Pearl Harbor to the Indian Ocean. But after they lost four of their six great fleet carriers at Midway, Japan's overstretched shipyards could never give the navy such power again. Although another fleet carrier was launched in 1943, the IJN now had to scramble to convert the existing hulls of merchant ships, cruisers, battle cruisers, and even the planned giant battleship *Shinano*. But there were never enough of them, none of these conversions could possibly equal an *Essex*-class carrier, and in any case, they would never again possess the trained aircrews of the past, which was largely why they remained on the defensive throughout 1943. Such was the disparity in aircraft carrier output that one scholar has estimated that even if Midway had been a Japanese victory (!), the United States would still have been able to put more carriers into the Pacific by the end of the next year.[5] Whatever the case, it was simply too little, too late for the Japanese carriers,[6] almost all of which were going to be sunk at sea during the two years following. The others lay wrecked in their home ports by July 1945, the result of the American strategic bombing campaign.

The story of the third large aircraft carrier fleet, the Royal Navy's, was a happier one, even though that service lost virtually all of its earlier vessels—*Glorious, Courageous, Furious, Eagle,* and *Ark Royal*—in the tough fighting off Norway and with the Malta convoys. But by the time those last two had been sunk in the Mediterranean, several of the newer, faster *Illustrious*-class carriers were already in service, and the rest followed soon after them—six in all (including the two *Implacable*-class ships). This surge of new warships together with the possession of so many of the other types of large units (battleships and cruisers) and its magnificent logistical array of bases, submarine cables, shipyards, garrisons, and Coastal Command airstrips kept the Royal Navy in a strong position even in the middle of this great war. Indeed, by some assessments it may have had the world's largest number of combatant ships until sometime late in 1943, and it never really ran short of carriers after the fateful absence of one to accompany the *Prince of Wales* and *Repulse*. There was no doubt, though, that given the extraordinary output of US warship-building yards, the American navy would very quickly overtake its old rival in every category of vessel—but especially carriers—by 1944 and be far superior to it by war's end, when the cuts to the Royal Navy were already reflecting Britain's grave economic problems. During the naval struggle itself, however, against two competent and deadly Great Powers on opposite sides of the globe, the Royal Navy's aircraft carriers made a sizable difference by ensuring control of the Atlantic sea-lanes, sustaining Malta, providing the greater part of the covering forces for Mediterranean landings, and by 1945 sending a very sizable British Pacific Fleet to participate in the Okinawa operations and prepare for the Allied invasion of Japan it-self.[7] By war's end, in effect, only two navies had any proper carriers at all, but one of those two was monstrously large.

There was, of course, a second major force of warship type being read-ied to join Nimitz's Central Pacific Fleet as well as the Atlantic Fleet, and that was the squadrons of new 16-inch-gunned battleships. The origi-nal battle-fleet calculations of War Plan Orange, for a supreme surface clash to take place somewhere in the Western Pacific between Japanese and American concentrations of heavy warships, had naturally been set back greatly by the devastation at Pearl Harbor. Yet the *operational con-cept* of a sort of modern Jutland-like contest between the most heavily armed warships afloat was axiomatic to perhaps the majority of Amer-ican and Japanese admirals and was to remain with the latter until the very final year of the war. It certainly stayed strong among some Ameri-can naval leaders, too, and there seemed very good reasons for continuing to have battleships, and lots of them, including in Atlantic waters. There was a deep respect for Germany's two *Bismarck*-class boats—its May 1941 foray into the mid-Atlantic had caused quite some alarm at the time—and right through until 1944 the US Navy shared the British Admiralty's con-cern over a disruption of convoys to Russia by the *Tirpitz,* thus sending its newer battleships like USSs *Washington* and *South Dakota* to deploy with the Home Fleet from time to time. In the early stages of Operation Torch, too, the USS *Massachusetts* had had a memorable shootout with the Vichy French battleship *Jean Bart* as it lay anchored in Oran harbor.[8]

As for having a very large US battlefleet in Pacific waters to counter Ja-pan's powerful squadrons, well, there was no doubt to planners through-out the 1930s that this was the correct naval strategy, and such a way of thinking was actually made more urgent by a sense of vulnerability af-ter the severe losses suffered at Pearl Harbor. Pushing one or two carriers forward aggressively, in the way Halsey liked to do in the early part of the Pacific campaign, seemed to them a highly risky enterprise against a Jap-anese foe that could clearly keep radio silence and strike out of the blue. American carrier and cruiser squadrons would be blown apart if ever they were trapped by Japanese heavy squadrons in some high-seas encounter, and amphibious operations in, say, the Solomons would be hugely vul-nerable if Tokyo ordered their disruption by a battleship squadron. Fi-nally, the more information that American naval intelligence gleaned about Japan's giant *Yamato*-class battleships, the more urgency there was in Washington to beef up the size of their own newer classes.

While the US Navy did indeed build ten new (that is, post–Washington Treaty) battleships, the tortuous story of their early construction, involv-ing so many amendments in defensive armor, main armaments, speed, and thus displacement, contrasts sharply with the much more decisive planning for the fleet carriers. The first two of these battleships—the *North Carolina* and *Washington*—suffered from some of the restrictions that applied to Britain's *King George V*–class battleships, and between 1935 and 1937–38 their intended main armament wavered from 14-inch to 16-inch guns before a decision was made for the bigger caliber (as noted in chapter 2). But neither they nor the next four *South Dakota*–class boats were really "fast" battleships, for that came only with the four slightly later *Iowa*-class vessels (again, with nine 16-inch guns but displacing 51,000 long tons when loaded), whose more powerful turbine engines gave them a top speed of near 33 knots so as to be able to keep up with the carriers. With the construction of these newer battleships, the United States was now clearly outbuilding Japan. As war broke out in the Pacific, though, American planners became extremely nervous at the thought of even these warships' armor being pierced by the 18-inch shells of the *Yamato,* and Congress was hustled into authorizing five giant, 65,000-ton *Montana*-class behemoths.[9] Ironically, just one month after these vessels were ordered, the Battle of Midway (June 1942) occurred and the *Montana*-class construction was immediately postponed. The program was finally scrapped in the summer following, just after the *Essex* had reached Pearl Harbor.[10] The shipyards had more pressing work to do.

While even the all-powerful United States did not need more super-dreadnoughts, then, the existing battleship-building program had already demonstrated the unrivaled capacity of the six largest American shipyards, including the government's own New York Navy Yard and Philadelphia Navy Yard as well as privately owned firms like Bethlehem Shipbuilding and the Newport News works. The admirals' dream of 1919, of a US battle fleet far larger than anyone else's, would be realized, although as it turned out by the time this force arrived there would be no real rival to it: the Japanese Navy was scrambling to convert many of its battleships and battle cruisers to carriers after Midway, the Royal Navy would construct only one more vessel (HMS *Vanguard*) after the *King George V*–class, the Italian fleet was done by 1943, and the *Tirpitz* was the last German heavy ship.

American battleships did see some action, of course, during the lengthy campaigning in the Pacific. The demolition of the Japanese battleship *Kirishima* by the radar-controlled gunnery of the USS *Washington* during the nighttime encounter in the Solomons in November 1942 has already been noted, and Admiral Jesse Oldendorf's battle squadron was to achieve a classic "Crossing the T" maneuver at Leyte Gulf and smash the hapless oncoming Japanese column (see chapter 9). But the greater part of the shooting carried out by the huge guns of American battleships was to be directed *onshore,* in pounding Japanese garrisons in their bunkers and

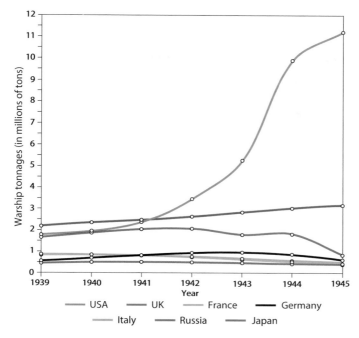

**CHART 5.** Overall warship tonnages of the Powers, 1939–45. French and Italian total tonnages were almost exactly equal throughout the years 1930 to 1943 in consequence of the Washington Naval Treaties. Produced using the dataset in Crisher and Souva, *Power at Sea*.

foxholes in one Pacific island group after another, as a softening up before the actual amphibious landings themselves—an important task in itself, yet one at which, the record repeatedly suggests, the older, repaired Pearl Harbor battlewagons performed rather better.[11] The last firings by US battleships in World War II were a series of bombardments carried out against Japanese shoreline steelworks and coastal cities in July–August 1945, a fine illustration of American naval dominance by then, but not the epic high-seas role that Alfred Thayer Mahan had envisaged for large surface fleets.[12]

In scrapping the last two *Iowa*-class and the five *Montana*-class monsters, then, the US Navy had proved its point—it could now outbuild anyone, even to the point of almost choking on its own productivity. Perhaps the same could be said about the highly ambitious heavy cruiser program as well: when war broke out in Europe, the navy immediately ordered fourteen of the large, well-designed *Baltimore*-class, of 14,500 tons and nine 8-inch guns, and would later even dabble with "super-heavy" cruisers displacing 27,500 tons, but only half of the navy's heavy cruisers saw active service in the Pacific and off Normandy, screening the carriers with their antiaircraft fire and (again) most usefully bombarding enemy beaches. At the time of Hiroshima, no less than fifty American cruisers of all sizes were being built or at least on order; all were canceled.[13]

Whichever category of US warship construction is examined, the reader comes away with a sense of overwhelming, actually crushing industrial might, but perhaps no warship-building scheme was as impressive as that for fleet destroyers and the slightly less powerful destroyer escorts, the two workhorses of the service. Overall, the US Navy listed 554 destroyers' names on its roster for World War II, including no less than 175 of the standard, reliable *Fletcher*-class—just coming up with suitable names for the smaller classes of surface warships and submarines became something of a challenge here.[14] From 1940 onward, congressionally allocated funds were poured into the expansion of existing shipyards or the creation of totally new ones along the east, west, and Gulf shorelines. The Seattle-Tacoma Shipbuilding Corporation, for example, put up a totally new yard (on an initial government grant of $9 million) for destroyer production only, was soon employing 17,000 workers, and delivered 40 ships to the fleet, thus becoming the third-largest source of destroyers. The redoubtable Bath Iron Works in Maine built 83 of these warships at a staggering pace, having reduced construction times from over 300 days to roughly 190 days per vessel. One wartime photo of the yard at its peak shows no less than 14 (!) *Geary*-class destroyers being built at the same time. The giant works was constructing these and various other warship classes so efficiently that a later historian calculated that it was making "a new fleet addition every 17.5 days."[15] This was a simply irresistible force.

It is difficult to know where to include the place of US submarines in this chapter on the 1942–44 surge in American industrial output, because their role in the weakening of Japan has a rather different chronology, as described in chapters 9–10. The submarines' devastation of the Japanese merchant fleet and sinking of many Japanese warships came later in the story simply because the service had to grapple first with the frustrating weaknesses of their Mark 14 torpedoes, a problem not solved until as late as September 1943. Yet the overall *production* story was much the same as that of the surface warships. When war began there were 111 boats in the fleet, many out of date, based chiefly in the Pacific. The naval budgets already foresaw the construction of several hundred more submarines of an increasingly larger size—1,500-plus tons for the *Gato*- and *Balao*-class submarines (the famous and far nimbler German *Mark VII* U-boats were a mere 750 tons). After Pearl Harbor, of course, orders for newer submarines soared, as did their production, the only constraint being the initial capacity of the yards to meet this demand. The famous Electric Boat Company at Groton, Connecticut, took on a major role here; after an initial $13 million grant from the navy, it steadily expanded its launch-

ing berths and built 74 boats, raising output from one a month to two a
month by early 1944. Later in that year, having committed 260 of its submarines to the Pacific theater, the US Navy started to cancel contracts for
all further boats; the production battle was over.[16]

However new and powerful these fleets of warships, their effectiveness
across the extreme distances of the Pacific Ocean would be heavily constrained if they were not frequently refueled, resupplied, and, if necessary,
repaired. Clearly, a chain of prime fleet bases such as the Royal Navy possessed in Atlantic waters, like Bermuda, Plymouth, Gibraltar, Freetown,
and so on, did not exist here. It was therefore deemed necessary by the
US Navy's logistical planners to build an extraordinary array of vessels
for the mobile service force in order to maintain the fleet in operations
and to meet all its needs, except of course for major damage repairs. The
fast-carrier task force itself had an exclusive support group (Sevron 10)
that was yet another testimony to organizational genius; each of the fast
oilers accompanying Task Force 58 during the post-Gilberts operations
contained over 80,000 barrels of fuel oil, 18,000 barrels of aviation gasoline, and 6,800 tons of diesel oil, thereby allowing the navy to conquer the
Pacific Ocean's famous tyranny of distance. The US Pacific Fleet also included tenders, tugs, minesweepers, barges, lighters, ammunition ships,
and hospital ships. Later on, a floating dry dock, pontoon assembly ships,
floating cranes, and even barrack ships were added to this gigantic assemblage and located centrally at Majuro Atoll after the capture of the Marshall Islands.[17]

The US Army and, especially, the Air Force needed something different in the Pacific War, namely, a string of very large military bases on specific islands where one could house and train troops before the next offensive as well as air bases for all manner of aircraft squadrons, fighters,
antisubmarine patrols, and especially the very-long-range bomber forces
that were going to be used in the strategic aerial offensive against Japan's industries and cities. Here again, America's civilian organizational
and industrial strengths were converted into military capacity through
the medium of another remarkable service, the US Navy Construction
Battalions (the so-called Fighting Seabees, or CBs). The brainchild of an
unusually gifted engineer, Admiral Ben Moreell, the Seabees were established in remarkably swift time after Moreell had gained Roosevelt's
support for the idea in December 1941. By the following year tens of thousands of skilled construction workers (qualified in more than sixty skilled
trades) were recruited as naval personnel, given weapons as well as tools,
and sent off to the fight—literally, as the first battalions and their bulldoz-
ers were landed into the middle of the bloody struggle for Guadalcanal.
Seabees were there, clutching carbine and monkey wrench, from Tarawa

to Okinawa (and Anzio and Normandy). Organizationally, this service was superb; by war's end, 325,000 men had been enlisted in the Seabees and had constructed more than $10 billion worth of infrastructure, including 111 major airstrips.[18]

Finally, there was the urgent need for landing craft to get troops onshore and for the larger types of specialized merchant vessel (Landing Craft, Ship; Landing Craft, Tank) that would carry the smaller boats, trucks, tanks, and other items of war across the oceans. In the larger scheme of the Anglo-American strategy of defeating the three Fascist powers, hardly any item in the Allied tool kit could be more important. Germany, Italy, and Japan had triumphed early on by successfully pushing *outward*, to the Atlantic and North Africa, to the borders of India, and down to the Solomons and New Guinea. But when the tides turned,[19] the strategy of the Western Allies was to push their vast new armies across the Atlantic, into the Mediterranean, onto the shores of France, and along a chain of Pacific islands in order to grapple with and defeat the enemies' forces. Since attacking strongly held harbors (Dieppe, Algiers, and Rabaul) was simply too costly, Allied planners had to assume that they would be putting vast numbers of troops onto open coastlines, rock-strewn tidal beaches, mango swamps, and coral reefs. And for this, thousands, if not tens of thousands, of basic, flat-bottomed landing craft would be needed, as would hundreds of the larger transporting ships. In fact, by 1943, with commanders in every operational field from Burma to Sicily screaming for more, it was the supply—or unavailability—of landing craft that began to determine Allied operational priorities along the various lines of advance.[20]

Fortunately, the solution to this problem was close at hand, thanks to yet another example of American industry and craftsmanship being capable of swiftly turning a peacetime mode of transportation into one of the simplest yet most important tools of victory: the flat-bottomed Higgins boat, originally constructed by Andrew Jackson Higgins's small company to provide a tender that would service oil industry structures in the weedy, marshy Louisiana bayous.[21] By modifying the 36-foot-long craft to give it a front ramp through which Marine landing troops could pour and then designing all sorts of variants to it, like landing craft to transport an army jeep or truck, or landing craft equipped with bazookas or flamethrowers for close-in assault, the Allies gave themselves the equipment, a humble Landing Craft, Vehicle, Personnel (LCVP), to place their armies onshore without the usual need to capture ports. Eisenhower and even Churchill sang the praises of the Higgins boats in helping to win the war, and the production record—once the Marine Corps had shown Higgins what was wanted[22]—was truly remarkable. One further great ad-

**TABLE 9.** US Naval Personnel (not Marines), 1939–45 (nearest hundred)

| 1939 | 1940 | 1941 | 1942 | 1943 | 1944 | 1945 |
|------|------|------|------|------|------|------|
| 125,200 | 161,000 | 284,400 | 640,600 | 1,741,800 | 2,981,400 | 3,380,800 |

Data from "Research Starters: US Military by the Numbers," National WWII Museum, New Orleans, accessed February 18, 2020, https://www.nationalww2museum.org/students-teachers/student-resources/research-starters/research-starters-us-military-numbers.

vantage of a Higgins-type boat is that it could be built en masse almost anywhere, but the fact remained that the original yard in New Orleans built more than all the other franchised firms put together. From seventy-five original employees in 1938, the Higgins Yard workforce swelled to over thirty thousand—there was a massive recruitment of unemployed Whites, women, retirees, and Blacks—by 1943 alone. Some 20,000 Higgins LCVPs were launched during the war. It is worth quoting at length from one admiring source here, because it captures perfectly our story of *the links between front-end war fighting and rear-end war production:* "By July 1943, Higgins had shattered every existing boat production record: he turned out more landing craft than all the other shipyards in America combined. In September 1943, when the US Army landed at Salerno and General Douglas MacArthur's forces landed in New Guinea, the navy owned 14,072 vessels. Of those, 12,964, or 92% of the fleet, had been designed by Higgins, and almost 9,000 had been built at the Higgins plant in New Orleans. A year later, when the largest fleet in history invaded Europe at Normandy, the boat that put the soldiers, their tanks, and their equipment on the beaches was the bow-ramp Higgins boat."[23]

Finally, a huge surge in the numbers of naval personnel paralleled everything else here. It simply had to; after all, taking the destroyers' manning needs alone and allowing a crew of around 300 men on each of the 550 destroyers equaled a requirement for over 165,000 sailors. An *Essex*-class carrier sailed with a complement of over 3,000 (including 870 aircrew), while a light fleet carrier like the USS *Princeton* embarked 1,570. To man all of its vessels and their shore establishments (eventually, around 50,000 women were also enlisted in the service), the US Navy relied on voluntary enlistments and then, increasingly, on conscription as it moved from a service of 35,700 officers and 301,000 men in December 1941 to one that would place approximately 390,000 officers and 3,800,000 men in uniform, including the Marines, by the end of the war.[24] This twelve-fold increase in fleet personnel was something that no other navy could match. And, once again, the leap in numbers after 1942 stands out, as shown in table 9.

Connecting the story of what was happening on the Pacific and other

battlefronts to this domestic mobilization of both manpower and industry on the American home front neatly explains to the reader what had
fundamentally changed in the course of just a year. In early June 1943, as
noted in chapter 7, so very little had been taking place, in terms of naval
actions, in the central Pacific area—the USS *Essex* had not even reached
Pearl Harbor. Exactly one year later, on June 9, 1944, a completely new
US armada of ships and men set out to conquer the critically important Marshall Islands; behind the three marine and single army division (130,000 troops) was a bombing and bombardment force of 12 escort
carriers, 5 battleships, and 11 cruisers. More to this point, giving distant
support was what Sir Basil Liddell Hart, in his succinct narrative of this
campaign, termed "the most powerful fleet in the world," consisting of
"7 battleships, 21 cruisers, and 69 destroyers, together with Admiral Marc
Mitscher's 4 carrier groups (15 carriers and 956 aircraft)."[25] But why be
amazed by such totals on the sea, when another source (John Ellis) points
out that "once American yards got into top gear the ratio of strengths became completely disproportionate, the Americans building five times as
many battleships as their opponents, ten times as many aircraft carriers,
six times as many cruisers, and six times as many destroyers"? Given such
disparities, is it really deterministic of that author to state that "it is hard
to see how the Americans, even with a markedly less competent leadership than they had in the Pacific, could ever have lost the war in that
theatre"?[26]

While all these powerful weapons systems—fleet carriers and light
fleet carriers, fast battleships, heavy and light cruisers, fleet destroyers,
and fast fleet trains—were brought together to give the US Navy maritime
predominance in the wide-ranging Pacific campaigns, American shipbuilding had an additional task for the Atlantic war. Here it was called
upon to produce en masse two rather different categories of vessel to help
specifically with defeating Karl Doenitz's U-boats: (1) escort carriers to
aid the British effort in producing enough of that type of ship for convoy duty and (2) merchant ships—lots more of them, chiefly in the form
of the standardized Liberty ship—to counter the losses of those vessels.
As noted above, very large numbers of US escort carriers were also sent
to the Pacific, where they performed a multitude of tasks, especially in
aerial coverage of landing beaches. In the Atlantic war, the task of these
small carriers' aircraft was pure and simple: to keep the U-boats from destroying the merchant convoys, preferably by killing as many of the attackers as possible as well as by shooting down or at least driving off the
Focke-Wulf Condor that shadowed the convoys. The first successful example of this, in the British-built HMS *Audacity*'s fierce clashes with enemy submarines and aircraft back in late 1941 (see chapter 5), became a

regular feature of the Allied convoy story from the middle of 1943 onward. With carrier-launched aircraft counterattacking, the U-boats simply had to go under; the Focke-Wulfs simply had to flee. By the next year,
there were over two dozen British and Canadian escort carriers operating in Atlantic waters as well as US vessels of this type patrolling their
own supply routes into the Mediterranean and successfully driving Doenitz's U-boats further into southern waters. By 1944, indeed, Royal Navy
escort carriers were working together to hunt down German submarines
across the Indian Ocean, while others were covering the landings in the
South of France. Closer to home (much closer), four of these American-
built *Attacker*-class boats were part of the successful air attack that damaged the *Tirpitz* in April 1944.[27] Both there and elsewhere, then, basic US
shipyard output during this war had its distant effects in the field; escort
carriers built with Lend-Lease funds in an Ingalls yard on the Mississippi
shore or in Tacoma-Seattle were by 1944 to be found underpinning the
Fleet Air Arm's operations across the Arctic, Mediterranean, and Indian
oceans.

Finally, American industrial productivity demonstrated itself to an extraordinary degree in its response to the Allied merchant shipping crisis
caused by the U-boat threat to the Atlantic convoys. As Churchill never
stopped reminding listeners, here was *the* battle that had to be won, for
without victory in this campaign Britain could neither be transformed
into the launching pad for the invasion of Europe nor continue to be the
giant aircraft carrier for the strategic bombing of Germany. And if it lost,
it would suffer a devastating strangulation of its imports, just as Doenitz planned. As with those other great grinding campaigns (the Eastern
Front and the bombing strategy), the fight over the security of the convoy
routes showed itself to be a battle of numbers, and this obviously was a
two-sided affair. On the one hand there was the key operational question
of how the U-boats could be kept at bay, and on the other there was the
vital matter of whether the Allied shipbuilding industry could produce
enough newer vessels not only to make up for shipping losses but also to
supply vast and increasing armies across two oceans.

The British Empire's contributions to this battle of numbers was large,
simply because of its already existing enormous holdings of merchant
ships of all types in 1939 (oil tankers, liners convertible to troopships, general cargo, and tramp ships), which were soon increased by those large,
modern merchant marines of Allied nations (for example, Norway) under German conquest. But since Britain's own overstretched shipbuilding industry was urgently directed to building escort vessels and aircraft
carriers and to repairing warships, the only country that could supply
the Allies' soaring need for more merchant ships was the United States

PAINTING 41. Three aircraft carriers at Ulithi Atoll, 1945.
By this late stage in the Pacific War, the giant American carrier
fleet (Task Force 58) possessed well over a dozen fleet carriers
and many smaller ones and could send subdivisions to rest at
Ulithi between operations.

itself. Already in 1940, British purchasing missions had put in an order for 60 rather simple coal-fired *Ocean*-class ships, but when in early 1941 the US Maritime Commission incorporated this into a larger order for 260 vessels, its designers came up with a much-improved steam-powered, oil-fired, 14,200-ton model (carrying 10,000 tons of cargo and needing only forty crew members). Named Liberty ships for publicity effect and applauded by Roosevelt as a program to help save democracy, it was already ramping up production when Pearl Harbor was attacked, at which point the businessman Henry Kaiser offered to the government his plan to build many more ships, and much faster.

Kaiser, whose construction company had earlier helped build the Bay Bridge and Hoover Dam, was nothing if not enterprising and ambitious. He conceived of prefabricated ships' parts being mass manufactured and then brought to his seven new yards (all on the West Coast) to be welded together, with the pace of delivery picking up the more vessels that were produced. Generally, his own yards built more cheaply and faster than any of the other Liberty ship firms, and in one eye-popping stunt the vessel *Robert E. Peary* was put together in four days and fifteen hours. The larger statistics were even more important. Of the 2,751 Liberty ships built by the United States in World War II, 1,552 were by Kaiser Shipbuilding. The four Kaiser yards clustered in Richmond, California, produced a staggering 747 (!) ships. Because of the simplicity of the design and production method, this program could obviously achieve full speed faster than, say, battleship launchings, and already by 1943 three Liberty ships were being completed each day.[28] It is worth adding that each of these simple, capacious vessels could transport up to 2,800 jeeps or 440 Sherman tanks.

This simply dazzling rise in American merchant-ship output by 1943–44 has led some scholars to suggest that virtually because of such output alone the Battle of the Atlantic was assured in the Allies' favor and that Doenitz's plan to break the latter's sea lines of communication really didn't have a chance once US productivity showed its full power.[29] That was clearly not the opinion of the British Admiralty at the time, nor is it of this author; the matter is much less simple than that, as discussed above (see chapter 7). What is abundantly clear, however, is that the phenomenal post-1942 surge in American shipbuilding output came *just at the right time,* in the same months as the U-boat attacks were being steadily beaten back and Allied shipping losses were consequently tumbling from the earlier dangerous high.

Wars are won, ultimately, by the fighting men on one side prevailing over the fighting men on the others, though it definitely helps those winners to have the battle of numbers greatly in their own favor. In all, the US

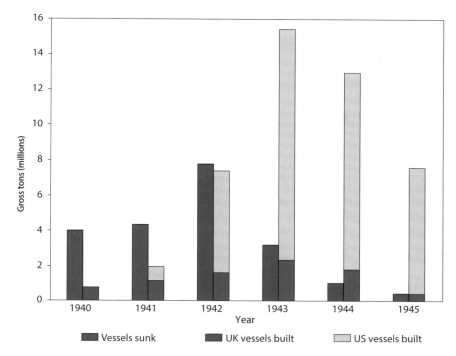

**CHART 6.** US/UK merchant tonnages built and sunk, 1940–45. Data from Ellis, *Brute Force*, 157.

Maritime Commission, the federal body that supervised the shipbuilding programs, ordered around 7,000 ships, of which some 5,500 were delivered before the approach of victory against the Axis caused the later orders to be canceled. The final figures exceeded everyone's most optimistic assumptions. Between 1942 and 1945 the United States launched a staggering 54 million gross tons of merchant shipping, whereas, by contrast, Japanese yards launched a mere 3.3 million gross tons, a freakish ratio of over sixteen to one.[30]

## The Explosion of American Airpower

And then there was the most important instrument of fighting strength of all during this war, that of airpower, which prevailed over both the land and sea struggles.[31] In this regard, as we have already argued, the United States clearly enjoyed many advantages from early on, even if its Army Air Corps had been kept small during the years of peace. Despite that period of austerity, it had always been the pioneer of long-distance navigation and flight and, even more important, possessed a cluster of aircraft

**TABLE 10.** US Aircraft Production, 1939–45 (nearest hundred)

| 1939 | 1940 | 1941 | 1942 | 1943 | 1944 | 1945 |
|------|------|------|------|------|------|------|
| 5,900 | 12,800 | 26,300 | 47,800 | 85,900 | 96,300 | 49,800 |

This single line, showing solely the US aircraft output, is from the comprehensive table of output figures in Kennedy, *Rise and Fall of the Great Powers*, 354. The drop in output in 1945 is clear.

companies—Lockheed, Boeing, and Grumman—that were readily structured for rapid expansion once American rearmament began in earnest. It was FDR, perhaps more than any other world leader, who had recognized the significance of airpower and had called upon Congress to authorize the building of what seemed to be impossible numbers of planes to make the country safe ("20,000 a year!" he had demanded in 1938, and later a total of 90,000 planes).[32] Yet since all the ingredients were available to the American nation, that is, aircraft firms; machine tools; assured supplies of aluminum, copper, and rubber; electricity; and skilled workers, plus a huge surplus of unemployed workers from the still-lingering Depression, then what seemed to be an impossible target became achievable, though once again after the necessary several years of buildup.

The astounding fact emerging from table 10 is that between 1942 and 1943—again, the key transformative period—US aircraft production leapt from the already impressive total of some 47,000 to the truly unbeatable figure of over 85,000 planes, as existing plants greatly expanded and newer factories sprouted across the country from Wichita to Texas. In the entire history of industrialization, from the early steam engines to the present day, it is hard to think of any equivalent, in terms of either speed or size or of such a surge in productivity. When represented as a bar chart (as in chart 7), this jump in output looks even more striking.

Staggering though this increase in *absolute* output was, its real significance for the war is best understood when compared with the aircraft production figures of *all* the great wartime Powers, since every one of them—the Fascist states and the USSR earlier than the democracies—also appreciated the need for as large an air force as possible. By the second half of the war in particular, with France and Italy knocked out, the five major combatants remaining were each producing enormous numbers of planes above every other weapons system; the German achievement here, under Albert Speer's reorganization, was quite remarkable given that Power's raw material shortages and the effects of Allied bombing. Even so, the American productive advantage over its foes was huge; in the key year of 1943, the United States built *three and a half times as many air-*

*craft as Germany and well over five times as many as Japan* (including increasing numbers of heavy four-engined bombers that its enemies never attempted to build en masse). Unsurprisingly, by 1943 but not before, the sheer weight of this American output was beginning to show (see table 11). Little wonder that Ellis describes the later aerial tussles during the Pacific battles of the year following as utterly lopsided, with the more realistic among the Japanese commanders realizing that they had little chance of winning a single encounter.[33]

To repeat, all those US aircraft did not immediately translate into highly trained, effective squadrons operating from frontline bases and ships, and the much-circulated photographs of rows of shining planes parked outside the giant factories at Willow Creek (Boeing) and Bethpage, Long Island (Grumman), did not of themselves mean swift victory in the air. For well into 1943 both in the Southwest Pacific Command and, especially, for the Battle of the Atlantic, there would remain a dire need for long-range bomber and antisubmarine-warfare aircraft. Yet by the second half of that year, and right into 1944, there would occur an uninterrupted flow of fighter, bomber, and transport planes from the American heartland to the frontline bases of the Pacific, Mediterranean, and northwest European theaters of war as well as to lesser theaters like India and Burma. Wherever the tides of war turned in the Allies' favor, they turned first in the air.

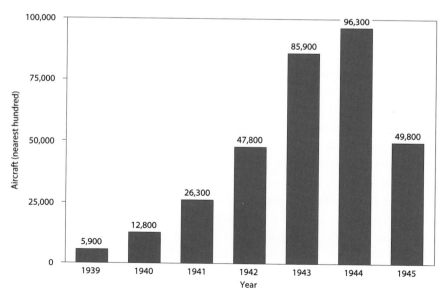

**CHART 7.** US aircraft production, 1939–45. Data from Kennedy, *Rise and Fall of the Great Powers*, 354.

**TABLE 11.** Aircraft Production of the Powers, 1939–45 (nearest hundred)

|                        | 1939      | 1940   | 1941   | 1942    | 1943    | 1944    | 1945      |
|------------------------|-----------|--------|--------|---------|---------|---------|-----------|
| United States          | 5,900     | 12,800 | 26,300 | 47,800  | 85,900  | 96,300  | 49,800    |
| USSR                   | 10,400    | 10,600 | 15,700 | 25,400  | 34,900  | 40,300  | 20,900    |
| Great Britain          | 7,900     | 15,000 | 20,100 | 23,700  | 26,300  | 26,500  | 12,100    |
| British Commonwealth   | 300       | 1,100  | 2,600  | 4,600   | 4,700s  | 4,600   | 2,100     |
| Total Allies           | ca. 24,200| 39,500 | 64,700 | 101,500 | 151,800 | 167,700 | ca. 84,800|
| Germany                | 8,300     | 10,200 | 11,800 | 15,400  | 24,800  | 39,800  | 7,500     |
| Japan                  | 4,500     | 4,800  | 5,100  | 8,900   | 16,700  | 28,200  | 11,100    |
| Italy                  | 1,800     | 1,800  | 2,400  | 2,400   | 1,600   | —       | —         |
| Total Axis             | 14,600    | 16,800 | 19,300 | 26,700  | 43,100  | 68,000  | 18,600    |

Data from Kennedy, *Rise and Fall of the Great Powers,* 354. Totals may not add due to rounding.

Fundamental to this surge was, of course, a concomitant explosion in the size and productivity of the American aeroengine industry, which by war's end had built well over 700,000 engines for everything from the single-engined Mustang to the new ultraheavy four-engined B-29 Super-fortresses. Giant factories mushroomed out of the ground across America, often in states that had known no aircraft industry at all before 1940, and were often run by earlier manufacturers of tractors, trucks, and automobiles that had now been subcontracted to work for established firms. There was no way, for example, that an established company like Pratt and Whitney could satisfy the US government's vast new demands for aeroengines without turning to and licensing production with the nation's commercial automobile firms like Ford, Buick, and Chevrolet, which were now suddenly desperate for work given the ban on wartime private car purchases. Thus, at one giant (government-owned) factory created in the small township of Melrose Park, Illinois, the Buick car company built Pratt and Whitney's famous R-1830 1,200-hp radial aircraft engines—in fact, over 74,000 of them, including most of those that were fitted on the four-engined B-24 Liberator bombers. It turns out, then, that those very-long-range Coastal Command Liberators that in 1943 closed the mid-Atlantic patrol gap in the fight against the U-boats were very probably manufactured in this Buick plant so recently erected in empty fields on the western edge of the Chicago suburbs.[34] And those very squadrons of Liberators flying over the convoys would have been paid for not by the British or Canadian air forces who flew them but through accounting them to Lend-Lease funds, that is, by the American taxpayer. The feedback loops here are eye-popping.

Yet it was another aeroengine that was probably Pratt and Whitney's most famous wartime creation, namely, the extraordinarily powerful (2,000 hp) and reliable P&W R2800, which achieved the distinction of being the engine that powered the Corsair dive-bombers, the USAAF's Thunderbolts, and above all, the navy's chosen fighter aircraft for the new carriers, the Grumman F6F Hellcat. Developed as the successor to the F4F Wildcat and benefiting from a careful study of some captured Mitsubishi Zeros, the Hellcat was not only supplied with this new engine but also equipped with full armor protection around the fuel tanks and cockpit and with six 50mm machine guns. Throughout 1942 Grumman designers and engineers worked steadily on improvements to the engine and to the plane itself, the first squadrons of which arrived on the USS *Essex* in February 1943. The rest is history. In their first serious tangles with Japanese Zeros over Tarawa in the Gilberts campaign that same November, Hellcats shot down thirty foes for the loss of one of their own. Hard to destroy but well equipped for destruction, Hellcats eventually shot down over 5,200 enemy aircraft, far more than did any other Allied fighter—in fact, a full 75 percent of all aerial victories claimed by the US Navy in the Pacific War were achieved by this aircraft. The famously lopsided Great Marianas Turkey Shoot (chapter 9) was, overwhelmingly, a Hellcat fighter's turkey shoot. Other factors contributed to this grotesquely unbalanced outcome, for Japanese operational leadership was poor and by this stage of the war the quality of the Japanese aircrews was severely deficient, but the main reason was that the Americans had by now far superior planes—and many, many more of them.[35]

## Comparative Resources and Military-Industrial Muscle

All of the above weapons statistics, whether it be the output of cruisers or fighter-bombers or fast battleships, point again and again to the sheer military-industrial muscle of the United States among the seven Great Powers of the war. In every stage of the productive process for armaments, whether measuring the inputs of vital raw materials or the outputs of vessels that were launched, the American advantage was unquestioned. In the possession of, or access to, raw materials especially, the disproportionality between the two sides in this global conflict was astounding, especially when one added to America's resources those of the entire British Empire (in particular, mineral-rich Canada and South Africa). Not for nothing was the war described as an existential fight between the have

**PAINTING 42.**
Douglas Devastators
on the flight deck of
USS *Enterprise.*
Ian Marshall's
modernist painting
here suggests the
sheer accumulated
firepower of the
American carrier fleet,
even under kamikaze
attacks.

and have-not powers, and here virtually everything favored the Allies. In an introductory chapter to his classic *History of the Second World War,* Liddell Hart wrote, "There were some twenty basic products essential for war. Coal for general production. Petroleum for motive power. Cotton for explosives. Wool. Iron. Rubber for transport. Copper for general armament and all electrical equipment. Nickel for steel-making and ammunition. Lead for ammunition . . . ," and so on. He continued, "The best placed of all the powers was the United States which produced two-thirds of the world's total petroleum supply, about half its cotton, and nearly half its copper." By comparison, Liddell Hart added, "Italy had to import the bulk of her needs in every product, even to coal. Japan was almost as dependent on foreign sources. Germany had no home production of cotton, rubber, tin, platinum, bauxite, mercury, and mica."[36] Given these gaps, it is again amazing in retrospect that the Third Reich managed as well as it did, yet at the end of the day its renowned battlefield efficiency could never make up the material differences.

Possession of these superior resources would benefit the United States only when translated into battlefield use, of course, but by the second half of the war it was easy to understand where and how that was occurring. Aluminum, for example, offered a wonderful tale of progression from raw material extraction to factory design and production to Allied success in combat. The powerful F6F Hellcat fighters that were shooting down so many Japanese aircraft by 1944 relied upon aluminum propellers, lightweight aluminum engine parts, and so many other key pieces supplied to the Grumman assembly plant by subcontractors, which in turn had received the aluminum sheets and slabs from a giant Alcoa smelting factory, which in its turn had received a steady flow of bauxite from South American sources (Suriname, British Guiana, and Trinidad), which in their turn had been safely transported through Allied naval convoys.[37] Here was a virtuous upward spiral indeed: control of this vital ore gave to the US war industry by 1942—that is, once the leading company, Alcoa, built itself the larger smelting and factory capacity—the wherewithal to support that sharp rise in aeroengine and aircraft output that then brought victory in the skies. And what America possessed in abundance, the other side did not. While American aluminum output soared sharply from 750,000 tons in 1942 to 1,251,000 tons in 1943, the Japanese increase and sum total remained but a tenth of that.[38]

It was a lopsided tale that repeated itself again and again, from rubber to iron ore and from copper to cotton. Behind all the American battlefield victories, there was this story of colossal resource advantage. There is therefore no need to detail this point for raw material after raw material,

**TABLE 12.** Armaments Production of the Powers, 1940–43 (in billions of 1944 dollars)

|  | 1940 | 1941 | 1943 |
|---|---|---|---|
| United Kingdom | 3.5 | 6.5 | 11.1 |
| USSR | (5.0) | 8.5 | 13.9 |
| United States | (1.5) | 4.5 | 37.5 |
| Total Allies | 3.5 | 19.5 | 62.5 |
| Germany | 6.0 | 6.0 | 13.8 |
| Japan | (1.0) | 2.0 | 4.5 |
| Italy | 0.75 | 1.0 |  |
| Total Axis | 6.75 | 9.0 | 18.3 |

Data from Kennedy, *Rise and Fall of the Great Powers*, 355. Figures in parentheses mean nations not yet at war.

except perhaps to note that the grotesque difference pertained more than ever for the most vital refined product of all, petroleum. In 1943 German crude oil production (including imports) had edged up to 9 million metric tons, whereas the American total was 200 million metric tons; no turn to synthetic fuels by German industry could close that gap, even before the latter source was badly reduced through targeted Allied bombing.[39] From the North African deserts to the Ardennes forests, German panzer columns often ground to a halt due to the lack of gas. And the Japanese petroleum deficit was even greater—well before US submarines had decimated Japan's oil tanker fleet, its navy and air force were suffering from completely inadequate fuel supplies. The war's have-not powers never escaped their plight. Lacking enough war-making materials, after 1942 they increasingly came to lack sufficient arms and fuel as well.

At the end of it, probably one basic statistic about relative weapons production in World War II should capture the reader's attention above all the others: the staggering leap in American total armaments output from a mere $1.5 billion in 1940 to $4.5 billion by the next year (1941) and then to an unbelievable $37.5 billion by the key year of 1943, as shown in table 12. To put this in another remarkable way, this meant that *while US arms production was only one-quarter of Nazi Germany's in 1940, it was heading toward being three times as much by 1943, a mere three years later.* And, of course, by adding once again to this vast American output that of its two great allies, Britain and the Soviet Union, the historian gets to the heart of the matter: by the middle of the war, the Axis powers were simply being eclipsed by the sheer economic heft of the Grand Alliance.

## Financing the War

Yet none of this prodigious American industrial output could have occurred without the monies to pay for it all. Roosevelt's happily named "Arsenal of Democracy" for the anti-Fascist coalition also was—needed to be—the paymaster of democracy by raising huge amounts of capital, through taxes and credit, to funnel toward those powerful and productive companies—Grumman, Boeing, Newport News Shipbuilding, and Kaiser—that were assembling the multitude of aircraft and ships that were now turning the tide in this global conflict and to cover the costs of the very large amounts of munitions and raw materials that were being provided to America's many allies under the Lend-Lease programs. World War II, like every other war in history, had to be paid for one way or another.

Prior to this modern example, the nexus between successful money-raising and successful war-making had never been better in evidence than it had a century and a half earlier, during Great Britain's twenty-three-year-long struggle against Revolutionary and Napoleonic France, when Great Britain repeatedly acquired enormous amounts of income both to pay for its own extensive fleets and armies and to furnish military supplies and financial support to its coalition partners. Britain then had raised these funds from three sources: a mixture of heavy taxes and duties upon its own nation, with impositions rising to record levels; from war loans that, because of superior credit, were constantly subscribed to by domestic purchasers; and through the sale of Treasury bonds to foreign investors.[40] The only difference this time was that virtually *all* of the income flow was raised from American sources, that is, from vastly increased taxes and from the sale of war bonds.

The spending part, in other words, was relatively easy, since, alarmed after the Fall of France, the US government began to spend on virtually everything: in 1940, the total spent on armaments was only $2.1 billion, and of that a mere $0.4 billion was spent on aircraft, $0.4 billion on ships, and $0.2 billion on combat and motor vehicles. By 1943, the arms bill was a colossal $52.4 billion, including $12.5 billion each on aircraft and ships and $5.9 billion on vehicles.[41] *Essex*-class carriers cost between $68 and $78 million each in 1942 (equal to approximately $1.2 billion by 2020). An *Iowa*-class battleship cost around $100 million when it was built ($1.6 billion today). A Boeing B-17 bomber was a mere $240,000, and each Liberty ship cost between $1.5 and $2 million each.[42] When one multiplies those respective costs by the number of items produced in the war—24 carriers, 10 battleships, 12,000 B-17s, and 2,700 Liberty ships—then what had seemed at first reading to be unbelievable grand totals of US government

**TABLE 13.** US GNP and Military Outlays at Current Prices, 1938–48 (in billions of dollars)

|  | Nominal GNP | Nominal military outlays | Percentage of GNP |
|---|---|---|---|
| 1938 | 84.7 | 1.0 | 1.2 |
| 1939 | 90.5 | 1.2 | 1.3 |
| 1940 | 99.7 | 2.2 | 2.2 |
| 1941 | 124.5 | 13.8 | 11.1 |
| 1942 | 157.9 | 49.4 | 31.3 |
| 1943 | 191.6 | 79.7 | 41.6 |
| 1944 | 210.1 | 87.4 | 41.6 |
| 1945 | 211.9 | 73.5 | 34.7 |
| 1946 | 208.5 | 14.7 | 7.1 |
| 1947 | 231.3 | 9.1 | 3.9 |
| 1948 | 257.1 | 10.7 | 4.2 |

Data from Harrison, *Economics of World War II*, 83. This collection, and especially H. Rockoff, "The United States: From Ploughshares to Swords," chap. 3 in Harrison, is another source with a wealth of statistical data.

expenditures becomes quite believable—indeed, *it has to be so.* If, say, the number of planes produced in American factories went from 6,000 in 1939 to a staggering 85,900 in 1943, then unsurprisingly the data also show that armaments spending also vastly increased, tenfold or twelvefold—after all, in that first year, only 1.4 percent of GNP had been devoted to military outlays, but by the second date (1943) over 43 percent was going to the military. And while this arms spending was constituting an ever-larger share of the measurable national product, and since all this money was being poured into goods and services and then into real wages, the GNP itself, in another feedback loop, was also significantly increasing. Mark Harrison's nifty calculation of the military outlays / GNP / percent of GNP shifts between 1938 and 1948 captures well the dynamic interconnections (see table 13).

How many statesmen of earlier great empires would have sighed in envy at such a story: despite colossal outlays on military hardware, which all too often had brought combatant nations to their knees, the fortunate Americans came away with a gross national product that was almost three-quarters larger at the end of the fighting than when they first began shooting. For none of the other Great Powers in this current war, whether allies or foes, was such a result remotely possible.[43]

How on earth was this American spending on the war paid for, avoiding hyperinflation on the one hand and default and collapse on the other?

From the beginning, government economic planners were aware of the dangers, even if the president and Congress had made clear that victory was an absolute necessity regardless of the cost and that real sacrifices were going to be asked of the people. In no way, of course, could any number of new taxes alone immediately pay for the soaring immediate expenditures of being at war. No matter how rich the United States was in 1940, it had to go into massive debt—although perhaps another way of understanding the matter would be to say that, precisely because America *was* so wealthy, it could assume a huge degree of domestic indebtedness without borrowing from and becoming dependent upon third parties. Relative to other material trends, the amount of debt held by the federal government at first rose slowly, from $43 billion in June 1940 to $49 billion in June 1941 and $72 billion in June 1942, but then it almost doubled during the following twelvemonth ($137 billion by June 1943) and added the same amount in the next year (to $201 billion), as the government's own out-payments on military goods surged. At war's end, then, the national debt held was about five times larger than it had been a mere four years earlier.[44] Americans had purchased Treasuries in unprecedented numbers; buying war bonds really did happen.

The other way this war was paid for—had to be paid for[45]—was through a panoply of taxes, both direct and indirect, and at increased rates that suggested the highest tax burdens would be carried by the well-to-do, but that somehow everyone would contribute a share to the national effort. How important, then, was the shock of Pearl Harbor, and the feeling that America was under threat, in inducing the conviction that economic sacrifices were now absolutely necessary. In 1941 the highest tax bracket of all (81 percent) had been applied only to the impossibly wealthy—the bracket started at incomes of over $5 million. By 1942 it applied to all incomes over $200,000, which presumably included a lot more Americans, and by 1944 the top tax bracket was raised to 94 percent (the federal income tax rate on the lowest bracket was by then 23 percent, well up from 1940's 4.4 percent).[46] At the same time, indirect taxes were raised on a whole variety of goods and services and on critical items like gasoline, though the government's motive here was as much to head off inflation—too much consumer money chasing too few goods—as it was to raise income. Where taxes alone might not cut consumption, regulations went into play. The production of private cars stopped in 1942; distance motoring was discouraged (to save on rubber stocks); nylon was needed for parachutes, not stockings; aluminum was used for planes, not refrigerators; and so on.

The war itself, and not the earlier New Deal measures, brought American unemployment to an end—even in 1938 the unemployment rate was still a stubbornly high 19 percent, but by 1943 it was at a historic low of

1 percent.[47] Just having 10 million more people earning a wage put a lot more money into the American people's pockets just as, ironically, they had fewer goods to purchase. Hence the importance, then, of the cleverly orchestrated publicity campaign (soldiers brought back from the Pacific War would urge an admiring public to "Buy War Bonds Now!") that fitted nicely into the fiscal calculation. By purchasing those bonds, the public provided another virtuous spiral that shored up the nation's strength and thus its capacity to bear the enormous burdens of total war. Here was trickle-down economics combined with fiscal control working to a degree and as a model that usually only existed in the textbooks on that subject. One government program, that is, the vast spending on armaments, produced a newly recruited and relatively well-paid workforce, but another government program, the propaganda campaign to purchase bonds, soaked up the surge in that workforce's earnings. Thus, for example, the thirty thousand men and women, often husband and wife, employed at Grumman's Bethpage plants, were repeatedly encouraged to pour as much of their earnings as possible into low-interest-bearing bonds; and, with personal taxes high and many consumer goods unavailable, they had every incentive to do so, at least until after the conflict's end. In sum, while on the one hand the war was acting like a vast bellows, stoking enormous industrial output, on the other hand the government's nifty mixture of taxation, price controls, and borrowing policies headed off the superinflation that could have come from giving the American worker so much newfound money. As those aircraft engineers and welders got richer, so too did the country, yet without any wild, uncontrollable, Habsburgian explosion of prices and indeed without much class conflict or the controversy over war profiteering that had occurred during World War I.[48]

A glance at how the other Great Powers fared confirms again that the American case was special. It clearly spent more on the war than any of the other combatant nations, and its massive spending could be seen not only in the sheer number of weapons produced (96,000 planes a year and all that) but also even in the very facilities built into individual US units of war: the roominess of the submarines, the air conditioning in the larger bomber aircraft, the ice machines on the carriers. The simple fact was that while America spent absolutely more on the war, it found it relatively easy to do so because it was so rich—in raw materials, in industrial muscle, in its high-technology base, in its capital resources, and in its numbers of easily trainable people. If it carried the largest weight, it also had by far the broadest shoulders. All the others found the burdens of war harder to bear, and thus the sacrifices demanded of them bit much more deeply. One useful comparative measure of the military burden borne by the Great Powers shows that by 1943 the British were devoting a full 55 percent of their national income to military outlays, the USSR over 60 percent, and Nazi Germany (even with huge plundering from neighboring lands to the east and west) a colossal 70 percent. The United States, although easily outspending all of them, devoted only 42 percent.[49] And wherever one searches for data on the economic and social costs of the war—for example, in nutrition levels—the evidence shows that while the other nations were hurting, the United States was not; while German food rations shrank, for example, Americans ate away. Thus, calorific intake per day, vitamin C per day, protein consumption, meat consumption—all were actually higher in 1943–44 than in, say, 1938.[50] Rosie the Riveter, as the artist Norman Rockwell's iconic painting suggested, was a rather well-fed riveter.

Finally, there were the huge amounts of US military supplies provided under the Lend-Lease Act (March 11, 1941) to the Allied powers, which in two cases—the Soviet Union and the United Kingdom—had enormous overall strategic importance in the winning of the war. Some 17 percent of the total war expenditures of the United States—contemporarily valued at $50 billion dollars, or $784 billion today—was shipped between 1941 and the act's conclusion in September 1945.[51] Since the USSR was rich in raw materials like coal and ores, the goods it needed, and got, were of the most immediate military sort: 427,000 trucks, including great numbers of the incredibly valuable Dodge and Studebaker type; 12,000 armored vehicles (including 4,000 Sherman tanks); 11,000 aircraft; and 2,000 locomotives, plus US-refined high-octane aviation fuel and over 4 million tons of foodstuffs.[52] Having command of the sea helped, of course. If it was the massed divisions of the Red Army that would eventually inflict by far the most of the Wehrmacht's losses, it was also incredibly important that Allied navies could protect the mercantile convoys—to Murmansk and to the Persian Corridor—carrying this flow of US war material (and British war material, including over 3,000 Hurricanes) for the Russo-German front. Indeed, there may be no better symbol of Churchill's Grand Alliance at work than the image of Georgy Zhukov's divisions advancing toward Berlin with the aid of thousands of 2.5-ton Studebaker trucks that had been brought in ships escorted by the Royal Navy.

Lend-Lease supplies to the British between 1941 and 1945 were even greater in type, size, and value—the total of $31.4 billion ($492 billion in today's figures) equaled more than 10 percent of all America's military production—and was of the utmost strategic importance, simply because of the "added value" of keeping the United Kingdom going as an almost full-size Great Power combatant for almost all of the war. The British had paid for and acquired large amounts of war goods, especially aircraft

(Catalina flying boats and Hudson bombers), early in the war, but by the time the act came into effect they had virtually run down all their reserves of dollar assets and gold; thus the vastly enlarged flow of "loaned" munitions and other supplies after March 1941 from a so-called neutral country was a godsend. Transport aircraft (especially for the paratroop corps and for William Slim's armies in Burma), long-range patrol aircraft, fighter squadrons, escort carriers, merchant ships, sheets of steel and aluminum, basic food supplies (wheat and flour), and all sorts of critically important fuels were either flown or carried in an unending flood from American ports to Britain—preserving this flow, after all, was what the Battle of the Atlantic was all about![53] Lancaster bombers flew on American-refined aircraft fuel, Spitfire fighters needed American-made aluminum, Higgins landing craft carried Britain's amphibious battalions to the beaches, Rolls-Royce Merlin engines (mass-produced by Packard) powered many a Royal Air Force squadron, and so on. And probably the most unneutral of all the Roosevelt administration's not-very-neutral measures was the decision to allow badly damaged British heavy warships (battleships, cruisers, and carriers) to be repaired and improved upon in US shipyards and to have the costs chalked up as a Lend-Lease item—a huge benefit to a battered Royal Navy, especially in the years 1941 and 1942.[54]

The strategic payoff for this buttressing of a valued ally (again, one thinks of the much earlier value to Britain in keeping Prussia and Austria going with supplies in their common fight against Napoleon) was that the United States had an almost equal-sized fighting partner against the Axis powers for much of the war. Side by side, American and British Commonwealth armies wrested control of North Africa and Sicily from the Axis and then fought their way together up the Italian peninsula. Side by side, their armies (two American, two British, and one Canadian) landed in Normandy also and then fought their way into the Third Reich. By night, 1,000 British heavy bombers pounded Germany, and each day, 1,500 American bombers did the same. The US Navy's "Two-Ocean War" (historian Samuel Morison's title) was not such an equally weighted parallel story as might be suggested; for while the Pacific campaign against Japan was almost all America's until 1944–45, by far the greater part of the naval-aerial contest in the Atlantic was an Anglo-Canadian war against the Kriegsmarine and Luftwaffe.

Of course the sheer economic heft of the US war effort by, say, 1944 dwarfed everyone else's—that is the point of this chapter. And of course it is also true that Britain's increasing economic dependence upon its American cousins came at a very considerable cost to its own longer-term status as a Great Power, although it is difficult to see what other choice it had in this matter.[55] But the critical point being made here is that by transfer-

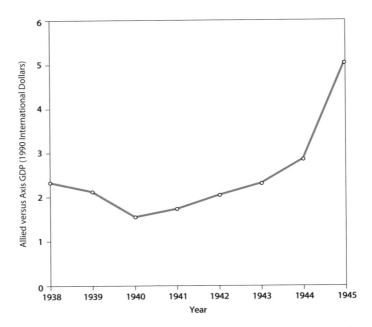

**CHART 8.** Ratio of GDP between Allied and Axis powers, 1938–45. This important basic graph is in "Military Production during World War II," Wikipedia, last modified April 7, 2020, https://en.wikipedia.org/wiki/Military _production_during_World_War_II#/media/File:WorldWarII-GDP-Relations -Allies-Axis-simple.svg.

ring under Lend-Lease arrangements such vast material assets from the American armaments cornucopia to the USSR and the United Kingdom (and to a lesser degree, China and France), the United States had created a sort of "force-multiplier effect" that made the overall Allied effort so large that it eventually swamped all Axis prospects (see chart 8).

All in all, one might consider this American spending on armaments and strategic materials such as steel and rubber for its Allies as yet an additional form of "War Keynesianism," for the pumping of capital into producing Studebaker trucks for the USSR or making large repairs to Royal Navy battleships meant further investment into US firms, more wages for American workers, and reduced unit costs per weapon, all of which in turn enhanced productivity and made America itself richer by far.

Scholars have sometimes had difficulty in showing the linkages between on the one hand the profound changes that drive and shape the course of history and on the other hand the day-to-day or even year-to-year events that occur, some of them dramatic, grand, and fast-moving. The historian of World War II, especially of the naval and aerial campaigns in the Pacific and the Atlantic, should have no such problem demonstrating linkages, particularly when it comes to coverage of the critical year of 1943. For it was in that year, or at least by the second half of it, that America's unequaled industrial productive power manifested itself to a degree that had simply not been there previously. With the North Atlantic convoys looking more and more protected and secure from U-boat attack, new US carriers and other vessels at last streaming into the Pacific, and Anglo-American heavy bombers commencing their destruction of the Third Reich's war industries, the course of the war really had changed, and Alanbrooke's remark just six months earlier that the Allies had now passed "the end of the beginning" seemed amply justified.

All this also, then, confirmed the insight and the correctness of Churchill's own emotional response back on December 8, 1941, as he pondered that evening the news of the Japanese attacks on American and British possessions in the Pacific. It was not the flood of bad news—Manila bombed, Pearl Harbor attacked, Hong Kong besieged—that gripped the prime minister's lively imagination at that time; no, it was the supreme fact that at last the United States would be coming into the fight. "We would win after all," he rejoiced. "Hitler's fate was sealed," while the Japanese "would be ground to powder." After all the long, hard struggle, victory was now assured, because—this was the prime minister's conviction—America's unequaled and irresistible strength was bound to prevail. The "giant boiler" (another of Churchill's colorful terms) that was the US economy had now been lit, with a capacity that knew few limits. There would be much tough fighting ahead, of that the prime minister was certain, but also certain was the final victory. "All the rest," he wrote, "was merely the proper application of overwhelming force."[56] Beneath all the further campaigns of the war, then, there beckoned victory, assured by a new order of global power. It would be America's.

## The Natural Culmination of Secular Historical Trends?

Is this vast expansion of American armaments output and the consequent near doubling of the US economy between 1941 and 1945 simply to be understood, then, as a natural consequence of the country's entry into total, modern war, impressive no doubt in all the statistical consequences—steel production quintupled, standards of living up 60 percent, and all that—but really quite understandable? For isn't this what happens within an industrialized economy where there are large underutilized resources that are then stimulated by massive fiscal injections? The Americans were lucky, no doubt, in that they were sitting upon enormous natural resources, especially oil and ores, which, like the country's large and underutilized human resources, could be made much more productive once the necessary sums of capital were applied. In all such things the United States was clearly much more fortunate that, say, Italy or France. So, when the amount of total federal purchases of goods and services shot up from $36 billion (1940) to $164 billion (1944),[57] of course total armaments production also went up, from $4 billion to $42 billion, the number of planes made went from 6,000 a year to 96,000 a year, and 35 new aircraft carriers and 122 escort carriers were sent off to the front. And *voilà!* The war was won—of course. And of course this amount of government spending, the unprecedented rates of personal taxation, and the unbelievable amounts of deficit and debt would not have been tolerated for one minute by the US political system but for the treacherous Japanese attack on Pearl Harbor. Without that shock, the picture of America's place in the world by 1945, and by midcentury, would surely have been very different. The country might still have remained economically rather moribund (as well as politically quite isolated), even if there had been further fiscal bouts of New Dealism by Roosevelt's government. Without the war, it might not have become so obviously the greatest of the Great Powers by 1945 after all.

All this is true. Of course it took the war—again, Lenin's "locomotive of history"—to change things. Of course it took World War II itself not only to blunt but to completely crush the Fascist states' aggressions, to weaken irretrievably the European colonial empires (even the British), and to leave the United States and, a bit more shakily, the USSR as the only large powers standing upright after 1945.

Yet there is more to it than this. There is a very different—yet not contradictory—way of viewing the explosion of US power during World War II, and that is to see it *as the natural culmination, though delayed by almost half a century, of the huge shifts in the world's balances once the American continent industrialized;* as the culmination, more or less, of Tocqueville's 1835 prophecy that this nation was one day destined to sway the destinies of half the globe.[58]

To see this argument properly, one would have to consider certain long-run economic and demographic statistics that take the reader's gaze away from all the eye-catching facts about American output during the mere five years of the war itself. In fact, the story would go back to the last two decades of the nineteenth century, when railways and telegraphs and huge internal migration really opened the Midwest and then the West to commercial and industrial takeoff. And it would probably best begin with the vast expansion of America's population itself, because this was a surge in numbers that—in contrast to any earlier, gloomy Malthusian models of demographic growth—interacted with significant rises in output, representing an expansion in population size that both fueled and raced to

**TABLE 14.** US Population, 1870–1930 (nearest million)

| 1870 | 1890 | 1910 | 1930 |
| --- | --- | --- | --- |
| 39 million | 63 million | 92 million | 123 million |

Data from "Population Distribution over Time," United States Census Bureau, accessed February 20, 2020, https://www2.census.gov/library/publications/decennial/1930/population-volume-1/03815512v1ch02.pdf.

supply an enormous, wealth-creating economic explosion. The growing numbers were those of an increasingly productive American workforce, without a vast peasantry (Russia) or destitute city multitudes (India and China) that slowed down real per capita GDP. This growth in the nation's numbers had in turn two chief consequences for its world power. The first was the rather simple one, that its population, while on a par with the larger European countries in the 1870s, was going to be far greater than any of theirs, even Imperial Germany's, within one person's lifetime (see table 14).

Second, while of course the Wall Street crash of 1929 and the sudden experience of poverty and unemployment for many Americans were great setbacks, the fact was that the massive natural increases in overall population in the decades before and after that event—16 million more people in the 1900s, 13 million more in the 1910s, 17 million more in the 1920s, and 18 million more in the 1930s—constituted a growing national strength, not a weakness.[59] When put to employment by American industry, this workforce was already turning the country into an economic giant compared with the others, even *before* World War I. This is a critical point. Whichever set of figures is chosen—energy consumption or total industrial potential of the Powers—one comes away with the same conclusion: America was a different sort of Power, an economic giant while still a military dwarf. Thus, its steel production in 1913 (31.8 million tons) was bigger than Germany's (17.6 million), Britain's (7.7 million), and France's (4.6 million) combined. More broadly, in that same year it had 32 percent of world manufacturing output, compared to Germany's 14.8 percent, Britain's 13.6 percent, and Russia's 8.2 percent.[60] World War I, which swept away Russia's economy and badly weakened Germany's, France's, and Britain's, simply increased the American share further, up to a colossal 40 percent or so. For one country to hold such a proportion was unheard of in world history, and yet everywhere one looked one saw evidence of its productive power—and wealth. "In 1929, for example, the United States produced 4.5 million motor vehicles, compared with France's 211,000, Britain's 182,000, and Germany's 117,000."[61] What seemed even more

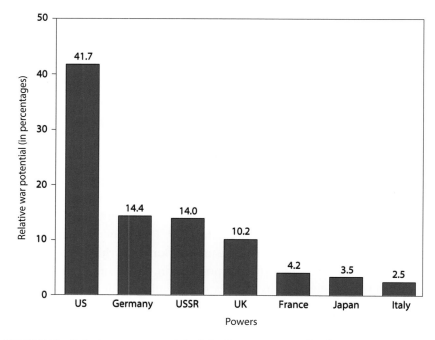

**CHART 9.** Relative war potential of the Powers, 1937. All other nations total 9.5 percent. Data from Kennedy, *Rise and Fall of the Great Powers*, 332. The original source is the superb essay by Hillman, "Comparative Strength of the Great Powers."

unusual, however, was the continued insistence of this nation's policy-makers on having such a miniscule army, perhaps only the twelfth-largest during the interwar years, and on trying to stay absent from most world affairs. Number one powers in the past didn't do that sort of thing.

Then came the great crash and an even more destructive event, the folly of US politicians in opting for trade protectionism when their economy was the most competitive of all. Comparatively measured, it looks as if America's share of world trade fell the most during the 1930s and also that the value of its manufactured goods tumbled the most (by 75 percent), the total of its workers thrown out of a job (15 million) was the largest, and its GNP eroded the most.[62] In consequence of all this, and to return to our attempts to measure the United States' *real* military muscle as World War II unfolded, it also seems clear that its comparative power, while remaining greater than anybody else's, could nonetheless easily be underestimated because so much of its capacity was dormant. As just one example, while it certainly produced more steel than Germany or the USSR or Japan in, say, 1938, those countries' plants were working to full capacity, *whereas two-thirds of American steel furnaces were idle.* Here, really, was Churchill's "sleeping giant" or "vast boiler" or any of the other colorful terms he employed to capture his understanding (perhaps better than anyone else's) of America's huge potential for war.

One final statistic (see chart 9), therefore, claims the crown.

The conclusion here is obvious. In any military struggle that lasted long enough to turn that war potential into hard fighting power, it would be folly for another country to take on the United States; it was simply in a different league. It is also easier to understand how, when the industrial capacities of the Axis had been ground to rubble in 1945, the American share of total world product went up to 50 percent, and perhaps a bit over. For the first and only time in history, one single country possessed half the planet's GDP (at least by this way of measuring output). Even Tocqueville might have been amazed. Little wonder that America could, among other things, build the largest navy the world had ever seen.

---

We may return here, then, to the matter of aircraft carriers and the transformation of the naval war after 1943. The arrival of the USS *Essex* at Pearl Harbor on June 1 meant far more than the deployment of a single warship, as this chapter makes clear. What it also meant was that, at long last, the United States' true Great Power potential was being revealed; the wraps had come off. Aircraft carriers were just a reflection of that larger change, and an excellent reflection at that, because such modern warships captured virtually all the dimensions of American productive power. And shortly following the *Essex*'s arrival into Pearl, there would come all the others: fleet carriers, light fleet carriers, and escort carriers in unimaginable numbers. If he had been looking across the harbor on that historic morning, and he most probably was, Admiral Nimitz would have been justified in feeling a huge sense of relief.

At the very end of that critical watershed year in the Pacific, the USS *Essex* returned again to Pearl Harbor for a short respite from the war. Since the first time it had sortied from the base, it and other carriers with it had been in almost continuous action against Japanese-held islands and air defenses—at Marcus and Wake islands in August 1943, Rabaul in October, the Gilberts in November, and Kwajalein in December—thus completely fulfilling the operational concept of fast-carrier attack forces on which the US Navy was pinning so much weight. By the time New Year's Day 1944 arrived in Hawaii, the *Essex* was being allocated along with a dozen other carriers to the new, giant Task Force 58 in preparation for a further, year-long series of amphibious and aerial strikes that would totally transform the Pacific War.

# PART IV

Narrative of the Great Naval War, 1944–45

**PAINTING 43.  Grumman F6F Hellcat and USS *Bonhomme Richard*, 1945.**
The "winning combination"—the USS *Bonhomme Richard* was the fourteenth
carrier in the *Essex* class, and the F6F Hellcat was the dominant fighter in the
Pacific War (75 percent of enemy planes were shot down by this plane).

# NINE

## Triumph of Allied Sea Power

### *1944*

To the historian of military affairs, what is striking about the major campaigns of the year 1944 is their sheer *size*—all of them, on the air, sea, and land, were bigger than anything else that had taken place in history. Simply put, those crude background figures of the total armaments production of the powers (see table 12 in chapter 8) showing the Grand Alliance's epic spending between 1940 and 1943 had now been translated into weapons and manpower forces that were overwhelming those of the significantly smaller German-Japanese empires in all theaters, and from all directions.[1] History really was with the big battalions. In the air, thousands of Anglo-American heavy bombers were tearing at the Third Reich's cities and industries. In the war at sea, the year 1944 was witness to the two largest amphibious ventures ever, made all the more impressive because these Allied campaigns were self-contained, ten thousand miles apart, and each of huge dimensions. In the Pacific, the twin drives of Chester W. Nimitz's command from Hawaii and General Douglas MacArthur's command from New Guinea were converging on the Philippines, brushing aside the Japanese forces holding the intermediate island groups. In the Atlantic, the Anglo-American aerial, amphibious, and land forces had at last been built up for the massive Normandy landings of that June. On the Eastern Front, millions of increasingly better-equipped Soviet soldiers pressed westward, the gigantic Operation Bagration of June–August being only the biggest of many advances. The grand story of this year of 1944 was therefore one of Axis retreat, with their forces fighting ferociously but being pushed ever further backward, toward their beleaguered homelands.

The strategic historian Sir Basil Liddell Hart, seeking to put a structure to his final work, his *History of the Second World War,* described the gigantic six-year conflict in terms of the waxing and waning of the oceanic tides. Like a huge, unstoppable flood, German forces had at first poured all over western Europe, surged into the Balkans and Mediterranean, and then rushed across thousands of miles of the Ukraine and southern Russia. The post-1941 Japanese deluge was, if anything, even more spectacular, overcoming Allied possessions everywhere from the Aleutian Islands to the borders of India. But the tides of Axis conquest turned, emphatically, during the course of 1943. So the chapters of Liddell Hart's book describing the campaigns of 1944 all suggest a certain tidal regularity and predictability: "The German Ebb in Russia," "The Japanese Ebb in the Pacific," and so on.[2] The Axis leaderships, it seemed, had no further prospect of staunching the inexorable advancing floods. Perhaps this sort of language makes the tale sound a bit too inevitable until, of course, the historian gets to describing and detailing the sheer size of the two great surges of Allied power across the central Pacific and up the English Channel in 1944.

## The Great Pacific Surge of 1944

While the campaign in the central Pacific during 1943 had closed successfully for the United States with its complete takeover of the Gilbert Islands, that year had been a quiet one overall. This next one was going to be anything but that; indeed, 1944 was the year when three colossal and irreversible blows were dealt to Japanese maritime power. The first was the Battle of the Philippine Sea in June, which crushed Japan's naval air force even more decisively than either Midway or the great raid on Truk of February 1944 had done and also permitted America's invasion of the strategically vital Mariana Islands. The second was the epic struggle at Leyte Gulf in October, ruining the Japanese main battle fleet and sinking most of its remaining carriers. The third advance was a more subtle and gradual one: the vast improvement in the destructive power of US submarine forces in the Pacific, so that they could at last really cripple the Japanese war economy. The naval victory at Leyte Gulf had, moreover, ensured that MacArthur's amphibious landings in the Philippines could unfold without interruption, in an operation that at last saw the fusion of those twin American "drives" across the Pacific that had begun back in 1942. In one twelve-month period—actually, in the mere months between June and November 1944—the Japanese were thrown out of the central Pacific and the approaches to their home islands were endangered.

Where there were *not* decisive advances for a very long time, and where there was no memorable battle, was in General MacArthur's Southwest Pacific Command (SWPC) area, that is, along the northern shores of New

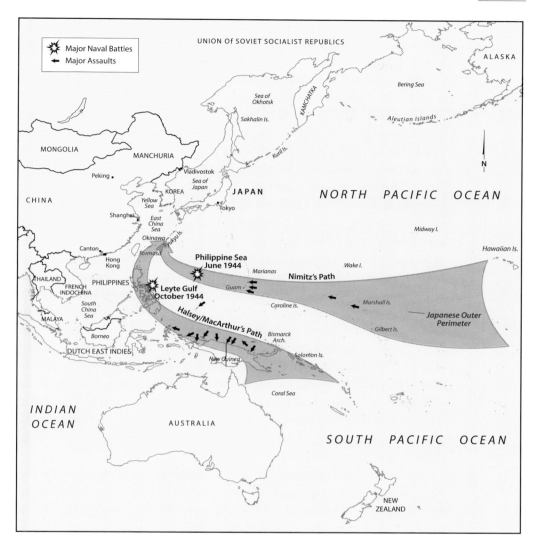

**MAP 13.** The twin American drives across the Pacific, 1943–44.

Guinea and the large offshore archipelagos beyond it. When MacArthur's US Army Command had begun fighting back in early 1942 with just a small number of American and Australian brigades, it was the only force stemming the Japanese advance. Holding on to Papua (Port Moresby), it had slowly pushed the enemy back, aided by the latter's many logistical and firepower weaknesses and the growing US strength in the air. Yet the jungle territories were terribly difficult to fight in, and the SWPC's own logistical problems were great, being at the end of the longest supply lines of the war, diagonally across the entire Pacific. Nimitz's central Pacific forces had it far easier in that respect, and they also benefited from the fact that their targets (the Gilberts and the Marshalls) were small and their Japanese garrisons isolated from each other. They also benefited from the revelation of what enormous power and flexibility the coming of the new, huge carrier task forces brought to the fight.

MacArthur's command, by contrast—and this was a sore point to him—did not have any large carriers of its own, though Admiral William Halsey and the USS *Saratoga* had stayed in the region a long while in 1943, and there were occasional temporary appearances of a carrier group from Pearl Harbor when a big operation was underway. In early 1944, for example, three-quarters of the new flat decks of Raymond Spruance's TF 58 pushed into the airspace around the Japanese base at the Admiralty Islands in order to knock out the defenses there. Hopeful that this might provoke a sortie from the Combined Fleet, this American strike was accompanied by no fewer than six of the newer fast battleships and nine brand-new heavy cruisers—the result at last of the massive naval shipbuilding plans of three to four years earlier. When the Japanese fleet failed to respond, the US heavy warships were at least given permission to bombard away against small military installations on nearby islands (Satawan and Ponape) in order to provide the gun crews with "a welcome change" from boredom.[3] Then the "big boys" of the US Navy swept northward again in order to prepare for the grand assault upon the Marianas. Behind them they left the smaller escort carriers, light cruisers, and destroyers that provided close air support to the US and Australian ground forces during their successful amphibious operations in the area—warships that may, in a way, have appeared as the poor relations to TF 58 but were much more fitting for the jobs in hand.

More encouragingly, MacArthur's land-based (that is, Army Air Force) bomber and fighter squadrons had grown in size by 1944 and could hit enemy bases and merchant convoys hard provided the range was not too great. Furthermore, even if this drive through the Southwest Pacific was slower, its very existence helped to keep the Japanese repeatedly off balance. They dared not keep their Combined Fleet in the south all the time lest Nimitz's forces make a bold drive in the direction of Japan itself, and they dared not base their navy out of, say, Okinawa lest there was a chance that MacArthur's forces actually drove sufficiently far westward as to cut the oil tanker route from the south. To some historians, then, though not for Fleet Admiral Ernest J. King, MacArthur's claims that these particular southern operations were important for the defeat of the Japanese Empire seem entirely plausible.[4]

Before this time of early 1944, then, it appeared that MacArthur was a plodder, as methodical and cautious (and self-righteous) a general as Bernard Montgomery was in the latter's campaigning along the North African coast and up the Italian Peninsula; that is, neither of them realized, once their respective enemy forces were crumbling and falling back, the chances of using sea power to make more ambitious amphibious leaps. Yet after the slowness shown in eastern New Guinea, leapfrogging was precisely what MacArthur's command began to do, consumed increasingly by the thought that Central Pacific Command's faster drive might turn their own area into a strategic backwater and might even make the reconquest of the Philippines seem unimportant. Fortunately for his position, both the Combined Chiefs of Staff in Ottawa in February 1944[5] and the US Chiefs had indicated a preference for moving on the Philippines— in preference to a Formosa landing or before a direct turn on Japan—and agreed to give MacArthur command of such a military operation, while the great carrier fleets would remain firmly under the navy. Even before detailed invasion planning could get underway, however, a few more steps in the great drive westward had to be taken, and if at all possible those Japanese main forces should be met with and crushed.

The type of warfare that followed, while hinted at already at Midway, had no equivalents in any earlier great contests, simply because the technology and weaponry had not been available then. The sheer distances of the Pacific Ocean plus the unequaled and fast-moving firepower of their new carrier task forces, supported by the fast fleet trains, gave the American planners a flexibility that they had never possessed before. Certain island groups might be identified as mere stepping-stones, of little strategic significance once they were taken over; thus, the northern Solomons and the Gilberts were neglected fairly soon after their seizure. Others, like Manus in the Admiralties (fully taken by May 1944), would remain of key importance as major naval refueling and repair bases, including for US submarine forces; and the Marianas were always a key target because Tinian and Saipan had been identified as flat enough to be converted into huge strategic bombing bases against Japan itself. Here was a freedom to pick and choose that a land general, tasked to conquer (say) Burma or Ukraine, did not possess. Certain Japanese-held islands, then, regarded earlier as important targets, could be hammered and then isolated and bypassed by American sea and air power when the planners realized how fast the advances might go; Rabaul, with its 100,000-strong garrison, had had its facilities crushed by Halsey's carrier attack and land-based air assaults and was thus left to wither on the vine. When US amphibious forces moved on the Marshall Islands in February 1944, having learned a lesson from the sheer bloodiness of Tarawa, they elected to leave alone the three more heavily garrisoned atolls of the group and instead, after far more thorough naval bombardments than in the Gilberts operation, to assault the three lightly held ones at Majuro, Kwajalein, and Eniwetok.[6]

Steadily, then, the American naval leadership was beginning to see that, in this gigantic Pacific campaign, physical possession of certain lands was of much less importance than the question of which of the foes had control of the open water—and the air space above. Perhaps the best example of all in this shift in assessments was that regarding Truk Atoll in the middle of the Carolines, a capacious anchorage often weirdly referred to as the "Gibraltar" of the central Pacific and sometimes used as a base for the Japanese Combined Fleet. But by February 17–18, 1944, when Spruance's giant Task Force 58 loomed down upon the atoll, the Imperial Japanese Navy (IJN) had prudently pulled back its heavier warships from Truk, and in fact, the US Navy had no intention of landing there, only of dealing its garrison and port facilities such a blow that they would be useless for the rest of the war. The whole series of strikes, appropriately called Operation Hailstone, were an indication of how much things had changed since, say, the early months of Guadalcanal. Spruance's force was by now the largest fleet in the world by far—15 carriers, 7 battleships, 10 cruisers, 28 destroyers, and over 560 planes—and its equipment so much superior; it was on the first day of aerial battles that the new Hellcats shot down 30 of the 80 Zero fighters scrambled for the loss of 4 of their own. Overall, the island base was flattened, the few smaller warships crushed, and over 200,000 tons of invaluable merchant shipping sunk. So defanged had Truk become that the Army Air Force later used it for easy target training purposes for brand-new B-29 crews in the Pacific.[7]

So far, the battleships and remaining fleet carriers of the Japanese Navy had not come out to oppose MacArthur's advance all along the New Guinea coast to Hollandia; had not stayed to fight for Rabaul, nor for Truk; and had remained at a distance when the Marshalls were taken. But by June 1944, as a Marianas invasion was looming and a subsequent threat to the Philippines came much closer, it was time to bring the Combined Fleet forward, spearheaded by Admiral Ozawa's still-considerable group of fleet carriers. The contest, though, was unfolding in a region—the Philippine Sea—studded with air bases and squadrons that could make up Japan's deficit in naval aircraft alone. What transpired was the largest carrier battle of the entire war, involving, again, some 15 American fleet and light fleet carriers, now opposed by 9 Japanese, and creating the war's biggest single aerial tussle over the Pacific, with a staggering 900 US carrier aircraft pitched against 450 carrier and 300 land-based Japanese planes.[8]

Within the two days of June 19–20, 1944, the Battle of the Philippine Sea was over, and it is easy to summarize its chief points. In the first place, this was, once again (that is, like Midway), a long-distance, carriers-versus-carriers contest, with no place for a showdown between the Japanese big guns (five battleships, eleven heavy cruisers) and the American ones (seven battleships, eight heavy cruisers). Each side had a battleship damaged a bit through a hostile air attack, but that was it. The giant new Japanese ships, like *Yamato,* and the fast and battle-keen *Iowa*-class boats of the Pacific Fleet were all too often mere observers to the action taking place above.

As a contest between what originally seemed to be two fairly equal naval air services, the Battle of the Philippine Sea remains remarkable. Above all, the extraordinarily unbalanced tally in losses that occurred on the first day of aerial combat between the naval squadrons still seems abnormal. There probably had been no larger set of dogfights in one day since the high point of the Battle of Britain (Eagle Day) back in September 1940, and here the same vista presented itself, of a sky full of aircraft trails, explosions, and planes on fire. And, like the Royal Air Force in its fight, the Americans benefited from having sophisticated radar and a Combat Air Control System to direct the squadrons. The first wave of Japanese aircraft ordered in by Ozawa was met by Hellcat patrols, and 25 (and then another 16) were shot down for the loss of 1 American plane. The second, more powerful wave totaled 107 planes, which were completely clobbered by the US fighters, and 97 of them were destroyed. There were 47 aircraft in the third wave, but these were warier about pressing on, and only 7 of them were shot down. A different group of 49 aircraft attempting to fly in to the Guam fields lost 30. By all accounts the Hellcats' performance was incredible, devastating in its speed and firepower, and very hard to destroy. The Mitsubishi Zero now looked like an out-of-date fighter (except on tight inward turns), and of course all the slower Japanese torpedo-bombers and dive-bombers were very vulnerable—no wonder the whole encounter was called the Great Marianas Turkey Shoot. The United States lost only 30 planes on that first day, the Japanese perhaps as many as 350, although calculating that figure is somewhat complicated by the other disaster that happened to the Japanese Naval Air Service, that is, the sinking of three of its six carriers.

The second stage of the contest was much messier, although no better for Japan. Ozawa was now ordering in land-based squadrons, which also suffered heavy losses, but it was the turn of Marc Mitscher's carrier command to overreach itself, sending out bombers (including Hellcats carrying 500-pound bombs) on a late-in-the-day attack against a retreating enemy fleet at a range that was simply too far. The incident cost some eighty aircraft that had to be ditched on the return flight. Yet that brought hardly any joy to the IJN, since their own carriers had the misfortune to run into now-potent American submarines and to lose both the large new carrier *Taiho* (Ozawa's flagship) and the renowned Pearl Harbor veteran *Shokaku,* blown apart by three torpedoes. A little later on, a mass of

US planes from TF 58 did find and sink a third Japanese light fleet carrier, *Hiyo*, as well as damaging the remaining three. Considering the huge number of Japanese aircraft destroyed overall on these two days—550 to 645, depending on the way of counting—plus the three carriers, this was as large a defeat as Midway. The latter battle had crushed a Japanese advance eastward toward Hawaii, while the Philippine Sea battle crushed a Japanese attempt to stop the Americans' advance westward. By this stage in the war, the IJN had lost no fewer than nine carriers and 90 percent of its naval air groups, with no prospect of replacing them. There being no sense in sending the Japanese battleships and heavy cruisers forward without air cover, the order was given to abandon the fight.

In consequence, of course, the critically important US invasion plans for Guam, Tinian, and Saipan could continue undisturbed, however tough the fighting on the ground was to be; the safety of the huge amphibious operation involving seventy-one thousand troops was, after all, Nimitz's chief strategic concern, which is why he defended Spruance when the carrier air enthusiasts in the fleet criticized the latter for keeping TF 58 too far back and failing to sink the main Japanese force.[9] Perhaps, indeed, those enthusiasts were right and the creation of the carrier task force had introduced a completely new form of naval warfare, and the more senior admirals were too cautious to understand that. But maybe it still was wise to be wary of Japanese subterfuges, decoys, and traps, then and in the future. Within another four months, at Leyte Gulf, that apprehension was to be well justified.

As plans for the recovery of the Philippines came to fruition, then, what was becoming obvious was that the US Navy had actually subdivided itself into three different forces: the traditional battleship navy, now being vastly strengthened by the arrival of the new *South Dakota*- and *Iowa*-class super-dreadnoughts; the carrier navy, self-evidently riding a wave of successes, also being reinforced by further new vessels; and the far less dashing but quite vital amphibious navy. Possessing all three naval elements made sense to the planners back in Washington, but the carrier lobby and the battleship lobby were each inclined to make large claims for their own importance. To the former, the sheer striking power of the massed aircraft squadrons of Nimitz's carrier navy argued that it would now be feasible for the American strategy to have its forces drive north after the Battle of the Philippine Sea and then capture Iwo Jima and Okinawa before a full invasion of Japan itself. Yet if the all-out advocates of the influence of bold-ranging, independent "naval air power"[10]—as opposed to mere "sea power"—felt that way, they were still in a minority in the navy at this time; and, in any case, cutting out the recovery of the Philippines would have aroused the bitterest opposition from MacArthur, still then laboring along the north shores of New Guinea (the important point of Hollandia was taken only in May 1944, as was Biak), determined to fulfill his promise to the Filipinos to "return." Furthermore, the acquisition of the Philippines would still keep open the China-coast option, and the very act of its invasion would flush out the Japanese battle fleet, many of whose units were now stationed in the south (Borneo) to be close to their limited fuel supplies. The American battleship admirals, like their Japanese equivalents, now looked to an attack on the Philippines to provoke an all-out big-gun shooting contest at last. Thus, for various motives, plans went ahead for an October 1944 invasion, with the first landings being along the eastern beaches in the vicinity of Leyte Gulf before moving on later to the city of Manila itself.[11] It was understandable, in turn, for the Japanese planners, who regarded continued possession of the Philippines as essential to the whole war, to assume that the Americans were coming that way.

None of this background helps explain, however, the extraordinarily elaborate nature of the Japanese plan (designation SHO-GO-1) for what would become the multipart Battle of Leyte Gulf, the greatest conflict between the two navies of the entire Pacific War. When Nelson's massed fleet of warships fought the Franco-Spanish fleets at Trafalgar (the battle with which Leyte Gulf is so often compared), his plan was to throw his whole force against the enemy. Even Admiral Tojo kept things simple in destroying the Russian Navy at Tsushima (1905), ordering his Japanese flotillas into immediate assault upon sight of the foe. But throughout World War II, Japanese naval planners seemed to prefer directing complex moves by many players—it had worked brilliantly in December 1941 (with moves against Pearl Harbor, Hong Kong, Manila, and the Malaya/Thai coast almost simultaneously), but it hadn't worked at Midway and had just failed disastrously at the Philippine Sea. Given modern fighting conditions, where the Americans were deploying submarine patrols, long-range aircraft, and radio-signal decrypts, it was exceedingly risky for the IJN to devise complicated stratagems and presume they *wouldn't* be detected. As it was here, for example, a decoy group of light carriers plus the *Zuikaku* (Admiral Ozawa's fleet) would come south from Japan and was intended to pull the dangerous main US carrier fleet up to the north and thus away from the landings at Leyte. As that ruse was hopefully working, a quite different force of battleships and cruisers under Admiral Takeo Kurita (including the two super-battleships *Yamato* and *Musashi*) would be coming up from the southwest, winding its way through the islands of the Sibuyan Sea in order to find and destroy the American landings. At the same time, another attack group of older battleships under Admiral Shoji Nishimura would emerge further to the south after

**PAINTING 44.** Japanese super-battleships *Yamato* and *Musashi* lurking in Brunei Bay, 1944. The irony of Ian Marshall's painting could not be greater: here are the two largest battleships in the world, looking like gigantic highwaymen. But they frequently had inadequate fuel supplies, which prevented them from operating. The *Musashi* was battered and crushed by US carrier aircraft at Leyte Gulf, and the *Yamato* was sunk during its suicide run toward Okinawa in April 1945.

its journey through the Surigao Strait to take on the American landing forces from that direction. What was more, the various Japanese forces would keep strict radio silence, understandable if they wished to surprise the Americans but risky in that they also lost contact with each other.[12]

In creating this elaborate scheme, the Japanese planners were seeking to compensate for their various weaknesses vis-à-vis the US Central Pacific Fleet. By this time, even Kurita and his fellow battleship admirals seem to have been fully aware that the tides of war had turned against Japan. Their naval air force was now but a shell of its former self, with few planes (about 100) and fewer trained aircrew on Ozawa's carriers. Still, they felt that if the latter really decoyed Halsey's powerful Task Force 58 away from Leyte, then even if they suffered heavily, the risks would be worth it. Moreover, despite all the losses at Truk and the Philippine Sea, Japan still possessed a number of land-based air squadrons that could, it was hoped, cover their own southern battle fleets and bomb the American amphibious forces. And there might be a real chance, if the dangerous American fleet carriers were off the scene, not only to crush the invasion but also, at last, to engage the new enemy battleships with their own giant dreadnoughts. Perhaps this was all overly optimistic, though in fact most Japanese admirals by now felt that they had very little choice but to commit everything they had as soon as their foe's amphibious craft touched down. In sum, given the unbalanced advantage the Americans now had with their hosts of fleet carriers, some sort of plot, like Ozawa's, was definitely needed. Besides, the enemy could make mistakes, and even at this late stage the Japanese could get lucky.

In fact, the American enemy, in the form of the impulsive Admiral Halsey, did make mistakes, and there were occasions during the harrowing four days of battle, October 23–26, when Japan's chances of delivering a severe blow came very close to success; when the decoy strategy worked very well, at least for a while; and when, as one consequence, a relatively small force of US escort carriers off Leyte found itself close to the heavy guns of Kurita's fast-approaching battleships. Moreover, what looked like a decisive American numerical advantage was considerably reduced by the fact that two of the four carrier divisions of TF 58 had been headed toward Ulithi for resupply when the Japanese counteroffensive suddenly opened up, and therefore they came rather late onto the scene. But the surprises were not all on Tokyo's side, and certain acts of small-ship initiative—the devastation of three of Kurita's heavy cruisers early on by a couple of American subs, USS *Darter* and USS *Dace,* and a stunningly brave defense of the escort carriers by their own small destroyers off Samar—frustrated Japan's planned ambushes. Even the scheme to have Nishimura's secondary battleship force secretly wind its way through the southern islands and emerge from the Surigao Strait was frustrated when it encountered a flotilla of Rear Admiral Jesse Oldendorf's rebuilt Pearl Harbor dreadnoughts "crossing the T" ahead of it and pouring full broadsides at the vulnerable and confused Japanese ships. Yet parts of their overelaborate decoy scheme almost did work, and Halsey fell so completely for the deception that he continued to send the main TF 58 fleet after Ozawa's force and away from the critical landings area until compelled to change course southward again. But he thereby failed to make battle contact at all. No wonder that naval academies in later years would so frequently war-game the many fascinating what-if aspects of the Leyte Gulf story.[13]

But if one wished to take one lesson from this extensive, multiact battle, it must be the way in which the sheer punishing force of American carrier-borne air attacks made every enemy warship, even the largest and best-armed of them, so very vulnerable. Here the fate of the giant, brand-new, 18-inch-gunned battleship *Musashi* on October 24, 1944, simply confirmed what had been increasingly clear since the sinking of the HMS *Prince of Wales* three years earlier: without their own strong aerial defenses, surface vessels had little or no chance against massed attacks from the air. Precisely in order to protect the 72,000-ton Japanese monster from attacking aircraft, the designers had given it a secondary armament of 6- and 5-inch guns and smaller-caliber weapons, but then, in a further 1944 refurbishment, they added no fewer than 130 25mm antiaircraft guns so that the ship did indeed look like a "castle of steel"—no wonder it needed a crew of 2,400 men. Moreover, having provided the *Musashi* with such thick armor as to resist 16-inch American shells, it was assumed that it was also invulnerable to torpedoes and bombs. But massed attacks upon a single warship, causing multiple fires that then spread, were something else. Once Kurita's battle force was detected picking its way through the inland seas, the *Musashi* especially was subject to repeated assaults from the Helldiver dive-bombers and Avenger torpedo-bombers from four US carriers, the *Essex, Franklin, Intrepid,* and *Enterprise;* overall, the vessel was overwhelmed by nineteen torpedo and seventeen bomb hits from 259 aircraft. American aerial photographs show the warship stopped in the waters of the Sibuyan Sea, surrounded by plumes of smoke and the splashes of bombs shortly before its end; and at 5:30 p.m. on that same day, the world's largest battleship, battered beyond recognition, slid below the waves and exploded underwater.[14] Meanwhile, further to the south the older battleships *Fuso* and *Yamashiro* were heading toward the enemy's trap laid in the Surigao Strait and would also be sunk.

One other Japanese warship casualty of the Leyte Gulf battles seems worthy of a tribute here: the fleet carrier *Zuikaku,* the very last of the six carriers that had attacked Pearl Harbor and a central combatant in and the only carrier surviving such epic battles as those at the Coral Sea (May 1942) and the Philippine Sea (June 1944). At the height of its fighting career, and with what were probably the best-trained naval aircrews in the world, it could brush away all opposition at sea—witness its part in the Indian Ocean foray of April 1942, where its aircraft nabbed the British carrier HMS *Hermes,* or the fatal blows its planes struck against the USS *Hornet* later that year. But here, in the complex Japanese master plan to defend the Philippines, it was an expensive decoy, Japan's sole fleet carrier but without proper air squadrons, offered along with the smaller carriers as a sort of sacrifice to pull the all-powerful TF 58 away from Leyte. When it eventually was found and attacked by US carrier planes, the *Zuikaku* was sunk swiftly by seven torpedoes and nine bombs.[15] Just before it rolled over, Admiral Ozawa left it, for the second time in four months transferring his flag to a light cruiser, since all three smaller carriers had also been sunk. One of the great fighting ships of World War II had been risked as part of an ingenious Japanese ploy; but it was a vessel that was sacrificed in vain, just as the overall plan failed.

The Battle of Leyte Gulf dealt an irreversible blow to Japan's position in the Pacific. Not only did it mean that the American reconquest of the Philippines could continue, but it also led to the end of the IJN per se. Total Japanese losses from all these fights and ancillary operations were four carriers (including the *Zuikaku*), three battleships (including the *Musashi*), and no less than eight heavy and four light cruisers, plus nine destroyers. By comparison, the US losses were negligible, the light fleet carrier USS *Princeton* being the biggest vessel sunk. The loss of the newly refitted *Musashi* especially chilled the battleship fleet—if it, with all of its antiaircraft guns, could not deal with the enemy's planes, which great ship could? Japan's large and proud fleet of heavy cruisers, the biggest of that type in the world, was now in shreds. Above all, the carrier navy was finished. That extraordinary force now lay as shattered as, say, the Spanish infantry after Rocroi or the French Army after Sedan. Remnants of the Combined Fleet crawled away, to Singapore in the south or back to Japanese ports. Some damaged craft were never repaired; some intact warships were later blown apart in harbor by American or British bombing; and others didn't go anywhere due to lack of fuel. After Leyte Gulf, Japan's navy never operated again, because it no longer had a navy.

It was therefore symptomatic of the Japanese war planners' desperation at the worsening military and naval situation that the first organized suicide planes, or kamikazes, were unleashed upon US warships and invasion vessels at this time. There was an easy military explanation for this shift to such a drastic form of fighting—an aircraft laden with explosives and piloted directly into the deck of an enemy vessel had a far greater chance of crippling the target than a bomb from a high-level aircraft or even a dive-bomber or a torpedo-bomber; and Japan still possessed thousands of (less than first-class) planes that could perform that mission and young, idealistic pilots to undertake the suicide task. Even a plane damaged by antiaircraft fire might still be driven ahead into its target. One single aircraft, like the Zero that was crashed into the escort carrier USS *St. Lo* off Samar on October 25, could trigger explosions that would be fateful. It was an early warning sign. That suicide plane was one from a special group, the Shikishima Attack Unit, which was deployed on such a mission for the first time; and thus the *St. Lo*, constructed only a year earlier in one of the new Kaiser shipyards, had the dubious distinction of being the first large American warship sunk in this way. At this time, however, the number of kamikazes was too small to stop the American operation—although the US Navy suffered damage to seven other escort carriers and many smaller ships from suicide planes during the overall Leyte Gulf encounter[16]—and the whole phenomenon remained a sign of Japan's desperation. It must have been bittersweet to some Japanese naval officers that the first organized kamikaze squadrons (brainchild of Rear Admiral Masafumi Arima, who died in an early attack, to give an example) were formed from within a naval air service once used to effortless domination of the Pacific skies and that the most used suicide plane itself was the Mitsubishi Zero, now less useful in aerial battles against the clearly superior Hellcats and Corsairs. Still, this was a taste of what was to come as US forces got closer to the Japanese homeland, and even the all-powerful Pacific Fleet—and especially its flattops—could be vulnerable if effective defenses were not established.

Leyte Gulf was, along with the Battle of Midway, the closest that the American and Japanese navies ever came to a grand Mahanian contest between rival battle fleets for control of the central seas. The total tonnage of the respective warships committed to the fray was indeed huge, larger than that in any other naval fight so far; and the American battleship admirals and their historians took some pride in the fact that a large enemy surface force had been sunk by the gunnery of Oldendorf's heavy ships, although, as noted above, because of Halsey's misjudgments none of the newer fast battleships had the chance to fire in combat.[17] It was, therefore, those Pearl Harbor veterans the USS *West Virginia* and USS *Tennessee,* recovered and refurbished, that had the distinction of being the last dreadnoughts ever to engage in battleship-versus-battleship action. Considering the overall fighting both here at Leyte Gulf and a little further back at the Philippine Sea, it seemed clear that it was becoming less and less likely for the big-gunned warships to clash in some epic shootout.

What the new fast battleships might be good at, though, given their huge amount of antiaircraft guns with proximity-fused shells, would be to act as close escort to their own carriers in the coming fights against the kamikazes. This was certainly not a role the battleship captains would rejoice in, but there was much logic to it.

By contrast, another branch of the US Navy, the Submarine Service, found 1944 to be the year that its promise as an effective strike force at last showed itself. Although it had swung into action only after an unconscionably late start due to defective torpedoes, it was eager now to exploit its many advantages. To begin with, it had a cadre of experienced captains and crews, many of whom had been on Pacific missions since early in the war. They all rejoiced, moreover, at the advent of much roomier and more reliable boats; the *Gato*-class subs, for example, displaced around 1,700 tons (much more when fully laden), were equipped with six forward-firing and four rear-firing torpedo tubes, and had a great range; based partly out of Hawaii and partly out of Australian ports like Fremantle, they could be sent out to cruise for weeks in search of plum targets. As time went on, they were also used for advanced picket duty, as transports for secret missions, and as rescue vessels for downed American airmen. They were sometimes invaluable in reporting back to Nimitz's headquarters early Japanese fleet moves. Above all, they made the Western Pacific and Southeast Asian waters dangerous, both to the enemy's warships and, equally critically, to his mercantile marine.[18]

The flood of new US submarines coming into Pacific waters throughout 1944 was symptomatic of that overall post-1943 burst in shipbuilding output detailed in chapter 8. In the case of these boats, the multiple locations of the shipyards demonstrated the country's continent-wide productivity at its best, and some parts of the story are astonishing. No fewer than twenty-eight of the navy's two-hundred-plus new subs were built in Wisconsin (!), at the Manitowoc Shipbuilding Company. Here again, it is possible to do a tracing history from the beginning of the story to the end. The USS *Hardhead*, for example, was a somewhat larger *Balao*-class submarine (2,400 tons submerged) that was launched at Manitowoc in December 1943, trained in Lake Michigan initially, carried on top of a huge barge through the locks and canals to the Mississippi, and finally commissioned in the Gulf in April 1944 before being sent to Pearl Harbor that June. On its first patrol in August 1944 it sank the Japanese light cruiser *Natori* in the San Bernardino Strait and had further success, chiefly against merchant ships, in every one of its later patrols until the war's end, although in the last few months it and its fellow subs found that they had run out of targets.[19] On so many occasions, the scarcely trained Japanese destroyers would react to the submarine's surprise attack by wildly strewing depth charges, but the American boats, although bulky compared to

German and British vessels, could go deep, move fairly fast under water, and stay down for a long time; a total of fifty-two US subs, roughly one in five of those deployed, were lost due to all causes during the entire war.[20]

More than the submarines of any of the other large navies, American boats were successfully deployed to work in conjunction with the US main surface forces during major fleet actions, both to act as vital lookouts and then as attackers. At the Battle of the Philippine Sea, it had been the two *Gato*-class subs (built in the greatly enhanced Groton yards) USS *Albacore* and USS *Cavalla*—and not the all-conquering American planes in the skies above—that had taken out the two large fleet carriers *Taiho* and *Shokaku*. And it was early in the very next big clash that two other Groton-built *Gato*-class subs, USS *Darter* and USS *Dace,* opened up the Battle of Leyte Gulf by sinking two and badly damaging a third Japanese heavy cruiser, in a foreshadowing of Admiral Kurita's many other losses. Equipped with radar and various other detection devices, with good surface speed and that six-torpedo-spread "punch," American submarines, sometimes in small clusters, ranged up and down the enemy's main maritime routes, hoping to find a prize target like a warship but happy to sink an oil tanker or two. It was during the later stages of just such an opportunistic patrol in late November 1944, the submarine's fifth to date, that the USS *Archerfish* detected ahead the gigantic shape of the super-battleship–turned–carrier *Shinano,* poorly escorted by three destroyers, and put a spread of four torpedoes into its side. The blow was fatal, and the boat sank fast. In earlier times in the war, the sinking of its largest aircraft carrier by far would have been a terrible shock to the IJN. Yet since Japan's proud Naval Air Service was by now chiefly reduced to providing training to new kamikaze pilots, the *Shinano*'s abrupt disappearance without having fought in battle meant much less. Its elimination was close to being the final nail in the coffin.[21]

Still, however remarkable the US submariners' record in sinking enemy warships during the Pacific War, in strategic terms it was their destruction of Japan's overseas merchant trade that counted most. Simply put, the American success in strangling Japanese shipping represented exactly what Karl Doenitz's U-boats had striven in vain for six years to do to British trade and the British wartime economy. As noted earlier, the IJN was strangely backward in regard to the critical issue of the protection of seaborne trade, believing (like the Royal Navy at the beginning of the war) that ASDIC would solve the submarine detection issue, and had never studied convoy operations at all; yet these weaknesses were of little importance if US torpedoes were defective, shot under their targets, or bounced off them. When those defects were overcome by late 1943, however, the American submarines came into their own, and Japanese merchant-ship losses began to soar, especially among the heavier cargo

**PAINTING 45.** USS *Archerfish* stalking the Japanese super-carrier *Shinano*, Honshu, 1944. This is a classic scene in US naval history; the scarcely visible *Balao*-class submarine is stalking the giant, 72,000-ton carrier and about to launch a spread of six torpedoes at it. The *Shinano* capsized within hours, the largest warship ever sunk by a submarine.

I. H. M.

ships and the oil tankers coming from the south—prime targets indeed. The loss statistics speak for themselves. In 1942, American submarines had sunk a mere 600,000 tons of Japanese shipping, a figure that its ship-building industry could replace without straining; but by 1944, Japanese merchant-ship losses had quadrupled, to around 2.4 million deadweight tons, and as imports plummeted, Japan's key industries were plunged into crisis. How could the war economy function, for example, without energy supplies, and yet the import of the latter was withering away quickly as the submarines' torpedoes slammed into oiler after oiler—between 1943 and 1944, according to Symonds's account,[22] oil imports fell by 48 percent and coal imports dropped by around 66 percent. Yet it had been in order to obtain secure sources of petroleum that Japan had recklessly gone to war in the first place. Moreover, if things looked bad for Japanese imports from the south (Dutch East Indies, Borneo, and Indochina) in the first half of 1944, they looked terrible after that October, when the American takeover of the Philippines began.

Taken all together, the IJN's warship losses at the battles of the Philippine Sea and Leyte Gulf were colossal—as we have seen, seven carriers alone, virtually its entire Fleet Air Arm along with all their aircraft and crews—and there was no flow of newer Japanese warships coming into the Pacific War, as there was from America's many yards, to make up for the losses. As with the Kriegsmarine at this time, every heavy warship lost was, well, a goner, not to be replaced. If one put that together with the US move into key islands of the Philippines and the severance therefore of Japan's maritime routes to the south plus the taking of the Marianas, the beginnings of the bombing of Japan's cities (and shipyards!), and the tightening submarine blockade, one had to conclude that the end was in sight. Perhaps diplomatic ways might be found to persuade Tokyo to agree to surrender. If it chose to fight on, however, the next forward steps by the American colossus would also be amphibious operations—Iwo Jima, Okinawa, and then the home islands—all leading to the collapse of Japan itself. But there would be no Japanese Navy there to come out and fight. At the close of 1944, then, not many foresaw what a tense and difficult time the next season of fighting the Pacific War would involve before that collapse occurred.

## The God Neptune Comes Ashore: The Normandy Operation and Allied Sea Power

To British strategic planners of this time, there must have been something deeply satisfying about the Allied invasion of France on June 6, 1944. It oc-

**PAINTING 46.** D-Day invasion fleet assembled at Spithead, June 1944. As occurred here and throughout the other harbors of southern England and South Wales, by June 6, 1944, a vast force of landing ships, supply vessels, and naval escorts was heading out, across the English Channel. In the foreground is the light cruiser HMS *Danae,* especially equipped for antiaircraft duties.

curred almost four years to the day after the final evacuation of Dunkirk, and yet the two events—the British expulsion and the Anglo-American return—were inherently connected. The Wehrmacht's victory in mid-1940 did not knock Britain out of the war, and three months later the Luftwaffe's huge aerial campaign was blunted. The invasion of Britain was then impossible. But any counterinvasion of German-dominated western Europe was also impossible—of this Churchill was convinced throughout—until three other strategic prerequisites were achieved. The first was to secure uninterrupted control of the sea-lanes supplying the British Isles, the great future base for the Allied invasion forces, but that had meant the defeat of the U-boat menace, which came only in the summer of 1943. The second was to attain command of the air, not just over France but also over the Reich, and that was properly secured, interestingly enough, only by early 1944.[23] The third and absolutely critical prerequisite had been of course the entry of the United States into the war and the commitment by the American government to a Germany First strategy, for only its vast productive power could guarantee that the Allies would be strong enough to push their way into France. Yet there was also a fourth great factor at work, though it was far to the east, namely, the vast Nazi-Soviet struggle that sapped so much of the Third Reich's resources and was still pinning down the majority of the German Army's divisions in 1944. When Eisenhower gave his June 5 order for Operation Overlord to take place the next day, all the advantages—control of the seas, aerial supremacy, and a huge invasion army—were his. And his German opponent was severely distracted and weakened by a great war on the Eastern Front.

The Allied victory in the "battle of the sea-lanes" had flowed from the defeat of the submarine wolf packs during the key convoy battles of May 1943 and the further punishment of the U-boats during the North African and Gibraltar convoy campaigns in the six months following.[24] Operationally, then, the Battle of the Atlantic during the first half of 1944 produced no surprises. Doenitz equipped his U-boats with more and more detection equipment, but of course anything with an electronic signal was equally likely to be picked up by Allied aircraft and warships; and whether the submarine chose to dive or to fight it out on the surface, its enemy could follow it nonetheless. Homing torpedoes would pursue any U-boat, though it twisted and turned; and a flying boat facing a sub that wished to fight it out on the surface might call in rocket-firing Beaufighters or naval escorts. Doenitz also equipped his fleet with the dangerous Zaunkoenig homing torpedo of his own, chiefly intended to find and sink the convoy escorts, but the British soon countered with an effective noise-making device (appropriately called a Foxer). Individual U-boats had individual successes against merchantmen in more-coastal waters, but they gained less and less access to the Atlantic and Gibraltar convoys, which as 1944 unfolded became bigger and bigger. Only half a dozen merchantmen were sunk in the Atlantic during the second half of 1944, and submarine losses were now far higher than those of their intended victims—in fact, 234 U-boats were sunk during the entire year, only a few less than in the grim 1943.[25] It was all rather weird, statistically speaking: November 1944 was the highest production month for U-boats of the entire war (so much for Allied strategic bombing), and Doenitz still had over 100 submarines at sea on any given day, but they scarcely came near a convoy, never in pack attacks, and most were sunk in other places. It had not been all that long ago when U-boat aces like Guenther Prien and Otto Kretschmer had run amok inside ill-defended Allied convoys, but that was becoming a distant memory to both sides.

The establishment of a well-escorted convoy system itself throughout 1944—with only approximately 10 percent of the shipping losses of 1942 and a further surge in US shipbuilding output—meant not only increasing safety for the tens of thousands of merchant sailors but also, of course, the victory of the Allied grand strategy for the defeat of Nazi Germany. If one anecdote serves to make that point, perhaps it can be the story of the (*Halifax*-designation) Atlantic convoy HX-300, which sailed in late July 1944 to the United Kingdom. It was the largest convoy of the entire war, some 166 merchantmen escorted by no less than 32 warships and continuous air patrols. Leaving from the harbors of New York, Halifax, Sydney, and Nova Scotia, this huge assembly was formed into nineteen parallel columns, with the whole body of ships roughly nine miles wide and four miles long. *There were no casualties.* But this of course was because there were no attacks—the U-boats were no longer in the Greenland Gap; thanks to long-range air patrols, there was no "gap." Even the hunter-killer groups, patrolling wider afield, were finding fewer and fewer opportunities. And the Luftwaffe had stopped attacking Atlantic convoys after March. As it was, most of the merchantmen unloaded in British ports, but nine were going on, in the next Arctic convoy, to North Russia, and a full forty-six were going to steam around the British Isles to French and Belgian harbors, bringing to the newly landed coalition armies vital supplies of food, fuel, and ammunition, not to mention "trucks, half-tracks, jeeps [and] locomotives" to keep those British and Canadian divisions moving in the direction of the Third Reich.[26] The thousands of trucks and jeeps may have been produced as far away as Michigan, but by two months after D-Day they were already crossing the Meuse; they had flowed along a giant umbilical cord, from factory to front line, across the broad, virtually U-boat-free North Atlantic. This really was an irresistible force.

HX-300 was, as its name suggests, the three hundredth Allied convoy that had sailed out of Halifax across the Atlantic since the initial categorization of the trade-protection system had been set up back in 1939–40. A further six enormous though not quite so grand HX convoys had crossed the Atlantic earlier that year, before the Normandy campaign had begun; and many more merchantmen had come up from the south, in the Freetown or Latin American / Caribbean convoys. The initial purpose of these orchestrated and protected clusters of cargo vessels, oil tankers, and ore carriers had simply been to sustain the beleaguered British Isles in the fight against Nazi Germany even when all the rest of Europe had fallen. But that early, heroic, "we stand alone" phase of the war was long over, and since 1942 the purpose had been to turn the United Kingdom into the largest preinvasion "forward base" in history, with several millions of

**PAINTING 47.** HMS *Starling*, Liverpool, 1943. The sloop *Starling* was the flagship of the famous Captain Johnny Walker, RN, and was the highest-scoring U-boat destroyer (with fourteen kills) of the war. Its sheer fighting power and speed compared with the little HMS *Pink* (see painting 8) could not be more obvious. After 1943, "hunter-killer" groups of four to six sloops protected most major convoys and rendered U-boat attacks impossible.

American, British Commonwealth, and associated soldiers waiting to be conveyed across the Channel.[27] And all this was to take place under the assured security provided by thousands of aircraft based upon so many (two hundred) newly built airfields that it must have appeared that eastern and southern England had been turned into one huge airstrip.[28]

It all fitted together, although perhaps only the Admiralty and British ports- and railway-authority planners knew how intimately it all worked. Those hundreds of thousands of American troops could be rushed across the North Atlantic at high speed in the giant Queen liners and then pour out onto the docksides and railway platforms of Greenock and Liverpool, while many thousands of brand-new aircraft (B-17s and B-24s, Mustangs and Lightnings, and medium bombers) flew overhead each month, via Newfoundland bases, in the careful hands of the Allied Transport Command's male and female pilots.[29] But the 3 million troops waiting in southern England campsites for the go-ahead invasion sign needed sustenance and armaments and gasoline as well as their tanks and trucks, just as the three thousand bomber aircraft in UK bases needed a constant inflow of fuel to be able to take to the skies. If those dark times when U-boat aces were blowing up Allied oil tankers in the mid-Atlantic were thankfully no more, then that great improvement also meant there were no fuel shortages to restrict the giant RAF and USAAF raids on Germany. By contrast, all of the Axis armed services suffered from growing and chronic fuel shortages during the later stages of the very conflict they had instigated in order to escape from their petroleum dependency.

Given the vast amount of literature that has gone into analyzing and explaining both the timing and the location of Operation Overlord in early June 1944, the summary here can be brief. The 1941 Churchill-Roosevelt understanding that Nazi Germany, with its far more advanced military-technical capacities, was the much more dangerous foe overall and thus had to be defeated as the first priority was soon followed by a long period of deep Anglo-American discords over *the when and the where* of the necessary invasion of Europe. The need for some display of progress to the US people led to the decision to occupy North Africa in late 1942 and to the further decisions to use the existing planes, troops, and landing craft to move upon Sicily and Italy from July 1943 onward. Yet Churchill and his generals could not hold out any longer from the American (and Soviet) pressure to open a second front in western France by 1944, and the only issue became how soon, practically, might the giant landings take place. Command of the sea-lanes had to be assured, of course, and it was not clear to the Allies until late in 1943—after the last big convoy fights of September—that the U-boat menace really had been suppressed; after that, what was needed was another six-months-plus uninterrupted flow of men and munitions to the United Kingdom, as described above. Achieving command of the air over a reequipped Luftwaffe took longer, and it wasn't until the coming of the long-range P-51 Mustang fighters and the decimation of Germany's aces in early 1944 that the Allied planners could be certain they would also have full aerial mastery. (In that sense, General George C. Marshall had been wrong to push for a 1943 cross-channel operation.) By this time, too, but only after Eisenhower had urgently pressed for it, the necessary number of the all-important landing craft had at last reached the invasion armies. Intelligence was good, and deception ploys well in hand. All that remained was to find a period of relatively calm weather to ease the difficulties of landing amid the tricky tides on the other side of the English Channel; as it happened, and very late in the day, atmospheric conditions were forecast to improve just enough by the morning of June 6, 1944.[30] The invasion was on!

Selecting the location for the gigantic operation was somewhat easier to accomplish, even if that also was not decided in detail until fairly late in the day. For all the attractiveness of crossing the Channel at the narrowest point, meaning an invasion of the Pas de Calais region, the area was simply too constricted, especially at sea, to allow for the physically huge forces that were going be committed to defeating the German Army in the field. The landing areas therefore had to be further to the west, along the Normandy coastline, which would in turn make it closer for those amphibious units coming from the west of England and from South Wales and much more convenient for direct trans-Atlantic supply. It also followed that it would be simpler for the American armies (two of them) to land on the westernmost beaches, with a completely new Canadian army landing in the middle zone and the British armies (two of them) landing on their individual beaches further up the Channel. This was not quite island-hopping along the lines of the Pacific campaign, and yet to some of the veteran Anglo-American divisions, and certainly to Admiral Bertram Ramsay and his joint planning team, this was going to be the fourth and by far the most important step in a long succession: North Africa, Sicily, Salerno, and now Normandy.

The multiple landing operations and ancillary measures carried out by the Allies in Normandy and beyond from June 6 onward were of enormous complexity, and yet that complexity never really caused a big problem for the mass amphibious forces. The very map of the five approach-and-withdrawal routes of escorting warships, landing craft, and bombardment groups excites admiration still, even today.

To be sure, it might be said that from the late-1942 North African landings onward, the Allied armies had been planning and rehearsing for this all along, the ultimate amphibious operation in the European war, and

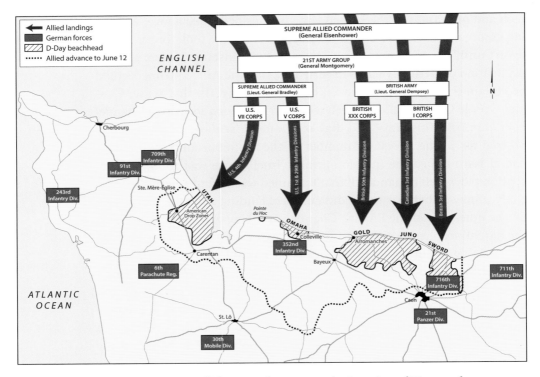

**MAP 14.** Five parallel approach routes to the invasion of Normandy.

that they had invested so much effort and resources into Overlord that it couldn't possibly go wrong. But Eisenhower and his planners didn't think like that, and after the scare they had received at Salerno the previous September, perhaps they were wise to be very cautious. The notorious Atlantic Wall of carefully constructed pill boxes, tank traps, beach obstacles, and offshore minefields was quite different from anything the initial landing forces would have encountered before—compared to the empty beaches of North Africa or the Italian coastal villages where the locals came down to help the GIs unload—and the defending troops would all be German, many of them veterans from Eastern Front campaigns. If their heavy Waffen-SS panzer divisions were let loose, they could slice their way right through the necessarily messy and crushed Allied beachheads before Eisenhower's troops had managed to gain a secure hold. And if—this was another big if—the weather was unkind and stormy, then not only would that make things difficult out in the Channel, but low clouds would completely negate the massive Allied preponderance in the air. Naval power could provide the battleships and cruisers to blow the roof off even the thickest German gun emplacements, and destroyers could steam right in close to shore in support of the pinned-down troops on Omaha

Beach, but much of the battle would be decided by the fighting on land; should formidable Wehrmacht divisions be allowed to establish strong defenses in the Normandy *bocage*, there might be a real stalemate, even a great setback. (Was Eisenhower thinking of such a prospect on the night before the landings, when he sat down and penned his hypothetical letter of resignation to Roosevelt and Churchill, accepting full responsibility for the failure of the operation?)[31]

In June 1944, then, the Allied invaders were both clever and lucky. With a dogmatic Fuehrer and deferential aides (Alfred Jodl, for example) convinced that the main attack would come in the Pas de Calais and with the British deception measures like the false Army Group Patton and the complete blurring of German radar screens encouraging the idea of a cross-channel invasion, the main Wehrmacht armored units were indeed located in the wrong place when huge numbers of enemy troops and vehicles began pouring onto the Normandy beaches. Yet there was nothing lucky about the highly detailed interdiction plans of the Allied tactical air forces to destroy all the bridges and railway junctions to the west of Paris and thus paralyze any longer-distance counteroffensive. Really, the invaders' superior firepower in all dimensions put the defenders at a disadvantage whichever way they located their dozen or so panzer divisions: if they scattered their tank battalions forward along the entire coastline from Brittany to the Scheldt, those units could be blown apart from the 15-inch shells of Allied battleships, carefully directed by spotters in the air or already onshore; yet if they held them back as a great reserve army, they might be ordered to deliver a blow to the invasion only to find they were clobbered by the thousands of available enemy aircraft. As it happened, both the naval bombardment vessels and the multiple Allied air squadrons were used to disrupt and drive back all German efforts to throw the invaders back into the sea. Once the precarious situation on Omaha Beach—the only one of the five that was in any way threatened—was stabilized by the end of the first day, the success of the great amphibious operation was pretty much assured. If there was much hard fighting on land ahead of the Allied armies and one hard surprise counterblast at the end of the year (in the Battle of the Bulge), the predominant sea power of the Anglo-American navies had fulfilled its task.

Yet if the "influence of sea power upon history" was shown beyond doubt by this vast amphibious landing, it is nonetheless interesting to observe what types of navies were needed on this occasion. Lots and lots of landing craft, to be sure, with each of the five invasion zones having its own close-in bombardment support group, but that could all be done by older battleships, veterans of Jutland and Pearl Harbor, not the *King George V*s and *Iowa*-class modern capital ships that were being sent off to the maritime contest in the Pacific. Nor did the Overlord landings re-quire modern fleet carriers—in contrast to those of Task Force 58 just then encircling Saipan—and thus already by this time three of Britain's *Illustrious*-class boats had been sent east, and the fourth was soon to fol-low. Thus the answer to the pointed question "Why were aircraft carriers not at D-Day?" is that the dozens of air bases along England's south coast, a mere twenty minutes' flying time from Normandy and with a sophis-ticated form of Combat Air Control already in place, constituted a giant aircraft carrier in themselves.[32] Not even the ubiquitous small escort car-riers were needed for this operation because of the blanket air cover pro-vided by the massive RAF and USAAF armadas.

The real demonstration of sea power's influence, though, had come well before the occasion of D-Day itself. The greatest contribution of the West-ern maritime nations to the defeat of Hitler's attempt to dominate Europe had been in maintaining the sea-lanes from the outside world to the Brit-ish Isles during the dark years of 1940–41 and in continuing to preserve naval mastery—even during the convoy crisis in the Atlantic of March–June 1943—so that Britain could become the giant springboard for the Al-lied bombers and armies that were unleashed upon the Third Reich in the latter part of the war. There is no need at this point to seek to join the de-bate over whether the Red Army or Anglo-American air-sea power was more responsible than the other for defeating the Nazi foe.[33] The fact is that Germany had made a huge effort to get control of the Atlantic world after France's fall in 1940, had been held in check by the British gate-keepers during the next year, and then had its naval, air, and land forces steadily crushed by the technologically and numerically superior West-ern states. The skeptical and often pessimistic Field Marshal Alanbrooke was perhaps justified in shaking his head at it all as he stood on a slope on the French side of the Channel in early July 1944, looking in wonder at the scene below. The grand plan for Overlord really had worked.[34]

## Wrapping Up the Flanks: The Arctic and the Mediterranean

While Operation Overlord constituted, to American satisfaction, that grand direct assault at last on the Third Reich's hold over western France, the larger map of maritime events in this region for 1944 would show two other enveloping drives, one around the north of the continent, and the second, far bigger (and amphibious) effort in the south. The Allies' na-val and aerial pressures in northern waters included the continued flow of critical supplies to Russia carried by the Arctic convoys (except in the high summer months), the elimination of the final great surface-vessel

threat to those routes—the *Tirpitz*—by the end of the year, and some significant close-in fighting against Germany's own convoys along the Norwegian coast. And the southern prong was of course the continuation of
the "Mediterranean strategy of World War Two"[35] even after the fall of
Italy, the naval parts of which were very considerable indeed, including
the original landings and then the large-scale amphibious flow of men
and supplies to stabilize the precarious position on the Anzio beaches,
the continued fight against the still-active German U-boat threat, and the
huge (chiefly US Navy) landings in the South of France, Operation Anvil. Apart from the brief scare at Anzio, which was of course about a potential setback on land, all these activities were, in the larger sense, about
the Western Allies going forward to envelop their German enemy from
the sea, while along the Eastern Front the Red Army was also inexorably heading toward Berlin. The best that the Wehrmacht could do in such
dire circumstances was to slow down these advances, though only for a
brief while.

The same Allied domination was also true in the north. Any reference
to the battleship *Tirpitz* being still a threat to the Russia convoys has to
be put in context; what its existence did do, ironically, was to display the
sheer size of the Allied sea power that could be brought to bear in this
theater of war, which was after all the core area of the Royal Navy's Home
Fleet. Thus, for example, in order to protect the important Arctic convoy JW-58 of some sixty merchantmen, which set out from Scotland in
late March 1944, the Admiralty allocated a close escort of three destroyers
and three corvettes, with two escort carriers embedded within this mass
of ships; plus an ocean escort of a cruiser flagship and no less than seventeen fleet destroyers; plus the distant cover of the Home Fleet itself, consisting of the battleships *Duke of York* and *Anson*, the fleet carrier *Victorious*, the cruiser *Belfast,* and escorting destroyers. As if that were not
enough, the Royal Navy also sent along its most successful anti-U-boat
force in the war, Captain Johnny Walker's Second Support Group of five
specially trained sloops. As it was, the *Tirpitz* was still too damaged by
the midget-submarine sabotage to be put to sea, and the Luftwaffe by this
time had been sent to fight elsewhere and was ineffectual, thus leaving
any attacks at all to the U-boats. Although there were eighteen of them
arrayed in three lines, these submarines found it impossible by now, as
they had in the North Atlantic, to do anything against the massed aerial and naval defenses of the convoy, and they lost three of their number
(plus six German planes) in trying.[36] It was less than two years since the
tragedy of Convoy PQ-17 in the same waters.

It was of course precisely because the Admiralty felt extremely frustrated at so large a portion of their fleet being tied down to guard against

**PAINTING 48. HMS *Roberts* shelling the Normandy shore, 1944.** The Royal Navy's shallow-draft coastal bombardment vessels harked back to the original monitors of the nineteenth century. With its huge 15-inch guns and stable platform, HMS *Roberts* was repeatedly deployed to bombard enemy positions during Torch, Sicily, Salerno, and here, off Sword Beach.

I. H. M.

any sortie by the *Tirpitz* that British forces tried, in all sorts of ways, to cripple the battleship permanently. It is worth noting again the difference that the coming of airpower had made to the Anglo-German naval struggle in this war, and of course the contrast with the stalemate of the 1914–18 war is glaring. What the critically significant change in the air balance over western Europe after 1941 did was much more than make the British Isles safe from amphibious attack; rather, it was now the Kriegsmarine that was made vulnerable. Driving the *Scharnhorst* and *Gneisenau* out of Brest by early 1942 was only the beginning, as the latter's permanent disablement due to further RAF bombing attacks showed. By 1944, when the *Tirpitz* was the only German capital ship left and British airpower had vastly strengthened, its end was almost preordained. One diligently compiled "list of the Allied attacks upon the German battleship *Tirpitz*"[37] counts twenty-six efforts over three years to disable the warship, including the ingenious (and partly successful) sabotage by midget submarines and two major aerial operations (one promising, one hopeless) by Fleet Air Arm carriers. While the latter showed, incidentally, how the overall balances had shifted—that a Royal Navy carrier task force could range up and down the Norwegian coast where none such had existed in April 1940—it was finally left to the Lancasters of RAF Bomber Command to first badly damage and then totally wreck the battleship with solid 6-ton bombs on November 12, 1944.[38]

By then, the Admiralty was already urgently arranging for the dispatch of all fleet carriers and the *King George V* battleships to the British Pacific Fleet; so, despite Hitler's lasting suspicions about the possibility, there would be no Allied invasion of Norway. At last, Whitehall's prewar Main Fleet–to–Singapore strategy was becoming a reality, and northern European waters by contrast returned to being a backwater, save for occasional light skirmishes around German coastal convoys. As to the remaining Allied convoys to Russia, they could continue their task without worry, well protected against U-boat and air attack though no longer needing any cover from heavy ships. And it had surely been more than coincidence that three of the Axis's "giant" battleships were sunk at this very time: the *Musashi* (October 24, 1944, by carrier aircraft), the *Tirpitz* (November 12, by heavy bombers), and the *Shinano* (November 29, by submarine). By this stage of the war, there really was no place for them to hide. Only the *Yamato* remained.

A full 1,500 miles to the south, in the more agreeable Mediterranean waters, Allied warships had also been able to show themselves off in very large force on two significant occasions in 1944. Both involved an amphibious strike in order to gain strategic advantage. The first of these was the highly controversial and, as it turned out, highly difficult landing at

Anzio on the western coast of Italy, a little to the south of Rome and behind the Gustav Line that the Wehrmacht was defending so doggedly.
There is little to say about this January–March 1944 operation—Operation Shingle by formal name—that has not been said a hundred times before in the literature about this contest.[39] The military leadership was un-
inspiring throughout, from Alexander and Mark Clark at the top to Major
General John Lucas, the ultracautious commander of the actual beachhead force, who thus gave over the advantage to Albert Kesselring and his
own aggressive subordinates for the adept German counterattacks once
it was clear that a major landing was underway. The heroes of this story,
on the Allied side, were undoubtedly the overstrained, near-exhausted
crews of the landing ships, steaming back and forth to Naples with battle casualties on the return leg and fresh reinforcements and supplies in
the other direction. The Anglo-American naval forces, which might have
been much larger, had been limited to light cruisers and destroyers for
coastal bombardments (including diversionary ones elsewhere), and the
now-ubiquitous escort carriers to provide local air coverage—notwith-
standing that the frequent Luftwaffe attacks, many using radio-controlled
bombs, sank and damaged a number of warships. But no call was made
for battleship fire support against the German ground forces, as had occurred at Salerno, and when at last the overcast weather cleared, the Allies preferred to use their huge advantage in the air, together with those
fresh troops pouring into the Anzio beachhead, to stifle and then push
back Kesselring's bold assault. It had not been a particular setback for naval power, but it had confirmed that there would be no easy way, no nifty
flanking amphibious move, that would push the German Army easily out
of Italy. The fall of Rome just a couple of months later, on June 5, 1944,
made rather silly by General Clark's intense and tasteless efforts to ensure
that US troops entered before the British did, was overshadowed by news
of Overlord a day later, and had little impact on the tough German retention of the rest of northern Italy over the following year.[40]

The second major amphibious operation was that carried out by the
American-French combined armies in July 1944 upon the South of France,
code-named Operation Anvil (and later Operation Dragoon). For logistical reasons—the ready supply of landing craft, as ever—it took place over
a month after Overlord, yet it was still judged strategically useful, as the
consequent military drive up the Rhone Valley would ease the general advance toward Germany, divert Wehrmacht forces, and of course liberate
more French territory. The total invasion forces for Anvil were therefore
substantial, 171,000 American and French troops overall, plus approximately 70,000 French Resistance fighters, and the eventual invasion number eventually swelled to an extraordinary 573,000 troops, numbers far

in excess of the German defenders. The Allied air forces were also huge, around 3,500 planes. By contrast, the Luftwaffe had also pulled back its squadrons by this time to defend the Reich and therefore had only 200 aircraft in the region; it offered little fight after launching a few glider bombs. The naval bombardment groups included four US battleships and one British, all elderly (HMS *Ramillies* had been authorized in 1913), and yet they engaged solidly with German-held fortifications all along the coast near Toulon for day after day, until the Wehrmacht chose no longer to resist there but to pull back, up the Rhone Valley. So, the operation was a clear success overall, even if the forces used were extravagant, and it brought the benefit of having opened up a further capacious supply line for the land invasion of Germany.[41]

One further, although by this stage smallish, consequence of the reconquest of the South of France was that it marked the end of Hitler's commitment of a sizable force of U-boats to the Battle of the Mediterranean (see chapter 5). To be sure, by 1943 operational conditions were becoming much more difficult for the German submarines. After Italy's fall they had moved their base from La Spezia to Toulon, using the port facilities even next door to the wreckage of the sunken French fleet, and as late as 1944 a few U-boats had run past the gauntlet of Gibraltar patrols and entered these crowded waters. Their tally of Allied merchantmen was not great, and the array of both naval and air antisubmarine forces was extensive and unrelenting, so that any U-boat that showed itself was, as the best recent account describes it, "hunted to exhaustion."[42] Their successful years had been back in 1941–42 with the sinking of the *Barham* and *Ark Royal* and their successful ravaging of the Malta convoys. By September 1944, the last operating boats were scuttled, with their crews returning overland to the Reich.

In sum, what one witnessed here was a repeated confirmation of the Allies' total command of the air and sea by this stage in the war and of the very ubiquity of their maritime advantage. They had been strong enough to land and support a multidivision invasion on the Italian coast in March 1944 plus a far larger one on the Normandy coast in June—in the same month as a substantial invasion of Saipan, on the other side of the globe—and to carry out a further large landing in the South of France in July. This did indeed sound like Liddell Hart's "ebb tides." The Grand Alliance's surge was advancing on all the Axis-held shores and lapping around all their islands.

---

It all fitted together, really. In 1942 the Allies could do little more than check their enemies' moves, in North Africa, at Stalingrad, at Guadalcanal, and in New Guinea. In 1943, they moved forward, cautiously, where they had the resources to do so. In 1944, their material superiority was clear, and victories followed one after another. The more than eleven thousand Allied aircraft that flew over the Normandy beaches and the Channel on D-Day were an indicator of hitherto unimaginable productive power and organization. The thousands of Higgins boat landing craft being unleashed onto enemy shores by the armies of Eisenhower and MacArthur alike were an amazing testimony to a Great Power at last quite capable of fighting a two-ocean war. The dozens of battleships and heavy cruisers supporting the amphibious forces with shocking firepower demonstrated wherein naval mastery lay. Behind and within each of the many multilayered weapons that the Allies deployed were aspects that told a far larger story. Those aluminum-based aeroparts, like the propellers and the pieces surrounding the Pratt and Whitney P-2800 engine that drove Hellcat and Thunderbolt fighters through the skies, represented new advances in aeronautical technology that hadn't been around even five years earlier. Mass-produced escort carriers were, like mass-produced Liberty ships, slipping down their launching ramps in such numbers that by 1944 their construction was being slowed. Those heavy, four-engined, very-long-range B-24 Liberators that closed the Atlantic gap could exist only because a huge technology base existed as a precondition. In sum, behind the battle stories of the Normandy invasion, the Marianas campaign, and Leyte Gulf, there had been a gigantic force against which the Axis, however hard it strove, simply could not prevail.

**PAINTING 49.  Allied fleet led by USS *Missouri*, Tokyo Bay, 1945.** A classic and symbolic vista of Anglo-American naval power in the Bay of Tokyo in September 1945, with Mt. Fuji in the background and the USS *Missouri* to the fore. The British battleship HMS *Duke of York* lies on the right.

# TEN

## The Allied Victory at Sea

### 1945

After the great campaigns and strategic victories for Allied sea power in 1943 and 1944, the naval story that followed was both a rather inevitable and a much less glamorous one, in European waters certainly, and even in the Pacific. Perhaps that was bound to be so, at a long war's end. The British and American fleets had steadily wiped the enemy navies from the sea and, as was always intended in the Anglo-American grand strategy, brought their own armies to their foes' doorstep. Yet neither the Third Reich nor the Japanese Empire gave up the fight willingly or sought a negotiated peace with the Allies, however overwhelming the force that the latter possessed on land, in the air, and at sea by the beginning of 1945. The Japanese plan at this stage in the war actually depended upon the Americans advancing further, and at very high cost. So the cumulative losses of all US servicemen in the Iwo Jima, Okinawa, and Philippines operations, as detailed below, was to make this year the costliest of all in the Pacific theater, well before the invasion of Japan itself.

And in the European and Atlantic theaters, even with British and Canadian armies moving on the ports of Northwest Germany, even with Baltic harbors closing because of either Allied bombing or Red Army advances, Karl Doenitz's Kriegsmarine fought on. While virtually all of Germany's heavier surface warships had been sunk or wrecked by this stage, German factories were still producing U-boats at this late hour, and many of the latter were still going to sea. If they no longer threatened the High Atlantic routes, that was just as well for the Allies, since some of the newer German boats were, remarkably, the most advanced and dangerous submarines ever produced in this war.

## The Limited Threat of the U-boats' Final Flourish

The German submarine campaign against Allied trade—and the coun-
tercampaign against the U-boats by Allied navies and air forces—was by
this stage in the war exhibiting some weird and very contradictory features: new U-boat numbers seemed scarily high, and the latest types of
vessels were so much more sophisticated and much harder to detect than
they had been two years earlier, yet merchant-ship losses were low, since
the North Atlantic had very few German submarines in it, and the most
dangerous zone for Allied shipping was in UK coastal waters, as it had
been back in September 1939. It all seemed quite bizarre.[1]

Despite the Allied bombing campaign, then, German production of U-
boats had continued well into 1945 at such a rate that by the end of April
1945 Doenitz still had 166 operational U-boats (out of a fleet total of 434),
which, as Jonathan Dimbleby notes, "was only twenty-two fewer than
he had following D-Day."[2] Moreover, the newer boats now included not
only the large and impressive Type XXI submarines (1,600 tons) but also
a few, albeit a very few, of the revolutionary newer submarines, ones difficult to detect because they were using a snorkel breathing apparatus, and
the even more dangerous electric-powered Type XXI (a true submarine
at last, and ultrafast), vessels that made it extremely difficult for the Royal
Navy's traditional escort warships to handle. Already in early 1945 some of
the newer U-boats were running in and out of British home waters completely undetected, and an alarmed—one is tempted to say, alarmist—
First Sea Lord, Admiral Andrew Cunningham, had gone to the Chiefs of
Staff Committee with a memo describing the submarine threat to Allied
command of the sea as so grave that he felt that by the spring, shipping
losses might be worse than those of 1943. And while the chiefs of staff did
not accept so bleak a picture, it was agreed that large numbers of destroyers and frigates designated for the Far East be retained for a while at UK
bases and that other countermeasures be taken. Here at last, it seemed,
were some of Hitler's oft-proclaimed "wonder weapons" that, along with
the V-1 and V-2 rockets, were intended to alter the course of the war.[3]

And yet of course Allied command of the sea was not seriously threatened by a U-boat resurgence at this time for many reasons, geographical
as well as military. Perhaps the most significant was the German Navy's
loss of its French Atlantic bases after the Normandy invasions, which was
yet another return to the 1939 circumstances. Unable to operate from
the Gironde, L'Orient, or Brest, the Kriegsmarine's submarines had once
again to transit around Scotland and the Faeroes to get to the wider seas;
and Doenitz's own headquarters, the radio stations, and his B-Dienst

offices all had to be pulled back. The Focke-Wulf squadrons in west-ern France were either scrapped or flew home. This all made Wilhelms-haven and Kiel more important once again and thus subjected to even heavier RAF bomber attacks; this also made even more important the U-boat bases in Norway, which is why the Royal Navy and Coastal Com-mand increased their forces in those waters. The antagonists fought on as fiercely as ever, but in much more limited space and in different ways. There were no more large wolf packs off Newfoundland controlled by the Commander U-boats' radio. And as had been the case already through-out 1944, the big Atlantic convoys, surrounded by layers and layers of es-corting ships and aircraft, brushed off the vain attacks by solo subma-rines. All the great U-boat ace captains of the first half of the war had been killed in combat or captured by now, and the newer skippers and crews were obviously inexperienced. Intensive Allied aerial minelaying in the Baltic disrupted training and sank many a new boat.

In sum, it had become a one-way, limited fight. Very large numbers of German submarines did not translate into large numbers of Allied ship-ping losses. In the eleven months from D-Day to the end of the war there were only thirteen merchant ships sunk along the North Atlantic routes. There were more losses to U-boat attack elsewhere during that time, in the Indian Ocean and South Atlantic and even up the St. Lawrence River, but those sinkings were, clearly, so broadly dispersed—and the sheer size of the Allied merchant shipping across the globe by this time was so huge—that such U-boat operations could never be strategic.

Since neither German aircraft nor submarines were contesting the cen-tral North Atlantic trade routes, the British Admiralty felt that it could, at last, relax the requirements for convoys there. One last great convoy, consisting of over one hundred ships, steamed from New York to Liver-pool in January 1945. By that stage the shipping routes themselves had changed, so that vessels leaving New York were permitted, for the first time since 1939, to travel *south* of Ireland and go directly to southern En-glish ports like Southampton. And the vast trans-Atlantic flow of Ameri-can servicemen and munitions heading to Brest and Cherbourg to supply the US Army's operations in Europe also required fewer escorts, and then no convoys at all. To the many experienced Allied convoy commodores and to the weary veterans among the British, Norwegian, Polish, Greek, and other merchant crews, so accustomed to the spectacle of ships blow-ing up around them, the scream of bombs, and the thunder of ack-ack fire, the quietness of the oceans must have seemed uncanny, indeed un-natural. So must it have seemed to the residents of port cities like Glasgow as the streetlights came on, the blackout curtains were removed, and the

**PAINTING 50.  U-boats surrendered at Lisahally, Northern Ireland, 1945.**
This remarkable sight, which must have been replicated in many other British
harbors after Germany's surrender, was a short-lived one. Very soon, the British
Admiralty would order all these U-boats to be sunk at sea.

I. H. M.

sandbags taken away. If the war had not ended completely, it was over in their parts of the world.

It ended later, though just a few months later, for their formidable wartime adversaries, the U-boats. It had become a local fight, for all the reasons described above, in familiar waters—down the eastern coast of Britain, off Norwegian harbors, and off the entrance to the Baltic; and then it was suddenly all over. By the conclusion of the naval war in Europe, all that was left standing of the proud German Navy was, amazingly, the heavy cruiser *Prinz Eugen,* plus the huge fleet of submarines. Perhaps it was because Hitler had designated Admiral Doenitz as his successor as Reichs Fuehrer that the U-boat Service and other ancillary units overwhelmingly complied with the surrender stipulations, after an earlier scheme to destroy all vessels (the Rainbow Order) was countermanded. At this time, the navy still had 470 submarines, of which 170 were "front" vessels in Norwegian ports. If a large number were rendered inoperable in harbor, and certain submarine crews scuttled their boats offshore so as to avoid handover, the remainder seemed willing to comply with the orders to sail to British ports like the Humber, dock their vessels, and be interned. Some other crews did leave their vessels intact at Kiel or Wilhelmshaven or in Norwegian bases and then try to go home; a few more, the lucky ones, turned themselves in at neutral harbors as far away as South America. In all, approximately 156 U-boats surrendered to the Allies, to later be towed out to sea and sunk. For a while, though, the sight of dozens of surrendered vessels, tethered together in British or Norwegian harbors, was a special one (see painting 50).

Along with the Japanese carriers, the German U-boats truly had been the most formidable of all the Axis weapons systems at sea. While the sheer size of the Allied merchant fleets (especially the British) plus the sheer productivity of the Allied shipyards (especially the American) kept pace with, and then outpaced, the sinkings, nonetheless the losses were simply awful; taken together, German, Italian, and Japanese submarines sank 15 million tons of Allied shipping, and the U-boats were responsible for the greater part of that. In addition, U-boats sank 175 Allied, again chiefly British, warships, battleships, carriers, cruisers, destroyers, and many more. It was testimony to the remarkable industrial strength of the Third Reich that a full 1,157 submarines were built during the five-and-a-half years of war. Over 700 were sunk, predominantly to British warships and aircraft, so while this fight was later joined, impressively, by the Canadian and US navies, it was overwhelmingly—once again—an Anglo-German maritime struggle.[4] In the later stages of the war, the submariners' losses were terrible (ten thousand men lost in the year of 1943 alone). No other branch of the Wehrmacht sustained such a staggeringly high ca-

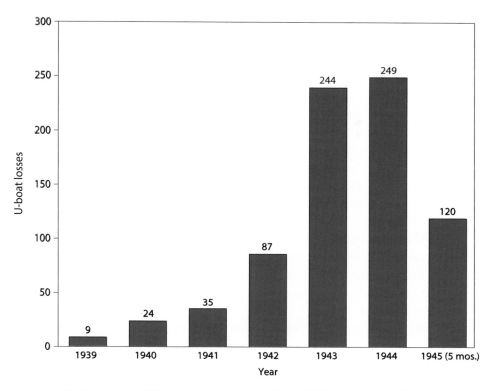

**CHART 10.** Annual U-boat losses, 1939–45. From Helgason, "Losses by Cause," accessed February 6, 2020, https://uboat.net/fates/losses/.

sualty rate (75 percent of the total U-boat crews) as it did. What really is remarkable is that it had fought so well and for so long during this, the lengthiest naval campaign of World War II. For the record, the annual losses of Admiral Doenitz's U-boat Service are noted in chart 10.

Even before the coming of the end of the European war, circumstances for the Royal Navy were changing fast. While a large new fleet was emerging to be sent off to the Pacific, the service itself was shrinking, and certainly in its antisubmarine, Atlantic world conformation. Overall, of course, the navy still looked enormous, for its personnel size had expanded more than fourfold since 1939 (to 940,000 officers and ratings), and wartime ship construction had largely kept pace with the many losses. Technically, it possessed 12 battleships (only 5 modern ones), 52 carriers (many of them escort carriers), 62 cruisers, and 257 destroyers. Its Fleet Air Arm and RAF Coastal Command were also greatly swollen.[5] But its real size and shape was now much changed from what it had been in 1941, or even at the beginning of 1944. For all the concern about the continued U-boat threat in home waters, that vast array of frigates, sloops, and corvettes that Max Horton had needed to fight the Battle of the Atlantic was shriveling fast. Many of the older, slower "little ships" were now tied up in Lough Swilly, Northern Ireland, or in the Mersey, their regular-service crews needed to man the smart new fleet destroyers and light cruisers being sent off to the Far East. In much the same way, the older slow (R-class) battleships were already being disposed of; by 1944 the *Revenge* and *Resolution* were mere training ships, and only the HMS *Queen Elizabeth* of its class was operating in a forward role by the spring of 1945. Many of the historic *County*-class heavy cruisers that had constituted, say, the main part of the navy's China Squadron as late as the 1930s were being retired and scrapped, unromantically and swiftly, less than a decade following.[6] They had no place in a Pacific war or in a service already feeling new fiscal constraints. And dozens of the Royal Navy's smaller escort carriers, so highly valued as they had been two summers earlier, soon found themselves being prepared for return to the US Navy (under Lend-Lease terms) or given to lesser navies. Many of the orders for the new light fleet carriers were canceled.

So the navy's pride and joy—its only substantive force by now, and in fact the *only* significant example of naval power in the world other than the US Navy by the spring of 1945—was the British Pacific Fleet that had been sent east under Admiral Bruce Fraser's command. Having made the decision to join the main campaign for Japan's final defeat, Churchill and the Admiralty now spared nothing in the allocation of forces; virtually the entire British large-warship construction of the wartime years was steadily sent east—the four *King George V* battleships, the five *Illustrious*-class fleet carriers, newer types of cruisers, and dozens and dozens of fast destroyers and frigates, all of them testing the navy's still-limited supply systems, in all a remarkable display of maritime power by a nation straining its fiscal utmost near the end of six years of total war.[7]

Before it made its way into the Pacific, however, a sizable advanced part of Fraser's fleet—the heavily escorted fleet carriers HMSs *Victorious, Indomitable, Illustrious,* and *Indefatigable,* under Rear Admiral Philip Vian's flag—delivered a double attack (Operations Meridian I and II) against the vast Japanese-occupied oil refinery complex at Palembang, in Sumatra.[8] This assault was made at Chester W. Nimitz's request, following a completely unsuccessful raid by Ceylon-based B-29s a few months earlier, and the target was a critical one, refining no less than 75 percent of Japan's aviation fuel—so there were many good reasons for the Royal Navy to seize this chance to demonstrate that it, too, had become a modern, long-range carrier force, following the American model. And the results of these two strikes of January 24 and 29, 1945, respectively, were solid enough. Despite unhelpful weather at sea and, more significantly, some strong Japanese air defenses, the forty-three Avenger bombers with eighty fighter escorts of the Fleet Air Arm forces flew well over a hundred miles overland to get at the two oil-refining complexes, knocked down numerous enemy planes in dogfights, and reduced output at the Pladjoe refinery by half. When forty-six Avengers returned for the second raid, to hit the nearby Sungai Gerong refinery, it was put out of production for six months. Considerable operational defects were also revealed during these extended carrier raids—much of the flying was ragged and confused, and the weak undercarriage of the British-made planes put many of them out of action, to Admiral Vian's fury—yet on the whole, Operation Meridian was a substantial plus. And far better to have such shortcomings revealed and hopefully corrected at this time than when operating alongside the experienced US fleet off Okinawa.

Inadequate oil and gas supplies had of course been a critical weakness of the Japanese war machine from the very beginning, and a major cause of Tokyo's decision to fight. Yet Japan's enormous territorial acquisitions in 1942 had never brought it the economic security it sought, and by late 1944 its fuel shortages were so acute that they were badly restricting operations by the remains of the main fleet. The Royal Navy's attack on the Palembang refineries had therefore been one part of a triple squeeze on Tokyo's shrinking oil stocks, the other two being the US submarine attacks on tanker shipping traffic (by far the most damaging) and the aerial strikes on the Japanese homeland by B-29s and carrier raids. There was a great irony here. Back in 1941 the Japanese military had argued that if it did not gain control of secure energy supplies in the East Indies, it would always be subject to an intolerable dependence upon the West that would keep the nation on its knees. But because it was losing the Pacific War, it was now being driven to its knees in any case by this growing lack of supply. Yet Tokyo still chose to fight on.

With the Palembang operation behind it, the British Pacific Fleet then proceeded to Sydney for further reequipping before it moved in long loops via Manus and on to Ulithi in the Carolines. It was not until the morning of March 23 that Admiral Fraser, having already formally presented the British Pacific Fleet to Admiral Nimitz for duty, led it further north as the new Task Force 57 of the Fifth Fleet.[9] By the time that happened, the fighting on Iwo Jima was tapering off, and it was the Royal Navy's turn to discover that there was no real Japanese surface fleet against which to give battle. Here was a service eager to avenge the sinking of Force Z back in 1941, and ironically, all four of the HMS *Prince of Wales*'s sister ships (the *King George V, Duke of York, Anson,* and *Howe*) were assembling to do it, but battleship contests in this war were now well and truly over. Yet there was still much for Fraser's squadron to do, for the kamikaze campaign against Allied warships was just then intensifying, and the final preparations for the assault on Okinawa were being completed. The Royal Navy would be not only a proper contributor to these final campaigns but also a front-row observer of the American crushing of Japanese power.

## The Crushing of Japan, from January to July 1945

The American-Japanese struggle in the closing year of the Pacific War actually involved three campaigns, each operating on its own level and at different speeds. The first was the story of the three major naval-operational events—of Iwo Jima, Okinawa, and then the preparations for the gigantic invasion of Japan itself. The second campaign narrative involved the continuation of the successful economic strangulation of Japanese merchant commerce by US submarines, which was taking place in parallel to that other form of economic warfare, the strategic bombing campaign (by the Twentieth Air Force) from the Marianas. But there was also, rather perversely, a third conflict narrative, which was of the Japanese kamikaze assault against the American amphibious landing areas and screening warships, an onslaught that was so long-lasting, sizable, and costly that it became a campaign in itself, with very large mutual losses.

Of course, the counterassault of the kamikazes' campaign, however striking in some of their individual blows, could never push back the American advance, no more than could some remarkable but brief German counteroffensives halt the Red Army's advance along the Eastern Front. Even on a day when the Japanese suicide planes seemed to be attacking in hordes, they were making only a small dent in the gigantic US armada cruising in the Western Pacific and always lost great numbers of aircraft on each occasion of their attacks. It is a tale, then, of ultimate American triumph, although for a great deal of the time it also seemed to be an account of the American admirals' frustration because their Japanese foe refused to bow to the logic—the military power—of the first two narratives and because the costs of the kamikaze counterattacks really did become high and were always threatening to get higher. This should have been an easier narrative, of the final stages of an American success, but the victory turned out to be harder to wrest, and consequently the historiography is a bit harder to parse.[10]

If these difficulties were not clear to Nimitz's command at the beginning of 1945, they had become abundantly so when the Iwo Jima campaign (February–April) unfolded shortly afterward. That this particular objective should be acquired had seemed unquestionable to the US na-

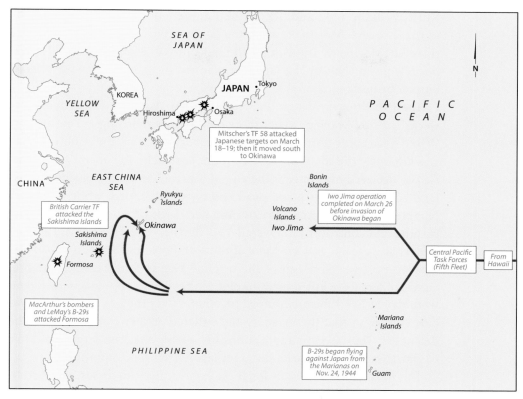

MAP 15. American operations in the Pacific, 1945.

val planners back in Hawaii. The island, just like Okinawa further west of it, appeared as a logical stepping-stone to victory, being so relatively close to Japan and providing valuable airfields (emergency landing strips for damaged bombers, and possibly useful air bases for fighter escorts). Moreover, targets like Iwo Jima and Okinawa were ones that could easily be surrounded and blockaded, in contrast to the far more open-ended task of invading a strip of the Chinese coastland. They would also—this hardly had to be said—come under the navy's sphere of control, whereas operations toward the Asian mainland (Formosa and so on) would come within General Douglas MacArthur's US Army domain.

Just because Iwo Jima itself was so small—a mere four miles in extent—did not mean it was for easy taking, since it was clearly Imperial Japanese Headquarters' intention to make the costs of acquisition very severe, perhaps high enough even to force the Allies to consider a negotiated peace before an invasion of Japan proper. To this end, Tokyo found it had enough time early in 1945 to expand the island's garrison up to twenty-five thousand troops and to instruct its commander, General Tadamichi

Kuribayashi, to fight and die for the Empire, but first to take a huge toll of the invaders. Moreover, when the latter arrived, consisting initially of three US Marine divisions, they did not possess overwhelming odds, especially given the way the Japanese planned to fight, foxhole by foxhole, bunker by bunker.

The Iwo Jima campaign did not last a few days, therefore, or a mere week. The first Marines went ashore on the early morning of February 19. While it was only four days later, on February 23, that the American flag was famously raised on the top of Mount Suribachi, the operation was officially declared over only at the end of March. The taking of this slim island cost the Marines 6,800 dead and 19,200 wounded, while the entire Japanese defending force was exterminated. Such US losses were both disturbing and controversial. Overall, the Marines' casualty rate in this battle was 30 percent, and for some of the battalions that went in first it was over 60 percent. Nineteen of the original twenty-four Marine battalion commanders were killed or wounded. If the American totals of dead and wounded at Iwo Jima are lumped together, it was the first time in the Pacific campaign that the invaders had suffered greater casualties than the defenders. The casualty implications for seizing the even larger objective of Okinawa or for future landings on Japan itself were daunting.[11]

The most obvious reason for these large American losses, apart from the defenders' determination to fight to the death, was the horribly difficult battle terrain. This was a struggle that took place as much underground, in a network of deep caves, as in the gullies and escarpments aboveground. Close-encounter fighting took away many American firepower advantages and equalized the losses, except on those occasions when the Japanese soldiers decided upon a "Banzai!" charge and gave the attackers the opportunity to wipe them out. To this degree, the heavy Marine Corps losses and the slowness of the fighting were understandable. It was quite another question, however, whether the American casualty totals during the *immediate days* of the landings themselves should have been as high. Both on the first day of the landing operation itself and in much subsequent writing, the Marines complained about the inadequate supporting naval bombardment and thus of the withering defensive fire they encountered from strongly held (and clearly undamaged) Japanese positions. As it only slowly became clear, neither the US warships' shells nor the bomb attacks from land-based and carrier planes made much of a dent in the Japanese network of deep caves and foxholes. Here was a circumstance entirely different from the success of those close-shore Allied naval bombardments in European theaters. Given this physical difficulty, then, as the official naval historian Professor Samuel Morison rather blandly observed, perhaps even three times as much shelling would not have made much difference against General Kuribayashi's deep-bunker policy.[12] Still, the fact was that the so-called softening up of the defenders through naval bombardments and aerial attacks was too short a process and that an additional two or three days of heavy inshore bombardments against the Japanese positions directly overlooking the landing beaches might have reduced some of the immediate amphibious casualties when those first assault waves landed. It would certainly have left the Marines less aggrieved.[13]

One reason why there was less time allocated for gunfire and aerial support off Iwo Jima, though, was because the ambitious commander of Task Force 58, Admiral Raymond Spruance, was keen at this time to launch a large-scale aerial assault on Tokyo and its industrial environs by his carrier forces. As the Japanese Air Force rose to defend Tokyo and its air bases, his argument went, it would be shot out of the sky and thus be unavailable for raids on Iwo. Furthermore, Spruance clearly also wanted to show that bombers from the new carrier navy, coming at their targets at lower levels, could inflict far more destruction on Japanese factories than Army Air Force B-29s flying around at 30,000 feet.[14] Unfortunately for those ambitions, when Spruance sent off Rear Admiral Marc Mitscher's carrier groups and attendant fast battleships to make their Tokyo run on February 23–26, very heavy seas hampered all the flight operations, and in any case much of the intended target area was, as was normal for that time of the year, covered by clouds.[15] In all, one doubts whether 250-pound bombs dropped from carrier aircraft could do much sustained damage against Japanese heavy industrial plants, while of course they did even less against Japanese airfield runways, for the latter were normally repaired swiftly (as the Battles of Britain and Malta and the bombing of Germany's air bases had all shown). Some Japanese coastal ships were sunk during this raid and some harbors damaged, and TF 58's planes did shoot down eighty-four enemy aircraft in this two-week operation, but it might well have shot down that number had it been operating around Iwo Jima instead. And had it been patrolling close to the landings, then of course its battleship escorts could have been available for a more sustained bombardment of the beaches. This was not a very effective demonstration of naval force.

As such, this particular "Tokyo Raid" was more a sign of some American admirals' frustration and ambition than it was anything else. As the Royal Navy's Home Fleet had found itself a little earlier in this war (say, after the *Scharnhorst* sinking), so the US Pacific Fleet now found itself, after Leyte Gulf, without a proper surface enemy. The American fast battleships, designed for a grand blue-water contest against Japanese equivalents, no longer faced a worthy foe and were reduced to providing antikamikaze fire for the carriers or shelling coastal targets. Meanwhile the imposing *Essex*-class fleet carriers, intended by their admirals to range widely across the seas as they had done at Midway and the Caroline Sea, now found themselves in protective support of much narrower amphibious operations. Little wonder, then, that Admiral William Halsey had eagerly raced his groups away whenever given orders to attack the China coast or Japan and that Spruance wanted to send the same vessels north against Tokyo in the month following.

Sea power was showing itself in many wondrous ways, therefore, though it was not exactly working in the manner that the classic texts had described. Since the beginning of the war the Japanese Navy had been clobbered at sea three times—Midway, the Marianas Turkey Shoot, and Leyte Gulf—but even in the latter case there had never been the giant fleet encounter that the battleship admirals of both sides had anticipated. The merchant fleets of Japan were at long last being decimated by US submarines or foundering upon the thousands of aerial mines that were being laid off Japanese harbors by the US Air Force, but even as food and oil imports shrank to nothing it was becoming evident that Japanese garrisons, and the home nation, would rather eat grass than surrender. The maritime advance across the Pacific had garnered island bases for the B-29 bombers, but in fact the high-level aerial bombing was not very effective militarily. And the land emplacements of Iwo Jima had been pounded by thousands of large-caliber shells, but those had had little effect upon a foe sitting fifty feet below the ground. Naval power could encircle, but not defeat, an enemy who had adopted a no-surrender policy.

Still, considering the final year of the US war against Japan, the taking of Iwo Jima was an important step in the *right* direction, that is, toward Tokyo. Even at this time, as historians have pointed out, a far larger amount of fighting was also still being done in the central and southern Philippines by the bulk of the forces under General MacArthur's command. This had little to do with strategy and much to do with MacArthur's "I shall return" pledges to the Filipino people, as well as with, later critics suspected, his desire to keep direct control of as many American divisions as possible and not have them reassigned to, say, the Okinawa fighting. In the early 1945 battle for Luzon, for example, MacArthur threw in ten infantry divisions and five independent regiments, which made this not only the biggest American campaign of the Pacific war but also one larger than had been committed in North Africa, Italy, or southern France.[16] It says a lot for the sheer size of the American deployments to the overall Pacific realm that such a large number of army divisions and land-based aircraft, as well as Admiral Thomas C. Kinkaid's long-suffering Seventh Fleet, could still be allocated to the Philippines theater at this time, in what was painstakingly slow campaigning (by one count, twenty-three separate amphibious operations were involved). As it was, Manila was not fully taken until March 4, 1945, and in the more distant southern parts of the giant archipelago, fighting was still going on at the end of the war. Overall, the US Army lost 16,300 dead and 55,500 wounded in the 1944–45 Philippines campaign. These were strategic dead ends, rather like those lingering German-held positions that the British sought to mop up in the eastern Mediterranean. The US Navy must have been relieved that it was so marginally involved here.

Rather more pertinent at this time were the frequent bombing operations (by B-29s from the Marianas, or carrier strikes) against Japanese positions in China or against the island of Formosa, all designed to suppress kamikaze and more regular aerial counterattacks that the Japanese were launching from those parts against the Iwo Jima and Okinawa amphibious forces. In the same way, US submarine operations continued against smaller enemy coastal traffic and fishing vessels in the Formosan straits; occasionally a US submarine would sink a valuable oil tanker or ore ship headed to a Japanese port, which was always a much bigger blow. Perhaps most important of all, though not entirely successful, were the American efforts to cut off the return flow of Japanese divisions from the Chinese/Manchurian mainland that Imperial Japanese Headquarters had belatedly ordered to reinforce the existing garrisons on Luzon, Okinawa, and Japan itself.

As the overall American strategic grip tightened in these early 1945 months, then, the taking of Iwo Jima before the larger move on Okinawa did make a lot of sense. It completed the chief US offensive in the Pacific but also marked an intelligible westward limit before Nimitz's forces would wheel northward toward the Japanese home islands. From early April onward, long-range P-51 Mustangs could be flown from the newly opened Iwo Jima airstrips to support bomber raids on Japan, although in fact the B-29s were meeting very little resistance by this time. Other Iwo Jima–based planes could now carry out reconnaissance and interdiction sweeps across the China Sea. Finally, a considerable number of B-29s, some damaged but most of them just short of fuel, could make emergency landings on the same airfields. If the claim that twenty-four thousand American aircrew were saved by such emergency landings in these months is rather strained, the fact that these bases were constantly in use seemed confirmation that the taking of the island was indeed a logical step in the grand plan of advance.[17]

Inevitably, though, the very arrival of the Americans on Iwo Jima made them a natural showcase for the display of Japan's kamikaze counterstrategy. In particular, the aerial campaign against US warships offshore became another grim and relentless feature of this struggle, and on some days, American casualties among the off-lying and escort vessels could be just as heavy as those suffered in the land fighting. At first, the sheer size as well as the unusual nature of the suicide attacks took the commanders of Spruance's Fifth Fleet aback, for there was simply nothing in American war planning that anticipated an enemy adopting mass aerial suicide attacks to try to alter a battle's outcome. It could be said that some warning had been given when those first "special attack" planes inflicted such damage on the American escort carriers and picket destroyers at Leyte Gulf and in the several months following (see chapter 9), but until this time the navy had clearly not given much thought to steps to combat this insidious form of assault.

And what exactly was a guaranteed form of protection against a swarm of one-way suicide fighters or a sneak night attack? The answer was to send out more and more combat air patrols from the increasingly strained escort carriers, which in turn became the chief desired target of the kamikazes. At the same time the US Navy pulled more and more destroyers and destroyer escorts from inshore bombardments and minesweeper patrols and sent them fifty or seventy-five miles out to sea to perform that most dangerous of military tasks—picket duty, that is—to be the first to spot and try to shoot down the incoming kamikazes and thus often be the first to take the hits, unless of course the suicide pilots were ordered only to go after larger targets.

If, then, American admirals at this time were found expressing frustration that it was taking so long for the military to conquer Iwo Jima and Okinawa (though, again, how *did* one ferret 25,000 enemies out of volcanic-rock tunnels?), that frustration was driven by a fury that, somehow, proud US warships had become vulnerable themselves, had become so many targets. Carriers, as noted, were the major attraction and any blow against them was always celebrated as a great victory in Japan, as was to happen after February 22, when a single nighttime kamikaze plane crashed into and sank the escort carrier USS *Bismarck Sea* with heavy loss of life (218 dead). Almost as bad was the attack the day before, when six planes emerged from low clouds to drop bombs and then crash onto the deck of the carrier *Saratoga,* causing huge fires that knocked it out of action for months. Badly hurt (with 123 sailors killed and 192 wounded), that veteran of so many battles nonetheless managed to limp back to the Bremerton yards (Puget Sound), a place where so many other damaged vessels of the Pacific War were repaired. Week by week, the US Navy's casualty list grew and, of course, did not cease when Iwo Jima was officially declared "clear" of fighting on March 16, for kamikazes could still come out of the blue, or the darkness, and strike anchoring or transiting landing ships and merchantmen.[18]

By this stage in the war, each side seemed intent on finding a new way of inflicting punishment upon its foe. Thus, on March 8, the new commander of the Twentieth Air Force in the Marianas, Curtis LeMay, frustrated at the ineffectiveness of high-level bombing, ordered his B-29 squadrons to attack Tokyo at night, at much lower levels (around five thousand feet), and to scatter napalm canisters over the city's flimsy infrastructure. The resultant firestorm here and the subsequent destruction by fire raids of cities like Nagoya and Kobe caused civilian deaths larger than any other bombings in history; Tokyo's total of a hundred thousand dead from the March 9–10 raid was greater than the deaths inflicted by the atomic bomb at either Hiroshima or Nagasaki. Perhaps uneasy about this unrestricted warfare, the Army Air Force came to argue that they were destroying the "housing units" of workers in Japan's armaments industry, but the fact was that US submarines had cut off most of the supplies to those factories, which by this time were empty.[19] Through massive aerial bombings, submarine blockade, and the occasional carrier aircraft attacks, Japan was being pulverized, and in this sort of war there seemed once again little room for large, traditional battle fleets.

Almost unrecorded in this tale of aerial, submarine, and amphibious operations, however, a giant logistical maritime endeavor was also taking place, without which all of the American military actions would have been impossible. Maintaining the strategic bombing campaign against Japan, for example, was a huge supply task. Each of those B-29 bombers carried as much as 6,900 gallons, or roughly 20 short tons, of fuel on every one of their long-range flights against Japan or Formosa. (Even a 10,000-ton oil tanker coming from the Gulf of Mexico via the Panama Canal and on to Saipan didn't carry that much supply to sustain 250- or 350-bomber air raids.) For the first time in its history, the wide expanses of the central Pacific were busy, as each week a fresh array of vessels of the US merchant marine, ammunition ships (with replacement shells, torpedoes, and bombs), oil tankers, Liberty ships carrying howitzers and tanks and trucks, and troopships with fresh divisions of Marines and army units all steamed in one direction, while a steady array of damaged warships limped home to America for repair and empty merchantmen returned for refilling. Here was a projection of American power that was quite stunning, both quantitatively and qualitatively.

## The Okinawa Campaign

While the capture of Iwo Jima had a certain utility, then, Okinawa's acquisition was always regarded as being of much more critical importance for the invasion of the Japanese home islands. Located only 350 miles southwest of Kyushu and with a flat central plain, it was the natural spring-board and refitting point for landing ships, aerial control, repair facilities, and even training facilities before the final US campaign. To both sides, the Battle of Okinawa was to be the last of a series of great insular tussles, almost like the last act of a drama that had unfolded, scene by scene, over the preceding two years: Tarawa as scene one, then Peleliu and Saipan as scenes two and three, and then Iwo Jima, all with the same grim, suicidal inevitability for the defenders. Marine and army veterans who had survived one campaign braced themselves when they were launched against the next target. The Japanese island garrisons were never leaving, were never going to receive reinforcements, and would fight to the death, for they had nowhere to retire to (unlike the Wehrmacht on the Eastern Front or the large Japanese armies in China). They too were essentially kamikaze units, undaunted by the odds.

In the same way, the sheer size of the American naval armada surrounding Okinawa was a retelling of the story of the Pacific War.[20] As 1,200 landing vessels commenced their Easter Sunday, April 1, assault on the central beaches of Okinawa, they were screened by 200 destroyers, 18 battleships, and over 40 carriers. What exactly did one do with 18 battleships and 40 carriers when there was no enemy fleet to fight?[21] Here, truly, was FDR's "navy second to none," but by this stage the greatest Mahanian battle fleet that ever existed lacked a proper foe. Instead, the American armada had to face the kamikazes, now able to fly a much shorter one-way journey from the Japanese homeland, carrying out what was the ultimate act of asymmetrical warfare. The Japanese display of suicidal warfare was to be practiced, moreover, through every vehicle of delivery, large and small, whether aircraft, speedboats, or even submarines.[22] And the largest and most striking of all was the battleship *Yamato.*

The giant vessel *Yamato* (named after the original Japanese people) was the lead battleship in a class of four equally powerful super-battleships; they were, in a very direct way, the apotheosis of that warship type begun a mere four decades earlier by Admiral John Fisher's 1906 *Dreadnought.* Yet there was to be no glory for any of these four later vessels. As noted earlier, *Yamato*'s sister ship *Musashi* was devastated by US aircraft during the Battle of Leyte Gulf. Then the *Shinano* was sunk by a single submarine, the USS *Archerfish.* The fourth vessel, called only *Keel No. 111,* was scrapped while on the stocks as early as 1942; the metal was needed for other purposes. The *Yamato,* too, was destined to be a fated ship, though its intimidating size would not have suggested it. Boasting nine enormous 18-inch guns and displacing over 70,000 tons, it was considerably larger than any of the *King George V*'s, or the *Richelieu,* or the *Bismarck,* or even the largest of the newer American battleships of the *Iowa*-class. Naval history buffs salivate over a what-might-have-been encounter between *Yamato* and the US fast battleships, but in fact the Japanese behemoth never once encountered an enemy capital ship, which might have allowed it to fight on its merits. Yet, in the very way it was destroyed, on the afternoon of April 7, 1945, this Japanese super-battleship made noteworthy naval history.

On April 6 the surface radar of the submarine USS *Threadfin* had made nighttime contact with the *Yamato* and its escort of one cruiser and eight destroyers as they headed toward Okinawa. The Japanese force was, intentionally, on a one-way mission. The battleships' instructions were to wreak havoc among the amphibious forces and, when it ran out of fuel (or was too damaged to maneuver), to beach itself on the island and use its guns to assist the defending garrison—this was about as far removed from the classical concepts of naval warfare as might be imagined! But, in any case, the *Yamato* didn't get that far, simply because, between noon and three o'clock in the afternoon on the seventh, it was torn apart by waves and waves of American naval dive-bombers and torpedo-bombers. Taking no chances, and eager to show that this was something the new carrier navy could do better than either the disappointed US battleships or the Army Air Force, Mitscher committed a strike by 280 planes from *nine* of his fleet carriers. Fifteen minutes apart, the squadrons relentlessly dropped their bombs and torpedoes. By the time of their sixth attack, the *Yamato* had virtually turned over, its lengthy bottom still taking hits as it faced skyward, until, at 2:30 p.m., an enormous explosion tore it apart. The Japanese flotilla also lost its cruiser and four of the destroyers. Mitscher's force suffered only ten aircraft lost.[23] Again, the disproportionality was staggering. A full four hundred years of battleship history, going back to John Hawkins's *Revenge,* had just ended. And the contentious Billy Mitchell, sacked twenty years earlier for suggesting that aircraft alone could sink the largest warships at sea, had been right.

The kamikaze *aircraft* assaults off Okinawa were altogether more successful, and their numbers often intimidating. On April 12, for example, the Japanese Air Force attacked the Allied ships with no less than 185 kamikaze planes, which were screened by 150 fighters to prevent their being shot down by US fighter patrols. It also threw 45 torpedo planes into the fray, plus 8 bombers carrying certain novel air-to-ship missiles.[24] These were almost Battle of Britain–sized numbers, and for a campaign that lasted almost as long. As with the kamikaze campaign off Iwo Jima, the attacks could come in the day and the night, and much more frequently since, as noted above, Okinawa was that much closer to the Japanese home islands. While no US battleships, fleet carriers, or heavy cruisers were to be sunk by this type of warfare, heavy losses did occur—

unsurprisingly—to the smaller warships on constant picket duty. Overall, no less than three American escort carriers and fourteen destroyers were sunk during the overall kamikaze campaign, and many more were damaged. For historians who count this encounter as a single though composite battle, the 4,900 American sailors killed and 4,800 wounded constituted the most losses suffered in a single battle for the US Navy, far more than those at Midway and Leyte Gulf and even Pearl Harbor.[25]

American destroyers took the bulk of these hits, and some were blown right in two, although others survived unbelievable amounts of damage. The most famous of these was the USS *Laffey,* known by legend as the ship that would not die. Moved into the Pacific theater after action off Normandy in the previous year, the *Laffey* was on outlier picket duty on April 16 when a Japanese "Val" dive-bomber called other planes to join it in a consolidated attack. Again and again the destroyer was strafed, bombed, and crashed into, with US aircraft from nearby escort carriers striving to give some protection. Hit by no fewer than six bombs and crashed into by four kamikazes, the warship still would not sink, which was a remarkable testimony to the structural strength of these American fleet destroyers of World War II, even though they were mass-produced at such speed. Almost as remarkable was this ship's repair and rebuilding to enable it to continue in active service—the *Laffey* was still in active service during the Korean War and even during the Cold War in the Mediterranean Fleet in the 1960s![26]

Yet the fighting careers of some of these vessels could be far briefer, even if also extremely action-packed. For example, the USS *Harding,* a *Gleaves*-class fleet destroyer commissioned in the Seattle-Tacoma yards in May 1943, was first deployed to convoy escort duty on the North Africa runs in late 1943, just as the tides of war against the U-boats were turning. A half year later it saw historic action supporting the US rangers on Pointe de Hoc on D-Day itself, and yet only two months after that it was participating in Operation Anvil and fought a ferocious nighttime battle against German E-boats off the South of France, sinking three of them. Even before its second year was over, USS *Harding* was sent home to be converted to be a destroyer minesweeper, taking up those minesweeping duties in Okinawan waters on March 24, 1945. Within a week, however, it also was urgently reassigned to the outer destroyer screen to intercept the kamikaze attacks. On April 16 the *Harding* was attacked by four Japanese suicide planes, one of which crashed into its bridge, killing twenty-two crewmen. Partially repaired at the Okinawa moorings, the destroyer then made its slow way back to Pearl Harbor, San Diego, and then Norfolk, Virginia. Unlike the *Laffey* and without much fanfare, USS *Harding* was decommissioned in November and then sold for scrap.[27] It had en-

**PAINTING 51.** *Fletcher*-**class destroyer USS** *Bennion*, **Ulithi, 1944.** The *Fletcher*-class destroyer, veteran of many campaigns in the Pacific War (Marianas, Leyte Gulf, Iwo Jima, and Okinawa), is seen having a brief rest in the US Navy's advanced naval base at Ulithi. The huge American shipbuilding effort produced 175 *Fletcher*-class ships during the war.

joyed less than two years of intense fighting at sea but limped home from Okinawan waters that hardly mattered in the grand scheme of things, because many more modern destroyers were streaming westward across the Pacific to replace it. Recall that by 1945, American shipyards had constructed 175 *Fletcher*-class and 96 *Gearing*-class fleet destroyers to replace the earlier *Gleaves*-class vessels (see chapter 8).

By the time of the Okinawa campaign, TF 58 had been joined by the four fast carriers of the British Pacific Fleet along with the rest of Admiral Fraser's force of two battleships, six cruisers, and escorting destroyers. The Royal Navy carriers were often compared slightingly to their American equivalents (they held fewer aircraft per carrier, had less range, and were a bit slower) but came into their own during the kamikaze attacks on account of their thick, steel-plated decks. It had taken Fraser's fleet some time to arrive on station in a full state of readiness, for all of the reasons noted earlier, in particular the lack of adequate fleet supply.[28] But by late March this considerable British force was placed under Spruance's general operational command, had been given the distinctive fleet name of Task Force 57, and was deployed to the southwest tangent, where they intercepted oncoming aerial assaults from Japanese bases in Formosa and China. With a break for refits and refueling, the British flotilla came back again in May and was later joined by many additional vessels for the pre-invasion operations off Japan. Designed for robust fighting off hostile European shores, and with those heavy steel decks, the British carriers easily withstood the Japanese suicide attacks. On May 4, for example, a kamikaze had struck the carrier HMS *Indomitable* but simply bounced off the deck (to the amazement of the American naval liaison officers on board). On the same day another suicide plane exploded onto HMS *Formidable*, sent up a huge plume of fire and smoke, and caused some damage; but the warship was repaired and operating again later in the day.[29] The contrast with what happened when a kamikaze smashed into the wooden decks of American carriers like the *Saratoga* was noted by many—with the official US naval historian Morison, present during this campaign, writing admiringly that "a kamikaze hitting a steel flight deck crumpled up like a scrambled egg."[30]

It was June 22 by the time the US Army and Marines finally wiped out the Japanese garrison on Okinawa, and because the defenders had almost all fought to the death, the losses on both sides were awful. A full 77,000 Japanese troops (110,000 if one counts the Okinawan conscript soldiers) were killed in the formal three months of the campaign, and perhaps another 10,000 more in the later mopping-up operations. Around 149,000 hapless native Okinawans died in the crossfire. But to MacArthur and Nimitz's planners the more frightening figure was the American casualty tally: over 12,000 servicemen were killed, 38,000 wounded in battle, and another 32,000 damaged (due to psychiatric cases, accidents, and exhaustion). As a result of the offshore kamikaze attacks, the navy's total dead (4,900) was, interestingly, larger in this campaign than that of the army (4,675) and the marines (2,938). The army's senior officer, Lieutenant General Simon Buckner, was himself killed by enemy fire near the very end of the fighting; the senior Japanese officer, General Mitsuru Ushijima, committed suicide at around the same time. This had been a grim battle, the worst so far in the Pacific War, not counting the debilitating Philippines fighting to the south.[31]

Not surprisingly, by May 1945 Washington was in a hurry, with its military leadership, including General George C. Marshall himself, most anxious about troop losses and overall morale, even at the crest of victory. Far away in the European theater, as Germany finally fell, what the US Army and Air Force planners desired most was to bring weary troops and airmen back home to their families rather than to have them reshipped to the Pacific, as was indeed happening. Both the Germans and the Japanese were taking longer, far longer, to crush in the field than might reasonably have been expected. And since, in the Pacific, the United States enjoyed a huge superiority in both naval and aerial force, it was vital to work those assets—the battleships and cruisers in shore bombardments, the great carrier raids, the submarine attacks, and the B-29 firebombing—as hard and aggressively as possible. Task Force 58, with its dependable and tough *Essex*-class carriers plus escorts, was steaming thousands of miles more without a break than the navy would have liked, while servicing the fuel-hungry destroyers at sea seemed an almost daily task. Admirals Spruance and Halsey could be interchanged at intervals (Halsey took over TF 58 again in June), but tired cruiser and destroyer skippers, let alone their crews, could not. Newer vessels were a welcome relief and brought swiftly into the frontlines, but only war-damaged or storm-battered warships could be allowed to limp back to Hawaii and then to West Coast ports.

In the weeks following the Okinawa campaign, the Allied aerial and naval grip on Japan tightened. The B-29 bombers, encountering everweaker Japanese defenses, now flew lower with their high-explosive and incendiary bombs; by this stage, the USAAF was starting to run out of significant military targets. At sea, the American submarine forces also closed in, and again the targets shrank in significance. Japan's longerrange shipping lines, especially those carrying oil and other strategic industrial supplies, had by now collapsed. Entering the Sea of Japan and other inland waters, US submarines ravaged the coastal trades and shot up fishing vessels. In 1944 Japan still had around 3 million tons of active shipping, but the losses that year and into 1945 were so severe that by July of the latter year the total of seaworthy ships had fallen away to almost nothing. An aerial minelaying campaign by a group of B-29s detached by LeMay for this purpose virtually paralyzed Japan's harbors; what few ships emerged were sunk by U-boats. Without food imports, the nation began to starve.[32]

After the war, certain American strategic bombing advocates as well as the US Submarine Service claimed that they could have compelled Japan to collapse and surrender without any need for the dropping of the atomic bombs or a military invasion. Given the stubbornness that still prevailed in Imperial Japanese Headquarters in August 1945, that seems unlikely. In any case, the first scenario implied the killing of perhaps millions of civilians through firebombing; the second, the deaths of millions through starvation. Those who argue that Hiroshima and Nagasaki were unnecessary measures need to consider how dire and painful and slow the other Allied weapons of pressure of mid-1945 actually were.[33] As it was, the US Army wasn't much interested in the submarine blockade or even its own Air Force's bombing campaign. It was planning to crush Japan's resistance on the ground, and in that regard, the atomic bombs probably saved the lives of millions of civilians who would have been sucked into the maelstrom of fighting following a land invasion.

By June of that year, the American and British navies were inflicting a further sort of punishment on their sagging foe in the form of offshore heavy-warship bombardments of coastal harbors, steelworks, factories, and cities. Covered by aerial patrols overhead and protected at sea by fleet destroyers, battleships such as USSs *Wisconsin* and *Iowa* (16-inch shells) and HMS *King George V* (14-inch shells) blasted away at Japanese targets unfortunate enough to be located near the sea; sometimes the escorting cruisers and destroyers were also allowed to join in the shelling. On July 14, for example, the Japanese ironworks at Kamaishi were the target, and on July 19 the industrial factories along the shoreline of Hitachi were shelled, although of course many of the factories already lacked materials for warlike production. These bombardments were actually continued until after the second atomic bomb was dropped and the formal "cease hostilities" order reached the fleets. Such a fate and humiliation had not happened to Italy and Germany in their last weeks, nor had anything like it been seen in World War I. Defeat was to be rubbed in by any and all means at hand; and, as the commanding admirals admitted, it gave their battleships one rare, last chance to fire their big guns at enemy targets.[34]

The naval bombardments along the coast, the devastating B-29 fire-bombing attacks from the sky, and the tightening of the submarine blockade were of course all intended as the softening-up steps before the actual invasion of Japan, which was to be the largest amphibious assault in all history. The American planners gave the grand two-stage invasion of Japan the rather melodramatic name Operation Downfall, with the first and smaller stage, the invasion of the southern part of the island of Kyushu (Operation Olympic) scheduled for the beginning of November 1945. Even the smaller operation was to be bigger than any previous assault from the sea, deploying forces in such numbers as stun the reader's mind: 670,000 American troops (eleven army and three marine divisions) initially, thousands of landing craft, thousands and thousands of aircraft, and so on. To the naval historian, though, it is the planned array of surface warships that again catches the imagination: engaged in everything from close-in beach bombardments to wider-ranging intercepts of kamikaze attacks from the mainland would be no less than twenty-four Allied battleships (new and old) escorted by four-hundred-plus destroyers

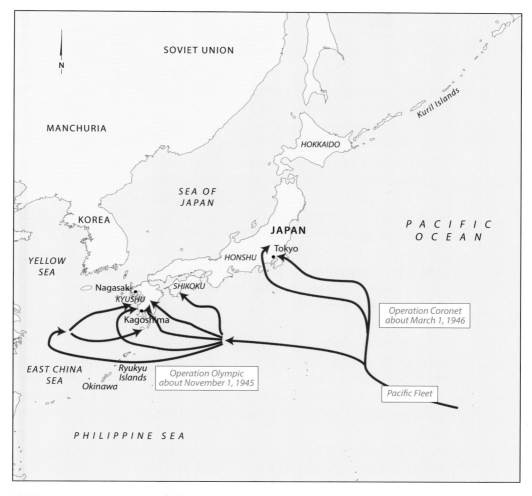

MAP 16. Operation Downfall: The planned invasion of the Japanese home islands, 1945–46.

and joined by some forty-two aircraft carriers. In retrospect, a force this size sounds quite excessive, but the American planners, remaining deeply impressed by the power of the kamikaze hordes off Okinawa, anticipated attacks against Operation Olympic from thousands and thousands of Japanese suicide aircraft, even primitive ones. Only by deploying an enormous modern armada to beat off these assaults and then actually taking the home islands by land forces would the enemy at last be forced to yield. But it would not be pretty, for this would be a campaign far larger than the Okinawa one, and the anticipated Allied casualties (even the lower estimates) were extremely disturbing to those in the know.[35]

By this stage the American planners, urged on by Washington, were beginning to appreciate the possible contributions that might be made by their allies in the final overthrow of Japan. The British naval performance at Okinawa had not been a small one, and ever more Royal Navy and Commonwealth warships were being added to that fleet. And there was much eagerness by Washington's allies—the Australians, Canadians, New Zealanders, and the Dutch but especially the British—to be involved in the final military stages of the campaign against Japan. Indeed, had the later invasion of Honshu (Operation Coronet) taken place as planned in March 1946, a vast Commonwealth Army would have been part of that endeavor. Even then, that army would have been only one-quarter the size of the American contribution (1 million, compared to 4 million soldiers), just as the Royal Navy's considerable Pacific Fleet, for all its reinforcements, would never come to be more than about a fifth of the gigantic American navy here.[36] By July 1945, the US Pacific Fleet alone totaled well over four hundred major warships, with more arriving by the month. (One wonders what the number of collisions was, quite apart from the losses inflicted by the frequent Pacific storms that blew in on the fleet.) And all this was a mere two years after the new USS *Essex* had first arrived at Pearl Harbor. Veteran crew members of the *Saratoga*, by this stage of the war repaired again but reduced to a simple pilot-training vessel back in Hawaii, must have been staggered as they read in their Fleet News of the sheer expansion in the size of the Pacific navy and recalled the time, not too long earlier, when they had operated as the sole American carrier in that ocean.

The dropping of the first atomic bomb on Hiroshima on August 6, followed by the second one on Nagasaki three days later, the USSR's hasty entry into the war, and the rapid Japanese surrender that followed changed all this, turning the plans for Downfall into archival history. For some days further, US surface warships and submarines patrolled around the shores of Japan, planes tangled with any Japanese aircraft (including kamikazes) that came out, and as mentioned above, some bombardments of shoreline establishments continued until, gradually, units on each side began to receive cease-fire instructions and to stop military activity. Steadily, American liaison groups began to enter Japanese ports to arrange for handovers of control facilities. Decisions were made as to which Allied squadrons would be sent off to Sydney and Pearl Harbor for rest and which would stay for the big surrender ceremony in Tokyo Bay.

The making and dropping of the atomic bombs had of course very little to do with sea power and everything to do with the newer stages of American technological and economic might. The idea that a single bomb dropped from a single plane could devastate an entire city in one blow and that a small number of such bombs might crush a nation could not be fitted into the traditional world of sea battles, convoys, grinding blockades, or swift destroyer actions. Atomic warfare existed in a different sphere, with both a very different destructiveness and a very different investment of resources. The entire Manhattan Project was estimated to have cost the hitherto unimaginable sum of 2 billion US dollars (an *Essex*-class carrier cost about $75 million), and no other combatant nation could have afforded as much. Yet it was *not* the most expensive weapons project of World War II, for that perhaps dubious accolade went to the gigantic B-29 Superfortress program itself, which is estimated to have cost the even larger sum of $3 billion.[37] But mere financial costs didn't seem to matter here. On one bright morning in early August 1945, the delivery vehicle and the bomb itself, horse and rider, brought the world into a new military era. To every American fighting man in that Pacific theater of war, the news that a brand-new weapon had led to an end to hostilities came as a huge relief. To their admirals, as we shall see, it came as a source of much puzzlement and concern.

The Pacific War ended with lots of symbolism, so as to emphasize this victory of Allied and especially American sea power. There were some precedents but only partial ones. The previous 1914–18 conflict at sea had concluded with an armistice, and it was only eight months afterward that the remains of the Kaiser's High Seas Fleet surrendered at Scapa Flow, an act partly replicated (as we saw) when the Italian battle fleet steamed into Malta in September 1943. By early 1945, Germany's surface navy was largely gone, so only its U-boats remained to surrender or be interned abroad. The six-years-long maritime war against the Third Reich ended with a whimper, so to speak.

By contrast, Japan's defeat was deliberately marked by the presence of the Allied victors in Tokyo Bay itself, where, in a solemn ceremony, MacArthur accepted the formal and unconditional surrender of the Japanese High Command on the morning of September 2, 1945. This event took place, surely a careful calculation of the US Navy's planners, on the deck of the huge new battleship USS *Missouri*—the name of President Truman's own state. A large-scale flyover of more than four hundred planes emphasized the victor's power. It was not, though, made into a crude triumphalist event, and both MacArthur's and Nimitz's statements on that occasion stressed reconciliation and, now that the war was over, a new world order of peace and justice. The victor's mode was determined but dignified. The Japanese delegation signed the surrender document quietly and then left. Various smaller ceremonies followed on various vessels. Feelings of relief and pride were manifest. At the close of this historic date and in the presence of that great fighting sailor, Admiral William Halsey, a British marine band on board the battleship *King George V* played the lovely Anglican hymn "The Day Thou Gavest, Lord, Is Ended." It was fitting.[38]

In the several weeks that followed, American carriers, battleships, and cruisers, with some warships of the British Pacific Fleet nearby, swung at their moorings in the great bay. Each day a hot Pacific sun crossed over the anchored flotillas and then settled in the hills to the west, eventually going down over Mount Fuji. No more appropriate symbol of the end of the Japanese Empire could be imagined.

# PART V

## Aftermath and Reflections

**PAINTING 52.** **HMS *Renown* and USS *Augusta*, Plymouth, 1945.** The two great warships have rendezvoused to mark President Harry Truman's return from Europe to the United States. The long lines of the historic British battle cruiser are well captured here, as is the clean and seaworthy shape of the US heavy cruiser. This was the *Renown*'s last mission at sea.

# ELEVEN

## Navies and Naval Powers in World War II

### *An Audit*

A t the beginning of August 1945, a mere seven years after the *Hood* and *Barham* had lain together in Malta's Grand Harbour (painting 1), two other large warships were anchored in another famous stretch of water, the Hamoaze estuary at Plymouth in southwest England. Across the way was the historic Royal Navy base of Devonport, but the Plymouth harbor's place in maritime history goes much further back, to the very time of Francis Drake and John Hawkins and the start of English sea power. It was appropriate, then, that one of the great gray vessels seen in painting 52 was the veteran battle cruiser HMS *Renown,* the seventh ship in the navy to bear that name, and a warship that had had a truly Elizabethan fighting performance throughout World War II. A keen-eyed observer might have noticed that, although its superstructure was festooned with celebratory flags and bunting, there was something wrong with several of the *Renown*'s gun turrets. Nothing was out of place, though, with the second ship, which was the almost equally interesting American heavy cruiser and presidential naval vessel, the USS *Augusta.*

The occasion for this event was President Harry Truman's return from the historic Potsdam Conference (July 17–August 2), on a journey that saw him flying from Berlin to England and then going by train to the port of Plymouth wherein lay the presidential command ship. Escorted by destroyers, the USS *Augusta* would then set out for a swift voyage back to Washington. It is worth noting not only that a lot of historic symbolism attended this brief presidential visit but that the two ships themselves carried an awful lot of history. The choice of vessels was no small coincidence, surely, as each warship had not only participated in some of the great naval campaigns of the war but had also been repeatedly selected to carry their own national leader to significant events. Perhaps some of the crew of the American cruiser could recall taking the president to the harbor at Argentia (Newfoundland) in 1941, where he and the prime minister had proclaimed the Atlantic Charter; recall its efforts as a headquarters ship at both the North African and Normandy landings; and recall, more recently, its role in bearing Roosevelt and his staff back from the Yalta Conference in early 1945. For its part, the *Renown,* the last of Admiral John Fisher's battle cruisers, had taken a major role in naval fights from the very beginning of the war in European waters to its close, as the lead warship for Force H out of Gibraltar, a stalwart in the Malta convoys, and a pursuer in the *Bismarck* chase; and on more benign occasions it had conveyed Churchill to both the Quebec and Cairo conferences.[1] There was a lot of history here.

Now, in Plymouth harbor, as the first part of the president's visit, Mr. Truman came on board the British battle cruiser to pay his formal respects to King George VI, with the latter resplendent in his uniform as a full admiral of the fleet. A day later, on August 4, 1945, the king in turn was invited to inspect the captain and crew of the USS *Augusta.* In attendance, too, was Clement Attlee, who had replaced Churchill as prime minister following the British general elections of July 1945. (It was symbolic that the great personal wartime leadership of the Grand Alliance was no more, with Roosevelt passed away and Churchill retired to the country.)

Later in the day the American warship weighed anchor, steamed past the tip of Cornwall, and headed into the Atlantic, carrying the leader of the free world with it. After he disembarked, Truman planned to go on to address a meeting of both houses of the American Congress and outline to them their grave new responsibilities. From the viewpoint of a gull or osprey circling high above, the USS *Augusta* would simply look like some other vessel, gray, metallic, and small, pushing through the Atlantic rollers. As the ship sailed from the Old to the New World, though, it just as surely represented a watershed in global history as had galleons leaving Leghorn, Genoa, and other Mediterranean ports for western destinations four centuries earlier.

But there was more to it than that, more even than the fact that the United States had emerged so decisively as the most powerful country the world had ever seen. For on the second day of his voyage on the *Augusta,* and thus (obviously) before he had reached port, Truman gave the final authorization for the dropping of the atomic bomb on the Japanese city of Hiroshima. Less than two days later, on the other side of the globe, a B-29 called Enola Gay dropped its bomb, and the world of international affairs—and navies within it—was transformed. A full seventy-five years afterward it still remains difficult for a reader to grasp the full historic dimensions of all this, not to mention the technological innovations that had emerged since the war's beginning; to grasp the fact that a single individual made a decision while on a ship in one ocean, somewhere just west of Ireland; the order was transmitted by wireless via Washington, DC, San Diego, and Pearl Harbor to the recently constructed US bomber base on Tinian, in the Mariana Islands on the other side of the planet; and a giant B-29 aircraft then took off, roared northward for six hours, and dropped a single bomb that destroyed an entire city. "Now I have become Death . . . , the Destroyer of the Worlds," murmured Robert Oppenheimer, the bomb project's chief administrator, recalling those ancient Hindu words when the news broke.[2] An established and comprehensible world order—even if a war-torn one—a world order that also had included an important place for cruisers and battleships, now seemed transformed.

A poignant fate now awaited the elderly battle cruiser *Renown*. Already in May 1945 it had been paid off from active service by the Admiralty, and a little later the turrets were removed from its secondary guns. But such work on the ship had abruptly ceased so that it could be used to represent the Royal Navy on the occasion of Truman's visit (all of the modern *King George V*–class battleships being of course with the Pacific Fleet at this time). Shortly afterward, with no further role envisaged for this famous vessel, it was ordered to move north to the Clyde, where it had been launched exactly forty years earlier. Partly dismantled, it waited there a little while longer and was scrapped in the summer of 1948. So many other elderly British warships were being scrapped around that time that its disappearance attracted very little attention. *Sic transit gloria.*

---

The war in which the *Augusta* and *Renown* had fought so well had been a long and hard one, and it had been particularly grueling at sea. But after all the fighting on the oceans and in the narrows was over and retrospective analysis was possible, the historian could ask this: how and to what extent did this particular 1939–45 maritime conflict accord with the grand theories of naval strategy? Perhaps it might be better to turn that question around and ask to what extent did the various schools of thought about naval strategy (see chapter 3) have their ideas validated during World War II at sea? And is it really possible to answer that question given the sheer number and variety of naval engagements during six years of fighting, from the torpedoing of the carrier HMS *Courageous* off Ireland in September 1939 to the Allied bombardments of the Japanese coast in June 1945?

The answer to the question is implied in the wording itself: the variety of the naval campaigns across most of the globe did not admit to any

single theory of maritime warfare being true of the whole. It makes more
sense, as we have sought to do in the previous chapters, to try to understand this second great war at sea as being composed of three separate
and only sometimes related multiyear struggles: a fight for mastery of the
Pacific realm that raged from late 1941 until mid-1945; the slightly shorter,
very intensive Battle of the Mediterranean from June 1940 until, say, the
invasion of southern France in July 1944; and the longest naval campaign
of all, the fight over the Atlantic sea-lanes throughout the entire European war. Only very few warships, it is safe to say,[3] had the opportunity
to fight in all three theaters in the course of this war; only they, perhaps,
through that experience, saw the multifaceted nature of this immense naval conflict. And only through fighting in all three areas would they have
appreciated how, time and again, geography played such a role. From the
tightness of the Mediterranean waters to the vast expanses of the Pacific
and back again to the vital convoy routes south of Greenland and Iceland,
distance and physical circumstance dictated the way the naval war was to
be fought.

Of the three great areas of naval fighting, probably that in the Pacific
is the easiest to summarize when assessing how closely it may be compared to the various schools of strategic thought. The Battle of the Pacific
was very much a Mahanian contest by intention, beginning with a Japanese main strike against the US battle fleet in Pearl Harbor, similar in so
many ways to Japan's preemptive strike against the Russian fleet in Port
Arthur in 1904. The problem that the Imperial Japanese Navy (IJN) then
had was that it had sunk or damaged so many of the American battleships that there were none left to constitute an opposing force for a surface gunnery shootout, as had occurred later in that previous war, at the
Battle of Tsushima (May 1905). This left the Japanese admirals of 1942 instead searching for ways to pin down the elusive US aircraft carriers and
thus pushing forward their own carriers to close a trap. When their overelaborate scheme at Midway led to the disastrous loss of so many fleet
carriers, the Japanese-American balance of forces became weird indeed,
from mid-1942 right through to the end of 1943. The IJN had lots of big
battleships but lacked fleet air squadrons and thus feared to push forward;
meanwhile, the US Pacific Fleet had no battleships and only a few precious carriers. All this changed with the arrival of a vast new American
navy early in 1944, but it was not until October of that year that the IJN
was able to attempt another elaborate trap, this time at Leyte Gulf with
various battleship groups, only to suffer blow after blow. American carrier
planes tore into parts of Japan's battle fleet, US submarines sank other big
ships, and a third group was battered by old-fashioned gunfire at the Battle of the Surigao Strait—it was hardly the case, then, that the overall Bat-

tle of Leyte Gulf was a great battleship encounter like Trafalgar or even Jutland, although it was a sort of Mahanian victory. Thereafter, the Japanese main fleet was no more, and the tables were completely turned. As the US Navy planned for the actual invasion of Japan, it could deploy over twenty battleships, but by then they faced no opponents. All that their great guns could fire at was targets along the Japanese shore or kamikazes. By that time in the war, too, the Japanese merchant marine had been crippled by American submarine attacks, so there was a certain Corbettian element to Japan's overall defeat. At the end of the day, it hardly mattered; one of these contestants was around six to eight times more powerful than the other, and the outcome of the war was not in doubt.

In contrast, it was the Battle of the Atlantic that, by common consent among historians, most closely resembled a maritime contest fought along Corbettian lines (again, using that shorthand term). From the very beginning of World War II, or, at the latest, after the Fall of France, the strategic test was clear to each side: could the Axis throttle the key lines of seaborne trade to the British Isles? If it managed to do that, Britain's own future was grim. It was never, then, a battle-fleet war. Even the few incursions that were made by large German surface vessels like the *Graf Spee, Scharnhorst* and *Gneisenau,* and *Bismarck* were really commerce-raiding ventures seeking to disrupt the Allied convoys, not a main challenge for command of the seas; and even those exciting gunnery battles (Barents Sea and North Cape) that took place along the northern-flank line of communication to Murmansk were just further fights between the weaker navy's commerce raiders and the protecting forces of an Allied convoy. In truth, the small size of the surface Kriegsmarine condemned it to adopt, of course reluctantly, a *guerre de course* strategy. By contrast, Karl Doenitz's U-boat arm rejoiced in pursuing a war against Allied trade and, for six grim years, did it so very well. Maybe it was only once, around March 1943, that it had threatened, as the Admiralty record stated, "to separate the Old World from the New," and that was a danger that was beaten off by an extraordinary array of Allied aerial-naval forces a mere three months later. The overall nature of the Atlantic campaign implied that, as the official historian Stephen Roskill had pointed out,[4] it could never have the character of great individual fleet actions like the Nile. Instead, victory or defeat here was measured only incrementally, through the steady statistical data of merchant-ship tonnage lost, U-boats sunk, and the overall tonnage of goods that got through to Britain not only to feed the islanders but also to build supplies for the move into Europe.

The ferocity of the three years of daytime (and often nighttime) battles in the narrower waters of the Mediterranean produced a myriad of examples both of significant surface actions for naval mastery and of a continuing struggle to fight through convoy supplies and maintain sea lines of communication. The shooting war in this sea had begun, after all, with the Royal Navy's ruthless bombardment of the French fleet at Mers-el-Kébir, an action easily compared to Nelson's preemptive attack on the neutral Danish navy in Copenhagen in 1801. The inconclusive Battle of Calabria that soon followed gave strong hints of how the surface war between the Italian and British battle fleets would unfold over the following seasons. From time to time a large Italian force would go forth, but it always hoped for a favorable circumstance in which it would get to a convoy before Admiral Andrew Cunningham's Mediterranean Fleet appeared or would catch only a part of the Royal Navy at sea; wary of its enemy's better gunnery and carriers, though, Italian admirals often called off a sortie before the fleets came close. The surprise nighttime defeat off Cape Matapan at the hands of radar-equipped British battleships was a shock. Perhaps the Regia Marina's best chance of surface domination in the Mediterranean came at the end of 1941, when so many of the Royal Navy's heavy warships had been sunk or damaged. But an aggressive Axis strategy, including the seizure of Malta, was not undertaken at that time, and by 1942, when both Churchill and Pound were willing to commit so many naval assets into this arena (the Pedestal Convoy, especially), it was too late. With the Anglo-American seizure of North Africa and the buildup of their bomber forces, and with the remaining Italian surface fleet running out of fuel, there was increasingly no role in the Mediterranean for Allied battleships, except as amphibious support vessels for further landings. The Luftwaffe's parting blows against the surrendering Italian fleet in September 1943 was more an act of spite than anything intended to influence the naval balance of forces; and the remainder of the French surface navy had already sunk itself, at Toulon, ten months earlier. There were no opposing big fleets left in these waters to prove Alfred Thayer Mahan's theories right or wrong in any case.

By contrast, throughout the Mediterranean fighting the Axis powers had endeavored to keep open the vital supply routes to Rommel's and Graziani's armies in North Africa, while the Royal Navy for its part had striven to reinforce Malta by convoys coming from either direction and even, at critical times of the war, to run convoys right through in order to supply the British Eighth Army in Egypt. Woodman counts no fewer than thirty-five large supply operations carried out by the Royal Navy to Malta in the years 1940–42 (and carrier operations to fly off relief planes, submarine runs, and fast minelayer runs are not in that total); most of them were fought through with heavy losses, and several turned back.[5] Corbett in his naval writings had often said that it would be just fine and that a successful naval strategy would be achieved if convoys reached their destination uninterrupted by the foe. In the contested Mediterranean arena, such a luxury was never in sight. Unlike in the North Atlantic campaign (where the majority of sailings did reach their destinations unscathed), not many convoys got through these waters between 1940 and 1942 without some loss.

In addition to surface fleet actions across the globe and a fight for the sea lines of communication, there was another, very different form of maritime warfare waged during the 1939–45 conflict, one that played an ever-larger role in the Allied march to victory—namely, that of amphibious war. It was a manifestation of Anglo-American sea power, surely, and it was a form of campaigning that occurred in every theater—Atlantic, Pacific, and Mediterranean—in which they fought and was of course the key to their eventual success. The Grand Alliance's proclaimed demand for the unconditional surrender of the Axis implied that if surrender wasn't offered, large invading armies would one day march on the foes' capital cities; that in turn would mean huge amphibious operations to seize their homelands and all positions leading to it. The list of Allied landings from the sea was a long one, from the early failures at Norway and Crete to the first advances in Guadalcanal and North Africa and then the push through the south-central Pacific and the central Mediterranean, followed by Normandy, Anvil, Iwo Jima, and Okinawa. When the atomic bombs were dropped, they cut short plans for the greatest amphibious operation of all, against the Japanese homeland. Operation Downfall, indeed. Here was the realization of Admiral Fisher's old dream, that armies were to be thought of as huge projectiles fired by navies onto the enemy's shore, as successful sea power morphed into victorious land power. And while many of the smaller instruments of amphibious warfare were to be scrapped after 1945, the operational know-how and command structures were retained and found to have a revived utility, both at Incheon and at Suez.

Just when, it then may be asked, was the war at sea essentially "won"? In a formal sense, of course, that didn't occur until the mass surrender of the U-boats at the beginning of May 1945 and the Japanese surrender three months later. But at a certain stage in the preceding fight it had become clear that one side faced defeat while the other could look forward to victory. The narrative chapters suggest that that stage in the war came rather later than some other histories suggest: that in the Pacific campaign, it is too early to call the June 1942 Battle of Midway the decisive turning point in the struggle and that the watershed was only properly crossed much later, nearer the end of 1943 when Chester W. Nimitz's new fleet moved in great force upon the Gilbert Islands. In the Atlantic, too, the British Admiralty scarcely dared hope that the end was in sight until it had understood the extent of the U-boat losses in May–June 1943 and Doenitz's re-call orders. In the Mediterranean and North Africa, possibly because the fighting had taken place in much tighter confines, it was easier to recognize "the end of the beginning" by the start of 1943. Of course, in a far larger materialistic sense, perhaps victory was going to one side as early as December 1941, when the entry of the United States and the survival of the USSR in the European struggle meant that roughly three-quarters of the world's military and economic power was now in play against a mere one-quarter of the whole on the Axis side. Yet even at this deeper level, as we have argued in chapter 8, it was not until the unfolding of the year 1943 that the great shift in the military-productive balances took place.

While they were always interrelated (simply because naval and aerial resources could be shifted from one theater to the other), the three large naval battlegrounds of World War II have generally been handled by historians as self-standing entities: the Pacific, including East Asia; the Mediterranean and Near East; and the larger Atlantic, including western Europe. And while giant fighting was occurring in all three of those regions throughout, say, the year 1943, naval historians need to remember that the struggle was a global one and was also taking place at the same time as *another* three massive campaigns: the battles along the Eastern Front; the Allied strategic bombing campaign; and the huge fight of the Japanese Army inside China. All six contests in this war interacted with each other (although the last-named of the six less so than the rest). Thus, the Nazi-Soviet struggle sucked large German manpower and industrial resources eastward and away from Doenitz's navy, while large flows of seaborne weaponry (aircraft and trucks) greatly assisted the Soviet fighting forces. The Anglo-American victory at sea helped the USSR win the war on the Eastern Front, just as the Soviet smashing of the Wehrmacht aided the victory at sea. Divining which effort claims the larger role is not a particularly useful exercise.[6] What is clear, though, is that in most areas of this global struggle the Axis position was fraying badly by the end of 1943. And sea power's responsibility for that happening, and thus the influence of sea power on history, was indisputable.

Great military conflicts, the historian Correlli Barnett has persuasively argued, are the "auditors" of all things, because it is only when societies are mobilized for a giant war that every part of the whole is tested: national direction, strategic decision-making, productive resources, scientific and technological capacity, the armed services, and their weapon systems.[7] In this light, it is clear that World War II not only tested all six of the navies that were described in chapter 2 but also provided an audit of their major warship types—different vessel systems revealed themselves to be more or less capable of responding in the newer fighting circumstances that unfolded after September 1939. It was perhaps more than merely symbolic that the European war at sea began with U-boats sinking a British carrier and a British battleship before the Admiralty had properly readied itself for another great maritime struggle and that the Pacific war at sea began with a surprise assault out of the air. The age of modern asymmetric weaponry had arrived.

Of all the warship types, it was the battleship, the core of every prewar navy, that had the greatest difficulty adapting to a new large-scale war at sea, but for different reasons depending on each of the navies in question. It surely could not have been foreseen, even by the acutest naval officer of 1939, how short was the time span—a mere five to six years—before their type would become redundant. At the war's beginning, all six navies were striving to get their latest battleships into the water as swiftly as possible, the *Littorios, King George Vs, Richelieus, North Carolinas, Bismarcks,* and *Musashis;* the very fact that the others were building them meant that each admiralty had to build more. The crushing of the French battle fleet took away one contestant. The slow peeling of the Kriegsmarine's few big ships—*Bismarck, Scharnhorst,* and *Tirpitz*—destroyed another surface navy. The Italian battleships were assaulted from the air, hemmed in, and then told to surrender by 1943. The Royal Navy's scarcely adequate fleet of dreadnoughts was juggled from theater to theater of war, took heavy losses and bruising damage, and yet performed well overall. But by the time the four modern *King George Vs* were being dispatched to the Pacific in 1944, the era of the all-big-gunned warship was coming to an end. Perhaps the Japanese were the ones chiefly responsible for that demise by having eliminated the US battle fleet so thoroughly at Pearl Harbor; for by the time the great new replacement ships had reached Nimitz's command, his carrier task forces had taken over the maritime war in the Pacific and were destroying much of the Japanese Navy in any case. As 1945 unfolded, then, both British and American battleships therefore came to have only two duties: to serve as antiaircraft platforms against kamikaze attacks on their own carriers, and to bombard shore installations. The era of grand fleet shootouts on the high seas was over. In truth, World War II had never been kind to such possibilities.

By contrast, this war at sea was one in which the cruisers of all navies found themselves being indispensable platforms of power projection almost throughout, acting as scouts for their battle fleets and as convoy escorts in dangerous waters, providing bombardment support to amphibious operations, or being in shooting matches against enemy cruiser squadrons (for example, the engagements at Cape Matapan, Second Sirte, and in the Southwest Pacific). The operational range covered by a single vessel like HMS *Sheffield,* from being with Norway patrols, Force H, *Bismarck* hunt, Malta convoys, and so on was actually not unusual, but cruisers paid a heavy price for being so often deployed. In consequence, the percentage of cruisers lost by most navies during World War II was probably higher than that of all other ships' types. About half the Italian cruisers were sunk. Germany's *Hipper*-class heavy cruisers and *Nürnberg*-class light cruisers were systematically damaged, shelled, bombed, and destroyed. Japan's big fleet of heavy cruisers had been decimated by the end of the Leyte Gulf battles. The Royal Navy lost no fewer than twenty-eight cruisers during the war, about 36 percent of its total. By the end of the conflict, almost all navies (Australian, Dutch, British, and French) had shifted away from using heavy 8-inch-gunned cruisers anymore—only the US Navy could keep them going—yet they still needed a sizable surface warship for many purposes in the years ahead, so whole new classes of light cruisers and antiaircraft (and later, antimissile *Aegis*-) cruisers entered their fleets.[8]

For more than any other warship type, though, this was a war in which fleet destroyers, and their somewhat smaller variant, destroyer escorts, distinguished themselves. Destroyers really earned that sobriquet of "workhorses of the fleet" throughout. The fast fleet destroyers found themselves being sent into action after action and were punished accordingly—the Kriegsmarine's loss of all ten of its destroyers in Narvik fjord was an extreme example of that, but shortly afterward the Royal Navy had over two dozen lost or heavily damaged at Dunkirk, and when the Battle of the Mediterranean commenced, the repeated fleet engagements or convoy battles between the British and Italian and German (U-boat) flotillas led to enormous numbers of warships lost, particularly in the Malta-Sicily narrows and off Crete; the seafloors of the Mediterranean must look in some places like some ghostly naval graveyard. The six-year Battle of the Atlantic, even if it was primarily fought by corvettes, sloops, frigates, and (US Navy) destroyer escorts, still took a considerable toll on Royal Navy and Allied destroyers. Japanese and American losses of this ship type were also very large indeed due to all the fights in the Solomons and the Bismarck Archipelago, the toll inflicted by kamikazes on the picket patrols, and the US bombing and submarine attacks on Japanese destroyers and other warships. The records suggest that the US Navy lost over 70 destroyers in World War II, although of course it also built over six times that number. The IJN lost a colossal 135 of its vessels, which was almost all of its destroyer fleet, by the conflict's end. The Kriegsmarine lost 27 destroyers, which was almost every one of its vessels in that type, while Italy lost a substantial 43 before its surrender. And the Royal

Navy's destroyer fleet, in action from the very beginning of the war until its close, lost a staggering 153 destroyers, which (like its cruisers) was over one-third of the whole.

Given that in all the naval theaters of war destroyers and destroyer escorts, together with their associated aircraft, spent a great deal of their energies seeking to kill enemy submarines and did so very well, it may be a bit surprising to argue that the 1939–45 conflict had also been "a good war" for that latter warship type too. After all, by the end of the fighting all three Axis submarine fleets were completely smashed up, destroyed, or abandoned. The Regia Marina had lost 85 of its submarines, almost all of them, in three short years of conflict, and the IJN lost about 127 of its boats (some 53 of them in 1944 alone). Meanwhile, the submarine branch of the German Navy, as we have seen, lost a staggering 780 U-boats throughout the war, most of them in the Battle of the Atlantic. Yet it was in that very struggle for control of the mercantile sea routes and in the extraordinary amounts of Allied shipping sunk by the U-boats that the power of this weapon system was evidenced. Only the U-boat had had the chance, albeit a brief one in 1942–43, to set back the Anglo-American plans for victory. And the fact that in the last few months of the war, the German Navy was bringing out revolutionary U-boat types, with snorkel breathing tubes, underseas recharging facilities, and terrific underwater speeds meant that the West's navies had only narrowly escaped what might have been another fierce battle on the seas. (Little wonder that, as with the other Nazi "wonder weapons," there was a scramble by the Americans and British after the war to acquire these new technologies.)

For the Silent Service, the Royal Navy's submarine branch, the conflict had been a satisfying one even if few knew about it. It lost a full seventy-six of its boats (32 percent) during the entire war, and the greatest number of those were in the narrow confines of the Mediterranean, which is why, interestingly, Italian forces sank more (thirty-seven) British submarines than the Germans did (twenty-four). The smaller British submarines were best for fighting the Kriegsmarine in the North Sea and at the entrance to the Baltic, but it was the larger ones that were sent east after 1942 to prey upon the Japanese merchant marine and an occasional heavy warship. By war's end, the service was destined to shrink again, for it seemed there were few potential enemies in sight. By contrast, the Submarine Services of the US Navy have claimed much more attention; after a slow start the American submarines tore apart the Japanese merchant marine and inflicted great losses on Japanese battleships, carriers, heavy cruisers, and many more warships—in the audit of war, US subs did very well indeed. By 1945 and afterward, its advocates were arguing that Japan could be defeated by submarine pressure alone, an argument that the dropping of the atomic bombs did not fully end. And the postwar story of the American Submarine Service became the more interesting when Admiral Hyman Rickover made it even more technologically advanced and strategic in the new Cold War setting by first introducing nuclear-powered boats and then endowing them with a ballistic missile capacity.

While such powerful and expensive naval weapons systems as cruisers and destroyers and (US) submarines seemed to have an assured future for the years following 1945, other surface types swiftly lost their perceived utility and thus their place in the Allied fleets. Almost all of the smaller escort carriers, regardless of their roles in the Battle of the Atlantic or supporting amphibious operations in the Pacific War, were swiftly scrapped, reconverted to merchantmen, or given or sold to lesser navies. Thousands of landing craft were scrapped or sold off to local commercial usage—for against what enemy would a vast landing-craft fleet, or the Seabees, be needed after the surrender of Japan? The most egregious of these "yard sales" of famous Allied warships was of the hundreds of the smaller sloops, corvettes, and destroyer escorts that had played such a critical role in the defense of the Atlantic merchant convoys throughout the entire war. By 1953, in fact, the Royal Navy had scrapped or sold off every one of its famous *Flower*-class corvettes—294 of them had been hastily built and pressed into extraordinary service during the war—so that it couldn't provide a single vessel of that type for the role of the HMS *Compass Rose* in the famous movie *The Cruel Sea* that was being made that year! (A surviving example was discovered with and borrowed from the Greek Navy, although it too was scrapped a few years later.)[9] So much for a nation's gratitude. The fact is that all of these warship types had been built and then committed to the great conflict in a most utilitarian way, like the thousands of Liberty ships that were built to carry emergency Allied supplies. With victory achieved, their purpose had gone. Audit of war, indeed.

Finally, World War II was the conflict in which the aircraft carrier had very definitely come into its own, and it had done so disproportionately, to the benefit of American sea power, with the Royal Navy quite some way behind even if it also enjoyed a late surge in its carrier fleet size and capacities. Of course long-range naval air was impossible for the three smaller navies that never possessed carriers to begin with, and even the German Air Force's specialist antiship Fliegerkorps X could be no equivalent to, say, Erich Raeder or Karl Doenitz controlling a squadron of navy flattops. The story of Japanese naval airpower in this war is one of the most extreme contrasts of all. At the very beginning of the Pacific campaigning, and for the first six months, Japan had the world's most effective and impressive carrier force. It stumbled at the Coral Sea and then suffered the huge loss of four fleet carriers and their aircrews at Midway. After that, in essence, it was all over—is it possible to point to any IJN action after June 1942 in which the Japanese carriers did well or achieved anything? It wasn't as if its navy completely lacked vessels, for it still had two fleet and four good light fleet carriers, and that at a time when Admiral William Halsey possessed only the USS *Saratoga*. But Japan had no great carrier admirals, and above all, it never recovered sufficient cadres of properly trained aircrews to match the skills and training of the American pilots; the advent of the P-38 Lightning and (especially) Hellcat fighters further increased the gap, as the Great Marianas Turkey Shoot showed. The fact that one part of the Japanese "plan" in the Leyte Gulf battle was to offer its five remaining carriers (almost all aircraftless) as a decoy—virtually as a sacrifice—to tempt the main US battle fleet northward while another part of the IJN made a surprise attack in the south was and is mind-boggling. Thereafter, nothing really remained. When the last carrier, the huge con-verted craft *Shinano,* was sunk by the USS *Archerfish* in November 1944, it was not ready for war and was carrying hardly any planes.

By that stage, and by contrast, the Royal Navy had finally assembled its own modern carrier task force to raid enemy targets in the East Indies and then become the core of the British Pacific Fleet. It wasn't that the Royal Navy hadn't deployed its modern carriers before then, but it had never been able to commit more than two or three of them at a time—for the Pedestal convoy, for Torch, for attacks on the *Tirpitz*—so it was never able to possess the independent, long-range airpower that, for example, Marc Mitscher's dozen carriers could show. Even as the Admiralty was rushing its newer light fleet carriers to the Far East in mid-1945, it really was too late; Japan was a crushed country, and the atomic bombs were about to fall. And as the war was ending, the new Labour government in London, confronting a massive financial crisis, began slashing most warship-building plans, including those for large carriers. A second-class economy could never really afford to possess a first-class carrier navy.

So, when naval histories record that the war was one in which mari-time airpower emerged supreme or in which the aircraft carrier replaced the battleship as the center of the fleet, it really is the story of Ameri-can carrier task forces in the Pacific that is meant by such words. The re-lentless successes of the fast-carrier groups from late 1943 onward is re-counted (chapters 9–10), as they pounded the shore bases and demolished the battleships of their enemies. Seventy-thousand-ton behemoths like *Musashi* or *Yamato* became mere targets when 300 carrier planes were thrown against them. There were many ways to measure the rise of Amer-ican power at the close of this great conflict, but the sheer number of the carrier groups off the Japanese coast is one of the best. Perhaps it was to make this point clear that a huge flight of some 450 naval planes flew over the American and British battleships as the Japanese surrender was being signed on board the USS *Missouri* on September 2, 1945. Even so, such a message was matched when, a few minutes later, a great array of giant B-29 Superfortresses also flew over Tokyo Bay, for the USAAF wanted to assert that it really had won the war. By that stage, of course, all of America's armed services were contending to show its unrivaled military might in the world.

———————

By that stage, too, the pre-1939 world of six naval powers was well over; in a matter of a few epic years, the multipolar maritime landscape that had been familiar for generations had gone. There is no need for detailed analysis of why the lesser naval nations failed their own audit of war. In France's case, it was scarcely its navy that could be blamed for the national eclipse. The Third Republic had fallen in a matter of weeks in May 1940 to a blistering German air and land assault, and its independent naval power fell with it. Had its admirals decided to accept Churchill's invitation to fight together, the first half of the war would have looked different, and the consequent story of the French battle fleet would have been very different too. There was nothing wrong with the design of the French warships themselves or the choices made by interwar French naval administrations about the types of vessels to construct; there simply was nothing that could be done within the service itself that could gainsay the vulnerability of French power vis-à-vis the Third Reich. France's naval position at this time was simply overwhelmed, as the country endured one of the great dramatic collapses of the century. Yet even those worried French admirals who elected to take their fleets into the Vichy regime could scarcely have imagined the further blows (Mers-el-Kébir, Toulon) that would crush their service.

It was almost comic, therefore, that Italy should have chosen to enter the war just as France was being forced from it, just when all the smaller states of northwestern Europe were being swallowed up by Germany and just as the Nazi-Soviet Pact was completing the division of middleish countries in the east. In a hegemonic struggle between ruthless larger nations, the best strategy for a medium power (if it could manage it) was to stay neutral, as Spain, Turkey, and Sweden demonstrated. By entering the war as it did and when it did, Mussolini's Italy put itself on the front line against a Churchill-led Britain desperate to show that it could fight on— fight, that is, throughout the Mediterranean, and fight aggressively with its battleships, carriers, submarines, and planes. The dominant English-language narrative about the Italian Navy in World War II, as it is about

the Italian Army in North Africa, is overwhelmingly negative and slighting; and the record is indeed a dismal one, from Taranto and Cape Matapan to the failure to neutralize Malta or to keep the Italian convoys safe.
Not taking Malta was critical, although it is clear from the British record
that the fight would have been severe, and an attempted invasion might
well have failed. But the fact that Italy's strategic leadership itself was
hopeless did not mean that the audit of its navy's performance is a completely negative one. The warships themselves, as we have seen, were often impressive, powerful, and fast, although they were rarely able to show
themselves off in the cramped operational circumstances of 1940–42. Its
antisubmarine patrols inflicted considerable damage on the Royal Navy's
flotillas, and the strike by its midget subs against Cunningham's battle
fleet in Alexandria harbor was superb. That latter blow, however, gives us
a clue to Italy's negative strategic function in this global conflict, that is,
while it could not win a naval war itself, the threat it posed to Britain's
Mediterranean interests pulled Royal Navy squadrons from the larger Atlantic realm and (especially) from the chances of playing much of a role
east of Suez. When the *Regia Marina* handed itself over in September
1943, therefore, it was not that it added anything to the Grand Alliance's
power so much as it removed a large distraction and at last eased the naval pressures on London. On the whole, though, it is doubtful whether
any more than that could have been achieved here by the ships of a nation possessing only 2.5 percent of the "relative war potential" of the Powers, that is, less than Japan, less than France, and much less than the really big players.

The audit of war over Germany's naval record in World War II has to
be much more nuanced than that. This was not a small-bit strategic actor, although ironically its fleet was nowhere as large as Italy's. The Third
Reich constituted a serious, ruthless, well-organized force for war at almost every level of military effectiveness (save for that flaw at the very top,
Hitler's own paranoid drive for global mastery). Germany's warships were
all strongly built, and their gunnery was excellent, although their large
destroyers and heavy cruisers were not very seaworthy in the Arctic ice
and Atlantic storms. German naval intelligence was usually good. Like
Italy, the navy lacked carriers, which made its admirals nervous when at
sea. Hitler's obsessions and interference cramped their freedom of action
on many occasions, while RAF Bomber Command repeatedly damaged
one heavy ship or another. Given the premature move to war in September 1939, the Kriegsmarine always suffered from a severe numerical defi-
ciency, made worse by the heavy losses incurred in the bold Norwegian
campaign. All of its Atlantic raids (*Graf Spee, Scharnhorst/Gneisenau,
Admiral Scheer,* and *Bismarck*) had a lone ranger quality to them, and

some were disastrous. After early 1942 every heavy German surface vessel was confined to the Baltic or northern Norway. How Raeder must have dreamed of possessing a battle fleet as large as Japan's, a country with only one-quarter of Germany's GNP. And what a nightmare a German fleet of some ten battleships and forty cruisers would have been to both British and American admiralties—but this was 1940, not 1914.

Germany's U-boat arm requires a different audit, especially in regard to the Battle of the Atlantic. From the beginning of the war to its end, its submarines were always frightening, and the losses they inflicted upon the Allies were vast: from the 3,500 merchant ships (of 14,500,000 dead-weight tons) to the long tally of Royal Navy battleships, carriers, cruisers galore, and dozens and dozens of destroyers. The most impressive part of Doenitz's U-boat campaign lay in its organizational power, especially in the wolf packs and in its sheer persistence. In the back-and-forth fight to control the Atlantic routes, the U-boat Service rarely gave up for long; even after the Allied convoy victories of May–June 1943, it is worth recalling, Doenitz immediately began figuring out how to counterattack, through homing torpedoes, better radar detection, and newer boats. And the Type XXI submarines of 1945 were scary indeed, their prospects ruined not by the Allied navies but by crushing bombing attacks on their production. The U-boat challenge to the Atlantic sea-lanes was the only German threat that was truly dangerous; and the argument that this campaign was going to be won by more shipbuilding launches alone or sending out more and more convoys *without* the crushing of the wolf packs in spring 1943 doesn't convince. If the Battle of the Atlantic was one of those key campaigns won by the Allies' "brute force,"[10] that did not mean simply that soaring US Liberty ship production explains the victory; it had involved the mobilization of massive Anglo-American industrial and technological power, which was then converted into an amazing array of new weapons systems and platforms, which then decimated the wolf packs. The German U-boat arm wilted and lost, but it is not surprising that Churchill stated that this was the only campaign that truly frightened him.

The German naval record, then, was persistent and impressive given the overall disparity of force. By contrast, the story of the Japanese Navy's almost completely lopsided performance in the Pacific War is so bizarre that, even seventy-five years later and after thousands of books and articles have been written about this campaign, it still remains a puzzle. During the first five months of the conflict the performances of the navy's various units were almost flawless: namely, the destruction of the US battle fleet in just one morning, the tearing apart of two great British capital ships—while maneuvering fast at sea—in just a few hours, the demolition of a large force of Allied destroyers and cruisers (Java Sea), the rampaging across the Indian Ocean by a long-range Japanese carrier group, and bold strikes and victories so threatening that while the Admiralty feared for the Suez Canal, the US government feared for California. In that short half a year, Japan acquired more space than any conqueror since probably Alexander. Its carrier task forces performed superbly. Its heavy cruisers and stupendous fleet destroyers seemed unbeatable, class for class. Its dive-bombers were terrifying, its Zero fighters unmatchable, and its airborne and shipborne torpedoes unequaled. If the historian was doing an audit of the IJN up until the end of April 1942, then its record would have seemed flawless, since virtually every one of its fighting units had appeared invincible.

Thereafter, it stumbled and stumbled. The mis-steps began at the Battle of the Coral Sea. Its carrier and flier losses at Midway were then so severe that the vaunted Naval Air Arm never properly recovered its capacities. It constantly underestimated the strength of the American forces on Guadalcanal, so that it never gained the initiative there. Its Aleutians invasion operation was inept and pointless. Its submarine fleets were misused. Its lack of radar was evident in nighttime gunnery battles again and again. Occasionally, but very occasionally, its surface ships showed just how terrifyingly deadly they could be, as when they crushed four Allied heavy cruisers in just one night (Savo Island), yet overall, and for more than three-quarters of the war, the service's performance was bad. The Imperial Japanese Army was still fighting well, and aggressively, across mainland China as late as 1944, and even in that spring its Fifteenth Army was pushing toward the Burma-Assam border, but the navy was flailing, about to be crushed again at the Philippine Sea and Leyte Gulf. What on earth did its navy staff think it was doing in those two latter operations, dispatching batches of its warships forward in so-called pincer movements and decoy operations when it should have been abundantly clear by then that extensive US submarine and air patrols, perhaps even American code breaking, would be warning the enemy of what was coming? One gets a sense that the Japanese admirals were just punching in the dark. Truly, after Admiral Isoroku Yamamoto's death, Japan seemed to possess no naval leader of insight, drive, and resourcefulness.

Was that it? Was it that every successful navy needs a Blake, an Anson, a Nelson, a Scheer, a Nimitz, a Halsey, a Cunningham—or a Tojo? That any navy's chances of victory are dim unless it possesses great fighting admirals at sea and great administrators ashore? There surely is a lot in that. After all, the stories of World War II and of this war across the Pacific are not just the stories of unfolding inexorable forces but also tales of personal misjudgments and multiple errors. What if Nagumo's carriers had regrouped for a *second* attack on Pearl Harbor, on December 8–9, 1941, and destroyed the fuel depot, the repair yards, and the submarine base? What if, indeed, they had come back a little later with a small amphibious army (part of the divisions that they were committing in the south) and occupied Hawaii? What if Japan's large submarine force had been trained for systematic attack upon the main Allied sea-lanes? What if the IJN had taken the protection of its own merchantmen as seriously as the Royal Navy did theirs? Why especially was it so slow to protect the precious oil tanker traffic from the East Indies that its battleships were virtually immobilized by the second half of the war? Why did the Combined Fleet "freeze" so badly after Japanese forces pulled out of Guadalcanal in January 1943 and not take advantage of those many months when Halsey had only one carrier left in the Pacific theater? Why was its navy training so relatively few fresh aircrews when the United States was training ten times as many?

Of course it can be said—in direct answer to that last question—that the overall American population was far larger than Japan's and that the extent of the air bases and pilot-training programs across the whole continent by, say, 1943 swamped anything Japan could offer. And that, further, it was not just in numbers of aircrews but in every other measure of military capacity that an aroused United States was pulling way ahead. However cleverly the IJN and the other armed forces fought, did they really have a chance against an enraged Great Power that was capable of doubling its aircraft production from 47,000 to 85,000 aircraft in a single year, from 1942 to 1943? Wasn't it Yamamoto himself who had said that Japan could run riot for the first six months of the war, and then, unless the United States was willing to negotiate a peace, the tide would turn? All that is true: the underlying odds—the "forces of production" (in Marx's term)—were always tilted heavily in America's favor. Yet it is hard not to conclude that the Japanese Navy and Air Force could have fought a far better defensive war in the Pacific than they did.

A deep and rather poignant irony looms, then, when one turns from Japan to attempt an audit of the Royal Navy's performance during World War II, for here by contrast was a fighting service, and a nation, that fought impressively throughout the entire struggle and yet still could not stave off relative decline, a country that could savor victory in Europe (V-E Day) and in the Pacific (V-J Day) and see its modern fleet swell in size but simply could not return to the position in the world that it had occupied back in September 1939.

No single term or nifty phrase can be used to sum up Britain's naval record for the 1939–45 struggle, simply because its own war at sea manifested itself in so many ways and occurred in so many places. Thus, any audit of the Royal Navy's victories and failures has to account for the fact that it was fighting against very different foes and different combinations of foes at very different times during World War II. To understand this properly, therefore, it may be best to think of Great Britain's performance as an extended drama in six acts.

The first act, the Anglo-French phase, was only against Germany and thus a one-power War" in which both the Kriegsmarine and Luftwaffe repeatedly showed their dangerous capacities with the swift sinking of HMS *Courageous* and then HMS *Royal Oak,* the stiff fights off Norway, and the Dunkirk debacle. On the plus side the *Graf Spee*'s threat was eliminated during this period, Germany's destroyer flotillas were greatly reduced, and much of the rest of the German surface fleet badly damaged. If that was all that was going to happen, the Royal Navy's dominance would scarcely be at risk.

The second act, June 1940 to December 1941, was the really tough time, simply because the Royal Navy lost its French ally and went from enjoying a two-to-one power superiority to struggling to keep seas safe against the Italian-German combination, one navy against two. Of the twin blows delivered against Britain's strategic situation in June 1940, it was surely the loss of the French ally that was the greater—had France remained intact, the Italians could certainly have been held in the Mediterranean, and the U-boats would have had much less access to the central and North Atlantic. This two-power war, as detailed in chapter 5, was the Royal Navy's own finest hour, and its losses correspondingly shot up. By the end of 1941—with Crete gone, the *Hood* gone, the *Ark Royal* gone, the *Barham* gone, and Cunningham's fleet immobilized—the service seemed on the ropes even before the news of the disasters in the Far East. Only the Atlantic theater offered relatively good news: the *Bismarck* was sunk, most other big German ships were damaged, the Atlantic routes were holding against the U-boats, and the US Navy was rendering more and more unneutral aid. All invasion fears were over, and the Fuehrer had made the military blunder of opening a vast second front in the East. Now the Wehrmacht itself had to fight more than one enemy.

The third act, roughly from January to November 1942, was one during which Britain experienced the strategic low point of the conflict before a slow recovery. It was the only one of the six phases in this struggle where the Royal Navy really had to fight a three-power war, and as the planners had feared back in 1937 or so, it couldn't do it. Even its large new American ally was being pummeled and driven out of the Far East, and the British defenses there couldn't hold. Hong Kong, Singapore, Borneo, and even Burma all fell. The enemy was at the borders of India and Australia, the garrisons of both were slim, and naval forces especially were slight. Then came the turnaround, marked by three separate events: Midway (June), Pedestal (August), and Torch (November 1942); by that latter month, things looked so much easier for the Allies. After Alamein there was no longer a Malta crisis. Germany's remaining surface navy resided only in Norway, leaving its U-boats alone to fight for the Atlantic. And enormous Lend-Lease supplies kept British wartime production growing.

Act four ran from Torch to the Italian surrender (November 1942–September 1943), with huge amphibious operations from Sicily to Salerno until the ferocious Battle of the Mediterranean was virtually over; most important Allied commanders then went home to prepare for D-Day. And in the Atlantic the key convoy battles (March–June 1943) really checked the U-boats. For the Royal Navy this was once again a two-power war against Italy and Germany, because the service still was not able to place a substantial fleet against Japan. And in the great amphibious operations (Torch, Sicily, and Salerno), there was now strong and important assistance from US naval forces.

Act five, from around October 1943 to November 1944, was a rather curious one for the Royal Navy, because it was almost just fighting a one-power war once again, against the Wehrmacht in all its various guises— that is, in a continuation of the Battle of the Atlantic, in the flurry of force off Anzio, and in the destruction of both the *Scharnhorst* and the *Tirpitz* in Norway, but chiefly in operations of the northwestern coast of Europe, from Normandy to the Scheldt. Britain's larger naval fleets were still not ready to engage in fighting against Japan. Its naval forces for D-Day were considerably larger than America's, but that was because the United States was assembling giant armadas in the central Pacific.

The sixth act in the Royal Navy's wartime drama was at last the long-awaited turn to the East, with growing attacks against the Japanese foe, from the Palembang air strikes to Okinawa patrols to the final coastal bombardments. It was fighting against a single Axis enemy, although of course that could hardly be described as a one-power war given that the main American role in crushing Japan was so evident. A large British Pacific Fleet was in action, but clearly as number two. There had been a final ripple of anxiety about Germany's advanced U-boats in home waters, but no more than that.

How, then, is one to achieve an overall audit of Britain's wartime naval performance? It is, in the first place, a remarkable fighting record, unequaled in length by any of the other five Powers. If the first phase and, frankly, the last phase were the easiest circumstances for the Royal Navy, it is clear that the second and third acts involved the most stressful times and showed the service at its pugnacious best and that it was not until the end of the fourth phase, in late 1943, that real relief came, with It-

aly knocked out of the war and the U-boats beaten at last. Britain battled against Italy continuously during acts two, three, and four, and then
it had Japan as an enemy all throughout acts three to six, although only
seriously in 1942 and again in the final phase (1945). But the fight against
the formidable German war machine lasted over *five*, if not quite six, of
these stages, even though the German Navy was the smallest of the three
opposing navies. (Not for nothing did most Britons regard World War II
as "the war against Germany.") It is also worth noting that it was only
during acts three and four (December 1941 to September 1943) that Britain
was fighting all three opponents. The plain fact was that, even at the rare
moments at which the Royal Navy found itself in easier circumstances
during this lengthy conflict—say, after it had weakened the Italian fleet at
Taranto—it was only a two-power navy and could never be more. While
its warships always fought doughtily, and sometimes magnificently, and
after all it was the main maritime opponent of two out of the three Axis
powers, the test of this total war had shown up the British limitations.[11]
And that should come as no surprise at all, for it had been a half century
since late-Victorian governments had been able to keep a real two-power
standard against the next two strongest navies in size.

The historian is left with mixed feelings, then, as he contemplates the
position of the Royal Navy in mid-1945, at the war's end. In six years of
fighting, it had lost a staggering number of ships (5 battleships and battle cruisers, 8 carriers, 28 cruisers, and 132 destroyers), yet in numerical
terms it still remained enormous. It had around a dozen battleships, although it was scrapping all of them except the four *King George Vs* (and
a brand-new HMS *Vanguard*). It was going to keep its *Invincible*-class
fleet carriers for a long while more, which would be joined now by the
*Colossus*-class light fleet carriers, but the escort carriers were going to
be disposed of in droves, with many returned to their US Lend-Lease
builder. The Admiralty's austerity-driven treatment of the Royal Navy's
historic cruiser fleets was predictably similar; with the inflow of the modern light cruiser flotillas, the older cruisers (as we have noted above) were
swiftly dispatched to the scrappers' yards, while the 6-inch-gunned vessels remained. Again, while the newer classes of destroyers and frigates
were preserved and deployed to peacetime stations from the West Indies
to Hong Kong, vast numbers of the Royal Navy's smaller and older vessels
were scrapped, sold off, or tied together in long lines of reserve fleets, and
only years later disposed of. Twice before, of course, after 1815 and again
after 1919–21, the Admiralty had deliberately cut down the enormous
numbers of its wartime forces, but this time it was different. It would
never grow large again.

It was, of course, a huge historical irony. Had the US Navy somehow *not* existed, this British Navy with its enhanced Fleet Air Arm would have been the most powerful naval force the world had ever seen. Yet that hypothetical condition did not exist in 1945, and America's giant power was evident to all. The Royal Navy was far, far larger than any other naval service in the world apart from that of the United States; the badly battered French Navy was way behind in third place, and perhaps Australia or Canada was in fourth.[12] But Britain's second place was a very distinct distance behind the world leader.

It did not shrink at breakneck speed, despite the scrapping of so many vessels and the repeated economies of the new Labour government (1945–51), although that is another story. Unease at the coming rivalry with Russia during the early Cold War, the demands of the Korean crisis, and Britain's continued presence in the Indian Ocean kept the fleet a substantial one for almost twenty years. Thus, in 1950 it still had twelve carriers and twenty-nine cruisers, while the pages of *Jane's Fighting Ships* for, say, 1952 still show a very considerable navy. It was not to be until after Suez (1956) and the defense-policy revolution of 1957 that the further drastic erosion occurred, and by 1970 the Royal Navy's surface fleet had shriveled to three carriers and three cruisers.[13] In the age of Soviet-American thermonuclear crises, there was not much place for secondary navies. With a newer and much smaller maritime force and a steady scrapping policy, then, there was soon after this scarcely a warship left in the Royal Navy that had fought, say, in the Battle of the Atlantic. The glories of World War II were a long way hence. History had moved on.

The audit of the US Navy's performance in World War II is also a story that unfolded in stages. Most of this less-than-four-year epic took place in one very large but unitary theater, the Central and Southwest Pacific; and the overwhelming proportion of every category of the navy's assets—carriers and carrier planes, battleships, so many of the cruisers and destroyers, all the subs, and virtually all of the US Marine Corps—were committed to the fight against Japan. It is to these Pacific War forces and their campaigning that the audit must chiefly be directed, and the US Navy under its authoritarian boss Fleet Admiral Ernest J. King would have wanted it no other way, for after all this was a war that operated under two grand unspoken compacts with which he was in full agreement: that the US Army and the Air Force (wanting to recruit and deploy huge forces for the defeat of Nazi Germany) would pay most attention to Europe, while the US Navy devoted most of its striving to the Pacific, and that the Japanese fleet would be destroyed by America, whereas the Italian and German navies would be defeated (chiefly) by the British. Measuring how well US sea power did in World War II is, then, chiefly an audit of its fight against Japan.

The first six months of America being at war (December 1941–May 1942) were simply awful: there was the devastation of the US main battle fleet and then the loss of the Philippines, a debacle from beginning to end, and for many General Douglas MacArthur's bluster made it even worse; while the blatant sinking of so many Allied merchantmen off America's eastern shores exposed the navy's failure to take anti-U-boat warfare seriously. Then came the amazing six-month recovery (Coral Sea, Midway, better control of the U-boats, clinging on to Guadalcanal, and Torch). The year 1943 was the year of the American Navy's most significant push into European waters, with its giant amphibious operations, to which Morison proudly dedicates his volume IX, "Sicily-Salerno-Anzio," and with the striking work by its escort carrier groups to protect the Atlantic–North Africa routes. There were some serious naval fights and step-by-step advances in Southwest Pacific Command's zone in that time as well, but it wasn't until near the year's end that the Gilberts campaign heralded the arrival of the new American fleets and air squadrons, growing in irresistible numbers. The year 1944 was a great one: in Europe the Normandy landings were remarkably well done, the U-boats were almost finished, and the Allied armies could advance toward Berlin; and in the Pacific there were gigantic victories for the US Navy, and only defeat and catastrophes for the Japanese—by the end of that year, the latter's main fleets were smashed and their trade routes cut, and yet they insisted on fighting on. Had the war ended with a call by Tokyo for peace in December 1944, the US armed forces in the Pacific, including its navy, would have felt completely triumphant. Instead, 1945 brought grim, harder work; the kamikazes, Iwo Jima, Okinawa, more kamikazes, the last bombardments, and the mixed blessing of the US Air Force's two giant bombs. Little wonder that the admirals wanted those 450 carrier planes to fly over MacArthur's grand, orchestrated surrender ceremony. To those contemporary auditors of victory, the US pressmen and television, and the Congress back home, the message should have been clear: "This was a war your navy had won."

The navy's losses during World War II were very considerable, yet regarded overall, they were not enormous. Only two battleships (*Arizona* and *Oklahoma*) were completely lost at Pearl Harbor, and the recovery of most of the rest of them to play roles in Pacific and Normandy bombardments was testimony to their toughness. The prewar carrier fleet took the heaviest losses of all (*Lexington, Yorktown, Hornet,* and *Wasp*), so with the 6 escort carrier losses and the USS *Princeton*, there were 11 carriers sunk, but only 7 heavy and 3 light cruisers, a full 96 destroyers and DDEs, and 53 submarines. By numerical contrast, the fleet that the navy ended up with by the war's end was five or six times as large as its original December 1, 1941, order of battle had been: what exactly did one do now, as the long-term occupation of Japan and Germany got underway and with no obvious naval rival in sight, with an armada of 22 battleships, 28 carriers and 71 escort carriers, literally hundreds of cruisers and destroyers and DDEs, and 95 submarines—in total 1,200 major combatant ships, 40,000 aircraft, and some 3.5 million active-duty personnel?[14]

Sir Basil Liddell Hart had once defined real victory as that in which a country emerged from a great conflict in a better position "after the war than before."[15] The United States after 1945 surely was that nation, since it was the only Great Power that had advanced unscathed (for the USSR, although emerging victorious, had also been badly battered); it was the only one of the six contenders that was never bombed on its home base and that never suffered civilian casualties. Economically, as its vast productive base had soared undisturbed by war, it may have briefly achieved a stunning 50 percent of total world GDP by 1945. It should have been most content in that position. So also should have been the US Navy, which enjoyed in the postwar years a staggering lead over all others in all categories of warships and in overall warship tonnage. In fact, as the compilation in chart 11 clearly demonstrates, it was not just that the postwar navy was bigger than the next largest navy, that of the British, but that it was *larger than all the rest of them combined*. Nothing like that had ever happened before in history.

It was a picture that, one imagines would have made Alfred Thayer Mahan, Henry Cabot Lodge, Teddy Roosevelt, and the naval expansionists of 1898 rejoice to witness. The post-1945 US Navy should have been very content indeed. And yet it wasn't. Here was irony, indeed.

As it turns out, virtually every history of the US Navy after World War II stresses not the service's triumph but the concatenation of problems, even existential problems, that it more or less immediately faced. In one well-known collection of essays on the US naval story, for example, the renowned scholar Dean C. Allard begins his chapter about this era with this sentence: "At the end of World War Two the United States Navy experienced one of the most difficult periods in its history."[16] There was, of course, a huge downsizing of ships and men to be done; given the pressing need to rebalance the national budget from wartime to peacetime and the fact that there was no observable enemy, that sort of need for reductions in combatant personnel and older warships was simply natural. But Allard and other scholars of this era were also alluding to some quite different, almost existential challenges. Those two atomic devices, carried secretly in a naval warship from San Diego to Tinian in late July 1945 but then unleashed from an air force bomber to crush the enemy's resolve, not only brought an end to the Pacific War but also brought the

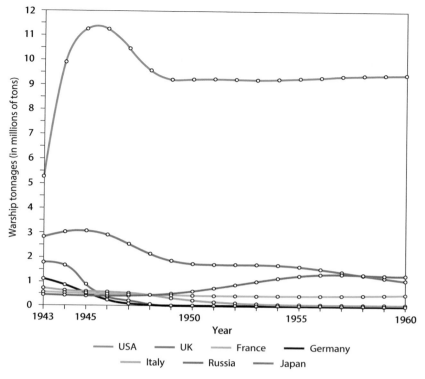

**CHART 11.** Overall warship tonnages of the Powers, 1943–60. Produced using the dataset in Crisher and Souva, *Power at Sea.*

United States to having to confront fundamental questions about its postwar grand strategy. What should its defense policy be, and how should its various armed services be treated in the new atomic age?

The navy, in the minds of some of the more worried of its admirals, faced four challenges, all in this same short time: the threat of excessive, unreasonable reductions to its main surface fleet (it was only twenty-three years after the Washington Treaty cutbacks); the completely novel factor of the A-bomb and its singular destructiveness; the steps being taken to establish an integrated Department of Defense, with a single secretary of defense and with the service Chiefs of Staff working out of a unified Pentagon building; and finally, a newly independent US Air Force, which was not only jostling for a large share of the defense budget but attempting to assert control over all "air assets."

The service's postwar struggles and its relative success in dealing with these dangers are not for this volume. There was a hard fight to beat off the air force's desire to control all air and space forces and another battle over the future of amphibious warfare and the Marines' special place

**PAINTING 53.** A nuclear-powered US aircraft carrier of the new age. For all its size, futuristic shape, nuclear-powered propulsion, and huge jets that thunder on and off its deck, this is the recognizable successor to the *Essex*-class carriers of the war. No other nation can afford such behemoths.

J. H. M.

in it. The navy's claims to procure its own weaponry and to be able to understand and conduct sea warfare best were fought out, against air force and army critiques, in acrimonious public congressional testimonies in the late 1940s. The battle over the authorization of the navy's first postwar carrier, the USS *United States,* was seen as existential—if it was scrapped, as a hostile secretary of defense wanted, what sort of future service was it to be? Even if its surface fleet had been significantly reduced (by June 1950 it was down to 237 major combatants), though, of what use were those vessels if the next great war was decided in a short, all-out nuclear exchange? One wonders how much worse it might have become for the navy but for a remarkable series of external events near the end of the decade: the "loss" of China to Mao's Communists in 1949 was a huge political shock; Stalin's pressures on eastern and southern European states, the Berlin blockade, and the decision to create NATO combined to show that the so-called Cold War really was underway; and then North Korea's attack on the South seemed to confirm that it was a global struggle, in many ways reminiscent of the Axis challenge to the West only ten years earlier. Finally, what on earth was the USSR up to, building a fleet of (so it was estimated) no less than 350 subs by 1950? This was not a time for defense cutbacks or for interservice squabbles over who could have new aircraft or A-weapons or, indeed, ships and amphibious forces. As the Korean War expanded and NATO commands (including in the Mediterranean) were built up, all US armed services grew again.[17]

Far from being existentially challenged by the atomic age, then, the US Navy became a nuclear navy, and in more ways than one: its new fleet of ever-larger fast carriers, with their squadrons of ever-more-powerful jet aircraft, themselves acquired nuclear-propulsion systems that in turn gave them extraordinary endurance at sea; and one class (SSBNs) of huge new submarines, also with nuclear propulsion, were equipped to carry the ultimate deterrence weapon, submarine-launched nuclear ballistic missiles. The navy thus came to have it all: a conventional surface fleet of cruisers, destroyers, and frigates, the largest in the world; a very large (US Marine Corps) amphibious force; a fast attack-submarine force (SSNs); a "strategic" submarine nuclear-missiles force (SSBNs); and a gigantic carrier fleet. Reconciled to sharing the Department of Defense's enormous budget with the other two services—each received roughly 32–34 percent of the whole each year—the navy's brief few years of crisis were over.

Thus after 1960 the US Navy could steam on, with the largest and most powerful carrier fleet in the world, funded by the world's largest defense budget by far. It had been less than twenty years since Pearl Harbor. Indeed, it was a mere twenty-two years since the pride of its Atlantic Fleet, the USS *Texas,* had paid the courtesy visit to Portsmouth in the high year of appeasement (see the start of chapter 2), when it was still an age of battleship navies. Now, however, the USS *Texas* was a rusting museum ship, disarmed and anchored near Houston, Texas; at least it had avoided the fate of the Royal Navy's battleships.

Fate, of course, always caught up with navies over time. Weapons, tactics, instruments, and the very structures of navies, Mahan had preached, are from age to age altered or even totally torn down, but the elements of sea power and the foundations of strategy would remain unchanged.[18] So was it now. A mere quarter century after it had been fought, World War II seemed, in so many ways, almost as far away as the Spanish-American War of 1898. The US Navy was a new force, of nuclear missile submarines, giant carriers, and sophisticated electronics. Its purpose still was to maintain command of the seas, though. It was now the age of Pax Americana.

# EPILOGUE

## The Sweep of History

In 1936, as we know, six navies coexisted within a traditional though precarious Eurocentric international order. Ten years later, US naval power predominated. The sheer size and speed of this change was remarkable. That long list with characteristics of the pre–World War II age that were deemed unlikely to end very soon—the Royal Navy being the leading naval power, aircraft still lacking much range and capacity, Japan being a rising threat, the United States being to the side of things (see chapter 2)—had gone. A hegemonic war had been fought, from which a giant number one maritime power had emerged. The chapters above tell the story of that transformation and seek to explain why. One final question remains: was such an outcome inevitable?

The simple answer here would be that those changes certainly weren't preordained, provided that Adolf Hitler had not dragged the European nations into war in 1939 and that the Japanese had not attacked the American battle fleet in Pearl Harbor two years later. But of course Hitler did start World War II in 1939, later invading the USSR and going to war against the United States in 1941; and of course the Japanese did attack Pearl Harbor. The result was total war between the revisionist and the status quo Great Powers, on land, in the air, and—the subject of this book—at sea. And the "great war at sea," as it deserves to be termed, was in consequence fought bitterly across three maritime fields of conflict: the Atlantic, the Mediterranean, and the Pacific, with all the resources each coalition could muster.

Because France fell so swiftly and the Russian Navy was to fight only in the Far North of Europe, the maritime struggle was essentially one between the Anglo-American navies on the one side and the Italian-German-Japanese navies on the other. Just by doing the warship count of each coalition on the eve of war, as detailed in chapter 2, the reader can observe how unfavorable the naval balance was to the Axis side. This was not as in Nelson's time, where the Franco-Spanish fleet frequently outnumbered his own. Yet that majority in warship numbers did not immediately and automatically translate into the Allies' victory at sea. The Royal Navy found it hard to prevail in the Atlantic and Mediterranean in the early years of the war, and when the US Navy joined the fight after December 1941, it was as a badly damaged force. Recovery wasn't easy. As late as, say, thirty months after the beginning of the conflict, in April 1942, an inquirer might ask in which theater of the naval war were the Allies doing well: off the eastern coasts of the United States, as the U-boats enjoyed their Second Happy Time? Hardly. In the Indian Ocean, where a Japanese carrier force inflicted damage left and right? Certainly not. In the Dutch East Indies, where the Japanese were as far south as New Guinea? Or in and around Malta, where the population was beginning to starve? These were grim times.

That may of course have been the lowest time of the war for the Allies, viewed overall. The Battle of the Coral Sea was only a month away, the U-boat attacks on the American seaboard would soon fall off, and the Pedestal convoy was just around the corner. Yet the point is that this massive oceanic struggle was not being easily won by the Allies, despite their apparent superiority in surface warships. Precisely because the fighting was so tough everywhere, the losses inflicted upon the British and American navies were severe on all fronts; and if the tide of the war was turning by the end of 1942, as the dour Alanbrooke thought it was, it was coming at great cost: the imposing prewar US Pacific battle fleet was long gone, most American carriers were gone, and a huge tally of Royal Navy capital ships, cruisers, and destroyers were no more. Nor had the critical battle against the U-boats in the North Atlantic been won.

So it is not surprising that our narrative of the naval battles and campaigning takes until 1943 to show the British and American fleets at last prevailing in all three oceans. The historical record shows a huge Anglo-American naval effort being projected into the Mediterranean by the time of the Sicily and Salerno landings after midsummer, while even larger US carrier and battleship fleets were being sent to encircle the Gilbert Islands; by late 1943 the numerous Atlantic and Bay of Biscay convoys were also being protected by all manner of guardians, escort carriers, close-in squadrons, hunter-killer groups, and flocks of very-long-range and medium-range aircraft. This is the stuff of the traditional fine narrative accounts of World War II at sea. The Axis navies did very well at first (Norway, Dunkirk, Crete, Pearl Harbor, and Singapore), because they were better prepared for the fight. Then the British and American forces recovered their balance, learned some lessons, replaced their losses, and started moving forward: after some hard fighting—in the Solomons, in the Malta convoys, in the mid-Atlantic gap, and into North Africa—the advantage shifted. It was a history of events once again, Lepanto, the Armada; *l'histoire d'événements.*

But there was more to the story than that. By the middle of 1943 a giant new productive force was affecting the war, sending toward the battlefields a flow of armaments and weapons far larger than the world had ever seen, all from one single nation that proved capable of doubling its aircraft output in one year and of dispatching a new aircraft carrier virtually every month to the Pacific fighting. This was not just a history of campaign events. This was the history of something far, far bigger. This was about a shift in the global power balances, perhaps in its way like certain other large shifts of the past, like the move from Venice to Antwerp around 1600 or the huge growth in steam manufacturing after 1815, but even faster and bigger. So that old-fashioned warlord Churchill had been right, instinctively. If the West's armed forces could just hang on and withstand the early Axis blows, however ferocious they were, then the entry of America ("that gigantic boiler") into the war would be decisive and its advance inexorable. Of course there was much more fighting to be done after early 1942, since the United States was only half-mobilized. But the outcome was no longer in doubt: Hitler, Mussolini, and the Japanese—their fate was sealed; they would be ground to a powder. All the rest, Churchill insisted, was merely the proper application of overwhelming force. The international order was moving.

It is curious, then, to think of Fernand Braudel, sitting in a German prisoner-of-war camp outside Luebeck after 1942, wrestling with his ideas about the structure of Philip II's Mediterranean world just as the underlying structures of his own Eurocentric order were being transformed, through major conflict and vast productive movement, to the other side of the Atlantic. The great French scholar struggled to describe historical continuity and change in a distant time, even as the external international system was advancing in yet newer directions. And was not all this, in another way writers have of expressing it, merely the historical "stream of time"? Whatever the surface whirls and eddies of the twentieth century, the broader currents were moving in a certain direction.

Still, it would be a very grave error to think that great contests are won solely by larger and larger forces moving inexorably toward victory, by global trends, or by sophisticated causation-chains. To be sure, if vast shifts occur in the economic substructure and productive forces (for example, if an entire American continent is mobilizing for war), and an overwhelming flood of ships, planes, and guns is being sent to the battlefields, then it is more than likely that the enemy's battalions will be crushed; indeed, if victory did not follow, the historian would be hard-pressed to explain that. But the deficit in all deterministic explanations—the substructure alters, therefore the superstructure is changed—is that they lack human agency. The victor's ships, planes, and guns need courageous men to steer them, insightful men to organize them, and clever men to give them superior battlefield performance. When the tides of war in the great Atlantic fight turned against the U-boats, it was because hundreds and hundreds of little ships, sloops, frigates, ore carriers, tankers, and cargo vessels, manned by tens of thousands of very brave crewmen (Americans, Britons, Norwegians, and Greeks), steamed back and forth from New York to Liverpool. If the vital strategic position of Malta held out, it was because the eventual winners, the Allies, were willing to take repeated heavy losses to both convoys and escorts and the home garrison. If victory in the great four-part Battle of Leyte Gulf went to the side with the most battalions (to employ Stalin's phrase), it was because American submarine commanders were extraordinarily skillful, American carrier air forces extremely professional, and American gunners remarkably well-trained; and also because the Japanese enemy committed fault after fault. Similarly, it was not just a "vast impersonal force" that came ashore on the five Normandy beaches at the very same hour on that morning of June 1944; it was the best-trained, best-organized, and best-directed army that the twentieth century had hitherto seen. A human factor was at hand.

It is not surprising that when those two mature official historians of the American and British naval effort, Samuel Morison and Stephen Roskill, came to write the final pages of their respective multivolume works, they preferred to focus on human agents rather than on broad underlying forces. Volume 14 of *U.S. Naval Operations* therefore concludes with a few brief vignettes and private letters about the surrender events in Tokyo Bay. Roskill, always wanting to pay tribute to the small ships and their crews, tells of the demobilization of various Royal Navy sailors and the retirement of their vessels. Without all these individuals, from admirals to ordinary seamen, the maritime war would not have been won. And yet without that sheer flow of new warships, aircraft, weapons systems, and technologies that boosted the fighting power of both navies after early 1943, those admirals and sailors would have found their victory two years later far harder to achieve.

History, so rich in its many genres and so complex in its many forms, has always been a multilayered thing, and the years between 1936 and 1946 prove to be no exception here. The deadly struggle between revisionist and status quo Great Powers exploded into an enormous fight across many stretches of sea, involving vast numbers of men, warships, and aircraft and leading to battle after battle. Small wonder that thousands of books and articles strive to cover all parts of this epic maritime struggle. But as this fighting unfolded, two broader developments began to make their mark. The first came out of the influence of science and technology, as one side, the Allies, brought out ever-newer weapons, firepower platforms, and detection devices that their enemies could not match. And this could happen only because of a second and even broader development, that of the vast latent resources of the continental United States being transformed into a giant factory for war. To those British sailors on North Atlantic convoys, nerves strained as another group of merchantmen was hit by a U-boat, and to those American picket destroyers in the danger zones off Okinawa, it would scarcely have been a consolation at that time to be informed that the broad sweep of history was going their way. And yet it was.

# APPENDICES

---

## 1943: The Pivotal Year of the War, by Three Measures

# APPENDIX A

## Sinking U-boats in the Dark, May 6, 1943

Was there a tipping point in the long Battle of the Atlantic, and if so, when did it occur? To make such a claim, one would have to be able to say that after that point, the U-boat threat to the Allied convoys would never be as dangerous or the monthly totals of merchantmen tonnage sunk ever as significant. One would have to show that from then on the damage inflicted on Karl Doenitz's predators increasingly outweighed what the wolf packs were able to render against the merchant traffic. It would be an occasion that the directors on both sides, in the Admiralty and at U-boat headquarters, would recognize or very soon come to recognize as a truly important one.

This is a very bold question to ask, therefore, especially when one recalls that the Battle of the Atlantic lasted a full six years, and that it was quite different in nature from the traditional tussles between surface navies. Yet it was that very cautious and sober scholar, the British official historian Captain Stephen Roskill, who remarked of the turning point discussed here that "this seven-day battle, fought against thirty U-boats . . . has no name by which it will be remembered; but it was, in its own way, as decisive as Quiberon Bay or the Nile." And it is not just Roskill, of course, but as noted earlier in the story of Convoy ONS-5 (chapter 7), a whole slew of naval historians who have called attention to Black May as being a terrible month for Doenitz's U-boat flotillas, and to this particular convoy battle as being the one in which the biggest reversal of fortunes between the two sides occurred. So this appendix makes no claim to a startling revelation.

What it would like to do is to recover for the book's readers those remarkable—some might say eye-popping—few hours in the early morning of May 6, 1943, off the coast of Labrador, when the destroyers and corvettes escorting the slow Return Convoy ONS-5 began to detect a slew of U-boats approaching through the dark. The actual timing and results of the various encounters between escorts and submarines are detailed in a brief and factual way in the fine Wikipedia summary of this battle:

> As May 5 faded into darkness, HMS [*Frigate*] Tay counted some seven U-boats surfaced in the convoy's path; but ONS 5 was entering the fog formed where the warm Gulf Stream meets the cold Labrador Current. . . . Visibility dropped to 1 mile [1.6 km] by 2202 and to 100 yards [91 m] by 0100. British centimetric radar enabled the escorts to see while the U-boats could not. . . . Many of the U-boats never returned to base to file their reports; so historians still struggle to correlate individual reports of the dozens of ships intervening briefly in no fewer than 24 attempted attacks on the night of 5/6 May.
>
> At 2309 HMS [Destroyer] Vidette made a radar contact at 5,100 yards [4.7 km] . . . , dropped a pattern of ten depth charges on a submarine seen submerging 700 yards [640 m] ahead. Historians suggest that the [first] attack destroyed U-531.
>
> At 0030 HMS [Corvette] Loosestrife made a radar contact at 5,200 yards [4.8 km]. . . . Loosestrife dropped a pattern of ten depth charges as it overran the diving U-boat. A reported slick of oil and debris is believed to have been produced by the destruction of U-192.
>
> At 0406 Vidette made an ASDIC contact at 800 yards [730 m] and made a hedgehog attack causing two explosions. Historians suggest that this attack destroyed U-630.
>
> At 0552 HMS [Sloop] Pelican . . . detected a radar contact at 5,300 yards [4.8 km] . . . , dropped a pattern of ten depth charges . . . [and then] dropped a second pattern of nine depth charges. . . . Historians suggest these attacks destroyed U-438.
>
> . . . Realizing his mistake, Doenitz called off the assault on May 6 and ordered [Wolfpack] Finke to retire.[1]

The Royal Navy destroyer HMS *Vidette* that accounted for two enemy submarines (*U-531* and *U-630*) was not one of the powerful *Tribal*-class fleet destroyers that accompanied the Home Fleet's battleships or even a smaller yet still dashing *K*-class like Lord Louis Mountbatten's HMS *Kelly*. It was instead one of the much older *V*- and *W*-classes that were built near the close of World War I. But since it was fast enough and solidly built, it was repeatedly modified for antisubmarine warfare during the interwar years, being one of the first escorts to receive ASDIC. In 1941, while being refitted at Gibraltar, it was given the standard 286M radar set, and in late 1942–early 1943 it underwent a lengthy conversion to become a long-range escort, probably with further radar included, although the full record is unclear. What is clear is that its radar operators had become quite accomplished by the time it joined Convoy ONS-5—a month earlier, in fact, sailing with Convoy HX-231, its radar had spotted a U-boat 6,000 yards away, and it drove the U-boat under with depth charges. This next time HMS *Vidette*'s fighting professionalism paid off. Readers will notice that the first submarine it sank (*U-531*) on that early morning of May 6 was detected on the surface by radar while a considerable way away, and in the Labrador coastal fogs (!), but the second kill (of *U-630*) was made after the destroyer's more traditional ASDIC (underwater) detection device made contact at a mere 800 yards. While the second submarine may have thought it would achieve surprise by approaching the convoy from below the surface, all the others followed the then-standard practice of attacking on the surface, trusting that the darkness and mists would make their approach undetectable. After all, that was the tactic that worked so well for U-boat attacks on all Allied convoys prior to the months of April–May 1943. After this time, however, as seems clear from the details in the quotation above, centimetric shipborne radar made U-boat attacks on escorted convoys extremely risky to the submarines and thus highly unlikely to succeed.

The battle had been turned, and as this record shows, it had been done on this particular night when one side could at last see the other. This predates the coming of ultra-long-range aircraft patrols, especially those by B-24 Liberators, arriving to support the late May Atlantic convoys onward; this huge but very different Allied counterstroke compounded Doenitz's problems, for these aircraft could spot and attack the U-boats by day. It is difficult to exaggerate what this all meant for the safety of future convoys. It was now terribly dangerous for German submarines to be on the surface in daytime, especially as more and more Allied patrol aircraft were being equipped with radar; and it was frightfully dangerous to attempt to attack the convoys in the dark at night if the Royal Navy's destroyers, frigates, corvettes, and even sloops were equipped with centimetric radar. Within a matter of months, the hunters had become the hunted. It was remarkable.

HMS *Vidette* was a lucky, or more likely, unusually accomplished, antisubmarine killer. Slightly later, while operating in a convoy on October 23, 1943, in conjunction with the destroyer HMS *Duncan*, it sank *U-274*. Six days afterward, again with *Duncan* and the corvette HMS *Sunflower*, it sank *U-282*. In 1943 alone, HMS *Vidette* operated as part of no less than twenty Allied convoys. In the year following, on August 20, 1944, while patrolling off the Normandy beaches, HMSs *Vidette*, *Forester*, and *Wensleydale* combined to sink the (hitherto extremely experienced and successful) submarine *U-413*. The destroyer continued to patrol Channel and home waters until the end of the European war, when it was paid off. Altogether HMS *Vidette* had five campaign honors during the war (including Malta convoys) and was credited with the aforementioned five U-boat kills. It was sent to the breaker's yard in April 1947, where its radar equipment was presumably stripped and destroyed. One closes the file of its wartime record—the reader may try https://en.wikipedia.org/wiki/HMS_Vidette_(D48)—with some humility.

# APPENDIX B

## A Hypothetical Causation-Chain, from a Bauxite Mountain in Suriname to Air-Sea Victory in the Western Pacific, 1943–44

A causation-chain, in which one action or step leads to the next, is a commonplace event in history or, for that matter, economics or chemistry. Indeed, especially memorable ones have lingered in our minds since childhood. "For want of a nail, the shoe was lost," the rhyme starts. And then, "for want of a shoe, the horse was lost," and with the horse gone, the knight was lost. When that all-important fighter fell, "the battle was lost," and with the battle lost, the entire kingdom was lost. But causation-chains also run in a positive direction, as any supply manager of a critically important product would testify. Complex industrial products, like automobiles or ships or cars, have thousands of parts that need to be fitted together in order to have a functioning whole; the front pages of the annual volumes of *Jane's Fighting Ships,* much relied upon for this book, are filled with advertisements from the manufacturers of everything from ships' brass railings to giant turbines, and all of those items were in turn dependent on the supply of subparts, basic pieces, and raw materials. And yet even those raw materials had to come from somewhere.

There is another form of causation-chain, familiar to readers of military history, which is best seen when examining the impacts of a new weapons system (although perhaps also newer command structures or sources of intelligence) on the outcome of a particular campaign. Thus, for example, what was the impact of the railroad and rifle upon the Elder Moltke's campaigning in the wars of 1866 and 1870, or the role of the improved version of the tank in the Western Allies' breakthrough of summer 1918? Again, how did the creation of carrier task forces give the Imperial Japanese Navy its great advantage in the early battles of the Pacific War? New and improved weapons, it is argued, change the course of a military struggle. The histories of battles and war are therefore replete

443

with sentences beginning with phrases like "With the coming of . . . ," "Following the advent of . . . ," "After the arrival of . . . ," "Reinforced by the new . . . ," and "With the replacement of (such-and-such) by . . ." In so very few of these battle narratives, however, is much attention given to where the newer item or artifact came from, so long as it was effective. Thus, while the newer lighter-weight carronades received by Wellington's armies and with which Nelson's warships were also equipped might be decisive in such-and-such a battle against the French, did the story of how the Carron Iron Works of Glasgow developed them matter very much? Did it matter to Georgy Zhukov where his vastly improved T-34 tanks of 1943–44 came from? Maybe not. But this author thinks asking such questions is always worthwhile.

In an earlier book, *Engineers of Victory*, I attempted to look at certain causation-chains in key World War II campaigning, like, for example, the various stages in the evolution of the Allied amphibious forces after 1943 (see chapter 4 of that book, "How to Seize an Enemy-Held Shore"). The chance to return to this inquiry in the present book has allowed further examples to be studied, and for the reader's benefit, one significant if scarcely known case is offered here in this appendix. My choice was affected by noticing how often books about the American war effort refer to the great significance of aluminum (in Britain, "aluminium") in the construction of much-lighter-weight aircraft frames and aeroengine parts, although usually little else is made of that fact. In the broadest sense, of course, all the combatant nations recognized the significance of this relatively new metal. (But did Stalin really declare to FDR, "Give me 30,000 tons of aluminum, and I will win the war"?) Granted the critical strategic importance of this item, then, what the chart below does is simply trace the causation-chain forward, from the extraction of the base metal from the Moengo bauxite hills in Dutch Suriname to the final part of this story, the systematic destruction of the Japanese fighter squadrons by the aluminum-clad F6F Hellcats in the Great Marianas Turkey Shoot. This is of course a reverse want-of-a-nail tale, a favorable rather than a disastrous causation-chain in wartime. For simplicity's sake, the author has reduced the story to a mere ten-piece chain, with each stage being a critical part of the process and the narrative.

The story itself is of course embedded in various sections of chapter 8 in this book, which cover the vastly expanded Alcoa factory's refinement of the bauxite into aluminum and then the supply of aluminum blocks and parts to the vital production of the powerful R-2800 Double Wasp aeroengine at Pratt and Whitney's Hartford plant. Chapter 9 then gives the military account of the so-called Turkey Shoot itself. What the cartoon below does, though, is let the reader see the whole story in a very

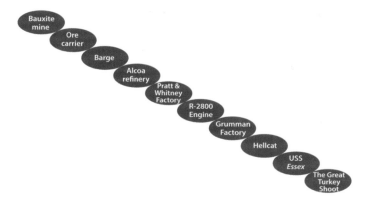

**CHART 12.** A hypothetical causation-chain, from a bauxite mountain in Suriname to air-sea victory in the Western Pacific, 1943–44.

simplified ten-part sequence. As a sketch, it links all parts of the chain together in very crude fashion, although of course each of the steps can be well documented. The various Dutch-owned bauxite ore fields [1], like those in adjacent British Guyana, lent themselves very easily to massively enhanced mining after December 1941 (even before that stage US military forces had moved in to provide a garrison here, rather as in Iceland). The specialized ore-carrier cargo ships, soon joined by newer and larger American models [2], were to take millions of tons of bauxite from South America to the Mississippi Delta terminals, with escorts provided by the Royal Navy until the US Navy took over. Huge river barges [3] brought the ore to the giant Alcoa aluminum refineries in Tennessee [4]. Slabs and pellets of aluminum were then dispatched to a whole array of parts manufacturers of airframe cladding, propellers, engine mountings, cowls, and panels, many of which sited themselves around East Hartford, Connecticut, so as to be closer to the key Pratt and Whitney aeroengine factories [5]. It was there that the fabulously powerful RM 2200 and later 2800 Double Wasp [6] engines had been designed and were now produced en masse before being shipped southward across Long Island Sound to the gigantic Grumman fighter factory [7] at Bethpage, Long Island, which had been a mere village before the war. The end result of this story of wartime production was that unrivaled fighter and fighter-bomber of the Pacific War, the Grumman F6F Hellcat [8], with its aluminum-clad airframe, lighter than steel and capable of taking enormous punishment from enemy machine-gun bullets. Assembled at Bethpage in the thousands, the Hellcats were flown across the country to naval bases at San Diego and Long Beach, where they were embarked in their squadrons on the newly built *Essex*-class fleet aircraft carriers [9], which were also be-

ing sent in large numbers via Pearl Harbor to participate in the great aerial battles against Japan. It is worth noting that the seven fleet carriers
alone in Raymond Spruance's Fifth Fleet at the Battle of the Philippine
Sea carried over 250 Hellcats, and the latter's extraordinarily one-sided
annihilation of Japanese planes in the air was quite rightly nicknamed the
Great Marianas Turkey Shoot [10]. There were few battles in all of aviation history that were more uneven. It all began, this cartoon suggests, on
a forest-clad hillside.

# APPENDIX C

## America as Number One: Overall Warship Tonnages of the Powers, 1930–60

The size of the competing navies during this period, as measured by their total warship tonnages, is shown in three tables embedded in the text above to capture the years 1930–39 (chart 1), 1939–45 (chart 5), and 1943–60 (chart 11). Each one told a particular tale: the multipolar naval world of the 1930s, with three very large fleets and three smaller ones; then the crushing impacts of the 1939–45 fight at sea, with four navies going under and the American Navy simply exploding in size after 1943; and finally, the staggering lead in warship tonnage of the US Navy—virtually a unipolar maritime world—in the first fifteen years of the Cold War.

Still, it is instructive to conflate the three shorter-term tables in a single one, covering before, during, and after the great naval contest, to permit the reader to see again the remarkable transformation. At no period in the history of the world have the naval balances changed so swiftly, and to such an extent.

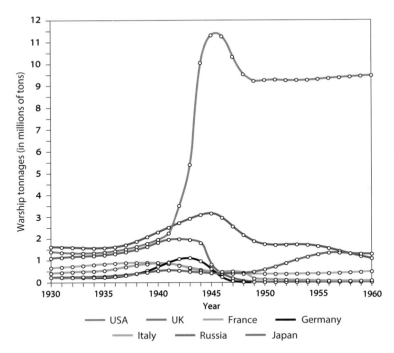

**CHART 13.** Overall warship tonnages of the Powers, 1930–60. Produced using the dataset in Crisher and Souva, *Power at Sea*. Put together, these three graphs, of the 1930s and the wartime and postwar periods, capture this book's core theme.

# Acknowledgments

A number of special people have assisted me with this book as it has evolved over the years. To begin with, I am greatly indebted to the research and other practical assistance afforded to me by some wonderful Yale assistants, Alex Mutuc, Noah Daponte-Smith, Nat McLaughlin, Elizabeth Hines, Brigitte Fink, Emma Mueller, and Owen Ogden; and by Arun Dawson of King's College London. I was especially helped by Emma, Brigitte, and Arun during the final push to completion. Arun produced and arranged many of the statistical tables in this book, and repeatedly checked things and researched my queries. Emma assisted on the citations, the layout, the arrangement, and the listing of the all-important Ian Marshall paintings and also did liaison work on the maps. Brigitte returned to take over all of that during the final few months of completion. My granddaughter Cathy Kennedy gave this manuscript, endnotes, and bibliography one final critical read.

All of the maps and graphs here were either reworked or created originally by map designer Bill Nelson, who was patience itself when we asked for so many adjustments.

I am so indebted to Jean Marshall, Ian's widow, and to his daughter Jessie Zarazaga for continued support, advice, and assistance while the original paintings for this volume were assembled and prepared.

During many an earlier summer, before the Covid-19 epidemic disrupted my research plans, I benefited greatly from my time in the naval history reading rooms of the Churchill College Archive in Cambridge, and I am grateful to the archivist Dr. Alan Packwood and his staff for their repeated assistance. I am also grateful to the Master and Fellows of St. John's College, Cambridge, for permitting this quondam Lady Margaret Fellow to return again and again to stay in college facilities. Financial support for my UK research trips was provided by the Maritime and Naval Studies Project at International Security Studies (ISS) at Yale, and I am also grateful to the provost and history department for permitting two periods of sabbatical leave. The permanent staff at ISS Yale, Elizabeth Vastakis, Kathleen Galo, and Kaitlyn Wetzler, were a constant support, and I was cheered on by its successive associate directors, Drs. Ryan Irwin, Amanda Behm, and Fritz Bartel. Finally, I doubt whether I could have accomplished this project without the continual help, in so many ways, of the ISS senior administrative assistant Igor Biryukov. To him, I am so very grateful.

My literary agent in London, Andrew Gordon of David Higham Associates, supported me throughout the writing of this book, as he has done for many previous works of mine, and he was of great encouragement whenever the project slowed down; my fondest memory now is of a congenial and supportive lunch with Andrew in High Holborn to discuss the book's final stages, just before (!) Covid closed down all the eateries in that great city. Also across the Atlantic, and for equally many years, my great pal and former colleague at the University of East Anglia, Eric Homberger, has encouraged, read, criticized, and suggested improvements; readers should know that chapter 2 of this book (on the warships and navies of the Powers) was due to Eric's insistence. No person other than myself, I hasten to add, is responsible for the final product, warts and all. If I have failed to acknowledge another scholar's work, I apologize; it has been a joy to give credit (in the endnotes) to so much earlier writing and research. I am sorry that so many fine though anonymous Wikipedia articles consequently lack their authors' names.

A book project like *Victory at Sea,* with its combination of detailed scholarly text and note apparatus on the one hand, and the production and printing challenges of showing off Ian Marshall's beautiful, multi-layered marine paintings on the other, could have been done by only a few publishers in the world today, and even fewer could do this as well as Yale University Press. I am so grateful to the staff of the press who assisted; the director of the press, John Donatich, for his encouragement; the insightful and helpful anonymous reader of this manuscript; and Gretchen Otto, of Motto Publishing. This work benefited enormously from the careful line editing of Alison Rainey throughout the text and illustrations and the indexing expertise of Joan Shapiro. I am especially indebted to Adina Berk, my own history editor at Yale University Press, for her many shrewd observations and, above all, encouragement and patience as this book steadily grew in ambition and size.

The continued patience of my wonderful Kennedy and Farrar family is also to be thanked, a thousandfold, for their cheerful encouragement and love. And a specially inscribed copy of this published book is due to my youngest grandchild, Charlie Kennedy, who on every visit to the North from his home in North Carolina would cheerily ask whether it was yet done. Now it is.

And my greatest debt of all is to my wife, Cynthia Farrar, for keeping me going, in both fair weather and foul storms, always rendering support and good, calming advice, and always being there. It is to Cynthia that, once again, this author dedicates his book.

We have ventured to make this a co-dedication from Ian Marshall (posthumously) to his wife, Jean, and from myself to Cynthia. Thus, from the author and from the painter, to two special women.

*New Haven and Branford, 2021*

# Notes

## Preface

1. I. Marshall, *Armored Ships: The Ships, Their Settings, and the Ascendancy That They Sustained for 80 Years* (Charlottesville, VA: Howell Press, 1990); I. Marshall, *Flying Boats: The J-class Yachts of Aviation* (Cheltenham, UK: History Press Limited, 2002); I. Marshall, *Cruisers and La Guerre de Course* (Mystic, CT: Mystic Seaport Museum, 2008); and J. Maxtone-Graham, *Passage East,* illus. I. Marshall (Cheltenham, UK: History Press, 1998).

2. C. Tilly, ed., *The Formation of the National States in Western Europe* (Princeton, NJ: Princeton University Press, 1975), 42.

3. F. Braudel, *The Mediterranean and the Mediterranean World in the Age of Philip II,* 2 vols. (New York: Harper and Row, 1972).

4. A classic article on this is G. Modelski, "The Long Cycle of Global Politics and the Nation-State," *Comparative Studies in Politics and Society* 20 (1978); and on the naval variant, G. Modelski and W. R. Thompson, *Sea Power in Global Politics 1494–1993* (Basingstoke, UK: Macmillan, 1988), passim.

5. P. Kennedy, *The Rise of the Anglo-German Antagonism 1860–1914* (London: Allen and Unwin, 1980), vi.

6. P. Kennedy, *The Rise and Fall of the Great Powers: Economic Change and Military Conflict from 1500 to 2000* (New York: Random House, 1987); *Preparing for the Twenty-First Century* (New York: Random House, 1993); *The Parliament of Man: The Past, Present, and Future of the United Nations* (New York: Penguin Random House, 2006).

7. P. Kennedy, *Engineers of Victory: The Problem Solvers Who Turned the Tide in the Second World War* (New York: Random House, 2013), passim.

## Chapter 1

1. See not only Braudel, *The Mediterranean World,* but also his later *Capitalism and Material Life, 1400–1800* (New York: Harper Colophon, 1975).

2. As explained in P. Padfield, *Tide of Empires: Decisive Naval Campaigns in the Rise*

*of the West 1481–1654: Volume I* (London: Routledge & Kegan Paul, 1979); *Tide of Empires: Decisive Naval Campaigns in the Rise of the West 1654–1763: Volume II* (London: Routledge & Kegan Paul, 1981); *Maritime Power and the Struggle for Freedom: Naval Campaigns that Shaped the Modern World, 1788–1851* (New York: Abrams Press, 2005) *Maritime Dominion and the Triumph of the Free World: Naval Campaigns That Shaped the Modern World, 1851–2001* (London: John Murray, 2009).

3. The argument in P. M. Kennedy, *The Rise and Fall of British Naval Mastery* (London: Ashfield Press, 1976).

4. W. Woodruff, *Impact of Western Man: A Study of Europe's Role in the World Economy, 1750–1960* (New York: St. Martin's Press, 1967); also important here is W. H. McNeill, *The Pursuit of Power: Technology, Armed Force, and Society since A.D. 1000* (Chicago: University of Chicago Press, 1982).

5. For that source, see not only K. Pomeranz, *The Great Divergence: China, Europe, and the Making of the Modern World Economy* (Princeton, NJ: Princeton University Press, 2000); but also the very full article "Great Divergence," Wikipedia, updated July 6, 2020, https://en.wikipedia.org/wiki/Great_Divergence. For a more economics-motivated approach, see I. M. Wallerstein, *The Modern World-System* (New York: Academic Press, 1974–1989).

6. See again McNeill, *Pursuit of Power;* and B. Simms, *Europe: The Struggle for Supremacy, from 1453 to the Present* (New York: Basic Books, 2013); and G. Parker, *The Military Revolution: Military Innovation and the Rise of the West, 1500–1800* (New York: Cambridge University Press, 1996).

7. McNeill, *Pursuit of Power;* and E. Hobsbawm, *The Age of Empire, 1875–1914* (New York: Pantheon, 1987), passim.

8. This fact about Europe's share of world population at its highest can be tracked at P. Kennedy, *Preparing for the Twenty-First Century;* or McNeill, *Population and Politics since 1750* (Charlottesville: University Press of Virginia, 1990).

9. Amply detailed in A. G. Hopkins, *American Empire: A Global History* (Princeton, NJ: Princeton University Press, 2018), passim.

10. An extremely interesting article at C. Baghino, *Port of Genoa: History and Informations,* trans. D. Canepa, www.guidadigenova.it/en/genoa-history/history-port-genoa/, accessed June 24, 2020, gives many useful details on the great rebuilding and expansion of the harbor facilities during the Fascist regime, and of the boom in trade, construction, and emigrants.

11. R. Ropponen, *Die Russische Gefahr* (Helsinki: Suomen Historiallinen Seura, 1976).

12. M. Beloff, *Imperial Sunset* (London: Methuen, 1969); P. Kennedy, *The Realities Behind Diplomacy: Background Influences on British External Policy, 1865–1980* (London: Allen and Unwin, 1981).

13. See the conclusion in A. J. P. Taylor, *The Struggle for Mastery in Europe, 1848–1918* (Oxford: Oxford University Press, 1971).

14. "Japanese Aircraft Carrier *Kaga,*" Wikipedia, last modified July 1, 2020, https://en.wikipedia.org/wiki/Japanese_aircraft_carrier_Kaga.

15. As the reader will discover, there are many delicious ironies here. *Kaga* was one those six carriers of the Pearl Harbor Task Force; its bomber squadrons actually carried out two waves of attacks, and its aircrews claimed they struck no less than six US battleships, USSs *Nevada, California, Oklahoma, West Virginia, Arizona,* and *Maryland. Kaga* also fought during the Japanese southward operations in early 1942. It met its match, though, at Midway, where it and three other of Japan's fleet carriers were sunk by their

American opposite numbers, without ever seeing their enemy—the new age of sea power had now burst through.

Another irony relates to the warships portrayed in this chapter; without being deliberately chosen for this reason, in fact all of them were sunk within a very short period of time as the naval war expanded in 1941–42. The *Zara* and *Fiume* were crushed by British nighttime gunnery fire at the Battle of Cape Matapan in March 1941; the *Hood* was sunk by plunging shells from the *Bismarck* in May 1941; the *Barham* was destroyed by four torpedoes from *U-331* in the eastern Mediterranean in November 1941; and *Kaga* was sunk at Midway in early June 1942.

16. C. Barnett, *The Collapse of British Power* (London: Eyre Methuen, 1972).

17. Z. Steiner, *The Lights That Failed: European International History 1919–1933* (Oxford: Oxford University Press, 2005), as well as *The Triumph of the Dark: European International History 1933–1939* (Oxford: Oxford University Press, 2011).

## Chapter 2

1. A. T. Mahan, *The Influence of Sea Power upon History 1660–1783* (Boston: Little, Brown, 1890; repr., London, 1965), x, 26–29.

2. P. Kennedy and E. Wilson, eds., *Navies in Multipolar Worlds: From the Age of Sail to the Present* (London: Routledge, 2020), passim.

3. Ibid.

4. The literature on the diplomacy around the Washington Treaty is enormous, but the naval data is easiest seen in "Washington Naval Treaty," Wikipedia, last modified April 1, 2020, https://en.wikipedia.org/wiki/Washington_Naval_Treaty, with bibliography, and the table reproduced here as chart 2.

5. Of the twenty-eight (!) Royal Navy cruisers sunk during World War II, only one (HMS *Exeter*, at the Battle of the Java Sea) would be lost to enemy surface fire. Similarly, almost all the fabled Japanese heavy cruisers were to be sunk by aircraft or submarines, not by enemy cruisers.

6. The situation is the same today: the hugely expensive US carriers never go to sea without being surrounded by a panoply of destroyers, *Aegis*-type cruisers, patrol planes, and often an attack submarine.

7. See, among many others, O. Parkes, *British Battleships, "Warrior" 1860 to "Vanguard" 1950: A History of Design Construction and Armament* (Hamden, CT: Archon Books, 1972); R. Sumall, "The Battleship and Battlecruiser," in R. Gardiner, *The Eclipse of the Big Gun: The Warship 1906–45* (London: Conway Maritime, 1973); N. Friedman, *Naval Weapons of World War One: Guns, Torpedoes, Mines and ASW Weapons of All Nations: An Illustrated Directory* (Barnsley, UK: Seaforth, 2011).

8. Full details of all (reported) battleship modernizations are in *Jane's Fighting Ships* (London: Sampson Low, Marston, 1939–), various pages. Each one of these warships usually has a detailed Wikipedia entry, "HMS *Rodney* (29)," Wikipedia, last modified December 29, 2019, https://en.wikipedia.org/wiki/HMS_Rodney_(29). (Note that since this chapter, more than any other, discusses warship types and individual warships, repeated reference is made to two sources.)

9. See again *Jane's Fighting Ships* in the various country sections; and a very superior comparative essay on battle cruisers: C. Hawks, "Battlecruisers, Large Cruisers, and Pocket Battleships of World War II," 2016, http://www.chuckhawks.com/battlecruisers.htm.

10. See again Parkes, *British Battleships*; and T. Gibbons, *The Complete Encyclopedia*

*of Battleships: A Technical Directory of Capital Ships from 1860 to the Present Day* (London: Crescent Books, 1983), passim.

11. L. Marriott, *Treaty Cruisers: The First International Warship Building Competition* (Barnsley, UK: Pen and Sword Press, 2005); and further details in *Jane's Fighting Ships 1939*.

12. *Jane's Fighting Ships 1939*, and I. Marshall's captions to the paintings in this book.

13. Such as Admiral Philip Vian's flotilla of *Tribal*-class boats that attacked the Bismarck during its final night, and the S-class destroyers that damaged and weakened the *Scharnhorst* in the turbulent waters off the North Cape.

14. C. Bekker, *The German Navy 1939–1945* (New York: Dial Press, 1974), trans. *Grosse Bildbuch der Deutschen Kriegsmarine, 1939–1945*, 162–67; on the absurdly top-heavy destroyer design, see the punchy article, C. Hawks, "The Best Destroyers of World War II," 2016, http://www.chuckhawks.com/great_destroyers_ww2.htm.

15. On which, see J. Lambert and A. Raven, *Warship Perspectives: Flower Class Corvettes in World War Two* (Lynbrook, NY: WR Press, 1999).

16. Submarine totals from table, *Jane's Fighting Ships 1939*, viii; as well as my own tally of the many Italian submarine classes; and the useful N. Friedman, *British Submarines in Two World Wars* (Annapolis, MD: US Naval Institute Press, 2019).

17. Kennedy, chaps. 7–9 in *British Naval Mastery*.

18. Such was the *Langley*'s demotion that by 1939 it had disappeared from the roster of US carriers in *Jane's Fighting Ships* and was listed with the miscellaneous vessels. For its full story, see "USS *Langley* (CV-1)," Wikipedia, last modified April 4, 2020, https://en.wikipedia.org/wiki/USS_Langley_(CV-1).

19. On the looming battle between battleship and carrier admirals, see C. G. Reynolds, chap. 1 in *The Fast Carriers: The Forging of an Air Navy* (New York: McGraw-Hill, 1968); for ship details, see N. Polmar, *Aircraft Carriers: A Graphic History of Carrier Aviation and Its Influence on World Events*, rev. ed., vol. 1, *1909–1945* (Washington, DC: Potomac Books, 2006).

20. Both C. G. Reynolds, *Fast Carriers*; and Polmar, *Aircraft Carriers*, have comparative comments on the US, UK, and Japanese carriers and aircraft; and see note 36 in this chapter.

21. See again Kennedy and Wilson, *Navies in Multipolar Worlds*. The French Navy's strategic dilemmas in the late 1930s are analyzed in R. Salerno, *Vital Crossroads: Mediterranean Origins of the Second World War, 1935–1940* (Ithaca, NY: Cornell University Press, 2002). For France's economic weaknesses in detail, see R. Frank, *Le Prix du Réarmement Français, 1935–1939* (Paris: Publications de la Sorbonne, 1982), passim.

22. Two useful summaries on the Italian Navy before and during World War II are F. de Ninno, "A Rising Power in the Age of Multipolarity: Italian Naval Policy and Strategy in the Age of Fascism," in Kennedy and Wilson, *Navies in Multipolar Worlds*, 23–32; and C. L. Symonds, chap. 5, "The Regia Marina," in *World War II at Sea: A Global History* (Oxford: Oxford University Press, 2018). Most writings, whether by Italian- or English-language authors, are highly critical, an exception being J. Sadkovich, *The Italian Navy in World War II* (Westport, CT: Greenwood Press, 1994), passim. For a more narrative account, see J. Greene and A. Massigniani, *The Naval War in the Mediterranean, 1940–1943* (London: Chatham, 2002).

23. The study by E. Groener, *German Warships, 1815–1945*, vol. 2, *U-boats and Mine Warfare Vessels* (Annapolis, MD: US Naval Institute Press, 1990), includes a calculation suggesting that by spending on more U-boats rather than on capital ships, that number could have been achieved. For a critical, brisk survey, see W. Rahn, "German Navies from 1848 to 2016," *Naval War College Review* 70, no. 4 (2017): 1–47.

24. And see the great detail in "Erich Raeder during World War II," Wikipedia, last modified March 27, 2020, https://en.wikipedia.org/wiki/Erich_Raeder_during_World _War_II. Despite that quote, Raeder had fantastical, expansionist ambitions throughout the war.

25. The two best English-language works are P. Dull, *A Battle History of the Imperial Japanese Navy, 1941–1945* (Annapolis, MD: US Naval Institute Press, 1978); and M. Stille, *The Imperial Japanese Navy in the Pacific War* (London: Osprey, 2014).

26. D. C. Evans and M. Peattie, *Kaigun: Strategy, Tactics, and Technology in the Imperial Japanese Navy 1887–1941* (Annapolis, MD: US Naval Institute Press, 1997), with much detail; and for further reading, a very good "Imperial Japanese Navy Air Service," Wikipedia, last modified January 19, 2020, https://en.wikipedia.org/wiki/Imperial_Japanese _Navy_Air_Service.

27. For the domination of the Japanese Army throughout, see S. C. M. Paine, *The Japanese Empire: Grand Strategy from the Meiji Restoration to the Pacific War* (Cambridge, UK: Cambridge University Press, 2017); also, a wide-ranging essay, much broader than its title suggests, is C. Boyd, "Japanese Military Effectiveness: The Interwar Period," in *Military Effectiveness*, ed. A. R. Millett and W. Murray, vol. 2, *The Interwar Years* (Boston: Allen and Unwin, 1987), 131–68.

28. On the American debate for or against intervention, see J. A. Thompson, chap. 4 in *A Sense of Power: The Roots of America's Global Role* (Ithaca, NY: Cornell University Press, 2015).

29. *Jane's Fighting Ships 1939*, 476. See also "North Carolina–class battleship," Wikipedia, last modified March 27, 2020, https://en.wikipedia.org/wiki/North_Carolina-class _battleship, for details of the extraordinary amount of design changes in the late 1930s.

30. *Jane's Fighting Ships 1939*, 476.

31. Ibid., 487–89. For the context and admirals, see C. G. Reynolds, preface and chap. 1 in *Fast Carriers*.

32. By the day of Pearl Harbor itself, the US Navy possessed six fleet carriers: three (!) were at Norfolk, Virginia; one was at San Diego; and only two were engaged on separate missions in the central Pacific.

33. On the British Empire's many political and strategic dilemmas after 1919, see M. Beloff, *Imperial Sunset*, vol. 1, *Britain's Liberal Empire, 1897–1921* (London: Methuen, 1969); and P. Kennedy, *Rise and Fall of the Great Powers*, 355ff.

34. For more details on these battleships, see *Jane's Fighting Ships 1939*, 23–39.

35. Ibid., 44–62.

36. The rather sad tale of both the Royal Navy's Fleet Air Arm and RAF Coastal Command is recounted in many works, inter alia: G. Till, *Air Power and the Royal Navy 1914– 1945: A Historical Survey* (Surrey, UK: Macdonald and Jane's, 1979); for technical details, T. Hone, N. Friedman, and M. D. Mandeles, *American and British Aircraft Carrier Development, 1919–1941* (Annapolis, MD: US Naval Institute Press, 1999); and more simply, "Fleet Air Arm," Wikipedia, last modified May 11, 2020, https://en.wikipedia.org/wiki /Fleet_Air_Arm; A. Hendrie, *The Cinderella Service: RAF Coastland Command 1939– 1945* (London: Casemate, 2006); and a superb "RAF Coastal Command during World War II," Wikipedia, last modified November 19, 2019, https://en.wikipedia.org/wiki/RAF _Coastal_Command_during_World_War_II.

37. Details of Royal Navy submarines are to be found in *Jane's Fighting Ships 1939*, 74–78; and Wikipedia as usual has significant entries under the categories of *S*-class, *T*-class, and *U*-class British submarines.

38. Kennedy, chaps. 7–8 in *British Naval Mastery*; and S. W. Roskill, *Naval Policy between the Wars*, vol. 1, *The Period of Anglo-American Antagonism, 1919–1939* (London:

Collins, 1978), early chapters; more recently, C. M. Bell, *The Royal Navy, Seapower and Strategy between the Wars* (Stanford, CA: Stanford University Press, 2000).

39. See the shrewd analysis in M. E. Howard, *The Continental Commitment: The Dilemma of British Defence Policy in the Era of the Two World Wars* (London: Maurice Temple Smith, 1972).

40. The Admiralty's expressions of this acute dilemma are nicely reported in A. J. Marder, "The Royal Navy and the Ethiopian Crisis of 1935–36," in *American Historical Review* 75, no. 5 (June 1971). On the larger picture of British overstretch, see Barnett, *Collapse of British Power.*

41. The best work on this 1939 decision is L. Pratt, *East of Malta, West of Suez: Britain's Mediterranean Crisis, 1936–1939* (Cambridge, UK: Cambridge University Press, 1975), passim. Among the vast literature on the Singapore Base policy, see J. Neidpath, *The Singapore Naval Base and the Defence of Britain's Eastern Empire, 1919–1941* (New York: Clarendon Press of Oxford University Press, 1981).

42. As in Barnett, *Collapse of British Power,* passim; and P. Kennedy, chap. 6 in *Rise and Fall of the Great Powers.*

43. For example, E. Mawdsley, *The War for the Seas: A Maritime History of World War II* (London: Yale University Press, 2019), 11; and J. A. Maiolo, "Did the Royal Navy Decline between the Wars?," *RUSI Journal* 159 (July 2014): 18–24.

44. See A. Clayton, *The British Empire as a Superpower, 1919–39* (Basingstoke, UK: Macmillan, 1986), passim, another interesting counter to all of the "empire is in trouble" literature.

45. For an array of studies of each Power's "military effectiveness," see again Millett and Murray, *Military Effectiveness,* vol. 2, *The Interwar Years.*

## Chapter 3

1. K. Marx, *The Eighteenth Brumaire of Louis Napoleon* (London: Electric Book Co., 2001).

2. A. T. Mahan, "Considerations Governing the Dispositions of Navies," in *National Review* 3 (July 1902): 701–19, which has also been reprinted in *Retrospect and Prospect: Studies in International Relations, Naval and Political* (Boston: Little, Brown, 1902).

3. P. Kennedy, "The War at Sea," in *Cambridge History of the First World War,* ed. J. M. Winter, vol. 1 (Cambridge, UK: Cambridge University Press, 2014); and Taylor, epilogue in *Struggle for Mastery in Europe.*

4. A. Lambert, *Seapower States: Maritime Culture, Continental Empires, and the Conflict That Made the Modern World* (New Haven, CT: Yale University Press, 2018), passim, borrowing the argument about the constraint of having land frontiers from Mahan's own disquisition in the foreword to *The Influence of Sea Power upon History* (Newport, RI: Naval War College Press, 1991).

5. Mahan, "Disposition of Navies," 710.

6. W. Wegener, *Naval Strategy of the World War,* trans. H. H. Herwig (Annapolis, MD: US Naval Institute Press, 1989), passim. Originally published as *Die Seestrategie des Weltkrieges* (Berlin: E. S. Mittler, 1929).

7. Ibid.

8. Kennedy, *British Naval Mastery.*

9. P. K. Kemp, ed., *The Papers of Admiral Sir John Fisher* (London: Navy Records Society, 1960–1964), 2:161.

10. P. Kennedy, "Imperial Cable Communications and Strategy, 1870–1914," in *The English Historical Review* 86, no. 341 (October 1971): 728–52.

11. Mahan, "Disposition of Navies."

12. The striking image of sentry boxes without sentries was first tossed out in the closing thoughts of Barnett's revisionist *Collapse of British Power,* although it is not unlike Liddell Hart's slightly earlier remark about "bases without fleets," as discussed in chapter 3 of this work.

13. The position and role of the Home Fleet is central to the three-volume S. W. Roskill, *The War at Sea, 1939–1945* (London: HMSO, 1954–61); but see also J. P. Levy, *The Royal Navy's Home Fleet in World War 2* (London: Macmillan, 2003), passim.

14. The Battle of the Atlantic lasts so long that there are references to important works and Wiki articles in every following chapter (5–10), beginning with those in notes 21–22 of chapter 5.

15. See the Arctic convoy references in chapter 6, note 5.

16. On the Italian position, see again de Ninno's clever article "A Rising Power in the Age of Multipolarity: Italian Naval Policy and Strategy in the Age of Fascism," in Kennedy and Wilson, *Navies in Multipolar Worlds,* 23–32.

17. See again the important if brief work by Pratt, *East of Malta, West of Suez,* passim.

18. Neidpath, *Singapore Naval Base,* among many others.

19. This is a rather different formulation from that of P. P. O'Brien, *How the War Was Won: Air-Sea Power and Allied Victory in World War II* (Cambridge, UK: Cambridge University Press, 2015).

20. W. Braisted, *The United States Navy in the Pacific* (Austin: University of Texas Press, 1958); and other references in chapters 2 and 5 here.

21. And see H. H. Herwig, *Politics of Frustration: The United States in German Naval Planning 1889–1941* (Boston: Little, Brown, 1976) for the actual German side.

22. See the conclusions in G. W. Prang, *At Dawn We Slept: The Untold Story of Pearl Harbor* (New York: McGraw-Hill, 1981), passim.

23. E. S. Miller, *War Plan Orange: The U.S. Strategy to Defeat Japan, 1897–1945* (Annapolis, MD: US Naval Institute Press, 1991), passim.

24. On this all the experts on the Japanese Navy in the Pacific war—Dull, Spector, Symonds, and Reynolds (see chapter 5)—appear to agree: if the Japanese carrier navy did extremely well in these campaigns, it was despite the battleship admirals and *not* with the latter's great support.

25. D. Landes, *The Unbound Prometheus: Technological Change and Industrial Development in Western Europe from 1750 to the Present* (Cambridge, UK: Cambridge University Press, 1969), passim.

26. For statistics on the growth of world population, output, and industrialization, see P. Kennedy, *Rise and Fall of the Great Powers,* 199ff; and Woodruff, *Impact of Western Man.*

27. See again *Jane's Fighting Ships 1939* for the various national sections. For the earlier period, see the table "Warship Tonnage of the Powers 1880–1914," in Q. Wright, *A Study of War* (Chicago: University of Chicago Press, 1942), 670–71.

28. There is no up-to-date analytical study of British shipbuilding in the interwar years, although there are some histories of the individual yards and shipbuilding areas (e.g., the Tyne), but there is some coverage in Roskill, *Naval Policy between the Wars,* vol. 2, *The Period of Reluctant Rearmament, 1930–1939;* and a little in Mawdsley, *War for the Seas.*

29. See again *Jane's Fighting Ships 1939,* 23–60; and Mawdsley, *War for the Seas,* 14–17.

30. *Jane's Fighting Ships 1939,* 476–90.

31. See the intriguing article by J. B. Parrish, "Iron and Steel in the Balance of World Power," *Journal of Political Economy* 64, no. 4 (October 1956): 368–88; and the further table on "Iron/Steel Production of the Powers 1890–1938," in P. Kennedy, *Rise and Fall of the Great Powers*, 200.

32. On the outstanding lead of the German and US machine-tool industries over all others, see A. S. Milward, *War, Economy and Society, 1939–1945* (Berkeley: University of California Press, 1977), 187–90 and 333–34. See also J. A. Maiolo, *Cry Havoc: How the Arms Race Drove the World to War, 1931–1941* (New York: Basic Books, 2010), 211ff.

33. Kennedy, chaps. 7–9 in *British Naval Mastery*.

34. This figure taken from H. Hillman's essay, "Comparative Strength of the Great Powers," in A. J. Toynbee and F. T. Ashton-Gwatkin, eds., *The World in March 1939* (London: Oxford University Press, 1952), 446.

35. Mahan, *Influence of Sea Power*, 88.

36. Ibid.; further analysis in Kennedy, introduction to *British Naval Mastery*.

37. For statistics on the nineteenth- and early-twentieth-century growth of economies, output, and defense budgets, see again Taylor, foreword to *Struggle for Mastery in Europe*; and P. Kennedy, chap. 5 in *Rise and Fall of the Great Powers*.

38. Most easily found at P. Kennedy, *British Naval Mastery*, 206.

39. For a brilliant work on the reexaminations of Jutland in the interwar years, see G. A. H. Gordon, *The Rules of the Game: Jutland and British Naval Command* (London: John Murray, 1996).

40. Mahan, *Influence of Sea Power*, 138.

41. It is fair to point out that Mahan did, of course, acknowledge the significance of commerce at sea—it was one of the underlying causes of Britain's success—although his tendency was to assume that once the big battle-fleet victory had been achieved, the enemy would be swept off the seas. It is also true that, by the time of his 1902 essay ("Dispositions of Navies"), he paid a lot more attention to the variable of geography in determining sea power.

42. J. Corbett's best early work here was *England in the Seven Years War: A Study in Combined Strategy* (London: Longmans, Green, 1907), followed shortly afterward by his theoretical classic *Some Principles of Maritime Strategy* (London: Longmans, Green, 1918), passim.

43. For further details on Corbett's line of thinking and a reference to his clash with the Admiralty on the writing of the official history, see G. Till, chap. 4, "Corbett and the Emergence of a British School," in *The Development of British Naval Thinking: Essays in Memory of Bryan McLaren Ranft* (London: Routledge, 2006), 81.

## Chapter 4

1. The 1939 setting of the naval conflict is described in Roskill, chaps. 5–7 in *War at Sea*, vol. 1, with many appendices; and in the early chapters of Symonds, *World War II at Sea*.

2. P. Auphan and J. Mordal, *The French Navy in World War II* (Annapolis, MD: US Naval Institute Press, 1959); Roskill, *War at Sea*, vol. 1.

3. On the sinking of the HMS *Courageous*, see "HMS *Courageous* (50)," Wikipedia, last modified October 23, 2019, https://en.wikipedia.org/wiki/HMS_Courageous_(50); as well as the withering comments on the "units of search" strategy by C. Barnett, *Engage the Enemy More Closely: The Royal Navy in the Second World War* (London: Hodder and Stoughton, 1991), 68–69.

4. For much detail of Prien's sinking of the HMS *Royal Oak,* see C. Blair, *Hitler's U-boat War,* vol. 1, *The Hunters, 1939–1942* (New York: Random House, 1996), 104–9.

5. Roskill, *War at Sea,* 1:115.

6. A fine map of the *Graf Spee*'s movements and another of the battle are in Roskill, *War at Sea,* 1:118.

7. "Battle of the River Plate," Wikipedia, last modified January 20, 2020, https://en .wikipedia.org/wiki/Battle_of_the_River_Plate; and a lively narrative in Barnett, *Engage the Enemy,* 84–88.

8. And the prewar rendezvous refueling arrangements were by this stage being broken. The few clandestine German supply ships operating under neutral flags could give respite to surface raiders like the *Graf Spee* for only so long.

9. Roskill, appendix Q in *War at Sea,* vol. 1, for the U-boat figures; Blair, *Hitler's U-boat War,* vol. 1, passim, for the repeated torpedo failures. See also M. Milner, "The Battle of the Atlantic," *Journal of Strategic Studies* 13, no. 1 (1990): 45–66, https://doi.org/10.1080 /01402399008437400, for the monthly merchant-ship losses.

10. The best overall account of the military and political situation in western Europe during the winter of 1939–40 and into June and July itself, including the balance of forces on each side, the Phony War, the Winter War/Finnish situation, British and German actions over Norway, and then the Fall of France, with Dunkirk, is probably Liddell Hart, chaps. 4–7 in *History of the Second World War* (London: Cassell, 1970), with excellent maps. Symonds, chaps. 3–4 in *World War II at Sea,* is fine, very succinct.

11. Admiral Raeder's memo to Hitler is quoted in Barnett, *Engage the Enemy,* 104.

12. On the overall theme of German military effectiveness (its strengths at the tactical and operational levels of war and its weaknesses at the top), see Millett and Murray, *Military Effectiveness,* especially the essays in the third volume.

13. For the weaknesses of the Fleet Air Arm, especially its aircraft, see again Till, *Air Power and the Royal Navy,* and the many more sources cited in chapter 2, note 36.

14. On the Luftwaffe numbers for Norway, see again Barnett, *Engage the Enemy,* 103.

15. Unsurprisingly, perhaps, Barnett's details on Churchill's awful role at the Admiralty in these weeks are eye-popping—see chaps. 4–5 in *Engage the Enemy;* but see also S. W. Roskill, *Churchill and the Admirals* (London: Collins, 1977). For another full-hearted criticism, see now J. Kiszely, *Anatomy of a Campaign: The British Fiasco in Norway, 1940* (Cambridge, UK: Cambridge University Press, 2017), passim.

16. Symonds, "Norway," chap. 3 in *World War II at Sea,* has a cool, detached, and succinct account of the whole campaign, including details on Allied warships and military units being sent back and forth. Liddell Hart, *History of the Second World War,* is good on the military side, much less so on the naval campaigning. Lloyd George's devastating speech, along with many others, is quoted from the momentous House of Commons, May 7th–9th, 1940, debates in "Norway Debate," Wikipedia, last modified January 24, 2020, https://en.wikipedia.org/wiki/Norway_Debate.

17. "Battles of Narvik," Wikipedia, last modified January 18, 2020, https://en.wikipe dia.org/wiki/Battles_of_Narvik#First_naval_Battle_of_Narvik.

18. "Battles of Narvik," the same Wikipedia page mentioned in the previous note, is by a Norwegian military historian and has much background on the land campaigns; see also the very lively chapter 4 of Barnett, *Engage the Enemy.*

19. Mountbatten's own very cool narrative of the actions with the E-boats and of HMS *Kelly* and the hazardous tow back to the Tyne is reproduced in "Mountbatten Brings Home HMS *Kelly,*" World War II Today, http://ww2today.com/9th-may-1940 -mountbatten-brings-home-hms-kelly. Roskill, *War at Sea,* 1:145, notes that this was the first-ever appearance of German E-boats.

20. The integrated Nortraship company became the largest shipping organization in the world, and 42 percent of its fleet consisted of modern oil tankers. "Nortraship," Wikipedia, accessed February 1, 2020, https://en.wikipedia.org/wiki/Nortraship.

21. "The overrunning of the West" is covered, with maps, in Liddell Hart, chap. 7 in *History of the Second World War.*

22. Ibid.; and on the crisis facing Admiral Ramsay and the unfolding of Operation Dynamo (the Dunkirk evacuation), see Roskill, chaps. 11–12 in *War at Sea,* vol. 1 (two large chapters).

23. It was fear of such an event repeating itself that in many later cases caused the evacuated troops to insist on remaining above the deck of the small vessels that rescued them, even if it made the latter dangerously top-heavy. This fear of being trapped below deck is well captured by scenes in the 2017 movie *Dunkirk.*

24. "HMS *Wakeful* (H88)," Wikipedia, last modified October 3, 2019, https://en.wikipedia.org/wiki/HMS_Wakeful_(H88); and "HMS *Grafton* (H89)," Wikipedia, last modified November 23, 2019, https://en.wikipedia.org/wiki/HMS_Grafton_(H89).

25. Unsurprisingly, there are many popular-history accounts of the Royal Navy destroyers' gallant actions off Dunkirk and of *Ivanhoe*'s fate and that of other ships, but see also the sober "HMS *Ivanhoe* (D16)," Wikipedia, accessed June 1, 2020, https://en.wikipedia.org/wiki/HMS_Ivanhoe_(D16). (There are individual Wikipedia entries for every one of the warships involved.)

26. "HMS *Havant* (H32)," Wikipedia, last modified January 25, 2020, https://en.wikipedia.org/wiki/HMS_Havant_(H32).

27. The *Foudroyant* wreck remains a noted site for scuba divers even today.

28. On the loss of the HMS *Glorious* and the destroyer HMS *Ancasta*'s damaging of the *Scharnhorst,* see the terse summary in Barnett, *Engage the Enemy,* 136–37.

29. For total troops evacuated (including day by day), see the table in "Dunkirk Evacuation," Wikipedia, accessed February 14, 2020, https://en.wikipedia.org/wiki/Dunkirk_evacuation.

30. For one example, see B. Cheall, *Fighting Through from Dunkirk to Hamburg: A Green Howard's Wartime Memoir* (Barnsley, UK: Pen and Sword, 2011); and a useful article, "Battle of Dunkirk," Wikipedia, last modified February 8, 2020, https://en.wikipedia.org/wiki/Battle_of_Dunkirk, has a massive bibliography itself.

31. C. Barnett, *Britain and Her Army, 1509–1970: A Military, Political, and Social Survey* (Harmondsworth, UK: Penguin Books, 1970), includes many disquisitions on British wars on the European continent.

32. For the reinforcements to the Home Fleet in 1940, especially the new *King George Vs* much desired by the Admiralty, see C. M. Bell, *Churchill and Sea Power* (Oxford: Oxford University Press, 2013), 200–202; and Roskill, *War at Sea,* 1:262–68.

33. Doenitz's U-boat losses by mid-1940 are given (together with new sailings) in great detail in Blair, *Hitler's U-Boat War,* vol. 1; D. van der Vat, *The Atlantic Campaign: World War II's Great Struggle at Sea* (New York: Harper and Row, 1988), 126; and Roskill, appendix K in *War at Sea,* vol. 1.

34. On the German dud torpedoes (many of which bounced off a large number of the heavy warships of the Royal Navy!), see the repeated evidence in both Blair, *Hitler's U-Boat War;* and van der Vat, *Atlantic Campaign.*

35. Although it was actually the British foreign minister Lord Grey who had coined the phrase that the army "was a projectile to be fired by the Navy," Admiral Fisher enjoyed quoting it; see his *Memories* (London: Hodder and Stoughton, 1919), 18.

36. See Liddell Hart's various essays—for example, chap. 1, "The Historical Strategy

of Britain," in *The British Way of Warfare* (London: Faber, 1932)—and also the many important studies and biographies on him; see the lengthy "B. H. Liddell Hart," Wikipedia, accessed August 1, 2020, https://en.wikipedia.org/wiki/B._H._Liddell_Hart, passim.

37. Luftwaffe versus RAF losses in the Battle of France are brilliantly diagnosed in R. J. Overy's revisionist "Air Power, Armies, and the War in the West, 1940," in the US-AAF Harmon Memorial Lecture #32 (1989), https://www.usafa.edu/academic/history/harmon32/.

38. The American alarm at the Fall of France is examined in Blair, *Hitler's U-boat War,* 1:165, which details the many acts of US support to Britain between mid-1940 and December 1941; and more data in A. Nagorski's new book *1941: The Year Germany Lost the War* (New York: Simon and Schuster, 2019).

39. "Two-Ocean Navy Act," Wikipedia, last modified November 30, 2019, https://en.wikipedia.org/wiki/Two-Ocean_Navy_Act; and S. E. Morison, *History of United States Naval Operations in World War II,* vol. 1, *The Battle of the Atlantic* (Boston: Little, Brown, 1984), 27ff. The eye-popping comparisons with the size of the Japanese Navy overall are also noted by Symonds, *World War II at Sea,* 179.

40. See chapter 8 for further details of these vessels.

41. For details of the carriers, see chap. 2, nn. 19–20; and in *Jane's Fighting Ships 1940* and *Jane's Fighting Ships 1941.*

42. Maiolo, chaps. 16–17 in *Cry Havoc,* 353–54, is excellent on the growing German awareness of the sheer size of US productivity.

43. Symonds, chap. 8, "The Rising Sun," in *World War II at Sea* is a wonderful account of Yamamoto's calculations.

44. Maiolo, *Cry Havoc,* passim; J. Lukacs, *The Last European War: September 1939/December 1941* (New Haven, CT: Yale University Press, 1976); B. C. Stoddard, *World in the Balance: The Perilous Months of June–October 1940* (Washington, DC: Potomac Books, 2011); and more details in the early chapters of Nagorski, *1941.*

45. Until "the New World, with all its power and might" (*nota bene* those words): these are of course the closing sentences of Churchill's historic "Never Surrender" speech in the House of Commons, June 4, 1940.

46. Being not more than a month in office as prime minister, Churchill kept referring a decision to sink the French fleet back to the British Cabinet. For details, see again Barnett, *Engage the Enemy,* 171–81; while Roskill, *War at Sea,* 1:240–45, is tightly restrained in his account here, as compared to his own later writings. Best now is D. Brown, *The Road to Oran: Anglo-French Naval Relations, September 1939–July 1940* (London: Cass, 2004).

47. For a brief summary, there is "Attack on Mers-el-Kébir," Wikipedia, accessed June 23, 2019, https://en.wikipedia.org/wiki/Attack-on-Mers-el-Kebir; but for gripping details, see A. J. Marder, chap. 5 in *From the Dardanelles to Oran: Studies of the Royal Navy in War and Peace, 1915–1940* (Oxford: Oxford University Press, 1974).

## Chapter 5

1. D. Low, "Very Well, Alone," *Evening Standard,* June 18, 1940.

2. HistoryExtra, "WW2: When Britain Stood (Not Quite) Alone," June 24, 2019, https://www.historyextra.com/period/second-world-war/britain-stood-alone-ww2-myths-brexit-debate/.

3. On the beginnings of American concerns after the Fall of France, and the swift se-

ries of measures of help, see the early chapters in Morison, *US Naval Operations,* vol. 1, passim.

4. This refers again to Wegener, *Naval Strategy of the World War* (chap. 3, nn. 6 and 7).

5. For the Battle of the Atlantic after the Fall of France, see Roskill, "The Campaign in the North-West Approaches," in *War at Sea,* 1:343ff.; Barnett, *Engage the Enemy,* 251ff., is an important critique. See also the nice survey in van der Vat, chap. 5 in *Atlantic Campaign.*

6. *The Halder War Diary, 1939–1942,* trans. C. Burdick and H. A. Jacobsen (Novato, CA: Presidio Press, 1988); and for the British defenses, see B. Collier, *The Defense of the United Kingdom* (London: HMSO, 1957), passim; and Levy, chap. 5 in *Royal Navy's Home Fleet.*

7. See the impressive detail in "Fliegerführer Atlantik," Wikipedia, accessed March 1, 2019, https://en.wikipedia.org/wiki/Fliegerführer_Atlantik. This source has lots of further references, which are only episodic in most navy-focused works, such as van der Vat, *Atlantic Campaign.*

8. The story of the HMS *Audacity* convoy is in Roskill, *War at Sea,* 1:477–79 (with, opposite p. 481, photos of the *Audacity* in convoy and of a typical fighter catapult ship).

9. For the Luftwaffe's juggling acts, see especially W. Murray, *The Luftwaffe, 1933–45: Strategy for Defeat* (Washington, DC: Brassey's, 1996).

10. There is much detail on German clandestine raiders at this time in Roskill, chap. 18 in *War at Sea,* vol. 1. But see also Symonds, chap. 6, "The War on Trade," in *World War II at Sea,* for a fine summary of all the categories of German raiders (clandestine, U-boats, and surface warships). See also note 24 below.

11. The raids of the *Scheer* and then the *Scharnhorst* and *Gneisenau* (see next note), with a composite map, are covered in Roskill, chap. 28 in *War at Sea,* which also has details of German clandestine raider operations.

12. Roskill's comments on the ocean raids by these German heavy warships (see previous note) are very sobering; he describes them as serious disruptions to the North Atlantic convoys.

13. The enthusiastic British literature on the "Sink the Bismarck!" story (Churchill's injunction, and a movie of that name) is overwhelming. There's a fine account in Barnett, *Engage the Enemy,* which devotes thirty pages, 284–314, to the story. The maps (31 to 33) in Roskill, *War at Sea,* vol. 1, are remarkable.

14. "Channel Dash," Wikipedia, accessed March 23, 2019, https://en.wikipedia.org /wiki/Channel_Dash, has exhaustive, hour-by-hour detail, but the best map of this ingenious operation is in Roskill, *War at Sea,* 2:153, with a defensive account of the Admiralty's difficulties. Still, what also impresses here is the constant threat to the German warships from RAF bombing, which plainly didn't disappear when they reached the Baltic.

15. American battleships were thus sent from time to time to join the Home Fleet in Scapa Flow, while the *Tirpitz* remained a threat to the Arctic convoys (chapters 6–7); but the last German battleship never met up with them and instead was hounded from port to port until its final destruction by RAF bombing in November 1944.

16. Or an even lower priority, given Hitler's mounting obsession by this time with the destruction of the European Jews and the defeat of the USSR. See the compelling account in A. Hillgruber, *Hitler's Strategie: Politik und Kriegsführung, 1940–1941* (Frankfurt: Bernand and Graefe, 1965).

17. J. B. Hattendorf, ed., *On His Majesty's Service: Observations of the British Home Fleet from the Diary, Reports, and Letters of Joseph H. Welling, Assistant U.S. Naval At-*

*tache, London, 1940–41* (Newport, RI: Naval War College Press, 1983), a remarkable personal account.

18. Still standard here are the accounts in Morison, *US Naval Operations,* 1:92–109.

19. For further details on the Lend-Lease programs, see chapter 8.

20. C. Williamson, "Industrial-Grade Generosity: British Warship Repair and Lend-Lease in 1941," *Diplomatic History* 39, no. 4 (September 2015): 745–72.

21. "Battle of the Atlantic," Wikipedia, last modified March 9, 2020, https://en.wikipedia.org/wiki/Battle_of_the_Atlantic. Probably the fullest detail now is to be found in Blair's epic history, *Hitler's U-boat War,* passim, although it is hard to beat the accounts, maps, and statistical tables in Roskill, *War at Sea,* vols. 1 and 2.

22. Blair, *Hitler's U-boat War,* vol. 1, is invaluable here in doing regular summaries of the losses and gains of each side; for example, "Assessments," 418–27, on the first twenty-eight months of the war (that is, to December 1941), and passim; and van der Vat, *Atlantic Campaign,* also has a "losses at sea" summary at the end of each chapter. There are also fine summaries in Liddell Hart, chap. 24, "The Battle of the Atlantic," in *History of the Second World War.* Finally, https://uboat.net/allies/merchants/losses_year.

23. Blair, chap. 3, "The June Slaughter," and "The October Slaughter," in *Hitler's U-boat War.*

24. There is a massive amount of popular literature on the "gray wolves" of the ocean, the German disguised raiders or auxiliary cruisers (*Hilfskreuzer*), and there are very detailed Wikipedia articles on every one of the most successful ones—the *Kormoran, Thor,* and *Atlantis.* An early solid account is D. Woodward, *The Secret Raiders: The Story of German Armed Merchant Raiders in the Second World War* (New York: Norton, 1955).

25. On the loss or capture of the U-boat aces like Prien, Kretschmer, and so on and the fight around Convoy HX-112, see, briefly, Symonds, chap. 6, "The War on Trade," in *World War II at Sea,* 129; and in much more detail, Blair, chap. 4 in *Hitler's U-boat War,* 248ff.

26. On the Arctic convoys generally, see B. B. Schofield, *The Russian Convoys: Heroes of the Murmansk Run—Allied Seamen Who Fought Stukas, Nazi Subs and Frozen Arctic Seas in WWII* (London: Batsford, 1966). (Admiral Schofield was a participant in the convoys.) The repeated chapters called "Home Waters and the Arctic" of Roskill, *War at Sea,* have much detail, with photos and maps; and there is a remarkable tribute, with use of original Admiralty reports, in chapter 23 (on the Arctic Convoys) of Barnett, *Engage the Enemy.*

27. A basic source here is "Operation Dervish (1941)," Wikipedia, accessed March 25, 2019, https://en.wikipedia.org/wiki/Operation_Dervish_(1941), with a British and a German bibliography.

28. See note 22 regarding the regular tallying of merchant-ship and U-boat losses by van der Vat and Blair, although both Roskill, *War at Sea,* and Barnett, *Engage the Enemy,* also give periodic summaries.

29. M. Simpson, "Force H and British Strategy in the Western Mediterranean 1939–1942," *Mariner's Mirror* 83, no. 1 (1997): 62–75; and Q. Hughes, *Britain in the Mediterranean and the Defence of Her Naval Stations* (Liverpool, UK: Penpaled, 1981).

30. B. R. Sullivan, *A Thirst for Glory: Mussolini, the Italian Military and the Fascist Regime, 1922–1936* (Ann Arbor, MI: University Microfilms International, 1984); M. Knox, *Mussolini Unleashed, 1939–1941: Politics and Strategy in Fascist Italy's Last War* (Cambridge, UK: Cambridge University Press, 1982); D. Mack Smith, *Mussolini's Roman Empire* (New York: Viking Press, 1976).

31. R. Hammond, "An Enduring Influence on Imperial Defence and Grand Strategy:

British Perceptions of the Italian Navy, 1935–1943," *International History Review* 39, no. 5 (2017): 810–35, https://doi.org/10.1080/07075332.2017.1280520.

32. On Force H bombarding Genoa, Leghorn, and Spezia, for example, see Roskill, *War at Sea,* 1:425.

33. "Battle of Calabria," Wikipedia, last modified September 12, 2019, https://en.wikipedia.org/wiki/Battle_of_Calabria, though scarcely covered in Roskill, *War at Sea,* vol. 1.

34. Given all of the celebratory British literature on the Taranto raid and the discussion of its being the precursor to Pearl Harbor, see "Battle of Taranto," Wikipedia, accessed March 15, 2019, https://en.wikipedia.org/wiki/Battle_of_Taranto, with Italian sources and US archives. It is surprising how cursory Roskill is in *War at Sea,* 1:300–301.

35. Roskill's coverage of the Battle of Cape Spartivento in *War at Sea,* 302–4, also makes plain his disapproval of Churchill's nagging of his admirals.

36. J. Holland, *Fortress Malta: An Island under Siege 1940–1943* (London: Orion, 2003).

37. Told rather wonderfully in "Operation Excess," accessed June 1, 2020, https://www.armouredcarriers.com/illustrious-malta-operation-excess-january-10-1941. Admiral Cunningham's quote is from Barnett, *Engage the Enemy,* 321.

38. Barnett, *Engage the Enemy,* 321. Holland, *Fortress Malta,* tells the Malta story; Barnett, *Engage the Enemy,* 322, tells the HMS *Illustrious* and Mediterranean Fleet side of this.

39. The rebuilt *Illustrious* would later be deployed on Arctic convoys and then would be back in the Mediterranean to cover the Sicily landings in 1943—a nice reversal of roles. It would end up operating with the British Pacific Fleet off Japan in June 1945. No other large fleet carrier had as many months of wartime fighting, from July 1940 to the end of the war, though the USS *Saratoga* came close.

40. "Battle of Cape Matapan," Wikipedia, last modified January 17, 2020, https://en.wikipedia.org/wiki/Battle_of_Cape_Matapan.

41. In the Pacific, the US Navy had, rather similarly, only two battleship shootouts: the USS *Washington*'s sinking of the *Kirishima,* and Leyte Gulf itself (at the Battle of Surigao Strait). This was not a war in which the big ships could shine.

42. Roskill, *War at Sea,* 1:440–49, analyzes the Royal Navy's tough fight off Crete, but for greater detail of the Greece-Crete campaign, see C. A. MacDonald, *The Lost Battle—Crete, 1941* (London: Macmillan, 1993). On Fliegerkorps X and the other formidable Luftwaffe groups that Goering and Hitler threw into (and then pulled out of) Mediterranean fighting between 1940 and 1943, see again Murray, *Luftwaffe,* passim.

43. For the loss of the HMS *Kelly* and many other British warships, see the graphic account in Barnett, chap. 12, "Catastrophe in the Mediterranean, 1941," in *Engage the Enemy.*

44. As quoted in a fine Wikipedia piece. See "Battle of Crete," Wikipedia, accessed June 2020, https://en.wikipedia.org/wiki/Battle_of_Crete.

45. Nagorski, *1941,* passim.

46. The Royal Navy's various fights and convoys in the Mediterranean in these months are covered in Roskill, chap. 24, "The African Campaigns," in *War at Sea,* vol. 1. For one of them, "Operation Substance," see Wikipedia, last modified December 23, 2019, https://en.wikipedia.org/wiki/Operation_Substance.

47. "Battle of Cape Bon (1941)," Wikipedia, last modified September 28, 2019, https://en.wikipedia.org/wiki/Battle_of_Cape_Bon_(1941).

48. For the Mediterranean Fleet's "Lowest Ebb," see Roskill, *War at Sea,* 1:538ff.; and Barnett, *Engage the Enemy,* 370–77.

49. For the Far East scene generally by 1941, see Morison, *US Naval Operations,* vol. 3, *The Rising Sun,* parts 1–2, which deals with the Pacific War.

50. On Roosevelt's oil embargo and details of Japan's oil dependency, see Liddell Hart, *History of the Second World War*, 206ff.

51. See Liddell Hart, chap. 17, "Japan's Tide of Conquest," in *History of the Second World War*.

52. Ibid.; and Symonds, chaps. 10–11 in *World War II at Sea*, provide excellent summaries.

53. The literature on the Pearl Harbor attack is of course enormous and told in great detail by many works—for example, Prang, *At Dawn We Slept*, which is an enormous 918 pages long, and was not his last book on the subject. There are nice narratives in another older work, J. Toland, chap. 8 in *The Rising Sun: The Decline and Fall of the Japanese Empire, 1936–1945* (London: Cassell, 1971), using many Japanese sources; and R. H. Spector, *Eagle against the Sun: The American War with Japan* (New York: Free Press, 1985), 1–100. Morison, *US Naval Operations*, 3:80–127, is actually rather brief.

54. C. G. Reynolds, *Fast Carriers*, but the carriers-versus-battleships debate is also well covered in both Spector, *Eagle against the Sun*; and Symonds, *World War II at Sea*, at appropriate times. Because the American carriers remained intact, Morison noted in *US Naval Operations*, 1:213, "the situation on 8 December was far less serious than it appeared to be at the time."

55. Historians are right to point out that this would have been a very large military operation, but would it have been much larger than the conquests of the Philippines, Malaya and Singapore, and the entire Dutch East Indies, had Imperial General Headquarters been willing to devote the resources to it? Was it more ambitious than the conquest of Burma?

56. Most thorough is M. Middlebrook and P. Mahoney, *Battleship: The Sinking of the Prince of Wales and Repulse* (New York: Scribner's, 1976); the best brief recent analysis, using a lot of original Admiralty sources, is Barnett, chap. 13 in *Engage the Enemy*; and Roskill, chap. 26, "Disaster in the Pacific, December 1941," in *War at Sea*, vol. 1.

57. Ibid., 565, with map opposite; Symonds, chap. 11, "Rampage," in *World War II at Sea*; Liddell Hart, *History of the Second World War*, 226.

58. Barnett, *Engage the Enemy*, on the British Admiralty's agonizing choices in 1941–42, is hugely critical and most impressive.

## Chapter 6

1. This picks up from the various sources on the Battle of the Atlantic that are referenced in chapter 5. Because of its centrality, there are multiple chapters in Roskill, *War at Sea*, vol. 2 (taking the story from 1942 onward). The two volumes of Blair's *Hitler's U-boat War* are amazing in their thoroughness.

2. And there would still be a large number of independent sailings, especially in southern waters, and especially by individual faster merchantmen not wanting to lose time by being in a convoy.

3. A general historical survey of convoys in modern times is presented in J. Winton, *Convoy: The Defence of Sea Trade, 1890–1990* (London: M. Joseph, 1983). My own brief discussion of Sir Julian Corbett on convoys is in chapter 3 of this work. There is a brief discourse about convoys in Morison, *US Naval Operations*, 1:19–26.

4. The Channel Dash is told, with grudging appreciation, in Roskill, *War at Sea*, 2:149–61 and map 15; and savagely in Barnett, *Engage the Enemy*, 443–55.

5. Schofield, *Russian Convoys*, passim; and, repeatedly, Roskill, *War at Sea*, vols. 2 and 3.

6. Barnett, *Engage the Enemy*, 707–10, is brief, but there is another fine article at "Convoy PQ 16," Wikipedia, accessed August 7, 2017, https://en.wikipedia.org/wiki/Convoy_PQ_16, passim.

7. The Convoy PQ-17 disaster has been the subject of enormous interest and controversy, most flamboyantly in the revisionist D. Irving, *The Destruction of Convoy PQ 17* (London: Cassell, 1968); rather painfully by Roskill, *War at Sea*, 2:134–46; and quite critically, again, in Barnett, *Engage the Enemy*, 711–22. For the German side, see Blair, *Hitler's U-boat War*, 1:638–45.

8. It is interesting to notice, then, how the hardworking destroyers, cruisers, and battleships of the Home Fleet were sent from Scapa Flow to support the key Malta convoy in Operation Pedestal in August, returned to offer cover to this Arctic convoy PQ-18 in September, and were then sent south again to play a role in support of November's Torch landings.

9. Instructively, see "Convoy PQ 18," Wikipedia, accessed August 11, 2017, https://en.wikipedia.org/wiki/Convoy_PQ_18. There is an astonishingly detailed layout of this convoy in "June–September 1942, Including DEFENCE of CONVOY PQ18," last modified July 18, 2011, https://naval-history.net/Cro3-54-00PQ18.htm.

10. The Battle of the Barents Sea attracted its own individual studies, starting with D. Pope, *73 North: The Battle of the Barents Sea* (London: Wyman, 1958); briefer and with more restraint in Roskill, *War at Sea*, 2:291–98; and succinctly in "Battle of the Barents Sea," Wikipedia, accessed August 13, 2017, https://en.wikipedia.org/wiki/Battle_of_the_Barents_Sea, with bibliography.

11. For a sobering account of the U-boat campaign off the Atlantic coasts, see again Morison, *US Naval Operations*, 1:114–57. All British accounts are greatly critical of King, whereas Blair, *Hitler's U-boat War*, vol. 1, springs strongly to his defense.

12. See Roskill, *War at Sea*, 2:102ff.; and with great detail, Morison, chaps. 6 and 9 in *US Naval Operations*, vol. 1.

13. E. Grove, "The West and the War at Sea," in *The Oxford Illustrated History of World War II*, ed. R. J. Overy (Oxford: Oxford University Press, 2015), 144, 150–52, ends the 1942 narrative on a chirpy tone; whereas van der Vat, *Atlantic Campaign*, 308–9, points to all the impending threats.

14. "Ship Losses by Month," accessed March 24, 2020, https://uboat.net/allies/merchants/losses_year.html.

15. I use "one last surge" because it is inconceivable to think of Hitler *at this time* being willing to send significantly more German units to support Rommel's drive toward Cairo after autumn 1942, given the epic struggle at Stalingrad and the need to parry the RAF's growing daylight and nighttime pressures in western Europe (the Hamburg Raid and others). Later, in early 1943, he was briefly willing to reverse course and send reinforcements to Tunis (see chapter 7), but by that stage the battle for Egypt—and Malta—was lost.

16. See the references in chapter 5. Generally, I have followed the narratives in the various works on the Battle of the Mediterranean, including Barnett, *Engage the Enemy*; Roskill, *War at Sea*, vol. 2; and various chapters in Liddell Hart, *History of the Second World War*.

17. Most recently, and thoroughly, M. Hastings, *Operation Pedestal: The Fleet That Battled to Malta, 1942* (London: HarperCollins, 2021); a good account in Barnett, chap. 16 in *Engage The Enemy*; and a lovely summation in Symonds, *World War II at Sea*, 313–20.

18. See Barnett, chaps. 8, 12, and especially 16, in *Engage the Enemy*.

19. There is no good "ship biography" of the *Wasp* (like those for the USS *Saratoga* and

*Warspite*), but the carrier's brief role in the Mediterranean in 1942 is covered in Morison, *US Naval Operations,* 1:194–97; and the "Malta Convoys" section in "USS *Wasp* (CV-7)," Wikipedia, accessed August 14, 2017, https://en.wikipedia.org/wiki/USS_Wasp_(CV-7).

20. The Torch operation, being so important, has a vast historiography, starting from Morison's very early 1947 volume, *US Naval Operations,* vol. 2, *Operations in North African Waters.* Also early on was the British military official history, I. S. O. Playfair, *The Mediterranean and Middle East: The Destruction of the Axis Forces in Africa,* vol. 4 (London: HMSO, 1954); and there is a very good summation at "Operation Torch," Wikipedia, accessed August 3, 2018, https://en.wikpedia.org/wiki/Operation_Torch, with fine maps and coverage of the diplomacy.

21. Including the battleships *Duke of York* and *Rodney* and the battle cruiser *Renown.* The landings on the Moroccan shore were covered by no less than three American battleships: the *Texas,* the *New York,* and the brand-new USS *Massachusetts,* which had a heavy exchange with the anchored *Jean Bart.* Here was an early example of the change in the role of both US Navy and Royal Navy battleships from being the center of a battle force that fought enemy heavy ships at sea to being the powerful artillery-support systems for all future amphibious operations.

22. The scuttling of the French fleet at Toulon is, amazingly, treated in the briefest way by all the normal Anglo-American works, for example, by Morison, *US Naval Operations,* 2:240; Roskill, *War at Sea,* 2:338 and notes; and Symonds, *World War II at Sea,* 362–63. Barnett, *Engage the Enemy,* surprisingly contains nothing. Ironically, by far the greatest detail is in "Scuttling of the French Fleet at Toulon," Wikipedia, accessed October 1, 2020, https://en.wikipedia.org/wiki/Scuttling_of_the_French_fleet_at_Toulon, although there is no bibliography.

23. Liddell Hart, *History of the Second World War,* 224, and chap. 17, on Japan's conquests in 1942, pointing again and again to the air factor. Of books on the fall of Singapore, there is no end, and there is a very large bibliography in "Battle of Singapore," Wikipedia, accessed August 7, 2018, https://en.wikipedia.org/wiki/Battle_of_Singapore (which has fine maps).

24. The Battle of the Java Sea and the other Japanese defeats of the ABDA (Allied navies) in Indonesian waters between February and May 1942 is eclipsed by the larger events of the fall of the Philippines, Singapore/Malaya, Coral Sea, and so on; so the standard works like those of Morison and Symonds have brief details and then move on.

25. The Japanese Navy in the Indian Ocean is treated well and succinctly in Symonds, *World War II at Sea,* 335ff.; while Mawdsley, *War for the Seas,* 192–93, also stresses the fatal British weakness in airpower here.

26. The most detailed account (with three maps) is in A. Boyd, chap. 8 in *The Royal Navy in Eastern Waters: Linchpin of Victory, 1935–1942* (Barnsley, UK: Seaforth, 2017).

27. It was, however, to take many more months before the British compelled the final surrender of the Vichy French forces here; see a very detailed account in "Battle of Madagascar," Wikipedia, accessed November 5, 2020, https://en.wikipedia.org/wiki/Battle_of_Madagascar; and curiously little (only p. 394) in Boyd, *Royal Navy in Eastern Waters.*

28. The scene is best set and the Coral Sea and Midway carrier actions nicely brought together in Morison, *US Naval Operations,* vol. 4, *Coral Sea, Midway, and Submarine Actions, May 1942–August 1942.*

29. There is a nice, succinct explanation of this incident, with maps, in Liddell Hart, *History of the Second World War,* 353–62; as a contrast, pungent and graphic, is Toland, *Rising Sun,* 345ff. The 1942 Battle of Midway is always included in any and all updated editions of E. S. Creasy's Victorian classic, *Fifteen Decisive Battles of the World: From*

*Marathon to Waterloo,* originally (New York: S. W. Green's Son, 1882); and often paired with the contemporaneous Battle of Stalingrad (in the 1964 revised amalgamation) J. B. Mitchell, ed., *Twenty Decisive Battles of the World* (New York: Macmillan, 1964).

30. Thus the words of Spector, *Eagle against the Sun,* 176, "The Americans still had a lot to learn," try to be a counter to the more triumphalist early histories of Midway (the earliest of which, in the US press, claimed that it was the USAAF's heavy bombers of the Southwest Pacific Command [SWPC] that had sunk the Japanese carriers.)

31. On the naval battles in particular, see again Symonds, *World War II at Sea,* chaps. 14–16, where he tries, interestingly, to weave the Malta, Torch, and Guadalcanal stories together; and Spector, chaps. 8–10 in *Eagle against the Sun,* who instead tries to interweave the New Guinea and Guadalcanal accounts. Morison, *US Naval Operations,* devotes the entire volume 5, *The Struggle for Guadalcanal* (370 pages!), to this campaign.

## Chapter 7

1. On the structures of Anglo-American strategic decision-making, varied official histories are invaluable. Especially good are M. Matloff and E. M. Snell, *Strategic Planning for Coalition Warfare, 1941–1942* (Washington, DC: Department of the Army, 1953), and its successor, by Matloff alone, *Strategic Planning for Coalition Warfare, 1943–1944* (Washington, DC: Department of the Army, 1959); M. E. Howard, "Grand Strategy," in *History of the Second World War,* vol. 4, *August 1942–September 1943* (London: HMSO, 1970); and, for a key figure in this process, A. Danchev, *Very Special Relationship: Field-Marshall Sir John Dill and the Anglo-American Alliance, 1941–44* (London: Brassey's Defence, 1986).

2. On the Mediterranean theater in 1943, see the two official naval histories; Roskill, chap. 6, "Sicily," and chap. 7, "Italy," in *War at Sea,* vol. 3, part 1; Morison, *US Naval Operations,* vol. 9, esp. 3–52 (this is a superb operational history for one that was composed so soon after the war); and Liddell Hart, chaps. 25–27 in *History of the Second World War.* There are pungent comments about the whole Mediterranean option in 1943 in Barnett, chaps. 20 and 22 in *Engage the Enemy.*

3. As a consequence, approximately 100,000 German and 130,000 Italian troops had surrendered by the end of the Tunisian campaign. "Tunisia Campaign," Wikipedia, last modified January 26, 2020, https://en.wikipedia.org/wiki/Tunisia_Campaign, gives a very fine summary. More fully, see the British official history, Playfair, *Mediterranean and Middle East,* passim; R. Atkinson, *An Army at Dawn: The War in North Africa, 1942–1943* (New York: Henry Holt, 2002); and Liddell Hart, chap. 25 in *History of the Second World War.* See also J. Ellis, chap. 6, "Tunisia and Italy," in *Brute Force: Allied Strategy and Tactics in the Second World War* (New York: Viking, 1990), on the sheer preponderance of Allied land, naval, and air forces in these campaigns.

4. To expand on the Allied invasions of Sicily, see Barnett, chap. 21 in *Engage the Enemy;* and Ellis, *Brute Force,* 306–19.

5. The Sicilian military campaign can be succinctly followed in Liddell Hart, chap. 26 in *History of the Second World War;* in much more detail in R. Atkinson, *The Day of Battle: The War in Sicily and Italy, 1943–1944,* vol. 2 (New York: Henry Holt, 2007); and in C. D'Este, *Bitter Victory: The Battle for Sicily, 1943* (New York: E. P. Dutton, 1988), passim. Symonds, chaps. 19–20 in *World War II at Sea,* is very good on the amphibious-warfare aspect.

6. On the somewhat different estimates for the Italian Navy by 1943, see Barnett, *En-*

*gage the Enemy,* 636; and Morison, *US Naval Operations,* 9:37–39. Since the main Italian fleet bases were under repeated aerial attacks from both American and British heavy bombers, which damaged a significant number of warships (e.g., on June 5 and again on the 24th, their bombs knocked the battleship *Roma* out of action), Morison's figures are more realistic.

7. For the Royal Navy's heavy warships deployed in this operation, see Barnett, *Engage the Enemy,* 638; and Roskill, *War at Sea,* vol. 3, part 1, 165.

8. And it had already decided to run no Russian convoys in the summer months (see below). Barnett, in *Engage the Enemy,* 662, is unnecessarily sarcastic about this buildup of British naval forces: "To deal with the Italian Navy in its present moral and professional decrepitude, the British Mediterranean Fleet alone would comprise 6 capital ships, 2 fleet carriers, 5 light carriers, 10 cruisers, 6 anti-aircraft ships and cruisers, 27 fleet destroyers, 44 escorts of all kinds, 24 submarines, 2 headquarters ships, 12 landing ships (infantry), and well over 300 ancillary vessels and craft from minesweepers and tugs to repair and depot ships."

9. For the Allied invasion of Italy and subsequent events, see, in addition to the above works by Atkinson (*The Day of Battle*) and Liddell Hart (*History of the Second World War*), "Allied Invasion of Italy," Wikipedia, last modified January 4, 2020, https://en.wikipedia.org/wiki/Allied_invasion_of_Italy, with a good bibliography.

10. On the surrender of the Italian fleet, see Barnett, *Engage the Enemy,* 669–70; Morison, *US Naval Operations;* and Roskill, *War at Sea,* vol. 3, part 1, 166–70. Admiral Cunningham's message to the Admiralty is in Barnett, 670.

11. Liddell Hart, "The Invasion of Italy—Capitulation and Check," chap. 27 in *History of the Second World War,* 473, is a good, succinct account, and the map on 448–49 is superb. See again Roskill, *War at Sea;* and Morison, *US Naval Operations,* for the amphibious operations and the naval bombardments in response to the beachhead crisis.

12. On the damage inflicted on HMS *Warspite* and on the Luftwaffe attacks more generally, see Morison, chaps. 13–14 and p. 296 in *US Naval Operations;* and Barnett, *Engage the Enemy,* 676–77.

13. On the altered importance and deadliness of Allied naval gunnery against land targets, see the interesting discourse in Morison, *US Naval Operations,* xi–xii. On Vietinghoff's report about the power of Allied naval bombardments, see Liddell Hart, *History of the Second World War,* 464.

14. This seems a fair comment even if, as shall be seen below, the German U-boat arm remained something of a menace until the end of the European war.

15. For general accounts of the Battle of the Atlantic, see the references in chapters 4–6. The respective UK and US official naval histories, although written very early (i.e., prior to the revelation of Ultra), are extremely thorough for all of the anti-U-boat campaigns in 1943, including the Gibraltar run/Bay of Biscay and the Arctic convoys. See Morison, *US Naval Operations,* vol. 10, *The Atlantic Battle Won,* passim; and Roskill, *War at Sea,* vols. 2 and 3, part 1.

16. Quoted in Roskill, *War at Sea,* 2:367.

17. There is an excellent summary in "Convoys HX 229/SC 122," Wikipedia, last modified January 25, 2020, en.wikipedia.org/wiki/Convoys_HX_229/SC_122, which includes the German propaganda quote. Also see M. Middlebrook, *Convoy: The Battle for Convoys SC.122 and HX.229* (London: Allen Lane, 1976); P. Kennedy, *Engineers of Victory,* 24–34; Winton, *Convoy,* 265–71 (with a map on 269); and J. Rohwer, *The Critical Convoy Battles of March 1943: The Battle for HX.229/SC122,* trans. Derek Masters (Annapolis, MD: US Naval Institute Press, 1977).

18. Rohwer, *Critical Convoy Battles,* has remarkable detail on what was carried in the sunken merchantmen.

19. P. Kennedy, *Engineers of Victory,* 34.

20. The Churchill quote is from Barnett, *Engage the Enemy,* 600 (and see 595–608 for his general discussion of "the grand crisis of the Battle of the Atlantic"). Pound's remark is in P. Kennedy, *Engineers of Victory,* 34.

21. See the impressive and almost hour-by-hour account in "Convoy ONS 5," Wikipedia, last modified October 17, 2019, https://en.wikipedia.org/wiki/Convoy_ONS_5, with tables and bibliography. This is the primary source for my appendix A. The older classic is R. Seth, *The Fiercest Battle: The Story of North Atlantic Convoy ONS 5, 22nd April–7th May 1943* (New York: Norton, 1961), and the escort commander's own account is in P. Gretton, *Convoy Escort Commander* (London: Cassell, 1964). The detailed coverage in D. Syrett, *The Defeat of the German U-boats: The Battle of the Atlantic* (Columbia: University of South Carolina Press, 1994), chap. 3, is outstanding.

22. The saga of the HMS *Pink* is told in P. Kennedy, *Engineers of Victory,* 46–47; and Syrett, *Defeat of the German U-boats,* 82–83.

23. The contacts were made in the dense fog of May 5–6, a fact Doenitz soon noticed but felt helpless to counter at this stage in the struggle. Details taken from "Convoy ONS 5," Wikipedia, last modified October 17, 2019, https://en.wikipedia.org/wiki/Convoy_ONS_5.

24. Roskill, *War at Sea,* 2:375.

25. This squadron, RAF Coastal Command 120, based in Iceland, was for quite a while into 1943 the only squadron flying very-long-range Liberators and, not surprisingly, was the highest-scoring squadron in the service. Had Coastal Command been given, say, six such squadrons at the time of the fabled but questionable "1,000-bomber" raids on the Third Reich, the tide in the Atlantic battle might have turned even earlier.

26. The many details on convoys SC-130 and ON-184 are in "World War 2 at Sea: Service Histories of 1,000 Royal and Dominion Navy Warships," National Museum Royal Navy, last modified May 3, 2013, http://www.naval-history.net/xGM-aContents.htm; Roskill, *War at Sea,* vol. 2; and Syrett, *Defeat of the German U-boats,* esp. 122–33 and 141–44.

27. On the defeat of the U-boats in this month, see K. Doenitz, *Memoirs: Ten Years and Twenty Days,* trans. R. H. Stevens and D. Woodward (Annapolis, MD: US Naval Institute Press, 1990), 341; see also T. Hughes and J. Costello, *The Battle of the Atlantic* (New York: Dial Press, 1977), 281; and M. Gannon, *Black May* (New York: HarperCollins, 1998).

28. These various Naval War Diary/Doenitz quotes are most easily found in Ellis, *Brute Force,* 155–56; P. Kennedy, *Engineers of Victory,* 51; and Barnett, *Engage the Enemy,* 611—each of these historians being struck by their brutal candor.

29. General Fritz Halder, in his penetrating 1941 *Kriegstagebuch* entries of the war on the Eastern Front, probably comes closest. Alanbrooke's private diaries are sometimes of the same quality. No Soviet general would have dared commit such candid comments (i.e., about the other side's many strengths and thus one's own side's weaknesses) to paper. Did any senior American admiral or general ever bother?

30. E. Mawdsley, "The Sea as a Decisive Factor in the Second World War" in *The Sea in History,* ed. Christian Buchet, vol. 4, *The Modern World,* ed. N. A. M. Rodger (Woodbridge, UK: Boydell Press, 2017), 538–39. This is otherwise a very judicious survey. And see, more generally, A. J. Levine, "Was World War II a Near-Run Thing?," in *World War II,* ed. L. E. Lee (Westport, CT: Greenwood Press, 1999), calling the March 1943 cri-

sis "a temporary alarm." Syrett's detailed study, *Defeat of the German U-boats,* is a very healthy corrective here.

31. Ellis, *Brute Force,* 161; Blair, *Hitler's U-boat War,* vol. 2.

32. Roskill, *War at Sea,* 2:379 (with graph of merchant-ship sinkings and output), puts it nicely in another way: "Had this victory of production not been won, the sacrifices of the escorting ships and aircraft, and of the merchant seamen, were all bound to have been in vain."

33. P. Kennedy, *Engineers of Victory,* 113–18, on the "unsustainable losses" of the 8th USAAF's bomber squadrons by October 1943.

34. E. Tufte, *The Visual Display of Quantitative Information* (Cheshire, CT: Graphics Press, 1983), passim.

35. For the battles of the second half of 1943 around the convoys (including observations on the U-boats' failed use of heavier antiaircraft guns and the neutralization of their Zaunkoenig, or "Gnat," homing torpedoes), see again Roskill, chap. 2 in *War at Sea;* Syrett, chap. 6 in *Defeat of the German U-boats;* and Winton, chap. 19 in *Convoy.*

36. This campaign is covered in Morison, chaps. 8 and 10 in *US Naval Operations,* vol. 10 (with a fine map of the continuous air coverage of Convoy UGS-10 from Norfolk, Virginia, to Casablanca on pp. 114–15); and, impressively, in Syrett, chap. 5 in *Defeat of the German U-boats.* See also the rather triumphalist J. G. Barlow, "The Navy's Escort Carrier Offensive," *Naval History Magazine,* November 2013, https://www.usni.org/magazines/naval-history-magazine/2013/november/navys-escort-carrier-offensive.

37. D. Baker, "American Escort Carrier Development: The Atlantic CVEs," accessed February 7, 2020, http://uboat.net/allies/ships/cve_development.htm; this article includes Admiral Ingersoll's assertion that "close-in air support (by carriers) of central transatlantic convoys was a waste of time." No Royal Navy commander of the intensely fought battles on the North Atlantic or Gibraltar convoy routes would have concurred. Morison, *US Naval Operations,* 10:111 and 117, recounts Ingersoll's "free roaming" decision but without offering his own judgment.

38. "UG Convoys," Wikipedia, last modified October 14, 2019, https://en.wikipedia.org/wiki/UG_convoys#Slow_eastbound_convoys_designated_UGS; and Syrett, *Defeat of the German U-boats,* 179, who actually counts eight U-boat tankers sunk. It hardly needs saying that this significantly restricted U-boat operations going further afield (i.e., to the South Atlantic) and even the boats pulling southward in search of fuel during the October–November North Atlantic battles.

39. Nicely put in Syrett's conclusion to *Defeat of the German U-boats,* 265; and in Morison, "General Conclusions about 1943," in *US Naval Operations,* 10:144–48.

40. For the battles along the UK–Gibraltar routes, see again Roskill, chap. 2 in *War at Sea;* and fine details in Syrett, chap. 7, "The Gibraltar Routes," in *Defeat of the German U-boats.*

41. "Battle of the Bay of Biscay," Wikipedia, last modified January 2, 2020, https://en.wikipedia.org/wiki/Battle_of_the_Bay_of_Biscay, passim; Roskill, *War at Sea,* 2:74–75; and V. P. O'Hara, *The German Fleet at War, 1939–1945* (Annapolis, MD: US Naval Institute Press, 2004), 277–82.

42. "Russian Convoys 1941–45," last modified September 7, 2011, http://www.naval-history.net/WW2CampaignsRussianConvoys.htm; and, generally, R. Woodman, *The Arctic Convoys, 1941–1945* (London: John Murray, 1994). Each has a little on the 1943 convoys, generally explaining why they were so few and uneventful. Roskill, *War at Sea,* vols. 2 and 3, part 1, have much detail in the pertinent "Home Waters and the Arctic" chapters.

43. In fact, it is estimated that by the end of the war a full 50 percent of the munitions supplied by the West to the USSR went via Siberia, around 27 percent via the Persian Corridor, and the remaining 23 percent via the Arctic convoys. All of this commerce, obviously, was seaborne for part of the way and thus depended on Allied naval mastery. Details about Lend-Lease to Russia, and trade via the Persian Corridor and the Siberian route, are in "Lend-Lease," Wikipedia, last modified January 26, 2020, https://en.wikipedia.org/wiki/Lend-Lease.

44. Apart from the useful "Battle of the North Cape," Wikipedia, last modified January 7, 2020, https://en.wikipedia.org/wiki/Battle_of_the_North_Cape, there is A. Konstam, *The Battle of the North Cape: The Death Ride of the* Scharnhorst, *1943* (London: Pen and Sword, 2011); A. J. Watts, *The Loss of the* Scharnhorst (Shepperton, UK: Allan, 1970); Roskill, *War at Sea,* vol. 3, part 1, 80–89 (with a fine map of the action); and many others.

45. For great detail about the Pacific War in 1943, see the two pertinent volumes in Morison's official history, *US Naval Operations,* vol. 6, *Breaking the Bismarck's Barrier,* and vol. 7, *Aleutians, Gilberts, and Marshalls.* There are punchy accounts in Spector, chaps. 11–12 in *Eagle against the Sun;* and in C. G. Reynolds, chaps. 5–6 in *Fast Carriers.* For a recent, brief account, see Symonds, chaps. 21–22 in *World War II at Sea.*

46. Liddell Hart, *History of the Second World War,* 498–99; and a summary in P. Kennedy, *Engineers of Victory,* 292.

47. See Morison, *US Naval Operations,* 7:22–36, for the Battle of the Komandorski Islands.

48. Again, in much detail, Morison, *US Naval Operations,* vol. 7, part 1. ("Mildly ridiculous" is on p. 61 of an overelaborate text.) Symonds, *World War II at Sea,* gives it a mere page, 471.

49. For this story of the doctrinal and personnel quarrels, lasting from 1942 until 1944, see C. G. Reynolds, chaps. 4–6 in *Fast Carriers.* (Reynolds leaves no doubt as to his own pro-carrier stance in this matter.) For MacArthur's opposition and determination to drive toward the Philippines, see Symonds, *World War II at Sea,* 472.

50. C. G. Reynolds, *Fast Carriers,* 59.

51. These small operations are covered in C. G. Reynolds, *Fast Carriers,* 80–86; and (almost apologetically, or so it reads) in Morison, *US Naval Operations,* 7:92–95.

52. The Marine Corps's agony at Tarawa has many narrators, of which the earliest were in Morison, *US Naval Operations,* 7:146–86, with full statistics and remarkable photographs; and in the chapters in J. A. Isley and P. A. Crowl, *The U.S. Marines and Amphibious War: Its Theory, and Its Practice in the Pacific* (Princeton, NJ: Princeton University Press, 1951). Even more detail is offered in P. A. Crowl and E. G. Love, *Seizure of the Gilberts and Marshalls* (Washington, DC: Department of the Army, 1955). See Spector, *Eagle against the Sun,* also tart.

53. For details of this American armada, see P. Kennedy, *Engineers of Victory,* 318–19; and Morison, appendix 2 in *US Naval Operations,* vol. 7. The sheer heft of the US forces assembled for the Gilberts operation is not specifically covered in Ellis, *Brute Force,* although much of his chapter 10 is devoted to the theme of the growing American preponderance.

54. C. G. Reynolds, *Fast Carriers,* 103, 119. (Interestingly, there is nothing about these internal quarrels in Morison.)

55. See Morison, *US Naval Operations,* vol. 6, parts 2–4; "Operation Cartwheel," Wikipedia, last modified December 16, 2019, https://en.wikipedia.org/wiki/Operation_Cartwheel, details the "thirteen subsidiary operations." The official US Army volume is this very thorough work: J. Miller, *Cartwheel: The Reduction of Rabaul* (Washington, DC: Department of the Army, 1959).

56. And with the express approval of Halsey, Nimitz, and Roosevelt.

57. Morison, *US Naval Operations*, 6:54–65, for "Battle of the Bismarck Sea," and 6:117–29, for "Yamamoto's Last Offensive." There exist a large number of specialists and often popular articles and movie reconstructions on the death of Admiral Yamamoto, which was given the formal title of Operation Vengeance.

58. The HMS *Victorious*'s radio call sign was "USS *Robin*," so there are lots of articles about the mysterious American carrier of that name operating in the Pacific in 1943. See "USS *Robin*," Armoured Carriers, accessed August 21, 2017, www.armouredcarriers.com /uss-robin-hms-victorious; and Roskill, *War at Sea*, 2:415–16.

59. The clobbering of Rabaul in November 1943 is covered by C. G. Reynolds, *Fast Carriers*, 104; and Morison, *US Naval Operations*, 6:323–36.

60. E. B. Potter, ed., *Sea Power: A Naval History*, 2nd ed. (Annapolis, MD: US Naval Institute Press, 1981), 314, on the final destroyer battles; and Morison, *US Naval Operations*, vol. 6, part 3.

61. The story of the delayed effectiveness of American submarines against Japan is summarized well in Potter, chap. 29, "Submarines in the Pacific War," in *Sea Power*. There is much more detail of these early difficulties in Morison, *US Naval Operations*, 6:66–85 (p. 84 for the January 1944 oil tanker remark). Symonds does not really begin his analysis of US submarine operations until 1944, *World War II at Sea*, 590.

62. The standard work in English translation is M. Hashimoto, *Sunk: The Story of the Japanese Submarine Fleet, 1941–1945* (New York: Henry Holt, 1954); but see Morison, *US Naval Operations*, 7:138, on the more successful Japanese submarine attacks during the Gilberts operations.

## Chapter 8

1. The sixth carrier, the USS *Enterprise*, was undergoing extensive repairs and modernization back in the United States throughout 1943, and the USS *Ranger* (technically the seventh carrier) was deemed too small for Pacific operations and was thus kept for Atlantic/North African operations.

2. See the still-standard work C. G. Reynolds, *Fast Carriers;* a useful summary in "*Essex*-Class Aircraft Carrier," Wikipedia, last modified January 16, 2020, https://en.wiki pedia.org/wiki/Essex-class_aircraft_carrier, passim.; plus N. Friedman, *U.S. Aircraft Carriers: An Illustrated Design History* (Annapolis, MD: US Naval Institute Press, 1983).

3. Details on the *Independence*-class light fleet carriers are in many standard sources, like *Jane's Fighting Ships*, and Friedman, *U.S. Aircraft Carriers*. Many of the naval classes mentioned here have summary statistics in "US Navy in Late 1941," WW2 Weapons, December 5, 2019, https://ww2-weapons.com/us-navy-in-late-1941.

4. "Escort Carrier," Wikipedia, last modified January 6, 2020, https://en.wikipedia .org/wiki/Escort_carrier; and for a lively read, A. Adcock, *Escort Carriers in Action* (Carrollton, TX: Squadron/Signal, 1996).

5. Standard works here are Dull, *Battle History of the Imperial Japanese Navy;* and Stille, *Imperial Japanese Navy*. The Japanese attempts to build or convert carriers after their Midway disaster and their failure to do very much is discussed in Ellis, *Brute Force*, 463 and many tables.

6. And this inexplicable delay affected not just the Japanese carriers, since the same was true of the vitally important class of destroyer escorts (DDEs)—Japan constructed far too few of those (cf. the Royal Navy) until late in the war, when it ran out of construction materials.

7. There are interesting comments on the travails of the Fleet Air Arm in C. G. Reynolds, *Fast Carriers*, 2–4 and chap. 9. But by 1945 it had 57 (chiefly escort) carriers, 72,000 men, and 3,400 planes, almost all of its *Casablanca*-class escort carriers having been built at a giant new Kaiser yard in Vancouver, Washington, as detailed in "*Casablanca*-Class Escort Carrier," Wikipedia, last modified January 21, 2020, https://en.wikipedia.org/wiki/Casablanca-class_escort_carrier.

8. On US battleships, the simplest reference may be "List of Battleships of the United States," Wikipedia, accessed August 17, 2018, https://en.wikipedia.org/wiki/List_of_battleships_of_the_United_States; and lots of data in the annual *Jane's Fighting Ships*.

9. They would mount no fewer than twelve 16-inch guns and enjoy thicker armor protection than anything known—except that their speed would drop again from 33 to maybe 28 knots, and they would be too broad to traverse the Panama Canal. This was not a sensible trade-off.

10. "*Montana*-Class Battleships," Wikipedia, last modified January 15, 2020, https://en.wikipedia.org/wiki/Montana-class_battleship; and on the steady replacement of the battleship by the carrier as the core element in a new US Navy, see again C. G. Reynolds, *Fast Carriers*, 39 and passim.

11. And three other "old ladies"—the World War I battleships USSs *Nevada, New York,* and *Arkansas*—formed a valuable part of the Western Naval Task Force that gave support to the US landing forces on D-Day.

12. For the 1945 bombardment of Japan, see Morison, chap. 10, "The War in the Pacific," in *US Naval Operations,* vol. 14.

13. "Cruiser Descriptions," WW2Pacific, last modified January 4, 2008, http://ww2pacific.com/ships2.html#ca. The giant cruisers, the *Alaska*-class, were to displace 27,500 tons and carry nine 12-inch guns.

14. The sources—whether in book form from the many warship publishers or in newer electronic-data form, on destroyers and the many other shop and aircraft types covered in this chapter—are very frequently loaded with technical data for enthusiasts, but many are useful, as, for example, "*Fletcher* Class," Destroyer History Foundation, accessed February 7, 2020, https://destroyerhistory.org/fletcherclass, for the most prolific and successful of the American destroyers in World War II.

15. "Builders: Seattle-Tacoma," Destroyer History Foundation, accessed February 7, 2020, https://destroyerhistory.org/destroyers/seatac; and "Builders: Bath Iron Works," Destroyer History Foundation, accessed February 7, 2020, https://destroyerhistory.org/destroyers/bath.

16. "Allied Submarines in the Pacific War," Wikipedia, last modified November 11, 2019, https://en.wikipedia.org/wiki/Allied_submarines_in_the_Pacific_War, maintains excellent data.

17. C. G. Reynolds, *Fast Carriers,* 128–30.

18. For the origin and performance of the Seabees, see P. Kennedy, *Engineers of Victory,* 328–33.

19. For use of this imagery about the turning tides of the war, see the section and chapter titles in Liddell Hart, *History of the Second World War;* and of course the first volume of Alanbrooke's war diaries, *The Turn of the Tide* (London: Reprint Society, 1957).

20. "LCVP (United States)," Wikipedia, last modified December 29, 2019, https://en.wikipedia.org/wiki/LCVP_(United_States), has some basic statistics (LCVP is, again, Landing Craft, Vehicle, Personnel).

21. The Higgins boats story is part of J. E. Strahan, *Andrew Jackson Higgins and the Boats That Won World War II* (Baton Rouge: Louisiana State University Press, 1994);

and for descriptions, "Research Starters: Higgins Boats," National WWII Museum, New Orleans, accessed February 7, 2020, http://www.nationalww2museum.org/students -teachers/student-resources/research-starters/research-starters-higgins-boats.

22. The irony was that it was the Japanese Army's use of nimble flat-bottomed boats in their riverine campaigns in China in 1937 that had given Marine observers the idea and basic design for this amphibious war craft.

23. Quoted from R. Coram, "The Bridge to the Beach," November–December 2010, https://www.historynet.com/the-bridge-to-the-beach.htm.

24. "US Navy Personnel in World War II: Service and Casualty Statistics," Naval History and Heritage Command, last modified February 21, 2017, https://www.history.navy .mil/research/library/online-reading-room/title-list-alphabetically/u/us-navy-personnel -in-world-war-ii-service-and-casualty-statistics.html.

25. Figures and quote from Liddell Hart, *History of the Second World War,* 618.

26. Ellis, *Brute Force,* 479ff. Ellis's remarkable book is again worth a special mention here. It is written with a passionate argument that, in the winning of World War II, the victorious Allies used an overwhelming—indeed, absurd—overkill of force in every regard. Ellis is also the author of that earlier work, *Cassino, the Hollow Victory: The Battle for Rome, January–June 1944* (New York: McGraw Hill, 1984), from which much of his passion derives. To prove his point, Ellis assembles in *Brute Force* a huge array of statistical data, especially tables, on wartime production, raw materials, force sizes, and ratios; see especially the sixty-three tables in the text and statistical appendices, which were of great use to this chapter of mine in particular.

27. "Escort Carrier," Wikipedia, last modified January 6, 2020, https://en.wikipedia .org/wiki/Escort_carrier, has basic details of the 151 carriers built during the war by the United States, of which 122 were CVEs.

28. K. Hickman, "World War II: The Liberty Ship Program," last modified July 21, 2019, http://www.thoughtco.com/the-liberty-ship-program-2361030; and see also "Kaiser Shipyards," Wikipedia, last modified October 26, 2019, https://en.wikipedia.org/wiki /Kaiser_Shipyards. Henry Kaiser, among other US businessmen, is adulated in A. Herman, *Freedom's Forge: How American Business Produced the Victory in World War II* (New York: Random House, 2012).

29. On the 1943 Anglo-American debate about the allocation of landing craft (i.e., which theaters would get priority for operations in the year to follow), see, briefly, Liddell Hart, *History of the Second World War.*

30. Basic details on the US Maritime Commission's work and achievements are in F. C. Lane, *Ships for Victory: A History of Shipbuilding under the U.S. Maritime Commission in World War II* (Baltimore: Johns Hopkins University Press, 1950); see also "United States Maritime Commission," Wikipedia, last modified January 2, 2020, https://en.wiki pedia.org/wiki/United_States_Maritime_Commission, passim. Ellis, *Brute Force,* 161 and 468–73, makes the Japanese comparison.

31. There is no outstanding general work on World War II in the air, but R. J. Overy, *The Air War, 1939–1945* (New York: Stein and Day, 1980), is a trove of invaluable information and statistical tables.

32. See J. S. Underwood, *The Wings of Democracy: The Influence of Air Power on the Roosevelt Administration, 1933–1941* (College Station: Texas A&M University Press, 1991); and more generally, M. Sherry, *The Rise of American Air Power: The Creation of Armageddon* (New Haven, CT: Yale University Press, 1987).

33. Ellis, *Brute Force,* 477, is almost withering in his comments about the incredible disproportionality of the two sides' forces from 1943 onward.

34. N. Goyer, "Pratt & Whitney, the Engine That Won World War II," Aircraft MarketPlace, July 30, 2009, http://www.acmp.com/blog/pratt-whitney-the-engine-that -won-world-war-ii.html, is full of detail.

35. "Grumman F6F Hellcat," Wikipedia, last modified January 13, 2020, https://en .wikipedia.org/wiki/Grumman_F6F_Hellcat, is an excellent summary, with a bibliography. Ellis, *Brute Force,* 489, covers the deficiencies among the Japanese aircrews by the second half of the war.

36. Liddell Hart, *History of the Second World War,* 23.

37. The sketch in appendix B seeks to capture this progression. "Alcoa, Tennessee," Wikipedia, last modified January 25, 2020, en.wikipedia.org/wiki/Alcoa_Tennessee, records a 600 percent rise in aluminum output as the war progressed; company publicity photos proudly show off rows of glistening B-29 bombers. Appendix B elaborates Alcoa's place in the hypothetical "From Aluminum Mountain to Marianas Turkey Shoot."

38. Ellis, *Brute Force,* table 49.

39. Ibid., tables 44 and 46.

40. P. Kennedy, *Rise and Fall of the Great Powers,* 129; and, more generally, J. M. Sherwig, *Guineas and Gunpowder: British Foreign Aid in the Wars with France, 1793–1815* (Cambridge, MA: Harvard University Press, 1969).

41. A. S. Milward, "Estimated Value of United States War Programme by Major Categories, 1940–1945," in *War, Economy, and Society,* 64.

42. And a B-24 Liberator slightly more, at $300,000 current cost; in the course of the war, and with ever more production sites opened, the unit costs for the more numerous items (not battleships!) tended to come down.

43. It also happened, to a lesser degree, in neighboring Canada, and for the same reasons: freedom from wartime damage, huge government spending stimulus, newer armaments industries, and favorable economic feedback loops.

44. "Historical Debt Outstanding—Annual 1900–1949," Treasury Direct, last modified May 5, 2013, https://www.treasurydirect.gov/govt/reports/pd/histdebt/histdebt_hist 03.htm.

45. "Had to be paid for," and for two critical reasons: first, the government needed those tax dollars, but second, to avoid giving the impression that the United States was simply printing its way out of the war, which would raise images of profligate Bourbon regimes of an earlier era.

46. R. A. Wilson, "Personal Exemptions and Individual Income Tax Rates 1913–2002," Internal Revenue Service, accessed February 20, 2020, https://www.irs.gov/pub /irs-soi/02inpetr.pdf.

47. For the shrinking US unemployment rate, see P. Jenkins, *A History of the United States,* 4th ed. (New York: Palgrave Macmillan, 2012), 208.

48. For US fiscal policy, see Rockoff, "From Ploughshares to Swords"; and for the more general political aspects, J. M. Blum, *V Was for Victory: Politics and American Culture During World War II* (New York: Harcourt Brace Jovanovich, 1976).

49. M. Harrison, *The Economics of World War II: Six Great Powers in International Comparison.* (Cambridge, UK: Cambridge University Press, 1998), 21.

50. See the tables at Harrison, *Economics of World War II,* 155 and 93.

51. See the very fine eighteen-page summary in "Lend-Lease," Wikipedia, last modified January 26, 2020, https://en.wikipedia.org/wiki/Lend-Lease, with extensive bibliography. There's far less literature on Lend-Lease as an overall policy, as compared with works on its application to the United Kingdom (very large) and to the USSR (large); see

next two notes. This particular article also covers Canadian aid to Allies, including the United States.

52. A. L. Weeks, *Russia's Life-Saver: Lend-Lease Aid to the U.S.S.R. in World War II* (Lanham, MD: Lexington Books, 2004). Many of the other works are on early Cold War diplomacy or on how little (or much) the Red Army gained from Lend-Lease.

53. A. P. Dobson, *U.S. Wartime Aid to Britain, 1940–1946* (London: Croom Helm, 1986), passim. Much of this literature is on the Anglo-American shift of power, as in R. B. Woods, *A Changing of the Guard: Anglo-American Relations, 1941–1946* (Chapel Hill: University of North Carolina Press, 1990), and not on the use or applicability of the leased materials themselves.

54. Readers of this book will notice reference from time to time of British capital ships—HMS *Warspite*, HMS *Victorious*, and HMS *Queen Elizabeth*—going off to US yards for serious repair and enhancement; see again Williamson, chap. 5, n. 19, in "Industrial-Grade Generosity."

55. Iconoclasts like Correlli Barnett argue that Britain no longer fought the war as a truly independent Great Power because it was on "life support" from its calculating American cousin. See C. Barnett, *The Audit of War: The Illusion and Reality of Britain as a Great Nation* (London: Macmillan, 1986), which builds on the closing ideas of *The Collapse of British Power*. The present author is less interested in that quarrel than in understanding how much help Britain was getting in, say, winning the Battle of the Atlantic in mid-1943. Almost all of the naval escorts were its own ships, or Canada's, unless it was transferred World War I US Navy older destroyers; but a very large number of Coastal Command's aircraft (B-24s, Catalinas, Hudsons, and Mitchells) were American, and almost all escort carriers (apart from six) were built in the United States. Many of the miniature radar sets (cavity magnetrons)—invented by the British, like so many other of the inventions in the war against the U-boats—were produced by Bell Labs. All the Liberty ships were built in Kaiser and other American yards, but the British built many other merchantmen. Then presumably all the contents of the merchant ships, like flour, timber, oil, and trucks, were American built and grown or produced, and after 1941 paid for under Lend-Lease. Accounting for the extent of US economic support and its impact is difficult.

56. Churchill's quote, from his own memoirs, is frequently cited. See, for ease here, P. Kennedy, *Rise and Fall of the Great Powers,* 347.

57. See table 3 in Harrison, *Economics of World War II,* 88.

58. A. de Tocqueville, *Democracy in America,* ed. J. P. Mayer, trans. G. Lawrence (Garden City, NY: Anchor Books, 1969).

59. For easy reference, see the first table of "Demographic History of the United States," Wikipedia, last modified January 16, 2020, https://en.wikipedia.org/wiki/Demographic_history_of_the_United_States.

60. Reproduced from tables 15 and 18 of P. Kennedy, *Rise and Fall of the Great Powers,* 200 and 202, respectively.

61. W. W. Rostow, *The World Economy: History & Prospect* (Austin: University of Texas Press, 1978), 210.

62. I have developed the argument about the United States itself being hurt the *most* (and by its own bad policies) by the 1930s Depression in P. Kennedy, *Rise and Fall of the Great Powers,* 327–31. It seems to me worth reemphasizing that point here, since there is still a tendency in World War II histories of not recognizing in what a condition of comparative *under*capacity the giant US economy was at this time.

## Chapter 9

1. See table 35 in P. Kennedy, *Rise and Fall of the Great Powers,* 355; and the overall argument of Ellis, *Brute Force.*

2. See the chapter titles in Liddell Hart, *History of the Second World War,* such as chap. 28 ("The German Ebb in Russia") and chap. 29 ("The Japanese Ebb in the Pacific").

3. Morison, *US Naval Operations,* vol. 8, *New Guinea and the Marianas, March 1944–August 1944,* 40–41. (It is notable that Symonds's otherwise fine *World War II at Sea* has nothing on these events in the Southwest Pacific in 1944.)

4. For Admiral King's hostility, see G. E. Baer, *One Hundred Years of Sea Power: The U.S. Navy, 1890–1990* (Stanford, CA: Stanford University Press, 1994), 243. Morison is more favorable in *US Naval Operations,* vol. 8, part 3.

5. Though brief and a bit outdated, Morison's small book *Strategy and Compromise* (Boston: Little, Brown, 1958), 83, is still good here; as is Liddell Hart, chap. 29 in *History of the Second World War.*

6. The Marshalls invasion is formally covered in Morison, *US Naval Operations,* vol. 7, *Aleutians, Gilberts and Marshalls, June 1942–April 1944,* part 3; and more briefly in Symonds, *World War II at Sea,* 509–13.

7. For the great blows against Truk, see especially the article "Operation Hailstone," Wikipedia, last modified January 27, 2020, https://en.wikipedia.org/wiki/Operation _Hailstone, with use of many action reports; and Morison, *US Naval Operations,* 7:315, with general discussion about the coming of fast-carrier airpower. (The reader will note in this chapter the frequent reference to Morison's official naval histories and to Wikipedia corroborating battle-specific articles as basic sources.)

8. The Battle of the Philippine Sea is summarized (with map) in Symonds, *World War II at Sea,* 543; and Morison, chaps. 14–16 in *US Naval Operations,* vol. 8.

9. There is a vast popular literature available; try D. H. Lippmann, "The Great Marianas Turkey Shoot," Warfare History Network, November 16, 2016, http://warfarehistory network.com/2016/11/16/the-great-marianas-turkey-shoot; as well as Morison, chap. 15 in *US Naval Operations,* vol. 8; and including map, Symonds, *World War II at Sea,* 543–53.

10. For the carrier critics of Spruance, see C. G. Reynolds, *Fast Carriers,* 190.

11. C. G. Reynolds, *Fast Carriers;* and, more delicately, Symonds, *World War II at Sea,* 552.

12. Morison's *US Naval Operations,* vol. 12, *Leyte, June 1944–January 1945,* is exhaustive, but there is a very smart (as usual) recent article, "Battle of Leyte Gulf," Wikipedia, last modified February 6, 2020, https://en.wikipedia.org/wiki/Battle_of_Leyte_Gulf.

13. Morison, *US Naval Operations,* vol. 12 (also using Japanese interviews) is fine here; and M. N. Vego, *The Battle for Leyte, 1944: Allied and Japanese Plans, Preparations, and Execution* (Annapolis, MD: US Naval Institute Press, 2006).

14. Leyte Gulf even merits inclusion in the updated edition of J. F. C. Fuller, *The Decisive Battles of the Western World and Their Influence upon History,* vol. 2 (London: Eyre and Spottiswoode, 1965).

15. For full detail, A. Yoshimura, *Battleship* Musashi: *The Making and Sinking of the World's Biggest Battleship* (Tokyo: Kodansha International, 1999); and a useful summary in "Japanese Battleship *Musashi,*" Wikipedia, last modified January 23, 2020, https://en .wikipedia.org/wiki/Japanese_battleship_Musashi.

16. "Japanese Aircraft Carrier *Zuikaku,*" Wikipedia, last modified January 22, 2020, https://en.wikipedia.org/wiki/Japanese_aircraft_carrier_Zuikaku (and a large bibliography on the Japanese Naval Air Service in general).

17. For the first Kamikaze attacks at Leyte, see Morison, *US Naval Operations,* 12:300.

18. See, for example, the praise of Oldendorf's "perfect trap" in Potter, *Sea Power,* 344–45.

19. The *Hardhead,* constantly upgraded with new technologies, was still on active service during the Cuban Missile Crisis! Later sold to and employed by the Greek Navy, it was not finally scrapped until 1993, a full fifty years after its launching. Potter, *Sea Power,* 335; and C. Blair, *Silent Victory: The U.S. Submarine War against Japan,* vol. 2 (Philadelphia: Lippincott, 1975), which gives enormous detail.

20. See "USS *Hardhead* (SS-365)," Wikipedia, last modified May 16, 2019, https://en.wikipedia.org/wiki/USS_Hardhead_(SS-365). This privately owned shipyard on Lake Michigan (which also turned to building landing ships for amphibious operations) consistently surprised the navy by fulfilling contracts in a much shorter time (and with a much lower cost) than was stipulated.

21. In most detail, again, Blair, *Silent Victory,* passim; see also Spector, *Eagle against the Sun,* 485; and a useful piece, "Allied Submarines in the Pacific War," Wikipedia, accessed August 22, 2018, with clear statistical tables.

22. See the lively account of the sinking of the *Shinano* in Symonds, *World War II at Sea,* 597–600; more details are found in the article "Japanese Aircraft Carrier *Shinano,*" Wikipedia, last modified December 23, 2019, https://en.wikipedia.org/wiki/Japanese_aircraft_carrier_Shinano.

23. See Symonds, *World War II at Sea,* 594, for these statistics.

24. See P. Kennedy, chap. 2, "How to Win Command of the Air," in *Engineers of Victory.*

25. See chart 10.

26. "U-boat Losses by Cause," last modified February 6, 2002, https://uboat.net/fates/losses/cause.htm, provides a brief list.

27. Morison's official *US Naval Operations,* 11:51, states that by July 1943 there were 238,000 US troops in England, by January 1944 there were 937,000, and by May 1944 there were 1,526,000.

28. There is great detail in the electronic source "Convoy HX 300," Wikipedia, last modified February 25, 2019, https://en.wikipedia.org/wiki/Convoy_HX_300; plus very brief coverage in Winton, *Convoy,* 307 (wrapping up his convoys story absurdly fast), and, interestingly, nothing in Roskill, *War at Sea.* The US armies in Europe would, from this time on, be supplied directly into Cherbourg and Brest.

29. A thorough institutional history in W. F. Craven and J. L. Cate, *The Army Air Forces in World War II,* vol. 7, *Services around the World* (Washington, DC: Office of Air Force History, 1983).

30. There is now a wonderful, vibrant literature on the US air forces (and airmen and airwomen) in Britain during the war; among them, see P. Kaplan and R. A. Smith, *One Last Look: A Sentimental Journey to the Eighth Air Force Heavy Bomber Bases of World War II in England* (New York: Abbeville Press, 1983), which captures how numerous they were; and see much more in various volumes of Craven and Cate, *Army Air Force.*

31. Eisenhower letter taken from David Eisenhower, *Eisenhower at War 1943–1945* (New York: Random House, 1986), 252.

32. There's a huge, breathless later email discussion about the Allies not having or needing carriers here: an easy summary is in T. Benbow, "Absent Friends? British Naval Aviation at D-Day," *Defence-in-Depth,* September 29, 2017, http://defenceindepth.co/2017/09/29/absent-friends-british-naval-aviation-and-d-day/.

33. O'Brien, *How the War Was Won;* and see the related, larger debate in "Did

the Soviet Union Win the War?," History Extra, last modified August 9, 2008, www
.historyextra.com/second-world-war/did-the-soviet-union-win-the-war.

34. A. Bryant, *Triumph in the West: A History of the War Years Based on the Diaries
of Field-Marshal Lord Alanbrooke, Chief of the Imperial General Staff* (Garden City, NY:
Doubleday, 1959).

35. Judiciously, as ever, M. E. Howard, *The Mediterranean Strategy in the Second
World War* (New York: Praeger, 1968).

36. "Convoy JW 58," Wikipedia, last modified March 19, 2018, https://en.wikipedia
.org/wiki/Convoy_JW_58, gives great detail; and almost jubilantly, Roskill, *War at Sea,*
vol. 3, part 1, 272–73.

37. As in "List of Allied Attacks on the German Battleship *Tirpitz*," Wikipedia, last
modified October 28, 2019, https://en.wikipedia.org/wiki/List_of_Allied_attacks_on
_the_German_battleship_Tirpitz, such attacks starting when it was being constructed in
Wilhelmshaven back in 1940; Roskill, *War at Sea,* 3:170–71. The successful Fleet Air Arm
attack was Operation Tungsten (April 1944) and the dismal one was Operation Good-
wood (three attacks, August 1944), leading to the decision to hand the sinking of the *Tirpitz* to RAF Bomber Command.

38. Of the vast literature, P. Bishop, *Target* Tirpitz: *X-craft, Agents, Dambusters; The
Epic Quest to Destroy Hitler's Mightiest Warship* (London: Harper Press, 2012); J. Sweet-
man, Tirpitz: *Hunting the Beast; Air Attacks on the German Battleship 1940–44* (Annap-
olis, MD: US Naval Institute Press, 2000); L. Kennedy, *The Death of the* Tirpitz (Boston:
Little, Brown, 1979); and P. M. Kennedy, "Sinking of the *Tirpitz,*" *Purnell's History of the
Second World War* 5, no. 15.

39. See L. Clark's *Anzio: Italy and the Battle for Rome, 1944* (New York: Atlantic
Monthly Press, 2006); the very extensive "Battle of Anzio," Wikipedia, last modified January 28, 2020, https://en.wikipedia.org/wiki/Battle_of_Anzio, with fine maps as usual;
Morison, *US Naval Operations,* vol. 9, *Sicily, Salerno, Anzio, January 1943–June 1944,*
part 4; and the briefer account in Roskill, chap. 12 in *The War at Sea,* vol. 3, part 1. Barnett, *Engage the Enemy,* 686, has by this stage little time for these (in his view) distract-
ing operations.

40. On Anzio and the German counterattack, see again Morison, *US Naval Operations,* 9:354; and Liddell Hart, *History of the Second World War,* 523–31. On Clark, and Allied and German generalship throughout, see the second volume of Atkinson's brilliant
trilogy, *The Day of Battle.*

41. Morison, *US Naval Operations,* vol. 11, part 2, "The Invasion of France"; but the
Anvil operation is also summarized in "Operation Harpoon (1942)," Wikipedia, last
modified November 1, 2019, https://en.wikipedia.org/wiki/Operation_Harpoon_(1942),
with good maps and bibliography.

42. "Mediterranean U-boat Campaign (World War II)," Wikipedia, last modified
November 13, 2019, https://en.wikipedia.org/wiki/Mediterranean_U-boat_Campaign
_(World_War_II); and Blair, *Hitler's U-boat War,* vol. 2, final chapters, generally on the
fading of the German submarine threats in all the outer oceans.

## Chapter 10

1. For what follows generally, see Roskill, *War at Sea,* vol. 3, part 2; Winton, *Convoy,* although appropriately it peters out swiftly after its 1943–44 narratives; Barnett,
chaps. 24–27 in *Engage the Enemy;* and more specifically, Blair, *Silent Victory.*

2. J. Dimbleby, *The Battle of the Atlantic: How the Allies Won the War* (New York: Oxford University Press, 2016), 449.

3. The Admiralty's alarm of January 1945 is detailed in Roskill, *War at Sea,* 3:289–90; this great source also details, on 290–302, the still-considerable U-boat activity in both British and Canadian waters until the end of the war, but those attacks never became as frightening as Cunningham had suggested.

4. The various statistics on the numbers of U-boats existing and surrendered at the end of the war, the U-boat losses, and the Allied merchant-ship and warship losses come from Roskill, *War at Sea,* 3:304–6; and Liddell Hart, *History of the Second World War,* 394.

5. The size of the Royal Navy by 1945 is a fluctuating figure, since newer warships were joining the fleet while older ones were being mothballed and scrapped, but Roskill, appendix S, "Strength of the Navies of the British Commonwealth on the 8th of May, 1945," in *War at Sea* is probably best.

6. The many reasons for the significant shrinking of the Royal Navy after the end of the war are discussed in chapter 11, and clearly it would be among the older classes of big-gun warships that the losses would be greatest. Still, it surprises this author that not one of the surviving *County*-class cruisers (HMSs *Norfolk, Suffolk, Cumberland,* and so on) was preserved as a museum ship; and only HMS *Belfast* survived at all from that great fleet of cruisers that the service had possessed at the beginning of this great war at sea.

7. Assessing the full importance and achievements of the British Pacific Fleet is made difficult by the very different stories that are told, so it may be best to start with the rather restrained if proud older official history in Roskill, *War at Sea,* vol. 3, part 2. The greatest detail is in D. Hobbs, *The British Pacific Fleet: The Royal Navy's Most Powerful Strike Force* (Annapolis, MD: US Naval Institute Press, 2011), passim; but both he and, even more, his fellow Royal Navy officer-historian Boyd (*Royal Navy in Eastern Waters*) strain at presenting an extremely positive account of all that was achieved. By contrast, Barnett, *Engage the Enemy,* 878–94, seems so affected by anger and frustration at recounting his tale of Great Britain's decline that he tends to focus more on the British Pacific Fleet's limitations and weaknesses (especially as compared to TF 58) than on what it did achieve.

8. With wonderful details and fine maps, Hobbs, chap. 4 in *British Pacific Fleet.*

9. Barnett, *Engage the Enemy,* 882. Fraser reported to Admiral Spruance, who allocated the Royal Navy carrier forces to handle attacks from the Formosa (i.e., western) flank. Symonds, *World War II at Sea,* 630–31, is rather slighting; Morison, *US Naval Operations,* vol. 14, is more factual and quite friendly. Clearly, the US Pacific Fleet was powerful enough for all operations here, though it was probably nice to welcome an ally.

10. Thus, the earlier official histories of all the US services are chiefly uncritical and tell a success story. So do early general accounts, like Potter, chaps. 28–30 in *Sea Power.* Later studies by professional scholars not only are more critical in themselves of what was being achieved, for example, regarding the necessity of the taking of Iwo Jima or the efficacy (and morality) of the various bombings of Tokyo, but are more willing to write about character defects—for example, Halsey's instability, McCain's incompetence, and Spruance's and Mitscher's narrow service prejudices, not to mention MacArthur's many flaws. Thus C. G. Reynolds, *Fast Carriers,* is very abrasive about so many of the leaders in the Pacific War; and Spector, *Eagle against the Sun,* also offers some very candid and critical accounts of particular aspects.

11. "Battle of Iwo Jima," Wikipedia, last modified February 11, 2020, https://en.wikipedia.org/wiki/Battle_of_Iwo_Jima; Spector, *Eagle against the Sun,* 497–503, on Iwo Jima. It was interesting to this author to see that the latest major synthesis, Symonds's ex-

cellent *World War II at Sea,* 603–12, contains a very critical assessment of many aspects of the American campaigning at this time—that is, the inadequate (perhaps futile) naval bombardment of Iwo Jima, the flaws in the strategic bombing assumptions, the horror of the Tokyo firebombing, and the tight commercial blockade that seemed to have no effect on Japan's determination to fight on.

12. Morison, *US Naval Operations,* 14:71–72. Overall, the official historian's coverage of the entire Iwo Jima operation is both thin (seventy-five pages) and laconic compared to the detail and passion he brings to the Okinawa campaign (over two hundred pages), which he observed at close range.

13. As argued in Spector, *Eagle against the Sun,* 499. Professor Spector himself served in the US Marine Corps, in Vietnam, before his academic career.

14. This is my reading of Spector, *Eagle against the Sun,* which is caustic toward Spruance's general ambitions; and of C. G. Reynolds, *Fast Carriers,* on the carrier admirals' repeated desire to justify themselves; and again, of Symonds (*World War II at Sea*) himself.

15. Morison, *US Naval Operations,* 14:57–59.

16. MacArthur's army thus remained by far the largest American force throughout the entire Pacific War, second only to the US armies in northwestern Europe, and it became even more so after the invasion of the Philippines. It is significant that Morison dutifully devotes an entire volume of *US Naval Operations,* vol. 13, *The Liberation of the Philippines,* to this mopping-up campaign. Spector, chap. 22 in *Eagle against the Sun,* casts a more critical eye over such a strategic diversion; and J. M. Scott, *Rampage: MacArthur, Yamashita and the Battle of Manila* (Norton: New York, 2018), is withering about the sheer awfulness of the reconquest of Manila.

17. Morison, *US Naval Operations,* vol. 13, *The Liberation of the Philippines,* is more positive here; Symonds, *World War II at Sea,* 610–11, less so, as is, once again, Spector, *Eagle against the Sun.*

18. Most detail here on the Okinawa naval campaign comes from Morison, *US Naval Operations,* vol. 14.

19. Symonds, *World War II at Sea,* 611.

20. The detail in Morison, appendix in *US Naval Operations,* vol. 14, gives a breakdown, namely of the many escort carriers offering aerial coverage over the beaches and then also of the giant Task Force 58, subdivided into flotillas of three, four, or five fleet and light fleet carriers (TF 58.2, etc.) but easily capable of being brought together when, for example, the *Yamato* approached. The list of warships here seems endless.

21. Spector, *Eagle against the Sun,* 532.

22. R. L. Rielly, *Kamikaze Attacks of World War II: A Complete History of Japanese Suicide Strikes on American Ships, by Aircraft and Other Means* (Jefferson, NC: McFarland, 2010).

23. The *Yamato* story is unbounded—represented in books, movies, war games, and Wiki articles. Morison, *US Naval Operations,* 14:199–209, is particularly good with maps and many eyewitness accounts.

24. Ibid., 14:221ff., is full of detail about this crescendo of attacks.

25. See the many details in "Kamikaze," Wikipedia, https://en.wikipedia.org/wiki/Kamikaze, accessed October 19, 2020, a very full article with a large bibliography.

26. And it was saved from the scrapper's yard. Nowadays the destroyer USS *Laffey* is a museum ship, anchored off Patriots Point, Charleston, South Carolina, next to the carrier USS *Yorktown.* USS *Laffey*'s story is retold in Symonds, *World War II at Sea,* with diagrams, and in many other sources.

27. "USS *Harding* (DD-625)," Wikipedia, last modified May 28, 2017, https://en.wikipedia.org/wiki/USS_Harding_(DD-625).

28. Roskill, *War at Sea,* vol. 3, part 2, 329. Morison, *US Naval Operations,* 14:102, 147, 211, is quite generous; Hobbs, *British Pacific Fleet,* is full of detail; whereas Barnett, *Engage the Enemy,* 891, is very brief on this rather favorable (to Britain, that is) episode.

29. Roskill, *War at Sea,* vol. 3, part 2, 352.

30. Morison, *US Naval Operations,* 14:265.

31. Symonds, *World War II at Sea,* 632; and "Battle of Okinawa," Wikipedia, accessed October 19, 2020, https://en.wikipedia.org/wiki/Battle_of_Okinawa, give many details.

32. Roskill, *War at Sea,* vol. 3, part 2, 367, has a detailed table on Japanese shipping losses (about which he says Japan was "well and truly defeated").

33. Morison, *US Naval Operations,* 14:352–53, puts this delicate point most elegantly.

34. On the shelling of the Japanese coastal cities, both official naval histories have brief, subdued accounts: Roskill, *War at Sea,* vol. 3, part 2, 373; and Morison, *US Naval Operations,* 14:307ff. (There are many other accounts, e.g., Hobbs, *British Pacific Fleet,* passim, on these late-in-the-day operations, but using the official histories is the most economical way to give reference—which is, indeed, why I have referenced Roskill and Morison so frequently in this chapter.)

35. Of the vast literature on the US plans to invade Japan, see D. M. Giangreco, *Hell to Pay: Operation Downfall and the Invasion of Japan, 1945–1947* (Annapolis, MD: US Naval Institute Press, 2009), a dense work; J. R. Skates, *The Invasion of Japan: Alternative to the Bomb* (Columbia: University of South Carolina Press, 1995); and, best, R. B. Frank, *Downfall: The End of the Imperial Japanese Empire* (New York: Random House, 1999).

36. Barnett, *Engage the Enemy,* predictably notes the disparity in his closing pages; and see the works in note 35 on the plans for the second invasion in spring 1946.

37. For the cost comparisons, see "Design and Development," in "Boeing B-29 Superfortress," Wikipedia, accessed October 19, 2020, https://en.wikipedia.org/wiki/Boeing_B-29_Superfortress.

38. The final pages of the final volume of Morison, *US Naval Operations,* 14:361–70, pertaining to the surrender ceremony are suitably dignified, moving, and elegiac—well worth a slow read.

## Chapter 11

1. The simplest way to track the two great ships' wartime experiences is in "USS *Augusta* (CA-31)," Wikipedia, last modified May 25, 2020, https://en.wikipedia.org/wiki/USS_Augusta_(CA-31); and "HMS *Renown* (1916)," Wikipedia, last modified July 7, 2020, https://en.wikipedia.org/wiki/HMS_Renown_(1916).

2. R. Rhodes, *The Making of the Atomic Bomb* (New York: Simon and Schuster, 1986); as well as the biography by K. Bird and M. Sherwin, *American Prometheus: The Triumph and Tragedy of J. Robert Oppenheimer* (New York: Alfred A. Knopf, 2005), on Oppenheimer's growing awareness of the transformative nature of atomic weapons.

3. As one example, the carrier HMS *Victorious,* from the *Bismarck* chase to Operation Pedestal (Malta) to being part of the British Pacific Fleet; another example is the destroyer USS *Harding,* from Atlantic escort to Normandy support ops to Mediterranean/South of France campaigning to antikamikaze picket duty off Okinawa.

4. This rather lovely Roskill quote is repeated from chapter 7.

5. R. Woodman, *Malta Convoys, 1940–1943* (London: John Murray, 2000).

6. Hence my feeling that the argument swings too far, however important the corrective of O'Brien, *How the War Was Won,* which impressed many readers when it came out in 2014.

7. This is part of the prolific Correlli Barnett's various works assessing the British performance before, during, and after World War II—*Audit of War,* an extremely influential work.

8. That is still a need felt by naval planners today, as the destroyers of the world's navies reach tonnages of 10,000 tons and more.

9. "*Flower*-class Corvette," Wikipedia, last modified July 4, 2020, https://en.wikipedia.org/wiki/Flower-class_corvette.

10. See again the pertinent chapters in Ellis, *Brute Force.*

11. Discussed in Barnett, *Audit of War;* and compare with the more mellow Barnett, *Engage the Enemy.*

12. Best seen in *Jane's Fighting Ships 1945,* and again in the *Jane's Fighting Ships 1946* annual.

13. E. J. Grove, *From Vanguard to Trident: British Naval Policy since World War Two* (Annapolis, MD: US Naval Institute Press, 1987), is the most thorough, with many statistics in chapter 1; and a thoughtful summing up of the postwar navy is in J. R. Hill, ed., *The Oxford Illustrated History of the Royal Navy* (Oxford: Oxford University Press, 1995).

14. The huge tally of the warships (including those still on order) of the US Navy in 1945 is in *Jane's Fighting Ships* (see note 12); D. Allard, chap. 15, "An Era of Transition, 1945–1953," in *In Peace and War: Interpretations of American Naval History, 1776–1978,* ed. K. J. Hogan (Westport, CT: Greenwood Press, 1978), 292, gives the personnel.

15. A repeated refrain of the great strategist, most cogently argued in his classic, Liddell Hart, *Strategy* (New York: Meridian, 1991), passim.

16. Allard, "Era of Transition," 290.

17. See Potter, chaps. 31–33 in *Sea Power,* with good further reading on 402–3.

18. Mahan's core argument, as he restates in *Influence of Sea Power,* 88.


## Appendix A

1. Retrieved from https://en.wikipedia.org/wiki/Convoy_ONS_5#Night_of_5-6_May, accessed on August 17, 2020.

# Bibliography

## Books

Adcock, A. *Escort Carriers in Action*. Carrollton, TX: Squadron/Signal, 1996.

Alanbrooke, Field-Marshal Lord. *The Turn of the Tide*. London: Reprint Society, 1957.

Allard, D. "An Era of Transition, 1945–1953." In *In Peace and War: Interpretations of American Naval History, 1776–1978*, edited by K. J. Hagan. Westport, CT: Greenwood Press, 1978.

Atkinson, R. *An Army at Dawn: The War in North Africa, 1942–1943*. New York: Henry Holt, 2002.

———. *The Day of Battle: The War in Sicily and Italy, 1943–1944*. New York: Henry Holt, 2007.

Auphan, T., and J. Mordal. *The French Navy in World War II*. Annapolis, MD: US Naval Institute Press, 1959.

Baer, G. E. *One Hundred Years of Sea Power: The U.S. Navy, 1890–1990*. Stanford, CA: Stanford University Press, 1994.

Barnett, C. *The Audit of War: The Illusion and Reality of Britain as a Great Nation*. London: Macmillan, 1986.

———. *Britain and Her Army, 1509–1970: A Military, Political, and Social Survey*. Harmondsworth, UK: Penguin Books, 1970.

———. *The Collapse of British Power*. London: Eyre Methuen, 1972.

———. *Engage the Enemy More Closely: The Royal Navy in the Second World War*. London: Hodder and Stoughton, 1991.

Bekker, C. *The German Navy 1939–1945*. New York: Dial Press, 1974.

Bell, C. M. *Churchill and Sea Power*. Oxford: Oxford University Press, 2013.

———. *The Royal Navy, Seapower and Strategy between the Wars*. Stanford, CA: Stanford University Press, 2000.

Beloff, M. *Imperial Sunset*. London: Methuen, 1969.

Bird, K., and M. Sherwin. *American Prometheus: The Triumph and Tragedy of J. Robert Oppenheimer*. New York: Alfred A. Knopf, 2005.

Bishop, P. *Target Tirpitz: X-craft, Agents, Dambusters; The Epic Quest to Destroy Hitler's Mightiest Warship*. London: Harper Press, 2012.

Blair, C. *Hitler's U-boat War*. 2 vols. New York: Random House, 1998.

———. *Silent Victory: The U.S. Submarine War against Japan*. Vol. 2. Philadelphia: Lippincott, 1975.

Blum, J. M. *V Was for Victory: Politics and American Culture During World War II*. New York: Harcourt Brace Jovanovich, 1976.

Boyd, A. *The Royal Navy in Eastern Waters: Linchpin of Victory, 1935–1942*. Barnsley, UK: Seaforth, 2017.

Braisted, W. *The United States Navy in the Pacific*. Austin: University of Texas Press, 1958.

Braudel, F. *Capitalism and Material Life, 1400–1800*. New York: Harper Colophon, 1975.

———. *The Mediterranean and the Mediterranean World in the Age of Philip II*. 2 vols. New York: Harper and Row, 1972.

Brown, D. *The Road to Oran: Anglo-French Naval Relations, September 1939–July 1940*. London: Cass, 2004.

Bryant, A. *Triumph in the West: A History of the War Years Based on the Diaries of Field-Marshal Lord Alanbrooke, Chief of the Imperial General Staff*. Garden City, NY: Doubleday, 1959.

Cheall, B. *Fighting Through from Dunkirk to Hamburg: A Green Howard's Wartime Memoir*. Barnsley, UK: Pen and Sword, 2011.

Clark, L. *Anzio: Italy and the Battle for Rome, 1944*. New York: Atlantic Monthly Press, 2006.

Clayton, A. *The British Empire as a Superpower, 1919–39*. Basingstoke, UK: Macmillan, 1986.

Collier, B. *The Defense of the United Kingdom*. London: HMSO, 1957.

Corbett, J. *England in the Seven Years War: A Study in Combined Strategy*. London: Longmans, Green, 1907.

———. *Some Principles of Maritime Strategy*. London: Longmans, Green, 1918.

Craven, W. F., and J. L. Cate. *The Army Air Force in World War II*. Vol. 7, *Services around the World*. Washington, DC: Office of Air Force History, 1983.

Creasy, E. S. *Fifteen Decisive Battles of the World: From Marathon to Waterloo*. New York: S. W. Green's Son, 1882.

Crowl, P. A., and E. G. Love. *Seizure of the Gilberts and Marshalls*. Washington, DC: Department of the Army, 1955.

Danchev, A. *Very Special Relationship: Field-Marshall Sir John Dill and the Anglo-American Alliance, 1941–44*. London: Brassey's Defence, 1986.

D'Este, C. *Bitter Victory: The Battle for Sicily, 1943*. New York: E. P. Dutton, 1988.

De Tocqueville, A. *Democracy in America*. Edited by J. P. Mayer. Translated by G. Lawrence. Garden City, NY: Anchor Books, 1969.

Dimbleby, J. *The Battle of the Atlantic: How the Allies Won the War*. New York: Oxford University Press, 2016.

Dobson, A. P. *U.S. Wartime Aid to Britain, 1940–1946*. London: Croom Helm, 1986.

Doenitz, K. *Memoirs: Ten Years and Twenty Days*. Translated by R. H. Stevens and D. Woodward. Annapolis, MD: US Naval Institute Press, 1990.

Dull, P. *A Battle History of the Imperial Japanese Navy, 1941–1945*. Annapolis, MD: US Naval Institute Press, 1978.

Eisenhower, David. *Eisenhower at War 1943–1945*. New York: Random House, 1986.

Ellis, J. *Brute Force: Allied Strategy and Tactics in the Second World War*. New York: Viking, 1990.

———. *Cassino, the Hollow Victory: The Battle for Rome, January–June 1944*. New York: McGraw Hill, 1984.

Evans, D. C., and M. Peattie. *Kaigun: Strategy, Tactics, and Technology in the Imperial Japanese Navy 1887–1941*. Annapolis, MD: US Naval Institute Press, 1997.

Fisher, J. *Memories*. London: Hodder and Stoughton, 1919.

Frank, R. *Le Prix du Réarmement Français, 1935–1939*. Paris: Publications de la Sorbonne, 1982.

Frank, R. B. *Downfall: The End of the Imperial Japanese Empire*. New York: Random House, 1999.

Friedman, N. *British Submarines in Two World Wars*. Annapolis, MD: US Naval Institute Press, 2019.

———. *Naval Weapons of World War One: Guns, Torpedoes, Mines and ASW Weapons of All Nations: An Illustrated Directory*. Barnsley, UK: Seaforth, 2011.

———. *U.S. Aircraft Carriers: An Illustrated Design History*. Annapolis, MD: US Naval Institute Press, 1983.

Fuller, J. F. C. *The Decisive Battles of the Western World and Their Influence upon History*. Vol. 2. London: Eyre and Spottiswoode, 1965.

Gannon, M. *Black May*. New York: HarperCollins, 1998.

Giangreco, D. M. *Hell to Pay: Operation Downfall and the Invasion of Japan, 1945–1947*. Annapolis, MD: US Naval Institute Press, 2009.

Gibbons, T. *The Complete Encyclopedia of Battleships: A Technical Directory of Capital Ships from 1860 to the Present Day*. London: Crescent Books, 1983.

Gordon, G. A. H. *The Rules of the Game: Jutland and British Naval Command*. London: John Murray, 1996.

Greene, J., and A. Massigniani. *The Naval War in the Mediterranean, 1940–1943*. London: Chatham, 2002.

Gretton, P. *Convoy Escort Commander*. London: Cassell, 1964.

Groener, E. *German Warships, 1815–1945*. Annapolis, MD: US Naval Institute Press, 1990.

Grove, E. J. *From Vanguard to Trident: British Naval Policy since World War Two*. Annapolis, MD: US Naval Institute Press, 1987.

*The Halder War Diary, 1939–1942*. Translated by C. Burdick and H. A. Jacobsen. Novato, CA: Presidio Press, 1988.

Harrison, M., ed. *The Economics of World War II: Six Great Powers in International Comparison*. Cambridge, UK: Cambridge University Press, 1998.

Hashimoto, M. *Sunk: The Story of the Japanese Submarine Fleet, 1941–1945*. New York: Henry Holt, 1954.

Hastings, M. *Operation Pedestal: The Fleet That Battled to Malta, 1942*. London: HarperCollins, 2021.

———. *Overlord: D-Day and the Battle for Normandy, 1944*. New York: Simon and Schuster, 1984.

Hattendorf, J. B., ed. *On His Majesty's Service: Observations of the British Home Fleet from the Diary, Reports, and Letters of Joseph H. Welling, Assistant U.S. Naval Attaché, London, 1940–41*. Newport, RI: Naval War College Press, 1983.

Hendrie, A. *The Cinderella Service: RAF Coastland Command 1939–1945*. London: Casemate, 2006.

Herman, A. *Freedom's Forge: How American Business Produced the Victory in World War II*. New York: Random House, 2012.

Herwig, H. H. *Politics of Frustration: The United States in German Naval Planning 1889–1941*. Boston: Little, Brown, 1976.

Hill, J. R., ed. *The Oxford Illustrated History of the Royal Navy*. Oxford: Oxford University Press, 1995.

Hillgruber, A. *Hitler's Strategie: Politik und Kriegsführung, 1940–1941*. Frankfurt: Bernand and Graefe, 1965.

Hobbs, D. *The British Pacific Fleet: The Royal Navy's Most Powerful Strike Force*. Annapolis, MD: US Naval Institute Press, 2011.

Hobsbawm, E. *The Age of Empire, 1875–1914*. New York: Pantheon, 1987.

Hogan, J. K., ed. *In Peace and War: Interpretations of American Naval History, 1776–1978*. Westport, CT: Greenwood Press, 1978.

Holland, J. *Fortress Malta: An Island under Siege 1940–1943*. London: Orion, 2003.

Hone, T., N. Friedman, and M. D. Mandeles. *American and British Aircraft Carrier Development, 1919–1941*. Annapolis. MD: US Naval Institute Press, 1999.

Hopkins, A. G. *American Empire: A Global History*. Princeton, NJ: Princeton University Press, 2018.

Howard, M. E. *The Continental Commitment: The Dilemma of British Defence Policy in the Era of the Two World Wars*. London: Maurice Temple Smith, 1972.

———. *Grand Strategy. August 1942–September 1943*, vol. 4 of *History of the Second World War*. London: HMSO, 1970.

———. *The Mediterranean Strategy in the Second World War*. New York: Praeger, 1968.

Hughes, Q. *Britain in the Mediterranean and the Defence of Her Naval Stations*. Liverpool, UK: Penpaled, 1981.

Hughes, T., and J. Costello. *The Battle of the Atlantic*. New York: Dial Press, 1977.

Irving, D. *The Destruction of Convoy PQ 17*. London: Cassell, 1968.

Isley, J. A., and P. A. Crowl. *The U.S. Marines and Amphibious War: Its Theory, and Its Practice in the Pacific*. Princeton, NJ: Princeton University Press, 1951.

*Jane's Fighting Ships*. London: Sampson Low, Marston, 1939–.

Jenkins, P. *A History of the United States*. 4th ed. New York: Palgrave Macmillan, 2012.

Kaplan, P., and R. A. Smith. *One Last Look: A Sentimental Journey to the Eighth Air Force Heavy Bomber Bases of World War II in England*. New York: Abbeville Press, 1983.

Kemp, P. K., ed. *The Papers of Admiral Sir John Fisher*. London: Navy Records Society, 1960–1964.

Kennedy, L. *The Death of the* Tirpitz. Boston: Little, Brown, 1979.

Kennedy, P. M. *Engineers of Victory: The Problem Solvers Who Turned the Tide in the Second World War*. New York: Random House, 2013.

———. *The Parliament of Man: The Past, Present, and Future of the United Nations*. New York: Penguin Random House, 2006.

———. *Preparing for the Twenty-First Century*. New York: Random House, 1993.

———. *The Realities Behind Diplomacy: Background Influences on British External Policy, 1865–1980*. London: Allen and Unwin, 1981.

———. *The Rise and Fall of British Naval Mastery*. London: Ashfield Press, 1976.

———. *The Rise and Fall of the Great Powers: Economic Change and Military Conflict from 1500 to 2000*. New York: Random House, 1987.

———. *The Rise of the Anglo-German Antagonism 1860–1914*. London: Allen and Unwin, 1980.

———. *Strategy and Diplomacy, 1870–1945: Eight Studies*. London: Allen and Unwin, 1983.

———. "The War at Sea." In vol. 1 of *Cambridge History of the First World War*, edited by J. M. Winter. Cambridge, UK: Cambridge University Press, 2014.

Kennedy, P. M., and E. Wilson, eds. *Navies in Multipolar Worlds: From the Age of Sail to the Present*. London: Routledge, 2020.

Kiszley, J. *Anatomy of a Campaign: The British Fiasco in Norway, 1940*. Cambridge, UK: Cambridge University Press, 2017.

Knox, M. *Mussolini Unleashed, 1939–1941, Politics and Strategy in Fascist Italy's Last War.* Cambridge, UK: Cambridge University Press, 1982.

Konstam, A. *The Battle of the North Cape: The Death Ride of the* Scharnhorst, *1943.* London: Pen and Sword, 2011.

Lambert, A. *Seapower States: Maritime Culture, Continental Empires, and the Conflict That Made the Modern World.* New Haven, CT: Yale University Press, 2018.

Lambert, J., and A. Raven. *Warship Perspectives: Flower Class Corvettes in World War Two.* Lynbrook, NY: WR Press, 1999.

Landes, D. *The Unbound Prometheus: Technological Change and Industrial Development in Western Europe from 1750 to the Present.* Cambridge, UK: Cambridge University Press, 1969.

Lane, F. C. *Ships for Victory: A History of Shipbuilding under the U.S. Maritime Commission in World War II.* Baltimore: Johns Hopkins University Press, 1950.

Lee, L. E., ed. *World War II.* Westport, CT: Greenwood Press, 1999.

Levy, J. P. *The Royal Navy's Home Fleet in World War 2.* London: Macmillan, 2003.

Liddell Hart, B. H. *The British Way of Warfare.* London: Faber, 1932.

———. *History of the Second World War.* London: Cassell, 1970.

———. *Strategy.* New York: Meridian, 1991.

Lukacs, J. *The Last European War: September 1939/December 1941.* New Haven, CT: Yale University Press, 1976.

MacDonald, C. A. *The Lost Battle—Crete, 1941.* London: Macmillan, 1993.

Mack Smith, D. *Mussolini's Roman Empire.* New York: Viking Press, 1976.

Mahan, A. T. *The Influence of Sea Power upon History 1660–1783.* Boston: Little, Brown, 1890. Reprint, London, 1965.

———. *Retrospect and Prospect: Studies in International Relations, Naval and Political.* Boston: Little, Brown, 1902.

Maiolo, J. A. *Cry Havoc: How the Arms Race Drove the World to War, 1931–1941.* New York: Basic Books, 2010.

Marder, A. J. *From the Dardanelles to Oran: Studies of the Royal Navy in War and Peace, 1915–1940.* Oxford: Oxford University Press, 1974.

Marriott, L. *Treaty Cruisers: The First International Warship Building Competition.* Barnsley, UK: Pen and Sword Press, 2005.

Marshall, I. *Armored Ships: The Ships, Their Settings, and the Ascendancy That They Sustained for 80 Years.* Charlottesville, VA: Howell Press, 1990.

———. *Cruisers and La Guerre de Course.* Mystic, CT: Mystic Seaport Museum, 2008.

———. *Flying Boats: The J-class Yachts of Aviation.* Cheltenham, UK: History Press, 2002.

Marx, K. *The Eighteenth Brumaire of Louis Napoleon.* London: Electric Book Co., 2001.

Matloff, M. *Strategic Planning for Coalition Warfare, 1943–1944.* Washington, DC: Department of the Army, 1959.

Matloff, M., and E. M. Snell. *Strategic Planning for Coalition Warfare, 1941–1942.* Washington, DC: Department of the Army, 1953.

Mawdsley, E. "The Sea as a Decisive Factor in the Second World War." In *The Modern World,* edited by N. A. M. Rodger. Vol. 4 of *The Sea in History,* edited by Christian Buchet. Woodbridge, UK: Boydell Press, 2017.

———. *The War for the Seas: A Maritime History of World War II.* London: Yale University Press, 2019.

Maxtone-Graham, J. *Passage East.* Illustrated by I. Marshall. Cheltenham, UK: History Press Limited, 1998.

McNeill, W. H. *Population and Politics since 1750.* Charlottesville: University Press of Virginia, 1990.

———. *The Pursuit of Power: Technology, Armed Force, and Society since A.D. 1000.* Chicago: University of Chicago Press, 1982.

Middlebrook, M. *Convoy: The Battle for Convoys SC.122 and HX.229.* London: Allen Lane, 1976.

Middlebrook, M., and P. Mahoney. *Battleship: The Sinking of the* Prince of Wales *and* Repulse. Scribner's: New York, 1976.

Miller, E. S. *War Plan Orange: The U.S. Strategy to Defeat Japan, 1897–1945.* Annapolis, MD: US Naval Institute Press, 1991.

Miller, J. *Cartwheel: The Reduction of Rabaul.* Washington, DC: Department of the Army, 1959.

Millett, A. R., and W. Murray, eds. *Military Effectiveness.* 3 vols. Boston: Allen and Unwin, 1987.

Milward, A. S. *War, Economy, and Society, 1939–1945.* Berkeley: University of California Press, 1977.

Mitchell, J. B., ed. *Twenty Decisive Battles of the World.* New York: Macmillan, 1964.

Modelski, G., and W. R. Thompson. *Sea Power in Global Politics 1494–1993.* Basingstoke, UK: Macmillan, 1988.

Morison, S. E. *History of United States Naval Operations in World War II.* 15 vols. Boston: Little, Brown, 1947–62.

———. *Strategy and Compromise.* Boston: Little, Brown, 1958.

Murray, W. *The Luftwaffe, 1933–45: Strategy for Defeat.* Washington, DC: Brassey's, 1996.

Nagorski, A. *1941: The Year Germany Lost the War.* New York: Simon and Schuster, 2019.

Neidpath, J. *The Singapore Naval Base and the Defence of Britain's Eastern Empire, 1919–1941.* New York: Clarendon Press of Oxford University Press, 1981.

O'Brien, P. P. *How the War Was Won: Air-Sea Power and Allied Victory in World War II.* Cambridge, UK: Cambridge University Press, 2015.

O'Hara, V. P. *The German Fleet at War, 1939–1945.* Annapolis, MD: US Naval Institute Press, 2004.

Overy, R. J. *The Air War, 1939–1945.* New York: Stein and Day, 1980.

———. *The Origins of the Second World War.* London: Taylor and Francis, 2016.

———. *The Oxford Illustrated History of World War II.* Oxford: Oxford University Press, 2015.

Padfield, P. *Maritime Dominion and the Triumph of the Free World: Naval Campaigns That Shaped the Modern World, 1851–2001.* London: John Murray, 2009.

———. *Maritime Power and the Struggle for Freedom: Naval Campaigns that Shaped the Modern World, 1788–1851.* New York: Abrams Press, 2005.

———. *Tide of Empires: Decisive Naval Campaigns in the Rise of the West 1481–1654: Volume I.* London: Routledge & Kegan Paul, 1979.

———. *Tide of Empires: Decisive Naval Campaigns in the Rise of the West 1654–1763: Volume II.* London: Routledge & Kegan Paul, 1981.

Paine, S. C. M. *The Japanese Empire: Grand Strategy from the Meiji Restoration to the Pacific War.* Cambridge, UK: Cambridge University Press, 2017.

Parker, G. *The Military Revolution: Military Innovation and the Rise of the West, 1500–1800.* New York: Cambridge University Press, 1996.

Parkes, O. *British Battleships, "Warrior" 1860 to "Vanguard" 1950: A History of Design Construction and Armament.* Hamden, CT: Archon Books, 1972.

Playfair, I. S. O. *The Mediterranean and Middle East: The Destruction of Axis Forces in Africa.* London: HMSO, 1954.

Polmar, N. *Aircraft Carriers: A Graphic History of Carrier Aviation and Its Influence on World Events.* Rev. ed. Washington, DC: Potomac Books, 2006.

Pomeranz, K. *The Great Divergence: China, Europe, and the Making of the Modern World Economy.* Princeton, NJ: Princeton University Press, 2000.

Pope, D. *73 North: The Battle of the Barents Sea.* London: Wyman, 1958.

Potter, E. B., ed. *Sea Power: A Naval History.* 2nd ed. Annapolis, MD: US Naval Institute Press, 1981.

Prang, G. W. *At Dawn We Slept: The Untold Story of Pearl Harbor.* New York: McGraw-Hill, 1981.

Pratt, L. *East of Malta, West of Suez: Britain's Mediterranean Crisis, 1936–1939.* Cambridge, UK: Cambridge University Press, 1975.

Reynolds, C. G. *The Fast Carriers: The Forging of an Air Navy.* New York: McGraw-Hill, 1968.

Reynolds, D. *The Creation of the Anglo-American Alliance, 1937–40: A Study in Competitive Cooperation.* Chapel Hill: University of North Carolina Press, 1982.

Rhodes, R. *The Making of the Atomic Bomb.* New York: Simon and Schuster, 1986.

Rielly, R. L. *Kamikaze Attacks of World War II: A Complete History of Japanese Suicide Strikes on American Ships, by Aircraft and Other Means.* Jefferson, NC: McFarland, 2010.

———. *Kamikazes, Corsairs, and Picket Ships: Okinawa, 1945.* Havertown, PA: Casemate, 2008.

Rohwer, J. *The Critical Convoy Battles of March 1943: The Battle for HX.229/SC122.* Translated by Derek Masters. Annapolis, MD: US Naval Institute Press, 1977.

Ropponen, R. *Die Russische Gefahr.* Helsinki: Suomen Historiallinen Seura, 1976.

Roskill, S. W. *Churchill and the Admirals.* London: Collins, 1977.

———. *Naval Policy between the Wars.* 2 vols. London: Collins, 1978.

———. *The War at Sea, 1939–1946.* 3 vols. London: HMSO, 1954–61.

Rostow, W. W. *The World Economy: History & Prospect.* Austin: University of Texas Press, 1978.

Ryan, C. *The Longest Day.* London: New English Library, 1962.

Sadkovich, J. *The Italian Navy in World War II.* Westport, CT: Greenwood Press, 1994.

Salerno, R. *Vital Crossroads: Mediterranean Origins of the Second World War, 1935–1940.* Ithaca, NY: Cornell University Press, 2002.

Schofield, B. B. *The Russian Convoys: Heroes of the Murmansk Run—Allied Seamen Who Fought Stukas, Nazi Subs and Frozen Arctic Seas in WWII.* London: Batsford, 1966.

Scott, J. M. *Rampage: MacArthur, Yamashita and the Battle of Manila.* New York: Norton, 2018.

Seth, R. *The Fiercest Battle: The Story of North Atlantic Convoy ONS 5, 22nd April–7th May 1943.* New York: Norton, 1961.

Sherry, M. *The Rise of American Air Power: The Creation of Armageddon.* New Haven, CT: Yale University Press, 1987.

Sherwig, J. M. *Guineas and Gunpowder: British Foreign Aid in the Wars with France, 1793–1815.* Cambridge, MA: Harvard University Press, 1969.

Simms, B. *Europe: The Struggle for Supremacy, from 1453 to the Present.* New York: Basic Books, 2013.

Skates, J. R. *The Invasion of Japan: Alternative to the Bomb.* Columbia: University of South Carolina Press, 1995.

Spector, R. *Eagle against the Sun: The American War with Japan.* New York: Free Press, 1985.

Steiner, Z. *The Lights That Failed: European International History 1919–1933.* Oxford: Oxford University Press, 2005.

———. *The Triumph of the Dark: European International History 1933–1939.* Oxford: Oxford University Press, 2011.

Stille, M. *The Imperial Japanese Navy in the Pacific War*. London: Osprey, 2014.

Stoddard, B. C. *World in the Balance: The Perilous Months of June–October 1940*. Washington, DC: Potomac Books, 2011.

Strahan, J. E. *Andrew Jackson Higgins and the Boats That Won World War II*. Baton Rouge: Louisiana State University Press, 1994.

Sullivan, B. R. *A Thirst for Glory: Mussolini, the Italian Military and the Fascist Regime, 1922–1936*. Ann Arbor, MI: University Microfilms International, 1984.

Sumall, R. "The Battleship and Battlecruiser." In R. Gardiner, *The Eclipse of the Big Gun: The Warship 1906–45*. London: Conway Maritime, 1973.

Sweetman, J. *Tirpitz: Hunting the Beast: Air Attacks on the German Battleship 1940–44*. Annapolis, MD: US Naval Institute Press, 2000.

Symonds, C. L. *World War II at Sea: A Global History*. New York: Oxford University Press, 2018.

Syrett, D. *The Defeat of the German U-boats: The Battle of the Atlantic*. Columbia: University of South Carolina Press, 1994.

Taylor, A. J. P. *The Struggle for Mastery in Europe, 1848–1918*. Oxford: Oxford University Press, 1971.

Thompson, J. A. *A Sense of Power: The Roots of America's Global Role*. Ithaca, NY: Cornell University Press, 2015.

Till, G. *Air Power and the Royal Navy 1914–1945: A Historical Survey*. Surrey, UK: Macdonald and Jane's, 1979.

———, ed., *The Development of British Naval Thinking: Essays in Memory of Bryan McLaren Ranft*. London: Routledge, 2006.

Tilly, C., ed. *The Formation of the National States in Western Europe*. Princeton, NJ: Princeton University Press, 1975.

Toland, J. *The Rising Sun: The Decline and Fall of the Japanese Empire, 1936–1945*. London: Cassell, 1971.

Toynbee, A., and F. T. Ashton-Gwatkin, eds. *The World in March 1939*. London: Oxford University Press, 1952.

Tufte, E. *The Visual Display of Quantitative Information*. Cheshire, CT: Graphics Press, 1983.

Underwood, J. S. *The Wings of Democracy: The Influence of Air Power on the Roosevelt Administration, 1933–1941*. College Station: Texas A&M University Press, 1991.

Van der Vat, D. *The Atlantic Campaign: World War II's Great Struggle at Sea*. New York: Harper and Row, 1988.

Vego, M. N. *The Battle for Leyte, 1944: Allied and Japanese Plans, Preparations, and Execution*. Annapolis, MD: US Naval Institute Press, 2006.

Wallerstein, I. M. *The Modern World-System*. New York: Academic Press, 1974–1989.

Watts, A. J. *The Loss of the* Scharnhorst. Shepperton, UK: Allan, 1970.

Weeks, A. L. *Russia's Life-Saver: Lend-Lease Aid to the U.S.S.R. in World War II*. Lanham, MD: Lexington Books, 2004.

Wegener, W. *Naval Strategy of the World War*. Translated by H. H. Herwig. Annapolis, MD: US Naval Institute Press, 1989. Originally published as *Die Seestrategie des Weltkrieges* (Berlin: E. S. Mittler, 1929).

Winton, J. *Convoy: The Defence of Sea Trade, 1890–1990*. London: M. Joseph, 1983.

Woodman, R. *The Arctic Convoys, 1941–1945*. London: John Murray, 1994.

———. *Malta Convoys, 1940–1943*. London: John Murray, 2000.

Woodruff, W. *Impact of Western Man: A Study of Europe's Role in the World Economy, 1750–1960*. New York: St. Martin's Press, 1967.

Woods, R. B. *A Changing of the Guard: Anglo-American Relations, 1941–1946*. Chapel Hill: University of North Carolina Press, 1990.

Woodward, D. *The Secret Raiders: The Story of German Armed Merchant Raiders in the Second World War.* New York: Norton, 1955.

Wright, Q. *A Study of War.* Chicago: University of Chicago Press, 1942.

Yoshimura, A. *Battleship* Musashi: *The Making and Sinking of the World's Biggest Battleship.* Tokyo: Kodansha International, 1999.


## Articles

Barlow, J. G. "The Navy's Escort Carrier Offensive." *Naval History Magazine,* November 2013. https://www.usni.org/magazines/naval-history-magazine/2013/november/navys -escort-carrier-offensive.

Crisher, B., and M. Souva. *Power at Sea: A Naval Dataset, 1865–2011.* https://qualitative datarepository.github.io/dataverse-previewers/previewers/SpreadsheetPreview.html ?fileid=2453823&siteUrl=https://dataverse.harvard.edu&datasetid=66002&dataset version=1.0. Edited by A. Dawson.

Hammond, R. "An Enduring Influence on Imperial Defence and Grand Strategy: British Perceptions of the Italian Navy, 1935–1943." *International History Review* 39, no. 5 (2017): 810–35. https://doi.org/10.1080/07075332.2017.1280520.

Kennedy, P. M. "Imperial Cable Communications and Strategy, 1870–1914." *English Historical Review* 86, no. 341 (October 1971): 728–52.

———. "Sinking of the *Tirpitz.*" *Purnell's History of the Second World War* 5, no. 15.

Low, D. "Very Well, Alone." *Evening Standard,* June 18, 1940.

Mahan, A. T. "Considerations Governing the Dispositions of Navies." *National Review* 3 (July 1902): 701–19.

Maiolo, J. A. "Did the Royal Navy Decline between the Wars?" *RUSI Journal* 159 (July 2014): 18–24.

Marder, A. J. "The Royal Navy and the Ethiopian Crisis of 1935–36." *American Historical Review* 75, no. 5 (June 1971).

Milner, M. "The Battle of the Atlantic." *Journal of Strategic Studies* 13, no. 1 (1990): 45–56. https://doi.org/10.1080/01402399008437400.

Modelski, G. "The Long Cycle of Global Politics and the Nation-State." *Comparative Studies in Politics and Society* 20 (1978).

Parrish, J. B. "Iron and Steel in the Balance of World Power." *Journal of Political Economy* 64, no. 4 (October 1956): 368–88.

Rahn, W. "German Navies from 1848 to 2016." *Naval War College Review* 70, no. 4 (2017): 1–47.

Simpson, M. "Force H and British Strategy in the Western Mediterranean 1939–1942." *Mariner's Mirror* 83, no. 1 (1997): 62–75.

Williamson, C. "Industrial-Grade Generosity: British Warship Repair and Lend-Lease in 1941." *Diplomatic History* 39, no. 4 (September 2015): 745–72. https://doi.org/10.1093 /dh/dhu040.


## Internet Sources

http://defenceindepth.co/2017/09/29/absent-friends-british-naval-aviation-and-d-day/
http://destroyerhistory.org/destroyers/bath
http://destroyerhistory.org/destroyers/seatac
http://destroyerhistory.org/fletcherclass

http://uboat.net/allies/merchants/losses_year.htm
http://uboat.net/allies/ships/cve_development.htm
http://uboat.net/fates/losses/cause.htm
https://uboat.net/fates/losses/1943.htm
http://uboat.net/ops/combat_strength.html
http://warfarehistorynetwork.com/2016/11/16/the-great-marianas-turkey-shoot
http://www.acmp.com/blog/pratt-whitney-the-engine-that-won-world-war-ii.html
http://www.armouredcarriers.com/uss-robin-hms-victorious
http://www.census.gov/history/www/reference/maps/population_distribution_over
    _time.html
http://www.chuckhawks.com/battlecruisers.htm
http://www.chuckhawks.com/great_destroyers_ww2.htm
http://www.euronet.nl/users/wilfried/ww2/1939.htm
http:// www.guidadigenova.it/en/genoa-history/history-port-genoa/
http://www.history.navy.mil/research/library/online-reading-room/title-list-alphabeti
    cally/u/us-navy-personnel-in-world-war-ii-service-and-casualty-statistics.html
http://www.historyextra.com/period/second-world-war/britain-stood-alone-ww2
    -myths-brexit-debate/
http://www.historyextra.com/second-world-war/did-the-soviet-union-win-the-war
http://www.historynet.com/the-bridge-to-the-beach.htm
http://www.irs.gov/pub/irs-soi/02inpetr.pdf
http://www.nationalww2museum.org/students-teachers/student-resources/research
    -starters/research-starters-higgins-boats
http://www.nationalww2museum.org/...ww2-by-the-numbers/us-milit.html
http://www.naval-history.net/WW2CampaignsIndianOcean.htm
http://www.naval-history.net/WW2CampaignsRussianConvoys.htm
http://www.naval-history.net/xGM-aContents.htm
http://www.thoughtco.com/the-liberty-ship-program-2361030
http://www.treasurydirect.gov/govt/reports/pd/histdebt/histdebt_histo3.htm
http://www.usni.org/magazines/naval-history-magazine/2013/november/navys-escort
    -carrier-offensive
http://ww2pacific.com/ships2.html#ca
http://ww2today.com/9th-may-1940-mountbatten-brings-home-hms-kelly
http://ww2-weapons.com/us-navy-in-late-1941
https://commons.wikimedia.org/wiki/File:Battleship_building_scatter_graph_1905
    _onwards.png

# Index

Page references in *italics* refer to figures and tables.

Royal Navy. *See* Britain
*Royal Oak*, HMS, 109, 112, 113, 141, 164, 419
Russia: Russo-Japanese War (1904–6), 100; steel output (1913), 327; WWI and geographic influences on, 68–69. *See also* Soviet Union (USSR)
*Ryujo* (Japan), 236

Salerno, Allied invasion Italy (1943), 242–54, *245, 249, 250–51*
*Salt Lake City,* USS, 278, *279*
Santa Cruz Islands, Battle of the, 236
*Santee,* USS, 272
*Saratoga,* USS: and Allied control in Pacific (1943), 285–86, 336; and Allied victory at sea (1945), 386, 392, 396; and audit of WWII naval power, 413; in Central Pacific Command, 293; damage to, 236; restrictions on warships of 1930s, 21, 46, 58; USS *Saratoga* and HMS *Victorious,* Nouméa, May 1943 (Painting 39), *288–89*; USSs *Saratoga* and *Lexington,* Puget Sound, 1936 (Painting 10), *44–45*
Savo Island, Battle of, 236
SC-122 (and HX-229) convoy(s), 258–60
SC-130 (and ON-184) convoy(s), 258, 262–63
Scapa Flow: HMS *Courageous* and Britain's Home Fleet losses to Germany, 108–10, 112, 113, 141; geographic influence on Britain's strategy, 70, 73, 76, 79, 201–2; Home Fleet redirected for invasion of Sicily, 246; Home Fleet redirected for Operation Pedestal, 468n8; during WWI, 397
*Scharnhorst*-class battle cruisers, 50, 52
*Scharnhorst* (Germany): Atlantic seaways threat of, 145, 149–50, 151, 153, 154, 177; 1943 attack by, 208; and audit of WWII naval power, 405, 409, 415, 420; and Battle of Norway, 113, 121, 127, 129; Channel Dash, 203; cruiser design, 32, 36, 77; damaged at North Cape, 456n13; *Luetzow* and *Scharnhorst,* Narvik Fjord, 1943 (Painting 12), ii–iii, *66*; production of, 92; *Rawalpindi* sunk by, 109; sinking of, 274; speed of, 200

Schepke, Joachim, 164
Schnorkel breathing apparatus, 372
*S-class* destroyers, 456n13
sea power, 3–15; European expectation to continue in power, post WWI, 3–10; independent "naval air power" vs., 340, 483n10; Mediterranean theater and Royal Navy's return to power (1942), 197, 212–25, *214–15, 220–21, 222;* military technology changes, WWI and interwar years, 10–15; Pacific Ocean and importance of control of open water/air space vs. land, 338, 352; Philippines campaign and three forces of US Navy, 340. *See also* Allied sea power control (1943); Allied sea power triumph (1944); Allied sea power victory (1945); warship types
*The Sea Strategy of the World War* (Wegener), 144
Seattle-Tacoma Shipbuilding Corporation, 300
*Sennen,* HMS, 262
Seven Years' War, *Influence* books (Mahan) on, 99–100
*Sheffield,* HMS, *142,* 410
*Shinano* (Japan), 296, 349, *350–51,* 366, 388, 413
Shingle, Operation, 367
shipbuilding: by Allied forces for defeat of U-boats, 304–9; for amphibious landings, 299; by British Navy, 296–97; British post-London Treaty warships, 129; *Essex*-class carriers and global power shift (1943), *292,* 293–94, 296, 303, 329; fleet distribution and need for, 77; German U-boat production (1944–45), 354, 372; ship-repair policy of Lend-Lease, 160–61; submarine output and Allied sea power triumph (1944), 348–49, *350–51,* 481nn19–20; technological advancement and production of, 90–96, *96;* US defense spending increased (1940), 133–37; and US expansion of Navy (1943), 294–305; US financing and investment in, 318; US shipbuilding yards (1943), 295, 298, 300–303, 305; warship tonnage of Powers, overall (1930–60), 447, *448;* war-